Antony and Cleopatra

From the prizewinning author of *Caesar* and *How Rome Fell*, a major new account of the charged love affair between Antony and Cleopatra, richly informed by military and political history. In this remarkable dual biography, Adrian Goldsworthy goes beyond myth to create a nuanced and historically acute portrayal of his subjects, set against the political backdrop of their time. Goldsworthy's masterfully told—and deeply human—story of love, politics, and ambition delivers a compelling reassessment of a major episode in ancient history.

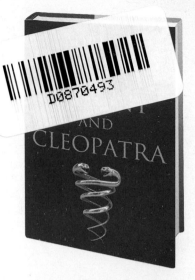

Cloth ISBN 978-0-300-16534-0

How Rome Fell
Death of a Superpower

In AD 200, the Roman Empire seemed unassailable. Its vast territory accounted for most of the known world. By the end of the fifth century, Roman rule had vanished in western Europe and much of northern Africa, and only a shrunken Eastern Empire remained. What accounts for this improbable decline? In this "meticulously researched, complex, and thought-provoking" book *(Washington Post Book World)*, Adrian Goldsworthy applies the scholarship, perspective, and narrative skill that defined his monumental *Caesar* to address perhaps the greatest of all historical questions—how Rome fell.

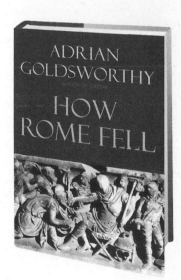

Paper ISBN 978-0-300-16426-8

Selected by the *Washington Post Book World* as one of the Best Books of 2009

For more information visit:
YaleBooks.com

Yale UNIVERSITY PRESS

CAESAR

LIFE OF A COLOSSUS

ADRIAN GOLDSWORTHY

YALE UNIVERSITY PRESS
NEW HAVEN AND LONDON

First published in the United States in 2006 by Yale University Press.
First published in Great Britain in 2006 by Weidenfeld & Nicolson.

Text design: www.carrstudio.co.uk.

Printed in the United States of America.

Library of Congress Control Number: 2006922060

ISBN-13: 978-0-300-12689-1 (pbk. : alk. paper)

A catalogue record for this book is available from the British Library.

The paper in this book meets the guidelines for permanence and durability of the
Committee on Production Guidelines for Book Longevity of the Council on Library
Resources.

10 9 8 7 6 5

CONTENTS

III – CIVIL WAR AND DICTATORSHIP, 49–44 BC

ACKNOWLEDGEMENTS

A number of people read through some or part of this book and I should begin by expressing my deep gratitude to them all. Thanks must go to my former undergraduate tutor, Nicholas Purcell, who very kindly agreed to have a look at a draft of the manuscript. Many useful comments came from Philip Matyszak, who knows more than I ever shall about the workings of the Roman Senate in this period. As ever, Ian Hughes was extremely thorough and helpful in checking and commenting on each chapter as it was written. Kevin Powell read the entire thing through and provided a number of useful comments. Ian Haynes was kind enough to look at Part Two for me and raised several points. To these, and anyone else who read some or all of the text, I offer my most sincere thanks. Thanks should also go to my agent, Georgina Capel, who negotiated a contract which gave me the opportunity to do this subject justice. Finally, I must thank Keith Lowe and the other staff at Orion for their work on, and enthusiasm for, this project.

MAP LIST

INTRODUCTION

The story of Julius Caesar is an intensely dramatic one, which has fascinated generation after generation, attracting the attention of Shakespeare and Shaw, not to mention numerous novelists and screenwriters. Caesar was one of the ablest generals of any era, who left accounts of his own campaigns that have rarely – perhaps never – been surpassed in literary quality. At the same time he was a politician and statesman who eventually took supreme power in the Roman Republic and made himself a monarch in every practical respect, although he never took the name of king. Caesar was not a cruel ruler and paraded his clemency to his defeated enemies, but in the end he was stabbed to death as a result of a conspiracy led by two pardoned men, which also included many of his own supporters. Later his adopted son Octavian – fully Caius Julius Caesar Octavianus – became Rome's first emperor. The family line perished with Nero in AD 68, but all later emperors still took the name of Caesar, even though there was no link by blood or adoption. What had simply been the name of one aristocratic family – and a fairly obscure one at that – became effectively a title symbolising supreme and legitimate power. So strong was the association that when the twentieth century opened, two of the world's great powers were still led by a kaiser and a tsar, each name a rendering of Caesar. Today the Classics have lost their central position in Western education, but even so Julius Caesar remains one of a handful of figures from the ancient world whose name commands instant recognition. Plenty of people with no knowledge of Latin will recall Shakespeare's version of his dying words, *et tu Brute* (in fact, he probably said something else (see p.508–9) but that is by the way). Of other Romans only Nero, and perhaps Mark Antony, enjoy similar fame, and from other nations probably only Alexander the Great, the Greek philosophers, Hannibal and, most of all, Cleopatra remain so high in the public consciousness. Cleopatra was Caesar's lover and Antony one of his senior lieutenants, and so both form part of his story.

Caesar was a great man. Napoleon is just one of many famous commanders who admitted that he had learned much from studying Caesar's campaigns. Politically he had a huge impact on Roman history, playing a key role in ending the Republican system of government, which had endured for four and a half centuries. Although he was fiercely intelligent and highly educated, Caesar was a man of action and it is for this that he is remembered. His talents were varied and exceptional, from his skill as an orator and writer, as framer of laws and as political operator, to his talent as soldier and general. Most of all there was his charm that so often won over the crowd in Rome, the legionaries on campaign and the many women whom he seduced. Caesar made plenty of mistakes, both as commander and as politician, but then which human being has not? His great knack was to recover from setbacks, admit, at least to himself, that he had been wrong, and then adapt to the new situation and somehow win in the long run.

Few would dispute Caesar's claim to greatness, but it is much harder to say that he was a good man, or that the consequences of his career were unambiguously good. He was not a Hitler or a Stalin, nor indeed a Genghis Khan. Even so one source claims that over a million enemies were killed during his campaigns. Ancient attitudes differed from those of today, and the Romans had few qualms about Caesar's wars against foreign opponents like the tribes of Gaul. In eight years of campaigning at the very least Caesar's legions killed hundreds of thousands of people in the region, and enslaved as many more. At times he was utterly ruthless, ordering massacres and executions, and on one occasion the mass mutilation of prisoners whose hands were cut off before they were set free. More often he was merciful to defeated enemies, for the essentially practical reason that he wanted them to accept Roman rule and so become the peaceful tax-paying population of a new province. His attitude was coldly pragmatic, deciding on clemency or atrocity according to which seemed to offer him the greatest advantage. He was an active and energetic imperialist, but having said that he was not the creator of Roman imperialism, merely one of its many agents. His campaigns were not noticeably more brutal than other Roman wars. Far more controversial at the time were his activities in Rome and his willingness to fight a civil war when he felt that his political rivals were determined to end his career. His grievances had more than a little justice, but even so when Caesar took his army from his province into Italy in January 49 BC he became a rebel. The civil wars that followed his assassination finally brought the Roman Republic to an end. Its condition may already have been terminal because of Caesar's own actions. The Republic fell and was replaced by the rule of emperors, the first of whom was his heir. During his dictatorship Caesar held supreme power and had generally governed well, bringing in measures that were sensible and statesmanlike and for the good of Rome. Previously the Republic had been dominated by a narrow senatorial elite, whose members all too often abused their position to enrich themselves by exploiting poorer Romans and the inhabitants of the provinces alike. Caesar took action to deal with problems that had been acknowledged as real and serious for some time, but which had not been resolved because of a reluctance to let any individual senator gain the credit for the act. The Republican system was pretty rotten and had been troubled by violence from before Caesar's birth, and civil war from early in his life. He won supreme power by military force, and we know that he employed bribery and intimidation at other stages in his career. His opponents were no different in their methods and were as willing to fight a civil war to destroy Caesar's position as he was to defend it, but that is only to say that he was no better or worse than they were. After his victory he ruled in a very responsible manner and in marked contrast to the senatorial aristocracy – his measures were designed to benefit a much broader section of society. His regime was not repressive and he pardoned and promoted many former enemies. Rome, Italy and the provinces were all better off under Caesar than they had been for some time. Yet if he governed responsibly, his rule also effectively meant the end to free elections, and however just his rule was, in the end monarchy would lead to emperors like Caligula and Nero. It was the wealthy elite at Rome who tended to write the histories and Caesar's rise meant a reduction in the power of this class. Therefore, many sources are critical of him for this reason.

Caesar was not a moral man; indeed, in many respects he seems amoral. It does seem to have been true that his nature was kind, generous and inclined to forget grudges and turn enemies into friends, but he was also willing to be utterly ruthless. He was an inveterate womaniser, disloyal to his wives and his numerous lovers. Cleopatra is by far the most famous of these – and the romance may have been genuine on both sides, but it did not stop Caesar from having an affair with another queen soon afterwards, or from continuing his pursuit of the aristocratic women of Rome. He was extremely proud, even vain, especially of his appearance. It is hard to avoid the conclusion that from a young age Caesar was absolutely convinced of his own superiority. Much of this self-esteem was justified, for he was brighter and more capable than the overwhelming majority of other senators. Perhaps like Napoleon he was so fascinated by his own character that this made it easier to enthral others. Also like the French emperor there were many contradictions in his character. Sir Arthur Conan Doyle once wrote of Napoleon that: 'He was a wonderful man – perhaps the most wonderful man who ever lived. What strikes me is the lack of finality in his character. When you make up your mind that he is a complete villain, you come on some noble trait, and then your admiration of this is lost in some act of incredible meanness.'[1] There is something of the same odd mixture with Caesar, although perhaps it was less extreme.

It is striking that while today academics are supposed to be trained to examine the past dispassionately, it is very rare to meet an ancient historian who does not have a strong opinion about Caesar. In the past some have admired, even idolised, him, seeing him as a visionary who perceived the huge problems facing the Republic and realised how to solve them. Others are far more critical and view him as merely another aristocrat with very traditional ambitions who scrambled to the top regardless of the cost to law and precedent, but then had no clear idea of what to do with his power. Such commentators tend to emphasise the opportunism that marked his rise to power. Caesar certainly was an opportunist, but the same has surely been true of virtually every successful politician. He believed strongly in the power of chance in all human affairs and felt that he was especially lucky. With hindsight we know that Octavian – these days more often referred to as Augustus – created the system through which emperors would rule the Roman Empire for centuries. Debate rages over the extent to which Caesar's years in control of Rome began what Augustus was able to complete, or were a false start and only provided an example that his adopted son consciously avoided in an effort to escape the same fate. Opinion remains fiercely divided and it is unlikely that this will ever change. The truth probably lies somewhere between the extreme views.

The aim of this book is to examine Caesar's life on its own terms, and to place it firmly within the context of Roman society in the first century BC. It is not concerned with what happened after his death, and there will be no real discussion of the differences between his regime and that which evolved in the years when Augustus held power. Instead the focus is on what Caesar did, and on trying to understand why and how he did it. Hindsight is obviously inevitable, but it does attempt to avoid assuming that the Civil War and the collapse of the Republic were inevitable, or the opposite extreme, which claims that there was nothing wrong with the Republic at all. There has been a tendency in the past for books to look at Caesar either as a politician or as a general. This distinction had no real meaning at Rome, in contrast to modern Western democracies. A Roman senator received military and civilian tasks to perform throughout his career, both being a normal part of public life. Neither one can fully be understood without the other, and here the two will be covered in equal detail. This is a long book, but it cannot hope to provide a full account of politics at Rome during Caesar's lifetime, nor does it attempt a complete analysis of the campaigns in Gaul and the Civil War. The focus is always on Caesar, and no more description is provided for events in which he was not personally involved than is essential. Many points of controversy are skimmed over – for instance, the details of a particular law or trial at Rome, or topographic and other questions related to military operations. However interesting, such points would be digressions unless they have a significant part to play in understanding Caesar. Those so inclined will be able to find out more about such things from the works cited in the notes collected at the end of this book. Similarly, as far as possible the main text avoids direct mention of the many distinguished scholars who have written about Caesar and discussion of their specific interpretations. Such things are a major and essential concern in an academic study, but are tedious in the extreme for the general reader. Once again the relevant works are cited in the notes at the end of the book.

For all his fame, and the fact that he lived in probably the best documented decades of Roman history, there are still many things we do not know about Caesar. Most of our evidence has been available for some time. Archaeological excavation continues to reveal more about the world in which Caesar lived – at the time of writing on-going work in, for instance, France and Egypt is likely to tell us a good deal more about Gaul in Caesar's day and the Alexandria of Cleopatra. However, it is unlikely that any discoveries will radically alter our understanding of Caesar's career and life. For this we are largely reliant on the literary sources in Latin and Greek that have survived from the ancient world, occasionally supplemented by inscriptions on bronze or in stone. Caesar's own *Commentaries* on his campaigns survive and provide us with detailed accounts of his campaigns in Gaul and the first two years of the Civil War. They are supplemented by four extra books written after his death by his officers, which cover his remaining operations. In addition we have the letters, speeches and theoretical works of Cicero, which provide us with a wealth of detail for this period. Cicero's correspondence, which includes letters written to him by many of the leading men of the Republic, was published after his death and contains a handful of short messages from Caesar himself. We know that complete books of correspondence between Cicero and Caesar, as well as another consisting of exchanges between Cicero and Pompey, were published, but sadly these have not survived. The same is true of Caesar's other literary works and published speeches. It is always important to remind ourselves that only a tiny fraction of one per cent of the literature of the ancient world is available today. There are some deliberate omissions from Cicero's published letters, most notably his letters to his friend Atticus in the first three months of 44 BC. Atticus was involved in the release of the correspondence, but this did not occur until Augustus was established as master of Rome. It is more than likely that the missing letters contained something that might have implicated Atticus in involvement in the conspiracy against Caesar, or more probably suggested either knowledge of it or subsequent approval, and that these were deliberately suppressed to protect himself. Another nearly contemporary source is Sallust, who wrote several histories, including an account of Catiline's conspiracy. During the Civil War Sallust had fought for Caesar and been reinstated to the Senate as a reward. Sent to govern Africa, he was subsequently condemned for extortion, but was let off by Caesar. More favourable to Caesar than Cicero, Sallust wrote with the benefit of hindsight and his opinion of the dictator seems to have become rather mixed. Ironically, given his own career – though he always strenuously denied any wrongdoing – his theme was that all of Rome's ills were caused by a moral decline amongst the aristocracy, and so inevitably this coloured his narrative. Cicero, Sallust and Caesar were all active participants in public life. Caesar in particular wrote to celebrate his deeds and win support for his continuing career. Neither he nor the others were dispassionate observers keen only to report unvarnished fact.

Most other sources are much later. Livy wrote during the reign of Augustus and so some events were still within living memory, but the books covering this period have been lost and only brief summaries survive. Velleius Paterculus wrote a little later and there is some useful material in his brief narrative of the period. However, a good deal of our evidence for Caesar was not written until the early second century AD, over one hundred and fifty years after the dictator's murder. The Greek writer Appian produced a massive history of Rome, of which two books cover the civil wars and disturbances from 133 to 44 BC. Plutarch was also Greek, but his most important work for our purposes was his *Parallel Lives*, biographies pairing a famous Greek and Roman figure. Caesar was paired with Alexander the Great as the two most successful generals of all time. Also of relevance are his lives of Marius, Sulla, Crassus, Pompey, Cicero, Cato, Brutus and Mark Antony. Suetonius was a Roman who produced biographies of the first twelve emperors, beginning with Caesar. Cassius Dio was of Greek origin, but was also a Roman citizen and a senator who was active in public life in the early third century AD. He provides the most detailed continuous narrative of the period. All of these writers had access to sources, many of them contemporary to Caesar and including some of his own lost works, which are no longer available. Yet we need always to remind ourselves that each was written much later, and we cannot always be sure that they understood or accurately reflected the attitudes of the first century BC. There are some notable gaps in our evidence. By a curious coincidence the opening section of both

Suetonius' and Plutarch's biographies of Caesar are missing and so we do not know with absolute certainty in which year he was born. Each author had his own biases, interest or viewpoint, and made use of sources that were in turn prejudiced and often open propaganda. Care needs to be taken when using any source. Unlike those studying more recent history, ancient historians often have to make the best of limited and possibly unreliable sources, as well as balancing apparently contradictory accounts. Throughout I have attempted to give some idea of this process.

Some aspects of Caesar's inner life remain closed to us. It would be interesting and revealing to know more about his personal and private relationships with his family, his wives, lovers and friends. In the case of the latter it does seem that for much of his life and certainly in his last years he had no friend who was in any way his equal, although he was clearly close to and fond of many of his subordinates and assistants. We also know next to nothing about his religious beliefs. Ritual and religion pervaded every aspect of life in the Roman world. Caesar was one of Rome's most senior priests and regularly carried out or presided over prayers, sacrifices and other rites. He also made the most of the family tradition that claimed descent from the goddess Venus. We have no idea, however, what any of this meant to him. He was rarely, if ever, restrained from doing anything because of religious scruples and was willing to manipulate religion for his own benefit, but that does not necessarily mean that he was entirely cynical and had no beliefs. In the end we simply do not know. Part of the fascination with Caesar is because he is so difficult to pin down and because mysteries remain, for instance, as to what he really intended in the last months of his life. In his fifty-six years he was at times many things, including a fugitive, prisoner, rising politician, army leader, legal advocate, rebel, dictator – perhaps even a god – as well as a husband, father, lover and adulterer. Few fictional heroes have ever done as much as Caius Julius Caesar.

PART ONE

❖

THE RISE TO THE CONSULSHIP

100–59 BC

I

CAESAR'S WORLD

'For, when Rome was freed of the fear of Carthage, and her rival in empire was out of her way, the path of virtue was abandoned for that of corruption, not gradually, but in headlong course. The older discipline was discarded to give place to the new. The state passed from vigilance to slumber, from the pursuit of arms to the pursuit of pleasure, from activity to idleness.'
– *Velleius Paterculus, early first century AD.*[1]

'The Republic is nothing, merely a name without body or shape.'
– *Julius Caesar.*[2]

By the end of the second century BC the Roman Republic was the only great power left in the Mediterranean world. Carthage, the Phoenician colony whose trading empire had dominated the West for so long, had been razed to the ground by the legions in 146 BC. At almost the same time, Alexander the Great's homeland of Macedonia became a Roman province. The other major kingdoms that had emerged when Alexander's generals had torn apart his vast but short-lived empire had already been humbled and had dwindled to shadows of their former might. Many of the lands in and around the Mediterranean – the entire Italian Peninsula, southern Gaul, Sicily, Sardinia and Corsica, Macedonia and part of Illyricum, Asia Minor, much of Spain and a corner of North Africa – were directly ruled by the Romans. Elsewhere Rome's power was acknowledged, however grudgingly, or at the very least feared. None of the kingdoms, tribes or states in contact with the Romans could match their power and there was no real prospect of their uniting in opposition. In 100 BC Rome was hugely strong and very rich and there was nothing to suggest that this would change. With hindsight, we know that Rome would in fact grow even stronger and richer, and within little more than a century would have conquered the bulk of an empire that would endure for five centuries.

Rome's rise from a purely Italian power to Mediterranean superpower had been rapid, shockingly so to the Greek-speaking world, which had in the past scarcely regarded this particular group of western barbarians. The struggle with Carthage had lasted over a century and involved massive losses, whereas the defeat of the Hellenistic powers had taken half the time and been achieved at trifling cost. A generation before Caesar's birth, the Greek historian Polybius had written a *Universal History* with the express purpose of explaining just how Rome's dominance had been achieved. He had himself witnessed the closing stages of the process, having fought against the Romans in the Third Macedonian War (172–167 BC), then gone to Rome as a hostage, living in the household of a Roman nobleman and accompanying him on campaign to witness the destruction of Carthage. Although he paid attention to the effectiveness of the Roman military system, Polybius believed that Rome's success rested far more on its political system. For him the Republic's constitution, which was carefully balanced to prevent any one individual or section of society from gaining overwhelming control, granted Rome freedom from the frequent revolution and civil strife that had plagued most Greek city-states. Internally stable, the Roman Republic was able to devote itself to waging war on a scale and with a relentlessness unmatched by any rival. It is doubtful that any other contemporary state could have survived the catastrophic losses and devastation inflicted by Hannibal, and still gone on to win the war.[3]

Caesar was born into a Republic that was some four centuries old and had proved itself in Rome's steady rise. Rome itself would go on to even greater power, but the Republican system was nearing an end. In his own lifetime Caesar would see the Republic torn apart by civil wars – conflicts in which he himself was to play a leading role. Some Romans felt that the system had not outlived Caesar, many naming him as its principal assassin. None doubted that the Republic was no more than a memory by the time that Caesar's adopted son Augustus had made himself Rome's first emperor. For all its earlier, long-term success, the Roman Republic was nearing the end of its life by the close of the second century BC with some signs that not everything was functioning properly.

In 105 BC a group of migrating Germanic tribes called the Cimbri and Teutones had smashed an exceptionally large Roman army at Arausio (modern Orange in southern France). The casualties from this battle rivalled those of Cannae in 216 BC, when Hannibal had massacred almost 50,000 Roman and allied soldiers in a single day. It was the latest and worst of a string of defeats inflicted by these barbarians, who had been provoked into

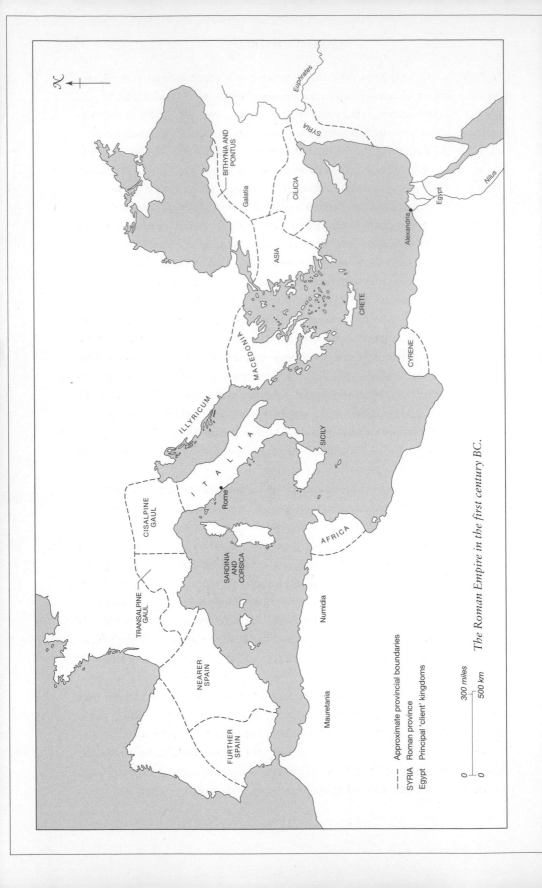

The Roman Empire in the first century BC.

Approximate provincial boundaries
SYRIA   Roman province
Egypt   Principal 'client' kingdoms

0   300 miles
0   500 km

Euphrates

SYRIA

BITHYNIA AND
PONTUS

CILICIA

Galatia

ASIA

Egypt

Nilus

Alexandria

CRETE

CYRENE

MACEDONIA

ILLYRICUM

I T A L I A

SICILY

Rome

AFRICA

CISALPINE
GAUL

SARDINIA
AND
CORSICA

Numidia

TRANSALPINE
GAUL

NEARER
SPAIN

Mauretania

FURTHER
SPAIN

fighting by the first Roman commander to encounter them back in 113 BC. The Cimbri and Teutones were peoples on the move in search of new land, not a professional army engaged in an all-out war. In battle their warriors were terrifying in appearance and individually brave, but they lacked discipline. At a strategic level the tribes were not guided by rigid objectives. After Arausio they wandered off towards Spain, not returning to invade Italy for several years. This temporary relief did little to reduce the widespread panic at Rome, fuelled by folk memories of the sack of the city in 390 BC by large, fair complexioned and savage warriors – in that case Gauls rather than Germans – but the Romans retained a deep-seated fear of all northern barbarians. There was widespread criticism of the incompetent aristocratic generals who had presided over the recent disasters. Instead they insisted that the war against the tribes must now be entrusted to Caius Marius, who had just won a victory in Numidia, ending a war that had also initially been characterised by corruption and ineptitude in high places. Marius was married to Caesar's aunt and was the first of his family to enter politics, and had already achieved much by being elected as one of the two consuls for 107 BC. The consuls were the senior executive officers of the Republic, charged with the most important civil responsibilities or military commands for the twelve months during which they held office. Ten years were supposed to elapse before a man was permitted to hold a second consulship, but Marius was voted into the office for five consecutive years from 104 to 100 BC. This was both unprecedented and of dubious legality, but did have the desired result, as he defeated the Teutones in 102 BC and the Cimbri in the following year.[4]

Marius' successive consulships violated a fundamental principle of Roman public life, but they could be interpreted as a necessary expedient to guide the State through a time of crisis. In the past the Republic had demonstrated a degree of flexibility, which had helped the Romans to deal with other emergencies. Far more disturbing was the recent tendency for political disputes to turn violent. In the autumn of 100 BC, a senator called Memmius, who had just been elected to the consulship for the following year, was beaten to death in the Forum by the henchmen of one of the unsuccessful candidates. This man, Caius Servilius Glaucia, along with his associate Lucius Appuleius Saturninus had employed threats and mob violence before to force through their legislation. They were widely believed to have arranged the murder of another of their rivals in the previous year. Memmius' lynching was blatant and prompted a swift backlash. Marius, who up until this point had been content to use Saturninus for his own purposes, now turned against him and responded to the Senate's call for him to save the Republic. Arming his supporters, he blockaded Saturninus and Glaucia's partisans on the Capitoline Hill, and soon forced them to surrender. Marius may have promised the radicals their lives, but the general mood was less inclined to lenience. Most of the captives were shut in the Senate House when a crowd mobbed the building. Some climbed onto the roof and started tearing off the tiles, hurling the heavy projectiles down into the interior until all the prisoners had been killed. To protect the Republic, normal law had been suspended and violence was crushed by greater violence. It was a far cry from the, admittedly idealised, picture of the perfectly balanced constitution presented by Polybius, although even he had hinted that Rome's internal stability might not always endure. To understand Caesar's story we must first look at the nature of the Roman Republic, both in theory and in the changing practice of the closing decades of the second century BC.[5]

THE REPUBLIC

Tradition maintained that Rome had been founded in 753 BC. For the Romans this was Year One and subsequent events were formally dated as so many years from the 'foundation of the city' (*ab urbe condita*). The archaeological evidence for the origins of Rome is less clear-cut, since it is difficult to judge when the small communities dotted around the hills of what would become Rome merged into a single city. Few records were preserved from the earliest periods and there were many things that even the Romans did not know with certainty by the time they began to write histories at the beginning of the second century BC. The tales of the City's early days probably contain some measure of truth, but it is all but impossible to verify individuals and particular incidents. Clearly, Rome was first ruled by kings, although it is hard to know whether any of the seven individual monarchs recorded in tradition were actual figures. Near the end of the sixth century BC – the traditional date of 509 BC may well be accurate – internal upheaval resulted in the monarchy being replaced by a republic.

The political system of the Roman Republic evolved gradually over many years and was never rigidly fixed. Resembling more modern Britain than the United States of America, Rome did not have a written constitution, but a patchwork of legislation, precedent and tradition. The expression *res publica,* from which we have derived our word republic, literally means 'the public thing' and can perhaps best be translated as 'the State' or the 'body politic'. The vagueness ensured that it meant different things to different people. Caesar would later dismiss it as an empty phrase.[6] The looseness of the system permitted considerable flexibility, which for centuries proved a source of strength. At the same time its very nature ensured that any new precedent or law, whether good or bad, could easily modify forever the way that things were done. At the heart of the system was the desire to prevent any one individual from gaining too much permanent power. Fear of a revival of monarchic rule was widespread and most deeply entrenched among the aristocracy, who monopolised high office. Therefore power within the Republic was vested in a number of different institutions, the most important of which were the magistrates, the Senate and the Popular Assemblies.

Magistrates had considerable power, the most senior formally holding *imperium*, the right to command troops and dispense justice, but this was essentially temporary and lasted only for the twelve months of office. It was also limited by the equal power of colleagues holding the same office. There were two consuls each year and six praetors holding the next most important magistracy. A man could not seek re-election to the same post until a ten-year interval had elapsed, nor could he stand in the first place until he had reached the age of thirty-nine for the praetorship and forty-two for the consulship. There was no division between political and military power and the magistrates performed military or civil tasks as necessary. The most important duties and military commands went to the consuls, the lesser to the praetors. Most senior magistrates were sent out to govern a province during their year of office. The Senate was able to extend a consul or praetor's *imperium* as a pro-magistrate – proconsul or propraetor respectively – on an annual basis. This was frequently necessary to provide the Republic with the number of provincial governors needed to control a large empire, but it did not alter the essentially temporary nature of power. An extension of more than two years was extremely rare. Therefore, while the offices themselves wielded great power, the individual consuls and other magistrates changed every year.

In contrast the Senate's importance was based less on its formal functions than its sheer permanence. It consisted of around 300 senators and met when summoned by a magistrate, usually a consul when one was present. Senators were not elected, but enrolled – and very occasionally expelled – in the Senate by the two censors, who every five years carried out a census of Roman citizens. It was expected that these would enrol anyone elected to a magistracy since the last census, although there was no legal obligation to do this. However, there were comparatively few offices to hold, and many senators, perhaps half, had never been elected to a magistracy. Senators had to belong to the equestrian order, the wealthiest property-holding class listed in the census. Their name, *equites* or 'knights', derived from their traditional role as cavalrymen in the Roman army. However, the vast majority of equestrians never sought to enter public life and the Senate tended to be drawn from an informal inner elite within the class. Wealthy, and given a prominent role in guiding the State, they were therefore men who had a strong vested interest in preserving the Republic. Debates were dominated by the ex-magistrates, for procedure dictated that the former consuls be asked their opinion first, followed by the former praetors and so on down to the most junior posts. Individuals who had served the Republic in a prominent position possessed huge influence or *auctoritas (see p. 524)* and the collective prestige of the Senate as a body was based to a large extent on the inclusion of such men. The Senate did not have the power to legislate, but the decrees resulting from its debates went to the Popular Assemblies for approval with a very strong recommendation. It also acted as an advisory council for the magistrates when these were in Rome, decided which provinces would be available for each year, and could grant *imperium* as a pro-magistrate. In addition, it was the Senate that received foreign embassies and despatched ambassadors, and also sent commissioners to oversee administrative arrangements in the provinces, giving it a critical role in shaping foreign affairs.

The various voting assemblies of the Roman people possessed considerable power within the Republic, but had little or no scope for independent action. They elected all magistrates, passed laws and had formally to ratify declarations of war and the peace treaties concluding a conflict. All adult male citizens were able to vote if they were present, but their votes were not all of equal value. In the *Comitia Centuriata*, which elected the consuls and had a number of other important functions, the people were divided into voting units based upon their property as registered in the most recent census. Its structure had its origins in the organisation of the archaic Roman army, where the wealthiest were best able to afford the expensive equipment required to fight in the more conspicuous and dangerous roles. Inevitably there were fewer members in the most senior voting units or centuries, simply because there were fewer rich than poor. Each century's vote was supposed to carry equal weight, but those of the wealthier classes voted first and it was often the case that a decision had already been reached before the poorest centuries had had their say. Other assemblies were based on tribal divisions, again determined by the census, and here the inequalities were similarly great if of a slightly different character. Each tribe voted according to a majority decision of those members present. However, the urban tribes, which included many of Rome's poor, usually contained on the day of any vote far more citizens than the rural tribes, where only the wealthy members were likely to have travelled to Rome. Therefore in most respects the opinion of the more prosperous citizens had a far greater impact on the outcome of all votes than that of the more numerous poor. None of these assemblies provided an opportunity for debate. Instead they simply chose from a list of candidates or voted for or against a particular proposal. Assemblies were summoned by a magistrate, who presided over them and dictated their business. Compared to the Assembly of Athens in the later fifth century BC, the democratic elements within the Roman system might seem tightly controlled, but that does not mean that they were unimportant. The outcome of voting, particularly in elections, remained unpredictable.

Only those registered as equestrians in the highest property class in the census were eligible for a political career. Reaching the magistracies depended on winning favour with the electorate. At Rome there was nothing even vaguely resembling modern political parties – although given the stifling impact of these, this may well have made it more rather than less democratic than many countries today – and each candidate for office competed as an individual. Only rarely did they advocate specific policies, although commenting on issues of current importance was more common. In the main voters looked more for a capable individual who once elected could do whatever the State required. Past deeds stood as proof of ability, but where these were lacking, especially at the early stages of a career, a candidate paraded the achievements of earlier generations of his family. The Romans believed strongly that families possessed clear character traits and it was assumed that a man whose father and grandfather had fought successful wars against Rome's foes would prove similarly capable himself. Aristocratic families took great pains to advertise the deeds of their members, past and present, so that their names sparked recognition amongst the voters. The combination of their fame and wealth allowed a comparatively small number of families to dominate the ranks of the magistracies and, in particular, the consulship. Even so, it was never impossible for a man, even one who was the first of his family to enter the Senate, to become consul. Someone who achieved this feat was known as a 'new man' (*novus homo*). Marius, with his unprecedented string of consulships, was the greatest of these, and for most 'new men' a single term was a sufficiently difficult achievement. Politics was highly competitive and even members of established families needed to work to maintain their advantage. The number of each college of magistrates declined with seniority, so that the struggle for office became even harder as a man progressed up the ladder. By simple arithmetic, only one-third of the six praetors elected each year could hope to become consul. This fierce competitiveness ensured that long-term political groupings were rare, and permanent parties unimaginable, for no one could share a magistracy.

In many ways the system worked well, providing the Republic each year with a new crop of magistrates, all eager to do great deeds on Rome's behalf before their twelve months of office expired. The formal power of *imperium* lasted only for this time, but a man's successes would greatly enhance his *auctoritas*. Like so many Roman concepts this term is hard to translate in a single English word, for it combined authority, reputation and influence with sheer importance or status. *Auctoritas* endured after an office was laid down, though it could be diminished by a man's subsequent behaviour or eclipsed by that of other senators. It determined how often and how early a man's opinion would be sought by the magistrate presiding over a meeting of the Senate, and the weight his view would carry with others. *Auctoritas* existed only when it was acknowledged by others, but men were aware of their status and could at times use it bluntly. In 90 BC the distinguished former consul and censor, and current senior senator (*princeps senatus*), Marcus Aemilius Scaurus was accused of taking bribes from a hostile king. His prosecutor was the undistinguished Quintus Varius Severus, who, although a Roman, had been born in the city of Sucro in Spain. As the key to his defence, Scaurus turned to the court and the watching crowd and asked a simple question. 'Varius Severus of Sucro claims that Aemilius Scaurus, seduced by a royal bribe, betrayed the *imperium* of the Roman people; Aemilius Scaurus denies the charge. Which of the two would you rather believe?' In reply Varius was jeered from the court and the charge dropped.[7]

Competition did not stop when a man won the consulship. His subsequent status depended on how well he performed in the office in comparison with other consuls. Leading an army to victory over an enemy of the Republic was a great achievement, especially if it was acknowledged by the award of a triumph on his return to Rome. In this ceremony the victor rode in a chariot through the centre of the city as part of a procession including his captives, the spoils won and other symbols of success, as well as his own soldiers parading in their finest equipment. The general was dressed in the regalia of Rome's most important deity, Jupiter Optimus Maximus, even to the extent of having his face painted red to resemble the old terracotta statues of the god. Behind him stood a slave holding the victor's laurel wreath over the general's head, but also whispering a reminder that he was a mortal. It was a great honour, commemorated for ever by hanging laurel wreaths (or carving their likeness) in the porch of a man's house. Such an achievement was highly valued, but it was also compared to the victories of other senators. It was important to have won better and greater battles over stronger or more exotic enemies for this enhanced a man's *auctoritas* in relation to other former generals. Most men had won and completed their first consulship by the time they were in their mid forties, and could expect to live on and remain active in the Senate for decades. Their continued prominence in public life depended on their *auctoritas*, and in time might further add to this. Competition was at the heart of Roman public life, senators struggling throughout their careers to win fame and influence for themselves, and prevent others from acquiring too much of the same things. The annual election of new magistrates and the restrictions on office-holding helped to provide many senators with the chance to serve the Republic in a distinguished capacity, and prevented any one individual from establishing a monopoly of glory and influence. All aristocrats wanted to excel, but their deepest fear was always that someone else would surpass all rivals by too great a margin and win a more permanent pre-eminence, raising the spectre of monarchy. Too much success for an individual reduced the number of honours available for everyone else to contest.

Although the Republic had become the great power of the Mediterranean world by the end of the second century BC, Rome itself remained the focus of all aspects of political life. There, and only there, could the Senate meet, courts convene or Popular Assemblies gather to elect magistrates or pass legislation. By 100 BC Rome was the largest city in the known world, dwarfing even its nearest rivals such as Alexandria. By the close of the first century BC its population may well have been around the million mark, and even in 100 BC there were certainly several hundred thousand people living there, perhaps half a million or more. We lack the evidence to be more precise, but these numbers at least give some sense of the order of magnitude. Huge though the population was, in an age before any form of transport faster than a man could walk or ride, Rome did not sprawl over as wide an area as more modern cities. Housing, especially in the poorer areas, was very densely packed. Yet at the heart of Rome in every sense was the open space of the Forum. This was a place of commerce, from the fashionable shops, which bordered on its great buildings and provided the luxuries that were the prize of empire, to the representatives of the big merchant companies and grain

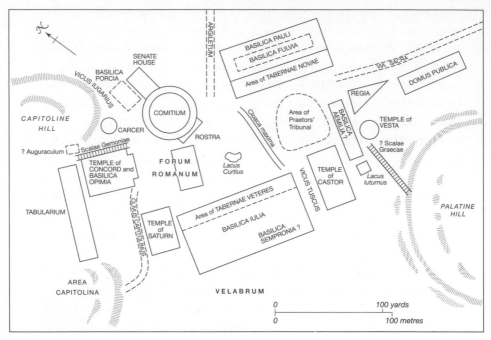

The City of Rome – central area, Forum etc. (after CAH² ix (1994) p.370). Some of the details are conjectural.

suppliers. It was also the place of law and justice, where the courts convened, advocates presented their cases and juries gave their verdict, all in open view. Through the Forum ran the Sacra Via, the route of triumphal processions. More than anything else, it was in and around the Forum that the public life of the Republic was conducted. Magistrates, such as the tribunes, aediles and praetors, had set places in the Forum where they sat to conduct business. When the Senate met it was with very rare exceptions in a building on the edge of the Forum, either the Senate House (Curia) or one of the great temples. Outside the Senate House was the Speakers Platform or Rostra, whose name was derived from its decoration with the prows of enemy warships during the wars with Carthage. From the Rostra speeches were made to informal meetings of the Roman people as magistrates and prominent men sought to persuade them to vote for or against a bill, or to favour someone at an election. At the command of a suitable magistrate, the same crowd of Romans could be told to convene as an Assembly of tribes (either the *Concilium Plebis* or *Comitia Tributa*) and pass legislation. Other than for elections, this almost always occurred in the Forum. In so many ways the Forum was the beating heart of Rome.[8]

THE PROFITS AND THE PRICE OF EMPIRE

The Roman Republic was frequently at war, for long periods virtually on an annual basis. Frequent war-making was not unusual in the ancient world, where states rarely needed much more reason to attack their neighbours than a belief that they were vulnerable. The great period of Classical Greek culture, with its flourishing arts, literature and philosophy, had come at a period when warfare between the Greek city-states was endemic. Yet from early on in its history Rome's war-making was distinctive in character, not simply because it was so successful, but through its talent for consolidating success on a permanent basis, as defeated enemies were absorbed and turned into reliable allies. By the beginning of the third century BC virtually all of the Italian Peninsula had come under Roman control. Within this territory some communities had been granted Roman citizenship and these, in addition to the colonies planted on conquered land, allowed the number of Roman citizens to grow in size far beyond the populations of other city-states. Other peoples were granted Latin status, conveying lesser, though still significant privileges, while the remainder were simply allies or *socii*. Comparatively early on, both Roman and Latin status had lost any real association with particular ethnic or even linguistic groups, and had become primarily legal distinctions. Over time, communities not granted such privileges could hope to gain them, progressing by stages from Latin rights to citizenship without the vote, and finally to full Roman citizenship. Each community was tied to Rome by a specific treaty, which made clear both its rights and obligations. Even more obvious was the fundamental fact that Rome was the superior partner in any such agreement and that this was not a settlement between equals. The most common obligation of all types of ally, including the Latins, was to supply Rome with men and resources in time of war. At least half of any Roman army invariably consisted of allied soldiers. In this way the defeated enemies of the past helped to win the wars of the present. Apart from confirming their loyalty to Rome in this way, the allied communities were also allowed a small, but significant, share in the profits of warfare. Since Roman war-making was so frequent – and some scholars have even suggested that the Republic needed to go to war to remind her allies of their obligations – there were plenty of opportunities for both service and profit.[9]

In 264 BC the Romans sent an army outside Italy for the first time, provoking the long conflict with the Carthaginians, who were of Phoenician origin, hence the Roman name of *Poeni* (Punic). The First Punic War

(264–241 BC) brought Rome its first overseas province in Sicily, to which was added Sardinia in the conflict's immediate aftermath. The Second Punic War (218–201 BC) resulted in a permanent Roman presence in Spain and involvement in Macedonia. The Republic's huge reserves of citizen and allied manpower and the willingness to absorb staggeringly high losses were major factors in securing the victory over Carthage. These conflicts also accustomed the Romans to despatching and supplying armies very far afield, something that was made possible by the creation of a large navy during the First Punic War. The Republic became used to waging war in several widely different theatres simultaneously. In the early decades of the second century BC, Rome defeated Macedonia and the Seleucid Empire. These, along with the Ptolemies of Egypt, were the most powerful of the Hellenistic kingdoms to emerge from the wreck of Alexander the Great's empire. The destruction of both Carthage and Corinth at the hands of Roman armies in 146 BC symbolised Roman dominance over the older powers of the Mediterranean world. More provinces were established in Macedonia and Africa, while elsewhere the conquest of the Po Valley was completed and a presence in Illyricum reinforced. Near the end of the century Transalpine Gaul (modern Provence in southern France) was conquered, establishing a Roman controlled land link with the provinces in Spain, just as Illyricum provided a connection with Macedonia. Soon Roman roads would be constructed linking one province to another in a monumental but highly practical way. Around the same time, the wealthy province of Asia was acquired. The link between Rome and her overseas provinces was at this time far less intimate than the bonds with the peoples of Italy, and there was no question as yet of widespread grants of Latin or Roman status to the indigenous populations. Communities in the provinces often provided troops to serve with the Roman army, but this was not their most important obligation, which took the form of regular tribute or taxation.

Many Romans benefited greatly from overseas expansion. For the aristocracy it provided plentiful opportunities to win glory during their magistracies by fighting a war. Campaigns against the tribal peoples in Spain, Gaul, Illyricum and Thrace were frequent. Wars with the famous states of the Hellenistic world occurred less often but were far more spectacular. With warfare so frequent, competition amongst senators focused on having won a bigger or more dangerous war than anyone else, and the honour of being the first to defeat a people was equally valued. Along with glory came great riches from plunder and the sale of captives as slaves. Some of this wealth went to the Republic, and some to the men serving in the army, but since greater shares went to the more senior ranks, it was the commanders more than anyone else who benefited. Victories won in the eastern Mediterranean were especially lucrative, and during the second century BC a succession of generals returned from such wars to celebrate more lavish and more spectacular triumphs than had ever been seen before. It was at this period that the city of Rome began to be rebuilt in a far more spectacular form as successful commanders used some of their spoils to construct grand temples and other public buildings as permanent reminders of their achievements. Competition for fame and influence continued to dominate public life, but it was becoming an increasingly expensive business as some men brought back massive fortunes from their victories. Senators from families who had not managed to win commands during the most profitable campaigns had increasing difficulty maintaining the costs of a political career. The gap between the richest and poorest senators steadily widened, reducing the number of men able to compete for the highest magistracies and commands.

It was not only senators who profited from the creation of the empire, but in general it was the wealthy who did best in the new conditions. The Republic did not create an extensive bureaucratic machine to administer the provinces, so that governors had only a small number of officials supplemented by members of their own households with which to govern. As a result, much day-to-day business was left to the local communities and a good deal was carried out by private companies controlled by wealthy Romans. These men were usually members of the equestrian order, for senators themselves were forbidden by law from undertaking such contracts. (This was supposed to prevent business interests from influencing the opinions they expressed in the Senate. However, many may have covertly invested money in companies run openly by equestrians.) Companies headed by such men bid for the right to collect taxes in a region, to sell war captives and other plunder, or to undertake massive contracts supplying the army with food and equipment. They were known as the *publicani* – the publicans of the King James Bible – for undertaking such tasks required by the Republic, but their primary motive was profit and not public service. Once a company had agreed to pay the Treasury a set sum for the right to collect the taxes in a particular region or province, it was therefore necessary for them to collect more than this from the provincials. The company's agents at all levels were inclined to take a cut of the profits, and inevitably the amount actually taken from the population of the province was often substantially higher than the sum received by the Treasury. Yet in the main the Republic was satisfied with this arrangement and resentment on the part of the provincials could, if necessary, be met by the force of the army. Apart from the *publicani*, many other Romans and their agents were active in business in the provinces. Merely being a Roman – and most Italians were taken for Romans by other races – gave merchants (*negotiatores*) considerable advantages, simply through association with the imperial power. The more influential men – once again usually the wealthiest or their representatives – were often able to draw on more direct aid from provincial governors. The activities of traders rarely feature other than peripherally in our ancient sources, but it is important not to underestimate their numbers or the scale of their operations. Such men profited greatly from Roman imperialism, even if it seems extremely unlikely that they had much influence on the decision-making process that directed the Republic's foreign affairs.[10]

Over the generations, an exceptionally high proportion of Roman men served in the army. Not until the government in Revolutionary France introduced mass conscription did a state of comparable size mobilise so much of its manpower over so long a period of time. Until the middle of the second century BC there appears to have been little popular resistance to this, and most men willingly undertook their military duties. For some active service was very attractive, in spite of the extremely brutal discipline imposed on the legions, for there was every prospect of plunder and winning honours. The Romans were also fiercely patriotic and valued this demonstration of their commitment to the Republic. The army recruited from the propertied classes, for each soldier was expected to provide himself with the necessary equipment to serve as a horseman for the very wealthy, a heavy infantryman for the majority, or a light infantryman for the poorer and younger recruits. The heart of the legions consisted of farmers, for land remained the most common form of property. Service lasted until the legion was disbanded, which often occurred at the end of a war. In the early days of the Republic, a spell in the army may well have taken no more than a few weeks, or at most months, for the foe was usually close by and the fighting small in scale and brief in duration. Ideally it allowed the farmer-soldier to win a quick victory and then return home in time to harvest his own fields. As Rome expanded, wars were fought further and further away and tended to last longer. During the Punic Wars tens of thousands of Romans were away from their homes for years. A number of overseas provinces demanded permanent garrisons, so that men unfortunate enough to be posted to somewhere like Spain often had to undergo five or ten years' continuous service. In their absence their own small farms risked falling into ruin, their families into destitution. The situation was worsened as the minimum property qualification was lowered to provide more manpower, since such recruits inevitably lived that much closer to the poverty line. Prolonged military service ruined many small farmers, and the loss of their land meant that such men would in future lack sufficient property to make them eligible for call up to the legions. Concern grew from the middle of the second century BC that the number of citizens liable for the army was in terminal decline.

The difficulties of many small farmers occurred at the same time as other factors were reshaping Italian agriculture. The profits of expansion brought fabulous wealth to many senators and equestrians. Such men invested a good deal of their fortunes in huge landed estates, often absorbing land that had formerly been divided into many smallholdings. Such estates (*latifundia*) were invariably worked by a servile labour force, since frequent war ensured that slaves were both plentiful and cheap. The size of a man's landholdings, the number of slaves who worked them and the lavishness of the villas built for when the owner chose to visit were all new ways in which men could compete in displaying their fabulous riches. In more practical terms, large estates could be devoted to commercial farming, which provided a steady, low-risk profit. In many respects it was a vicious circle, as repeated wars in distant provinces took more citizen farmers away from their land and often left them and their families in penury, while the same conflicts further enriched the elite of society and provided them with the means to create more big *latifundia*. It has proved very difficult archaeologically to quantify the shifts in farming patterns in Italy during the period, and in some areas at least it seems that small-scale farming continued. Nevertheless, significant change clearly did occur over wide areas, and it is certain that the Romans themselves perceived this to be a serious problem.[11]

POLITICS AND BLOODSHED

In 133 BC Tiberius Sempronius Gracchus, one of the ten annually elected tribunes of the plebs, launched an ambitious reform programme aimed at dealing with this very problem. The tribunes differed from other magistrates in that they had no role outside Rome itself. Originally the office had been created to provide the people with some protection against the abuse of power by senior magistrates, but by this time it was essentially just another step in a normal career path. Tiberius was in his early thirties, from a highly distinguished family – his father had been censor and twice consul – and was expected to go far. In his tribunate he focused on the public land (*ager publicus*) confiscated over the centuries from defeated Italian enemies. In both law and theory this was supposed to have been shared out in comparatively small lots amongst many citizens, but in practice large swathes had been absorbed into *latifundia*. The tribune passed a law confirming the legal limit of public land each individual was permitted to occupy, and redistributing the rest to poor citizens, thus raising these to the property class eligible for military service. Some senators supported Gracchus, but many more stood to lose directly from the confiscation of improperly held public land, as did many influential equestrians. Unable to secure approval for his law in the Senate, Tiberius violated tradition by taking it directly to the Popular Assembly. When a colleague in the tribunate tried to stop proceedings by imposing his veto, Gracchus organised a vote and had the man deposed from office. This may or may not have been legal, since in theory the people could legislate on anything, but it struck at the very heart of the Republican system by challenging the assumption that all magistrates of the same rank were equal.

Some senators who may have sympathised with the aims of Gracchus' legislation became worried that the tribune's ambitions had more to do with personal dominance than altruistic reform, for Tiberius stood to gain vast prestige and *auctoritas* if he was successful in improving the lot of so many citizens. The fear grew that he was aiming at something even more spectacular than the very successful career expected for a man of his background. That Tiberius, his father-in-law and his younger brother Caius were the three commissioners appointed to oversee the distribution of land raised more hackles by giving them so much patronage. Some began to accuse him of seeking *regnum*, the permanent power of a monarch. The final straw came when Tiberius, claiming the need to ensure that his laws were not immediately repealed, stood for election as tribune for 132 BC. His success was not certain, since by the very nature of his reforms many of the citizens most indebted to him had been settled on farms too far from Rome for them to attend an election. However, emotions spilled over when the consul presiding over the Senate refused to take action against the tribune. A group of angry senators led by Tiberius' cousin, Scipio Nasica, stormed out of the meeting and lynched the tribune and many of his supporters. Gracchus had his head staved in with a chair leg. His body, along with those of many of his supporters, was thrown into the Tiber.

This was the first time that political disputes had ended in widespread and fatal violence, and Rome was left in a state of shock. (A few stories of the early years of the Republic told of demagogues or other men who had threatened the State being lynched, but these had long been consigned to ancient history in the Roman mind.) In the aftermath of the riot much of Tiberius' legislation remained in force, even as some of his surviving supporters came under attack. The tribune's brother Caius was serving with the army in Spain at the time and on his eventual return to Rome was permitted to continue his career. Embittered by the fate of Tiberius, Caius was still in his early twenties and it was not until he was elected to the tribunate in 123 BC that he embarked upon his own series of reforms, which were far more radical and wide ranging than those of his brother. In part this was because he had more time, managing to gain a second term as tribune for 122 BC without provoking any serious opposition. Many of his reforms were concerned with sharing the spoils of empire more widely. Caius confirmed his brother's legislation and extended his drive to restore the number of property-owning citizens by establishing a colony on the site of Carthage. He also won many supporters amongst the equestrian order by establishing a court to try senators accused of malpractice while serving as provincial governors (the *quaestio de rebus repetundis*) and forming the jury from equestrians. Up until this point a senator had only ever been tried by his peers. Less popular with Romans was Caius' move to extend citizenship to many more Latins and Italians, and his attempt to win a third term as tribune failed. From the beginning both Caius and his opponents were more prepared to employ intimidation and threats than anyone had been ten years before. Matters came to a head when a scuffle resulted in the death of one of the consul Opimius' servants. The Senate passed a decree – known to scholars as the *senatus consultum ultimum* (ultimate decree) due to a phrase used by Caesar, though it is not known what it was called at the time – calling upon the consul to defend the Republic by any means necessary. Normal law was suspended and the partisans of both sides armed themselves. Opimius added to his force a group of mercenary Cretan archers who were waiting just outside Rome, suggesting a degree of premeditation in his actions. Caius and his outnumbered supporters occupied the Temple of Diana on the Aventine Hill, but the consul refused all offers of negotiation and stormed the building. Gracchus died in the fighting and his head was brought to Opimius who had promised a reward of its weight in gold.[12]

We cannot know whether the Gracchi were genuine reformers desperate to solve what they saw as the Republic's problems, or ambitious men out solely to win massive popularity. Probably their motives were mixed, for it is hard to believe that a Roman senator could be unaware of the personal advantages to be gained through such sweeping legislation. Regardless of their personal motivation they highlighted existing problems within society, most notably the plight of the many poor citizens, and the desire of those excluded from power, whether the equestrian order or the population of Italy, to have some greater share of it. The impact of the Gracchi's careers on public life was not immediate – the vast majority of tribunes continued to be elected for only a single term and political violence was rare – but it was to prove profound. In a system so reliant on precedent, many fundamental principles had been shattered. The brothers had shown how great influence, if temporary and somewhat precarious, could be obtained by appealing to the growing consciousness of social groups in a new way. It was only a question of time before someone else would possess both the initial prestige and the desire to emulate them. Things were not helped by the inertia of the Senate in dealing with the problems that the Gracchi had highlighted, and its preference for doing nothing, rather than allowing anyone to gain credit through providing a solution. On top of this, the closing decades of the second century were not distinguished by widespread competence and honesty on the part of many magistrates.

A dynastic struggle in the allied Kingdom of Numidia in North Africa resulted in a succession of scandals, as senators were bribed on a lavish scale to favour the claim of Jugurtha. The massacre of thousands of Roman and Italian traders at the town of Cirta caused outrage at Rome, forcing an army to be sent against Jugurtha, but the war was waged in a lethargic way and in 110 BC this force was defeated and surrendered to the enemy. A consul of greater ability was sent to take charge after this, but the whole episode had seriously damaged the faith of the wider population in the ability of the senatorial elite to lead. Exploiting this mood, Caius Marius campaigned for the consulship for 107 BC, contrasting himself, a tough and experienced soldier who had succeeded only through personal merit, with the scions of the noble houses who relied on their ancestors' glory rather than their own ability. Marius won comfortably and, through the aid of a tribune who passed a law in the Assembly to override the Senate's allocation of provinces, was given the command in Numidia. A further attempt to frustrate him came when the Senate refused to let him raise new legions to take to Africa, instead granting him permission only to take volunteers. Marius outmanoeuvred them by seeking volunteers from the poorest class, men not normally eligible for military service. It was an important stage in the transition from a militia army conscripted from a cross-section of the property-owning classes, to a professional army recruited overwhelmingly from the very poor. The change was not instant, but its significance was to be deep and contributed much to the end of the Republic.[13]

Marius eventually won the war in Numidia by late 105 BC, but by this time the menace of the Cimbri and Teutones hung heavy over Italy. The early contacts with these tribes had again been marked by scandals and incompetence on the part of magistrates, many of them from the old established families. There was a strong feeling, evidently amongst the better off as well as the poor, for it was the former who dominated the voting in the *Comitia Centuriata*, that only Marius could be trusted to defeat the barbarians. This led to his unprecedented run of consulships, a far more serious breach of precedent than Caius Gracchus' consecutive tribunates. Saturninus and Glaucia offered support to Marius and at the same time hoped to capitalise on his success. In 103 BC Saturninus was tribune and passed a law granting land in North Africa to many of Marius' veterans from the war in Numidia. Caesar's father was one of the commissioners appointed to oversee the implementation of either this bill or more probably a similar one passed by Saturninus in 100 BC. The reliance on recruits from the poorest sections of society did mean that these men had no source of livelihood when they were discharged back to civilian life. Part of Saturninus' legislation in 100 BC was aimed at providing for the discharged soldiers of the operations against the Cimbri. Saturninus used the tribunate in much the same way as the Gracchi, bringing forward popular measures to distribute land, particularly land in the provinces, and renewing a measure that made wheat available to all citizens at a set price irrespective of the market. The latter had been introduced by Caius Gracchus, but abandoned after his death. Yet from the beginning Saturninus and Glaucia were less reputable than the Gracchi and far more inclined to resort to violence. In the end they went too far, losing the support of Marius who, acting under the Senate's ultimate decree just as Opimius had in 122 BC, led their suppression. The Republic into which Caesar was born was not coping well with some of the problems facing it.

II

CAESAR'S CHILDHOOD

'Born into the most noble family of the Julii, and tracing his ancestry back to Anchises and Venus – a claim acknowledged by all those who study the ancient past – he surpassed all other citizens in the excellence of his appearance.' – *Velleius Paterculus, early first century AD.*[1]

'In this Caesar there are many Mariuses.' – *Sulla.*[2]

Caius Julius Caesar was born on 13 July 100 BC according to the modern calendar. The day is certain, the year subject to just a little doubt, as by chance the opening sections of both Suetonius' and Plutarch's biographies of Caesar have been lost. A few scholars have dated his birth to 102 or 101, but their arguments have failed to convince, and the consensus of opinion remains firmly with a date of 100. By the Roman calendar Caesar was born on the third day before the Ides of Quinctilis in the consulship of Caius Marius and Lucius Valerius Flaccus, which in turn was the six hundredth and fifty-fourth year 'from the foundation of the City'. Quinctilis – the name is related to *quintus* or fifth – was the fifth month of the Republic's year, which began in March (*Martius*). Later during Caesar's dictatorship the month would be renamed Julius in his honour, hence the modern July. The Ides of Quinctilis, as in March, fell on the fifteenth, but the Romans included the day itself when they counted back or forward from such dates.

Names revealed much about a person's place in Roman society. Caesar possessed the full *tria nomina* or 'three names' of a Roman citizen. The first name (*praenomen*) served much the same purpose as its modern equivalent, identifying the individual member of a family and being used in informal conversation. Most families employed the same first names for their sons generation after generation. Caesar's father and grandfather were both also named Caius, as presumably had been many more first sons of this line of Julii Caesares. The second or main name (*nomen*) was most important for it was the name of the 'clan' or broad group of families to which a man belonged. The third name (*cognomen*) specified the particular branch of this wider grouping, although not all families even amongst the aristocracy were distinguished in this way. Caesar's great rival Cnaeus Pompey and his own lieutenant Mark Antony both belonged to families who did not possess *cognomina*. A few individuals acquired an additional, semi-official nickname, which, given the Romans' robust sense of humour, was often at the expense of their appearance. Pompey's father was known as Strabo or 'Squinty', as was a distant cousin of Caesar's, Caius Julius Caesar Strabo. Caesar's name was never added to in this way. As a boy he received the full three names, but had he been born a girl he would have been known only by the feminine form of the *nomen*. Caesar's aunt, sisters and daughter were all called simply Julia, as indeed was any female member of any branch of the Julian clan. If a family had more than one daughter, in official contexts their name was followed by a number to distinguish them. This disparity between the sexes says much about the Roman world. Men, and only men, could play a role in public life and it was important to know precisely who each individual was in the competitive world of politics. Women had no political role and did not need such specific identification.[3]

The Julii were patricians, which meant that they were members of the oldest aristocratic class at Rome, who in the early Republic had monopolised power, ruling over the far more numerous plebians. Little is known about the dozen or so members of the clan who won election to the higher magistracies in the first two centuries of the Republic. Unlike other more successful patrician clans such as the Fabii and Manlii, the Julii do not appear to have preserved and promoted the achievements of their ancestors as effectively. Several of these other families continued to be very influential while the patricians' exclusive hold on power was gradually eroded as the plebians demanded more rights, and wealthy plebian families forced their way into the ruling elite. From 342 BC one of each year's consuls had to be a plebian. By the end of the second century BC the majority of the most influential families amongst the senatorial elite were plebian. A few honours continued to be open only to patricians, who in turn were barred from becoming tribunes of the plebs, but on the whole the differences between the two were minimal. Merely being patrician did not guarantee political success for a family. There was no process for creating new patricians, and over the centuries a number of families died out altogether or faded into obscurity. The Julii survived, but enjoyed little prominence in public life. A Julius Caesar – the first man known to have had that cognomen – reached the praetorship during the Second Punic War. A much later author claimed that this man took the name because he had killed an enemy war elephant in battle and that it was copied from the Punic word for elephant. Another story was that the name meant 'hairy' and that the family were renowned for their thick heads of hair. The story may be an invention. It does seem that around about the same time the line divided into two distinct branches, both called Julius Caesar but registered in different tribes in the census. In 157 BC Lucius Julius Caesar reached the consulship, the only Caesar in the second century BC to manage this. He was not an ancestor of Caius, but came from the other, marginally more successful branch of the family. In the early years of the first century a number of Julii Caesares would begin to enjoy greater electoral success. In 91 BC Sextus Julius Caesar was consul, as was Lucius Julius Caesar in 90. The latter's younger brother, Caius Julius Caesar Strabo, was aedile in the same year. Aediles were junior magistrates whose responsibilities included the supervision of public festivals and entertainments. Lucius and Caius were from the other branch of the family, and so distant cousins of Caesar's father. Strabo was widely respected as one of the leading orators of his day. Sextus Julius Caesar is something of a mystery, as it is unclear from which branch of the family he came. It is even possible that he was Caesar's uncle, the younger, or perhaps more probably older, brother of his father Caius, but there is no positive evidence for this and he may instead have been a cousin.[4]

Although the Julii had made less of an impact on the Republic's history than other clans, their antiquity was widely acknowledged. They were said to have settled in Rome in the middle of the seventh century BC after the capture and destruction of the neighbouring city of Alba Longa by Tullus Hostilius, the Romans' third king. Yet the association with Rome's earliest days did not begin with this event, for the family claimed that their name was derived from Iulus, the son of Aeneas, the leader of the Trojan exiles who had settled in Italy after the fall of Troy. Aeneas himself was the son of the human Anchises and the goddess Venus, so that the ancestry of the Julii was divine. As yet the myths of these early times had not crystallised into the form they would take in the Augustan age, when the poet Virgil and the historian Livy would recount the stories in some detail. Even Livy would acknowledge that there were differing versions of the story of Aeneas and his descendants. He was unsure whether it was Iulus or another son of Aeneas who had founded Alba Longa and became its first king, establishing the dynasty that would in time produce Rhea Silvia, the mother of Romulus and Remus. There is little suggestion that in the early first century BC many

Romans were aware of such a possible association between the Julii and Romulus. In contrast the clan's claim of descent from Venus was fairly widely known and presumably not of recent invention. Part of the oration delivered by Caesar at his aunt's funeral in 69 BC is recorded by Suetonius:

> My Aunt Julia's family is descended on her mother's side from kings, and on her father's side from the immortal gods. For the Marcii Reges – her mother's family – descend from Ancus Marcius; the Julii – the clan of which our family is part – go back to Venus. Therefore our blood has both the sanctity of kings, who wield the greatest power amongst men, and an association with the reverence owed to the gods, who in turn hold power even over kings.[5]

Caesar clearly assumed that his audience would not be surprised by such statements. Some scholars have pointed out that the name *Rex* (King) may have been derived from a role in religious ceremonies early in the Republic rather than connection with the monarchy. This is almost certainly correct, but such distinctions are unlikely to have been too clear in the first century BC.

Virtually nothing is known about Caesar's grandfather, Caius Julius Caesar, but it is just possible that he may have held the praetorship. His wife was Marcia, daughter of Quintus Marcius Rex, who had been praetor in 144 BC. They had at least two children, Caesar's father Caius and his aunt Julia, who was to marry Caius Marius. As we have seen it is also possible that there was another son, Sextus, who reached the consulship in 91 BC. Caius embarked upon a public career with some success, holding the quaestorship either just before, or soon after the birth of his son. His wife was Aurelia, who came from a highly successful family of plebian nobles. Both her father and grandfather had reached the consulship, in 144 and 119 BC respectively, and three of her cousins, Caius, Marcus and Lucius Aurelius Cotta would also achieve this distinction. Marriage into this family probably did much to help the political prospects of Caius Caesar, but these were boosted even more as a result of his sister's marriage to Marius. As already noted, Caius was one of ten commissioners tasked with overseeing part of the colonisation programme created by Saturninus for Marius' veterans in 103 or 100 BC. In due course he would be elected praetor, but the year in which he achieved this is unknown, and estimates have varied from 92 BC to as late as 85 BC. An early date seems more likely, for the year as magistrate was followed by a period as governor of the province of Asia and the most likely time for this is about 91 BC. Caius died early in 84 BC, and we cannot know whether or not his connections would have been enough to lift him to the consulship. If his praetorship had indeed been as early as 92 BC, then he would certainly have been old enough to seek the highest magistracy – and if Sextus Caesar was in fact his brother, then his electoral success in 91 BC would surely have encouraged his brother. However, if Caius ever stood for the consulship then he evidently failed. Ultimately, our evidence for Caesar's family is so poor and confusing that there is very little that we can say with any certainty, beyond the overall conclusion that his father's career was reasonably successful, if unspectacular. We cannot say whether his achievements satisfied or disappointed Caius himself and his immediate family.

Caius and Aurelia are known to have had three children, Caesar and two sisters, both of course called Julia. It is more than possible that other children were born but failed to survive into adulthood for the rate of infant mortality was staggeringly high at Rome (and indeed throughout the ancient world), even amongst the aristocracy. Cornelia, the mother of the Gracchi, is said to have given birth to twelve babies, of whom only three – Tiberius, Caius and their sister Sempronia – survived. This was probably exceptional, but two or three children reaching maturity does seem to have been a steady average for senatorial families. There were exceptions; the Metelli, a plebeian noble family of considerable wealth and influence, seem to have been especially fertile and as a result figure heavily amongst the ranks of the senior magistracies in the last hundred years of the Republic.[6]

EARLY YEARS AND EDUCATION

Little has been recorded about Caesar's earliest years, but some things can be inferred from what is known more generally about the aristocracy in contemporary Rome. As in most societies until the comparatively recent past, babies were usually born at home. The birth of a child was an important event for a senatorial family and tradition demanded that it be witnessed. When the event seemed imminent, messages would be sent to inform relatives and political associates, who would usually then go to the house. Traditionally their role had been in part to act as witnesses that the child was truly a member of the aristocracy, and an element of this remained. Neither the father nor these guests would actually be present in the room where the mother was confined, attended by a midwife and probably some female relations as well as slaves.

In a few cases a male doctor might attend, but he was the only man present with the mother. Although the procedure would later bear his name, there is no ancient evidence to suggest that Caesar was delivered by Caesarean section, although the procedure was known in the ancient world. In fact, it is extremely unlikely, since the operation was usually fatal for the mother and Aurelia lived on for decades. (One much later source claims that one of Caesar's ancestors was born in this way.) Indeed, no source indicates that his birth was anything other than normal – breech deliveries or other difficult births were seen as a bad omen and are recorded for some individuals, most notably the Emperor Nero. Once the baby was born the midwife would lay it down on the floor and inspect it for abnormalities or defects, at the most basic level assessing its chance of survival. Only after this would the parents decide whether or not to accept and try to raise the child. In law this decision was to be made by the father, but it seems extremely unlikely the mother was not involved, especially when she was as formidable a character as Aurelia.[7]

Once a child had been accepted fires would be lit on altars in the parents' house. Many of the guests would perform the same ritual when they returned to their own homes. Birthdays were important to the Romans and were widely celebrated throughout someone's life. When a boy was nine days old – for obscure reasons the same ceremony occurred a day earlier for a girl – the family held a formal ceremony of purification (*lustratio*). This was intended to free the child of any malign spirits or pollution that may have entered it during the birth process. On the preceding night a vigil was held and a series of rites performed, culminating on the day itself in sacrifices and the observation of the flight of birds as a guide to the child's future. A boy was presented with a special charm, usually of gold, known as the *bulla*. This was placed in a leather bag and worn around the boy's neck. As part of the ceremony the child was named, and the name subsequently registered officially. Ritual and religion surrounded every Roman, especially an aristocrat, throughout every stage of his life.[8]

Normally the mother played the dominant role in the early years of raising a child. It is unlikely that Aurelia breast-fed any of her babies, for much earlier in the second century BC the wife of Cato the Elder was seen as exceptional for doing this. This and other stories suggest that it was no longer normal for an aristocratic woman to breast-feed her children.[9] Most probably a wet nurse was found amongst the substantial slave household maintained by any aristocratic family, even one of such comparatively modest wealth as the Caesars. Selecting a nurse and other slaves to care for the infant were important tasks for a mother, who supervised them closely and performed many tasks herself. Another tale celebrating the importance Cato attached to his role as father tells of his care to be present whenever his wife Licinia bathed their son. This rather implies that the mother's presence was taken for granted on such occasions. Mothers were not supposed to be distant figures to children looked after principally by servants, but even so their authority was considerable. Tacitus, writing in the late first or early second century AD, discussed the mother's role in raising children in a passage that presented Aurelia as an ideal:

> In the good old days, every man's son, born in wedlock, was brought up not in the chamber of some hireling nurse, but in his mother's lap, and at her knee. And that mother could have no higher praise than that she managed the house and gave herself to her children. . . .. In the presence of such a one no base word could be uttered without grave offence, and no wrong deed done. Religiously and with the utmost diligence she regulated not only the serious tasks of her youthful charges, but their recreations also and their games. It was in this spirit, we are told, that Cornelia, the mother of the Gracchi, directed their upbringing, Aurelia that of Caesar, Atia of Augustus: thus it was that these mothers trained their princely children.[10]

Aurelia's influence on her son was clearly very strong and lasted well beyond his childhood. Caesar was forty-six when he finally lost his mother, who had lived on as a widow for three decades. In itself this was not uncommon amongst the aristocracy for husbands were often considerably older than their wives, especially in the second, third or even fourth marriages that senators might contract for political reasons. Therefore, assuming that the wife survived the rigours of child bearing, it was more than probable that she would outlive her spouse, and so a senator was far more likely to have a living mother than father by the time that he began to reach important office. Mothers, especially those like Aurelia who conformed so closely to the ideal of motherhood, were greatly admired by the Romans. One of their most cherished stories was told of Coriolanus, the great general who, mistreated by political rivals, had defected to the enemy and led them against Rome. On the point of destroying his homeland he withdrew his army, moved less by a sense of patriotism than by a direct appeal from his mother.[11]

For the aristocracy education was managed entirely within the family. Many Romans took pride in this, contrasting it with the prescriptive State-controlled systems common in many Greek cities. At Rome, it tended to be those of middle income who sent their children to the fee-paying primary schools, which took children from about the age of seven. For the aristocracy, education continued to occur in the home and, at least initially, boys and girls were educated alike, being taught reading, writing and basic calculation and mathematics. By Caesar's day it was rare for senators' children not to be brought up to be bilingual in Latin and Greek. Early tuition in the latter probably came from a Greek slave (*paedagogus*) who attended to the child. There would also be much instruction in the rituals and traditions of the family and in the history of Rome. This last invariably emphasised the role played by the boy's ancestors. These and other great figures from the past were held up as object lessons in what it meant to be Roman. Children learned to admire such quintessentially Roman qualities as *dignitas*, *pietas* and *virtus*, all words with a far more powerful resonance than their English derivatives, dignity, piety, and virtue. *Dignitas* was the sober bearing that displayed openly the importance and responsibility of a man and so commanded respect. This was considerable for any citizen of Rome, greater for an aristocrat, and greater still for a man who had held a magistracy. *Pietas* embraced not merely respect for the gods, but for family and parents, and the law and traditions of the Republic. *Virtus* had strongly military overtones, embracing not simply physical bravery, but confidence, moral courage and the skills required by both soldier and commander.[12]

For the Romans, Rome was great because earlier generations had displayed just these qualities to a degree unmatched by any other nation. The stern faces carved on funerary monuments of the first century BC, depicting in detail all the idiosyncrasies and flaws of the man in life and so unlike the idealised portraiture of Classical Greece, radiate massive pride and self-assurance. The Romans took themselves very seriously and raised their children not simply to believe, but to know that they were special. Their pride in themselves and in belonging to the Republic was very strong amongst even the poorest citizens, and even more pronounced in those of greater wealth and more privileged birth. Roman senators had long come to see themselves as the superiors of any foreign kings. Young aristocrats were brought up to know this, but also to believe that they and their family were distinguished even amongst the Roman elite. Caesar's family, with few ancestors who had reached high office and done great deeds in the service of the Republic, still doubtless had some achievements to recount, as well, of course, as the great antiquity of the line and its divine origins. With this sense of importance came a massive sense of duty and of the obligation to live up to the standards expected by the family and the wider community of the Republic. Children were raised to see themselves as intimately connected with their family's and Rome's past. As Cicero would later declare, 'For what is the life of a man, if it is not interwoven with the life of former generations by a sense of history?'[13]

Caesar was raised to think of himself as special. In itself this was nothing unusual, but as the only son to carry on the family line, and with a particularly forceful and admired mother, he from the beginning doubtless developed an unusually high, though probably not unique, sense of his own worth. Roman education had an essentially practical purpose of preparing a child for its role as an adult. For an aristocratic boy this meant a career in public life and the chance to win new glory for the family, as well as becoming one day the head of his own household, the *paterfamilias*, in charge of raising the next generation. From around the age of seven boys began to spend more time with their fathers, accompanying them about the business. At the same stage a girl would watch her mother as she ran the household, overseeing the slaves and, at least in traditional households, weaving clothes for the family. Boys saw their fathers meet and greet other senators, and were permitted to sit outside the open doors of the Senate's meeting place and listen to the debates. They began to learn who had most influence in the Senate and why. From an early age they saw the great affairs of the Republic being conducted, and so naturally grew up feeling a part of that world and expecting to participate in it once they were old enough. Informal ties of favour and obligation bound Roman society together in a system known as patronage. The patron was the man with wealth, influence and power, to whom the less well off (or clients) came to ask for help, which might take the form of securing a position, winning a contract, assistance in business or legal disputes, or even at its most basic level gifts of food. In return the client had duties to assist his patron in various ways. Most would come to greet him formally each morning. The number of clients a man had added to his prestige, especially if they were distinguished or exotic. Senators might well include entire communities, including towns or cities in Italy and the provinces, amongst their clients. It was quite possible for a patron, even some less distinguished senators, to in turn be the client of an even more powerful man, although in this case the name itself would not have been used. A great part of a senator's time was spent in seeing his clients, in doing enough for them to ensure their continued attachment, while in turn ensuring that they provided him with the support he wanted. Much of Roman politics was conducted informally.[14]

At the same time more formal education continued, perhaps involving attendance at one of the twenty or so schools teaching *grammatica* or, probably more often, similar instruction at home or with other children at the house of a relative. Caesar was educated at home and for this stage of his life we know that his tutor was a certain Marcus Antonius Gnipho. Originally from the Hellenistic East and educated at Alexandria, Gnipho had been a slave, but had subsequently been freed by the Antonius family, presumably out of their satisfaction at his teaching of their children. He was highly respected as a teacher of both Greek and Latin rhetoric. In this secondary stage of education there was detailed study of literature in both languages as well as practice in rhetoric. Literature occupied a central role in learning and the aristocracy had the advantage of being able to afford copies of manuscripts in a world before the printing press made the copying of books so much easier. Many senators maintained extensive libraries in their houses, which their young relatives and associates were able to use. Caesar's own future father-in-law Calpurnius Piso possessed a very large collection of books, mainly dealing with Epicurean philosophy, remnants of which have been discovered in the ruins of his villa near Herculaneum. It was also common to entertain visiting scholars and philosophers, further adding to the cultural environment in which young aristocrats were raised. For Caesar, like many other young aristocrats, it was not enough simply to read great literature – he was also inspired to compose his own works. Suetonius mentions a poem praising Hercules as well as a tragedy entitled *Oedipus*. The quality of these immature works may not have been especially high – though probably no better or no worse than those written by other aristocrats who later went on to greater things – and they were suppressed by Caesar's adopted son, Emperor Augustus.[15]

Some learning by rote continued, as children memorised such things as the Twelve Tables, the ultimate basis of Roman law. In 92 BC an edict closed down schools teaching rhetoric in Latin, stating that instruction in Greek was superior, even for teaching a man to make speeches in Latin. It is possible that this measure was in part intended to prevent the oratorical skills useful in public life from becoming too common, for such schools were most likely to have taken pupils from those families outside the Senate. Some skill at public speaking was essential in the Roman political environment, so this continued the emphasis on what would be useful rather than on acquiring purely academic learning. Cicero, who was six years older than Caesar, recalled how in 91 BC he had gone 'almost every day' to listen to the finest orators speaking in the Popular Assemblies and in the courts. He also described how 'I wrote, read, and declaimed all the time with great energy, but was not content to restrict myself just to rhetorical exercises' and soon began observing the activities of one of the leading jurists of the day. Caesar seems to have been particularly influenced by the oratorical style of his relative Caesar Strabo, so may well have heard him in action.[16]

Physical training was directed by similarly utilitarian aims to academic education. In the Hellenistic world athletic perfection was pursued as an end in itself and was not direct preparation for the duties of an adult. In the *gymnasia* exercise was carried out naked and in many cities these institutions tended to celebrate homosexuality, both aspects very alien to the Romans. For them exercise was intended to promote physical fitness and had a strongly military flavour. Most usually on the Campus Martius – the plain of Mars the war god, where the army had mustered when Rome was still a small city – young aristocrats learned how to run, swim in the Tiber and fight with weapons, most particularly the sword and javelin. They were also taught to ride, and Varro, a near contemporary of Caesar's, tells us that at first he rode bareback rather than with a saddle. Much of the instruction in all these skills was supposed to be given by the father or another male relative. It was highly significant that all this occurred in public view. Boys of a similar age, who would in time go on to be competitors in the scramble for political office, trained in full view of each other, and even at this early stage in life might begin to forge a reputation. Caesar was slightly built and not particularly robust, but his great determination seems to have made up for this. Plutarch tells us that he was a natural horseman and we also read that he accustomed himself to riding with his arms folded behind his back, guiding the trotting horse with his knees. In later life his skill at arms was also praised, and the Romans believed that all good commanders should handle sword, javelin and shield as well as they controlled whole legions.[17]

THE LULL AND THE STORMS

After the savage suppression of Saturninus and Glaucia in the autumn of 100 BC, Roman public life had returned to something like normality. Marius' reputation had suffered through his earlier association with the pair, even though he had led the forces of the Republic against them. There were rumours that he had been tempted to join Saturninus. One of the wilder stories claimed that on the night before the final confrontation he had received both the radical leaders and a delegation from the Senate in his house at the same time. Marius is supposed to have feigned a nasty attack of diarrhoea, using this pretext to dash suddenly out of the room and leave one group whenever he wanted to talk to the others. Yet apart from his questionable role in this affair, Marius was simply not skilful enough at the political game to make the most of his wealth and military glory. The daily business of greeting friends and associates, of doing favours to as many people as possible and so placing them under an obligation without making them feel inferior, occupied a great part of a senator's time, but were not things at which Marius excelled. Plutarch tells us that few people chose to seek his assistance, even after he had constructed a new house for himself close to the Forum, declaring that visitors should not have to walk too far to see him. We do not know how much contact the young Caesar had with his famous uncle during the nineties BC, but it seems doubtful that he learned much from him about how to gain influence in the Senate.[18]

The legislation of the Gracchi and Saturninus had provoked much opposition, but in the end it was the fear of the power and influence that these radical tribunes would win through their actions that contributed most to their violent deaths. Ultimately, most of the Roman elite preferred to allow some of the major problems facing the Republic to go unanswered rather than see someone else gain the credit for dealing with them. Yet the issues remained, many of them connected with the fundamental question of who should benefit from the profits of empire. A magistrate proposing a new distribution of land, State-subsidised corn for the urban poor or an extension of the public role of the equestrian order as jurors could expect to find ready support. The success of the radical tribunes in the last decades had demonstrated this clearly, just as their violent ends had shown how difficult it was to maintain popularity with such disparate interest groups over the long term.

One group whose favour offered less immediate advantage to a senator were the Italian allies or *socii*. Tiberius Gracchus had incurred the hostility of the Italian aristocracy by his land law, since many of these men held large sections of *ager publicus*. Directly, such men had no power at Rome but they were able to influence sufficient important senators to oppose the tribune. Caius Gracchus had sought to win over the Italians by granting Roman citizenship to them, but in the process had alienated many of his Roman supporters. The Roman elite disliked the idea of the wealthiest new citizens adding to the competition for public office, while the poor, especially the urban poor, feared that crowds of Italians would overwhelm them at games and entertainments and make their votes of less value in the assemblies. The failure of Caius' legislation seems to have increased existing resentment of their treatment amongst Rome's Italian allies. These communities invariably supplied at least half of the soldiers in any Roman army – and it is possible that in recent decades the proportion had risen even higher – and suffered casualties accordingly. Yet they do not by this time seem to have shared the spoils of expansion to the same degree. The arrogant behaviour of some Roman magistrates in their dealings with the *socii* offered a further source of resentment. In 125 BC the colony of Fregellae, which possessed Latin status and so was comparatively privileged, had rebelled against Rome and been brutally suppressed. Many Italians seem to have reached the conclusion that only when they became Roman citizens would Rome's rule be made more palatable. Some drifted to Rome and somehow managed to get themselves enrolled as citizens, but during the early first century a series of especially strict censors did their best to remove the names of such men who had no real claim to be Romans.[19]

In 91 BC the tribune Marcus Livius Drusus once again advocated granting citizenship to the allies. This was the centrepiece of a series of reforms strongly reminiscent of those of the Gracchi – ironically, since Drusus' father had been one of Caius' chief opponents. Like the brothers, Drusus came from an extremely wealthy and influential family, which allowed him to be bolder in his legislation, while also adding to fears of what his long-term ambitions were. There was considerable opposition to the tribune, particularly to his plan to extend the franchise. However, before the citizenship law could be voted on by the Assembly, Drusus was fatally stabbed with a leather worker's knife while greeting callers in the porch of his house. The identity of the murderer was never established, but it was clear that his law would never now be passed. A large number of Italian noblemen, some of them close associates of Drusus, soon resolved to take things into their own hands. The result was the rebellion of large sections of Italy in what became known as the Social War – the name comes from *socii*, the Latin for allies. The rebels created their own state, with a capital at Corfinium and a constitution heavily based on the Roman system, having as its key magistrates two consuls and twelve praetors elected every year. Coins were minted showing the bull of Italy goring the Roman wolf and a large army speedily mobilised, its equipment, training and tactical doctrine identical to those of the legions. By the end of 91 BC heavy fighting had broken out, with considerable losses on both sides. Allegiances in the struggle were complex and at many points it resembled more closely a civil war than rebellion. Many Italian communities, including virtually all the Latin towns, remained loyal to Rome, while numbers of captured Roman soldiers were willing to enlist in the Italian armies and fight against their fellow citizens.[20]

Caesar was too young to take part in the Social War, but a number of those who would play major roles in his story, notably Cicero and Pompey, had their first taste of military service during this conflict. It is quite possible that Caesar's father served in some capacity, but the sources are silent on this. If he was indeed governor of Asia in 91 BC then he would have missed the start of the war, but probably returned before it was complete. The Lucius Julius Caesar, who was consul in 90 BC and proved an uninspired commander in his operations against the rebels, was a member of the other branch of the family. Sextus Julius Caesar, who as already mentioned may or may not have been Caius' brother, had held the office in the previous year and also took part in the conflict. He died of disease while a proconsul in command of an army. The sheer scale of the fighting in the Social War, added to the deaths of several magistrates at the hands of the enemy and the incompetence shown by others, ensured that many experienced senators received commands as pro-magistrates. Marius played a major role in the first year of fighting, winning a number of small actions and, perhaps more importantly, avoiding defeat. He was now in his late sixties, which the Romans considered very old for a general in the field, and there was some criticism of his conduct as too cautious. Whether because of this, or through failing health, he does not seem to have played any active role in the war after 90 BC. Two other commanders, Lucius Cornelius Sulla and Cnaeus Pompeius Strabo, were credited with doing more than anyone else to ensure Rome's military victory. Yet the Social War was won as much through diplomacy and conciliation as by force, and from the beginning the Senate had started to grant what the Italians had unsuccessfully demanded in the first place. Allied communities who had remained loyal were given citizenship, as were those who quickly surrendered and, very quickly, those who had been defeated. The readiness with which the Romans extended the franchise to virtually the entire free population of Italy south of the River Po underlined the essential pointlessness of the conflict. The way in which it was done also illustrated the reluctance to alter the existing political balance in Rome itself, for the new citizens were concentrated in a few voting tribes to minimise their influence.[21]

Sulla had gained much credit for his role in suppressing the rebels and by the end of 89 BC he returned to Rome and won election to the consulship for the following year, defeating as one of his main competitors Caius Julius Caesar Strabo. In many ways Sulla's career foreshadowed that of Caesar. Both were patricians, but ones whose families had long since fallen from prominence so that their own progress in public life was almost as hard fought as that of any 'new man'. Sulla began his career rather later than was normal, but served as Marius' quaestor in Numidia and played the principal role in arranging the betrayal and capture of Jugurtha. It was an achievement that he constantly paraded, fuelling a growing jealousy in his former commander who felt that this diminished his own glory. Although during the war with the Cimbri Sulla at first served under Marius, he soon transferred to the army of his colleague and relations between the two men seem never to have been cordial after this. As consul in 88 BC the Senate gave Sulla the war with King Mithridates VI of Pontus as his province. Mithridates ruled one of the Hellenised eastern kingdoms, which had grown in power with the decline of Macedonia and the Seleucids. While the Romans were busy with the war in Italy, the king had overrun the Roman province in Asia and ordered the massacre of the Romans and Italians in the region. This success was followed by an invasion of Greece. For Sulla this command was a great opportunity to campaign amidst the famous, and extremely wealthy, cities of the east and he set about forming an army to take with him. There seems to have been little shortage of recruits, for wars in the east were renowned for the easy fighting and rich plunder.[22]

In ordinary circumstances Sulla would simply have gone to the war and done his best to add new lustre to his family name. However, a tribune named Sulpicius passed a bill through the Assembly giving the eastern command to Marius in place of Sulla. It was one of a series of laws in which he tried to follow in the path of the Gracchi and Saturninus by using the tribunate for a wide-ranging reform programme. Another bill was designed to spread the newly enfranchised citizens more evenly amongst the voting tribes. Marius was happy to use Sulpicius as he had once used Saturninus, and Sulpicius was equally content to benefit from association with the popular war hero. It is unlikely that either would have hesitated to break with the other if this offered more advantage, especially once their immediate objectives had been achieved. We must always remind ourselves that politics was about individual success and not parties. For the moment Marius had clearly decided that he needed once again to fight a war in order to win back the adulation he had enjoyed after defeating Jugurtha and the northern barbarians. Sulpicius as a tribune with great sway in the Assembly could provide him with the opportunity to fight another war. Marius was sixty-nine and had not held an elected magistracy since 100 BC, while Sulla's own record had demonstrated his competence so that there was no reason for such a break with the traditional methods of allocating commands. However, the Gracchi had confirmed that the Popular Assembly could legislate on any matter. Sympathy and all precedents were with Sulla, but technically there was nothing illegal about this. Sulpicius backed up this legality with mob violence and one story maintained that Sulla only escaped with his life by taking refuge in Marius' house.[23]

Sulla had been unfairly treated, his *dignitas* as an aristocrat, senator and consul severely dented. If his bitterness was understandable, his response was shocking. Leaving Rome he went to his army and told the soldiers that now that he had been supplanted in the eastern command, it was inevitable that Marius would raise his own legions to fight the war. Rather than let this happen, he called upon the legionaries to follow him to Rome and free the Republic from the faction that had seized power. None of the senatorial officers, save one, responded to his appeal, but this reluctance was not shared by the remainder of the army. Whether through fear of being denied the chance of booty from the war, or even a sense of the injustice of their commander's treatment, the legions followed Sulla to Rome. It was the first time that a Roman army had marched against the city. Two praetors sent to confront the army were roughly handled, their robes were torn and the fasces, carried by their attendants to symbolise that they held *imperium*, were smashed by the angry legionaries. Later, other senatorial delegations asking the consul to halt and allow time for a peaceful settlement were received cordially, but ignored. When the entry into Rome of a small force was stopped by hastily organised forces loyal to Marius and Sulpicius, Sulla responded with greater force, his men fighting their way through the streets and burning down a number of houses in the process. Opposition was initially fierce but poorly equipped, and was soon crushed. Sulla outlawed twelve of the opposing leaders, including Marius and his son, as well as Sulpicius, making it legal for anyone to kill them and then claim a reward. The tribune was betrayed by one of his own slaves and killed. (Sulla gave the slave his freedom and then had the man thrown to his death from the Tarpeian Rock for disloyalty to his former master. Such a severe gesture was well in keeping with Roman traditions of respect for both law and duty.) The other fugitives avoided pursuit and escaped. Marius, after a series of picturesque adventures – no doubt much embellished by later legend – eventually reached Africa where he was welcomed by the communities of his veterans established there after the Numidian war. Sulla took some measures to restore normality and then left with his army to fight Mithridates, not returning to Italy for almost five years.[24]

The two consuls for 87 BC swiftly fell out and one, Lucius Cornelius Cinna, was declared an enemy of the Republic and expelled from office after attempts to undo Sulla's legislation. Copying Sulla, Cinna fled to one of the armies still engaged in stamping out the last embers of the Italian revolt and persuaded the soldiers to support him. Soon he was joined by Marius who had returned from Africa with a mass of volunteers, who were little more than a rabble. Most notorious of all were the Bardyaei, a band of freed slaves who formed Marius' personal bodyguard and often acted as executioners. Near the end of the year Marius and Cinna marched on Rome and were ineffectually opposed by the consul Cnaeus Octavius, a man of high principle but very modest talent. The ambiguous behaviour of Pompeius Strabo, who was still at the head of his army and had been angling for a second consulship for several years, only made matters worse. Sulla had sent Quintus Pompeius, his fellow consul for 88 BC, to take charge of Strabo's legions. Quintus and Strabo were distant cousins, but that did not prevent the former from being murdered by the latter's legionaries, almost certainly with their commander's approval. Strabo may well have been unsure of which side to join and probably made overtures to both. In the event he joined Octavius, but failed to support him effectively and their forces were defeated. Strabo died soon afterwards, perhaps from disease or just possibly after being struck by lightning.

Octavius refused to flee when the enemy entered the city and was killed as he sat in his chair of office on the Janiculum Hill. His severed head was brought to Cinna, who had it fastened to the Rostra in the Forum. It was soon joined by the heads of a number of other senators. In our sources Marius receives the chief blame for the wave of executions that followed, but it seems likely that Cinna played as full a part. The famous orator Marcus Antonius – the grandfather of the Mark Antony who would follow Caesar – was killed, as were the father and older brother of Marcus Licinius Crassus, and Lucius Caesar and his brother Caesar Strabo. A few men were given sham trials, but most were simply killed as soon as they were caught. Sulla's house was burned to the ground in an important symbolic gesture, for a senator's residence was not only the location for so much political activity but was a visible sign of his importance. His wife and family were sought out, but managed to evade capture and eventually joined him in Greece. If Sulla's seizure of Rome had been shocking, the brutality of this second occupation was far worse. Marius and Cinna were elected consuls for 86 BC, but the former died suddenly a few weeks after taking up the office. He was seventy.[25]

The role, if any, of Caesar's father in these events is unknown. Nor is it possible to say whether or not the young Caesar was actually in Rome on either of the occasions when the city was stormed, or saw the corpses floating in the Tiber and the heads hanging from the Rostra. The education of young aristocrats was highly traditional and they were supposed to learn much by watching their elders conducting their daily affairs. Yet in these years public life was so disordered and often violent that they were inevitably absorbing a very different impression of the Republic to earlier generations. Worse was to come.

III

THE FIRST DICTATOR

'Lists of proscribed people were posted not only in Rome, but in every city in Italy. There was nowhere that remained free from the stain of bloodshed – no god's temple, no guest-friend's hearth, no family home. Husbands were butchered in the arms of their wives, sons in the arms of their mothers. Only a tiny proportion of the dead were killed because they had angered or made an enemy of someone; far more were killed for their property, and even the executioners tended to say that this man was killed by his large house, this one by his garden, that one by his warm springs.'
– Plutarch, early second century AD.[1]

Caesar's father died suddenly, collapsing one morning while in the act of putting on his shoes. His son was nearly sixteen, but had probably already formally become a man, laying aside the purple-bordered *toga praetexta* – worn only by boys and magistrates – and replacing this with the plain *toga virilis* of an adult. As part of this ceremony the boy also removed the *bulla* charm from around his neck and laid it aside forever. For the first time in his life he was shaved, and his hair was cut in the short style appropriate for an adult citizen, rather than the somewhat longer fashion acceptable for a boy. There was no fixed age for this ceremony, and like so many other aspects of Roman education it was left to each family to decide. Usually it occurred between the ages of fourteen and sixteen, although cases are known of individuals as young as twelve and as old as eighteen. Equally often the ceremony took place at the Liberalia festival, which occurred on 17 March, though again there was no legal obligation to hold it on this day. Apart from ceremonies within the household, an aristocratic child would be paraded through the heart of the city by his father and his father's friends, symbolising the son's admission as an adult into the wider community of the Republic. After passing through the Forum, the group would ascend the Capitoline Hill to perform a sacrifice in the Temple of Jupiter, making an offering to Iuventus, the deity of youth.[2]

After his father's death Caesar was not simply an adult, but also the *paterfamilias* or head of the household. There were few close male relatives to guide his future career, but the young man from the beginning displayed considerable self-confidence. Within a year he broke off the betrothal arranged for him at some earlier date by his parents. This was to a certain Cossutia, whose father was an equestrian not a senator. Her family was very wealthy, and would doubtless have provided a large dowry, but although this money would have been very useful for launching a political career the alliance offered few other advantages. It is possible that the couple were actually married, rather than simply betrothed, for the word used by Suetonius often means an actual divorce, while Plutarch clearly counted Cossutia as one of Caesar's wives. Their age makes this a little unlikely, but certainly not impossible. Whatever the precise nature of the union, it was broken. Instead Caesar wed Cornelia, the daughter of Cinna, a fellow patrician, consul for four consecutive years from 87–84 BC, and the most powerful man in Rome.[3]

It is not clear precisely why Cinna chose to honour Caesar in this way. Clearly the execution of two Julii Caesares did not count against him, which in itself illustrates just how separate the two branches of the family were. Marius was the boy's uncle, which doubtless brought favour, but the importance of this link had diminished to some extent with Marius' death early in 86 BC. In the last weeks of his life it is true that he and Cinna had nominated the boy for the post of *Flamen Dialis*, one of Rome's most prestigious priesthoods. The previous incumbent, Lucius Cornelius Merula, had been made suffect (acting) consul in 87 BC by Octavius to replace the dismissed Cinna. When the Marian and Cinnan forces captured Rome, Merula had anticipated execution by committing suicide. The *flamen* had to be a patrician married to a patrician by an ancient, rarely used form of the wedding ceremony known as *confarreatio*. Caesar was too young to take up the post in 86 BC and the arrangement of the marriage to the patrician Cornelia in 84 BC was in part to prepare him for his priesthood. Yet it is hard to believe that Cinna's daughter was the only available patrician girl to be married to the *flamen* designate, or that the desire to ensure that Caesar was qualified for the priesthood overruled the normal priorities of a senator looking for a son-in-law. Indeed the youth was in fact not really eligible for the priesthood at all, because a *flamen* was supposed to be the son of patrician parents married according to the ritual of *confarreatio* and Aurelia was plebian. Cinna must have had a high opinion of the young Caesar.

If so, then the decision to make him *Flamen Dialis* seems more than a little peculiar. The flaminate was one of Rome's most ancient religious orders. There were fifteen of these priests all told, each dedicated to the worship of a particular deity, but three were of far greater importance and prestige than the rest. These were the priests of Quirinus (*Flamen Quirinalis*), Mars (*Flamen Martialis*), and Jupiter (*Flamen Dialis*). Jupiter was Rome's most important god, and his *flamen* was correspondingly the most senior. The great antiquity of the flaminate was attested by the host of strange taboos binding him, for the *flamen* and his wife were considered to be permanently engaged in the propitiation of the god, and so could not risk any form of ritual pollution. Amongst many other things, the *Flamen Dialis* was not allowed to take an oath, to pass more than three nights away from the city, or to see a corpse, an army on campaign or anyone working on a festival day. In addition he could not ride a horse, have a knot anywhere within his house or even in his clothing, and could not be presented with a table without food since he was never to appear to be in want. Furthermore, he could only be shaved or have his hair cut by a slave using a bronze knife – surely another indication of antiquity – and the cut hair, along with other things such as nail clippings, had to be buried in a secret place. The *flamen* wore a special hat called the *apex*, which appears to have been made from fur, had a point on top and flaps over the ears. These restrictions made a normal senatorial career impossible.[4]

The prestige of the *Flamen Dialis* was very great, and in the last century holders of this priesthood had asserted their right to sit in the Senate and hold magistracies that did not require them to leave Rome. This required them to be exempted from the oath normally taken by any magistrate at the beginning of his term of office. The restrictions preventing the *flamen* from holding military command could not be bypassed so easily. Merula's consulship was unlikely to have occurred without the peculiar circumstances of Cinna's deposition in 87 BC. He claimed later that he had not wanted to stand, but was presumably voted into office by the *Comitia Centuriata* in the normal way. The taboos imposed by his priesthood ensured that he could not play a very active part in events, and it may be that this was why Octavius had wanted him as a colleague. When Cinna and Marius seized Rome, Merula had voluntarily laid down his consulship but swiftly realised that this would not be enough to save his life. He went to the Temple of Jupiter on the Capitoline Hill and there removed the *apex* hat, formally laying down his office, before cutting his wrists with a knife. He died roundly cursing Cinna and his supporters, but was careful to leave a note explaining that he had been careful to avoid polluting his priesthood.[5]

Caesar and Cornelia were married by the peculiar *confarreatio* ceremony. The name came from that of emmer wheat – *far* in Latin – which was used to make a loaf for a sacrificial offering to *Jupiter Farreus*. This was carried ahead of the bride, and may well have been eaten by the couple as part of the ritual. Ten witnesses needed to be present and the ceremony was supposed to be conducted by two of Rome's most senior priests, the *Pontifex Maximus* and the *Flamen Dialis*. Since the latter post remained vacant after Merula's death this part of the ritual cannot have been fulfilled. Given that Caesar was marked out for this post and therefore that his wife would become the *flaminica*, their wedding was also marked by the sacrifice of a sheep. Afterwards, their heads veiled, the couple sat on seats covered in sheepskin.[6]

The selection of Caesar for the vacant priesthood was a considerable honour, which would make him an important figure in the Republic and a member of the Senate at a very young age. Yet this prominence came at the price of severely limiting opportunities for his future career. At best Caesar might hope to reach the praetorship like his father, but he could not have left Rome to govern a province and certainly would have had no opportunity for military glory. Given the family's fairly modest achievements in the past, a career of this sort may have been considered ample reward for the boy, for certainly no one would have guessed at his eventual achievements. However, there is no evidence that it was felt that lack of talent or poor health would anyway have prevented the lad from doing well in the normal way – Caesar had not yet begun to suffer from the epileptic fits to which he would be prone in later life. The marriage with Cornelia also suggests that the boy was not seen as wholly lacking in merit. Cinna and Marius clearly agreed on the appointment in the first place, and the former maintained the decision after his ally's death, but in the end we cannot know their reasons, or indeed the attitude of the young Caesar towards it. Whatever their thinking, there does not seem to have been any great urgency about the whole business, and although one of our sources claims that he was actually invested with the flaminate, it is most probable that the other authors were right to say that this did not actually occur. At first his youth may have been an obstacle. More importantly Cinna himself could not make the actual appointment, which had to be done in accordance with a strict procedure by another of Rome's senior priests, the *Pontifex Maximus*. At the time this was Quintus Mucius Scaevola, who was not a friend of the new regime, having already survived a murder attempt by one of Cinna's henchmen. An ex-consul and a famous jurist – the *Pontifex Maximus* was not bound by such oppressive rules as the *flamen* and so could follow an active public career – Scaevola may have objected to Caesar on technical grounds, given Aurelia's plebian status, or perhaps simply refused to bow to pressure from Cinna. Ultimately this was a very minor issue and Cinna's preoccupation with other, far more important matters ensured that it was left unresolved.[7]

WAITING FOR SULLA

The years when Cinna and his supporters dominated Rome are not recorded in any detail by our sources. Yet it is probably not merely this lack of information that suggests he made no attempt at major reforms. Although he had appealed to the newly enfranchised Italians and to other discontented groups before his victory, Cinna made little attempt to satisfy their demands afterwards. Rome's first period of civil war – and indeed the latter conflicts – had little to do with conflicting ideology or policies, but were violent extensions of the traditional competition between individuals. Cinna had no revolutionary ambitions to reform the Republic, but craved personal power and influence within the existing system. Therefore, once he had won these things through the use of force, his chief priority was to retain them. Already consul for 86 BC, Cinna made sure than he was elected to the office for 85 and 84 – quite probably only his name and that of a chosen colleague were allowed to be put forward as candidates. As consul he held *imperium* and so had a legal right to command the armies that he would need to protect himself from Sulla or any other rival. As a magistrate he was exempt from prosecution, for it seems that there was some activity in the courts at Rome, although a few prominent advocates appear to have chosen to cease appearing. Cinna and Marius had killed some senators and caused others to flee abroad, but the majority of the Senate remained in Rome and continued to meet. Many senators were not strong supporters of Cinna and his associates, but equally had no particular love for Sulla. The Senate's debates appear to have been comparatively free and at times it voted for measures that were not particularly pleasing to Cinna, for instance, when it began negotiations with Sulla. Yet it could not restrain him or prevent his consecutive consulships, for in the end he controlled an army and the Senate did not. In Cinna's Rome the Senate convened, the courts functioned and elections were held, creating at least a veneer of normality. There was a remarkable elasticity in the main institutions of the Republic, which tended to continue running in some form under almost any circumstances, interrupted only temporarily by riot and bloodshed. Senators' lives revolved around the doing of favours to win support, gaining influence and seeking office. Whatever the circumstances, they naturally continued to try and do these things as far as was possible.[8]

Cinna's position was incompatible with a properly functioning Republic, for in the end his position rested on his army and he showed no signs of giving this up, while his repeated consulships denied others the chance at high office and also limited the number of magistrates available to govern the provinces. Yet Cinna could not feel secure while Sulla remained at large and in command of his legions. Marius had been allocated the war against Mithridates as his province in 86 BC, but had died before he had even set out. His replacement as consul, Lucius Valerius Flaccus, also inherited his province and did at last go to the east with an army. It was soon evident that Sulla was not about to allow himself to be replaced, but Flaccus may well have attempted to negotiate with him with a view to their joining forces against Mithridates. However, Flaccus was promptly murdered by his own quaestor, Caius Flavius Fimbria, who took over the army and tried to defeat Pontus on his own. Showing less talent for warfare than he had for treachery and murder, Fimbria eventually committed suicide after his soldiers had mutinied. Over the next few years, the Senate made a few approaches to Sulla, hoping to reconcile him with Cinna and avoid further civil war, but neither of the leaders showed much enthusiasm for this. Sulla maintained that he was a properly elected magistrate, sent as proconsul by the Senate to wage war against an enemy of the Republic, and must be acknowledged as such and left to complete his task. By 85 BC as it became clear that the war with Mithridates was drawing to a close, Cinna and his associates threw themselves into raising troops and massing supplies for what they saw as the inevitable clash with Sulla.[9]

Lucius Cornelius Sulla was a man of striking appearance, with exceptionally fair skin, piercing grey eyes and reddish hair. In later life his appearance was marred by a skin condition that speckled his face with red patches. (An obscure piece of military law from several centuries later also claims that he had only one testicle, and that his achievements make it clear that such a defect was no bar to becoming a successful soldier.) Sulla could be very charming, winning over soldier and senator alike, but many aristocrats remained deeply uncertain of him. In spite of his late entry into public life he had been reasonably successful, and demonstrated his military skill on repeated occasions. His consulship came when he was fifty, which was unusually old for a first term, and in the preceding decade it had taken two attempts for him to win the praetorship. Many senators probably found it hard to forget the poverty of his youth and the decay of his family. It is common for those who flourish under any system to feel that the failure of others is deserved. Sulla had been poor and revelled in the company of actors and musicians, professions considered extremely disreputable. Such behaviour was bad enough in his youth, and far worse for a senator and magistrate, but Sulla remained loyal to his old friends throughout his life. He was a heavy drinker, enjoyed feasting and was widely believed to be very active sexually, taking both men and women as lovers. For much of his life he publicly associated with the actor Metrobius, who specialised in playing female roles on stage, and the pair were believed to be having an affair. The inner elite of the Senate were fairly grudging in their acceptance of Sulla's political success, although at times evidently preferring him to some of the other alternatives. This in itself may not have mattered to him, but he was unshakeable in his determination to have his success publicly acknowledged and not be robbed of his achievements. In 88 BC he marched on Rome claiming that he was the legitimate representative of the Republic and that he needed to free Rome from the unlawful domination of a faction. Afterwards he always presented himself as a proconsul of Rome, denying the validity of Marius' and Cinna's declaration proclaiming him an enemy of the State. Sulla was a man whose self-proclaimed epitaph would be that he had never failed to do good to a friend or harm to an enemy.[10]

As far as Sulla was concerned his *imperium* and command were legitimate, and his opponents had acted illegally and as enemies of the Republic. Therefore it was both his right and duty to suppress them by any means necessary. It was also important for him to protect his own *dignitas*, for his achievements deserved respect for himself and his family. The Romans openly stressed the great part played by luck in all human activities, especially warfare, and – anticipating Napoleon – believed that being lucky was one of the most important virtues of a general. Commanders were not supposed to rely on blind chance, and were to make every preparation possible to ensure success, but in the chaos of war the best plans could fall apart and victory or defeat depend on chance. Sulla paraded his good fortune throughout his career. Being fortunate implied divine favour, in his case the support of Venus and, on occasions, Apollo and others. Sulla claimed that he had had prophetic dreams before many of the great events in his life, in which a god or goddess urged him to take the action he planned and promised him success. Marius had similarly been inspired by oracles foretelling his great future, most famously that he would hold seven consulships. Both men were ruthlessly ambitious, but the belief that their success was divinely ordained and therefore right, further boosted their already considerable self-confidence. Nor should modern cynicism blind us to the fact that such claims of divine favour often made highly effective propaganda.[11]

Sulla had used force once already to defend his position. The brutality of Cinna's own capture of the city cannot have led him to anticipate any milder behaviour from his enemy. In 85 BC Sulla signed the Peace of Dardanus concluding the war with Mithridates. It was not a complete victory by Roman standards, for the King of Pontus remained independent and still possessed considerable power, but he had been expelled from Roman territory and his armies humiliatingly defeated in battle. Sulla was not able to return to Italy immediately, for there was much administrative work to be done to settle the eastern provinces. In 84 BC Cinna had decided to fight his rival in Greece rather than Italy, but there were severe delays when the weather in the Adriatic turned bad and one convoy of soldiers was blown back to Italy. Soon afterwards the soldiers mutinied – probably through a reluctance to fight other Romans, although our sources are contradictory on this point – and Cinna was killed by his own men. The leadership of his supporters was taken over by Cnaeus Papirius Carbo, who was his fellow consul in this and the preceding year. In 82 BC he would hold a third term as consul with Marius' son as his colleague, in spite of the fact that the latter was too young for the post. A growing number of senators had already either decided that Italy was no longer safe for them, or perhaps guessed which way the wind was blowing, and had fled to join Sulla in the east. More would rally to his cause when he finally landed at Brundisium (modern Brindisi) in southern Italy in the autumn of 83 BC.[12]

The odds against Sulla were huge, but his opponents consistently failed to make the most of their numbers, and army after army was defeated, or on one occasion persuaded to defect en masse. Few of the leaders opposing him displayed much military talent. After a lull during the winter months the campaign resumed and Sulla was able to take Rome in 82 BC. A sudden enemy counter-offensive led to a desperate battle outside the Colline Gate. During the fighting Sulla himself narrowly escaped being killed and one wing of his army collapsed, but in the end the remainder of his troops carried on to win a victory. As their fortunes failed the enemy leaders became more vindictive. The Younger Marius ordered the execution of Scaevola, the *Pontifex Maximus*, an action that his mother Julia is supposed to have condemned. Marius himself was besieged in Praeneste and either killed or committed suicide when the city surrendered. When his head was taken to Sulla the victor commented that such a stripling ought to have 'learned to pull an oar before he tried to steer the ship'. Carbo escaped to Sicily to continue the resistance, but was defeated and executed by one of Sulla's subordinates.[13]

Just as the Marian capture of Rome had greatly surpassed Sulla's march on the City in the scale of massacre and execution it brought, now both were eclipsed by the savagery of Sulla's return. Addressing the Senate in the Temple of Bellona on the outskirts of Rome, the victor's speech was accompanied by the screams of thousands of captured soldiers – mostly Italians who were treated more harshly than Romans – being executed a short distance away. It was not simply the rank and file of the enemy who suffered. Most prominent leaders were executed as soon as they were taken or anticipated this outcome by taking their own lives. Many more senators and equestrians seen to be hostile to Sulla were killed by his men in the aftermath of victory.[14]

At first the executions occurred without warning, but complaints from a nervous Senate wishing to know just who was going to suffer led to the process becoming more formal. Sulla ordered that the proscriptions – lists of names of men who thereby lost all protection of law – be posted up in the Forum, and copies were subsequently sent to other parts of Italy. Those proscribed could be killed by anyone and a reward claimed on presentation of their severed heads to Sulla, who had them displayed on and around the Rostra. Usually the victim's property was confiscated and auctioned off, much of it being purchased at a knock-down price by Sulla's associates. The victims were principally either senators or equestrians. Several lists were posted and, though we have no precise figure, the total amounted to some hundreds. Most had opposed Sulla, but other names were added simply because of a man's wealth. One equestrian who had taken little interest in public life is supposed to have seen his name on one of the lists and declared that his Alban estate wanted to see him dead. He was soon killed.[15] Many private hatreds were exercised, and there were more than a few cases of names being added to the lists after the man had been killed in order to legitimise murder. Sulla does not appear to have supervised the process too closely, but he did form a bodyguard of the freed slaves of many of the proscribed and these were widely accused of abusing their new-found power. The proscriptions formally ended on 1 June 81 BC, but their horror lived on and scarred the Romans' collective consciousness for the rest of the century.[16]

Sulla's power came directly from his control of an army that had defeated all his rivals, but the man who had done so much to defend his legitimacy as proconsul soon gave himself a more formal position to justify his domination of the State. At times of severe crisis the Republic had occasionally set aside its fear of the rule of one man and had appointed a dictator, a single magistrate with supreme *imperium*. It had always been a temporary post, laid down after six months, but Sulla discarded these restrictions and set no time limit to his office. He was named *dictator legibus faciendis et rei publicae constituendae* (dictator to make laws and reconstitute the State) by a vote in the Popular Assembly. His office was unprecedented, as was the violence he used to crush any opposition. On one occasion he casually ordered the execution of his own senior officer in the Forum because the man persisted in standing for the consulship in defiance of the dictator's orders.[17]

FUGITIVE

Caesar was about eighteen when Sulla's army took Rome for the second time. He had not taken any part in the civil war. His father-in-law Cinna was dead and there is no evidence to suggest a particularly close relationship with the Younger Marius. More importantly he was probably already expected to follow the rules laid down for the *Flamen Dialis* even if he had not yet formally been invested with the priesthood. The same restrictions that prevented him from going to war should have meant that he was in Rome when the city was taken and the great battle fought outside the Colline Gate, and that he witnessed the bloodbath of the proscriptions. The *flamen* was not supposed to see a corpse, but it must have been difficult to have avoided doing so at this time. Whether he saw them or not, the youth must have been aware of the heads of so many prominent Romans being displayed in the city's heart. At one point it seemed as if his own would shortly join them.

Caesar himself was neither important enough nor sufficiently wealthy to warrant his inclusion in the proscriptions. However, he was married to Cinna's daughter Cornelia and such a connection was not one to win favour with the new regime. Sulla instructed the youth to divorce his wife. He had given similar orders to other men, at times arranging a more favourable match for them, often involving some of his own female relations. The most famous case was of Cnaeus Pompey, the son of Pompeius Strabo and one of Sulla's most effective commanders, who was told to divorce his wife and instead marry the dictator's stepdaughter. The latter was both already married and heavily pregnant, but this did not prevent a rapid divorce and equally speedy union with Pompey. We know of at least one other man who put aside his wife on the instructions of Sulla. Caesar was the only man to refuse, and to persist in that refusal in spite of threats and offers of favours, quite possibly including a marriage link to the dictator's family. Given recent events this was remarkable boldness, most of all for a youth who could easily be removed and anyway had connections with the opposition. Why he did this is unknown. The marriage to Cornelia does appear to have been a happy one, but it may just as easily have been innate stubbornness or pride.

Sulla's threats became stronger. Cornelia's dowry was confiscated and added to the Republic's Treasury as punishment. At some point the flaminate was also taken from Caesar. This may have happened anyway given that it had been bestowed by Marius and Cinna, but our sources tend to associate this with the dispute over Cornelia. Alternatively someone may have been scrupulous enough to point out that Caesar was not technically eligible in the first place. Rome had survived without a *Flamen Dialis* since 87 BC, and there was evidently no urgency to appoint a replacement, for the post would in fact remain vacant until 12 BC. There seems to have been little enthusiasm amongst the aristocracy for such a restrictive honour. Plutarch tells us that Caesar also tried to stand for election to an unspecified priesthood, but was secretly opposed by Sulla and so failed in the attempt. This may simply be a confused version of the story of the flaminate, although this was not bestowed by election, or an invention intended to emphasise the confidence displayed by the young Caesar in the face of the mighty dictator.[18] Whatever the extent of his public opposition to Sulla, this was a dangerous path and soon led to orders being issued for his arrest, which was usually a prelude to execution. It is unclear whether Sulla himself gave these instructions, and it may actually be that the initiative was taken by some of his subordinates. If so, then the dictator soon seems to have learned of it and did not at first do anything to restrain his men.[19]

Caesar fled from Rome and sought sanctuary in Sabine territory to the north-east. The dictator's forces were active throughout Italy – he would soon give orders for the demobilisation and settlement of some 120,000 veterans, which gives an indication of the sheer size of his army. Caesar could not hope simply to vanish, blending into one of the small communities. He had to move virtually every night to avoid patrols, and there was always the risk of betrayal since it is probable that the rewards given to those who brought in fugitives during the proscriptions were still in force. The young aristocrat who in recent years had probably had to follow the strictly regulated routine of the flaminate now had to live rough. He may have had some slaves with him, perhaps even some friends, but such a lifestyle was at marked contrast to his earlier years. To make matters worse he contracted malaria. While suffering from an attack, he had to move by night from one shelter to the next safe house when he was intercepted and taken by a group of Sullan soldiers. These men, under the command of a certain Cornelius Phagites who may have been a centurion, were sweeping the area for the dictator's enemies, and according to Suetonius had been hounding him for days. Caesar offered them money to let him go, eventually buying his freedom for 12,000 silver denarii – almost one hundred years' pay for an ordinary soldier, although centurions received considerably more.[20]

In the end Caesar was saved by his mother. Aurelia persuaded the Vestal Virgins, along with some of her relations – most notably her cousin Caius Aurelius Cotta as well as Mamercus Aemilius Lepidus – to plead with the dictator for her son's life. Cotta and Lepidus had both sided with Sulla in the civil war and would each win the consulship in the next few years. The lobbying of such influential men, combined with Caesar's lack of real importance, won a pardon. Not only was Caesar's life spared, but he was permitted to begin his public career. This was a considerable concession, since the sons and grandsons of the proscribed were barred from holding any office or entering the Senate. Legend maintained that when Sulla finally relented, he declared that 'they could have their way and take him, but they ought to realise that the one they so desire to save will one day destroy the party of the best men (*optimates*), which I and they have both defended; for in this Caesar there are many Mariuses.' This may be no more than a later myth, but it is certainly not impossible that the dictator recognised the massive ambition – and perhaps also the talent – of the cocksure youngster who had stood up to him.[21]

Sulla laid down his dictatorship at the end of 80 or beginning of 79 BC. He had enlarged the Senate, adding 300 new members from the equestrian order, and done much to restore its prominent guiding role in the Republic. The tribunate, which Sulpicius had used to give his eastern command to Marius, was crippled, no longer able to propose legislation to the Assembly. Even more importantly a tribune was barred from holding any further magistracies, effectively ensuring that only the unambitious would now seek it. Legislation confirmed the traditional age limits on office-holding, and expressly forbade consecutive terms in the same post, while the activities of governors in their provinces were regulated. Sulla, who had always claimed to be a properly appointed servant of the Republic, had used his supreme power to re-establish a very conservative vision of the Republic. Even more importantly he had filled the Senate with his own men. If the system was to work, then it would depend on those men playing their part and acting within the traditional boundaries that Sulla's laws had sought to restore. The system did not require a dictator to oversee it and so Sulla retired. For a while he walked through the streets of Rome just like any other senator, accompanied by his friends, but unprotected by bodyguards. It was a sign of the respect and fear felt for him that he did this without being molested in any way. However, one story claims that he was followed about by a youth who continually shouted abuse, so that Sulla declared that this young fool would prevent any future dictator from giving up power. This may well be another invention. Much later Caesar said that 'Sulla was a political illiterate when he resigned from the dictatorship'.[22]

Soon afterwards Sulla retired to a rural estate. He had recently remarried, his wife having died from the after-effects of giving birth to twins. Sulla was a member of the priesthood of augurs and had scrupulously followed the rules of the order by divorcing his dying wife because his house could not be polluted by death at a time of festival. He refused even to see her during this period but, in another display of both stern adherence to duty and personal affection, gave her a lavish funeral. Later he encountered a young divorcee at the games. What began as a flirtation initiated by the woman, soon proceeded in a proper aristocratic way as the intrigued Sulla made discreet enquiries about her family and then arranged the marriage. After his retirement there were many rumours of wild parties as Sulla lived in the country with his wife and many of the theatrical friends he had kept since his youth. He died suddenly at the beginning of 78 BC.[23]

Rome had had her first taste of civil war and dictatorship. The young Caesar – and it is important to remember that all these events occurred while he was in his teens – had seen the personal rivalries of leading senators spill over into savage bloodshed. Consuls and other distinguished men had been executed or forced into suicide, showing that even the most prominent men in the Republic could have their careers violently and suddenly terminated. Caesar himself had narrowly avoided death. He had also stood up to the overwhelming power of the dictator, refusing to back down, and he had survived the experience. Senators' sons were raised to have a very high opinion of themselves and Caesar was no exception to this. The experience of the last few years can only have reinforced this sense of his own unique worth. He had resisted tyranny when everyone else was cowed into submission. Perhaps the rules that bound others did not apply to him?

IV

THE YOUNG CAESAR

'This is what I wish for my orator: when it is reported that he is going to speak let every place on the benches be taken, the judges' tribunal full, the clerks busy and obliging in assigning or giving up places, a listening crowd thronging about, the presiding judge erect and attentive; when the speaker rises the whole throng will give a sign for silence, then expressions of assent, frequent applause; laughter when he wills it, or if he wills, tears; so that a mere passer-by observing from a distance, though quite ignorant of the case in question, will recognise that he is succeeding and that a Roscius [a famous actor of the day] is on stage.' – *Cicero, 46 BC.*[1]

A number of portrait images of Caesar survive as busts or on coins, some either made during his lifetime or copied from originals that were, but all portray him in middle age. They show the great general or the dictator, his features stern and strong, his face lined and – at least in the few more realistic portraits – his hair thinning. These images radiate power, experience and monumental self-confidence, and at least hint at the force of personality of the man, although no portrait, whether sculpted, painted or even photographic can ever truly capture this. Ancient portraits often seem especially formal and rather lifeless to the modern eye and it is all too easy to forget that many were originally painted, for we have a deeply entrenched vision of the Classical world as a place of bare stone and marble. Even enhanced by paint – and the great statue painters were as revered as the great sculptors – a portrait bust revealed only some aspects of character. In Caesar's case they do suggest a keen intelligence, but do not hint at the liveliness, wit and charm that his contemporaries commented upon so often.

It is also difficult when looking at portraits of the mature Caesar to imagine his features softened by youth, though some sense of his appearance is provided by our literary sources. According to Suetonius, Caesar 'is said to have been tall, with fair skin, slender limbs, a face that was just a little too full, and very dark, piercing eyes'. Plutarch confirms some of this when he notes that Caesar was slightly built and pale, which made his feats of physical endurance during his later campaigns all the more remarkable. Much of this is highly subjective and it is hard to know, for instance, just how tall he was. Suetonius' comment may well mean no more than that Caesar did not strike people as particularly small even though he was rather slim. We really have no idea of what sort of stature first-century-BC Romans considered to be tall or indeed of average size. In most respects there was nothing especially unusual in Caesar's physical appearance, for there were surely plenty of other aristocrats who had dark eyes, dark brown or black hair (presumably, since we have no explicit comment on its colour) and pale complexions. It was his manner that most marked out the young man as unusual. We have already encountered the extraordinary boldness with which he stood up to Sulla, when everyone else seemed terrified into submission. Caesar revelled in standing out from the crowd, and dressed in a highly distinctive way. Instead of the normal short-sleeved senator's tunic, which was white with a purple stripe – the evidence is unclear as to whether this ran vertically down the centre or horizontally around the border – he wore his own unconventional version. This had long sleeves that reached down to his wrists and ended in a fringe. Although it was not normal to wear a belt or girdle with this tunic, Caesar did so, but perversely kept it very loose. Sulla is supposed to have warned the other senators to keep an eye on that 'loose-girded boy'. It is just possible that this style was intended to serve as a reminder of his earlier designation for the flaminate, given that the *flamen* was not permitted to have knots in his clothing, but it may simply have been mere affectation. Whatever its purpose, the result was the same. Caesar dressed so that he was recognisably a member of a senatorial family, but at the same time marked himself out as not quite the same as his peers.[2]

Appearance and grooming were very important to the Romans, and especially the aristocracy. It was no coincidence that the bath-house, a complex devoted to the comfort and cleanliness of citizens, required some of the most sophisticated engineering ever devised by the Romans. The very nature of political life, where senators frequently visited or were visited by potential allies and clients, and where they walked through the streets to attend public meetings, ensured that dress and bearing were always under scrutiny. Caesar was very much the dandy, his turnout impeccable even if his clothing was a little eccentric. The same was true of many other young aristocrats in a Rome whose wealth ensured that expensive and exotic materials were readily available. Young men of senatorial families had the money to spend on such things, as well as great numbers of slaves to pamper to their needs. Those who lacked the funds for such a lavish lifestyle were often willing to place themselves in debt so that they could keep up with those who could. Yet even amongst the 'fashionable set' in Rome, Caesar's fastidiousness about his appearance was seen as excessive. To be closely shaven and have short, neatly trimmed hair was entirely proper, but rumours circulated that Caesar had all his other body hair removed. In many ways it was perhaps the contradictory nature of his character that perplexed observers. Most of the fashionable young aristocrats in Rome spent as lavishly on wild living as they did on their own appearance. In contrast Caesar ate sparingly and drank little and never to excess, although his guests were always well entertained. He thus presented an odd mixture of traditional frugality and modern self indulgence.[3]

Caesar's family was not especially wealthy by aristocratic standards and the loss of Cornelia's dowry had doubtless been a heavy blow. A senator's prominence and wealth were usually indicated by the location of his house, with the leading men in the Republic living on the slopes of the Palatine along the Sacra Via, the road taken by processions through the heart of the city. Marius had signalled his success over the barbarians by purchasing a house in this area, close to the Forum. Some of the great houses were very old, but it seems to have been rare for the same family to remain in one house for many generations. In part this was because the Roman aristocracy had no concept of primogeniture and instead tended to divide property between their children, often along with political associates whom it was felt important to honour by a legacy. To facilitate this, houses and other property appear to have been bought and sold with great frequency. The house that the orator Cicero would own at the height of his career had originally been owned by Marcus Livius Drusus until his murder in 91 BC. Cicero had bought it from another senator, Marcus Licinius Crassus, a prominent supporter of Sulla who is known to have bought up a lot of property during the proscriptions. The same house had at least two other, unrelated owners in the decades following Cicero's death in 43 BC. This was a grand building in a position that indicated the great prominence of its occupant. In contrast the young Caesar had a smaller place in the unfashionable district known as the Subura. Situated in a valley between the Esquiline and Viminal hills, and some distance from the main Forum, the Subura was dominated by large areas of slum housing, where many of the poorest occupants lived in badly built blocks of flats off narrow streets and alleys. It was an area of constant bustle, teeming with people and notorious for a number of disreputable activities, most notably prostitution. The occupants were probably mainly citizens, including many former slaves, but may well also have included substantial foreign communities. There is evidence for a synagogue in the area at a later date and it is not impossible that one already existed in Caesar's day.[4]

Much of a senator's business was conducted in his home and this was reflected in the design of houses. A porch for meeting visitors, including the clients who were expected formally to greet their patron each morning, and for displaying the busts or ancestors and the symbols of honours and achievements won by them or the present resident was essential. Equally important were rooms for more private discussions and places to entertain dinner guests. The usual layout with a central, enclosed courtyard did offer some privacy, but ambitious men were reluctant to shut out the world. Livius Drusus' architect is supposed to have offered to construct his house so that he would be free from all outside gaze, prompting the reply that if it were possible he would prefer it built so that everything he did was visible.[5] For all their wealth, status and influence, men in public life could not afford to close themselves off from the life and business of the wider city. Therefore, though he doubtless lived on the fringes of the Subura, and certainly is most unlikely to have had a house in the very poorest part of the region, Caesar cannot have been entirely detached from what was going on around him. It may even be that daily contact with the less well off taught him some of the skill he would later show in handling crowds and in talking to the rank and file of the legions.

Living in the Subura may have proved advantageous, allowing the foppish aristocrat to understand better the wider population, but the reason for living there is unlikely to have been anything other than his own modest means. The young Sulla had been even worse off, having to rent a flat in an apartment block since he could not even afford a house, and paying only a little more for his accommodation than the freedman who lived above him. Caesar's house indicated both his lack of funds and his comparative unimportance in the Republic. To an extent his desire to stand out conflicted with this, as did his willingness to spend beyond his means. Usually this was to further his career, but occasionally it seemed little more than whim. Suetonius tells us that he decided to have a country villa constructed on one of his estates. However, when the foundations had already been laid and building was underway, he was dissatisfied with the design. He immediately ordered the structure to be demolished and a new one built in its place. The date of this incident is uncertain, and it may well have occurred somewhat later in his career, but it helps to illustrate the point that, at least in certain things, Caesar demanded perfection. For much of his life he was an enthusiastic collector of fine art, gems and pearls, which was a rather expensive hobby given his circumstances.[6]

A CROWN AND A KING

Caesar had gone abroad soon after escaping from Sulla's men and did not return to Rome until after the dictator's death. During these years he began the military service that was the legal preliminary to a public career. He served first with the governor of Asia, the propraetor Marcus Minucius Thermus. Caesar's father had governed the same province about a decade before, so that the family name was already a familiar one to the provincials and the son inherited a number of important connections with leading men in the region. Thermus was a prominent Sullan and Caesar became one of his *contubernales* ('tent-companions'), young men who messed with the commander and performed whatever duties he allocated to them. Ideally this provided the governor with a pool of useful subordinates for minor staff functions, while at the same time teaching the youths about soldiering and command. The *contubernales* were supposed to learn by observation, just as younger boys learned how the Republic worked by accompanying prominent senators in the daily duties at Rome. Like so many aspects of an aristocrat's early years, the details of where and with whom he would serve were not centrally controlled by the State, but arranged by individual families. The connection between Caesar and Thermus is obscure and may well have been indirect, via someone else with whom both parties had bonds of political friendship.[7]

Under normal circumstances Asia was a peaceful and prosperous province, making it the sort of posting where a Roman governor and his staff could expect to make a handsome profit during their service. Yet it was only seven years since Mithridates of Pontus had overrun the whole area and ordered the communities to massacre all the Romans living amongst them. Sulla had defeated Mithridates and for the moment the king was once again at peace with Rome, but some of his recent allies had yet to be defeated. One of Thermus' main tasks was to defeat the city of Mytilene, which was besieged and eventually taken by storm. During the course of the fighting the nineteen-year-old Caesar won Rome's highest award for gallantry, the civic crown (*corona civica*). Traditionally this decoration was given only to those who had risked their own life to save that of another citizen. The rescued man was supposed to plait a simple wreath of oak leaves – a tree that was sacred to Jupiter – and present this to his saviour as an open acknowledgement of his debt. However, by Caesar's day it was normally awarded by the magistrate commanding the army. The wreath was worn at military parades, but winners of the crown were also permitted to wear them during festivals in Rome. None of our sources preserve any details of the exploit that led to Caesar being awarded the crown, but the *corona civica* was never lightly bestowed and commanded immense respect. During the crisis of the Second Punic War, when the Roman Senate had suffered huge casualties and needed to replenish its numbers, men who had won the *corona civica* were one of the main groups chosen for admission. It is just possible that Sulla had decreed a similar measure, so that aristocratic winners of the crown were immediately enrolled in the Senate, but even if this was not true, the decoration was guaranteed to impress the electorate and help a man's career.[8]

Not all of Caesar's first term of overseas service was so creditable. Before the storming of Mytilene, the propraetor had sent him to the court of King Nicomedes of Bithynia (on the north coast of modern Turkey) to arrange for the despatch of a squadron of warships to support the Roman campaign. Bithynia was a client kingdom, allied to Rome and obliged to make such contributions. Nicomedes was elderly and had doubtless encountered Caesar's father, which probably ensured that the welcome given to the son was especially warm. The youth seems to have revelled in the luxury he encountered, and was accused of lingering far longer than was necessary to perform his task. Caesar was young, had led a comparatively sheltered life because of the burdens of the flaminate, and was getting his first taste of the wider world and of royalty. He was also moving amongst those steeped in the Hellenic culture that was so admired by the Roman aristocracy. Any of this might explain his tarrying overlong at the king's court, but gossip soon spread that the real reason was that Nicomedes had seduced the youth. Stories began to circulate portraying Caesar as a very willing lover, claiming that he had acted as the king's cup-bearer at a drunken feast attended by a number of Roman businessmen. Another tale had him being led by the royal attendants into the royal bedroom, dressed in fine purple robes and left reclining on a golden couch to wait for Nicomedes. The rumours spread rapidly and were fed when Caesar returned to Bithynia not long after leaving, claiming that he needed to oversee the business affairs of one of his freedmen.[9]

It was a scandal that would dog Caesar throughout his life. The Roman aristocracy admired most aspects of Greek culture, but it never openly accepted the celebration of homosexuality that had been espoused by the nobility of some Greek cities. Those senators who took male lovers tended to do so discreetly, but even so would often be held up to public ridicule by political opponents. The dislike of homosexuality appears to have been fairly widespread in most social classes at Rome, and it was seen as something that weakened men. In the army homosexuality within the camp was a capital offence from at least the second century BC. During the campaign against the Cimbri, Marius awarded the *corona civica* to a soldier who had killed an officer after the latter had tried to force his attentions on him. The legionary's conduct was held up as an example of virtue and courage, while the officer's death was seen as fitting punishment for his excessive passion and abuse of authority. This was in spite of the fact that the dead man was a relation to the consul. Senators were not subject to such rigid rules as ordinary soldiers, but faced at the very least criticism and mockery if they showed a fondness for male lovers. During his censorship Cato the Elder expelled a senator because the man had ordered the execution of a prisoner at a banquet merely to please the boy with whom he was then enamoured. The man's fault was his abuse of *imperium*, but his motives were felt to have made the crime worse. Particular contempt was reserved for the boys or young men who were the objects of passion, and the passive partners in sex. Such a role implied extreme effeminacy and, if anything, was felt to be worse than the behaviour of the older, more active lover. That Caesar was said to have been submissive in this way made the rumours all the more damaging, for this meant that the young aristocrat had acted in a way that was thought unfitting even for a slave. The enthusiasm with which the stories claimed he had taken on the role compounded the crime.[10]

Ultimately, it was a very good piece of gossip, playing on well-established Roman stereotypes. The Romans were suspicious of easterners, seeing the Asiatic Greeks as corrupt and decadent, in no way resembling the admired Greeks of the Classical past. Kings were especially disliked, and royal courts seen as places of political intrigue and sexual depravity. Thus the tale of the ageing, lecherous old ruler deflowering the young, naive aristocrat on his first trip abroad had a wide appeal. It helped that the story involved Caesar, a youth whose unusual dress and massive self-esteem had doubtless made him cordially disliked, since as yet neither he nor his family could boast sufficient achievements to justify such vanity. It was deeply satisfying for others to think that this overconfident young man had behaved so submissively to gratify some decrepit old lover. Later in Caesar's career, as he acquired more and more political enemies, the affair with Nicomedes offered them plentiful ammunition to use against him. The story was widely repeated throughout Caesar's life, so that at times he was dubbed the 'Queen of Bithynia'. Another of his opponents styled him 'every woman's husband and every man's wife'. Whether or not men like Cicero, who joyfully repeated the charges, actually believed them to be true is hard to say. Whatever they believed, they wanted the allegations to be true and relished hurling them at a man that many disliked, and some came to loathe. Political invective at Rome was often extremely scurrilous, and the truth very rarely got in the way of a juicy story of rampant or perverted desires. Yet it was not just his opponents who mocked Caesar over this episode, for in later years his own soldiers also enjoyed repeating the joke. Interestingly, this does not appear to have diminished in any way from their respect for their commander, and their mockery was affectionate, if characteristically crude.[11]

The story that Caesar became Nicomedes lover persisted, but it is now impossible to say whether or not it was actually true. Caesar himself fervently denied this, on one occasion offering to take a public oath that there was not a fragment of truth in the allegation, although all this achieved was to increase the ridicule. In later life he was extremely sensitive about the subject, one of few that led him to lose his temper in public. At the time, his rapid return to the royal court had fired the rumours. Was this an indication of his infatuation, a sign of his naivety that such an action might be interpreted as it was, or a conscious decision to ignore the gossips when there was no truth in the rumours about him? The last is a distinct possibility given Caesar's urge not to be confined by some of the rules that bound others. In the end we simply cannot know. Perhaps the nineteen-year-old did feel and succumb to an attraction to an older man – 'experimenting with his sexuality' would probably be the fashionable modern euphemism. If so, then this was the only occasion on which this happened, for it is absolutely certain that homosexuality did not play a part in the rest of Caesar's life. Given the nature of political debate at Rome, it was striking that the affair in Bithynia was almost the only insult of this sort that others were ever to hurl at him. Other rumours of a similar nature, including a scurrilous work by the poet Catullus, did not win widespread belief, though they clearly bothered Caesar himself. Caesar's sexual exploits were a rich source of gossip and scandal, and earned him an extremely dubious reputation, but his frequent affairs were always with women. The lack of restraint he displayed in his relations with his female lovers makes it all the more unlikely that he also slept with men or boys, but that this was not commented upon by contemporaries. Caesar's appetite for women was almost insatiable and his conquests – who often came from the most distinguished families – very numerous. The knowledge of this doubtless added further to the delight others took in repeating the accusation that the great womaniser had once played the woman himself for Nicomedes. Once again, whether or not the story was true mattered far less than that it struck a raw nerve and embarrassed Caesar. All in all, it is more than probable that there was no real truth in the story, although of course absolute certainty is impossible.[12]

Caesar had married Cornelia when he was at most sixteen, but it is extremely improbable that this resulted in his first sexual experience, even if it most probably did for his bride. It was common for an engaged girl to live in the house of her future husband until they were sufficiently old to wed, so that Cossutia (whom Caesar forsook in order to marry Cornelia) may well have been numbered amongst the household of the Caesars for a year or two. However, it would have been most unusual for the couple to have anticipated their wedding, and Cossutia was probably anyway some years younger. Yet we should never forget that the Romans accepted slavery as a normal aspect of life, and that in any aristocratic house there would be large numbers of slaves who were literally the property of their owners. Household slaves were often chosen for their physical appearance, for their duties ensured that they would be highly visible to their masters and the latter's friends. Good-looking house slaves invariably fetched high prices at auctions. Should a slave girl or woman – or indeed boy – attract the owner's attention they had no legal right to resist, for in the end they were property and not human beings. It was assumed to be quite normal for aristocratic Romans to take pleasure with their slaves in this way, and rarely warranted special comment. That paragon of old-fashioned virtue, Cato the Elder, had regularly slept with a slave girl after the death of his wife. During the civil war Marcus Licinius Crassus had fled to Spain and was sheltered by one of his father's clients. Living in a cave to evade detection by Marian agents, his host regularly sent him food and drink, but soon decided that such hospitality was insufficient given the youth of his 'guest', who was in his late twenties. Therefore he sent two pretty slave girls to live in the cave with Crassus and cater to the natural requirements of a virile young man. An historian who wrote much later in the century claimed to have met one of these slaves, who even in her old age had fond memories of those days. Slaves had no choice in such things, for the owner could use force if he chose and punish them or sell them on a whim. Yet doubtless some female slaves welcomed the attention of their master or their master's sons and hoped to benefit from a more privileged position. If so then it was a dangerous hope, for they were likely to incur the jealousy of other slaves, as well as, perhaps, the owner's wife if he were married. It was so normal for owners to make love to their slaves that it seems very likely that Caesar's first sexual experiences were with female slaves owned by the family. Like many other young men he may also have visited the more expensive brothels with which Rome was so plentifully supplied, for again this was to a fair extent viewed as normal and acceptable. It is tempting to read a note of incredulity into Caesar's statement in his *Gallic War Commentaries* that the German tribesmen thought it 'a most shameful thing to have carnal knowledge of a woman before they were twenty years old'.[13]

THE STUDENT AND THE PIRATES

Sometime after the fall of Mytilene, Caesar transferred to the staff of the governor of Cilicia, Publius Servilius Vatia Isauricus, who was operating primarily against the pirates that infested the area. However, in 78 BC the news of Sulla's death reached the eastern provinces and prompted Caesar to return to Rome. The city was once again facing the threat of civil war, as the consul Marcus Aemilius Lepidus came into conflict with the main body of the Senate. Lepidus was soon engaged in raising an army to seize power by force just as Sulla, Cinna and Marius had done. Caesar is said by Suetonius to have contemplated joining the rebels, and even to have been offered great incentives by Lepidus. However, he soon decided against siding with the consul, doubting both the latter's ability and ambition. This may simply be one of a number of stories invented in later years under the assumption that Caesar was always aiming at revolution. Yet in itself it does not seem unreasonable. Caesar had suffered at Sulla's hands and, although he had escaped execution and in the end been pardoned, he had little reason to feel a great affection for a Senate packed with the dictator's supporters. We should also remember that he had grown up in the years when Rome had been stormed three times by legions supporting ambitious senators. It was a real possibility that this might occur again, and if so, then it was better to be associated with the winning side than the losers, so it may simply have been a question of opportunism, deciding whether or not it was advantageous to join with Lepidus.[14]

In the end Caesar chose a more conventional political path, appearing for the first time as an advocate in Rome's courts. The seven courts established by Sulla in his codification of earlier practices were each presided over by a praetor and had a jury drawn from the Senate. Trials were very public affairs, held either on raised platforms in the Forum or sometimes in one of the grand basilicas, and in either case open to public view. Roman law had no concept of the State prosecuting an individual, and charges had always to be brought by an individual, though he might be acting on behalf of others or indeed an entire community. During their term of office magistrates were not subject to prosecution, but all were aware that they were vulnerable to being attacked in the courts once they had laid down *imperium*. In theory the fear of subsequent prosecution was intended to prevent their abusing their office. There were no professional lawyers as such, for although a class of prosecutors (*accusatores*) existed, they came from outside the aristocracy and were not highly esteemed. Instead the parties would usually be represented by one or more advocates who were normally men pursuing a career in public life. Their status and *auctoritas* greatly added to the force of the case they made. Appearing on someone's behalf in court was an important way of cementing political friendships or placing other men under an obligation, and also of being seen by potential voters.

In 77 BC Caesar prosecuted Cnaeus Cornelius Dolabella for extortion during his term as proconsul of Macedonia. Dolabella had gone out to his province after his consulship in 81 BC and had won a triumph for his military exploits. He was a supporter of Sulla, as is indicated by his electoral success under the dictator, but it would be a mistake to understand the court case as motivated by this connection. Caesar was not seeking to attack the Sullan regime, but was simply choosing a prominent man to prosecute. The trial of an ex-consul, and a man who had triumphed, was bound to attract more public interest than that of someone more humble, and offered to place the young prosecutor in the limelight, if only for a short time. The case was most likely inspired by complaints made by some of the provincial communities in Macedonia who had suffered under Dolabella's rule. As non-citizens they could not bring charges against him themselves, so instead had to go to Rome and persuade a Roman to take the case on for them. Why they chose Caesar is unknown, but it may have been the result of some tie of friendship with the community leaders, perhaps inherited from his father or an earlier ancestor. It is more than likely that Dolabella had abused his power to enrich himself, for such behaviour was all too common amongst Roman magistrates in this period. Men spent lavishly to win election at Rome and frequently went to their province desperate to pay off their massive debts. Governors were not salaried, although they received modest expenses, but they were the supreme power in their province, able to bestow or withhold favours to provincials or businessmen. The temptation to take bribes was great, as was the urge to confiscate as plunder anything they desired. The poet Catullus would later give 'How much did you make?' as the first question a friend asked him after his return from a junior post on the staff of a provincial governor. The difficulty for provincials of using the law against their rulers, since they had to travel to Rome and find advocates, further encouraged corruption on a massive scale. In 70 BC the orator Cicero prosecuted a particularly notorious governor of Sicily, who is supposed to have declared that a man needed three years in a post – the first year to steal enough money to make himself rich, the second to provide the money to hire the best legal defence team, and the third to accumulate the bribes for the judge and jury to ensure that he escaped justice.[15]

Something of the odds usually stacked against the provincials were evident at Dolabella's trial. His prosecutor was Caesar, twenty-three years old, of little achievement and from a poorly connected family. The proconsul was defended by Rome's leading orator, Quintus Hortensius, and the very distinguished Caius Aurelius Cotta. The latter was a cousin of Caesar's mother, but it was not uncommon for relations to represent opposing parties in court. This was considered to be entirely proper, allowing them both to honour or create new obligations to other senators, and did not indicate any bad blood between the advocates. Caius had been one of the men who persuaded Sulla to pardon Caesar and was to win the consulship for 75 BC. Cicero later recalled watching Hortensius and Cotta in action at this and other trials:

> In those days there were two orators who so surpassed all the rest that I craved to emulate them – Cotta and Hortensius. One was relaxed and gentle, phrasing his sentences readily and easily . . . the other ornate and passionate . . . . I saw too in cases where both were on the same side, as for Marcus Canuleius, and on behalf of Cnaeus Dolabella the ex-consul, that although Cotta was the principal advocate, even so Hortensius played the greater part. The bustle of the Forum needed a powerful orator, a man of passion and skill, and with a voice that carried.[16]

Caesar was therefore facing one of the most formidable teams then active in the courts. This was not surprising since acting for the defence was considered to be a more honourable role than prosecution. Prosecutors were essential to allow the legal system to function, but their success often meant the ending of the career of another senator. A governor found guilty of extortion in theory faced the death penalty, for Rome had few prisons and tended to punish all serious crimes with execution. In practice the condemned man was allowed to flee the city with all his movable possessions and go into comfortable exile. Massilia (modern Marseilles), the old Greek colony on the coast of Gaul and now part of the Roman province of Transalpine Gaul, was one of the favourite locations for this. Yet for all its consolations such exile was permanent, for the man could never return to Rome. Prosecution was therefore an aggressive action and defence was held to be more honourable. By the standards of the senatorial aristocracy it was better to support a friend facing charges, even if he were guilty, than to seek to end another man's career. Almost always the defending counsels were older, more experienced men who had long since proved their skills in the courts. It was considered worthier for such men to demonstrate their loyalty to political allies. Prosecution was usually left to the young and ambitious, who hoped to win the fame that would assist them in climbing the political ladder.

When the case came to trial Caesar delivered a speech that greatly impressed onlookers. Caesar subsequently published a version of this speech – a not uncommon practice, which Cicero was to follow throughout his career. Although it has not survived, we know from ancient commentators that it was widely admired. It may well have been this speech that showed how much Caesar had been influenced by the rhetorical style of Caesar Strabo – in another of his published speeches he actually copied a substantial section of one of the latter's orations. The words of a speech were only part of the performance – for performance it was as Cicero admitted when he compared the gifted orator to a famous actor (see the opening quote, page 61). How the orator stood, how he dressed and held himself, letting his toga fall in just the right way, his expressions, the power and tone of his voice were all vital aspects of an advocate's job. During the trial Caesar impressed the crowd watching proceedings as well as those taking part, while the publication of the speech helped to build on the reputation he had won. His voice was a little high pitched, but his delivery evidently gave it force and power. He did well out of his first appearance as an advocate, even though the prosecution ended in failure with Dolabella's acquittal. The outcome was probably not unexpected, since most governors charged with extortion were exonerated. As usual the defence had been composed of men with far greater experience and *auctoritas* than the prosecution with the almost inevitable result. The fame won by Caesar was probably little consolation to the Macedonians who had persuaded him to undertake the case, but they had at least demonstrated their capacity to bring a former governor to trial, even if he had escaped conviction.[17]

Caesar did a little better in his next appearance in the same court, although once again the accused evaded punishment. This was the trial of Caius Antonius in 76 BC for his rapacity while serving in the war against Mithridates. The court was presided over by the praetor Marcus Licinius Lucullus, the brother of Lucius who had been the only senator to accompany Sulla on his march on Rome in 88 BC. Caesar made a very good case against a man whose guilt seems to have been patent, but Antonius appealed to the tribunes of the plebs, prompting one or more of these to veto the proceedings. As a result the trial broke up without delivering its verdict and Antonius escaped, although his subsequent career proved extremely chequered – he was expelled from the Senate by the censors in 70 BC, restored in 68 and even managed to reach the consulship in 63, holding office jointly with Cicero. Although once again the provincials had seen a corrupt Roman official go unpunished, Caesar had further added to his reputation. However, Suetonius claims that his activities had incurred the hostility of influential men, notably the associates of Dolabella, prompting him to decide to go abroad in 75 BC, ostensibly to study.[18]

Caesar travelled first to Rhodes, where he planned to study with Apollonius Molo, the most distinguished teacher of oratory of his day. Apollonius had been sent to Rome by the Rhodians as part of an embassy a few years before, when he had been permitted to address the Senate in Greek – the first person ever to be granted this privilege. By the early first century BC it was common for young Roman aristocrats to round off their education by attending the famous schools of philosophy and rhetoric in the Greek East. In rather a similar way to Caesar, Cicero had left Rome for further study after being active in the courts for a couple of years. In his case he spent time in Athens and in several cities of Asia Minor in 78–77 BC, before also going to Rhodes to learn from Apollonius. Cicero describes him as:

> . . . famous as an advocate in important cases and as a speech writer for others, and also skilled at dissecting and correcting mistakes and very wise teaching. He focused in particular, as far as it was possible, on cutting out the redundant and over florid aspects of my style, which was then characterised by the over enthusiasm and lack of restraint of youth, as if it were a river, to confine it within its banks.[19]

It is not known in what specifics Caesar received tuition from the famous teacher.

Before Caesar reached Rhodes his ship was intercepted by pirates near the island of Pharmacussa off the coast of Asia Minor. Piracy was a major problem throughout the Mediterranean in the early decades of the first century BC. In part this was a legacy of the Romans' own successes, which had destroyed the Kingdom of Macedonia, crippled the Seleucid Empire and helped the decline of Ptolemaic Egypt. All of these great Hellenistic powers had once maintained powerful navies, but with their decay piracy flourished in the Aegean and eventually became endemic throughout the Mediterranean. Further encouragement and direct support came from Mithridates of Pontus, who saw these freebooters as useful allies against Rome. The rugged coastline of Cilicia in Asia Minor was home to many pirate strongholds, and the campaigns of Servilius Isauricus, under whom Caesar himself had served, and others had made little headway in controlling the problem. The pirates were extremely numerous, at times operating in large squadrons and even launching plundering raids on the coastal communities of Italy itself. Although they were not united under a single leader, but had many chieftains, there does seem to have been a considerable degree of mutual co-operation between the different pirate communities. At the height of their power in the late seventies BC the pirates were even able to raid Ostia, and on another occasion kidnapped two Roman praetors along with all their attendants. Although they did occasionally kill Roman prisoners – allegedly telling one haughty aristocrat to disembark when they were at sea, in a story to some extent anticipating the walking of the plank so beloved of the fiction dealing with a later generation of pirates – their main aim was to ransom them. [20]

The young patrician was a valuable prize and his captors decided to demand a payment of 20 talents of silver for his release. Caesar is supposed to have laughed at the amount, declaring that he was worth far more than that and pledging instead to pay them 50 talents. He then sent off most of his travelling companions to the nearest cities in the provinces where they could raise loans to obtain the necessary money. This left Caesar attended only by his doctor and two slaves in the pirates' camp. According to Plutarch he was in no way overawed by his fierce captors, but:

> . . . he held them in such disdain that whenever he lay down to sleep he would send and order them to stop talking. For thirty-eight days, as if the men were not his watchers, but his royal bodyguard, he shared

in their sports and exercises with great unconcern. He also wrote poems and sundry speeches which he read aloud to them, and those who did not admire these he would call to their faces illiterate Barbarians, and often laughingly threatened to crucify them all. The pirates were delighted at this, and attributed this boldness of speech to a certain simplicity and boyish mirth.[21]

After his friends returned with the ransom, which had been dutifully provided by allied communities eager to oblige a man who might in time become a useful connection at Rome, Caesar was released. The city of Miletus on the western coast of Asia seems to have provided the bulk of the money and Caesar immediately hurried there. He was twenty-five years old and a private citizen who had never held elected office, but this did not prevent him from persuading and cajoling the provincials to gather and crew a number of warships. Taking charge of this force, he led it straight back to Pharmacussa to attack his former captors. Complacently the pirates were still in the camp on shore, their ships beached and in no position to resist. Caesar's improvised squadron took them prisoner and captured their amassed plunder, including his own ransom. The 50 talents was presumably repaid to the donor communities, while Caesar took the prisoners to Pergamum where they were imprisoned. He then went to the Roman governor of Asia to arrange for the pirates' execution. However, the propraetor Marcus Iuncus showed little interest in imposing the punishment that Caesar had repeatedly promised to inflict. He was currently occupied in organising Bithynia into the Roman province, for Nicomedes had recently died and bequeathed his realm to Rome. Iuncus saw the opportunity to profit by selling the pirates as slaves, and was also eager to appropriate some of their captured plunder for himself. When it became clear that he would not act quickly at the behest of some young patrician, Caesar hastened back to Pergamum and ordered the prisoners to be crucified. He had no legal authority to do this, although no one was likely to question the execution of a group of raiders. In this way Caesar fulfilled his promise. However, he had clearly developed some regard for the men during his time with them, and anyway wished to show his merciful nature, so that he had each pirate's throat cut before they were crucified, sparing them a lingering and extremely painful death.[22]

Thus runs the story. In so many ways it encapsulates the legend of Caesar, who was always in charge whatever the situation. Here is the young aristocrat who mocked his captors, scorned the ransom they demanded, and never once lost his poise. Once again we have the same self-confidence that had faced down Sulla the dictator, as the patrician failed to be cowed by overwhelming force. There is also the charm, which could win over a band of cut-throats as easily as Roman citizens or soldiers. After his release Caesar acted swiftly, his force of character making others do his bidding even though he had no power to command them, and won a sweeping victory. Caesar had promised to capture and execute the pirates, and that is precisely what Caesar had done, in spite of the reluctance to act of the propraetor who actually governed the province. It was a display of his fearlessness, determination, speed of action and ruthless skill, while the final act provided an instance of the clemency he would later parade as one of his greatest attributes. It is a very good story and one which doubtless leant itself to embellishment with each retelling. Given that Caesar's travelling companions had left him and that only his slaves and doctor were present during his time with the pirates, it is interesting to wonder who first told the tale. Was this an early instance of Caesar's skill in celebrating his own achievements? Perhaps not, but even if the rumours only began in the communities after his release or were spread by his friends, Caesar doubtless did little to discourage this version of events. How much was true and how much romantic invention is obviously impossible to say.

At the end of this adventure Caesar finally reached Rhodes and studied with Apollonius. He proved an adept pupil, his rhetorical style fluent and deceptively simple. Cicero and others considered him one of the best orators of the period and suggested that he might even have achieved first place if he had concentrated on oratory to the exclusion of other pursuits. Yet for Caesar skill with words remained a means to the wider aim of political success. He was exceptionally good at it, but then he was also proving himself very good at other things, most notably soldiering. There was another opportunity to demonstrate this during his time as a student on Rhodes. Open war had once more broken out with Mithridates in 74 BC and a detachment of Pontic troops had launched a raid into Asia, plundering the territory of peoples allied to Rome. Caesar laid aside his studies and took a ship to the province, where he raised troops from the local communities and with this hastily formed force defeated the invaders. The action – once again so swift, confident and competent – was believed to have prevented some allies from defecting to Mithridates since the Romans had proved unable to defend them. Once again it is worth emphasising that he was a private citizen without any legal authority to act in this way. No one would have held him responsible for the damage being done in Asia if he had simply sat quietly at Rhodes. Yet for Caesar it was his duty to act since there was no properly constituted Roman officer available. It was also a splendid opportunity for him to make a name for himself. Serving the Republic and winning personal glory in the process were entirely proper ambitions for the senatorial aristocracy.[23]

IN ROME AGAIN

Towards the end of 74 or early in 73 BC Caesar was appointed to a priesthood, but one that was far less restrictive than the office of *Flamen Dialis*. The college of pontiffs, fifteen strong and headed by the *Pontifex Maximus*, voted to admit him to the vacancy created when one of their number died. This was Aurelia's relation Caius Aurelius Cotta, who had in the past pleaded for Caesar's life with Sulla and then been on the opposing side at Dolabella's trial. Pontiffs were supposed to pass on their religious knowledge by word of mouth, so that it was normal to have a broad age range within the college. It is more than likely that the family connection was one of the reasons for Caesar's selection, but it is also an indication that the young man was already displaying talent. One of the pontiffs was Servilius Isauricus under whom he had served after winning the *corona civica*. Given that the majority of the pontiffs were also very much Sulla's appointees it is also an indication that Caesar was not perceived as a dangerous radical. The appointment was a great honour, marking the holder out as an up and coming man likely to do well in public life. The fifteen pontiffs, along with the equal number of men belonging to the other two important orders, the augurate and the quindecemvirate, represented an elite within the senatorial class. In the main only members of noble families, who included consuls amongst their ancestors, were given these posts and the admission of anyone else was a great distinction. If they lived long enough, the majority of these priests gained the consulship.[24]

The news of his appointment prompted Caesar to abandon his studies and immediately return to Rome to be formally admitted to the priesthood. Travelling with only two friends and ten slaves in a small boat, he had once again to pass through seas infested with pirates, who had been given little cause to love him by his recent escapade. At one point during the voyage the Romans thought that they had sighted a pirate vessel, prompting Caesar to remove his fine outer clothes and strap a dagger to his thigh. Presumably he hoped to blend with his attendants and the crew and escape at any favourable opportunity. In the event it proved unnecessary, as he soon realised that he had mistaken a wooded shoreline for the silhouette of a ship. Once back in Rome, he was soon active in the courts again, and seems to have prosecuted Marcus Iuncus in the extortion court. Most probably he was acting on behalf of the Bithynians, for he preserved his connection with their royal family in particular. At some later date he represented Nicomedes' daughter Nysa in a legal dispute, and gave a strong speech recounting his debt to the Bithynian king. This is said to have prompted the retort from Cicero of 'No more of that please, when everyone knows what he gave to you and what you gave to him.' The scandal clung to Caesar, but does not seem to have damaged him politically. The outcome of Iuncus' trial is unknown, but it is more than probable that he was acquitted, since so many obviously guilty former governors managed to escape punishment. As with his earlier appearances in court, the outcome of the case was in some ways less important for his own career than his personal performance. [25]

Sometime near the end of the decade he stood for his first public office and was successfully elected as one of the twenty-four military tribunes. This was probably for either 72 or 71 BC, although our sources are vague. The military tribunes were very different from the tribunes of the plebs, for their role was exclusively military. Each legion of the army had around six tribunes and, since there were now many more than four legions in existence at any one time, many of these officers were appointed. However, there was considerable prestige attached to the elected posts and this was seen as often the first opportunity to test a young aristocrat's popularity with voters. None of our sources mention a posting to a province at this time, which suggests that Caesar served his time in Italy itself, for the great Slave War was raging at that time. In 73 BC a small group of gladiators led by a Thracian called Spartacus had escaped from their training school outside Capua, sparking a huge slave rebellion throughout the Italian Peninsula. Spartacus won a series of stunning victories, smashing one Roman army after another, and it was not until 71 BC that he was finally defeated by Marcus Licinius Crassus. Caesar may well have served under Crassus and if so it would mark the first known connection between the two men.[26]

Crassus had won the praetorship for 73 BC and was given the command against the slaves in the following year after both the consuls had been defeated in battle. He was about forty, but had gained considerable experience of high command during the civil war. Forced to flee Italy after the murder of his father and brother by the Marians, Crassus at first sought refuge in Spain. This was the occasion when he is supposed to have been hidden in a cave, where one of his family's clients provided him with food and two slave girls as companions. Later he joined Sulla and fought with distinction for him, saving the day at the battle of the Colline Gate outside Rome in 82 BC.

Crassus became bitter because he believed that the dictator never gave him sufficient credit for his achievements, but in other respects he did very well out of Sulla's rule, acquiring property on a massive scale from the victims of the proscriptions. A shrewd and utterly ruthless businessman, he soon became one of the richest men in Rome. His conduct of the campaign against the slaves was similarly efficient. To restore the discipline of troops dismayed by earlier disasters, he ordered the decimation of a number of units. One soldier in ten was chosen by lot and beaten to death by his comrades, who then underwent the symbolic humiliations of eating barley rather than wheat and pitching their tents outside the rampart of the army's camp. Cornering the slaves in the toe of Italy, Crassus had a huge line of fortifications built to trap them. Spartacus managed to break out, displaying once again the truly remarkable skill and force of character that had allowed him to turn a disparate horde of runaway slaves into a highly effective army. The Romans pursued and in the end brought the slaves to battle and destroyed them. Crassus ordered 6,000 male prisoners to be crucified at regular intervals all along the Appian Way from Rome to Capua. There was no talk of slitting their throats to be 'merciful', for the Slave War had terrified the Romans and this ghastly spectacle was intended to show all slaves the folly of further rebellion.[27]

So little is known about Caesar's spell as military tribune that we cannot know whether he actually took part in the Slave War, and if so what part he played in the affair. Years later, when he led his legions against the German tribes for the first time, Caesar would encourage his soldiers by recalling that there had been many Germans amongst the defeated slave army, but his own account makes no mention of personal service in the earlier conflict. This is not necessarily a strong indication one way or the other, since the *Commentaries* rarely include autobiographical detail. On balance it is more probable than not that he did serve in the war, and presumably that he displayed the competence he had shown in the past, though perhaps he did nothing especially distinguished that might have earned mention in the sources. It is known that during his time as military tribune he spoke in favour of a proposal for some restoration of the powers of the tribunes of the plebs, which Sulla had taken from them. There was clearly widespread enthusiasm for this amongst the electorate and Caesar was most likely wanting to gain popularity by associating himself with this cause. Such opportunism was common amongst those seeking to climb the political ladder and need not be taken as a sign of deep hostility to the Sullan regime or to a Senate still packed with the dictator's supporters. Caesar's relation

Caius Aurelius Cotta had brought in a bill during his consulship in 75 BC that permitted former tribunes of the plebs to seek other magistracies, preventing the office from being a political dead end as Sulla had intended.[28]

The possibility of an early connection with Crassus is intriguing, for the latter was highly skilled in using his wealth to gain political influence by assisting those whose ambitions outstripped their funds. In the next decade Caesar certainly benefited from substantial loans from Crassus and it is possible that he received some similar aid earlier on. Yet we should not exaggerate Caesar's importance, for he was one of many senators assisted in this way by Crassus, and few could have guessed at his eventual success. He was flamboyant, talented – as demonstrated by his military service and activity in the courts – and had a gift for self-publicity which helped to attract the attention of the electorate, while the scandal surrounding him at least ensured that his name was widely known. Such things were assets for a man aspiring to a career in public life, but to a greater or lesser degree they were also displayed by many of his contemporaries. Nor were they automatic guarantors of success. Personal talent did appeal to the voters, but it was not the sole, nor even the most important factor in winning their favour. Though he might dress distinctively and display an immensely high opinion of his own worth, Caesar's career so far had been conventional in most important respects. His independent actions against the pirates and the Pontic raiders in Asia had been exceptional, but were proper enough for a dutiful citizen and, even more importantly, successful. Such behaviour was a good indicator of *virtus*, a quality that lay at the heart of the Roman aristocracy's self-image. By the time that he was thirty Caesar had shown considerable promise – something that his admission to the pontificate indicated – and was in no way considered a revolutionary. It remained to be seen how far up the political ladder he might climb, his talent balancing his comparative poverty and the mediocre achievements of his recent ancestors.

V

CANDIDATE

Caesar ' . . . spent money very freely, and some thought that he was only buying brief and passing fame at massive cost, when in fact he was securing things of enormous value at a knock-down price. . . . In this way the people became so well disposed towards him that they all sought new offices and honours as repayment for his generosity.'– *Plutarch, early second century AD.*[1]

In 70 BC Caesar was thirty years old. He was extremely well educated, even by the standards of the Roman aristocracy, a gifted orator and a soldier of proven courage. In the domestic sphere his life was also going well. He and Cornelia had now been married for some fifteen years. The couple had spent over a third of this time separated, when Caesar went abroad for his education and military service, but the marriage was certainly a successful one by the standards of the Roman nobility, and it may well also have been a happy one. At some point Cornelia had given birth to a daughter, who was of course named Julia. This was Caesar's only legitimate child, but despite her importance the date of her birth is not known. Estimates have varied from as early as 83 to as late as 76 BC, but somewhere near the end of this range seems most probable. Julia was married in 59 BC, by which time she was probably in her mid to late teens. Caesar's periods of absence overseas make it most likely that his daughter was conceived between 78 BC after his return from the east and before he left Rome again in 75 BC.[2]

Caesar treated Cornelia with great respect, most famously in his defiance of Sulla's order to divorce her. In Roman tradition wives were to be honoured, but were not necessarily the objects of great passion for such emotions were seen as irrational and even rather shameful. The marriage bed was the place to produce the next generation of Roman children to continue the family name, but physical pleasure for its own sake should be sought elsewhere. This is not to say that some married couples – perhaps even the majority –

were more or less deeply in love and enjoyed an active sex life, but simply that by the ideals of Roman aristocratic society this was not seen as an especially important aspect of marriage. It was widely accepted that aristocratic husbands would take sexual pleasure elsewhere and not require their wives to cater for their more shameful desires. This was especially true in the case of a younger man, what the Romans called an *adulescens*. Although this is the root of our word adolescent, for the Romans it referred to any man not yet fully matured and could well extend into the late thirties. Such 'youths' were granted a degree of leeway in their behaviour not extended to those who had reached full manhood, who as leaders of the Republic were expected to act more responsibly. Taking discreet pleasure with female slaves or with prostitutes was rarely criticised.[3]

Many young aristocratic men also kept mistresses after they were married. There was a distinct group of high-class prostitutes or courtesans who relied on lovers to provide them with a house or apartment, attendants and wealth. Such women were usually well educated, witty, charming, and perhaps skilled in singing, dancing or playing a musical instrument, so that they provided the lover with company as well as sexual gratification. These affairs were never intended to be permanent and successful courtesans passed from one lover-provider to the next. This added further spice to the affair for the lover had to struggle to win the favour of the mistress and then keep devoting sufficient attention and gifts to retain it. Famous courtesans were often associated with some of the most important men in Rome, for it was not only young senators who might choose to maintain a mistress. The nature of the relationship between lover and courtesan was such that the woman could gain considerable influence. In 74 BC it was widely believed that the consul Lucius Licinius Lucullus gained an important provincial command through winning over Praecia, the mistress of a prominent senator, with gifts and flattery. This man was Publius Cornelius Cethegus, a useful illustration of a man who held no formal office, but enjoyed massive, if temporary, influence in the Senate through a mixture of *auctoritas* and shrewd knowledge and exploitation of senatorial procedure. Concubines could also play a political role in other ways, as was shown in the case of another famous individual called Flora. At one time the young Pompey was deeply in love with her. In later life she was said to have often boasted that she was always left with scratch marks on her back after the two of them had made love. However, when he discovered that a friend of his called Geminius was repeatedly trying to seduce Flora, he willingly gave her up to him. Scrupulous in his generosity to his friend, who thus became indebted to him and a useful political supporter, Pompey never again visited Flora. This was held to be a particularly great sacrifice for him as he was still greatly attracted to her. For her part Flora was also supposed still to have been in love with Pompey, and claimed that she was unwell for a long time afterwards. The concubine's position was at heart precarious, for even if at times some were able to win great influence they had no legal status and were successful for only as long as they could command their lovers' affections.[4]

Courtesans and slave girls were generally acceptable as the objects of male aristocrats' affections, since this did not in any way threaten the established social order or the integrity of family lines. Most courtesans were of a low social status, prostitutes who had done well for themselves. Often they were slaves or former slaves who had worked as entertainers of various forms. For some time in the mid forties BC Mark Antony was deeply enamoured of a mime actress and dancer called Cytheris, a former slave who had been freed by her patron and given the name Volumnia. Antony paraded her in public and gave her the place of honour at dinner parties, treating her almost like a real wife, much to the private dismay of Cicero. The same woman later became the mistress of Caesar's assassin Brutus, as well as other prominent senators. Any children born of such a union between an aristocrat and his mistress were illegitimate and so did not take the father's name or have any legal claim to be supported by him – in the case of the babies born to slaves these were literally the property of their owners. Yet if an aristocratic husband might take lovers in this way, society did not grant the same licence to his wife, for it was important that there should be no question mark over the paternity of her offspring. Chastity, in the sense of remaining faithful to her husband and only her husband, was one of the central attributes of the ideal Roman matron. In earlier times a woman spent her whole life under the power of – literally 'in the hand of' (*sub manu*) – either her father or her husband, who had the power to execute her if they chose. By the first century BC this traditional, strict form of marriage where the husband gained all the rights of the woman's father was rarely used. Marriage had become looser and divorce more common, but a wife was still expected to remain absolutely faithful to her husband, even if that husband frequently took other lovers.[5]

Caesar may well have amused himself with courtesans, slave girls and any other available women during his twenties and thirties. Our sources make no explicit mention of this, but since such behaviour was common this may not be especially significant. Suetonius does tell us that Caesar frequently paid very high, even extravagant, prices to purchase physically attractive slaves, noting that even he was ashamed of the cost and so had it concealed in his account books. Whether such servants were entirely ornamental or also intended to provide their owner with sexual entertainment is not stated. However, Suetonius does tell us that it was the 'fixed opinion' that Caesar's passions were 'unrestrained and extravagant' and that he seduced 'many distinguished women'. He lists five by name, all of them wives of important senators, but implies that there were others. One of the named women was Tertulla, the wife of Crassus, under whose command Caesar may have served during the Slave War. She had originally been married to one of Crassus' older brothers, but when the latter was killed during the civil war he had chosen to marry the widow. She was probably a few years older than Caesar and her marriage to Crassus was successful by aristocratic standards, producing children. There is no indication of when the affair occurred or of how long it lasted, a vagueness common for this side of Caesar's life. Nor do we know whether Crassus himself became aware of the liaison, although the notoriety of Caesar's amours make this distinctly possible. He certainly took no action against his wife's lover and readily employed Caesar as a political ally.[6]

Caesar's affairs with married women were numerous, but usually do not appear to have lasted for very long before he sought out a new lover. One definite exception to this pattern was his relationship with Servilia, which seems to have endured for the greater part of Caesar's life. Suetonius tells us that he 'loved her before all others'. Servilia's first husband was Marcus Junius Brutus, but he had supported Lepidus' coup in 78 BC and been executed when it failed. The widowed Servilia had already given birth to a son in 85 BC, who was also named Marcus Junius Brutus. This was Shakespeare's 'noblest Roman of them all', the man who would be one of the leaders of the conspiracy that would assassinate Caesar in 44 BC. The irony did not end there, for Servilia was also half-sister to Cato the Younger, one of Caesar's bitterest opponents for over twenty years. Caesar was very fond of Brutus, an affection which remained even after the latter had fought against him in 49–48 BC. This encouraged persistent rumours that he was in fact Brutus' father, Plutarch even suggesting that Caesar himself believed this. Given that he would only have been fifteen when Brutus was born, this must surely be a myth, but the existence of these tales does suggest that the liaison between Caesar and Servilia began at an early date, probably during the seventies. It continued in spite of the fact that Servilia remarried, and did not prevent Caesar from having numerous affairs with other women. The affair between

Servilia and Caesar was evidently passionate on both sides and long lasting, even if the intensity varied over the years. This does suggest more than mere physical attraction. Servilia was an extremely intelligent woman, deeply interested in politics and keen to promote the careers of her husband and son. Her three daughters were each married off to prominent senators. After Caesar's death she was included in the councils held by Brutus to decide on what the conspirators should do next, her opinion overriding that of distinguished senators including Cicero. The orator was suitably disgusted at a woman invading the male world of politics, but on other occasions had been eager to seek her advice on topics seen as more within the female sphere. He and his family had consulted her when they were seeking a suitable husband for his daughter, Tullia. When the latter died in childbirth, Servilia wrote in sympathy to the distraught Cicero. Although as a woman she could hold no office or formal power, Servilia carefully maintained connections and ties of friendship with many prominent families.[7]

Attractive, intelligent, well educated, sophisticated and ambitious – the description could as easily be of either Caesar or Servilia, although in the case of the latter the ambition was indirect and aimed at securing prominence not for herself but for the male members of her close family. The pair do seem very alike in many ways, which may in part explain the closeness and longevity of the bond between them. The length of the affair in itself suggests that Caesar felt a deeper love for Servilia than for any of his other lovers. Apart from her affair with Caesar, Servilia appears otherwise to have remained faithful to her second husband, Decimus Junius Silanus. This was in contrast to her sister – as usual, confusingly also called Servilia – who was divorced by her husband because of her frequent extramarital affairs. Caesar was a serial seducer of married women. If he felt strong love for any or all of these lovers, it rarely seems to have lasted, or at least was never exclusive. The sheer scale of his activities stood out in Roman society, which at this time did not lack adulterers or rakes. Therefore it is important to try to understand why he behaved in this exceptional way. The obvious answer, that he enjoyed having sex with lots of attractive women, should not be completely ignored purely because it is so basic. Yet this in itself is inadequate, since sexual pleasure could be taken less controversially with slaves or mistresses of lower social status. The more distinguished courtesans offered witty companion- ship in addition to satisfying more physical needs. Seducing married women from senatorial families brought many risks, not least that of notoriety, which could be used against you by political opponents. Tradition, though not law at this date, permitted a husband to kill his wife's lover if he caught them in the act. Such direct violence was unlikely, but a cuckolded husband might well become a bitter political enemy.[8]

The risks involved may have added to the thrill. It is even possible to see Caesar's womanising as an extension of political competition, sleeping with other senators' wives to prove that he was the better man in the bedroom as well as the Forum. Perhaps there was even a conscious desire to smother the stories about his submission to Nicomedes by gaining notoriety for predatory and blatantly heterosexual adventures? Yet none of these reasons seem enough to explain why it was primarily with aristocratic women that Caesar sought satisfaction. That such lovers were almost invariably married was almost inevitable, since the daughters of senatorial families played such an important role in creating and strengthening political bonds. Girls were married young, and those who were divorced or widowed while still young or middle-aged would tend to be swiftly placed into a new match. Only women of mature years who had surviving children were normally permitted to live on as widows without remarrying. Caesar's mother Aurelia followed this path, as did Servilia after the death of her second husband, but in most respects there simply was no group of single aristocratic women at Rome amongst whom Caesar might seek lovers. However, the very nature of Roman public life, where senators held a series of posts many of which required them to serve overseas for years on end, did mean that married women were left on their own for long periods.

Aristocratic wives enjoyed considerable freedom in first-century-BC Rome. Many had considerable means independent of their husbands, including the dowry they had brought at the time of marriage, which was always supposed to remain separate from, although complementary to, the income of the household. As we have seen, by this era girls were educated in the same way as their brothers, at least in the academic sense and during the early years. Therefore they learned to be bilingual in both Latin and Greek and gained a deep appreciation of literature and culture. Unlike their male siblings, girls rarely had any opportunity to travel abroad to further their education by studying in one of the great centres of Greek learning. Since many philosophers and teachers visited Rome for long periods this was only in part a disadvantage, and there were schools teaching a whole range of cultural accomplishments. Sallust's description of one senator's wife is illuminating:

> Amongst these was Sempronia, who had often committed many outrages of masculine audacity. This woman was well blessed by fortune in her birth and physical beauty, as well as her husband and children;

well read in Greek and Latin literature, she played the lyre, danced more artfully than any honest woman should, and had many other gifts which fostered a luxurious life. Yet there was never anything she prized so little as her honour and chastity; it was hard to say whether she was less free with her money or her virtue; her lusts were so fierce that she more often pursued men than was pursued by them.. . . She had often broken her word, failed to pay her debts, been party to murder; her lack of money but addiction to luxury set her on a wild course. Even so, she was a remarkable woman; able to write poetry, crack a joke, and converse modestly, tenderly or wantonly; all in all she had great gifts and a good many charms.[9]

Sempronia was married to Decimus Junius Brutus, a cousin to Servilia's first husband. Her son was to become one of Caesar's senior subordinates in Gaul and during the Civil War, but would later turn against him and become one of his assassins. Caesar doubtless knew her, although whether he was one of the men who sought her favours – or was sought by her – is unknown.

Sallust's description of Sempronia is couched in terms of outrage at her immorality and wildness, but many of her accomplishments were not seen as bad in themselves. Plutarch wrote admiringly of another aristocratic woman who was widowed at a young age and then remarried:

Even apart from her beauty, the young woman had plenty of attractive qualities, in that she was well read, a good player of the lyre, skilled in geometry, and capable of profiting from the philosophical lectures she regularly attended. She also combined these qualities with a character that was free from the unpleasant curiosity which these intellectual interests tend to inflict on young women. . . [10]

Sophistication, learning, wit and even some skill in music or dancing were not in themselves seen as bad things in a woman, so long as they were combined with chastity in the sense of remaining loyal to her husband. Yet in Caesar's day many women did not display this virtue. As a generation they were better educated than their mothers and certainly than their grandmothers, but were still expected to concern themselves with little more than running the household. Given in an arranged marriage while little more than a child, and then perhaps passed on from one husband to the next as death or changing political alliances dictated, a woman was fortunate if she found happiness and fulfilment in this way. Unable to vote or seek office, those like Servilia had to direct their deep interest in politics into promoting the careers of male relations. Independently wealthy in a Rome where all the spoils and profits of empire were available for sale, there was a temptation for many women to compete in luxurious living. Some added spice to their lives by taking a lover or lovers.

On balance it seems likely that Caesar looked for at least a measure of companionship and witty, sophisticated conversation from his mistresses. Some of the most distinguished courtesans may have offered this, but in this respect very few could have competed with the daughters of Rome's great families. His affairs provided him not merely with sexual gratification, but other forms of stimulation. Other thrills already mentioned – the element of danger in carrying out an affair with a married woman, the added pleasure of cuckolding men whom he would meet and compete with in public life on a daily basis – doubtless contributed to his enjoyment. For the women he loved there was his charm, which few people were ever able to resist when in his company. He was Caesar, the one who dressed distinctively, setting fashions that many younger men copied, who took such care over his appearance and deportment, and always marked himself out as special. To receive his full attention even for a while was doubtless very flattering, something that the notoriety of his amorous exploits may well have made even more attractive. Whatever its root, his repeated success with so many women makes it clear that he was very good at seduction. The urge to go from one affair to another was in part merely a reflection of the great energy and ambition he showed in all other aspects of his life. It may also be that he was always searching for someone who was enough of his match to keep him interested over a long period. Servilia, so like him in many ways, evidently came closest to his ideal than any other Roman woman, hence the longevity of their relationship. Yet for all the passion on both sides, each retained a measure of detachment and independence. Though Servilia may well have mourned her lover after the Ides of March, this in no way prevented her from seeking to promote her son's cause in its aftermath. Similarly, for all the enthusiasm and effort devoted to his womanising, Caesar seems never to have allowed this to interfere with his ambition for office and status. It is also possible that some of the stories about him were false. Once he had gained this reputation, his simply being seen with a woman was probably enough for the gossips to assume that they were having an affair.

CHANGING TIMES: THE RISE OF POMPEY

The years after Sulla's death were on the whole a successful time for Caesar, as he gradually moved into public life. Although he had incurred the dictator's wrath, he had been accepted back into the fold and saw no reason for joining those still choosing to fight against Sulla or the regime he created. He did not join Lepidus' rising in 78 BC, nor does it ever seem to have occurred to him to go to Spain where many of Marius' and Cinna's supporters still continued to fight the civil war. These men were led by Quintus Sertorius, probably one of the greatest generals Rome ever produced, whose talent for winning over the Spanish tribes allowed him to resist the Senate's armies for the greater part of a decade. Sertorius and his followers were exiles and refugees from the proscriptions, barred by Sulla's decrees from returning to Rome or ever resuming a political career. There was little alternative for them but to fight on, although on several occasions Sertorius expressed a deep longing to return home, even to live as a private citizen. Despite crossing Sulla, Caesar's family connections had prevented him from facing a similar ban on political activity. As a result there was no need for him to follow the desperate path of open rebellion against the State.[11]

Sulla cast a long shadow over the Republic in these years. The Senate was very much his creation, purged of all his opponents who had failed to defect to him in time, and packed with his partisans. As a body he had strengthened the Senate's position, restoring the senatorial monopoly over juries in the courts and severely limiting the power of the tribunate. Other legislation, for instance a law restricting the behaviour of provincial governors, was intended to prevent any other general from following the dictator's own example and turning his legions against the State. Making such actions formally illegal was obviously of questionable practical value, as the continuing war in Spain and the rebellion of Lepidus indicated. Sulla could undo neither the precedents he had set nor the consequences of his actions. Italy was still in a state of upheaval as a result of the Social and civil wars. Large areas had been devastated by the rival armies, while the newly enfranchised Italians had yet to be fully and fairly integrated into the wider citizen body. Great swathes of land had also been confiscated so that Sulla could give his discharged veteran soldiers farms of their own, dispossessing many peasants. The problems faced by the Italian countryside had only been made worse by the years of marauding by Spartacus' slave army.[12]

Sulla's Senate had not coped all that well with the series of crises it faced after the dictator's retirement. The Slave war had seen army after army led by duly elected magistrates routed and even destroyed by the enemy. Unorthodox measures were employed to gain final victory, the two consuls laying down their commands and being replaced by Crassus, who had only been elected to the more junior magistracy of the praetorship. This was somewhat unconventional, but paled in comparison to the rapid rise to prominence of Cnaeus Pompey. The son of Pompeius Strabo, Pompey was born in 106 BC and served under his father's command during the Social War. Following Strabo's death, he spent some time in the camp of Cinna, but was treated with suspicion and eventually retired to his family's vast estates in Picenum. When Sulla landed in Italy in 83 BC, Pompey decided to join him, as did a growing number of others who had fallen from favour with the current regime or who guessed the likely outcome of the war. Unlike these other refugees, the twenty-three-year-old Pompey chose to appear not as a suppliant, but as a useful ally. Using his own money and drawing predominantly on the population of Picenum, he raised first one and then two more legions of soldiers. This was illegal in every respect, since Pompey had never held any office granting him *imperium* to raise or command troops, and was merely a private citizen. He was not even a member of the Senate, but through his family's wealth and influence and his own force of personality he was able to get away with it. Unlike his father, who had been one of the most unpopular men of his generation, Pompey was adored by his soldiers, who seem to have had no qualms about his lack of authority to lead them. On their march south to join Sulla the young general and his private army both soon proved that they knew how to fight with skill and ferocity.

Sulla had no scruples about employing Pompey's services and sent him in succession to fight on his behalf in Italy, Sicily and Africa. In each campaign the dashing young commander defeated the opposition with ease. Sulla – perhaps partly ironically, though it is hard to tell with such a complex character – hailed him as Pompey 'the Great' (*Magnus*) and permitted him to celebrate a triumph, an unheard of honour for a man with no legal *imperium*. For all the glory he won in these years, Pompey also acquired a reputation for cruelty, stories being told of how he derived a sadistic pleasure from executing the distinguished senators he had captured. For some he was not 'the Great', but the 'young executioner'. In marked contrast to Caesar, Pompey obediently divorced his wife to marry the dictator's own step-daughter. The latter was already married and heavily pregnant and died soon after the wedding to Pompey, but it was nevertheless a mark of great favour. For all the honours granted by the dictator, Pompey was not enrolled in the Senate and remained a private citizen, able to call upon his own private army. He did, however, take a keen interest in politics and supported Lepidus' campaign for the consulship for 78 BC, greatly assisting the latter's victory. Yet when Lepidus turned against the Senate Pompey quickly distanced himself from him. Faced with rebellion, but lacking significant forces with which to oppose it, Sulla's Senate turned to Pompey and his legions. Acting with all the vigour he had shown in earlier campaigns, the twenty-eight-year-old general rapidly crushed Lepidus and his forces. His accustomed cruelty was also again on display, most notably when he executed Servilia's first husband, Marcus Brutus.[13]

Following this success, Pompey encouraged the Senate to send him to Spain to deal with Sertorius, supporting the army that was already operating there under the command of a more conventionally appointed governor. His cause was helped by the reluctance of the consuls of 77 BC to be sent to the region. This time Pompey was invested with proconsular *imperium*, legitimising his status. A senator who supported him quipped that he was going not as a proconsul but *pro consulibus* – 'instead of both consuls'. In Spain Sertorius proved a much tougher opponent than the military incompetents Pompey had faced in the past, and for the first time he suffered some reverses. The experience was humiliating for one so accustomed to success, but the young general had the capacity to learn from his mistakes, developing a respect for his opponent without ever becoming overawed by him. The war in Spain was bitter and protracted, but as the years passed Pompey and the other senatorial armies gradually made headway against the Marian forces. Even so, had Sertorius not been murdered by one of his own subordinates in 72 BC, the war could easily have gone on for several years. Instead, bereft of his genius and instead guided by his assassin, a man whose ambition and pride greatly outstripped his talent, it was all over in a matter of months. Pompey returned to Italy in the following year, arriving just in time to intercept and destroy a few thousand slaves who had escaped the defeat of Spartacus. This minor success soon prompted him to declare publicly that it was he and not Crassus who had brought the Slave War to an end.

The bad blood between Pompey and Crassus dated back to the civil war when both had fought for Sulla. Crassus was six or seven years older and resented the honours and attention lavished on the flamboyant younger man. He was understandably bitter at an attempt to rob him of the credit he had deserved for his victory over Spartacus. The incident also revealed a rather petty streak in Pompey, which on other occasions moved him to try and steal the glory of others. There was no need for this, given that the war in Spain had been a far more prestigious conflict than the suppression of Spartacus, bringing him a second triumph compared to the lesser honour of an ovation granted to Crassus. Yet Pompey revelled in the acclaim of the Senate and citizens and was jealous of anyone else who distracted the attention from him even for a moment. People tended to like Pompey, his round face being considered open and attractive even if not classically handsome. Those who knew him better were more cautious, knowing that his public statements often did not match his actions and that he was not always a reliable friend. In contrast Crassus was respected rather than liked, but scrupulously honoured his obligations to others, while never forgetting any debt or favour owed to him. In some ways Pompey was rather immature, something that had been most clearly illustrated at the time of his first triumph when he had planned to ride in a chariot pulled by elephants. Only the discovery that an archway on the processional route would not accommodate such a monstrous vehicle and team had dissuaded him from such a bizarre display. He revelled in the name Magnus, as well as the tendency of flatterers to compare him to Alexander the Great. At times he could be extremely devious, which was no bad thing in a general during a war, but he was not particularly good at playing the political game at Rome. This was mainly through lack of experience, for he had spent the greater part of his life in near constant military service. From the age of twenty-three he had led his own army, for much of the time in independent operations far from any superior. Pompey was used to commanding rather than manipulating and persuading. Unlike other young aristocrats he had spent little time watching the day-to-day business of the Senate and Forum, learning from older senators just how public life was conducted. However, on his return from Spain he decided that now was the time to enter politics formally.

In 71 BC Pompey was thirty-five, but had never held any elected post and was still numbered amongst the equestrian order, for he had never been enrolled in the Senate. He now announced that he wished to stand for election to the consulship for the following year. This was directly contrary to Sulla's regulation of the public career, which had confirmed earlier legislation. According to this a man could not seek election to the consulship until he was aged at least forty-two and had already held the posts of quaestor and praetor. Crassus, who also declared his candidature around the same time, met the age qualification, but Pompey's entire career to this date violated both the letter and spirit of Sulla's rules. Both men were encamped with their armies outside Rome, entirely legitimately, since they were waiting to celebrate their ovation and triumph respectively. Neither made any overt threat, but ever since Sulla had turned his legions on the city to deal with his political opponents the fear was very real that others might do the same. When Pompey and Crassus put aside their personal differences to launch a joint campaign for the consulship there was little desire to oppose them. Crassus had clearly earned the office by his success against the slaves, while Pompey was seen as a hero by a large part of the population. It was irregular for someone outside the Senate to seek to join this body and become consul simultaneously, but it would have seemed absurd for someone who had already enjoyed a string of senior commands to have had to go through all the junior magistracies. Exempted by the Senate from the age and other qualifications – as both men needed permission to stand for election without actually entering the city, since they could not do this without laying down their *imperium*, which would have meant disbanding their legions before the triumphal procession – he and Crassus were duly elected by a landslide.

Sulla had permitted Pompey a somewhat anomalous position outside the rules he laid down for a career in public life, something that the Senate had felt unwilling or unable to challenge in subsequent years. A degree of flexibility had always been important within the Republican system, especially at times of military crisis. The extraordinary honours and exemptions granted to Pompey were personal and did not mean that regulations were abandoned and that everyone else could follow his example. However, even before they were elected he and Crassus had declared that they were intending to do away with key aspects of Sulla's system. The first thing that they did in their year of office was to restore full traditional rights and powers to the tribunate. It was a popular measure, hence Caesar's desire to associate himself with this cause during his time as military tribune. Another measure passed in 70 BC, doubtless with the approval of Pompey and Crassus, was actually put into force by one of Aurelia's relations, Lucius Aurelius Cotta, who provided a solution to the controversial question of composition of juries. From now on until the end of the Republic juries were drawn in equal numbers from senators, equestrians and the property class registered immediately below them, the *tribunii aerarii*. Once again this measure carried a good deal of popular support and was seen as a sensible compromise. Another long-running problem was also to a great extent resolved in this year with the election of two censors. These men were the consuls of 72 BC, both of whom had been defeated by Spartacus without this affecting their subsequent careers too adversely. Although the census would not be complete for over a year, it resulted in a massive increase in the number of male citizens properly registered and able to vote. The last even partially complete census had been carried out in 85 BC and included only 463,000 names, but in the new list the total was almost doubled to 910,000. As part of the process, censors were also required to examine and amend the senatorial roll, adding new names and expelling from the House any whose actions or morals had rendered them unfit to guide the Republic. No fewer than sixty-four men were punished in this way.[14]

Although Pompey and Crassus had combined to seek office and co-operated in the restoration of the tribunate, their mutual dislike and envy swiftly resurfaced. The younger man had begun their year of office in spectacular style. He became consul, joined the Senate and celebrated a triumph all on the same day. Then the new censors decided – no doubt with considerable encouragement from Pompey – to revive an old-fashioned ceremony where the equestrian order paraded with horses and weapons to demonstrate their willingness to perform their traditional role as cavalrymen in the legions. In the middle of this Pompey arrived, proceeded by the twelve lictors who attended him as consul and cleared a way through the watching crowd for him to approach the censors. When asked in the formal words of the ceremony whether he had fulfilled his duty to the Republic, the consul replied in a loud voice that he had served wherever Rome required and always under his own command. As the crowd cheered, the censors accompanied him back to his house. It was a great piece of political theatre, and this and his triumph with its celebratory games were impossible for Crassus to match. Instead he decided to dedicate one-tenth of his wealth to Hercules, paying for a huge public feast at which ten thousand tables were laden down with food, as well as the allocation of three months supply of grain to every citizen. Hercules, the great hero, was closely associated with victory and triumph and the last man to commemorate his military success in this way had been Sulla. As each attempted to upstage the other, relations between the consular colleagues became frigid in the extreme, until at the end of their term they made a public gesture of reconciliation in response to the appeal of an otherwise unknown Caius Aurelius. Both then retired to private life, neither wishing to go out and govern a province as was usual after one of the senior magistracies.[15]

CAESAR'S QUAESTORSHIP

Little is known of Caesar's activities in 71–70 BC. During Pompey's and Crassus' consulship he is known to have supported a bill put forward by the tribune Plotius (or Plautius), which was intended to allow exiled supporters of Sertorius and Lepidus to return home. He made a speech in favour of this law, which had a personal dimension as it permitted the return of his brother-in-law Lucius Cornelius Cinna. Only a single sentence from this oration is preserved, Caesar declaring that 'in my opinion, as regards our relationship, I have lacked neither toil, nor deeds, nor diligence'. The duty owed to the extended family as well as friends or clients was very important. Some scholars have speculated that he played a larger role behind the scenes, perhaps encouraging Pompey and Crassus to join forces in their desire for the consulship. It has even been suggested that he arranged the reconciliation between the two, under the assumption that Aurelius was somehow related to his mother's family. While none of this is impossible, it remains pure speculation since none of our sources suggest any involvement on his part.[16]

We do know that it was around this time that Caesar himself stood for the quaestorship and it is probable that securing this was his main concern. In 70 BC he was thirty, the minimum age Sulla had decreed for election to this magistracy. It was an important point of pride for an aristocrat to win office in 'his year' (*suo anno*), that is at the time when he first became eligible. This, as well as other factors, make it most likely that Caesar was elected as one of the twenty quaestors in the autumn of 70 BC and began his year of office early in 69 BC. The consular elections were normally held near the end of July, although there was no rigidly fixed date. There were around 150 days a year when it was permissible to hold an Assembly of the Roman people, but this could be reduced by additional festivals or the declaration of periods of public thanksgiving during which no State business could be conducted. The more junior posts such as the quaestorship were decided in a different assembly that was summoned fairly soon after the consular elections. Canvassing could begin as much as a year before the election, but was particularly intense in the last twenty-four days before actual voting. It was during this time, after they had formally registered with the magistrate overseeing the election, that those seeking office donned a specially whitened toga – the *toga candidus*, hence our word candidate – intended to make them stand out as they moved around the Forum. As they walked through the crowded centre of the city candidates greeted their fellow citizens, especially those whose property and status made their vote most influential. A specially trained slave known as a *nomenclator* usually stood behind the candidate, ready to whisper the names of anyone they approached, so that his master could greet them properly. Reliance on these slaves was almost universal, but good politicians made sure that their dependence on this aid to memory was never obvious. It was important for a candidate to be seen, but in many ways it was even more important with whom he was seen. Other senators who supported his candidature were expected to accompany a man for some of his canvassing, and their *auctoritas* helped to sway the voters. Less subtle propaganda took the form of signs painted on buildings expressing support. Many of the tombs that stood along the sides of the main roads into Rome included in their inscription a prohibition against such marks of support being posted or painted on them.[17]

Quaestors were elected by the Comitia Tributa, the Assembly of the thirty-five tribes of Roman citizens. When meeting to elect magistrates rather than vote for or against pieces of legislation, the Comitia was normally held in the Campus Martius, the mainly open area of parks and exercise grounds outside the formal boundary of the city to the north-west. This seems to have been because a higher turnout was expected for an election, and it would have been impossible to squeeze so many voters into the confines of the Forum. It is probable, though not certain, that candidates were given a chance to address the Assembly before the presiding magistrate gave the order 'Divide, citizens' (*Discedite, Quirites*). The members of each tribe then went to their allocated section of the *saepta*, a temporary complex of fenced enclosures. To vote, each member of the tribe in turn would leave the tribe's enclosure, walking across a narrow raised gangway known as a 'bridge' to the *rogator*, the official appointed to oversee the process for each tribe. The voter then placed his written ballot into a basket, watched over by other officials known as the 'guards' (*custodes*), who would later count them and report the result to the presiding magistrate. Each tribe voted as a unit, their decision being announced in an order previously established by lot. The number of voters in each tribe varied considerably, with even the poorest members of the four urban tribes being able to attend without much difficulty. Given that the majority of Roman citizens now lived far from Rome, only the wealthier members of some of the other tribes were likely to be able and willing to travel to Rome for an election. The vote of these men was very significant, as was that of poorer men who now lived in Rome, but who were still enrolled in one of the rural tribes. In spite of the disparity between the numbers present at the election, the vote of each tribe carried equal weight. It was important for an aristocrat to carry the vote of his own tribe – in Caesar's case the Fabia tribe – and great effort was made to know and do favours for fellow tribesmen. Elections were not decided by an overall majority, but concluded as soon as enough candidates to fill the available posts had each received the vote of eighteen tribes. It was literally a 'first past the post' system.[18]

Caesar's prospects were good. He had won acclaim in the courts and served with distinction fighting in the East. Even the rumours about Nicomedes and his own scandalous womanising at least helped to make his name widely known, as did his distinctive style of dress. If his family was not amongst the inner circle of nobles in the Senate, the Julii Caesares had provided a number of magistrates in recent years. Some of these were from the other branch of the family, but this still meant that the name had been kept in the public eye. His mother's relations were doing very well, with two consulships in the last five years and another member holding the praetorship in 70 BC. With twenty posts as quaestor available each year this was the easiest elected magistracy to win. The enfranchisement of the Italians had brought many sons of wealthy local families to Rome in search of a career, but a member of an established Roman family and patrician had little to fear from such competition. Caesar was duly elected. It was an important moment, for Sulla's political reforms ensured that all quaestors were automatically enrolled in the Senate. Quaestors performed a range of financial and administrative tasks, but the majority served as deputy to a provincial governor, who was in turn either an ex-consul or ex-praetor. Caesar was sent in this way to Further Spain (Hispania Ulterior), the westernmost province of the Iberian Peninsula.[19]

Before he left Rome some time in 69 BC, Caesar suffered two personal blows with the death of his aunt Julia, followed shortly afterwards by the death of his wife Cornelia. Aristocratic families held very public funerals for their members, using the opportunity to celebrate the achievements of their whole line, reminding voters of what they had done and hinting at the promise for the future. Actors dressed in the regalia of office and wearing the funeral masks of distinguished ancestors formed part of the procession, which went first to the Forum, where an oration would be delivered from the Rostra. Polybius tells us that

> ... who makes the oration over the man [or, in this case, woman] about to be buried, when he has finished speaking of him recounts the

successes and exploits of the rest whose images are present, beginning from the most ancient. By this means, by this constant renewal of the good report of brave men, the celebrity of those who performed noble deeds is rendered immortal, while at the same time the fame of those who did good service to their country becomes known to the people and a heritage for future generations.[20]

At Julia's funeral Caesar spoke from the Rostra about her distinguished ancestry, of the Julii's descent from the goddess Venus, and the royal connections of her mother's family. These were useful reminders to the watching crowd of his own lineage. More controversially he included in the procession symbols of Marius' victories, and perhaps even an actor to represent him. Sulla had banned the public honouring of his rival, but only a few of the watchers protested, and they were swiftly shouted down by the rest. Though Sulla had won the civil war, he had not won over many, even of Rome's elite, to accept all of his decisions, as had been indicated by the widespread popularity of the restoration of the tribunate. For a lot of Romans Marius remained a great hero, the man who had restored Rome's injured pride in Africa and then saved Italy from the Northern menace. Cicero, who roundly condemned Marius' role in the civil war, frequently and enthusiastically praised his victories over Jugurtha and the Cimbri in his speeches, knowing that his audience would warmly concur. Caesar's gesture was generally welcomed and this emphasis on his own close connection to the great hero was very good for his own popularity.[21]

It was not uncommon for elderly women from the noble families to receive a grand public funeral. Caesar's decision to grant the same honour to Cornelia was highly unusual, and Plutarch says that he was the first Roman to do this for such a young woman. The gesture proved popular, as many people took it as a sign of the genuine sorrow of a kind-hearted man. Although the popular image of the Romans sees them as stern and phlegmatic, in truth they were often a deeply sentimental people. Funerals, like so much of an aristocrat's life, were conducted in public and had an impact on politics. No close male relative of Caesar had died during his young adulthood, and in one sense the funerals of his aunt and wife provided great opportunities for self-publicising. Caesar seized the chance and exploited it to the best of his ability. This does not necessarily mean that his sorrow was not genuine, for sentiment and politics often co-existed happily at Rome. His marriage to Cornelia had been successful, perhaps also happy and loving. However, none of our sources suggest that it was the loss of his wife that sparked off his womanising and it is most probable that he had already had a number of affairs while married to her. We do not know if he paraded the symbols of her father Cinna, as he had so recently done with the latter's ally Marius. Marius had far greater emotional appeal to the wider population, so the connection with him was far more important for Caesar.

Caesar left for Further Spain in the spring or early summer of 69 BC, quite probably travelling out with the governor he was to serve, Antistius Vetus. It was common for governors to select their own quaestor from those who had been elected. It is possible that this had happened in Caesar's case and that the two already had a connection. Certainly, they seem to have got on well, and Caesar would take Vetus' son as his own quaestor when sent to govern Further Spain after his praetorship seven years later. One of the quaestor's most important tasks was to oversee the accounts for the province, but he could be called upon to act as the governor's representative in a wide range of activities. Much of a governor's time was spent in touring the main towns of the region, listening to petitions, resolving problems and dispensing justice. Vetus sent Caesar to perform this function in some places. Caesar performed all his tasks well, and over twenty years later would remind the locals of his services to them. A quaestorship offered the chance to acquire clients amongst the notable men of a provincial population.

We are told that Caesar was first subject to an epileptic fit while serving in Spain, although it is not clear whether this was in 69 BC or during his own spell as governor in 61–60 BC. Another incident probably dated to the quaestorship, although Plutarch sets it later, and occurred when he was visiting Gades (modern Cadiz) to hold court. Caesar is supposed to have seen a statue of Alexander the Great in the Temple of Hercules and been visibly distressed, because he had done so little at an age when the Macedonian king had conquered half the world. More disturbing still was a dream in which he raped his mother Aurelia. Understandably dismayed by this, Caesar consulted a soothsayer whose interpretation was that 'he was destined to rule the world, since the mother whom he had ravished represented Mother Earth, the parent of all'. Suetonius claims that this explanation prompted him to leave the province early, so eager was he to return to Rome and resume his career. If this is true, then it is likely that he acted with the approval of Vetus, since there never seems to have been any criticism or suggestion that he abandoned his post. His review of the provincial accounts may well have already been complete and so his primary duty fulfilled. On the whole he had done his job well, but the activities of a quaestor rarely held much fascination to the electorate back in Rome.[22]

MONUMENTS AND GLADIATORS : CAESAR AS AEDILE

On his way back to Italy Caesar paused in Transpadane Gaul, the area of the Po Valley. This was part of the province of Cisalpine Gaul, the only province that formed part of the Italian Peninsula. It was populated by a mixture of descendants of Roman and Italian colonists and the Gallic tribes, the leading families of which were by now culturally very Roman. The grants of citizenship that came in the aftermath of the Social War had stopped at the line of the Po, and communities to the north possessed only Latin status. This was deeply resented, especially by the rich and powerful who had most to gain from full citizenship. Caesar encouraged these sentiments, for the future votes of wealthy new citizens would have been well worth having. The suggestion that his agitation was so strong as to push the Transpadanes to the brink of rebellion, and that this was only prevented by the chance presence of legions nearby, seems extremely improbable. It is most likely a later invention based upon the assumption that Caesar was always aiming at revolution. The man who had refused to join either Lepidus or Sertorius seems unlikely to have wanted to start a rebellion on his own. At this stage in his career, there was simply no need to take such a risk.[23]

On arrival back in Rome, one of Caesar's first actions was to remarry. His new bride was Pompeia, grandchild on her mother's side of Sulla and on her father's side of the latter's consular colleague in 88 BC, Quintus Pompeius. Therefore, for all the parading of the connection with Marius and his support for legislation aimed at dismantling Sulla's regime, it would be far too simplistic to see Caesar as fixedly pro-Marian or anti-Sullan. Roman politics rarely, if ever, divided so starkly, even when civil war raged. When senators married it was almost invariably with a view to the useful associations they would gain as a result of the union. Not enough is known about Pompeia's relatives to understand precisely how Caesar thought the marriage would help to foster his career – the web of inter-connections between aristocratic families was complex in the extreme. Unlike his marriage to Cornelia, this one would not have been through the *confarreatio* ceremony. A good deal is known about the rituals associated with conventional marriages at Rome, although we do not know whether all of these were followed at Caesar's wedding in 67 BC. As with most aspects of private and public life at Rome, there were sacrificial offerings and taking of omens. Brides were traditionally supposed to wear orange slippers and a home-woven dress, fastened with a girdle tied in a complex 'Herculean' knot for the groom to undo on the wedding night. If Pompeia followed the usual conventions she would have had her hair bound into six plaits and covered with the bright orange veil (*flammeum*) – a reminder of Cornelia who would have had to wear such a covering whenever she left the house if Caesar had actually been made *Flamen Dialis*. In a torch-lit procession, she would then be escorted from her family home to the groom's house, where the latter would be waiting. On arrival the door posts of the house would be decorated with wooden fillets, and anointed with oil or animal fat. The bride was then carried over the threshold, a gesture that was believed to go back to the rape of the Sabine women, when the first Romans had only been able to find wives by kidnapping the daughters of a neighbouring community. The first Roman brides had therefore entered their new homes unwillingly. This ritual – though without a general consciousness of its supposed origin – has survived into the modern world, but Roman practice differed in that it was the bride's attendants rather than the groom who actually carried her.

The bridegroom was waiting with a torch and a vessel full of water, symbolising his willingness to provide her with the essentials of life. There rarely appears to have been a particularly long ceremony to formalise the marriage. The traditional formual was simplicity itself, with the bride declaring 'Where you are Caius, I will be Caia' (*Ubi tu Caius*, *ego Caia*), the masculine and feminine forms of a common name symbolising the joining of the couple. There was a symbolic bridal bed laid out and ornately decorated in the reception hall of the house, although the couple would obviously not actually occupy this but retire to a proper bedroom in due course. (Some Greeks believed that a Roman groom had all the lights extinguished so that the room was in complete darkness before he joined his wife in the proper marriage bed. This was supposed to be a mark of respect for an honourable woman, so that she would never seem like a prostitute, only wanted for sexual pleasure. This may well have been no more than a story told about the quaint Romans by the Greeks.) On the next morning the new wife for the first time sacrificed to the household gods (the *lares* and *penates*) of her new home. She and her husband would also entertain guests to a special feast.[24]

Pompeia was only distantly related to Pompey the Great and there was little love lost between the two branches of the family, so Caesar's marriage gave him no close link to Rome's greatest and most popular living general. For the first two years after his consulship Pompey seemed content, even though his performance in the Senate was lacklustre. By 67 BC he was clearly missing the adulation that his victories had brought him and began to manoeuvre for a new command. The spectacular nature of his career so far ensured that this could not simply be a standard consular province, but needed to be far grander. Piracy continued to plague the Mediterranean and a tribune called Aulus Gabinius proposed a bill creating an extraordinary command to deal with the problem once and for all. This was not entirely unprecedented, since the Senate had sent one of the consuls of 74 BC, Marcus Antonius – the father of Caesar's subordinate Mark Antony – with a roving brief to combat pirates. However, he had achieved little, suffering a serious defeat in 72 BC and dying soon afterwards. The situation had deteriorated even further, threatening the supply of foreign grain on which Rome depended. If its intention was nothing new, the details of Gabinius' law were extremely radical, granting the new commander control of vast numbers of ships and troops, as well as *imperium* that stretched throughout the Mediterranean and for a distance of 50 miles in from the shore. His power was at the very least equal to that of all the governors whose provinces included land in this area, and it may possibly have been superior. While Gabinius made no explicit mention of Pompey in his initial proposal, it was clear to all that he was the obvious and really the only choice. Many leading senators opposed the measure, declaring that it was a mistake in a free Republic to give so much power to any one man. As usual the forces of inertia within the Senate ensured that many preferred letting a serious problem continue rather than allowing someone else the credit for solving it.[25]

Caesar is said to have been the only senator to speak in favour of the bill, doubtless being summoned by Gabinius to speak from the Rostra as the tribune tried to persuade the crowd in the Forum to support his bill. When the order was given for the people to reconvene as the Assembly of the tribes, they enthusiastically passed it. It seems unlikely that no other senator supported the law, but Caesar may well have been one of its more vocal supporters. As in the past he was keen to associate himself with popular causes, while his own experiences with pirates gave him a personal knowledge of the threat they posed. When the law was passed the price of grain at Rome is supposed to have dropped immediately to a more normal level as the market expressed its confidence in Pompey. Many prominent senators proved ready to assist him in his task, so that the twenty-four legates or senior subordinates granted to him by the law were a very distinguished group. This in itself does suggest that Caesar's support for Gabinius was probably not unique. The faith in Pompey proved entirely justified as he set his organisational genius to the problem. Dividing the Mediterranean into sectors, the seas west of Italy were swept free of pirates in a matter of weeks. It took only slightly longer to defeat the raiders infesting the eastern half of the Mediterranean. One reason for the speed of this success was Pompey's willingness to accept the surrender of the pirates and their families, settling them on good farmland and often in new communities where they could support themselves without recourse to violence. Once again Pompey was the adored hero of the Republic, although the pettiness in his character surfaced as he tried to deny the proconsular governor of Crete credit for defeating the pirates on that island. His success merely whetted his appetite for further glory.[26]

In 66 BC another tribune, Caius Manilius, brought a bill before the Popular Assembly, making use of the powers that Pompey and Crassus had restored to this magistracy. Since 74 BC the command in the on-going conflict with Mithridates had been held by Lucius Licinius Lucullus – a post, which as already noted, he is supposed to have secured through the assistance of the courtesan Praecia (see p. 83). Lucullus was one of Sulla's men, probably the only senator to stay with him when he first marched on Rome in 88 BC. He was a bold and skilful general, but his strategic and tactical gifts were not matched by comparable skill as a leader. During his campaigns, Lucullus had achieved victory after victory over Mithridates and his ally King Tigranes of Armenia. Yet he had never won the love of his officers and soldiers in the way that commanders like Marius, Sulla and Pompey were able to do. Even more dangerously, he closely regulated the activities of Roman businessmen and the *publicani* tax collectors in Asia. This was bitterly resented by these influential groups who had grown accustomed to exploiting the locals under governors who demanded no more than a cut of the profits. Lucullus had been anxious to avoid alienating the provincials for fear that they might then come to see Mithridates as a potential liberator from Roman oppression. Yet for many wealthy businessmen profits came before such concerns, and from 69 BC onwards Lucullus' command was steadily reduced as regions were taken from him and given to other governors. His strength eroded, much of the ground he had won earlier in the war was lost and final victory began to seem ever more distant. Under such circumstances the idea of sending Pompey out to take charge and settle the business once and for all was very attractive. Caesar once again spoke in favour of the bill, which was easily passed. Pompey replaced Lucullus, again giving the impression of arriving at the last minute to take the credit for a war that had already been virtually won.[27]

It is highly unlikely that Caesar's support for the laws granting Pompey extraordinary commands in 67 and 66 BC made much difference to the outcome of the voting on these issues. There were plenty of former quaestors around, as well as several junior senators who flouted convention in their dress and behaviour. It is still useful to remind ourselves that at this point in his life Caesar was still not all that important. His record so far suggested that he was an up and coming man, likely to have a reasonable career, but once again he was not unique in this. Speaking out for both the *Lex Gabinia* and the *Lex Manilia* was unlikely to win him the deep gratitude of Pompey, for his had been a very minor role. Yet both laws had been controversial, attracting great attention as a number of leading senators spoke out against them in the Senate and in the Forum. Caesar seized the opportunity to be noticed and to be associated with the success of the laws and of Pompey. There was a chance that some small share of the latter's popularity would rub off on him. More importantly he had voiced opinions held by a broad range of citizens, including many equestrians and other moderately prosperous Romans whose vote counted for so much in the assemblies. To espouse popular causes in this way was to be a *popularis*. Although often portrayed in older studies as almost a well-defined political party or grouping, this was no more than a style of politics that relied on winning the support of the people. The Gracchi had been *populares*, as had Marius at times, as well as Saturninus and Sulpicius. Although they raised many of the same issues, these men did not hold a fixed set of common views. Caesar had from early in his career inclined towards a *popularis* path, but in the same way this did not automatically mean that he made common cause with anyone else who acted in the same way, as many did. Politics remained essentially an individual struggle, since everyone else was a competitor. It was not just a question of winning popular acclaim, but of winning more than anyone else.[28]

Another way in which Caesar sought to woo the electorate was by lavish expenditure. He was appointed curator of the Appian Way, and spent a good deal of his own money to pay for the renovations and improvements he had made to the road and its associated structures. Potentially this offered a good return for his money, for the Appian Way remained one of the most important roads to Rome, so that voters travelling to the city by this route would be given a reminder of what Caesar had done for them. The willingness to spend his own wealth on his fellow citizens doubtless contributed to his election to the post of curule aedile for 65 BC. There were four aediles altogether, but two were exclusively plebian posts and therefore could not be held by a patrician like Caesar. The curule aediles, who could be either patrician or plebian, had the right to sit in a magistrate's official chair, just like praetors and consuls. Sulla had not made the aedileship a compulsory part of a public career if a man wanted to hold a more senior magistracy, since there were so few posts available, but he had set thirty-seven as the minimum age at which it could be held. Caesar was only thirty-five when he became aedile, and it is most probable that he had been granted a special exemption by the Senate to allow him to stand two years earlier than was normal. Such special favours seem to have been reasonably common, so much so that in 67 BC a tribune had passed a law barring the Senate from granting such dispensations unless a quorum of 200 senators were present. The influence of his mother's family, and his own distinction as a holder of the *corona civica* and a pontiff probably explain Caesar's own exemption. (However, the date of his aedileship has been used by those scholars who prefer to date Caesar's birth to 102 BC. Yet this does not tie in with the little evidence we have, for instance it would have been odd for him to have become quaestor two years late.)[29]

The aediles were concerned almost exclusively with the running of Rome itself, supervising the upkeep of temples, the cleaning and maintenance of roads, aqueducts and sewers, and overseeing the grain supply, the markets and even the brothels of the city. In addition they sometimes took on a judicial role, but one of the main attractions to an ambitious politician was the aediles' responsibility for public entertainments and festivals. The two curule aediles were specifically responsible for the seven days of games and shows honouring the Mother goddess Cybele in April (the *Ludi Megalenses*) and the 'Roman Games' (the *Ludi Romani*), a further fifteen days of entertainment in September. Although the Treasury provided an allowance to the magistrates to meet the costs of these productions, it had long become customary for the aediles to supplement this from their own funds. Each lavish spectacle staged by an aedile wanting to make a name for himself set a new standard for his successors to match or surpass. Caesar threw himself into the preparations for the games with all the panache of a natural showman and a determination that no expense should be spared. Much of his private art collection was displayed in the Forum and the basilicas surrounding it, as well as temporary colonnades erected for the purpose. At this time Rome still lacked the monumental theatres that were a feature of Hellenic cities and it was necessary to rig up seating and a temporary auditorium. The other curule aedile, Marcus Calpurnius Bibulus, joined him in footing the bill, but complained that all the credit seemed to go to his colleague as they jointly put on beast fights and dramatic productions. Bibulus is supposed to have remarked that it was just like the Temple of Castor and Pollux, the Heavenly Twins, which was invariably known as the

Temple of Castor for brevity's sake. In the same way it seemed people were talking about the aedileship of Caesar, never of Caesar and Bibulus.[30]

Caesar decided during his aedileship to stage gladiatorial games in honour of his father, who had died some twenty years before. The origin of gladiatorial displays lay in funeral games. At first these had been private, family affairs, but near the end of the third century BC they became public spectacles, with rapid escalation in their scale and splendour. The tradition that such fights could only be staged to commemorate a death of a family member continued down to Caesar's day, in contrast to beast fights, which could be presented as part of a number of different celebrations. Yet it had become little more than a pretext for this form of violent entertainment, which had proved so popular in Rome and throughout Italy. Even so, it was certainly a most unusual step for Caesar to declare funeral games after such a long lapse of time. Yet in many ways the sheer scale of his plans was more exceptional. He began to collect so many gladiators from the schools across Italy that the Senate became nervous. Spartacus' rebellion was still fresh in everyone's memory, while there may even have been fears of what an ambitious man like Caesar could do with so many armed men at his command in Rome itself. Probably as importantly, other senators were reluctant to allow such lavish displays, which would raise the expectation of the audience and so make it more expensive and difficult for everyone else to woo the people in future. As a result, a law was passed limiting the number of gladiators that could perform in any games staged by an individual. It is still reported by our sources that 320 pairs of gladiators appeared in Caesar's games, and that all were equipped with ornate silvered armour. Similarly lavish weapons were also used by the beast fighters in the entertainments staged jointly with Bibulus.[31]

During his aedileship Caesar spent huge amounts of his own money, supplemented by Bibulus' cash in their joint projects. The people of Rome revelled in the shows and games put on for free enjoyment. They disliked any hint of stinginess in those staging the games and would hold this against a man in his future career, just as they would gratefully remember someone who was responsible for a truly impressive spectacle. Yet it was not simply a question of throwing money at the projects, for even expensive games could sometimes fall flat if they were not presented well. Caesar never lacked style in anything he did and his games were a great success. From his point of view, the money that had gone to produce this result had been very well spent. It was his personal money only in the sense that he had borrowed it. Even before he had held any elected office, Plutarch tells us that Caesar was said to have debts of over 1,300 talents – a total of over 31 million sestertii in Roman currency. (To put this into proportion, the minimum property qualification for a member of the equestrian order at a slightly later date, and probably also at the time, was 400,000 sestertii.) This was a staggering sum, which was then massively increased by his spending as curator of the Appian Way and as aedile. Caesar was gambling on his political future being bright and lucrative enough to cancel out his debts. His creditors were taking the same risk, but presumably had confidence in Caesar to do well. The greatest part of this money was most probably owed to Crassus. Caesar was not the only rising senator he funded in this way, but it is unlikely that he gave others as much leeway to keep on borrowing more and more.[32]

There was one last gesture during Caesar's aedileship. At some point during the year, most probably before one of the sets of games, he gave orders for Marius' trophies commemorating his victory over the Cimbri and Teutones to be re-erected in the Forum. Sulla had ordered them to be torn down and probably destroyed, so Caesar most likely had a facsimile set up. As with Julia's funeral, there was a warm response from much of the population to this gesture. Enough people still remembered the fear that the northern barbarians would spill south into Italy and sack Rome again. Marius had saved Rome from this fate, and that was a deed most felt worthy of celebration. One exception was Quintus Lutatius Catulus, consul in 78 BC and like Caesar a pontiff. His father had been consul with Marius in 102 BC and proconsul in 101 BC and had deeply resented the popular hero receiving most of the credit for their joint success. Catalus was now probably the most respected member of the Senate, even if he was not formally the *princeps senatus*, the man whose name appeared first on the senatorial roll. Emphasis on Marius diminished the glory of Catulus' own family. He resented this, but if the stories are true he was also beginning to see Caesar as a reckless and potentially dangerous politician. In the Senate Catulus declared that 'No longer, Caesar, are you undermining the defences of the Republic – now you are launching a direct assault.' Yet for all the elder statesman's *auctoritas*, Caesar replied in a speech that was utterly reasonable and convinced most senators of his innocence. They were probably right, for his career was still in most respects conventional, if flamboyant. Yet revolution was in the air.[33]

VI

CONSPIRACY

'As soon as riches came to be held in honour, and brought glory, *imperium*, and power, virtue began to grow dull; poverty was seen as disgraceful, innocence as malevolence. Therefore because of wealth, our youths were seized by luxury, greed and pride; they stole and squandered; reckoning their own property of little worth, they coveted other peoples'; contemptuous of modesty and chastity, of everything divine or human, they were without thought or restraint.' – *The senator and historian Sallust, writing in the late forties* BC.[1]

Late in 66 BC the consular elections for the following year were won by Publius Cornelius Sulla and Publius Autronius Paetus. Sulla was a nephew of the dictator and had become very wealthy during the proscriptions. Brother-in-law to Pompey, he may have enjoyed some popularity by association with the great commander, but Sulla's success owed far more to his money in elections that were marked by widespread bribery and intimidation. This in itself was nothing unusual.

Throughout the period a long succession of laws were passed to deal with electoral malpractice, but the frequency of such legislation makes clear its ineffectiveness. A recent bill had stipulated that candidates found guilty of such crimes lost not only the office they had secured, but were expelled from the Senate, denied the right to display the symbols of any public office and barred from entering politics again. The two runners-up in the election, Lucius Aurelius Cotta and Lucius Manlius Torquatus, promptly prosecuted the victors under this bribery law. Cotta was the man who as praetor in 70 BC had brought in the law altering the composition of juries in the courts. By this time he was a year or two overdue for his consulship, which may well have made his defeat rankle even more. Both of his brothers had also already been consul, while Manlius came from a very distinguished patrician line, in contrast to the two victors in the election. Autronius relied more for his defence on using a gang of supporters to intimidate the members of the court, or, failing that, to break up proceedings. Sulla may or may not have made use of similar tactics – years later Cicero defended him on another charge and blamed all the earlier violence on Autronius. In spite of this the prosecutions were successful, and both men were stripped of their office and expelled from public life. Cotta and Torquatus became the consuls for 65 BC, either because they had gained the most votes after Sulla and Autronius or perhaps following a second election.

The matter does not seem to have ended there. Autronius and Sulla were reluctant to accept their permanent expulsion from politics. There was talk of a plot to assassinate Cotta and Torquatus when they assumed the consulship on 1 January 65 BC. Other leading senators were also to be murdered and the conspirators were then to install themselves in the supreme office. Forewarned of the planned coup, the new consuls were allowed an armed guard by the Senate and the day passed without any violence. Officially a veil of silence was cast over the whole affair, so that Cicero, a praetor in 66 BC, could claim a few years later that he had known nothing about it at the time. In the absence of fact, rumour flourished, especially as the years went by and it was useful to blacken rivals' names by alleging their involvement in these murky events. It was later alleged that Autronius' chief ally was Lucius Sergius Catiline, whom we shall encounter later in this chapter. He had just returned from governing Africa as a propraetor and had wanted to become a candidate for the consulship after the dismissal of Sulla and Autronius. The refusal of the presiding magistrate to permit this is supposed to have prompted him to join Autronius in planning to seize power by force. Another man whose name was mentioned was Cnaeus Calpurnius Piso, who had been elected to the quaestorship for 65 BC and was seen as a wild, intemperate man. When the Senate decided soon afterwards to send him to Spain as a propraetor – a most extraordinary appointment for such a young and junior magistrate – this was seen as an indication of their fear of what he might do if allowed to remain in Rome. The stories doubtless grew in the telling, especially after Piso was murdered in his province by some of his own Spanish soldiers. Some claimed these auxiliaries had been prompted by the governor's tyrannical rule. This was plausible enough, although it should be remembered that of the many oppressive Roman governors only a handful managed to get themselves assassinated. Yet others suggested that the Spanish soldiers were loyal to Pompey, having served under him against Sertorius, and had either been instructed – or decided on their own initiative – to dispose of a potential rival. It was an indication of the nervous mood of these years that such wild tales were circulating.[2]

It is in this context that we need to place the version given by Suetonius, in which Crassus and Caesar were in league with Autronius and Sulla. The plan was to massacre their opponents in the Senate, give the consulship to the convicted pair and make Crassus dictator, with Caesar as his deputy, who bore the archaic title of Master of Horse (*Magister Equitum*). Caesar was supposed to have given the signal for the onslaught by letting his toga fall from his shoulder, but did not do so when Crassus failed to turn up, moved by 'conscience or fear'. The sources named by Suetonius for this incident were all written later by authors hostile to Caesar. The same was true of another tale he mentions, describing how Caesar planned an armed rebellion in concert with Piso, but that this was thwarted by the latter's murder. As with other claims that he plotted to seize control of the Republic by force from his earliest years, it is likely that these are no more than later propaganda. Caesar, recently elected aedile for 65 BC, had no reason to wish for revolution. He was certainly extremely unlikely to have joined any plot aimed at assassinating his relative Lucius Aurelius Cotta. Similarly, Crassus, who had just won the censorship with Catulus as a colleague, had little to gain from armed rebellion. There was politically motivated rioting during and after the consular elections, and there may even have been a plot of some sort, but the involvement of Caesar or Crassus is surely a later invention.[3]

There has been a tendency amongst historians ancient and modern to see these years as dominated by rivalry between Crassus and Pompey. In 67 BC Catulus had argued that the command against the pirates gave too much power to any one man. When Pompey was also given responsibility for the war with Mithridates, he came to control far larger forces and could draw on the resources of a far wider area than Sulla at the start of the civil war. Men writing under the rule of the emperors expressed surprise when Pompey chose to lay down this great power on his eventual return to Italy at the end of 62 BC. It was assumed that anyone with the strength to make himself sole ruler at Rome would inevitably crave such dominance. With hindsight we know that this belief was wrong, for Pompey preferred to pursue his ambitions by more conventional means. Cicero's letters from these years betray no hint that he was worried about the great general following Sulla's example. It seems unlikely that many other senators expected a fresh civil war, but that is not to say that they considered it to be utterly impossible. Anyone active in public life in these years was old enough to remember the appalling violence of the eighties BC, of proscription lists marking famous men for death and of severed heads decorating the Rostra. All this had happened in the very heart of Rome and who was to say that it could not happen again? Pompey had been one of the bloodthirsty lieutenants of Sulla, the 'young executioner'. He appeared to have mellowed as he matured, but he had still spent only a small part of his career in Rome, taking part in the day-to-day business of public life. Everyone knew the figure of the dashing commander, who was adding victories in Asia to those he had already won in Africa, Spain, Sicily and Italy, but how many truly knew the real man and so could be sure how he would behave? The circumstances were very different to the situation that had faced Sulla and effectively backed him into a corner. Yet if someone were to seize power in Rome by force, as the disgruntled consul Cinna had done, who was to say that this would not be the reason, or the pretext, for Pompey to return sword in hand at the head of his army. Such a scenario was all the easier to imagine when elections and trials were being disrupted, and competition between leading senators seemed more desperate than in the past.[4]

In contrast to Pompey, people knew Crassus, who spent far more time in Rome and was very active in public life. One of the richest men in the Republic – his fortune probably second only to that of Pompey – Crassus was fond of saying that no man could call himself rich unless he was able to afford to raise his own army. In spite of his wealth, his lifestyle was remarkably frugal in an age of luxury and indulgence. Men like Lucullus and Cicero's great rival the orator Hortensius paraded their riches in their magnificent houses, villas and gardens, while dining in lavish style on exotic foods. They were famous for the efforts they devoted to construct saltwater ponds, in which they raised sea fish, often as much as pets as for food. Crassus did not waste his money on such whims, and instead devoted great effort to augmenting his already vast fortune. He had interests in many businesses, maintaining close links with the *publicani* and other companies active in the provinces. Most visibly he dealt in property, maintaining hundreds of skilled slaves to develop buildings and increase their value. They included a force trained as a fire brigade, something that did not at this time otherwise exist at Rome. Large parts of the city consisted of narrow streets separating tall, densely packed and often cheaply constructed *insulae* thrown up by landlords keen to profit as much as possible from rents. Fires started easily and spread rapidly, especially in the heat of the Italian summer. Crassus was able to buy up great swathes of Rome at a knock-down price by waiting for a conflagration to begin and then purchasing properties in the path of the fire. Once the deal was done, he called in his fire brigade to fight the flames, usually by demolishing buildings to create a fire-brake. Some of his new purchases were saved, while his slave artisans were ready to build afresh on the sites of the demolished structures. He seems to have dealt particularly in grander houses for the better off, although like other prominent Romans he may also have owned many blocks of slum flats. The means of acquiring much of his property displayed both determination and ruthlessness. At some point, probably in 73 BC, he was known to have been spending much time with a Vestal Virgin named Licinia. She was formally accused of unchastity, a crime that in the case of the Vestals was punished by being entombed alive. The case was dismissed when Crassus announced that he was intent on buying a house from Licinia, whose name suggests she might well have been a relative. So convinced was everyone of his enthusiasm for acquiring new properties that this was accepted as far more probable than the idea that they were having an affair. Licinia was acquitted, but Crassus is supposed to have kept hovering around her until she finally sold him the house.[5]

Crassus was not just a property tycoon who owned great estates and silver mines as well as housing, and his fortune did not exist purely for its own sake, but to serve his political ambitions. As we have seen, it is probable that Caesar benefited from loans to fund his grand attempts to buy popular favour. Crassus loaned money readily to many men pursuing a public career. He rarely charged them interest, although he was relentless in collecting the loan as soon as the agreed date for its repayment had arrived. Instead he concentrated on accumulating political capital, doing favours for other men and so placing them in his debt. In these years a large proportion of the 600 or so senators, perhaps even the majority, either owed money to Crassus or had benefited from one of his interest-free loans in the past. Few of these men came from the greatest families, who usually had wealth enough of their own. Many, like Caesar, were ambitious men from the fringes of the inner circle of families, still more were minor senators who never held a magistracy, but were members of the Senate and could vote even if they were rarely called upon to speak. Amongst these men Crassus had great influence, from the generosity with which he permitted others to draw upon his wealth. He was equally willing to do favours in other ways if this placed other men in his debt. Crassus was exceptionally active in the courts, even in comparison with men like Cicero whose career relied primarily on his skills as an advocate. The latter claimed that Crassus had:

> with no more than a mediocre rhetorical training and even less natural talent, still by effort and industry, and particularly by judicious use on behalf of his clients of favours owed to him, he was for many years

one of the leading advocates. His speeches were characterised by clear Latin, carefully chosen and arranged words, free of too much adornment, his ideas were clever, but his delivery and voice undistinguished, so that he said everything in the same style.[6]

Plutarch also emphasised how careful Crassus was in preparing a speech before each appearance in court. Effort then, rather than natural flair, best characterised his advocacy, but it was still highly effective, and his willingness to take on cases that others had refused placed many men under obligation to him. Similarly, the readiness he showed to canvass on behalf of electoral candidates was another way of doing favours that might be returned at a future date. His enthusiasm to make new connections meant that at times he appeared fickle, acting on behalf of a man one day in court or the Forum and then siding with someone else opposed to him a little later. Crassus worked hard at politics, in contrast to Pompey who, when in Rome, rarely appeared in the Forum. Pompey's wealth and *auctoritas* were greater than those of anyone else, but he was seen as reluctant to use them, disliking crowds and rarely appearing as an advocate. Crassus was always visible, speaking for or supporting other men, and taking care to greet even the humbler men by name whenever he met them. He never won the affection of the crowd, but his influence ensured that he was treated with respect. Prosecutions of prominent men were a normal and frequent part of public life, but no one attacked Crassus in this way. Plutarch mentions one tribune of the plebs who was notorious for his fierce attacks on leading men. When asked why he had never targeted Crassus, he replied because 'that one has straw on his horns', referring to an Italian practice of fixing straw to the horns of dangerous bulls as warning for people to keep their distance. This may have been a play on words, since the Latin word for hay has the same root as the word for moneylender.[7]

Crassus clearly had grand plans for his censorship in 65 BC. He announced plans to enrol as citizens many of the inhabitants of Cisalpine Gaul. Caesar had already associated himself with the agitation for this in the region, and Crassus was keen to earn gratitude and future support from so many new voters. Other senators feared the influence that this would give him and his colleague Catulus was resolute in his refusal to accept the new citizens. Crassus also attempted to annex Egypt as a province and levy taxes – quite how is unclear, because such matters were not normally dealt with by censors. The country was in turmoil, plagued by dynastic disputes amongst the decadent Ptolemies and internal rebellion. Suetonius tells us that Caesar, buoyed by the popularity won during his aedileship, also attempted to persuade some popular tribunes to vote him an extraordinary command as governor of Egypt. It is possible that he and Crassus were working in concert in this matter. Equally they may both simply have seen the same opportunity for enriching themselves by taking charge of this famously wealthy region. In any case there was far too much opposition for either plan to be successful. Crassus and Catulus were so bitterly at loggerheads that both men agreed to resign as censors after only a few months in the magistracy. They had failed to undertake their main role, carrying out a new census of citizens and their property, and it would be decades before a new census was properly carried out. A key institution was failing to cope with the changed circumstances of public life.[8]

CATO, CATILINE, AND THE COURTS

In 64 BC Caesar for the first time served as a magistrate presiding over a trial. This was a common duty for aediles and former aediles, who were regularly called in to act as judges in the courts when there were too many cases for the praetors to deal with. In 64 BC there was an overflow of trials for the murder court (the *quaestio de sicariis*), prompted in part by the activities of one of the quaestors, Marcus Porcius Cato. The latter is said to have taken his duties far more seriously than most of the young men who held this first post on the *cursus*. Appointed to oversee the Treasury, Cato was not content to follow the usual practice and leave the day-to-day administration to the clerks permanently employed to perform this. Instead, he went into every aspect of business in detail, supposedly shocking the professional staff with his rigour and knowledge. The clerks resisted strongly, trying to use some of the other quaestors of the year to block him. Cato replied by sacking the most senior member of staff, and prosecuting another man on charges of fraud. During his year of office he also looked into several anomalies from the time of the dictatorship. Sulla had allowed favoured supporters to take 'loans' from the Republic's funds. Cato chased these up and made sure that the money was now repaid. A group he singled out for particular attention were those who had taken the reward money of 12,000 denarii (equal to 48,000 sestertii) offered for killing the proscribed. These men were publicly named, and made to return this 'blood money'. The quaestor's actions met with general approval, for the horror of the proscriptions was still fresh in people's minds. Realising the mood of the times, prosecutors rapidly came forward to charge all of these men with murder. It was questionable whether this was legal, since Sulla's proscription law had granted protection to those acting on his behalf against decreed enemies of the Republic. These trials questioned the basis and legitimacy of the dictatorship itself, in the same way that the widespread enthusiasm for the restoration of the status and powers of the tribunate had reflected a desire for things to return to the days before Sulla when there had been a 'proper' Republic. The Romans were struggling to come to terms with the violence and turmoil of their recent past.[9]

Presiding over these trials was doubtless a welcome task for Caesar. His own experiences during the years of dictatorship gave him little sympathy for those who had taken part in and profited from the proscriptions. Politically it was also no bad thing to be involved again in a popular cause. Although a judge did not control the jury in his court, he could certainly favour one side in the case and Caesar seems to have been enthusiastic in the condemnation of men whose guilt was anyway attested by official Treasury records. Amongst the condemned was Lucius Luscius, one of Sulla's centurions who had acquired a massive fortune of 10 million sestertii during the proscriptions. Another was Catiline's uncle, Lucius Annius Bellienus, whose victims had included Quintus Lucretius Ofella, the man who had tried to stand for the consulship in defiance of Sulla's specific order. Catiline himself was also put on trial and was clearly guilty, though Cicero's later invective may well have been exaggerated. This claimed that he had paraded through the streets waving the head of his own brother-in-law, who had been a close relative of Marius. Nevertheless he was acquitted. Whether this was with the collusion of Caesar as the presiding magistrate is unclear, but Catiline was far more important and had more influential friends than others condemned in these trials. His connections may well have been enough to sway the jury, especially if backed by bribes or favours. Catiline may not have needed the assistance of Caesar, but the latter may well have felt it in his interest not to show too much enthusiasm for this particular case. The fact that the two were associated politically over the next years indicates that the trial did not result in any personal enmity, but how much can be read into this is harder to say. In spite of his association with Marius, Caesar does seem to have avoided acting as an avenger of personal wrongs during this affair. Suetonius notes that he pointedly refused to prosecute Cornelius Phagites, the officer who had arrested him during his flight from Sulla's anger (see p.59) and only released him on payment of a generous bribe. Cornelius had fulfilled his part of the bargain and Caesar, who stressed that he never neglected anyone who had aided him, may have felt that this was more important than the original arrest.[10]

This was not the first prosecution Catiline had survived. His connections amongst the senior members of the Senate had already allowed him to survive a trial for mal-administration and corruption during his time as propraetor of Africa. Again he was probably guilty, but the presence of men like Catulus supporting him in court allowed him, like so many other governors, to escape punishment. In this case even his prosecutor was most obliging to the defence. Like Sulla and Caesar, Catiline came from an ancient patrician family that had dwindled over the centuries until it was on the margins of public life, struggling to compete with wealthier and more recently distinguished rivals. The civil war had helped him to restore his fortunes, as he became eventually an eager partisan of Sulla. In the following years scandal dogged his career as he was accused of seducing a Vestal Virgin, amongst other amorous exploits. He subsequently married Aurelia Orestilla – as far as is known no relation to Caesar's mother – who was wealthy but of dubious reputation. Sallust acidly commented that 'no good person ever praised anything about her apart from her looks'. Wild rumours circulated that in his passion for her he had murdered his own teenage son because she did not care to live in the same house as this nearly adult heir. Catiline was seen as disreputable, as a womaniser whose friends, both male and female, tended to come from the wilder members of the aristocracy. Yet he also possessed great charm, and had the knack of commanding ferocious loyalty in his associates. The similarity to Caesar is striking, and it is tempting to see Catiline almost as what Caesar might have become. For all the scandals, Catiline's career up to this point had been broadly conventional, with the exception of the civil war years where the normal rules did not apply. There was an eagerness and desperation about his will to succeed that is again reminiscent of Caesar. Having been barred from standing for election to the consulship in 66 BC, he did not stand again in the next year, probably because he was still on trial in the provincial extortion court. Yet he again became a candidate at the end of 64 BC. Both Crassus and Caesar seem to have supported his campaign.[11]

In contrast to Catiline, Marcus Porcius Cato seems at first sight to have been Caesar's opposite in every respect. He was the great-grandson of Cato the Elder, a 'new man' elevated to the Senate for distinguished service in the Second Punic War, who had gone on to be both consul and censor. His ancestor had always contrasted himself with the effete aristocrats of the established families, disdaining their love of Greek language and culture, and living a simple life guided by the stern principles of duty. He was the first to write a prose history of Rome in Latin, pointedly refusing to name individual magistrates since he wished to celebrate the deeds of the Roman people and not commemorate the achievements of the nobility. It was an interesting illustration of the way senatorial families marketed themselves that the great-grandson could make himself famous and highly respected through emulating the manners and lifestyle of his famous ancestor. Cato combined his personification of traditional Roman values – which may or may not actually have reflected any historical reality in an earlier generation, but were nevertheless widely admired if not emulated – with a particularly rigorous adherence to the Stoic philosophy. This doctrine emphasised the pursuit of virtue above all else, but in his case was taken to an almost obsessional extreme. Cato was never touched by scandal or accused of luxurious living. In contrast to Caesar's fastidiousness and unconventional fashions, Cato cared little about his appearance. It was common for him to walk the streets of Rome barefoot, while he is even supposed to have conducted official business as a magistrate wearing a toga, but without the normal tunic beneath. On journeys he never rode a horse, preferring to walk, and was supposedly easily able to keep up with mounted companions. Again in contrast to Caesar, Plutarch noted that Cato had never had sex with a woman until he slept with his bride. In this case his self-control was not matched by his spouse, whom he later divorced for infidelity. Nor was it to be found in his half-sister Servilia, who for so long was Caesar's lover.[12]

In behaviour Caesar and Cato often seem poles apart, but in some ways they were both striving for much the same ends. Ambitious politicians needed to be noticed so that they could stand out from the crowd of other men all seeking the same offices. Here Cato had an advantage, for his family connections were better than Caesar's. When a man won a magistracy, he had to outshine all the other men who were holding the same post. Ability counted, but it was important to attract attention to one's deeds. In his quaestorship Cato made sure that everyone knew that he was doing things differently, bringing to the job not simply talent but his particular brand of rigid virtue. Pursuing those who had killed during the proscriptions and profited from them was a popular move, drawing attention and winning approval. In opposite ways – Caesar through his neatness and trend-setting, Cato through his apparent careless scruffiness – these two advertised themselves as distinct from their peers. The same was true of the former's taste for luxury and lavish spending on games as well as the latter's thrift.

Cato and Caesar were both recognised early on as men who already had won wide recognition and fame and who were likely to go far. Though so opposite in style, they were playing the same game.

OLD CRIMES AND NEW PLOTS

At the end of 64 BC the elections were once again fiercely contested. Caesar was not involved as a candidate, for he would not be eligible to stand for the praetorship until the following year, but he was certainly present to support the campaigns of others. This was an important way of earning support for the future, and it was always a welcome thing to place the incoming magistrates in your debt. The race for the consulship was especially tight. Catiline was finally able to stand for this office, and he was associated with the almost equally disreputable, but far less gifted Caius Antonius. The other notable candidate was Marcus Tullius Cicero, the famous orator. Cicero was a 'new man', relying on his own talent for success. He had won fame through his appearances as a legal advocate, especially in celebrated cases where, for instance, he had opposed one of Sulla's minions in 80 BC, and prosecuted a notoriously corrupt, but wealthy and well-connected governor in 70 BC. Like Caesar he had supported the Manilian Law to give Pompey the eastern command, and continually associated himself with the supporters of the popular hero. He and Pompey had briefly served together under the command of Pompeius Strabo during the Social War as, ironically, had Catiline. Cicero also presented himself as the champion of the equestrian order and had been careful to stage good entertainments during his time as aedile. Yet playing the *popularis* in this way did not endear him to the leading aristocrats in the Senate, the 'good men' (*boni*) as they liked to call themselves, and no 'new man' had reached the consulship for a generation. In the event there was enough suspicion of Catiline to make the orator seem a better choice. Cicero won comfortably, while Antonius scraped into second place.[13]

When Cicero and Antonius formally took up office on 1 January 63 BC, they were immediately confronted with a radical land bill proposed by the tribune Publius Servilius Rullus. This involved a huge allocation of plots of land to poor citizens, beginning with the State-owned territory in Campania – almost all that was left of the *ager publicus* after the re-distributions initiated by the Gracchi. Since this would be inadequate for the numbers involved, the Republic was then to buy the extra land needed. The law guaranteed a good price to sellers, declared that all sales should be voluntary and explicitly exempted the farms of Sullan veterans settled on confiscated land after the civil war. It was clear that even property in the provinces might be sold to raise the funding required. A commission of ten (*decemviri*) with propraetorian *imperium* for five years were to oversee the implementation of this programme, these being elected by the vote of a smaller assembly consisting of seventeen instead of thirty-five tribes. The project was on a massive scale, and the powers of the board of ten correspondingly great, but the problem it addressed was very real. Rural Italy had suffered badly in recent decades and there were clearly large numbers of poor citizens whose situation was desperate in the extreme. Many of the dispossessed had drifted to Rome, where they often struggled to find enough paid employment to provide for themselves and their families. There were opportunities and work in the city, but not all who went there found success. Rents were high, living conditions could be extremely squalid in the crowded *insulae* and debt was a terrible burden for many of the poor, who unlike the nobility could not hope to make themselves rich through public office.

The Rullan land bill would not have solved all of these problems on its own, but it would have done something to alleviate them. At first it was supported by all ten of the year's tribunes. It is also extremely likely that Crassus and Caesar were enthusiastic backers of Rullus and probably both hoped to win election to the board of ten. Pompey's attitude is harder to judge. On the one hand the bill would probably have provided farms for his veterans when he brought them back from campaigns that were now nearly complete. Yet if Crassus had played a key role in the programme then this would also mean that they and many other citizens were indebted to his great rival. Some of the tribunes were his keen supporters, which makes it seem unlikely that he actively opposed the bill, but he may simply not have had the time to develop too fixed an opinion as he was still so far from Rome. Cicero was set against the proposal from the very start, and throughout his life consistently disliked similar legislation. Many prominent senators were also opposed to Rullus and the new consul may have felt that this was a also a good chance to ingratiate himself with these men, whose enthusiasm for him had so far been lukewarm at best. In a series of speeches to the Senate and meetings of the People in the Forum, Cicero savaged the proposed law. The ten commissioners were demonised as 'kings' for their extraordinary powers, and dark motives alleged for the shadowy men who were claimed to be really behind the bill. These sinister figures – never named, but it is generally assumed that he meant Crassus and probably Caesar as well – wished to set themselves up as rivals to Pompey. At least one of the tribunes had already broken the consensus and declared that he would veto the bill. Cicero's rhetoric won the day, and the land law was abandoned.[14]

In the coming months Caesar prosecuted Caius Calpurnius Piso, an ex-consul who had recently returned from governing Cisalpine Gaul. Amongst the charges of extortion and maladministration was the accusation that he had unjustly executed a Gaul from the Po Valley. Once again Caesar was championing the cause of the inhabitants of this region, but with no more success than his previous efforts. Piso was successfully defended by Cicero, who added the *auctoritas* of his current office to his formidable oratory. Yet the fact that Caesar had brought the case, and doubtless also the skill and enthusiasm with which he pressed it, earned him the lasting enmity of Piso. Later in the year Caesar appeared on behalf of a Numidian client, a young nobleman who was trying to assert his independence from King Hiempsal. The king's son Juba was present in exchanges that became increasingly heated. At one point Caesar grabbed Juba by the beard. It may have been the deliberate gesture of an orator seeking to exploit most Romans' latent xenophobia, but is more likely to have been a genuine burst of anger. For all Caesar's impeccable manners and aristocratic poise – this was the guest who graciously accepted even the humblest hospitality and criticised his companions when they complained – throughout his life he was prone to occasional bursts of temper. Whatever his motive, the dispute was settled in favour of the king. Caesar did not abandon his client, but kept him hidden in his own house until he was able to smuggle him out of Rome.[15]

On several occasions during 63 BC Caesar was associated with one of the tribunes of the year, Titus Labienus. The two men were probably old acquaintances, being of a similar age and both having served in Cilicia and Asia under Servilius Isauricus in the seventies BC. Labienus seems to have come from Picenum, an area dominated by the estates of Pompey's family, and it is likely that there was some connection. As tribune, he passed a bill granting extraordinary honours to Pompey. The great commander was granted the right to wear the laurel wreath and purple cloak of a triumphing general whenever he went to the games and the full regalia if he attended a chariot race. Caesar is said to have been the instigator and chief supporter of these measures. Suetonius also credits him with having inspired the prosecution brought by Labienus against Caius Rabirius, an ageing and fairly undistinguished member of the Senate. The charge was an archaic one of *perduellio* – something like high treason – and referred to events that had occurred not long after Caesar's birth thirty-seven years earlier. Rabirius had been one of the men who followed the consuls to massacre the supporters of Saturninus and Glaucia. Labienus' uncle was amongst those who died. A very late, and quite probably unreliable, source claims that Rabirius actually displayed Saturninus' head at a dinner held soon afterwards. The prosecution may well have charged him with killing the tribune, whose person was sacrosanct by law, but since a slave was rewarded for this deed this must be extremely unlikely. In 100 BC the Senate had passed its ultimate decree (the *senatus consultum ultimum*), instructing Marius and his fellow consul to protect the Republic by whatever means were necessary. Caesar and Labienus do not seem to have been challenging the Senate's right to pass this decree, or of magistrates to obey it, but were concerned with how it should be implemented. The belief that Marius had accepted the surrender of the radicals, who were subsequently killed by a mob that had climbed onto the roof of the Senate House, seems to have formed part of the case. The *senatus consultum ultimum* gave magistrates the power to use force against citizens who were threatening the Republic, but it was less clear whether these lost all legal protection once they had given in and were no longer in a position to do harm.[16]

Many of the details of the trial are obscure. This is especially true of the prosecution's case, which is known principally from the speech Cicero made in Rabirius' defence. Much the same is true of the Rullan land bill, which again is largely known through Cicero's detailed and extremely hostile rhetoric. The whole affair was distinctly odd, in the first place simply because of the enormous lapse of time. It seems doubtful that there were many witnesses left alive, particularly considering the great loss of life amongst Rome's elite during the civil war. There was also no modern procedure for conducting a trial on a *perduellio* charge. Sulla had established a permanent court to deal with cases of a similar, but lesser crime of *maiestas* – effectively an offence against the majesty of the Roman people, rather like the idea found in some modern sports of 'bringing the game into disrepute'. However, Caesar and Labienus deliberately chose the older crime, the legislation dealing with which was believed to date back over five hundred years to the time of Rome's kings. The archaic procedure included death by crucifixion, a penalty no longer imposed on a citizen by any other law, and did not appear to permit the normal voluntary exile for the guilty. A board of two judges (*duumviri*) was appointed by lot to try the case. Caesar was one, and his distant cousin Lucius Julius Caesar, who had been consul the year before, the other. While this seems highly suspicious, there is no particular reason to assume collusion with the praetor who oversaw the selection process and it may simply have been coincidental.

Rabirius was found guilty by both judges and condemned to death. He was allowed to appeal to the Roman people, in the form of the *Comitia Centuriata*. Not only Cicero but also the orator whom he had supplanted as the greatest in Rome, Quintus Hortensius, defended the old man against Labienus. This was most probably the occasion on which Cicero delivered the speech that he subsequently published. In it he emphasised that Saturninus richly deserved his fate, pointed out that Rabirius was not the man who killed him, although repeatedly claiming that he wished his client could boast of the deed. He attacked the cruelty inherent in the revival of this long forgotten law, and, as was fairly standard in the Roman courts, blackened Labienus' name, hinting cryptically at his 'well-known' immorality. With more justification the consul complained that he had only been given an unusually short time in which to speak. His efforts do not seem to have convinced the voters who had assembled for the Comitia, in spite of the fact that some are supposed to have been moved to sympathy for the accused because of Caesar's blatant hostility as judge. Soon it was obvious that the vote would condemn Rabirius, but then the whole unorthodox business came to a fittingly bizarre conclusion. Its structure drawn from the early Roman army, the *Comitia Centuriata* had always met on the Campus Martius, outside the formal boundary of the city. In those days Rome had still been small and its enemies nearby. The gathering for voting purposes of all those obliged to do military service inevitably left the city vulnerable to a surprise attack. Therefore, to guard against this threat, it was the practice to station sentries on the vantage point offered by the Janiculum Hill. As long as these men were in place and keeping watch, a red flag was flown from the hilltop and the *Comitia Centuriata* could go about its business. If the flag was lowered, it was a sign that Rome was in danger, and that her citizens must immediately break up the Assembly and take up their arms. The custom remained in Caesar's day, and would continue for centuries afterwards, even though its function had long become obsolete. Before the Comitia completed its voting on Rabirius' fate, the praetor Quintus Caecilius Metellus Celer gave the order for the flag to be lowered. The Assembly was dissolved without giving a verdict. No one ever made any effort to reconvene the trial.[17]

None of the sources explain why Metellus acted in this way. Was he acting to protect Rabirius, or instead providing Labienus and Caesar with a face-saving way of ending the whole affair without having to convict and punish an elderly and unimportant senator? It is clear from the willingness with which they abandoned the case afterwards that condemning him was never their principal aim. They had questioned whether the *senatus consultum ultimum* overrode all other laws and citizens' rights, but had provided no clear answer or altered the law in any way. In practical terms the most that they may have achieved was to inject a note of caution into the actions of any future magistrate operating in response to such a decree. Personally the trial was a success for both Labienus and Caesar. The Comitia that met to pass judgement on Rabirius was most probably packed with their supporters and with those who were stirred by the case and the broader issue, so should probably not be seen as typical in its composition. Many citizens lacked the time, interest or opportunity to attend – it would indeed have been physically impossible to fit all those eligible to attend into the location where the *Comitia Centuriata* met. Yet even so this Assembly more than any other was weighted in favour of the better off. That it was clearly willing to condemn Rabirius does indicate that many of these citizens sympathised with the prosecution's case. Once again, Caesar was making sure that he was prominent in public life and associated with popular causes. His popularity was demonstrated later in the year when another meeting of the *Comitia Centuriata* elected him praetor for 62 BC, for which he was for the first time eligible.

The praetorship was an important post, which brought with it the certainty of receiving a provincial command after the year of office as long as a man wanted such a post. Competition for it was fierce, and more than half of former quaestors would never win the higher office. However, as things turned out, this success was far less dramatic than another electoral victory Caesar won during the last months of 63 BC. The post of *Pontifex Maximus*, head of the college of fifteen pontiffs of which he was a member, became vacant on the death of the current incumbent, Quintus Caecilius Metellus Pius – yet another representative of the prolific Metelli whose already considerable prominence had been further boosted by their support for Sulla. The dictator had placed the selection of the appointments to this and other senior priesthoods in the hands of the Senate. However, at some point in the year Labienus had passed a bill reverting to the former practice of appointment by popular election. A cut-down Tribal Assembly, with seventeen tribes chosen by lot rather than the full thirty-five was given this task. It is not clear when this law was passed, and whether Metellus' death was anticipated or the legislation rushed through in its aftermath. Three market days, which effectively meant twenty-four days in total, had to elapse between the publication of a bill and its being put to the vote of an assembly. Caesar spoke in favour of the bill and soon after it became law announced his candidature.[18]

The *Pontifex Maximus* was an office of immense prestige, in many ways the most important of all Roman priesthoods. As a result it was eagerly sought by many of the Republic's leading men. Catulus was standing for the post, as was Publius Servilius Isauricus, Caesar's old commander from Cilicia. Both were older and far more distinguished than Caesar in terms of the offices and honours they had held. Had the appointment still been controlled by the Senate, it is virtually certain that Catulus would have been appointed. In an election the outcome was far less certain, for the voters remembered Caesar's lavish spending as aedile, and his constant support for popular causes. He also seems to have spent lavishly during the campaign, giving gifts and doing favours to win over the key men in each tribe. His rivals were doing the same, and in one sense the reliance on the vote of only seventeen tribes instead of the full assembly made it easier to employ bribery. As the campaign went on, Catulus became deeply concerned that the upstart Caesar had turned into a serious challenger. Great though his *auctoritas* was, it would certainly be dented by an electoral defeat, especially one inflicted by a man so much his junior. Knowing that Caesar's debts were huge even before the campaign had begun, Catulus wrote to him offering him a considerable sum of money on condition that he withdrew from the race for the priesthood. Caesar interpreted this as a sign of weakness and immediately took out new loans to have more to spend on wooing the tribes. It was a desperate gamble. His creditors were relying on his prospects for the future, chiefly the high office and the opportunities for profit that these would bring. In itself the office of *Pontifex Maximus* brought no real financial reward, but Caesar could not afford any electoral failure. If he could no longer win over the voters, then he would begin to look like a very poor risk for his creditors. These might well press him for repayment of his debts, before his fortunes failed altogether and he was utterly ruined.

When the day of the election came – there is no record of when this was, but it must have been near the end of 63 BC – Caesar knew that the result would for him decide more than simply whether or not he won the post. Aurelia was there, and kissed him in parting before he left. Caesar told her that he would either return home as *Pontifex Maximus* or he would not return at all. This is one of the rare mentions of Aurelia from these years, but once again indicates the vital role she played in her son's life. It is notable that the story has Caesar speaking in this way to his mother rather than to his wife Pompeia or to any of his lovers. Although we cannot be absolutely certain, it does seem that Aurelia lived in her son's household. Perhaps in some way she symbolised the debt that Caesar owed to his family, making every success not simply significant to him, but part of restoring its importance and status. The contest for the priesthood was a gamble, and the price of failure very serious, certainly sufficient to retard his public career and possibly to terminate it. Yet before taking the gamble Caesar had done everything that he could to promote his success. Backing down from the challenge, as Catulus had tried to persuade him to do, was against Caesar's instincts, for he was a gambler at heart, though never a wild one. He had raised the stakes by spending even more, but he had also judged that his prospects of success were good and hence that the risk was justified. Failure was a real possibility, but Caesar seems to have estimated that the odds on his success were good. Given Catulus' hostility to him in the past, most recently following the erection of Marius' trophies, his offer suggested that his main rival had reached a similar conclusion.[19]

In the event Caesar prevailed. Plutarch describes the voting as very close, but Suetonius suggests a landslide victory, where more votes were cast for Caesar in Catulus' and Servilius' own tribes than they received in the entire Assembly. It was a great victory for him, particularly since he had overcome such strong rivals. As *Pontifex Maximus* he would in future take a central role in many aspects of State religion and ritual. He could not command the other pontiffs, for a majority of the other members of the college could overrule the *Pontifex Maximus*, but nevertheless his prestige and *auctoritas* were immense. Also, unlike the office of *Flamen Dialis*, there were no restrictions that hindered a political and military career. Physically it marked an important change, for the post came with a house, the *domus publica*, on the edge of the Sacra Via. Caesar had moved from the relative obscurity of the Subura to a place close to the heart of the Republic. The *domus publica* lay at the eastern end of the Forum and adjoined the Temple of Vesta and the Regia, where the records and texts of the pontiffs were housed and where they assembled as a college. The name Regia or 'palace' suggests a connection with Rome's monarchy, and excavations have shown that there was certainly a building on the site from a very early period and that subsequent phases and rebuildings all broadly conformed to the same, unusual design. There is a fierce debate over the precise nature of the early buildings and whether it had ever been a royal residence or palace as such, but this need not concern us. In the Late Republic the *domus publica* and the Regia were hallowed for their great antiquity and long association with the sacred.[20]

The contest for the priesthood was critical for Caesar, but in spite of its surprising result, its significance was far less than the consular elections.

Catiline was once again a candidate, as was Servilia's husband Decimus Junius Silanus. This was Silanus' second attempt – a few years before Cicero had dismissed him as a nonentity. As consul, Cicero was now in charge of overseeing the election. Encouraged by one of the other candidates, he had himself created and ensured the passage of a new, even harsher law against electoral bribery, which carried the penalty of ten years' exile. It did nothing to stop the already rampant bribery, perhaps begun by Catiline, but soon copied by all of the other candidates. Cato announced that he would prosecute whoever won the election, on the basis that no one could have prevailed in such a contest honestly. He did make an exception of his brother-in-law Silanus. While this may seem hypocritical to the modern eye, the Roman aristocracy placed huge importance on family connections and fully understood. Catiline's fortunes were at a dangerously low ebb and he was clearly desperate, presenting himself as a champion of the poor, whose plight he could well understand because of his own poverty. He openly talked of the domination of the Republic by a clique of unworthy and vulgar individuals who looked only to their own interests. When challenged in the Senate by the consul, he spoke of two Republics – the great mass of the population were a powerful body without a head to guide them, while his opponents were a head without a body, since there was no real substance to their support. He declared that he would become the head that the mass of the population so urgently longed for. It was clear that many were rallying to him, and his agents were especially active in the rural areas. He does seem to have been slowly losing the friendship of the many leading men who had in the past supported him in court. Crassus and Caesar probably continued to back him throughout the campaign. Cicero postponed the elections once, and when they were finally held in late September he arrived accompanied by a bodyguard of *equites* voted to him by the Senate. He also made sure that everyone could see that he was 'secretly' wearing a breastplate under his toga. The successful candidates were Silanus and Lucius Licinius Murena, who had served as one of Lucullus' senior subordinates in the Mithridatic War.[21]

Catiline had clearly considered using force even before the election, but had presumably hoped to succeed by conventional means. His failure left him with little choice other than facing political extinction and exile, for, like Caesar, his debts were massive and many were due by 13 November, when he would face bankruptcy. Unlike Caesar his gamble was very much a longshot and he seems to have been undecided as to how to put his plan into operation. One of his followers, Caius Manlius, was busy raising an army in Etruria, but Catiline remained in Rome, attending the Senate as if nothing was happening. Manlius was a former centurion who had served with Sulla, but since the dictatorship had lost the fortune he had made in the civil war. He appears to have been a capable man, but was from outside the senatorial class and so could never be more than a subordinate. Catiline had a number of aristocratic followers, but these were chiefly characterised by their dubious reputations and conspicuous lack of ability. It was hard for many to take such incompetents seriously, and this, combined with Catiline's continued presence in Rome, helped to foster uncertainty amongst the Senate. There were rumours of plots and rebellion, but as yet nothing had happened to suggest that there was any substance behind them. Cicero was better informed, for he had assembled a network of spies who observed the conspirators. One of the most important sources was Quintus Curius, who had boasted of the plans in an effort to impress his mistress Fulvia. She was a member of an aristocratic family and married to a senator, and Cicero was able to persuade her to convince her lover to betray his fellow conspirators. As a result the consul knew much of what was going on, and was able to safeguard himself against a murder attempt. The ability to thwart the conspirators was all very well, but it did not permit the consul to stand up in the Senate and publicly prove that a plot was underway. As yet, they had not actually done anything to warrant his acting against them. Catiline was clearly exploiting this public uncertainty, but it may also be that he had not quite made up his mind when and how to act.[22]

On the night of 18 October, Crassus and several other senators received anonymous letters, which warned them to flee because a massacre of leading men was going to occur on the 28th. They took the letters straight to Cicero, who had them read in the Senate. More reports of Manlius' activities in Etruria reached the city, and on the 21st Cicero brought this information before the Senate, which passed the *senatus consultum ultimum*. He claimed that the rebel army would openly declare itself on 27 October. This occurred, although the threatened massacre did not. Various forces, including a number of armies who had been waiting outside Rome until their commanders were allowed to celebrate triumphs, were despatched to deal with the rebels. On 8 November the Senate met once again and Cicero harangued Catiline to his face, accusing him of past crimes and declaring that he knew all about his current plans. Although at the time he returned the invective, dismissing the consul as a 'naturalised alien' with all the contempt a patrician could show for a 'new man', this meeting finally stirred him into action. He left Rome that night, claiming that he was going into voluntary exile to spare the

Republic from internal conflict. In a letter sent to Catulus, he complained of the wrongs done to him by his enemies and how he had been robbed of the proper rewards for his efforts and ability. In a properly Roman way, he commended his wife and daughter to Catulus' protection. It was soon discovered that Catiline had not in fact fled abroad, but had instead joined Manlius and the army. Both men were declared public enemies. He left behind in Rome a number of supporters, who began to negotiate with some ambassadors from the Allobroges, a Gallic people who were in the city to complain of their desperate plight. The conspirators hoped to persuade the tribe to rebel and open a second front to distract forces loyal to the Senate. Instead the Gauls went to Cicero and betrayed them. One man was caught when the Allobroges led him into an ambush, and the four other key figures arrested shortly afterwards. Confronted with damning evidence, the initial declarations of innocence were soon replaced by admissions of guilt. It was now a question of what to do with them.[23]

VII

SCANDAL

'The Republic, citizens, the lives of you all, your property, your fortunes, your wives and your children, together with this heart of our glorious empire, this most blessed and beautiful of cities, have, as you see, on this very day been snatched from fire and the sword. The great love that the immortal gods hold for you has combined with the toil and the vigilance that I have undertaken, and with the perils that I have undergone, to bring them out of the very jaws of destruction and restore them to you safe and sound.' – *Cicero, 3 December 63 BC.*[1]

Caesar's attitude throughout these months seemed to many to be deeply ambiguous. Along with Crassus, he had backed Catiline's candidacy. He probably knew Catiline quite well, but then the world of Rome's aristocracy was so small that most senators knew each other. Although Cicero's speeches from 63 BC and afterwards painted Catiline as an irredeemable monster, he had not always thought of him in this way. As recently as 65 BC, he had considered defending him in court, 'hoping that this will encourage them to join forces in our canvassing' for the consulship in 63 BC.[2] Caesar had persisted in his open support for Catiline for much longer and, as previously noted, the similarities between them were striking. Both men were inclined to support 'popular' causes and keen to associate themselves with Marius. When he reached Manlius' army, Catiline paraded an eagle that had been the standard of one of Marius' legions. Caesar would also have seemed a likely man to join a conspiracy of debtors, for his lifestyle was similar in many ways. When Cicero addressed the crowd in the Forum, he described many of the conspirators as: 'the men you see with their carefully combed hair, dripping with oil, some smooth as girls, others with shaggy beards, with tunics down to their ankles and wrists, and wearing frocks not togas'.[3] This image could almost be an exaggerated portrait of Caesar himself, who had probably set the fashion for wearing long sleeves and whose loose girdled tunic hung low. In later years Cicero was suspicious of almost everything Caesar did, but even then is supposed to have said that: 'On the other hand, when I look at his hair, which is arranged with so much nicety, and see him scratching his head with one finger, I cannot think that this man would ever conceive of so great a crime as the overthrow of the Roman constitution.'[4] Like many of the conspirators Caesar was a dandy, a man whose sexual exploits and massive debts were equally notorious, but unlike them he was also very successful. He had gained each office in the *cursus* as soon as he was eligible, and had just had the spectacular success in the competition for the post of *Pontifex Maximus*. Caesar had no need for revolution, which is not to say that he might not have joined the rebels if he had thought it likely that they would succeed.

Crassus was in a similar position, for he had openly backed Catiline in the elections. Probably, like Caesar, Crassus would have made sure that he was on the winning side, whichever it might be, but the uncertainty of the situation made this a nervous time for anyone suspected of involvement in the plot. Even while his agents were openly raising an army, Catiline remained in Rome. After he left, it was known that other conspirators had remained behind to cause mischief in the city. With the consul announcing almost on a daily basis that he had uncovered new plans for assassinations and arson attacks, it was unsurprising that senators looked at many of their fellows with suspicion. Both Caesar and Crassus had to be very careful in their behaviour. Therefore Crassus immediately took the anonymous letter to Cicero as soon as he had received it. Even so, following the arrest of the conspirators, an informer was brought into the Senate who claimed that he had been sent by Crassus with a message to Catiline, telling him not be worried by the arrests, but to press on with his enterprise. According to Sallust:

> But when Tarquinius named Crassus, a man of enormous wealth and great influence, some found the accusation incredible, while others thought it was true, but reckoned that at a time of crisis it was better to win over than to alienate such a powerful man; a good number of them were in Crassus' debt from private deals, and they all loudly called out that the accusation was false. . . [5]

A vote was taken declaring the statement false and placing the informer in custody, pending investigation. The historian Sallust says that he himself later heard Crassus say that the informer had acted on the instructions of Cicero, who had wanted to force him to make an open breach with Catiline and the rebels instead of sitting on the fence. Certainly, the whole incident seems to have worsened the already poor relations between the two men.[6]

Cicero was under great pressure in these weeks. Even at the time he was aware that this was his finest hour, the moment when the 'new man' from Arpinum would save the Republic. Throughout his life he would revel in recounting his great success, but it was not a victory that came easily. From the beginning it had been difficult to persuade all senators that the threat of rebellion was real, especially since for a long time there were few hard facts that he could report openly. Eventually, the arrest and interrogation of the key conspirators in Rome convinced the entire Senate that the threat was real and serious. It was now a question of dealing with it, but Cicero was hindered by the fact that his own year of office as consul had only a few more weeks to run. Like any Roman magistrate he was eager to ensure that the main threat was defeated in that time, both to ensure that it was done properly and because he wanted to gain the credit for this achievement. It was extremely inconvenient when Cato fulfilled his promise and prosecuted Murena, consul elect for 62 BC. Murena was clearly guilty of electoral bribery, but Cato was displaying his characteristic lack of timing. At a time of crisis it would obviously have been dangerous to have removed one of the two senior magistrates due to begin guiding the Republic in just a few weeks. Therefore, Cicero took the time off to defend Murena, emphasising the dire threat faced by the State and the valuable service that his client, as an experienced military man, could do for the threatened Republic. His speech was later published, and although it was said at the time that fatigue made his delivery less perfect than his normal standard, Murena was acquitted. Largely ignoring the charges, he mocked the motives of the prosecutors, depicting Cato as a naive idealist, trying to impose impractical philosophical principles in the real world. Cato is supposed to have responded by grimly saying 'what a witty chap our consul is'. Cicero always preferred to speak last after the other defence counsels, in this case Hortensius and Crassus. It was an indication of the complex web of obligations and friendships in Roman politics that Crassus and Cicero found themselves working together in court on this and other occasions. Both men liked to defend, gaining the gratitude this brought from the client, his family and his close associates.[7]

The trial had been an added burden to the consul's load in these desperate weeks. Soon after the accusation against Crassus, there was an attempt to persuade Cicero to implicate Caesar in the conspiracy. The men behind this were Catulus, still indignant at his defeat in the race for the senior priesthood, and Caius Calpurnius Piso, whom Caesar had unsuccessfully prosecuted earlier in the year. Cicero refused to go along with this. He may simply not have believed it, for he probably knew Caesar fairly well, most likely having seen a lot of him in the seventies BC when he was close to the Cotta brothers. Alternatively it could have been expediency, reckoning that it was dangerous to force a man like Caesar into a corner and make him join the revolutionaries. Later, in a work not published until after both Crassus and Caesar were dead, Cicero would write that both had been closely involved with Catiline, but it is not at all clear that this is what he believed at the time, or that he was right. In the dying months of 63 BC, he decided anyway that he would openly trust the loyalty to the Republic of both men, whatever his personal view. After the interrogation of the five key conspirators in the Senate each man was given into the charge of a prominent senator who was to keep him in custody until the Senate had decided their fate. Crassus and Caesar were amongst those selected to perform this task, Cicero very deliberately showing his faith in them in this way. None of this prevented Piso and Catulus from continuing to spread rumours about their personal enemy Caesar.[8]

The captives were a motley crew. Two, Publius Cornelius Lentulus Sura and Caius Cornelius Cethegus, were amongst the sixty-four senators expelled from the Senate by the censors of 70 BC. Lentulus had been consul in 71 BC and had been steadily rebuilding his public career since his expulsion. In 63 BC he had won the praetorship for the second time, but was stripped of the post following his arrest. He was not the only man to claw his way back to prominence through standing for election again. Cicero's consular colleague Antonius had also been expelled by the same censors. So had Curius, the man whose mistress Fulvia had persuaded to turn informant (p.128). Lentulus believed firmly in his destiny, continually citing a prophecy that proclaimed that three Cornelii would rule Rome – Sulla, Cinna and soon himself. His wife was a Julia, sister of Lucius Julius Caesar, who had been consul in 64 BC. Her son from an earlier marriage was Mark Antony, then around ten years old. Catiline throughout the rising refused to recruit slaves, preferring to rely on citizens. Lentulus not only argued against this, but did so in writing, in a letter that was subsequently captured and read out in the Senate. All of the conspirators seem to have done their best to incriminate themselves. Most at first met the interrogation with simple denial – Cethegus claiming that the large cache of weapons discovered in his house was simply his collection of antique militaria – but soon caved in when confronted with damning letters sealed with their own seals and written in their own hands. Their guilt was firmly established when they were brought before the Senate on 3 December. Two days later, on the 5th, the House met again to decide on their fate.[9]

THE GREAT DEBATE

The Senate assembled in the Temple of Concord rather than in the Senate House. This was not unusual, for the House met in a range of temples as well as the Curia itself. The choice of the deity Concordia may have seemed especially appropriate, or even ironic, in the circumstances, but may also have been based on its position at the western edge of the Forum near the slope of the Capitol Hill. This was an easier area to defend for the large numbers of armed men, many of them young equestrians, who attended the consul and took up positions to guard the meeting. Cicero as presiding magistrate would have begun the session with a formal prayer, before addressing the House and asking that it decide what should done to the prisoners. In the past, consuls acting under the *senatus consultum ultimum* had taken it upon themselves to execute those seen as enemies of the Republic without consulting the Senate. Yet in the main such killings had occurred in the heat of the fighting, when the 'rebels' could be seen as posing an active threat. The five conspirators were already under guard, unlike the earlier occasions when the decree had been passed. There were rumours that Cethegus had attempted to communicate with his slaves and arrange for an armed gang to free the prisoners, but even so this could not be presented as a lynching in the heat of the moment. The trial of Rabirius had recently called into question just what actions could be justified by the ultimate decree, and this may have made Cicero particularly cautious. The Senate was not a court, but if a clear consensus of its members approved a course of action then this would add moral force to what the consul did. Cicero declared himself willing to conform to whatever was the Senate's decision, but clearly believed that the prisoners both deserved and needed to be executed.

There was no fixed order of speaking in the Senate, but there was a hierarchy in the sense that it was customary to call first upon the consuls, then the praetors and so on to the lesser magistrates. The order in which individuals from each group would speak was decided by the presiding magistrate, who called upon them by name. Junior members of the House, especially those who had never held a magistracy, were rarely asked to speak. However, every senator present could vote and, uniquely in Roman voting systems, each vote carried equal weight. When the division was called, senators walked to opposite sides of the house to signify whether they were approving or rejecting the motion. It was common during a debate for those supporting a speaker to move over and sit next to him. The backbenchers, who rarely spoke, but could still vote, were sometimes referred to as *pedarii*, which roughly translates as 'walkers'. It had been very noticeable at the meeting on 8 November that when Catiline had taken his seat the senators had quickly moved away, leaving him isolated physically as well as politically.[10]

On 5 December Cicero began the debate by calling upon Servilia's husband Silanus to give his opinion. It was usual to seek the opinion of the consuls elect before the former consuls or 'consulars', since these men might well have to put into effect measures decided by the House. Silanus declared that the prisoners should suffer 'the ultimate punishment', which was interpreted – and clearly intended to mean – execution. Murena was called next and concurred, as did all fourteen ex-consuls present on the day. Crassus was notable by his absence, continuing his somewhat ambiguous behaviour. In contrast Caesar was there and boldly gave his opinion when called upon as praetor elect. Up until now all the speakers had opted for the death penalty, and the murmurs – perhaps louder cries as we do not know how raucous or dignified and sedate meetings of the Senate were – of approval from the rest of the House suggested that this was the near universal view. Caesar, given the doubts expressed about him in recent days, might have been expected to give his vigorous assent as proof of his loyalty to the Republic. Yet not long before he had attacked Rabirius for the illegal killing of Roman citizens, and throughout his career had championed popular causes, criticising the arbitrary use of power by Senate or magistrates. It would have been inconsistent now to express a contrary view, but it seems unlikely that Caesar ever considered this. Standing alone had never bothered him since the days when he had defied Sulla. The aristocracy celebrated men who single-handedly had persuaded the Senate to change its mind. One of the most famous was Appius Claudius Caecus in 278 BC, who was supposed to have convinced the Senate not to negotiate with the victorious Pyrrhus, but to keep fighting. When it was a choice between merging with the crowd and playing a conspicuous role, Caesar always chose the latter. In this case it may well also have been a matter of conscience and genuine belief. Winning fame and doing what he believed to be right were not mutually exclusive.[11]

The text of Caesar's speech has not survived, but Sallust gives a version that appears to reflect the key arguments, even if it does so in Sallustian style and probably at rather shorter length. As with any written speech, it is hard now to conjure up the full impact of the orator speaking these words before an audience. Caesar was praised for gestures, the elegance and forcefulness of his stance and bearing, and the tones of his slightly high-pitched voice. In Sallust's version the great performance began with these words:

> Chosen fathers of the Senate, all men who decide on difficult issues ought to free themselves from the influence of hatred, friendship, anger and pity. For when these intervene the mind cannot readily judge the truth, and no one has ever served his emotions and his best interests simultaneously. When you set your mind to a task, it prevails; if passion holds sway, it consumes you, and the mind can do nothing.[12]

Throughout the speech he was calm and sweetly reasonable, and he gently mocked the previous speakers who had tried to outdo each other with graphic descriptions of the slaughter, rape and pillage that would have followed Catiline's victory. There was never a trace of the man who had grabbed Juba's beard in his rage. The guilt of the accused was unquestioned, and no punishment could possibly be too harsh for them. Yet, returning to his opening theme, the Senate held too responsible a position to permit its members to give in to their emotions. They must decide what was best for the future of the Republic, knowing that they would set a precedent today. Caesar carefully paid tribute to Cicero by declaring that no one could ever suspect that the current consul would abuse his position. What they could not guarantee was that all future office holders would always be so restrained. He reminded them of how Sulla's proscriptions had begun with a few deaths of men who were generally thought guilty. Soon the slaughter had escalated into an appalling bloodbath, with victims being killed for 'their town houses or villas'.[13]

For Caesar the death penalty was unRoman (although, of course, the recent *perduellio* trial with its archaic procedure had threatened its use). He gently chided Silanus, praising him for his patriotism, but suggesting that he had become carried away by the enormity of the prisoners' crimes. Under normal circumstances Roman citizens – at least well to do citizens – were always permitted to go into exile if found guilty of a serious offence, making the death penalty effectively a theoretical punishment unknown in practice. Caesar wondered why Silanus had not also suggested that the men be flogged before they were killed, answering his own question by saying that of course such a thing was illegal. He praised the wisdom of their ancestors, the past generations of senators who had systematically removed the death penalty and other brutal punishments in regard to citizens. Anyway, death was 'release from woes, rather than a punishment . . . it brings an end to the ill fortune of life and leaves no place for worry or joy'.[14] Caesar's solution was different. It would obviously have been absurd to let the men go so that they could join Catiline. Rome had no real prison intended to keep prisoners for long periods of time, for most laws carried either fines or exile as punishment. Caesar proposed that the prisoners be given into the hands of different Italian towns, who would be bound to hold them in captivity for the rest of their lives. Any town failing in its charge was to suffer a heavy penalty. The men's property was to be confiscated by the State, effectively blocking their children from going into public life and seeking revenge. It was also to be decreed that neither the Senate nor People should ever consider permitting the conspirators to be recalled, in the way that Caesar himself had campaigned for the return of Lepidus' supporters. This, according to him, was a far harsher penalty than death, since it would make the conspirators live with the consequences of their crimes.[15]

During the speech Caesar appealed to the example of past generations. This was conventional, for the Roman aristocracy had a great reverence for their ancestors, children listening from an early age to stories of their great deeds on behalf of the Republic. Yet the proposal he was making was both radical and innovative. Never before had the Romans held citizens in permanent captivity – hence the need to create a new method to do this. Although he stipulated that it should be unlawful for anyone to seek the release and restoration of the condemned, it was questionable that such a provision could be enforced. The Gracchi and other tribunes had repeatedly asserted the right of the Popular Assembly to vote on any issue. Whether anyone was ever likely to espouse the cause of the conspirators was questionable, but this could certainly not be ruled out altogether. The problem facing the Senate was a new one, for never in the history of the ultimate decree had it been a question of using its powers calmly against men already held in custody. Caesar had spoken about the precedent that the Senate would set by its decision and he now proposed a new solution to what was in many ways a new problem. It was intended to avoid the recriminations that had followed the suppression of the Gracchi and of Saturninus. The conspirators were guilty of planning appalling crimes, but even so they should not be stripped of all the rights of citizens. They were no longer in a position to harm the Republic and imprisonment would ensure that they would never be able to do so in the future.[16]

Throughout his speech Caesar was calm and measured, always rational as he appealed to the senators not to let their emotions overrule their duty to the Republic. Such a call to place Rome before their own feelings was bound to appeal to men raised with such a strong sense of the obligations inherent in belonging to one of the great families. The certainty that had marked the start of the meeting began to crack, and then crumble away. Quintus Tullius Cicero, the consul's younger brother, was another of the praetor designates and spoke after Caesar, fully agreeing with his viewpoint. He may well, in the conventions of the Senate, have moved to sit with Caesar as an indication of this. Another of the praetors for 62 BC, Tiberius Claudius Nero – the grandfather of Emperor Tiberius – took a slightly different tack, suggesting that it was too early to decide on the prisoners' fate while Catiline was still at large with an army. Instead, they should be held in custody and a future date fixed for another debate, which would decide their fate.[17] Many others were wavering. At some point Silanus spoke up claiming that he had been misinterpreted and had not advocated the death penalty at all, but the 'ultimate punishment' *permitted by the law*. Such vacillation seems to have been typical of a man who clearly did not want to be seen as responsible for anything controversial.

Cicero, seeing the earlier consensus slipping away, decided to act, and at this point delivered a long speech, the text of which he subsequently published as the *Fourth Catilinarian Oration*. Given that the original must have been at least partially composed during the debate itself, it was probably a little less polished than the version we have today. However, it would be a mistake to underestimate the rhetorical training and skill of the great orator, and it is likely that even speaking off the cuff, Cicero's use of language, rhythm and structure were of an exceptionally high order. He made sure from the beginning that everyone was reminded that he was consul, the man leading the Republic at this time of crisis and also, ultimately, the one who would carry the responsibility for whatever action they decided to take. Reviving the tone of the earlier debate, before Caesar's restrained and reasonable intervention, he spoke of slaughter, rape and the sacking of temples:

> Take thought for yourselves, therefore, gentlemen; look to the preservation of your fatherland, save yourselves, your wives, your children and your fortunes, defend the name of the Roman people and

their very existence; stop protecting me and cease your concern for me. Firstly, I am bound to hope that all the gods which watch over this city will recompense me as I deserve; and secondly, if anything happens to me, I shall die calm and resigned.[18]

He turned to the two proposals, that of Silanus, which he continued to interpret as meaning execution, and that of Caesar. The first punishment accorded with tradition – Cicero mentioning the Gracchi and Saturninus whom he claimed had been killed for far lesser crimes – the second was unprecedented and impractical. How, Cicero asked, were the towns tasked with guarding the prisoners to be chosen? It seemed unfair for the Senate to choose them, but could communities be expected to come forward of their own free will? Yet he did not challenge the severity of Caesar's proposal, emphasising that life imprisonment and confiscation of all property were in many ways more savage punishments than a swift death.

Cicero was also studiously polite to Caesar himself, who had demonstrated by his speech and actions his 'devotion to the Republic'. He contrasted him, a genuine '*popularis* with the good of the people at heart', with other rabble-rousing demagogues. At this point there was a sly dig at Crassus, when he noted that 'one who posed as a *popularis*' was absent, 'presumably so he did not have to vote on whether or not to kill Roman citizens'. Crassus – still unnamed, but there could be no doubt over his identity – had in the last two days taken charge of one of the prisoners, voted a public thanksgiving to Cicero and approved the rewards granted to informers. Then he tried to use Caesar's very presence to weaken his argument. If he accepted that it was proper for the Senate to pass judgement on the conspirators at all, then he must have acknowledged that they had in fact ceased to be citizens, and so lost all protection of law. If the Senate chose his proposal, Cicero knew that Caesar's personal popularity would make it easier for them to persuade the crowd gathered in the Forum that this was just. Yet he also claimed to be convinced that the wisdom of the people would allow them to accept the necessity of executing the prisoners. This led him back to the enormity of their crimes and 'how he trembled at the vision of mothers crying, girls and boys fleeing, and the rape of Vestal Virgins'.[19] He reassured them of the precautions he had taken to protect this meeting and defend the city, making it clear that they were free to do what they thought right. As consul, he was willing to take on himself the consequences of their decision and any stigma or hatred that the executions might bring in the future. He would personally pay any price to serve the Republic.

The consul's speech rekindled the emotions of some senators, but the meeting remained divided and uncertain. More opinions were called for, and Cato's view was sought as one of the tribunes elect. Once again we have to rely principally on Sallust's account for its content, but Plutarch tells us that the speech itself was written down and subsequently published by clerks working for Cicero who followed the whole debate. In his version the thirty-two year old began by stating that his fellow senators seemed to be forgetting that Catiline was still at large and the conspirators still potentially a threat to the Republic. The State's very survival was in doubt, and they would be foolish if 'in sparing the lives of a few villains, they brought destruction on all good men'.[20] He disdained Caesar's view that death was a merciful end to suffering, recalling instead traditional tales of the punishment meted out to evildoers in the afterlife. He was equally critical of the suggestion of sending the prisoners into captivity in different towns. Why should they be any more secure there than in Rome, and what was to prevent them being freed by Catiline's rebels? On this occasion, as throughout his life, Cato advocated the same stern, unyielding and severe course. Mercy was out of place and dangerous until the threat to the Republic had been averted:

> Be assured . . . that when you decide the fate of Publius Lentulus and the rest, you will at the same time be passing judgement on Catiline's army and all the conspirators. The more vigorous your action, the less will be their courage; but if they detect the slightest weakness on your part, they will be here immediately, filled with reckless daring. . .
>
> Citizens of the highest rank have conspired to fire their native city, they stir up to war the Gauls, bitterest enemies of the Roman people. The leader of the enemy with his army is upon us. Do you even now hesitate and doubtfully ask yourselves what is to be done with foemen taken within your walls?[21]

Just like Caesar, Cato spoke of the example of Rome's history, in an effort to bolster his view with the support – in each case rather spurious – of tradition. It was not unusual for men arguing opposite courses of action to claim that Rome's long-standing customs supported them. At Rome innovations almost invariably arrived wrapped in a cloak of tradition. Sallust portrays the debate as essentially a struggle between Caesar and Cato. Thus it foreshadowed the Civil War, when Cato would be Caesar's bitterest and most implacable opponent. This was a common view, especially as the years went on. Cicero was deeply annoyed when Brutus wrote an account which minimised his own role, while stressing that of Cato. This version had great attraction, becoming one of those incidents where one man had swayed the whole Senate and shown it the path of duty. Cato was clearly conscious of playing this role at the time, just as Caesar had been, and he certainly had a considerable impact on the debate. All of the former consuls and many other senators applauded Cato's proposal as soon as he finished speaking and sat down. Caesar was undaunted and continued to argue his own case. The two men were sitting not far from each other and Cato's replies became increasingly bitter, though he failed to provoke his opponent. Unlike Cicero, he freely cast aspersions on Caesar's conduct in recent months, demonising him and claiming that his unwillingness to support the death penalty showed his sympathy for, and perhaps complicity in, the conspiracy. While this was going on, a note was brought in and quietly given to Caesar, presumably by one of his slaves. Cato saw this as an opportunity, declaring that his opponent was obviously in secret communication with the enemy. Caesar, who had quietly read the note, did not respond, but demurred when Cato demanded that he read the message aloud. Cato sensed a guilty conscience and became even more forceful, encouraged by approving shouts from all sides. Finally, Caesar simply handed the note to Cato, who was staggered to see that it was in fact a very passionate love letter from Servilia. With a despairing cry of 'Have it back, you drunk!', he hurled the message back to Caesar, whose patrician dignity and calm, self-confident style had not wavered throughout the exchange. It was a slightly odd form of abuse, for Caesar was renowned as abstemious when it came to alcohol, whereas Cato himself was a heavy drinker.[22]

The incident provides an interesting sideline on the relationship between Caesar and Servilia. Clearly it is indicative of great ardour, and the need for contact and communication when they were apart. Sending a love note to a meeting of the Senate, where Caesar would be sitting close alongside both her husband and her half-brother, was an act of considerable boldness on Servilia's part. Perhaps she, or both of them, were thrilled by the danger of such an act. Silanus' attitude is very hard to gauge and it is unclear whether or not he knew that his wife was having an affair with Caesar. If he did find out, then he made no attempt to act against his rival. Caesar's political friendship was worth having, particularly for a man who had only managed to gain the consulship at the second attempt and who did not have a great reputation for ability. It has even been speculated that he may have encouraged his wife in an effort to gain Caesar's support. Deep though their love evidently was, neither of the lovers were likely to miss an opportunity for personal gain.

In the end the vote – taken on Cato's proposal rather than that of his brother-in-law Silanus' because it was felt to be better worded – was overwhelmingly in favour of executing the prisoners. Lucius Caesar, Lentulus' brother-in-law, supported this resolution, as it seems did Cethegus' actual brother, who was himself a senator. Caesar did not change his position, and was mobbed by an angry crowd as he left the Temple of Concord. As was usual during a debate, the doors had been left open and it was clear that much of what was going on was being reported to the many who had gathered outside and in the rest of the Forum. Fear of the conspiracy, and particularly the stories of plans to set fire to Rome – a dire threat to the many who lived in its crowded, densely packed and readily flammable *insulae* – had created a deeply hostile mood. Cicero continued to give his open support for Caesar, ensuring that he was not harmed. The final act was played out in the nearby Tullianum, the small cave-like prison where prisoners were held for short priods, pending punishment. The conspirators were taken there. Lentulus had been stripped of his praetorship, but even so was granted the distinction of being led by the consul in person. The five were taken inside and then strangled out of public view. Cicero emerged shortly afterwards and announced simply, 'They have lived.' (*vixerunt*). In spite of the Senate's vote, he was one who could be held accountable for this action.[23]

THE AFTERMATH: CAESAR'S PRAETORSHIP, 62 BC

It did not take long for the first attacks to be made against Cicero over this issue. The new tribunes took up office on 10 December 63 BC, and amongst them was Quintus Metellus Nepos, a man whose reckless reputation is supposed to have prompted Cato to stand for the tribunate in this year as soon as his candidature was announced. He soon began to denounce Cicero's 'illegal' punishment of the conspirators. On the last day of December, the consuls formally laid down their office, and it was customary for them to make a speech recounting their achievements. Nepos and one of his colleagues, Lucius Bestia, used their tribunician veto to stop Cicero from doing this, an almost unheard of insult. He could not prevent the outgoing consul from taking the customary oath and Cicero employed this chance to state that he had saved the Republic. Nepos was Pompey's brother-in-law and had served for some time as one of his legates in the East, but had returned to Rome and was seen as representing the general's interests. The war was over and Pompey's return imminent, but there was a question of how he would return. Already there was talk of summoning back the Republic's most famous and successful commander to crush Catiline's rebel army.[24]

On 1 January, Caesar took up office as praetor and immediately launched an attack on Catulus. The Temple of Jupiter on the Capitoline Hill had been burnt down in 83 BC, and five years later Catulus as consul had been allotted the task of overseeing its restoration. The project had not yet been completed and the praetor summoned Catulus before a meeting of the people in the Forum to account for this dereliction, accusing him of embezzling the funds allocated by the Senate. In a studied insult, he stopped the ex-consul from mounting the Rostra and made him speak from ground level. Caesar proposed to bring in a bill that would transfer the task to someone else, most probably Pompey, for Caesar continued to seek popularity through vocal support for the great hero. However, enough supporters of Catulus arrived to pressure the praetor into backing down. As was often the case in Caesar's career up to this point, actually succeeding in his projects was less important that publicly becoming associated with a cause.[25]

Caesar then actively supported Nepos, who was proposing a bill to recall Pompey and his army and give them the task of restoring order in Italy. Cato, his fellow tribune, violently opposed them, lambasting them in the Senate and swearing that, while he was still breathing, Pompey would never enter the city with soldiers under command. On the day of voting on this bill, Nepos in the normal way held an informal meeting of the Roman people. He took his seat on the podium of the Temple of Castor and Pollux. This high platform was often used as an alternative to the Rostra, for there was more room for a crowd at this eastern end of the Forum. Caesar had his chair of office placed beside the tribune to show his support. Amongst the crowd were numbers of burly men, including some gladiators, stationed to defend the tribunes if there was trouble. This soon arrived in the shape of Cato and his fellow tribune Quintus Minucius Thermus, who were there to veto proceedings and had come supported by their followers. Cato strode up to the podium and he and Minucius climbed the steps. Cato took a seat between Nepos and Caesar, momentarily disconcerting them by his boldness. A fair proportion of the crowd was now cheering him on, but others were still loyal to Nepos and the tension grew. Recovering, Nepos ordered a clerk to read the bill aloud. Cato used his veto to forbid this, and when Nepos himself took up the document and started to read, he snatched it from his hands. Knowing the text by heart, the tribune then began to recite it, until Thermus slapped his hand over his mouth to stop him. Nepos then signalled to his armed supporters and a riot ensued, beginning with sticks and stones, but culminating in some fighting with edged weapons. Cato and Thermus were both roughly handled, but the former was physically protected by Murena, the consul whom he had so recently prosecuted. In the end Nepos' partisans and supporters were dispersed. That same afternoon the Senate convened and passed the *senatus consultum ultimum*. A proposal to strip Nepos of his tribunate was, however, abandoned on the recommendation of Cato himself. However, after summoning another public meeting in the Forum and accusing Cato and the Senate of a plot against Pompey, but saying that they would soon pay the price for this, Nepos fled from Rome. A tribune was not supposed to leave the city during his year of office, but he went even further and sailed from Italy altogether to join Pompey in Rhodes. In the relief at his departure, no one chose to question its legality.[26]

Caesar had badly misjudged the situation. All our accounts portray Nepos as the prime mover behind the violence in this episode, and as a dangerously impulsive and volatile individual, but Caesar had enthusiastically supported him, at least in the beginning. Nepos was a supporter of Pompey because his half-sister Mucia was married to the general, and because he hoped to benefit from his return. Caesar was no relation to Pompey, and had never had any direct connection with him – although he had been sleeping with Mucia during her husband's absence on campaign – but was continuing his policy of praising and supporting Rome's great hero as a means to increase his own popularity. This time it had gone too far and the Senate decreed that he be expelled from the praetorship, which he had only held for a matter of weeks. At first Caesar tried to brazen it out, continuing to appear in public with the trappings of office and carrying out his duties. Again he had failed to understand the general mood, and the deep anger that the recent events had caused. Hearing that some senators were ready to oppose him with force, he dismissed the six lictors who attended him. These men carried the fasces, the bundles of rods and an axe that symbolised a holder of *imperium*, and his power to inflict corporal and capital punishment. He then removed his *toga praetexta*, worn on official occasions by senators, and quietly slipped off to his house, the *domus publica*, making it known that he intended to retire from public life. On the next day a crowd gathered in the Forum outside his house, loudly proclaiming that they were ready to help him restore his fortunes. Caesar went out and spoke to them, calming their mood and persuading them to disperse. Orchestrated or spontaneous – or quite possibly a mixture of both – it was a dignified and responsible performance which persuaded the Senate to restore him. Although his political instincts had failed him a few times during these days, Caesar had shown his ability to realise that he had made a mistake and the skill of recovering from it.[27]

By now Catiline had been defeated by an army nominally under the command of Cicero's former colleague Antonius, but in fact led by one of his subordinates. Cato's claim that strong action would terrify the rebels had proved ill-founded, for the majority stayed loyal to Catiline and died with him. Whatever they may have thought of him in life, there was grudging acknowledgement that Catiline had died well, showing all the courage expected of a member of the aristocracy. Yet although he was gone and the rebels defeated, there was still a climate of suspicion and recrimination at Rome. Rewards were available to those providing valuable evidence to the authorities, and this may in part explain the spate of denunciations. Quintus Curius, the man whose mistress had persuaded him to betray the rebels and who had been rewarded with restoration to the Senate, now named Caesar amongst a list of men said to have been part of the conspiracy. Another informer, Lucius Vettius, repeated the charge, claiming that he possessed a letter written by Caesar to Catiline. In the Senate the restored praetor answered Curius by appealing to Cicero, who testified that Caesar had provided him with some information and throughout proved his loyalty. As a result, Curius lost his informer's bounty. Vettius, an equestrian of little importance and questionable reputation, could be dealt with more easily. Caesar as praetor commanded him to appear before the Rostra, then had him beaten up and thrown into prison. He was most probably released soon afterwards, but no more public accusations were levelled at Caesar.[28]

THE 'GOOD GODDESS'

Little else is recorded of Caesar's praetorship, and it is more than probable that, at least by his standards, he kept a low profile and simply went about his main task of acting as a judge. Near the end of the year he became embroiled in a scandal of illicit and adulterous love, but just for once he was the innocent party. Every year the festival of the *Bona Dea*, or Good Goddess, was celebrated in the house of one of the senior magistrates. In 62 BC Caesar's residence was chosen, probably because he was the senior pontiff as well as a praetor. Although the celebration occurred in a magistrate's house, neither he nor any other man was permitted to be present, for the ceremonies were performed exclusively by women, chiefly the aristocratic matrons of Rome and their female attendants. After performing sacrifices and other rituals, music and feasting continued throughout the night. The Vestal Virgins presided over the rites, and according to Plutarch the magistrate's wife did much of the organising of the celebrations. In this case Aurelia may have played more of a role than Pompeia, and Caesar's sister Julia was also present.

Pompeia had a lover, the thirty-year old quaestor-elect Publius Clodius Pulcher, and the couple had decided that the celebrations offered a perfect cover for an assignation. Clodius disguised himself as a girl harp-player, one of the many professional entertainers, mostly slaves, who took part in the festival. During the night he was let into the house by Habra, one of Pompeia's personal maids, who was in on the secret. She then ran off to fetch her mistress, leaving Clodius to wait for some time. Growing impatient, he began to wander and bumped into one of Aurelia's slaves, who promptly tried to persuade the young, and apparently shy, musician to join the rest of the company. Unable to shake off her persistent attentions, Clodius at last said that he could not come as 'she' was waiting for 'her' friend Habra. Betrayed by his voice, which was obviously masculine, the slave ran off screaming that there was a man in the house, causing instant confusion. Clodius fled into the darkness. Aurelia reacted with the calm efficiency that it seems was a hallmark of her own character as well as her son's. She immediately halted the ceremony and had the sacred implements used in the rites covered up, lest they suffer pollution by being seen by a man. Slaves were sent to lock all the doors of the house, to prevent the intruder from escaping. Caesar's mother then led them as they searched the house by torchlight, eventually finding Clodius hiding in Habra's room. The woman took a good look at him to make sure who he was – the world of the Roman aristocracy was small and most members of it recognisable to each other, before driving him from the house. Aurelia then sent the women back to their own homes to tell their husbands about Clodius' sacrilege.[29]

In the following days, Caesar divorced Pompeia. There was no provision for divorce in Rome's earliest law code, the Twelve Tables still memorised by aristocratic children in Caesar's day, but it was nevertheless hallowed by long tradition. Like so many other aspects of Roman society, it was seen as a matter for individual families. By the Late Republic it seems that either the husband or wife could unilaterally divorce the other. In its simplest form a husband would simply say 'Take your things for yourself!' (*tuas res tibi habeto*). Caesar may or may not have used this traditional phrase, or he may have sent a letter to Pompeia, but in any case the marriage was quickly broken. No reason was publicly given for the divorce, but this was nothing unusual even if the preceding circumstances were. The union seems never to have been as close as his marriage to Cornelia and, although the couple had spent most of their marriage together, had failed to produce any children. There is no record of either of Caesar's other wives taking a lover, but in this case Caesar's charm had not been sufficient to keep Pompeia faithful. Perhaps he had spent too much time in these years with Servilia and his other mistresses, or it may be that his substantially younger wife resented living in a household that seems to have been dominated by her mother-in-law. Nor should we underestimate the attractions of Clodius, who was intelligent, handsome – his family were renowned for their looks – and charming, with a rakish reputation that made him even more intriguing. The description could as easily apply to Caesar, as could the willingness to seduce other men's wives. Whatever the reason for Pompeia's unfaithfulness, Caesar was unwilling to grant his wife the same licence he gave himself. Such an attitude was common for a man of his class and era.[30]

The ending of a marriage was important for the individuals concerned, but the scale of the shock that this episode sent through the Republic should not be underestimated. Never before had the Bona Dea festival been polluted in this way. Some senators, Cicero and Caesar amongst them, were privately sceptical about the gods, or at least many aspects of traditional religion, but publicly none doubted the importance of the rituals that pervaded so many aspects of public life. Rome's success was said to be based on the favour of the gods, and no ceremony necessary to continue to assure this blessing could be seen to be neglected or improperly performed. The Senate established a special commission to investigate the affair and decide what action needed to be taken. The festival itself was restaged on another night and properly conducted. After seeking advice from the Vestals and the college of pontiffs, it was decided to place Clodius on trial. Caesar seems from the beginning to have wished to brush the whole affair under the carpet, but although head of the college, the *Pontifex Maximus* had more of a chairman's than a controlling role. In the subsequent tribunal he declined to give evidence against Clodius, claiming ignorance of the whole affair. When publicly challenged as to why he had divorced his wife if he thought that she had not been caught in an adulterous liaison, he replied with the famous phrase that he had done so because 'Caesar's wife must be above suspicion.' Clodius was an up and coming man, with powerful friends, who were doing their best to ensure that the court would exonerate him. Caesar may have felt that it was an unnecessary risk to gain the personal enmity of such a man, or perhaps he even felt that Clodius might be a useful ally in the future. With hindsight we know that this is what in fact happened, but it may not have been so obvious at the time. For all his frequent prosecutions and attacks on men like Catulus, Caesar's whole career was based on trying to win friends rather than destroy enemies. It was for his favours and generosity that he was famous, unlike Cato who was known more for his unflinching severity – he was one of those pressing for strong punishment of Clodius.

Political concerns were never far from a senator's mind, but we should not forget the personal element. Throughout much of history, being held up as a cuckold has been deeply embarrassing. It would also have been most unlike a Roman defence counsel not to have thrown Caesar's own philandering reputation against him had he appeared as a witness in the case. Perhaps he genuinely felt that it would have been hypocritical of him to attack another man for something that he had so often done himself, if in less bizarre and sacrilegious circumstances. However, in spite of his own reluctance, both Aurelia and Julia appeared as witnesses, testifying to Clodius' guilt. Cicero also appeared, stating that he had met Clodius on the day of the ceremony in Rome, hence destroying the defendant's claim that he had been far from the City at the time when the offence was committed. In spite of his obvious guilt, Clodius was acquitted after he and his friends mounted a concerted campaign of intimidation and bribery. For the final session the jurors requested and were granted guards for their protection. When they voted thirty-one to twenty-five for acquittal, it prompted the scornful Catulus to say, 'Why did you ask us for a guard? Were you afraid of being robbed?' It is the last anecdote recorded about the old senator, who died not long afterwards.[31]

SPAIN

Long before the trial was over, Caesar had left Rome as propraetor to govern Further Spain (Hispania Ulterior). Smuggled out in his entourage was the Numidian client he had unsuccessfully defended against King Hiempsal, who for months had remained concealed in Caesar's house. Also accompanying him were his quaestor Vetus, the son of the man for whom Caesar had performed the same role. Another member of his staff, holding the title of *praefectus fabrum*, a sort of general staff appointment, was a Lucius Cornelius Balbus, a Spaniard from a well-to-do family that had gained citizenship through Pompey's gratitude. The new governor had doubtless left the city and the scandal behind with some relief, but at one point it had looked as if Caesar would be prevented from going. A number of his creditors had become impatient, perhaps simply because payment was due, but his temporary expulsion from the praetorship earlier in the year may have made them question his long-term prospects. Moves were made to prevent his leaving, but Caesar turned to Crassus who stood surety for 830 talents, a massive sum but only a fraction of his total debt. This is the first occasion when it is explicitly recorded in our sources that he had taken out a loan from Crassus, but it is more than probable that Caesar had often drawn on his massive wealth in the past. Even so it was a near thing, and he ended up leaving the city before the Senate had formally announced the provinces for the year. This was a mere formality, since these had already been allocated, but it was a breach of convention. Ironically, one of the first problems he had to deal with when he reached Spain was widespread debt, which may have been forcing many to swell the numbers of bandits that infested the region. Caesar decreed that a debtor should pay two-thirds of his income to his creditors until the debts had been made up, but were to be left the remaining third to support themselves and their families.[32]

A provincial posting was a chance for enrichment. Caesar had on a number of occasions prosecuted returning governors for corruption and extortion. It was soon claimed by his senatorial opponents that he had needlessly provoked a war in Spain, even attacking allied communities simply so that he could plunder them. The charges were fairly conventional, and plenty of Roman governors acted in this way, but there is not enough evidence to decide whether or not Caesar was guilty of such behaviour. In 61 BC large tracts of Spain were still showing the scars of the war against Sertorius. Raiding and banditry had for generations been ways of life in the Iberian Peninsula, especially amongst communities in the more mountainous regions who struggled to support themselves by farming. North Western Lusitania, where Caesar principally operated, was not a wealthy region at this time, and it is doubtful that any commander could have made himself rich through plunder by campaigning there. Nor is it likely that he lacked opportunities for mounting a military operation, for all of our sources emphasise the lawlessness of much of the area. What is clear is that Caesar eagerly took up these opportunities, responding in an extremely robust manner. Almost as soon as he arrived he raised ten new cohorts of troops, augmenting the existing garrison by 50 per cent. Marching into the mountainous area between the rivers Tagus and Duero, he summoned one of the fortified hilltop communities to surrender and be resettled on the plains. They refused, as he had expected, so Caesar took the place by storm. He then moved against the neighbouring towns, avoiding an attempted ambush when the Lusitanians tried to lure him into a trap by using their herds as bait. Caesar ignored these and instead attacked and defeated their main army. Ambush was a common tactic for the hill peoples of Spain, and his forces avoided another ambush by not following the obvious route through the difficult country. Later Caesar returned, fought on ground of his own choosing, and won. Following up his success, he pursued the Lusitanians to the Atlantic coast, where they took refuge on a small island. The first attempt to take this failed, but Caesar summoned warships from Gades (Cadiz) and forced the defenders to surrender. He then sailed along the coast, and the sight of his forces – oared warships were largely unknown in the area – was enough to overawe at least one community into instant capitulation.[33]

There were many traces of the Caesar so familiar from his own *Commentaries* on the later campaigns in Gaul and the Civil War. Swift but calculated action, refusal to be daunted by natural obstacles or initial reverses and the ruthless exploitation of success. Also there was the willingness to accept surrender and treat the conquered generously in the hope of turning them into productive, tax-paying members of the province. His victory had not in itself completed this process, but did mark an important stage in it. Caesar was hailed as *Imperator*, the formal acclamation which entitled a governor to request a triumph on his return to Rome. Yet his term of office was not solely devoted to war, and he did much to reorganise the civil administration of the province, arbitrating in disputes between the local communities. He also appears to have suppressed the practice of human sacrifice in some of the local cults. How effective he was in the long term is harder to say, for other governors of the province had acted against this in the past. Such offerings were known – perhaps even fairly common – throughout much of Iron Age Europe and elsewhere. The last occasion the Romans had made such an offering had been only a few years before Caesar's birth, when the threat of the Cimbri and Teutones had seemed very real. It was, however, one of the few religious practices that the Romans actively suppressed in the provinces. Caesar's governorship of Spain is not well documented, but seems to have been marked by his usual frenetic activity. He probably profited from his time there, though certainly on nothing like the scale to do much more than dent his massive debts, won accolades from the locals and had the prospect of triumph on his return. This posting had given Caesar what he wanted, but he was always looking to the future, and left his province to return to Rome before his successor had actually arrived. This was a little unusual, but certainly not unique – Cicero would do the same when he finally went out to his province over a decade after being consul. His quaestor was probably left in charge.[34]

On the way out to Spain Plutarch claims that Caesar and his party passed through a small Alpine village. His friends jokingly asked whether even in such a squalid setting men still scrabbled for power and office. Caesar declared quite seriously that he would rather be the foremost man in a place like that, than the second in Rome. The story may or may be apocryphal, but as Plutarch realised it says much about Caesar's character. He had already done well politically, and could by now almost count on having a good career. This was no less that he had always expected of himself, but being successful was not in itself enough and Caesar was aiming for the very top. He craved to achieve more than anyone else had ever done.[35]

There was room at the top, for as the decade drew to a close only Crassus could be seen as a serious rival to Pompey. Some of the wealthiest men in the Republic, notably Lucullus, had largely withdrawn from public life into luxurious retirement. The Senate of these years contained some 600 members, but was scarcely crammed with talent. The legacy of the civil war, which had culled the ranks of the prominent and capable, was still very obvious. It is striking that only fourteen former consuls were present at the Catilinarian debate, an occasion of such importance that a strong turnout would be anticipated. Crassus deliberately avoided the meeting, while Pompey and several other consulars were away on campaign. Assuming as a very rough guide that a man might expect to live for at least twenty years after being consul, the total is still less than half the number that we might expect. Compared to earlier periods, there were far fewer distinguished senators whose *auctoritas* allowed them to guide the Senate's debates. This was one reason why men like Caesar and Cato were able to assume such prominence while still in their thirties.

VIII

CONSUL

'Caesar had accustomed himself to great effort and little rest; to concentrate on his friends' business at the expense of his own, and never to neglect anything which was worth doing as a favour. He craved great *imperium*, an army, and a new war so that he could show his talent.' – *Sallust, late forties* BC.[1]

'Yet what would history say of me in six hundred years time? For that is a thing which I fear more than the idle chatter of men alive today.' – *Cicero, April 59* BC.[2]

On 28 and 29 September 61 BC Pompey the Great celebrated his third triumph, which commemorated his victories over the pirates and Mithridates. The festivities coincided with his forty-fifth birthday and included displays and processions of unprecedented scale and magnificence. His first triumph had been twenty years before, but this time there was no ridiculous plan for riding in a chariot pulled by elephants. Pompey was older, more mature and had no need for such theatrics, for the splendour of his victories dwarfed the achievements of the great generals of the past. Even so, triumphs were never occasions for restraint or modesty. Like any Roman aristocrat, Pompey took care to quantify his success and the processions included placards declaring that he had killed, captured or defeated 12,183,000 people, taken or sunk 846 warships, and accepted the surrender of 1,538 towns or fortified places. Each kingdom, people or place he had overcome was listed in turn on the great floats carrying the spoils he had taken from them. Then there were paintings showing famous episodes from the wars. Other signs told of how every soldier in the army had been given 1,500 denarii – equivalent to more than ten years' pay – and proclaimed that the vast sum of 20,000 talents of gold and silver had been added to the State Treasury. Pompey boasted that as a result of his efforts, the annual revenue of the Republic had more than doubled, from 50 million to 135 million denarii. At the end of the procession was an enormous float presented as a trophy of victory over the known world. People were saying that Pompey had triumphed over all three continents: Africa as part of his first triumph, Europe and specifically Spain in his second, and now Asia in his third. Ahead of Pompey walked over 300 senior hostages, including kings, queens, princesses, chieftains and generals, all wearing their national costume. The general himself rode in a chariot decorated with gemstones and wore a cloak captured from Mithridates, which he claimed had once been owned and worn by Alexander the Great. Appian, writing over a century and a half later, thought this unlikely, but Pompey revelled in the parallels often drawn between himself and the greatest conqueror in history.[3]

There is no doubting the scale of Pompey's achievement. The suppression of the pirates had been a dazzling display of meticulous planning and rapid action, but proved to be merely a prelude to even greater successes. Mithridates of Pontus had proven one of Rome's most resilient enemies. Sulla had expelled him from Greece and recovered the province of Asia, but the need to return to Italy had prevented him from achieving total victory. Lucullus had done more in the seven years he held command in the region, savaging the king and his allies in a series of battles. In the process he became fabulously rich from the spoils of war, but alienated the *publicani* operating in Asia as tax collectors, as well as many of his own soldiers. A successful general never lacked for opponents in the Senate, for senators were instinctively nervous of anyone else gaining too much glory, wealth and *auctoritas*. There were growing complaints that the war was going on too long, and even that Lucullus was deliberately prolonging it to enrich himself still more. His large province was broken up, and sections given to new governors, starving him of the men and material with which to wage war. With Lucullus weakened, Mithridates was given a chance to win back some of the ground he had lost. Everything changed when Pompey arrived in 66 BC. Backed by resources on a scale of which his predecessor could only have dreamed, he had irrevocably smashed the king's power by the end of the year. It would be going a little far to say that Lucullus had already won the war – unlike the Slave War, which had certainly been decided by Crassus before Pompey arrived and tried to steal the credit – but he had certainly contributed a great deal to the eventual Roman victory.

His assigned task complete, Pompey showed no desire to go back to Rome straightaway, but instead sought new opportunities to win glory with the forces under his command. Over the next two years he took advantage of any opportunity to lead his legions further than any Roman army had gone in the past. They marched against the Iberians and Albanians, round the eastern shore of the Black Sea and into what would become southern Russia. Intervening in a civil war between rival members of the Judaean royal family, Pompey laid siege to Jerusalem and took it after three months. All of these spectacular achievements were celebrated in his triumphal procession. Pompey had throughout these campaigns given abundant evidence of his abilities as a commander, and may also, as in earlier campaigns, have occasionally led charges in person, emulating Alexander's heroic style of leadership. In Jerusalem he and his commanders had gone into the Holy of Holies in the Great Temple, something forbidden to all save the high priests. As a mark of respect, none of the treasures were removed, but the gesture, as was intended, provided a new tale to tell at Rome of the unprecedented deeds of Rome's great general. For the Romans, the spectacular was often combined with the practical, and Pompey spent much of his time organising the administration of Rome's old provinces in the region and the new ones he had created. Active campaigning largely ceased when news arrived in 63 BC that Mithridates was dead – killed by a bodyguard after he had tried to poison himself but discovered that the antidotes he had taken throughout his life rendered him immune. Even so Pompey remained in the east for over a year settling the region. His organisational talents were considerable and many of the regulations he established would remain in force for centuries.[4]

The wild activities of Metellus Nepos during his tribunate increased the apprehension over what Pompey would do on his return to Italy. Nepos was his brother-in-law, had served under him as a legate, and so his readiness to use violence and intimidation in his effort to allow Pompey to retain command of his army was deeply worrying. Crassus is said to have exploited the mood by taking his family abroad. It is difficult to know how far Nepos had been acting under instructions, but clearly Pompey cannot have been pleased with a result that raised many senators' suspicion of him without achieving any benefit. In the spring of 62 BC he wrote to the Senate as a whole and privately to leading senators assuring them of his desire for peaceful retirement. Another of his legates, Marcus Pupius Piso, was already in Rome canvassing for the consulship for 61 BC. Pompey asked the Senate to postpone the elections till the end of the year so that he could be present and support his friend. Opinions were divided, but Cato prevented any vote by manipulating the procedure of the House. When asked his opinion in the debate, he kept on talking until the day ended and the meeting closed without a result. No one attempted to discuss the issue again. In the event

Piso won the consulship anyway, but this was the first of a series of snubs that Pompey was to suffer. It did not prevent him from continuing his efforts to reassure the Senate of his good intentions. When he finally landed at Brundisium in December 62 BC he immediately demobilised his legions, instructing the soldiers to gather again only when it was time for them to march in his triumph.[5]

Until he had celebrated his triumph, Pompey could not actually cross the *pomerium*, the sacred boundary of the city, so he took up residence in his villa in the Alban Hills outside Rome. By the middle of the first century BC, substantial parts of Rome were actually outside the *pomerium*. On several occasions the Senate chose to meet, or public meetings were called, at locations in these areas to permit Pompey to attend. When he had become consul in 70 BC Pompey had the experienced senator and prolific author Marcus Terentius Varro write him a pamphlet explaining senatorial procedure. His return to political life showed that he still had much to learn after almost six years away on campaign. The first speech he made fell flat, pleasing no one. It was especially unfortunate that he had arrived at the height of the controversy over the trial of Clodius for sacrilege, with fierce debate over the procedure to be used and in particular the selection of jurors. Piso, Pompey's former legate, was a friend and supporter of Clodius, while his consular colleague was an equally determined opponent. Not a well trained or especially gifted orator, Pompey attempted to show his firm support and respect for the Senate when his opinion was asked on such issues, but his speeches met with little enthusiasm. Cicero, smarting over Pompey's refusal to praise him with sufficient enthusiasm for his suppression of Catiline, was scathing in his judgement of the man he had so often supported in the past. On 25 January 61 BC he wrote to his friend Atticus that Pompey 'is now openly and ostentatiously trumpeting his friendship for me, but secretly he is jealous and does not conceal it very well. In him there is no real courtesy, straightforwardness, statesmanlike talent, or indeed a sense of honour, constancy, or generosity.'[6] Cicero was delighted when Crassus began eulogising him in the Senate, probably largely because Pompey had failed to do so.[7]

In the domestic sphere things were little better. Pompey had divorced his wife Mucia almost as soon as he had returned to Italy. She and Caesar had had an affair in her husband's absence, but he had not been her only lover and her infidelities were a matter of public scandal. Politically this had unfortunate consequences, alienating Pompey from her half-brothers Metellus Nepos and Quintus Caecilius Metellus Celer, for the Metelli as a family were never slow to respond to real or apparent slights. After he had been attacked by Nepos, Cicero had had to go to great lengths to placate Metellus Celer even though it had been his brother who had begun the dispute. Celer was a strong candidate for the consulship in 60 BC, making him an especially dangerous enemy. Nevertheless, the divorce gave Pompey the opportunity for making a new political alliance, and he clearly wished to demonstrate again his commitment to the senatorial elite and show that he was no revolutionary. He approached Cato and asked that he and his son be allowed to marry his nieces, the daughters of Servilia. To the dismay of both the girls and their ambitious mother, Cato rejected the proposal, a gesture that added to his reputation for placing the stern dictates of virtue ahead of political advantage. Although he lost the prospect of an alliance with the wealthiest man and most successful commander in the Senate, the incident added to the legend that Cato was consciously building by his actions and behaviour.[8]

Pompey had two main objectives in these years. The first was to secure grants of land to the discharged veterans of his armies. In 70 BC a law had been passed to provide for the men who had fought under him in Spain, but had failed to achieve much as the Senate had not provided the resources to make an adequate distribution of land possible. His second aim was to secure the ratification of his Eastern Settlement, the scheme of laws and regulations that he had established after his victory over Mithridates. It was normal for such things to be done by a senatorial committee, but Pompey had gone ahead without this authority. The fact that he had done the job extremely well did not prevent considerable criticism. Lucullus, who had been forced to wait years for his own triumph and was still deeply bitter of his replacement in the command by Pompey, came out of his self-imposed retirement from public life to oppose him. He was especially critical of anything that had altered his own rulings. Pompey wanted his entire Eastern Settlement to be ratified in a single law. Lucullus, Cato and many other leading senators demanded instead that each individual ruling be discussed and dealt with on its own. During Piso's consulship in 61 BC nothing was achieved, in part because of his preoccupation with the trial of Clodius. Realising that Metellus Celer was practically certain to win the consulship for 60 BC, Pompey indulged in massive bribery to ensure that he was given a more amenable colleague. The man chosen was another of his former legates, a 'new man' called Lucius Afranius. Although he may have been a capable officer, Afranius was better known as a dancer than for his skill as a politician. As consul he proved an abject failure, his fellow 'new man'

Cicero viewing him as little more than a joke in the poorest taste. More talented was Lucius Flavius, one of the tribunes of the year who was eager to do Pompey's bidding. He proposed a land law, which was intended to provide farms for the veterans and a substantial number of the urban poor. Metellus Celer led the opposition, and was so bitter in his invective that the tribune ordered him led off to prison. The consul was a shrewd enough player of the political game to know how to exploit the situation and promptly convened a meeting of the Senate in the prison itself. Flavius responded by placing his tribunician bench of office in front of the entrance to stop anyone from getting in. Undaunted, Metellus ordered his attendants to knock a hole in the prison's wall to admit the senators. Pompey realised that Flavius was losing the contest and instructed him to release the consul. The episode showed the same almost farcical respect for convention as the confrontation between Cato and Nepos in 62 BC on the podium of the Temple of Castor and Pollux. In this case, things stopped short of actual violence. Further attempts to intimidate Metellus by denying him the right to go to a province failed and the bill was eventually dropped.[9]

After two years Pompey had achieved neither of his key objectives. The confirmation of the Eastern Settlement and the provision of land for veteran soldiers were both sensible measures, that would have been of benefit to the Republic. Metellus opposed the land bill primarily because he resented doing anything for the man who had divorced his half-sister Mucia, but also because of the prestige of standing alone and out of his innate stubbornness. His grandfather had won fame through being the only senator to refuse to take an oath to obey one of Saturninus' laws, suffering a period of exile as a result. Lucullus was motivated by memory of the wrong he felt that Pompey had once done to him in 66 BC. Cato and others were more inclined to thwart Pompey as a means of cutting him down to size and preventing him from dominating the Republic through his great wealth and fame. Pompey was not the only senator to feel frustration in these years. Crassus, who had at first enjoyed his rival's discomfort, found that many of the same senatorial clique were as willing to block a measure of great importance to him. Early in 60 BC a dispute erupted between the Senate and the equestrians who headed the great companies of the *publicani*. These had bought the rights to collecting taxes in Asia and the other eastern provinces only to discover that in the aftermath of so many years of warfare they were unable to raise sufficient revenue to cover the sum they had pledged to the State Treasury. Faced with the prospect of making a loss, rather than the usual handsome profit derived from tax collecting, the dismayed *publicani* wanted to renegotiate the terms of their contract, reducing the amount that was due to the Treasury. Crassus, who was closely associated with the leading *publicani* and probably had a stake in a number of companies, was an enthusiastic supporter. Cicero thought that the demand was outrageous, but nevertheless was willing to go along with it since the wealthy equestrian order ought to be placated and kept on the side of the Senate. A new bribery law had just imposed severe fines on equestrian as well as senatorial jurors, causing deep offence amongst the order. Cato was never one to restrain his own outrage and vigorously opposed the *publicani*, persuading the Senate to reject their appeal. Cicero despairingly commented that Cato 'in the best spirit and with unquestionable honesty . . . does harm to the State: the resolutions he puts forward are more fitting for Plato's ideal Republic, than the cess-pit of Romulus'.[10]

Pompey and Crassus, the two wealthiest and in some ways most influential men in the Republic, were both finding themselves thwarted by members of the handful of noble families that dominated the Senate. Pompey, in particular, had been rejected when he attempted to become part of this inner elite. Necessary, sensible and popular reforms, along with more questionable measures that may have been politically expedient, were all being blocked by a small minority of aristocrats. The inertia at the heart of the Republic was alienating many citizens at all levels of society. Decades later, one of Caesar's former commanders would begin his history of the Civil War in the year when Metellus Celer and Afranius were consuls. With hindsight many would see 60 BC as the year when the disease infecting the Republic became terminal.[11]

COMING HOME

In the summer of 60 BC Caesar returned from Spain. He was forty and – presumably with the same dispensation he had enjoyed to hold earlier offices two years before the normal time – now eligible to stand for the consulship for 59 BC. He had clearly been preparing the way for his candidature for some time. Unable to canvass in person he seems to have written to leading senators, including Cicero. Caesar was a prolific letter writer, making it all the more unfortunate that so little of his correspondence has been preserved. He is said to have been able to dictate to several scribes at the same time, while it was noted that he was the first man who while in Rome regularly wrote to friends and political allies who were also in the city. It may well be that he had divorced Pompeia in a written note. It was probably also by letter that he reached an agreement with another of the candidates to run a joint campaign. This was Lucius Lucceius, a man of considerable wealth but little reputation or charisma. The combination of his money and Caesar's popularity was a strong one. In early June 60 BC, before he had even reached Rome, Caesar was seen as the favourite in the race for the consulship, Cicero commenting that he had a 'following wind'. Caesar's letters to Cicero had evidently pleased the orator, for he wrote to Atticus that he hoped to 'make Caesar better', which he saw as a good service to the Republic.[12]

Caesar, just like Pompey two years before, arrived outside Rome, but could not cross the *pomerium* until he had celebrated the triumph awarded for his campaigns in Spain. A triumph, with its spectacular procession and accompanying celebrations, would further enhance his election prospects. The Roman electorate and society in general admired military glory above almost everything else, and in practical terms a consul was very likely to find himself placed in command of an important war, so that proof of martial talent was obviously a good thing. Cicero at times liked to claim that a great record as an advocate in the courts was almost as highly valued as martial exploits, but evidently knew in his heart that this was not the view of most voters. However, by law, candidates for office had to present themselves in person at a meeting in the Forum. It took time to prepare properly for the triumphal celebration, which could then only be held on a day allotted by the Senate. The date for the election had already been set, and Caesar would be unable to stand unless he crossed the *pomerium* and so gave up the right to his triumph. He requested an exemption to the rule to allow him to become a candidate without appearing in person. Presumably this was done by a letter to the Senate, or through an intermediary, since there is no record of the Senate convening at one of the temples outside the *pomerium* to permit him to attend. Suetonius tells us that there was widespread opposition to this petition. Our other sources unsurprisingly single out Cato as the main focus of this. He once again used the tactic of simply continuing to speak until time for the debate ran out and the meeting had to close without voting on the issue. The Senate would not assemble again until after the list of candidates had been formally announced – the House was only permitted to meet on certain days and could not, for instance, convene on the same day as any of the Popular Assemblies. Cato's tactic of 'talking out' a proposition had worked in the past and this time ensured that Caesar could not celebrate his triumph and stand for the consulship for the next year.[13]

Cato's filibuster worked, but not in the way that he had intended. When Caesar realised what was happening he immediately gave up his triumph and entered the city, crossing the *pomerium* so that he could present himself as a candidate. It is difficult to understate the importance of this decision. A triumph was one of the greatest honours a Roman aristocrat could win, something permanently commemorated by the display of its symbols on the porch of his house. Pompey, whose whole career had been deeply unorthodox, had triumphed three times, but this was exceptional, and in this period it was very rare for a man to win the honour more than once. Not only that, but triumphs were awarded to no more than a tiny minority of propraetors in the first century BC and were fairly rare even for proconsuls. It was the clearest indication that Caesar was looking ahead, absolutely convinced that far greater deeds and opportunities lay ahead of him. A triumph for his victories in Spain would have been very welcome and he did his best to secure it, but the consulship was a far greater prize.

Cato's motives are also worth consideration, for at first glance his action seems to have been pointless, while with hindsight it was also highly ill-judged. At best he would have delayed Caesar's candidature for a year. Caesar would have held his triumph, which could only have increased his already good electoral prospects. Perhaps Cato hoped that during the next twelve months, Caesar's debts would finally overwhelm him and his career implode. Yet he had just returned from his province and, like all Roman governors and especially those who fought a successful war, had doubtless profited. His debts were too huge to have been paid off, and Caesar obviously felt the need for Lucceius' finances in his election campaign, but all in all he must have been in a more secure financial position on his return to Rome compared with when he had left. As a private citizen Caesar would be open to prosecution, so perhaps it was hoped that he might be charged in the extortion court. Yet, most former governors faced with such charges were acquitted and, as we have seen, Caesar may well genuinely not have been guilty – not that that was necessarily the key factor in many legal cases. There was a more personal reason for delaying Caesar's candidature for a year. Cato's son-in-law, Marcus Calpurnius Bibulus, was also standing for the consulship. This was the man who had been so overshadowed by Caesar during their aedileship in 65 BC. Bibulus' talents were modest, and made to seem all the more so by comparison with the flamboyant and extremely capable Caesar. Yet the system, with the minimum ages for each office, ensured that a man was likely to compete and hold office with the same men throughout his career. Both Caesar and Bibulus had been praetors in 62 BC, although there is no record of any conflict between them. Postponing Caesar's bid for the consulship would mean that for once Bibulus would have a chance of taking the limelight himself. It also avoided the danger that the 'new man' Lucceius, boosted by his ally's popularity, would actually beat Bibulus into third place. Losing an election was a humiliating blow to a member of a noble family.

Therefore, there were certainly advantages to be gained for Cato's family in blocking Caesar's request. The conflict between their personalities should also not be ignored. It is no exaggeration to say that Cato loathed Caesar, believing that he had seen past his outward charm. Servilia's continuing affair with this man exacerbated her half-brother's feelings. The Roman aristocracy saw nothing wrong in senators pursuing personal hatreds, as long as their actions did not become excessive. Viewed in this light, Cato was simply taking an opportunity to do one of his enemies a bad turn. Furthermore, every time that he changed the Senate's mind or stopped it from doing something added to Cato's reputation. He was still only thirty-five and had held no magistracy higher than the tribunate, but was already well established as one of the dominant voices in the Senate. This was because he was Cato, paragon of old-fashioned virtue as exemplified by his famous ancestor, and never to be dissuaded from his views or afraid to state them even if they were contrary to the mood of the majority. It does seem unlikely that in 60 BC he represented Caesar as a danger to the Republic. Cicero's letters make it clear that such a view was not widespread before the elections. The only hint that there was some suspicion came when the Senate allocated the provinces that the consuls of 59 BC would receive after their year of office, something that a law of Caius Gracchus had stipulated that they must do before the election. In this case the Senate decided that both men would be sent to deal with 'woodland and country lanes of Italy' (*silvae callesque*). It was true that rural Italy had suffered much in recent decades, but even so such a task was pitifully beneath the dignity of one, let alone both, consuls. The suggestion that this was intended merely to keep the consuls in reserve, in case a major war erupted in Gaul, is unconvincing, since this was not normal Roman practice. Instead it was an insult and, the sources maintain, one aimed at Caesar, although it should be noted that Bibulus was as likely to suffer as a result of it.[14]

Consuls were elected by the *Comitia Centuriata*, whose structure differed markedly from the Tribal Assemblies. Caesar had already been successful in the Comitia when he was elected praetor, but competition was inevitably stronger for the two consulships than for the eight praetorships for each year. Consular elections were usually held at the end of July, so that Caesar had only a few weeks to canvass in person. The *Comitia Centuriata* met on the Campus Martius, amidst rituals that had strong associations with the military system of Rome's early history – for instance, the raising of a red flag on the Janiculum Hill already mentioned in connection with the trial of Rabirius (see p.123). The presiding magistrate, one of the consuls of the current year, also gave his instructions to the Assembly in a traditional form, which made them sound much like military orders. First there was an informal meeting or *contio* before proceedings began, although it is not known specifically whether or not the candidates were given the chance to make a speech as one last plea to the electorate. The consul would open the business with a prayer, followed by a set formula that ordered the people to choose the two new consuls. The voters were divided into centuries based upon their property as recorded in the last census. Individual centuries were composed of men from the same tribes, but only to this extent was there a tribal element. Voting began with the seventy centuries of the First Class, followed by the eighteen equestrian centuries. Each century chose two names from the list of candidates to fill the two vacancies for consul. There were 193 centuries altogether, and the outcome of elections could be, and often was, decided during the voting of the Second Class. Members of the First Class, had to have significant property, although just how much is unclear for this period. It would be a mistake to see all of them as very wealthy. Some were almost as well off as equestrians, but others had relatively modest means. There is no real trace of the members of this class having a strong sense of their corporate identity or forming a social class in the modern sense. The decision of the centuries voting first influenced subsequent voting, since there seems often to have been an urge to choose the men who were expected to win. Especially influential was the decision of one century from the First Class chosen by lot to speak first. This was the *centuria praerogativa*, and it was generally believed that the man whose name was placed first in the vote of this century was bound to win the election.[15]

Like other elections, the voting of the *Comitia Centuriata* took place in the *saepta* or 'sheep-pens' on the Campus Martius. Sometimes known also as the *oviles*, this temporary structure of wooden enclosures for each of the voting units was open to the elements and covered a wide area. We do not know how many citizens normally chose to participate. Over 900,000 male citizens were listed in the census, and at least several hundred thousand of these lived in Rome itself, at least for some parts of the year. Yet it seems extremely unlikely that the majority even of these residents could all have voted even if they had wanted to, given the size of the *saepta*. Estimates have been made of the number of voters who could have been accommodated within the voting enclosures, usually modified by entirely conjectural notions of how long the voting would have taken, for the whole process had to be complete by sunset. These vary from as many as 70,000, to 55,000, or as few as 30,000. Each commentator has tended to suggest that these are maximum figures and that the real numbers would usually have been much lower. Although it would be unwise to place any real reliance on such guesswork, it is safe to assume that only a minority of those eligible actually did vote. Yet it is hard to say whether it was always substantially the same voters who did assemble – this tends to be assumed, but we really do not know. A consular election was certainly a great event, and significant numbers of citizens deliberately travelled to Rome from all over Italy to take part. Inevitably these tended to be the better off, but since the wishes of the equestrian order and First Class carried such weight this made them all the more important. It is very clear that election results were unpredictable and that it was exceptionally rare for there to be two candidates for the consulship both of whom were seen as certainties. The *praerogativa* century was selected by lot on the day of the election, adding an additional element of uncertainty to proceedings.[16]

During his own campaign Cicero had thought about visiting Cisalpine Gaul to canvass amongst the wealthy citizens there and throughout his life tried to maintain links with many parts of Italy. Where past favours and friendship did not suffice, money might win the day. There were men in each tribe who were recognised as able to sway the vote of their fellow tribesmen, whether they voted as a whole or each in their own century. In 61 BC it was widely reported that many of these men had visited the garden of Pompey's house to receive payment for their support for his candidate Afranius. In 60 BC the bribery was less blatant, but still employed by all candidates. Lucceius' money acted for himself and Caesar, while Bibulus drew not only on his own resources, but was aided by a number of prominent senators. Cato approved, just as he had refrained from prosecuting his brother-in-law from electoral bribery in 63 BC when he had attacked Murena for the same thing. Like any senator, he wanted his family to succeed. Suetonius claims that he and Bibulus' other backers were also motivated by fear of what Caesar might do if as consul he had a colleague who was closely tied to him politically. This may well simply be the view of hindsight – the connections and status of Bibulus' family probably were far more important factors.[17]

On the day of the election Caesar came first by a very comfortable margin. Bibulus secured the second place, so that Lucceius ended up with little return for his expenditure. Many of the voters must have named Caesar and Bibulus on their ballots. Having reached the most senior magistracy, it was now a question of what Caesar would do and how he would behave in his twelve months of office.

THE LAND LAW

In December 60 BC, just a few weeks before Caesar would take up the consulship on 1 January 59 BC, Cicero received a visitor in his country villa. The caller was Lucius Cornelius Balbus, the Roman citizen from Gades in Spain who had recently served on Caesar's staff and was now starting to act as his political agent. Balbus spoke mainly of the agrarian law that Caesar was planning to introduce in his consulship. Throughout his life Cicero had a landowner's aversion to any redistribution, and his opposition had done much to block Rullus' bill three years before. This time he had a choice between opposing the new law, absenting himself for a while to avoid committing himself, or supporting it. As Cicero wrote to Atticus, Caesar expected him to back the bill. Balbus had 'assured me that Caesar will follow my own and Pompey's opinion in every issue, and that he will strive to reconcile Crassus to Pompey'. If Cicero followed this course he had the prospect of 'a very close alliance with Pompey, and, if I want, with Caesar as well, and a reconciliation with my enemies, peace with the mob, and security in old age'. Caesar was preparing carefully for his year of office and trying to gain as many political allies as possible. Cicero, in spite of his successes as consul, remained a 'new man', never entirely accepted by the established families of the Senate, and his execution of the conspirators in 63 BC left him vulnerable to attack for overstepping his powers. For the last decade he had consistently presented himself as Pompey's loyal supporter. Now Pompey was clearly associated with Caesar's land bill and both men wanted to secure Cicero's oratory to help their cause. [18]

After some thought, Cicero refused to commit himself. This was certainly a disappointment for Caesar, but not a critical one, since he had already secured two allies who were far more powerful. Balbus had hinted to Cicero of the prospect of an alliance between Pompey and his arch-rival Crassus. At some point during these months, Caesar was able to achieve just that, bonding himself to both men so that, as Suetonius put it, 'nothing could be done in the Republic, which displeased any one of the three'.[19] This political alliance is known to scholars as the First Triumvirate – the Second

Triumvirate being formed between Mark Antony, Octavian and Lepidus in November 43 BC to oppose Caesar's murderers. Triumvirate simply means board of three, but unlike the latter alliance, which was formally instituted by law with the three men receiving dictatorial powers, the association between Crassus, Pompey and Caesar was informal. At first it was also secret. The fact that in December 60 BC Balbus spoke only of the possibility of reconciliation between Pompey and Crassus should not be taken as an indication that the triumvirate had not yet been formed, merely that it had not yet become public knowledge. Caesar had been closely associated with Crassus for some time, and the latter had invested heavily in him when he chose to act as surety for the debts that nearly prevented Caesar from leaving to govern Further Spain. Caesar had time and again been a vocal supporter of measures favouring Pompey. He had doubtless also met him – the world of the Roman aristocracy was a small one, and the two had both been in Rome for much of 70–67 BC – although there is no record of any particular intimacy. Caesar had seduced Pompey's wife during his absence overseas, which had surely not endeared him to her husband, but then he had also slept with Crassus' wife without it preventing their political collaboration. Both Pompey and Crassus had been frustrated in the last few years, discovering that their wealth and influence were not sufficient to get everything that they wanted. Pompey needed a more gifted and determined consul than Piso or Afranius to do his bidding. Caesar had sacrificed a triumph to reach the consulship immediately. For this to have been worthwhile, he needed an opportunity for far greater military adventures after his year of office was over, something that the 'woods and paths' of Italy would certainly not provide. To make this possible he wanted influential supporters. If he had joined with either Pompey or Crassus individually, it was likely that the mutual antipathy of these two would have ensured that the other opposed him. With Cato, Bibulus and their associates certain to resist his every move, he simply could not afford another powerful enemy. Therefore, the elegantly simple answer was to unite Pompey and Crassus, knowing that their combined weight ought to be irresistible. Cato and the other nobles who had blocked and embittered the two greatest men in the Republic had created the opportunity to do this. Even so, it doubtless took all of Caesar's persuasiveness and charm to convince the old enemies that he could deliver what they wanted if only they combined to support him.[20]

The negotiations to create the triumvirate may have begun by letter, but it is unlikely that any real decision was made until Caesar returned to Italy in the summer of 60 BC. Agreement may not have come until after the consular elections, when Caesar's success strengthened his bargaining position. It is not clear whether Pompey and Crassus openly joined forces to canvass on his behalf. Even had they done so, this might not have been seen as especially significant, since it was quite normal for personal enemies both to support the same candidate if each had individual ties of friendship with him. Co-operation between the three men was not widely suspected until January 59 BC at the earliest. Later, it became even more obvious and provoked outrage and the usual cries of the end of the Republic. Varro, the polymath who had in 70 BC advised Pompey on senatorial procedure and later served as his legate, wrote a pamphlet decrying the 'three-headed beast'. Over a century and a half later, Plutarch was adamant that the friendship between the triumvirs, especially between Caesar and Pompey, was the root cause of civil war and the end of the Roman Republic. It was the way in which Caesar could gain so much power that in the end he could overcome even Pompey. It was a judgement based on hindsight, but certainly not a unique one, though it suggests an inevitability about future events that is questionable. Yet in one sense Plutarch had understood that the triumvirate was not at heart a union of those with the same political ideals and ambitions. Pompey, Crassus and Caesar were all seeking personal advantage. Pompey wanted land for his veterans and the ratification of his Eastern Settlement, and Crassus relief for the tax collectors of Asia. Caesar was very much the junior member, who needed powerful backers if he was to achieve anything in the face of a recalcitrant consular colleague and gain an important provincial command afterwards. He was effectively the tool of the other two, for they needed a magistrate to introduce and force through the legislation they needed. For this he would be rewarded. Each of the three knew that the others would benefit from the arrangement, but were content for this to happen so long as they achieved their own aims. It was ultimately a marriage of convenience, to be broken by any of the members as soon as it ceased to be to his advantage. To see it as anything more solid or permanent risks misunderstanding the events of this and subsequent years. Dio speaks of the three men taking solemn oaths, but this is most probably just later propaganda. The secret swearing of oaths was always viewed as a sinister act by the Romans. Catiline was supposed to have done this with his followers. In later centuries this would also be one of the accusations against the early Christians.[21]

The two consuls were equal in power, but each took precedence over his colleague on alternate months. Caesar had come first in the polls on election day, and so when he and Bibulus took up office on 1 January 59 BC, it was he who held precedence and so began the Republic's year with prayers and sacrifices. Each consul was accompanied by twelve lictors carrying the fasces which symbolised a magistrate's power. The consul with precedence in that month was said to hold the fasces. Normally the lictors went ahead of a magistrate, clearing a path through the crowd if this was necessary. As a mark of respect to his colleague, Caesar stated at the beginning of the year that whenever Bibulus held the fasces, his own lictors would follow behind him. Instead only a single lesser official, the clerk or *accensus*, would precede him. It was just one of a number of reasonable gestures that Caesar made at the very beginning of the year. He also wanted his deeds and words, as well as those of everyone else, to be a matter of public knowledge. Therefore, speeches in the Senate and at public meetings were to be recorded by scribes and published in the Forum. In the past this had only been done occasionally, for instance, for some of the debates during Cicero's consulship.[22]

Yet his immediate priority was the land bill, and it is probable that this was read in the Senate and debated on either 1 or 2 January. Haste was necessary, for a bill needed to be published twenty-four days before the Tribal Assembly was called to vote upon it. If Caesar was to have this vote in January while he himself held the fasces, then every day was precious, for the Senate could not meet on the 3rd or 4th. Considerable effort had already been devoted to preparing the bill and securing its passage before the end of the previous year. We have already seen that Balbus had been sent to canvass for Cicero's active support. Caesar had been careful to learn from the failed land bills of Rullus and Flavius. The publicly owned land in Campania – the *ager Campanus,* which supplied the Treasury with a healthy revenue – was formally exempted. Clauses also made it clear that private property was to be respected. A commission would oversee the purchase and distribution of the land to both Pompey's veteran soldiers and large numbers of the urban poor. The commissioners were only permitted to purchase land from owners willing to sell, and would do so at the value recorded in the last census. The funding for this was to come from the vast surplus provided by Pompey's victories. Other clauses of the law expressly recognised all existing land occupation, lest fears grow up that there would be investigations into whether or not it was legally owned. It also barred the new settlers from selling their land for twenty years, to emphasise that it wanted to set up stable and permanent new communities. There were to be twenty commissioners, so that no one or two men should have overwhelming patronage in their hands, although there does appear to have been an inner council of five members to take some decisions. The commissioners would be elected, and the law expressly excluded Caesar from being amongst their number, so there would be no question of his proposing legislation from which he would derive tangible benefit. Roman laws tended to be long and complex – one of Rome's most enduring legacies to the world is cumbersome and tortuous legal prose. Before Caesar read the entire text to the Senate, he announced that he would alter or remove any clause to which an objection was raised.[23]

The bill was well crafted and sensible. There was little or nothing within it that could be reasonably criticised, and the senators were aware that anything they said in the debate was to be published. It was most probably on 2 January that Caesar began to ask individual senators their opinion. Crassus was the first of the ex-consuls and presumably gave his approval, as did Pompey who would have been asked second. The others were somewhat sullen, but unwilling to go on record as opponents of the bill. The same was true of the former praetors. It was only when Caesar reached the ex-tribunes and called upon Cato to speak that there was anything other than unenthusiastic support or equivocation. Even Cato was forced to acknowledge that the bill was a good one, but he felt that it was badly timed and claimed that it would be a mistake to bring in any innovation during this year. Some of the earlier speakers had managed to delay proceedings by introducing tangential matters, but Cato was the true master of manipulating the conventions of the House. Having been asked his view he gave it, and then continued to give it, speaking without interruption as the minutes stretched into hours. It was obvious that he planned once again to keep on talking until the Senate had to end its session for the day and so prevent a vote from being taken. He had employed the same tactic in the past and always succeeded.

This time Caesar's temper snapped and he ordered his attendants to arrest Cato and lead him off to prison. Extreme though this action seems, there was no other way of stopping a member of the House from continuing to speak once he had been asked his opinion, since someone like Cato could not simply be shouted down. It was a sign of Caesar's frustration and rapidly proved to be a mistake. Cato knew how to milk the situation by playing the part of the righteous defender of the Republic who refused to bow to 'tyranny'. In the Senate at least, there was widespread sympathy for him, even though for a while the debate continued. One senator, Marcus Petreius, the man who had defeated Catiline in battle in 62 BC and had already undergone thirty years of military service, got up and left the House. Caesar demanded to know why he was leaving before the session had ended and received the tart reply from the grizzled veteran that he would rather be in prison with Cato than here with Caesar. The consul was already realising that he had misjudged the situation. He is supposed to have hoped that Cato would call upon one of the tribunes of the plebs to veto his arrest. However, the prisoner was enjoying the moment too much to provide Caesar with an easy way out. In the end the consul had to order his release. The day had been spent without the Senate ever voting on a motion supporting the bill.[24]

Cato had won a victory and added once again to his reputation. Yet, like many of the successes of his career, it was a hollow triumph that in the long run made things worse. This time he was not facing a Piso or Afranius who could easily be diverted or blocked. Caesar, who had done so much to appear conciliatory, now declared that since the Senate would do nothing, he would go directly to the Roman people. Probably the next day he held a meeting in the Forum, and once again made every effort to be reasonable. He summoned his colleague Bibulus to the Rostra and asked him his opinion of the land bill in full view of the crowd. It is always difficult to know precisely who attended these public gatherings and whether they were genuine reflections of the views of the wider population or more like modern party rallies. On the one hand there was little to stop any citizen – or indeed non-citizen – who was in Rome from turning up and watching proceedings. On the other hand the space in the Forum was limited and could not possibly have contained more than a small fraction of the city's vast population. It seems doubtful that more than 5,000 people could actually have heard a speech being made, although parts of the Forum could probably have contained bigger crowds than this. Most scholars assume that the magistrate calling the meeting would ensure that the gathering was packed with his supporters. This is quite possibly true, although there is no real evidence for how this was organised, and we should probably be a little cautious about making their control of such gatherings absolute. In this case, the mood of the crowd was certainly favourable to Caesar. Nevertheless, Bibulus repeated Cato's argument that whatever the merits of the bill, there should be no innovations in his year of office. Caesar kept trying to persuade his colleague, and told the crowd that they could have the law if only Bibulus would consent. He lead the chant that called upon his fellow consul to agree, but the pressured Bibulus only shouted out that, 'You shall not have this law this year, even if you all want it.' After this crass comment, Bibulus stormed off.[25]

Roman magistrates were not elected to represent anyone, and neither they nor senators were answerable to any sort of constituency. In this way Roman politics differed markedly from the theory – if not necessarily the practice – of modern democracies. Yet in the end the will of the Roman people was supposed to be sovereign and for a consul to express such disdain for the voters was a serious error. Caesar had pressured him into making the mistake and now built upon this success. He summoned no more magistrates to his meeting – or meetings, as there may well have been more than one – but instead called upon distinguished senior senators. This was entirely normal practice, and Caesar began with Crassus and Pompey. Both enthusiastically supported the bill, for the first time giving a clear public indication of their association with the consul. Pompey spoke of the need to reward with land the soldiers who under his own command had fought so well for Rome. He also reminded them that the spoils won by his armies had given the Republic ample funds to make the distribution practical. Caesar worked on the crowd once again, getting them to beg Pompey to ensure that the bill became law. Always susceptible to adulation, he announced in reply to Caesar's questioning that if anyone 'took up the sword' to stop the bill, then he was 'ready with his shield' (or in another version 'with his sword and shield'). The threat was more than a little clumsy. It delighted the cheering crowds, but made many senators nervous. Cato and Bibulus had blocked Caesar in the Senate, but raising the stakes in the struggle had not deterred him or his backers. In the end, Caesar was at least as stubborn and determined as they were. Like Tiberius Gracchus in 133 BC, having failed to gain the Senate's approval, Caesar took his law directly to the voters. A date was set in the last days of January for a Tribal Assembly to vote on the land bill. Caesar had handled his public meetings well and all indications suggested that it would be approved. Although they presented themselves as the true defenders of the Republic, it is doubtful that Cato and Bibulus spoke for more than a small minority of citizens. In fact, their views were probably only shared by a minority, if perhaps a larger one, of the Senate, but in that case it included many of the most distinguished and influential nobles.[26]

THE CONSULSHIP OF JULIUS AND CAESAR

In the early hours of the day when the Tribal Assembly was to vote on the bill, supporters of Caesar, Pompey and Crassus began to position themselves in key places around the Forum. Amongst them were probably some of the veterans from Pompey's army, who had a vested interest in the passage of the bill. Some carried arms, which were at least partially concealed. It is doubtful that there were enough of them to control all access to the Forum, and as the sun rose many other citizens came to join the crowd gathering in front of the Temple of Castor and Pollux. The choice of this location for a public meeting before the Assembly suggests that large numbers were anticipated, as there was more space in this end of the Forum than around the Rostra itself. It should be remembered that the proposed distribution of land does seem to have had widespread support and, even more, that those actively opposed to it, rather than simply unconcerned, were very few. Pompey's open support had convinced many who might have been less sure of Caesar's motives. Whether those present felt intimidated – or even protected – by the burly men standing in groups around the Forum, is harder to say. Caesar made a speech from the podium of the temple, once again explaining the need for his law. In the middle of this, his consular colleague arrived. Bibulus was accompanied by his attendants and lictors, and with him were Cato, three of the year's tribunes and a band of supporters. The crowd parted in front of them as the consul made his way to join Caesar. Dio says that this was in part out of natural respect for the supreme magistracy, but also because they thought that he had come round and would no longer oppose the law. Once he had reached Caesar on the platform of the temple – and perhaps remembered his own grim joke about their joint aedileship – Bibulus made it clear that his attitude had not wavered in the slightest. The presence of the tribunes suggests that he and Cato planned to veto proceedings and prevent an assembly from being held. He may also have considered announcing that he had seen unfavourable omens, which would also have broken up the meeting. However, matters may already have gone too far for this, since such pronouncements were supposed to precede the order for the citizens to separate into their tribes, which Caesar may already have given.[27]

The response of the crowd was immediately hostile. Doubtless the ensuing violence was led by the armed supporters. Bibulus was pushed off the steps of the temple as he tried to speak against Caesar. His lictors were overpowered and the fasces they carried smashed – an important symbolic humiliation for a magistrate. According to Appian, Bibulus bared his neck and shouted out that he would rather stain proceedings with his death since he could not stop Caesar. His attempt at heroism ended in farce, when a basket full of dung was dumped over his head. Missiles were flung and several attendants wounded, as were one or more of the tribunes in some versions.

Several of the attendants were injured by missiles. No one was killed, which may suggest that the violence was tightly controlled by Caesar and his allies. Covering the consul in manure rather than actually injuring him rather adds to the impression of well-orchestrated and restrained use of force. This was in marked contrast to most of the other periodic outbursts of violence since 133 BC. Cato was unhurt and was the last to leave, all the while shouting at his fellow citizens to persuade or intimidate them to his own point of view. Appian claims that he was actually carried out by some of Caesar's supporters, but later sneaked back in and only gave up when he realised that no one would listen to anything he said. The Assembly then convened and approved the bill by a comfortable majority. The new law included a clause requiring every senator to take an oath to abide by its clauses and not to seek its repeal. Failure to do so would result in exile. Within a short period – perhaps five days, which was the period for a similar clause in another law – all had taken the oath. Metellus Celer, the consul who had summoned the Senate to join him in his prison cell a year before, was reluctant, but finally relented. Cato is said to have been persuaded by Cicero that he was of more value to Rome in the city than as an exile. Bibulus had summoned the Senate as soon as was possible after the day of the vote to protest at Caesar's behaviour. The meeting was most likely held on 1 February when he assumed the fasces. However, Bibulus' hope that the Senate would condemn Caesar, perhaps pass the *senatus consultum ultimum* and strip him of his office as had been done to Lepidus in 78 BC, proved unfounded. No senator was willing to oppose Caesar or his law, given the enthusiasm shown for both by so many of the people. Many of the members of the House were anyway closely attached to his backers, Pompey and Crassus.[28]

Bibulus retired to his house and did not again appear in public as consul for the rest of the year. He busied himself writing scurrilous pamphlets and denunciations of Caesar, Pompey and their supporters, which he ordered posted up in the Forum. Yet he remained out of sight. Soon it was common to speak of the 'consulship of Julius and Caesar', rather than Bibulus and Caesar. Suetonius repeats verses popular at the time:

> Not long ago an act was passed during Caesar's year, not that of Bibulus.
> I don't remember anything done in Bibulus' consulate.

Yet Bibulus was not entirely inactive, and still attempting to block Caesar. The consuls had the task of fixing dates for those festivals that did not have to be celebrated on a certain day. Bibulus chose to place these on days when the Popular Assemblies were allowed to meet, preventing this from happening. However, his colleague was not obliged to acknowledge this, and Caesar routinely ignored him. He could not prevent Bibulus from declaring the celebration of periods of thanksgiving already voted by the Senate to successful commanders. No public business could be conducted during such periods, and some of the year was lost to Caesar and his allies in this way. Yet these methods were not sufficient to block all activity in the year, and so Bibulus routinely sent messengers to every meeting and assembly held by Caesar to announce that he had seen unfavourable omens and that therefore business had to be suspended. This practice of 'watching the skies' was hallowed by antiquity, but lacked the force of such an announcement made in person. In this case it was a sham, and everyone realised this, but archaic ritual could still have an impact in public life, as with the lowering of the flag on the Janiculum, which ended the trial of Rabirius. It did raise the question of whether or not any of Caesar's laws were valid, although the Romans themselves seem to have been unsure of the answer. Caesar himself was *Pontifex Maximus*, and Pompey an augur, the college of priests with particular responsibility for interpreting omens.[29]

Caesar refused to accept Bibulus' declarations, for there were too many measures that he needed to get through. For all the obstructions his year of office was crammed with new legislation, the precise chronology of which is uncertain. The land law had helped to achieve one of Pompey's goals, and at some point his Eastern Settlement was also finally ratified by a vote of the Tribal Assembly. It may have been in a meeting to discuss this that Lucullus spoke out against Caesar. The consul replied with such a fierce tirade and with threats of prosecution that the senior senator flung himself on the ground to beg for mercy. For Crassus there was a one-third reduction in the sum due from the *publicani* for the right to collect the Asian taxes. However, Caesar did formally warn the companies not to bid in such a reckless way in future. He may have benefited directly from this relief, for Cicero later claimed that Caesar was able to reward his agents with shares from the major companies. He had long taken an interest in how Rome's provinces were governed, with most of his famous appearances in court being prosecutions of oppressive governors. Now he framed a law that closely regulated the behaviour of provincial governors, clarifying and improving a law passed by Sulla as dictator. This proved highly successful and would remain in force for centuries. Cicero later described it as an 'excellent law'. Both Caesar and Crassus had in earlier years tried to secure special commissions to Egypt. Pompey, who had personally reorganised great swathes of the eastern Mediterranean, also took a deep interest in the area.

In 59 BC they ensured that the Roman Republic formally recognised the rule of Ptolemy XII, an illegitimate son of Ptolemy XI. Ptolemy XII, who was nicknamed Auletes or 'the flute-player', was deeply unpopular with the Egyptians, but had paid a massive bribe to Pompey and Crassus. Suetonius claimed that this amounted to 6,000 talents, or a staggering 36 million denarii. Some of these laws were presented in Caesar's own name, so that each was a Julian law (*lex Julia*) on whatever the subject happened to be. Others were put forward by sympathetic tribunes. The most notable of these was Publius Vatinius, who comes across as a charming rogue in our sources. On one occasion he led a crowd to Bibulus' house and tried to make him come out and announce his unfavourable omens in public. There was even talk of arresting him. Vatinius supported Caesar, but it would be wrong to see him merely as the consul's tool, for like any senator he had ambitions of his own. He helped Caesar because this brought him personal benefits, including some of the shares in the tax-gathering companies mentioned above. Cicero claims that in later years Caesar would wryly comment that Vatinius had done nothing 'for free' during his tribunate.[30]

For all his legislative activity, Caesar had time for other things during 59 BC. He remained deeply in love with Servilia, and in these months presented her with a pearl worth 1.5 million denarii – perhaps paid for from Ptolemy's bribe. Caesar had now been single since the divorce of Pompeia in 62 BC. None of our sources tell us whether Caesar and Servilia felt any desire to marry. Since both the divorce from Silanus and any union with Caesar would have required Cato's approval, it was obviously not a realistic possibility. Julia, Caesar's only child, was also now of marriageable age. In late April or early May 59 BC two weddings were announced. Caesar took as his wife Calpurnia, the daughter of Lucius Calpurnius Piso, who was obviously favoured for the next year's consulship and would win this easily with the backing of the triumvirs. It was a move that secured a sympathetic successor to protect Caesar's interests. This marriage was politically successful and, as far as we can tell, reasonably happy, although the couple spent the vast majority of their time apart, since Caesar was to spend the bulk of the remainder of his life on campaign overseas. The second marriage was between Julia and her father's political ally, Pompey the Great. Pompey was six years older than Caesar, and the age difference between husband and wife was great even by Roman standards. He had also divorced his last wife for infidelity with, amongst others, his new father-in-law. The marriage clearly had a political motivation and was announced suddenly. Julia was already engaged to Quintus Servilius Caepio, the marriage scheduled for just a few days later. Caepio was understandably upset when the betrothal was broken, prompting Pompey to give him his own daughter Pompeia as a wife, a move which in turn involved the severing of her engagement to Faustus Sulla, the dictator's son. The creation of such a close family link between Caesar and Pompey is usually seen as an indication that the consul was becoming worried over the loyalty of his ally. Dio and our other sources certainly felt that the initiative came from Caesar. He had taken a lot of chances to force through the legislation Pompey wanted and would need powerful friends in Rome when he himself set out for a province. Caesar also needed Pompey's support in order to secure an appropriate province for himself. Yet the marriage may equally have been an indication of the triumvirate's success. Caesar had proved himself and a more permanent tie was now worthwhile. Pompey's new wife was young, attractive, intelligent and seems to have had much of her father's charm. The forty-seven-year-old husband rapidly fell deeply in love with his teenage bride. His affection appears to have been returned and the marriage was undoubtedly a happy one. Pompey had always thrived on adoration, and willingly returned devotion with devotion.[31]

THE BACKLASH

From the middle of April to well into May, most senators tended to leave Rome and visit their rural estates. As a result, there were rarely any meetings of the Senate or assemblies during these weeks. Probably before this unofficial recess began, Caesar had already put forward another agrarian law. This time it dealt specifically with the publicly owned land in Campania, which had been exempted from his first law. The commissioners for the first law had already been elected and begun their work, and it may be that they had found too little other land available for immediate purchase. Perhaps Caesar had always thought that its distribution would also be necessary at some point, or maybe the realisation that his first law was on its own inadequate came more gradually. If we knew this, we would certainly have a clearer idea of whether he had genuinely hoped to win over the Senate to support his first land law, or had merely wanted to put them in the wrong in the eyes of the electorate. Now 20,000 citizens – or rather 20,000 families since only married men with three or more children were eligible – were selected from Rome's poor and settled on farms in Campania. The same commissioners who oversaw the first law were probably placed in charge of this. The emphasis on men with families is very interesting, for it was a consistent feature of similar colonisation plans under the emperors, and was evidently believed to encourage more serious and deserving colonists. Senators were once again bound by a solemn oath to uphold this law and not seek its repeal.[32]

Around the same time as this new land bill, the tribune Vatinius also put forward a proposal to give Caesar a special five-year command, combining the provinces of Illyricum and Cisalpine Gaul into one. These provinces were garrisoned by three legions and were also conveniently close to Italy. He was given the privilege of choosing his own legates, at least one of whom would be granted propraetorian *imperium*. Both laws were passed, probably at the end of May. By a vote of the Senate, Caesar's province was increased to include Transalpine Gaul, which had become vacant on the death of its current governor, Metellus Celer, who had not actually reached his province when he fell ill and died. A five-year command, with powerful armies – there was an additional legion in Transalpine Gaul – and opportunities for military adventure in the Balkans, or in Gaul itself, where trouble had been simmering for some years, was just what Caesar had wanted. Bibulus could be left to cope with the 'woods and country paths', although in fact he does not seem to have taken up this post and did not actually take command in any province for nearly a decade. Yet, although each of the triumvirs had achieved his objective, their success was as yet unsecured, and the danger remained that the hostility against them could produce opposition in the future. In the worst possible scenario, a magistrate in the next or subsequent years would move to have all the acts of Caesar's consulship declared invalid. As a result the triumvirs remained nervous and inclined to react strongly to any open criticism.

In early April Cicero's old consular colleague, Caius Antonius, was accused of extortion during his governorship of Macedonia. In 63 BC this wealthy province had actually been voted to Cicero himself, but he had voluntarily given it to Antonius to keep the latter on his and the Republic's side during Catiline's conspiracy. Although he had no high opinion of Antonius, and probably guessed at his obvious guilt, the orator chose to defend him. The prosecution was backed by Caesar and probably Crassus as well. The prosecution carried the day and Antonius went into luxurious exile. During his defence, Cicero made the mistake of openly criticising the triumvirs and lamenting the poor state of the Republic. That was in the morning. In the afternoon his personal enemy Clodius – the same man who had invaded the Bona Dea festival to seduce Caesar's wife Pompeia – was transferred from patrician to plebian status. Caesar as *Pontifex Maximus* presided over the ceremony, with Pompey officiating as augur, which involved Clodius' adoption by a plebian. Clodius had been angling unsuccessfully for this for several years, wanting to stand for the tribunate, an office from which patricians were banned. He had already taken to spelling his name in the more vulgar form of Clodius rather than Claudius. As if to emphasise the farcical nature of this ceremony, the plebian adopting Clodius was younger than he was.[33]

Cicero spent much of the remainder of the year swinging between nervousness and sudden optimism. For much of the rest of April he was at his villa in Antium, 'lying low', as he put it. He was not alone, and attendance in the Senate apparently slumped as many members of the House simply stayed away. On one occasion, Caesar is supposed to have asked an elderly senator why so few were present at a meeting. The old man, a certain Considius, apparently replied that the others were afraid of Caesar's armed followers. When the consul asked why Considius himself continued to attend, he was told that as an old man he was past fear, given that he had very little future ahead of him anyway. Cicero welcomed the Campanian Law, because he thought that it might alienate many senators from the triumvirs. He pointed out that this redistribution would take away a significant source of revenue. This was certainly true of taxation levied in Italy, but Pompey's conquests had more than compensated for this. Once more there were attempts to win him over to join the triumvirs. Caesar offered him a post as a legate with him in Gaul, but neither this nor any alternative quite swayed him from his belief that they had acted wrongly. There was also mild bitterness at Cato, whom he felt had only made things worse by his actions earlier in the year, and at the principal nobles whose support for him could not be relied on if he took a stand. By late April he began to hope that the balance in public affairs was changing and wrote to Atticus, saying that 'if the power of the Senate was hateful, you can guess what will happen now control has passed not to the people, but to three immoderate men. In a short time you will see not only those of us who made no mistakes praised, and even Cato, for all his errors.'[34] On 18 April Cicero had heard that Clodius planned to stand for the tribunate, but was publicly declaring that he would annul all of Caesar's laws. This was probably because he had been denied a lucrative posting to Egypt and been offered a less attractive one to Armenia instead. Gossip claimed that Caesar and Pompey were now denying that they had ever performed the adoption ceremony. This was encouraging but in May he wrote with some despair of Pompey, even suggesting that he was planning to establish a tyrannical rule. Later in the year a young senator accused Pompey of this openly in the Forum and came close to being lynched, although whether by the triumvirs' partisans or the wider crowd is unclear. Cicero's description of this man, Caius Cato, as 'a youth of little political sense, yet still . . . a Cato', provides a clear indication of the power of a famous name at Rome.[35]

As the summer drew on, Cicero reported that the most vocal opponent of the triumvirs was Caius Scribonius Curio, son of the consul of 76 BC. Like Caius Cato, Curio was still a young man, and it is striking that the triumvirs faced little open criticism from distinguished senators and former magistrates. It was another indication of the weakness of the senior ranks of the Senate in these years, largely as a result of the civil war and more recent disturbances. Sometimes, however, it was a crowd of ordinary citizens who chose to protest. Pompey was hissed when he took his seat in a place of honour at games held by Gabinius, the man who as tribune had secured him the command against the pirates and subsequently served as his legate. At a play an actor was cheered when he emphasised the line 'You are *great* through our misery', which was evidently meant to be taken as an attack on Pompey the Great. According to Cicero:

> When Caesar came in the cheering died away; but then young Curio followed him and there was applause of the kind Pompey used to get in the days when the Republic was still secure. Caesar was very irritated. They say that a letter flew to Pompey at Capua. They are upset with the *equites* who rose and cheered Curio – they [the triumvirate] are now enemies of everyone.[36]

Bibulus' vitriolic and often filthy edicts were read with glee by many citizens, and Cicero spoke of the crowd that was usually clustered around them in the Forum. Their enjoyment need not have been a sign of particular sympathy for the housebound consul – throughout the ages political satire has often amused even those who disagreed with it. The Romans had a robust sense of humour and enjoyed such crude invective. Caesar was the target for much of his colleague's insults, but seems not to have been bothered by it. Pompey never coped well with criticism and on 25 July was moved to make a speech in the Forum defending himself against these slurs. Cicero found the sight pathetic, for he continued to hope for a renewal of friendship with the man he had praised so often, but noted that all Pompey achieved was to attract even more attention to Bibulus' pamphlets. Pompey was by this time continually assuring Cicero that he need have no fears of Clodius. The latter had evidently dropped his plans to attack Caesar's laws – if indeed he had ever seriously considered this and was not aiming at the tribunate all along. By the autumn Cicero felt, or perhaps wanted to believe, that Pompey regretted the disturbances of earlier in the year and his alienation from the nobles in the Senate.[37]

In late summer or early autumn a strange episode occurred, which is still not fully understood. Vettius, the man who in 62 BC had accused Caesar of complicity in Catiline's conspiracy and been beaten and imprisoned for his pains (see p.145), was brought before the Senate and declared that he knew of another 'plot'. He had become friendly with Curio and eventually told him that he planned to murder Pompey – or both Pompey and Caesar in another version. Curio told his father, who promptly told Pompey, and the Senate was summoned and called Vettius in for questioning. Now he accused Bibulus of inciting Curio to murder Pompey, and perhaps Caesar as well. He named several other conspirators, among them Servilia's son Brutus, now in his mid twenties. He, and at least one of the other men named, could perhaps be seen to possess a motive, since Pompey had executed their fathers during the civil war. One of Bibulus' servants was supposed to have supplied the dagger that the young conspirators were to use. At the time Cicero believed that Caesar was behind Vettius, and that he had wanted to neutralise Curio for criticising the triumvirs. Yet it seems extremely unlikely that he would have wanted his lover's son implicated. Curio defended himself well against the attack, while Pompey had already thanked Bibulus some months before for warning him against assassins. Vettius' story was treated with great suspicion and he was placed into custody, for having by his own admission been discovered with a concealed dagger in the Forum. On the following day Caesar and Vatinius called him to the Rostra at a public meeting. This time Vettius made no mention of Brutus. Cicero, doubtless hinting at Caesar's relationship with Servilia, noted slyly that 'it was obvious a night, and a night-time plea had intervened'.[38] Instead he claimed that Lucullus and a number of other men were involved, one of them Cicero's own son-in-law. No one was inclined to believe him and he was to be put on trial, but was found dead in his cell before this could begin.

How Vettius died is unclear. Plutarch says that it was called suicide, but that marks of strangulation were visible on his neck. Suetonius, who claimed that Caesar was behind the whole affair, says that he had Vettius poisoned A few years later Cicero shifted the blame for this episode onto Vatinius rather than Caesar. More recently, scholars have varied in their opinions as to who was really behind it. Some have blamed Caesar, but others have speculated about Clodius, and even Pompey himself. On the one hand, the business may have helped to make Pompey nervous, for he had always had a morbid fear of assassination, and confirm him in his loyalty to the triumvirate in spite of the barrage of abuse from Bibulus and his unaccustomed popularity. Yet the naming of Brutus makes it very unlikely that Caesar inspired the whole thing. More probably he simply sought to profit from the affair once it had been revealed. The omission of Brutus' name on the second day indicates that the informer had come under pressure. Vettius may have been acting on his own account, craving a return to the limelight or hoping to restore his fortunes with the reward an informer might win. Caesar obviously did try to use him, but quickly realised that there was little to be gained and that Vettius could not be relied upon. It is plausible enough that he gave the orders to kill the prisoner, who was after all a man who had attacked him in the past, but this cannot be proven.[39]

Bibulus did manage to delay the consular elections from July to October. However, in spite of the fact that he had the right to preside over these, he remained at home and the task was left to Caesar. The consuls elected for 58 BC were Caesar's new father-in-law Calpurnius Piso and Gabinius, both of them favourable to the triumvirs. How things went in the next months would be critical for Caesar's fortunes, for the longer that his legislation was respected then the harder it would be for anyone to raise serious questions over its validity. At the end of his year as consul, Caesar lingered for some months in or near Rome to see how events were likely to take shape. Clodius had been elected to the tribunate and, since his own transferral to plebian status was bound up with the legality of Caesar's actions as consul, was now clearly going to devote much effort to confirming their validity. Dio says that he forbade Bibulus from delivering a speech when he finally emerged on the last day of his consulship – just as Metellus Nepos had stopped Cicero at the end of 63 BC. Two of the new praetors attacked Caesar, and he answered their criticisms in a meeting of the Senate. Three speeches he delivered in these debates were published to present a lasting defence of his actions in 59 BC. Sadly these have not survived. However, after three days the House had come to no decision. An attempt by one of the new tribunes to prosecute him was blocked by the majority of the college. It was not until March 58 BC that Caesar finally left for Gaul, where a situation had arisen that required his immediate attention.[40]

Caesar had achieved a great deal during his consulship. An extensive programme of land resettlement was now under way and would continue throughout the decade. Pompey had secured his Eastern Settlement and Crassus had gained relief for the tax farmers. Caesar, through allying himself with the other two, had been able to do all this in the face of opposition that his initially conciliatory actions had not been able to win over. It had been a turbulent year, with tensions running high on a number of occasions. Cicero wrote in his letters of his fears of tyranny and impending civil war. Neither had happened, but many of the conventions and precedents that regulated public life had come under great strain and been further eroded. Bibulus' and Cato's determination to block Caesar at all costs had done as much damage as his own determination to push on at all costs. Yet for the moment Caesar had won, and had gained the chance to win military glory on a grand scale. Now he had a long and important provincial command it was a question of winning victories for the Republic. If his military successes were grand enough – and Caesar was determined that they would be – then surely even his bitterest opponents would have to accept him as a great, perhaps the greatest, servant of the Republic, and the more dubious acts of his consulship could be forgotten or pardoned. The passage of the *Lex Vatinia* giving him Cisalpine Gaul and Illyricum, and the subsequent addition to his province of Transalpine Gaul, had delighted Caesar. Elated by this success, he declared in the Senate that, since 'he had gained his greatest desire to the great grief of his enemies, he would now mount on their heads'. Whether this was an intentional double entendre or not, one senator retorted that that would be a hard thing for a woman to do, referring to the old story of Caesar and Nicomedes, which Bibulus' edicts had revived. Caesar quipped cheerfully back that it should not be difficult, since 'Semiramis . . . had been queen of Syria and the Amazons in days of old had held sway over a great part of Asia.' It seems fitting to end the account of this year with a crude joke, as well as an episode that shows Caesar's confidence and self-satisfaction.[41]

PART TWO

❖

PROCONSUL
58–50 BC

IX

GAUL

Caesar 'also fought fifty pitched battles, the only commander to surpass Marcus Marcellus, who fought thirty-nine.' – *Pliny the Elder, mid first century AD.*[1]

'Caesar possessed the highest skill and elegance of style, but also the most perfect knack of explaining his plans.' – *Aulus Hirtius, 44 BC*[2]

Caesar was forty-one when he set out from Rome for his province. He would not return to the city for nine years. The remainder of his life was dominated by warfare to a degree that it is difficult to exaggerate. From this moment on, there were only two years in which he was not involved in major military operations. In 50 BC this was because Gaul was conquered and he was busily engaged in settling the region. In 44 BC he was murdered just days before setting out for grand new campaigns against first Dacia and then Parthia. In most years he fought at least one, and often several, major battles or sieges. Pliny claimed that altogether Caesar led his army in fifty battles, while Appian says that thirty of these engagements occurred during the campaigns in Gaul. It is impossible to confirm or deny the precision of these numbers, since in any period of history there is rarely agreement as to just what constitutes a battle and what is merely an engagement or skirmish. The fact remains that these authors reflected the widespread belief that Caesar had fought more often and with more consistent success than any other Roman general. Alexander, with whom he was frequently compared, took part in only five pitched battles and three major sieges, although he was in many smaller encounters. Hannibal, who was up against a very different opponent, fought more big battles, but probably did not surpass, or perhaps even equal, Caesar's total of major engagements. It was not until the era of Napoleon, with the increased intensity of warfare, that a few army leaders began to see more days of serious combat than Caesar and the other great commanders of the ancient world.[3]

The contrast between Caesar's life before and after 58 BC could not be more marked. Up until then, he had spent at the very most some nine years outside Italy, and perhaps half that time in some sort of military service. This was fairly typical for a Roman senator, if anything perhaps slightly below the average, although not in comparison with men like Cicero who relied on constant appearances in the courts to keep themselves in the public eye. Once again, it is worth emphasising that for all his flamboyance, association with dubious characters and the controversial nature of some of his actions during the consulship, the overall pattern of Caesar's career had been broadly conventional. Having reached the consulship two years before the normal age, he was just marginally younger than the average proconsul. Compared to Alexander the Great, Hannibal or Pompey his opportunity came very late in life. Alexander was dead by the age of thirty-three, and Hannibal fought his last battle at forty-five. Napoleon and Wellington were just a year older than Hannibal when they clashed at Waterloo, though Blücher was seventy-three. In contrast Robert E. Lee was in his fifties when the American Civil War broke out, as was Patton when America entered the Second World War. Neither by Roman nor modern standards could Caesar have been considered elderly in 58 BC, but neither would it have been obvious to any of his contemporaries that he was about to prove himself as one of the greatest commanders of all time. In the past he had shown talent, courage, and self-confidence during his spells of military service, but plenty of other ambitious men had displayed similar ability. As always in Caesar's story, we need to be very careful not to allow hindsight to impose a sense of inevitability on events. The scale of Caesar's successes in Gaul was startling, even in a Rome so recently dazzled by Pompey's achievements. Yet the balance between success and failure was often narrow, and he might easily have been killed, or have died from accident or disease before he could return. That he would eventually come back as a rebel to fight against his former ally and son-in-law Pompey was unlikely to have occurred to anyone. When Caesar went to Gaul he had plans and ambitions, and doubtless considered many possible outcomes, but in the end he was trusting to fortune for his future.

THE WAR COMMENTARIES

Caesar had worked hard to win the opportunity for such a great command, running up huge debts, taking great political risks and making many enemies. He needed colossal victories if all this was to become worthwhile, but he also had to make sure that people knew about his achievements if he was to gain real advantage from them. Pompey's campaigns against the pirates and Mithridates had been recorded by Theophanes of Mytilene, a Greek scholar who had accompanied his staff. Caesar had no need of the literary services of other men and would record his victories in his own words. He had already published a number of his speeches as well as several now lost works, some of which he had written as a youth. The Emperor Augustus later suppressed these immature works, including a tragedy entitled *Oedipus*, and also his *Praises of Hercules* and *A Collection of Maxims*, and none of the speeches have survived other than in fragments. There was a tradition for Roman generals to celebrate their achievements by writing commentaries – a genre that was seen as distinct from history, and was often viewed as the material for subsequent historians to use. Caesar eventually produced ten books of *War Commentaries*, with seven covering the operations in Gaul from 58–52 BC, and three more dealing with the Civil War against Pompey from 49–48 BC. After his death, several of his own officers added four more books covering the operations in Gaul in 51 BC, the campaigns in Egypt and the East in 48–47 BC, Africa in 46 BC, and Spain in 45 BC. No other commentaries have survived in anything other than the tiniest fragments, making it difficult to know whether or not Caesar's books conformed to the established style.[4]

Caesar's *Commentaries on the Gallic War* was from the beginning acknowledged as one of the greatest works of Latin literature. Cicero had great respect for Caesar's oratory and was similarly generous in his praise of the *Commentaries*:

> They are admirable indeed . . . like naked forms, upright and beautiful, pared of all ornamentation as if they had removed a robe. Yet while he wished to provide other authors with the means for writing history, he may only have succeeded in pleasing the incompetent, who might like to apply their 'gifts' to his material, for he has deterred all sane men from writing; for there is nothing better in the writing of history than clear and distinguished brevity.[5]

These words were written in 46 BC, when Cicero was becoming increasingly uncomfortable with Caesar's dictatorship, so it may be that there was just a hint of double meaning when he said that 'men of sound judgement' had been put off from writing their own narratives of his achievements. Nevertheless, it is clear that his praise for the literary quality of the books was entirely genuine, perhaps especially because the stark simplicity of their narrative contrasted so much with his own style of rhetoric. On one occasion Caesar declared that an orator should 'avoid an unusual word as the helmsman of a ship avoided a reef'. Apart from necessary technical or foreign terms, he adhered staunchly to this principle and produced a narrative that was clear and fast-paced. Rarely, if ever, is it emotional or melodramatic, for he allowed the drama and importance of the events to speak for themselves. Referring to himself always in the third person, while his soldiers are *nostri* or '*our* men', he tells the story of the army of the Roman people under their properly appointed commander, as they struggle against ferocious enemies and even nature itself. At every stage Caesar presents his actions as entirely in the interest of the Republic. Although the modern reader may sometimes balk at the catalogue of unabashed imperialism, massacre, mass execution and enslavement contained in the *Commentaries*, a contemporary Roman would not have found these things shocking. Indeed, it must have been hard, even for one of Caesar's political opponents, not to get carried along with the excitement of the narrative.[6]

Many political and military leaders have written their own versions of the events in which they were involved, but few have matched the literary standard of Caesar's *Commentaries*. In recent times Churchill probably comes closest, in the sheer power of his words and the speed with which he produced his account so soon after the Second World War. Yet there is one major difference, both from Churchill and the vast majority of other famous generals, for all of them wrote for posterity, knowing that their own careers were substantially over and wishing to imprint their chosen version of events on future opinion. In contrast Caesar was far more concerned with the contemporary audience, and wrote to help further his career and gain even more opportunities for glory (which had also been true of Churchill with his earlier writings). It is not absolutely clear when the seven books of *Commentaries on the Gallic War* were written and released, but it is often asserted that they came out altogether in 51–50 BC. The conjecture – and it is no more than this in spite of the certainty with which it is often asserted – is that in the months of tension that would eventually culminate in the Civil War, Caesar was hoping to win as much support as possible in Rome. Yet this had been true from the moment he left for Gaul in 58 BC, for neither he, nor any other man pursuing a public career, could afford to be forgotten by the electorate and the influential groups in the city. It would have been strange for him to wait so long. Moreover, differences in the treatment of some individuals and apparent contradictions of detail between the various books make it more than likely that each was published separately.

A better case can actually be made for each book having been produced after the year of campaigning it describes, in the winter months before operations could resume. Even the advocates of the later collective release assume that Caesar sent an annual report to the Senate and that this was widely circulated, and sometimes suggest that this was similar to the form of the *Commentaries* as we have them. There is no reason to believe that in most cases Caesar lacked the time during the winters in Gaul to produce a book. Hirtius, one of his own senior subordinates who later added the eighth book of *Gallic Commentaries*, reflected Cicero's praise for Caesar as a stylist, but also noted the great speed with which he wrote these books. Another officer, Asinius Pollio, believed Caesar intended eventually to rewrite them, which could also be an indication that they were rapidly produced to fulfil an immediate political need. Neither comment proves that each book was published individually – it would obviously have been a considerable task to compose all seven books in the months at the end of the Gallic campaigns – but on the whole it does seem extremely probable.[7]

Another widespread assumption is that the *Commentaries* were aimed first and foremost at the senatorial and equestrian classes, but once again this may be questioned. In his consulship he had ordered the publication of all senatorial proceedings, which was evidently not for the benefit of senators. Levels of literacy in the Roman world are very difficult to judge, so that we do not know how many readers there were outside the wealthy elite. However, more practically we can judge that any system where each copy of a book had to be written out by hand did mean that books were a rare and expensive luxury. Yet Cicero noted the enthusiasm with which men of humble station, such as artisans, devoured history books. There are hints in our sources that the public reading of books was common and could be very well attended. It does seem probable that Caesar, the man who had always been a *popularis* and reliant on the support of a wide section of the community, was keen to engage this audience. It is striking that senatorial and equestrian officers do not figure very prominently in the *Commentaries*, and at times are shown in an unflattering light. In contrast, the ordinary soldiers of the legions consistently show courage and prowess. In most cases even when they are criticised, it is usually for excessive enthusiasm that leads the legionaries to forget their proper discipline. Even more than the ordinary rank and file soldiers, the centurions who lead them are most often painted in heroic colours. Only a few of these officers are named, but generally it is the centurions as a group who keep calm at times of crisis and fight and die for the approval of their commander. This favourable portrayal of centurions and soldiers may well have pleased patriotic aristocrats and equestrians, but it was surely even more appealing to the wider population. Caesar cultivated these Romans and did not simply speak to the elite. It is probable that some groups mattered to him more than others, for instance those citizens enrolled to vote in the First Class in the *Comitia Centuriata*, but we know so little of life outside the circles of the elite that it is hard to be sure.[8]

From the start of the campaigns in Gaul, until the very end of the Civil War, we know far more about Caesar's activities, but the overwhelming majority of this information comes from his own account in the *Commentaries*. For the campaigns in Gaul in particular, there is scarcely any information in other sources that does not seem to have been derived from Caesar's version. If we have reason to doubt the basic truthfulness of the *Commentaries* then we have nothing with which to replace them.

Napoleon was a great admirer of Caesar as a commander, placing him on the list of Great Captains whose campaigns should be studied by any aspiring general, but even so he doubted the truthfulness of some aspects of his account, and spent some time during his exile criticising them. However, given the flexible attitude to the truth in his own bulletins and memoirs, he may simply have seen this as natural. Caesar wrote for a political purpose, to build up his reputation as a great servant of the Republic and show that he deserved his pre-eminence. Therefore, the *Commentaries* were works of propaganda and showed everything he did in the most favourable light. According to Suetonius: 'Asinius Pollio believes that they were composed without too much diligence or absolute concern for truth, since often Caesar was too willing to believe the versions which others gave of their actions, or gave a twisted version of his own, whether on purpose or merely from genuine forgetfulness. . ..'[9]

Pollio served under Caesar in the Civil War, but was not with him in Gaul, and it is more than likely that his comments were mainly aimed at Caesar's account of that later conflict. The claim that Caesar was too ready to accept the accounts others gave of their actions, may well have had a bitterly personal note, since Pollio was one of the few survivors from a disastrous landing in Africa led by a man given favourable treatment in the *Commentaries*. Yet if he was right that Caesar also distorted some of his own actions, then to what extent could this have occurred? Archaeology has confirmed some of his account of operations at Gaul, but it is a clumsy tool with which to reconstruct the details of military operations, still less the motivation and thought behind them. More importantly it is clear that throughout the conflict in Gaul, the many senators and equestrians serving with Caesar's army regularly wrote to their family and friends. In later years Cicero's brother Quintus became one of Caesar's legates. The surviving correspondence includes little military detail, but it is striking that Quintus was even able to send a letter to his brother while the army was in Britain for a few months in 54 BC. There was clearly a constant flood of information going back to Rome from the army. In 56 BC Cicero attacked Caesar's father-in-law Lucius Calpurnius Piso's record as proconsul of Macedonia in the Senate. Piso had flouted convention by not sending regular dispatches to the Senate, but nevertheless Cicero claims that he and everyone else in the House was well informed about the proconsul's activities and failures.

Most of the critics of Caesar's truthfulness employ details from his own narrative against him. Defeats are mentioned, as are a number of controversial actions. Ultimately, Caesar could not risk widespread invention or blatant distortion because these would readily have been spotted by his audience. He could, and clearly did, present everything in the most favourable light possible, passing the blame for defeats onto others, justifying his actions with apparently calm reason, and not highlighting operations that achieved little. Yet in the end he had to stick closely to facts – particularly those facts that were of most concern to a Roman audience – if the *Commentaries* were to achieve their aim of winning over public opinion. Caution must be used in dealing with Caesar's narrative, as with any other source, but there is good reason to believe that, at the very least, his account recounts the basic events accurately.[10]

CAESAR'S ARMY

The army garrisoning Caesar's province in 58 BC was twice the size of the force that he had taken over in Spain, and in due course it would double and then treble in size. He had had about five years of military service, with no prior experience of warfare in this region, but, as we have seen, neither of these things were especially unusual for a Roman commander. Caesar coped well with the challenge, but it is a mistake to assume that from the very beginning he showed the sureness of touch that has led to his universal recognition as one of the greatest commanders of all time. He had to get to know his new army and learn best how to use it, and this process was not instant. However, his most senior officers were all men whom he had selected himself and brought with him to the province.

The most important were the legates – the name *legatus* meant representative and was used both for ambassadors and senior officers who 'acted on behalf of' a governor – who were invariably senators. As far as we can tell none of these men had any more experience of soldiering than Caesar himself. He had asked Cicero to accompany him in this role, which is a good indication that useful political connections were often of greater importance than head-hunting military talent. The orator had turned Caesar down, but from the beginning of the campaigns he had at least five, and possibly six or even ten, legates on his staff. The most senior was Labienus, who was actually granted propraetorian *imperium* of his own and not merely delegated power. The man who as tribune in 63 BC had co-operated with Caesar and brought the prosecution against Rabirius receives more attention in the *Commentaries* than any other legate, and proved himself to be an exceptionally gifted soldier. However, in 58 BC he may well have had no more prior experience of warfare than Caesar, and his talent blossomed and flourished only on arrival in Gaul. Labienus had served in Asia back in the seventies under the command of Publius Servilius Vatia Isauricus. He and Caesar may have crossed paths during these years, although it is equally possible that Labienus did not arrive in the province until after Caesar had returned to Rome. Extensive service under Pompey has been conjectured, but there is no actual evidence to support this. Similarly, many scholars have assumed that Labienus had held the praetorship in 60 or 59 BC, but again this is plausible rather than actually attested.[11]

Balbus was another old associate of Caesar's and was once again his *praefectus fabrum*, but it seems that he did not spend too long in Gaul before returning to Rome to act as one of Caesar's key agents. Another man who served Caesar in the same role was Mamurra, who came from Formiae and made himself notorious for the massive fortune he acquired by dubious methods during his time in Gaul. The tribune Vatinius, who had secured the five-year command for him, seems to have been in Gaul for a while, but this may have been later in the decade. Quintus Pedius seems to have been with Caesar from the start. The identity of Caesar's other legates in 58 BC is unclear, but if they were not already with him, then several men were soon to join him. One was Aulus Hirtius, the man who would eventually add the eighth book to the *Commentaries*. Another was Servius Suplicius Galba, who had served under Pomptinus during the rebellion of the Allobroges and so had recent experience of warfare in Gaul. Quintus Titurius Sabinus and Lucius Aurunculeius Cotta were probably also both there from the start. (In spite of the *cognomen* Cotta, he is unlikely to have been a relation on Caesar's mother's side, since their *nomen* was Aurelius.) Cotta had written a treatise on the Roman constitution, and there was a pronounced literary feel to Caesar's staff. From 58 to 56 BC, this also included Crassus' younger son Publius, who was a keen student of literature and philosophy and an intimate of Cicero for that reason. This was an indication of the continuing closeness between Caesar and Crassus, which had not needed cementing with a marriage alliance. In his mid twenties, Publius Crassus was to prove a bold and gifted commander, but began the campaign as the commander of the army's cavalry (*praefectus equitum*), before being promoted to legate in the following year. Another young man of talent who served with Caesar probably from the start of the campaign was Decimus Junius Brutus, son of Sempronia who had notoriously been closely involved in Catiline's conspiracy. Finally Caesar also had the assistance of a quaestor, but his identity is unknown.[12]

The most striking thing about Caesar's legates is their comparative obscurity. Crassus, and to a slightly lesser extent Brutus, belonged to distinguished families, and both their fathers had become consul. Labienus was a 'new man' and had not yet held a magistracy more senior than the tribunate, as had Vatinius. Cotta's family seem not to have been prominent for many generations, while even less is known of the background of Sabinus and several other officers. On the whole the great noble families, especially those who had done well under Sulla and afterwards, chose not to accept employment with Caesar. This is in marked contrast to the very distinguished list of legates who had served under Pompey in the command against the pirates. Most of the legates in Gaul seem to have been looking to restore or improve their family's situation, and not a few were to do so. This was probably also true of many of the less senior officers. In his account of 58 BC Caesar talked of 'the military tribunes, prefects, and others who had accompanied Caesar from the city to earn his friendship, but had no great military experience'. Men who were already well established did not need to tie themselves to Caesar in 58 BC. No one knew that he would prove to be such a great commander and that he would not march to defeat or his own death on some Gaulish hillside. They might guess that he would prove generous with whatever success he did have, for his reputation was already established in this respect. Seeking a closer link with Caesar was a gamble more likely to appeal to those unable to succeed any other way. As far as we can tell Caesar seems to have welcomed almost anyone, eager as he always was to do as many favours as possible and so place more men under obligation to him.[13]

Caesar chose his own senior officers, but the army he was to command was already in existence. Altogether, Illyricum, Transalpine and Cisalpine Gaul contained a garrison of four legions – the *Seventh*, *Eighth*, *Ninth* and *Tenth*. It is not known when and by whom these had been raised, but it is quite likely that they had been formed several years before and had already seen active service. On paper a legion in this period consisted of a little under 5,000 men, but as in all armies in all periods of history, units on campaign were often seriously under strength. We hear of one of Caesar's legions during the Civil War that was only able to muster just under 1,000 effectives. A legion had no permanent commander, but its most senior officers were the six tribunes, who were usually equestrians. Some were young aristocrats who had not yet been enrolled in the Senate, while others were semi-professional officers, who sought continued appointments in successive legions. Twenty-four tribunes were elected by the Roman people each year, this traditional number being intended to supply the army of two legions, which was allocated to each consul in earlier centuries. Caesar had himself been elected in this way, but there were now usually too many legions in service at any one time to rely on this method. Most, if not all, of Caesar's tribunes were appointed by him, although some may already have been with the four legions. The *Commentaries* never mention a tribune actually commanding a legion, and Caesar normally gave this task to his legates and his quaestor. However, the tribunes clearly had important staff and administrative roles, and could command sizeable detachments.[14]

Beneath a tribune was a centurion, which is better thought of as a grade rather than a specific rank. There were sixty centurions in a legion. Each commanded a century of eighty men – the title had probably never meant anything more specific than around one hundred men – and six centuries combined to form a cohort of 480, which was the basic tactical unit of the army. Our sources are silent on the matter, but it is highly probable that the most senior of the six centurions commanded the cohort in battle. There were ten cohorts in a legion, and the first cohort had greater prestige than the rest for it protected the silver or gilded eagle that was the standard of the entire legion. The centurions of the first cohort had immense prestige and they, probably along with centurions who commanded the other cohorts, formed the 'centurions of the first grade' (*primi ordines*), who were often included in the commander's briefings. Centurions have sometimes been portrayed as 'sergeant-major' types, grizzled veterans promoted only after long service in the ranks, but there is actually very little evidence to support this view. Never in the entire *Commentaries* does Caesar mention promoting an ordinary legionary into the centurionate, but then he says nothing at all about their origins, presumably because he assumed that his audience would know this. Many men may have been directly commissioned as centurions, something that we know was common under Rome's emperors, when we even hear of equestrians serving in this way. The administrative role that was an important part of the job evidently required a good standard of literacy and numeracy, neither of which may have been common amongst the ordinary soldiers. Once in the rank it is certain that centurions were socially and economically very distant from the ordinary legionaries, for their pay was several – perhaps as much as ten – times greater. Probably most centurions already came from the more prosperous classes and not the very poor who formed the bulk of the rank and file. If so, then the prominence they receive in the *Commentaries* becomes all the more interesting. It may well be that they were drawn from amongst the First Class, which played such a decisive part in the voting in the *Comitia Centuriata*. Appointments to this grade, and subsequent promotions, would then have taken on an importance beyond the purely military for a commander like Caesar, fitting in with the wider networks of patronage that underlay so much of Roman society. Yet unlike the more senior officers, centurions do seem to have stayed with the army for long periods, and it would not be a mistake to see them as essentially professional officers.[15]

The legions of earlier centuries, which had been drawn from a cross-section of society and had excluded all those with insufficient property to afford their own equipment, were now a distant memory. Marius had openly recruited from the *capite censi*, those so poor that they were counted simply as numbers in the census, but he had probably just acknowledged a trend that was already well established. There was now little to attract the better off and well educated to the legions. Discipline could be brutal, with floggings common, and execution the penalty for more serious dereliction of duty. A legionary received an annual salary of 125 denarii (500 *sestertii*) – a figure that helps to put Caesar's staggering debts into perspective – which compared unfavourably with the money that could be earned as a farm labourer, although it did have the advantage of being regular. Poorer citizens saw the army as either a viable career, or as a pathway to a better life. A general who was generous with the rewards or promised to secure grants of land for his veteran soldiers could win an intense loyalty from his legionaries, as Marius, Sulla and Pompey had already demonstrated. Centurions often transferred from one legion to another, but there is no mention of ordinary soldiers doing the same. Legionaries were long service professional soldiers, although it is unclear just how long men normally spent in the army. Augustus would later set the term of service at sixteen years, later extending it to twenty with another five as a veteran, which meant being exempted from some duties and fatigues. The legion was their home, and the better units developed a fierce pride in their corporate identity. Each legion also contained many men with technical skills, who would in turn train others. There were no special units or cohorts of engineers or artillerymen, specialists simply being detached from their cohorts whenever they were required to build a bridge or besiege a town. The engineering skill of the Roman army in this period was extremely high.

The legionary was a heavy infantryman who fought in close order, but in Caesar's day he looked rather different to the classic image perpetuated by Hollywood and the rather loose use of images by re-enactors in television documentaries. The famous banded or segmented armour had probably not yet been invented, for the earliest known fragment of such a cuirass dates to AD 9. (However, since until this was discovered it was generally assumed that this armour was not introduced till the middle of the first century AD it is just possible that it was known in Caesar's day.) Instead the legionary wore mail armour and a bronze or sometimes iron helmet. Roman helmets left the wearer's eyes and ears uncovered, although some protection was provided for the rest of the face by the wide cheek pieces. Enclosed helmets of the type sometimes used in earlier centuries by Greek armies offered better protection, but a legionary needed to be able to hear and see so that he could respond to orders. Further protection was provided by the large semi-cylindrical shield or *scutum*. This was some 4 feet in height and from 2–2 feet 6 inches in width and probably oval in shape, although the rectangular tile shape of the classic 'Hollywood' legionary may already have been adopted. It is highly likely, although unproven, that legions already carried distinctive insignia on their shields, either painted or in raised decoration. The shields themselves were made from three layers of plywood glued together, covered in calfskin, and with the edges protected by bronze binding. The shield was flexible and offered good protection, but was heavy at some 22 lb. It was held in battle by a single horizontal hand-grip behind the central boss, and could be used offensively, the soldier punching the boss forward to overbalance his enemy.

The legionary's main weapons were the *pilum* (javelin), and the *gladius* sword. The *pilum* had a 4-foot wooden shaft, topped by a narrow 2–3-foot iron shank, which ended in a small pyramidal point. When thrown all the weight of the weapon concentrated behind the small head, allowing this to punch through an opponent's shield, while the long slim shank gave it the reach to keep going and wound or kill the man himself. Contrary to deeply entrenched myth, the metal was not intended to bend. By the first century AD the *gladius* sword used by the Roman legionary was short, with a blade usually under 2 feet in length. However, in Caesar's day a longer blade – at least 2 feet 6 inches in length and sometimes longer – was in use. Made of high quality steel, the heavy blade was well adapted to both cutting and thrusting, its long point being well suited to penetrating armour and flesh. The legionary was well equipped and trained as an individual fighter, but the greatest strength of the Roman army lay in the discipline and command structure that made them so effective collectively.[16]

For support troops, the legions relied on foreign soldiers, who were known collectively as the *auxilia*. Many of these were locally recruited allies – Caesar would draw heavily on the tribes of Gaul, especially for contingents of cavalry. In most cases these men were led by their own chieftains, but at least some Gauls do seem to have served in units led by Roman officers, and may have been drilled and equipped by the army. In his account of the Civil War Caesar mentions that in 49 BC he had '3,000 cavalry, which he had had with him in all his past campaigns'. He also tells us that he had 5,000 auxiliary infantry, although it is unclear if these had also served with him from 58 BC onwards. Neither group is specifically mentioned in his account of the campaigns in Gaul, and they may have been allies, mercenaries or regular soldiers foreshadowing the organised and permanent regiments of auxiliaries of the Imperial period. He does make a few references to units of specialists, including Cretan and Numidian archers, and slingers from the Balearic Islands. The Cretans and Balearics were famous for their skill with their respective weapons and had appeared as mercenaries in many armies for several centuries. The Numidians were more famous for their light cavalry and it is quite possible that Caesar also had some of these with him. It is only through a single comment that we know that there were some Spanish cavalry with the army. The number of allied soldiers varied from year to year, while the total force of professional mercenaries and auxiliaries is likely to have been more static. Allied contingents were on occasions substantially larger, but even so it was always the legions that remained the heart of Caesar's army.[17]

'THE WHOLE OF GAUL IS DIVIDED'

In 58 BC it was not obvious where Caesar's campaigns would lead him. He had first been granted Cisalpine Gaul and Illyricum as his province, and Transalpine Gaul was only added after the sudden death of its governor. Caesar's original intention may well have been a Balkan campaign, probably to curb the growing power of the Dacian King Burebista, who was carving out a powerful empire around his heartland in what is now Transylvania. The region was wealthy, and scarcely explored by Roman armies, offering the glory attached to defeating a people never before encountered. He may well have been planning to advance in that direction, both in 58 BC and in later years, but events continued to provide him with ready opportunities for military adventures in Gaul, and the Balkan expedition never took place. Even so, it never left Caesar's mind, for he was planning to move against Dacia in 44 BC when he was assassinated.[18]

In the first century BC Gaul comprised the area of modern France, Belgium and part of Holland, running from the Rhine to the Atlantic coast. In no sense was Gaul a nation. As Caesar famously said in the opening sentence of the *Commentaries on the Gallic War* its population was divided into three ethnic and linguistic groups. In the south-west, bordering on the Pyrenees, were the Aquitanians, whom he believed had much in common with the Iberians of Spain. In the north, especially the north-east, were the Belgians, while central Gaul was the home of the peoples whom the Romans referred to as Gauls (*Galli*), but who named themselves Celts. Each of these groups was in turn subdivided into numerous individual peoples, who for all their similarity in language and culture were often mutually hostile. The basic political unit was the clan (*pagus*), and several of these usually made up a tribe (*civitas*). (Neither English word is entirely appropriate, and some scholars would prefer state to tribe, but no one has really come up with anything better.) The importance of the tribe seems to have increased markedly in the century before Caesar's arrival in Gaul, and some scholars would like to see them as comparatively recent inventions. More probably, the changing political and economic climate in Gaul had simply given new importance to loose ties of kinship and ritual that were very long established. Even so, the degree of unity between the clans of one tribe varied considerably, and there were a number of cases during the Gallic Wars when individual *pagi* acted independently. Kings appear in some tribes, and perhaps also at the clan level, but not in others and the majority seem to have been governed by councils or senates, with the day-to-day running of affairs

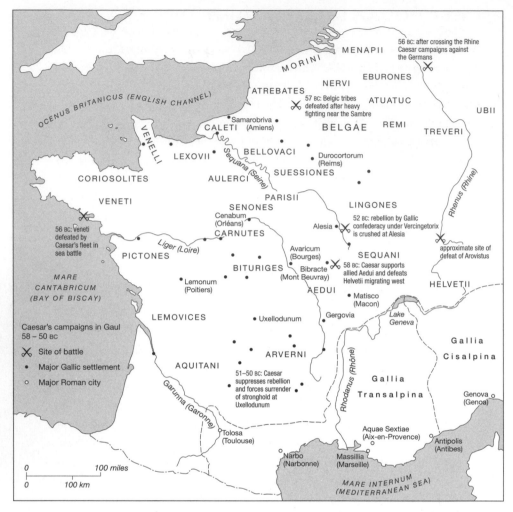

Gaul and its tribes

being placed in the hands of elected magistrates. Rome's oldest ally, the Aedui, had a supreme magistrate called the Vergobret who held office for a single year. No man could be elected twice to this post, nor could any member of his family hold the office during his lifetime, thus preventing any individual or group from monopolising power. The similarity of this ideal to the Roman Republican system is striking, and in many ways the tribes of Gaul resembled the city-states of the Mediterranean world, though perhaps at an earlier stage of development.[19]

There is an on-going academic debate over the extent to which we can see the Gauls and other peoples who spoke 'Celtic' languages as part of one people with broadly uniform customs and culture, but this need not concern us here. Caesar notes both similarities and differences between the various tribes, but did maintain a very clear distinction between the peoples of Gaul and the German tribes. The River Rhine was presented as the dividing line between them, although he concedes that the picture was a little less clear than this and that some Germanic groups were well established in lands on the west bank. Archaeology does not support such a clear division, suggesting strong similarities in settlement patterns and material culture – pottery, metalwork, etc. – between Gaul and central Germany. There was more of a difference between the southern/central regions and the northern areas of Germany, where there were few substantial fortified settlements. Yet it would be a mistake on this basis to reject the testimony of Caesar and other ancient authors, for archaeology is often a clumsy tool for revealing ethnic or political boundaries. There were distinct Germanic and Celtic languages, and doubtless huge numbers of dialects and regional variations within each broad group. Some tribes that spoke a Germanic language may well have lived in similarly sized and laid out settlements to peoples living in Gaul, as well as using objects of a shape and style that were much alike. This does not mean that either group would have perceived the other as fundamentally like themselves and not as foreigners. They were more likely to see peoples who spoke the same or a similar language, who revered the same deities in much the same way, and who had lived around them for a long time as kindred. This would not in itself have prevented hostility and warfare between the two groups, nor ruled out peaceful relations with a more 'foreign' people. Neither the Gauls nor the Germans were nations in any meaningful sense, and personal identity and loyalty had far more to do with tribe and clan, and within these, family, neighbour or chieftain.[20]

Contact between Gallic tribes and the Mediterranean world had a long history and was often marked by warfare. A band of Gauls had sacked Rome in 390 BC, while other tribes had overrun and settled in the Po Valley. Later, the Romans began to colonise the same region, resulting in a series of wars that ended in the early second century BC with the subjugation and absorption of the Gallic tribes. Around 125 BC the Romans began the conquest of Transalpine Gaul to create a secure land route to their provinces in Spain. One of the proconsuls involved in these campaigns was Cnaeus Domitius Ahenobarbus, the great-great-great-grandfather of Emperor Nero. Described by a contemporary as having 'a face of iron and a heart of lead', he is said to have impressed the tribes by riding on an elephant, but his most enduring legacy was the Via Domitia, a great strategic road running to

Spain. The region was the scene of much fighting during the migration of the Cimbri and Teutones, but there was no more concerted Roman expansion before Caesar's arrival. There was considerable consolidation, with the establishment of fortified outposts and a colony at Narbo (modern Narbonne) in 118 BC. The latter soon became an important trade centre as goods produced by the great *latifundia* estates of Italy flooded over the Alps. Wine was the main product, and the trade can be traced by the discovery of sherds from the amphorae used to transport it. The sheer quantity involved is staggering, and one scholar has estimated that during the first century BC some 40 million wine amphorae were traded in Gaul. If anything this figure is probably too low. Each vessel was usually around 3–3 feet 6 inches high and contained 35–45 pints. The main trade routes followed the Rhône-Saône valleys, or went west to the Atlantic coast via the Aude and Garonne. In return for wine and other luxury goods, traders sought raw materials, including tin from south-western Britain, and most of all, slaves. One source claims that a Gaulish chieftain would exchange a slave for a single amphora of wine. This may have been a misunderstanding of the social obligation on a host to demonstrate his wealth and power by giving a guest something of far greater value than his gift, but nevertheless illustrates the importance of wine to the Gaulish nobility. Some of this trade may have been undertaken by local middlemen, but Roman merchants were evidently a familiar sight in much of Gaul. This was a time of great commercial opportunity for Romans, and enterprising businessmen penetrated deep into lands that had never yet seen a Roman army. At one site in Noricum there was a Roman trading community with its own small forum established outside a native town by the start of the first century BC.[21]

Trade with the Roman world encouraged a trend towards centralisation in many of the tribes of Gaul. The late second and first centuries BC saw the growth in large walled towns, which Caesar calls by the somewhat vague term *oppida*. Many tribes were minting coinage of a standard size and weight based on Hellenistic models, which suggests that long-distance trade was common. Some sites show traces of large-scale manufacturing activity, and were laid out to an organised plan. Entremont, a hill town stormed by the Romans around 124 BC during the conquest of Transalpine Gaul, was built in stone in a very Greek style. The cultural influence was not overwhelming though, for a Hellenistic-style shrine also had niches built into the walls to take the severed heads of enemies. Those communities lying on the main trade routes benefited most from this and their towns were corresponding large. The Arverni lay on the western route, while the

Rhône-Saône valleys were contested between the Aedui and Sequani. The principal town of the Aedui at Bibracte (modern Mont Beuvray) enclosed an area of 135 hectares within its walls, and excavations there have revealed vast quantities of wine amphorae. Towns like this tended to be the focus of tribal government, but never quite acquired the central role of Greek and Roman cities. Leaders whose power was based on rural areas were still able to dominate their tribe.[22]

In the end it was the aristocracy which dominated all the tribes of Gaul to a greater or lesser extent. Caesar dismissed the ordinary people as little more than slaves, so closely were they tied to powerful chieftains. The nobility he divided into the knights (*equites*) and the priests, known as druids. Neither group was drawn from a set caste, and families could contain both druids and knights. The druids did not fight and their power rested on their long years of training, which made them experts in matters of religion, law and tribal custom. Caesar says that they deliberately wrote none of their beliefs down, since they felt that reliance on the written word weakened the power of memory and also might diminish their own authority. As a result, very little is known with certainty of druidic beliefs – something that has given plenty of scope over the centuries for the vacuum to be filled with romantic invention. At the time Greek philosophers liked to see the druids as primitive Stoics, and Caesar does say that they believed in the immortality of the soul, something that he claimed encouraged warriors to disdain death in battle. Once a year the druids of much of Gaul met at a shrine in the territory of the Carnutes, but their ability to act as a force to unify the tribes was extremely limited. They also presided over sacrifices and could punish a man by barring him from such rituals. The type of offering varied, but Caesar and our other ancient sources are adamant that the Gauls practised human sacrifice on certain occasions. He speaks of large wicker figures that were filled with people – usually criminals or enemies, but if there were none of these then others had to take their place – and set on fire. Some scholars dismiss such stories as Greek and Roman propaganda, but we should not forget that the Romans themselves had offered human victims to the gods at the time when the Cimbri threatened Italy, and the Senate only outlawed the practice in 97 BC. Roman society remained quite content to watch people being killed for entertainment in the arena, but balked at killing them for the sake of religion. The archaeological record does not provide incontrovertible evidence for widespread human sacrifice by the Gallic tribes, although such practices are clearly attested amongst the Germanic and British peoples. However, it is certain that many Gaulish rituals certainly made use of human body parts, and it is in most cases impossible to tell whether or not these were acquired through ritual killings. In addition head-hunting was certainly common amongst Gaulish warriors and probably amongst many north European peoples. The shrine at Entremont, and a similar one at nearby Rocquepertuse, provide graphic illustration of this.[23] Strabo tells us that:

> when they [the Gauls] depart from the battle they hang the heads of their enemies from the necks of their horses, and, when they have brought them home, nail the spectacle to the entrances of their houses. Poseidonius says that he himself saw this spectacle in many places, and that, although at first he loathed it, afterwards, through his familiarity with it, he could bear it calmly. The heads of enemies of high repute, however, they used to embalm in cedar-oil and exhibit to strangers, and they would not deign to give them back even for a ransom of an equal weight in gold.[24]

Poseidonius was a Greek philosopher who travelled in southern Gaul in the early years of the first century BC, gathering material for his ethnographic study. He later settled in Rome and it is quite possible that Caesar met him. A Gallic coin from the middle of the century actually depicts a warrior holding a severed head in one hand. Archaeologists have also discovered a gruesome trophy at Ribemont-sur-Ancre, where the corpses of many armed warriors and some horses had been fixed to a wooden structure, so that they stood upright. The heads of all these men were missing, and it is now unclear whether they were defeated enemies or some form of sacrificial offering. Caesar mentions that mounds of spoils taken from an enemy were often dedicated to the gods and could be seen in many places, for the Gauls respected the rituals and would not dare to steal anything from them. He also states that before his arrival the tribes would go to war 'well-nigh every year, in the sense that they would either make wanton attacks themselves or repelling such'. Strabo described the whole Gallic race as 'war-mad', and it is clear that the knights were a warrior aristocracy. A man's status was judged by the number of warriors he maintained at his own expense and who were personally bound to him by solemn oaths. The strength and fame of their retinues acted as deterrents against anyone inside or outside the tribe from attacking them, or the communities loyal to and protected by them.[25]

Much of the military activity in Gaul seems to have taken the form of raiding, but at times warfare between the tribes could be on a very large scale, as in the struggle between the Aedui and Sequani for control of the trade route along the Rhône-Saône valleys. It is very unlikely that the growth in trade with the Mediterranean world caused the tribes of Gaul to become warlike, but it certainly acted as a spur to war-making. The goods that flooded into Gaul were primarily aimed at the aristocratic market. Wine played an important role in the feasting that bonded chieftain and warrior together, and luxury goods helped to increase a man's status or could provide spectacular gifts for loyal followers. The tribes along the trade routes had best access to such goods, and could also levy tolls on trade, and the bulk of the profits went to the aristocracy, giving them the wealth to support bigger and bigger bands of warriors. Leaders needed not just riches, but a high martial reputation if they were to encourage to join and then retain famous warriors in their train. Successful raiding was one of the best ways to achieve this, and also win plunder, some of which could be given to followers to confirm their loyalty. Individual leaders and whole tribes were willing to use force to control the trade routes. In addition the slaves, which seem to have been traded so freely for wine, had to come from somewhere, encouraging raiding to take captives. An aristocrat with a strong following of warriors might often turn this against enemies of his tribe, but there was also the temptation to use force in a bid for power inside the tribe. Kings had largely disappeared amongst the tribes of central Gaul, and even elsewhere their powers were limited, but the dream of monarchic or tyrannical power still fired the imagination of many powerful leaders. The institutions of the tribe, the magistrates and senatorial council, were not always strong enough to control such men.[26]

In contrast to the Roman legions, Gallic armies were clumsy forces, which rarely had the logistical ability to remain in the field for a long campaign and were difficult for their commanders to manoeuvre. Warriors were individually brave, but, apart from the retinues of great men, rarely drilled or trained collectively, and the emphasis was generally on individual prowess. The semi-professional warriors who followed powerful chieftains were comparatively few in numbers, sufficient for a raiding expedition, but never more than a small inner core in a tribal army, which consisted mainly of all those men able to provide themselves with weapons. The Romans may well have copied mail armour as well as their commonest helmet designs from Gallic originals, but they were able to manufacture them in far greater quantities. Every legionary had a sword, shield, cuirass and helmet, but only the wealthy and some of the semi-professional warriors were likely to have had all of these things. The vast majority of warriors fought without any protection apart from a shield. Swords do seem to have been fairly common, but tended to be longer than the Roman style – itself a copy of a Spanish design – and used more for slashing than thrusting. Most of the tribes raised horses for riding, which were of a smaller size than most modern mounts but of good quality. Gallic cavalry were famous, and the mounted arm of the professional Roman army would subsequently copy many aspects of equipment, training and terminology from them. However, while very effective in a charge, the cavalry of the tribes, which inevitably consisted of the wealthier warriors, often showed little enthusiasm or aptitude for such important roles as patrolling.[27]

Gaul was not in the most stable of conditions when Caesar arrived. The Roman province of Transalpine Gaul was still recovering from the rebellion of the Allobroges, who had received no reward for aiding Cicero in 63 BC and had felt no alternative but to revolt. This had been suppressed by 60 BC, but the on-going struggle between the Aedui and the Sequani was a serious matter, since it affected the security of the province and the continuance of profitable trade. Both tribes were allied to Rome, but also displayed a willingness to seek outside help in winning the conflict. Around 71 BC the Sequani had summoned the Germanic King Ariovistus to bring his warriors to their aid. About ten years later he inflicted a serious defeat on the Aedui, many of whose principal noblemen were killed in the fighting. In return he was granted land on which his followers could settle. Soon afterwards the Aedui were also raided by the Helvetii from what is now Switzerland. Around the same time Diviciacus, a druid who had held the office of Vergobret, came to Rome seeking assistance. The Senate sent a delegation of envoys to the region, but took no direct action. In 59 BC, during Caesar's own consulship, Ariovistus was recognised as both king and a 'friend of the Roman people'. For the moment this diplomatic activity had brought a measure of stability to the frontiers around Transalpine Gaul, but it is worth emphasising that Caesar was entering a dynamic situation. The balance of power between – and often within – the tribes was frequently changing. By no stretch of the imagination were the tribes of Gaul mere victims, passively awaiting the onslaught of Roman imperialism. Yet they were certainly disunited and divided, and these weaknesses would be ruthlessly exploited by Caesar.[28]

X

MIGRANTS AND MERCENARIES: THE FIRST CAMPAIGNS, 58 BC

'At the moment fear of a war in Gaul is the main topic of conversation [in Rome]; for "our brothers" the Aedui have just fought and lost a battle, and the Helvetii are without doubt armed for war and launching raids into our province.' – *Cicero, 15 March 60 BC.*[1]

On 28 March 58 BC a people known as the Helvetii began to gather on the banks of the River Rhône near Lake Geneva. Some 368,000 people were said to be on the move, about a quarter of them men of fighting age, and the remainder women, children and the elderly. They wished to leave their homes in what is now Switzerland and cross to the western coast of Gaul, where they planned to settle on new, more extensive and fertile lands. Their route lead directly through the Roman province of Transalpine Gaul. News had reached Caesar of the impending migration earlier in the month, and immediately prompted him to hasten to his province. Until then he had been waiting just outside Rome, keeping a close eye on the struggles in the Senate and in the Forum. The Helvetii wished to move through Transalpine Gaul, taking the easiest route to their destination. The northernmost frontier of Caesar's great province was under threat, and public opinion would not be kind to a proconsul who dallied outside Rome while there was a crisis in the region placed under his command. After the chances he had taken to secure himself this command, Caesar could not afford failure of any kind. He hurried north, travelling with that phenomenal speed that so often amazed contemporaries. Covering on average 90 miles a day, he was on the Rhône eight days later. A crisis could also be an opportunity.[2]

The migration was not the result of a sudden impulse, but the outcome of years of planning. It had first been conceived by Orgetorix, described by

Caesar as by far the 'noblest and wealthiest' man in the tribe, but he seems to have played upon existing frustrations. The Helvetii were a numerous and martial people who found their homeland increasingly restrictive, hemmed in by mountains, the Roman province beyond the Rhône, and the Rhine to the east. 'With things as they were their freedom to range was restricted, and there were few opportunities of waging war on their neighbours; since they were men who craved war, they were greatly frustrated.'[3] Raiding was endemic in Gaul, and it was the capacity to launch plundering forays with greater ease that the Helvetii desired. However, Caesar claims that Orgetorix had an ulterior motive, believing that uniting the tribe to this purpose would help him to make himself king. The Helvetii, like many of the other tribes, had ceased to be a monarchy and appear to have been ruled by a council of chieftains and by elected leaders or magistrates. Orgetorix had won over many other nobles and evidently possessed considerable power and support, for coins were minted at this time which carried his name in the form ORCIITIRIX. With the approval of the tribal leaders he was sent on a diplomatic mission to visit other tribes and prepare the way for the migration. Finding it easier to deal with individual chieftains rather than magistrates or tribal councils, he won over Casticus of the Sequani and Dumnorix of the Aedui. These two tribes dominated central Gaul, and the Helvetii would pass through or near their territory on the journey to the west. Their support, or even their non-intervention, would make the migration easier and help the Helvetii to establish themselves once they had arrived. Orgetorix encouraged both Casticus and Dumnorix to hope for supreme kingship in their own tribes, most likely promising them support from Helvetian warriors in the aftermath of the migration. Casticus' father had in fact been sole ruler of the Sequani, and been formally acknowledged as a 'friend of the Roman people' by the Senate. Dumnorix was the younger brother of the druid Diviciacus, and had built up a considerable following in the tribe. The three leaders secretly took a solemn oath – always a sinister thing in Roman eyes – binding themselves to aid the others in their enterprises. Dumnorix also married the daughter of Orgetorix, continuing his fondness for marriage alliances – his mother had already been married off to the leading man amongst the Bituriges, his half-sister and other female relatives to various chieftains in the neighbouring tribes. Allied together, the three leaders of what would be the strongest tribes in central Gaul, felt that no one would be able to oppose them.[4]

The preparations of the Helvetii were thorough. Their leaders judged that at least two years – 60 and 59 BC – were needed to make themselves ready to move. Draught cattle were gathered, some apparently bought or taken from their neighbours, and the greatest amount of cereal crops planted to produce a surplus that would feed them on their journey. Worrying reports of the plan came to the notice of the Senate in Rome, no doubt forwarded on by friendly leaders in the tribes as well as the governor of Transalpine Gaul. In 60 BC it was decided to send a delegation to Gaul, including a number of men with experience in the area and family connections amongst the tribes. Contact seems to have been made with the German King Ariovistus, who had been brought into Gaul to aid the Sequani against their rivals, but who had now settled with his warriors and their families on a large tract of tribal land. Otherwise we know little of the Roman delegation's activities, but the situation did soon appear to be turning in Rome's favour. In spite of the diplomatic success of Orgetorix, word reached the other Helvetian nobleman of his wider ambitions and he was placed on trial for aspiring to tyranny. The penalty for this crime was to be burned alive, and Orgetorix decided to intimidate the other leaders. On the day appointed for his trial he arrived accompanied by his warriors, dependants and all tribesmen bound to him by social obligation or debt, which gave him a force of over 10,000 men – perhaps an eighth of the entire military strength of the Helvetii. It was to be a contest between the budding institutions of a state and traditional patterns of aristocratic leadership. No actual trial could occur under such circumstances, but the other leaders were not permanently overawed and soon began to muster a full levy of the tribe with which to crush him once and for all. However, before civil war could actually break out, Orgetorix died amidst rumours of suicide. Preparations for the migration continued in spite of this, and his death did not in any way alter the tribe's determination to go through with its plans. The Romans may not have fully appreciated that the momentum was still there even after the removal of the leader behind the plan. By May 60 BC Cicero felt that the prospect of a major war in Gaul had been averted, much to the displeasure of the consul Metellus Celer, who had been granted Transalpine Gaul as his province.[5]

This is Caesar's explanation for the migration, a product of the tribe's desire for greater opportunity to raid and the personal ambition of Orgetorix. Not all scholars have been willing to accept this at face value and have suggested that he concealed the truth in order to justify his own subsequent actions. They note, for instance, that the *Commentaries* make no mention of Ariovistus, the Germanic king who had fought for the Sequani and subsequently settled in their lands. This leads to the suggestion that the main intention of the Helvetii was to assist the other tribes in defeating Ariovistus and his Germans. In Caesar's own consulship the German leader was named a 'friend of the Roman people' by the Senate and those fond of conspiracies suggest that he needed the neutrality or even complicity of Ariovistus to deal with the Helvetii in 58 BC. Once they had been defeated, he cynically turned on the German and drove him from Gaul. In this version, Caesar did not want the Helvetii to evict Ariovistus and so deny him the excuse for intervention in Gaul.[6]

None of this is convincing, for it is mainly reliant on hindsight. In the first place it is inherently unlikely that Caesar could have got away with such a massive distortion of the facts in his account, given that this was subject to hostile – and often informed – criticism. It is also unlikely that Rome would have viewed the expulsion of Ariovistus by the Helvetii entirely favourably. Their province of Transalpine Gaul was at present bordered by the Aedui and Sequani, both of whom had allied status. Ariovistus had recently been brought into the system. The province itself had just suffered a major rebellion on the part of the Allobroges and ideally required a period of stability if trade and revenue were not to suffer. The arrival of a strong tribe threatened to disturb this existing network of alliances. There was also the question of what would happen to the Helvetii's own homeland once they left. If the abandoned land were then settled by newcomers, perhaps from one of the German tribes, then this might pose a new threat to the Roman province. On the whole the Romans were suspicious of the movements of peoples, so common in Iron Age Europe, and sought to prevent these from occurring in the lands near to their own provinces. Nor was it in their interest for the tribes of Gaul to unite independently of Rome.

Therefore Caesar would have had ample justification for intervention even if the Helvetii had intended to fight Ariovistus, and did not need to conceal this. On balance, his own account is far more plausible. Casticus and Dumnorix clearly both believed that they would gain from the arrival of the migrants, and doubtless expected support from Orgetorix against all their opponents, whether foreign or within their own tribe. Those leaders of the Sequani who had invited Ariovistus into Gaul in the first place, and the many chieftains who would appeal to Caesar for aid over the coming years, acted with the same motives. Association with a strong external force boosted a chieftain's prestige, and might well be converted into direct military assistance. It is misleading to speak of pro- or anti-Roman factions within the tribes – or for that matter pro- or anti-German or Helvetian groups. Each individual leader sought whatever aid he believed would be of most benefit to him, and all were engaged in the struggle for dominance within the tribe. Some leaders, and indeed the ruling councils of some tribes, decided that they were better off allied to Caesar and Rome, while other men and peoples who were their rivals acted differently.[7]

Yet in the spring of 58 BC there is every sign that Caesar was wrong-footed by the Helvetii. Perhaps he had been surprised by the timing of the migration, or maybe its sheer scale. He had four legions at his command, but only one of these was in Transalpine Gaul. The remaining three were camped near Aquileia on the border of Cisalpine Gaul nearest to Illyricum. It is not known who stationed the troops there, but even if it had not been Caesar, then he had made no effort to alter this disposition. Even when he hastened to the Rhône he made no effort to send new orders to these troops. It is hard to avoid the conclusion that he was still thinking very much in terms of a Balkan campaign. Perhaps it was only when he arrived near Geneva that he appreciated the full scale of the problem. The Helvetii and the allied clans who joined them in the migration had piled their possessions into wagons and set off with great purpose. Behind them they left the smouldering ruins of their towns and villages, deliberately put to the torch to discourage anyone from wavering if the journey became difficult. Caesar may have exaggerated when he claimed that every single settlement was burned, and indeed in the implication that not a single tribesman remained behind, but the upheaval was clearly a massive one.

The figure of 368,000 migrants was said by Caesar to have been taken from captured records that the Helvetii themselves had made using Greek characters – Gallo-Greek inscriptions using the Celtic language but Greek alphabet are fairly common finds from southern Gaul and attest to the long presence and influence of Massilia. Any numbers found in an ancient text must always be treated with a degree of caution, since it is so easy for them to become distorted over the centuries as manuscripts were copied and recopied. In cases of this sort, the Roman desire to quantify military victory in the numbers of enemies killed and cities captured encouraged deliberate exaggeration. It is certainly a very high figure, suggesting a density of population considerably higher than would be expected, even in a region so overcrowded as to produce a migration. Yet in the end we know so little about ancient levels of population that it is unwise to be too dogmatic, and if we reject Caesar's figure then we have nothing with which to replace it. Modern suggestions of more 'plausible' totals can never be anything more than conjectural. In the end, even if Caesar did exaggerate, or was genuinely mistaken, a substantial number of people and animals were on the move, probably in many separate parties rather than one immensely long column, which would have presented huge practical and logistical problems. However, at certain points, such as river crossings and mountain passes, there would have been a tendency for the different groups to cluster closer to each other.[8]

Caesar is unlikely to have known precisely how many migrants were waiting to cross the river into his province, but they certainly far outnumbered the single legion he had at his disposal. One of his first orders instructed the legionaries to break down the bridge crossing the river at Geneva. He also levied as many troops as he could find in the province, the tribes there providing him with contingents of cavalry. Soon after his arrival he was visited by a delegation of Helvetian leaders who asked permission for their people to move through the Roman province, promising that they would not plunder as they went. Caesar was unwilling to grant the request. In the *Commentaries* he takes this opportunity to remind his audience of a battle some fifty years earlier, when one of the clans of the Helvetii had defeated a Roman army. From a Roman viewpoint this had been an unprovoked attack, made worse when the survivors were forced to undergo the humiliation of passing under a yoke of spears, symbolising their loss of warrior status. This had been in 107 BC, in the midst of a series of disasters inflicted on Roman armies by the Cimbri and Teutones. Caesar wished to revive the fear of those years – something which was still just within living memory – amongst his Roman audience. They could then be reassured that Marius' nephew was there to defend them.

Yet at the beginning Caesar did not have the means to do this. Instead he played for time, telling the Helvetian representatives that he would consider the matter, and inform them of his decision if they returned on the Ides – the 13th – of April, which was probably in one or two weeks time. During the interval he set the legion to constructing a line of defences running along the Roman bank of the Rhône from Lake Geneva to the edge of the Jura Mountains. It was the first of many engineering feats that his army would perform and was swiftly accomplished. For 19 Roman miles (each somewhat shorter than the modern mile at 1,618½ yards or 1.48 km) they raised an earth rampart some 16 feet high. This was strengthened at key points where the river could be forded by forts garrisoned by detachments of the legion and the other troops Caesar had raised. It is possible that the rampart was not absolutely continuous, having gaps whenever natural features ensured that it was impossible to cross, but there is insufficient evidence to confim this suggestion. Such a line was not a novel concept for a Roman army in this period. Crassus had made use of a similar fortified barrier in the campaign against Spartacus, and Pompey had done the same in the Mithridatic War. Such lines were practical, presenting an obstacle that would at the very least slow down an enemy, but also were a strong visible statement of intent and determination.[9]

When the Helvetii returned for Caesar's decision, he bluntly informed them that 'according to the custom and precedent of the Roman People, he could not permit anyone to journey through the province, and that he would stop them if they tried to force their way through'.[10] The new fortifications were there to demonstrate that he meant what he said. However, it was difficult for such a great mass of people suddenly to change direction and purpose. The period of waiting by the river had also probably been very frustrating and many of the Helvetii were determined to keep going, especially after the years of preparation and the willing destruction of their old homes. Small groups began to cross the Rhône, either using the fords or rigging up rafts to carry themselves, their animals and vehicles. It is possible that these were deliberate probes sent by the chieftains to test the strength of Caesar's defences, but more likely that they reflected the loose central authority and individual independence that seems to have been characteristic of many of the tribes of Gaul. They were certainly not full-fledged assaults on the line of fortifications. Most of the crossings took place under cover of darkness, but a few parties were bold enough to risk the attempt in daylight. None succeeded, for Caesar's men were able to concentrate and meet each group in turn, overwhelming many of them with missiles as they struggled to cross. Eventually the Helvetii admitted defeat, but by this time some of their leaders had decided on another course, taking the alternative, more difficult route out of their lands. This meant taking the passes through the Jura Mountains into the lands of the Sequani. It would not have been practical if the latter had decided to resist them, but the tribe was persuaded by Dumnorix the Aeduan to let the Helvetii through. He was presumably able to do this through his own reputation and some of his many marriage connections with powerful men. Orgetorix was dead, but it would still be useful for Dumnorix to be able to call on the support of the powerful Helvetii once they were established in their own lands. Even before they began to lumber off in this new direction, Caesar received reports of their plans.[11]

'A NEW WAR'

It was probably at this point that Caesar finally resolved on a full campaign in Gaul against the Helvetii. The reason he gave in the *Commentaries* was that the Helvetii planned to settle 'on the borders of the Santones, who lived not far away from the borders of the Tolosates, a tribe within the province. He understood that if this occurred, it would put the province in great danger, with many warriors, hostile to the Roman people, living close by a region which produced a rich harvest of grain, but was undefended.' His own recent actions had ensured the hostility of the Helvetii, but from a Roman standpoint his reasoning was sound. As we have seen, at the very least the incursion of the new settlers would have upset the existing balance system where a combination of Roman diplomacy and military strength had ensured the security of the province. Leaving his senior legate Labienus in charge of the defences on the Rhône – probably another indication that the Helvetii were travelling in lots of separate groups, and that it took time for such a sprawling mass of people, animals and vehicles to move off in a new direction – Caesar hastened to Aquileia and his main army. Two new legions, the *Eleventh* and *Twelfth*, were enrolled to add to the three already stationed there and the one left behind on the Rhône.

The *Commentaries* give the impression that this was only done on Caesar's arrival, but the practicalities of recruitment and organisation make it more likely that he had already given the order for this some time before. The troops may originally have been intended to strengthen the army for operations in the Balkans, but the immediate threat of the Helvetii provided a better pretext for his audience. He had no authority to raise new legions, for only the Senate was supposed to instruct a governor to do this, but lack of specific power had never stopped Caesar in the past. As a youth and a private citizen he had raised allied troops to combat the pirates and oppose the Pontic invasion of Asia, while he had also raised ten cohorts – equivalent in numbers to a legion – during his term as propraetor in Spain. Never doubting that he knew what was in the interest of Rome and the provinces, Caesar simply acted and then trusted in his own ability to make things work. Since it had not authorised their existence, the Senate would not provide money from the Treasury to pay and supply the new legions, which meant that the proconsul would have to find the funds to do this from the revenue he raised in his province and any profits to come from victories. The bulk of the soldiers in the new formations were almost certainly from Cisalpine Gaul and so not actually Roman citizens and therefore legally ineligible for service in a legion. In the past Caesar had championed the desire of the population of the region for enfranchisement, and as governor he consistently treated them as if they were in fact citizens. This was the first major example of this deliberate policy.[12]

Soon, Caesar was ready to lead all five legions back to Transalpine Gaul. The quickest route was through the Alps, which although largely surrounded by Roman provinces was still unconquered. In a week the Roman column crossed the mountains, beating off successive ambushes from the fiercely independent tribes who resented this incursion and doubtless also saw the welcome opportunity for gaining some plunder. It was a harsh introduction to campaigning for the raw recruits, but the march seems to have been made without serious loss. Once over the mountains Caesar moved into the territory of the Allobroges, joining up with the troops he had left in the province. He now had six legions at his disposal, with a total of something like 25,000–30,000 men, and a force of allied cavalry that would soon muster about 4,000 men, along with some light infantry. Added to this were the slaves who accompanied each legion to care for the baggage train, doubtless some also owned by the officers, and quite possibly also some camp followers. All of these needed to be fed, as did the thousands of cavalry mounts and draught and pack animals. Keeping his army supplied has always been one of the first concerns of any army commander. The operations against the Helvetii had developed so unexpectedly that Caesar had had little opportunity to prepare for this task by massing all that he needed in conveniently placed supply dumps in Transalpine Gaul. The main force is unlikely to have brought substantial supplies of food with it in its rapid march from Aquileia. It was still only spring, and the harvest would not become available for some months – Caesar notes in the *Commentaries* that it occurred late in these northern climes – so that the army could not expect to gather too much of what it needed from the land it marched through. Therefore messages went to Rome's allies, particularly the large and powerful Aedui, to gather stocks of grain and make them available for his troops.

In the meantime the Helvetii had crossed through the Pas de l'Ecluse into the lands of the Sequani and were entering the borderland of the Aedui. Representatives of the tribe came to Caesar complaining of plundering attacks by the migrants. 'The Aedui had always deserved well and that it is not right for our lands to be devastated, our children carried off into bondage, and our towns to be sacked almost under the eyes of a Roman army.' Similar complaints also came in from the Ambarri, a tribe allied to the Aedui, and the Allobroges, who had not that long before rebelled and been defeated. It is unknown whether or not the leaders of the Helvetii had consciously decided to launch these plundering attacks. Even if they had not, it would have been extremely difficult to control such a large and disparate group broken up into many individual parties. Given the delays imposed on their journey, some of the migrants may have been running short of supplies. Equally the hostility could have begun with the local peoples, nervous of the incursion of so many strangers. That violence resulted was unsurprising, but the need to defend or gain revenge for attacks on an ally was for the Romans a classic justification for aggressive warfare. It should also be said that this made practical sense. If Rome was unwilling or unable to guard its friends, then why should any tribe, especially the so recently discontented Allobroges, feel that it was worth maintaining the alliance? As consul, Caesar had passed a law regulating the behaviour of provincial governors and restricting their freedom to lead their army outside their province. In the *Commentaries* he demonstrated that it was entirely right for him to do just that.[13]

Caesar caught up with the migrants near the Saône. For twenty days the tribesmen had been ferrying themselves across the river on rafts and small boats lashed together, and three-quarters of them were already on the far bank. It was another indication that we should not think of the Helvetii as moving in one ordered column, but in many separate groups spread over the landscape and only bunching when the path became narrow. Still on the same side of the river as the Romans were the Tigurini, the clan that had been responsible for the humiliating defeat of the Romans in 107 BC. Caesar makes sure that he reminds his readers of this defeat once again, and adds that he had a personal stake in avenging it, since the grandfather of his father-in-law Calpurnius Piso had died in the battle. After his scouts had reported this to Caesar, he decided on a surprise attack, leading his army out before dawn. The result was not a battle, but a massacre, as the Romans fell upon the scattered and unsuspecting groups of tribesmen and their families. Many were killed and the rest dispersed, abandoning their wagons and possessions. The Romans then bridged the Saône and crossed it in a single day.[14]

As the Roman army closed with the rest of the Helvetii, their chieftains sent another delegation to the proconsul. To further emphasise the connection with 107 BC, Caesar claims that it was headed by the same man who had been their war-leader in that year, a certain Divico, who by this time must have been very elderly. The tribe offered to settle on whatever land Caesar suggested and promised to keep the peace with Rome. Yet they also showed that they were not dismayed by the surprise attack on the

Tigurini, and warned the Romans not to despise their military strength, reminding them of the battle half a century before. They had learnt 'from their parents and ancestors, to win battles through courage, not by guile or stealth'.[15] A Roman audience would have seen this as dangerous pride which refused to acknowledge and submit to Roman might. Caesar told them that the defeat of Cassius' army in 107 BC had only occurred because the Helvetii had attacked without warning, when they were not even at war with the Romans. Apart from this old wrong, he reminded them of their recent attacks on Rome's allies. He advised them against overconfidence, declaring that the immortal gods often granted short spells of success to criminals before they met with terrible punishment. (Caesar was *Pontifex Maximus*, yet this is one of very few references to the gods in his writings.) Only if they gave him hostages for their good behaviour and made restitution to the Aedui and others who had suffered from their depredations would he be willing to grant them peace. Retorting that the Helvetii 'took, but never gave' hostages, Divico and his delegation stormed off. It is difficult to see how Caesar could reasonably have granted the request for land, since Gaul was already densely inhabited. He had no right to allocate them any territory outside his own province, and it would have been unthinkable to settle them inside. Wherever they went the Helvetii would inevitably cause disruption and this was not in the interest of the Romans.[16]

The convoys of the Helvetii moved onwards, and Caesar followed them, sending his 4,000 cavalry out in advance. Amongst them was a sizeable force of Aedui led by Dumnorix, the same chieftain who had allied with Orgetorix and then aided the Helvetii. Advancing too carelessly, the allied cavalry were ambushed and beaten by a force of Helvetian cavalry a fraction of their size. The rout began with Dumnorix and the Aedui. Encouraged by this easy success, the enemy rearguard started to move more slowly and offered to fight more often. Caesar was unwilling to risk too many skirmishes with them, but kept the enemy under observation and stopped any parties from breaking away and plundering the landscape. His army followed the Helvetii, shadowing their every move so that his advance guard was never more than 5 or 6 miles from their rearguard. By this time he was some distance out of his province, and growing more worried about the supply situation. When he was near the Saône this had been less of a problem as he had been able to have food brought to him in the many barges plying this trade route. However, the Helvetii had moved away from the river, and so he had had to do the same. The Aedui had promised him grain – he was after all fighting against an enemy who had invaded and plundered their lands – but as yet nothing had arrived and repeated requests brought no results, in spite of frequent promises that it was on the way. In a few days time the soldiers were due to be issued with grain that Caesar did not at present possess. For short periods of time, soldiers on campaign have sometimes been persuaded to keep going on minimal rations, but usually only strong leadership made this possible. Caesar and his men were still relative strangers, while one-third of the army was very inexperienced.[17]

Eager to avert a disaster, Caesar summoned the leading men of the Aedui, headed by the druid Diviciacus and Liscus, the man who currently held the post of Vergobret, the annually elected supreme magistrate of the tribe. Berated by Caesar over their failure to fulfil their obligations to an army that was fighting to protect them, Liscus blamed powerful men within the tribe who had deliberately held up the collection and transport of the grain, claiming that they thought it better to be dominated by their fellow Gauls the Helvetii, rather than the Romans. These chieftains were passing information to the enemy and intimidating anyone who dared to oppose them. Liscus had named no names, but Caesar was clearly already suspicious about Dumnorix and guessed that he was the man behind this. He dismissed the other chieftains and spoke privately with the Vergobret, who was now willing to talk more freely and readily confirmed the proconsul's suspicions. Dumnorix was aiming at kingship – coins dating to this period and carrying the name DUBNOREIX were probably minted by him – backed by a large force of warriors maintained with the profits from controlling the tolls on trade along the Saône. His complicity with the Helvetii was now fully revealed and Caesar felt that he had sufficient evidence to warrant stern punishment, but was hesitant since he valued the loyalty of Diviciacus. Therefore, he summoned the druid to an even more closed conference in his headquarters tent. He dismissed the interpreters he normally used and relied on Caius Valerius Procillus, an aristocrat from Transalpine Gaul whose father had won Roman citizenship for the family. Caesar, who had spent enough time in the courts at Rome, presented the facts and the case against Dumnorix, and suggested that either his brother or the Aedui needed to try him for these offences. Diviciacus told how his younger brother had depended on him for his success in public life, but had since turned against him as a rival. Some of Dumnorix's frustration is understandable, for the druid had recently held the office of Vergobret and the rule was that no other member of his family could win the post during his lifetime. Nevertheless, Diviciacus pleaded with Caesar not to punish his ambitious sibling, in part through affection, but mainly because he thought that it would be very damaging to him personally if he was seen to back the Romans against his own brother. His appeal was tearful and persistent. Dumnorix was summoned to the tent and in front of his brother presented with his crimes. The proconsul informed him that he was to be given another opportunity for the sake of his older brother, but that in future he must avoid even the hint of suspicion. Such face-to-face diplomacy was to be a common feature of Caesar's time in Gaul. As in Roman public life, much of what a governor did was at a very personal level. Caesar was famous at Rome for his readiness to forgive and his willingness to do favours. In Gaul he would sometimes follow the same principles. Yet nowhere was he ever naively trusting. After the meeting he gave orders that Dumnorix be kept under constant observation and everything he did reported to him.[18]

Although the hindrance to the grain supply had been removed, it was not an instant solution to his problems, and it would still take time for the Aedui to bring the grain to his army. Caesar needed to force a quick outcome to the campaign, and on the same day as he had held these meetings he believed that he had spotted the opportunity. His scouting patrols came back to report that the Helvetii had camped some 8 Roman miles away, next to some high ground. Caesar sent out another patrol to carry out a detailed reconnaissance of the position, looking in particular at how readily the slopes of the hill might be climbed from each side, especially that furthest from the enemy. This party returned to report that the ascent was straightforward. Caesar decided to launch a full-scale attack on the enemy camp, hoping to achieve the same sort of surprise he had gained against the Tigurini. Labienus was given command of two legions – persumably two of the experienced ones – and would march out in the small hours of the morning to seize the hill. Two hours later Caesar would lead out the rest of the army and march the 8 miles to the enemy camp. When Labienus saw him beginning his assault, he was to attack with his legion from the high ground. Both forces were to follow the same route for most of the way, being guided by men who had taken part in the previous day's patrol and seen the ground in daylight.

It was a bold plan, but a perfectly feasible one, using a method of preparation that in its essence would not be unfamiliar to a modern army. Caesar had plenty of experience of raids and surprise attacks, rather more than he had of pitched battles, for warfare in the Spanish Peninsula tended to be of this type. Marius had similarly managed to secrete a strong detachment of men in dead ground behind the Teutones at Aquae Sextiae in 102 BC. Operations at night have always been risky, for the potential for confusion and units getting lost is always there. In this case things began very smoothly. Labienus moved out and disappeared into the darkness. After the appointed interval Caesar followed with the main force. The cavalry led the column, and sent out patrols to screen the advance. These scouts were placed under the command of one Publius Considius, an experienced officer with a fine military reputation. He had served under Sulla and Crassus and was therefore probably at least in his forties. Caesar does not give his rank but he was probably a tribune or prefect, although it has sometimes been suggested that he was a centurion. It is possible that he was a relation of the senator Considius, who the year before had declared that, unlike many others, he was too old to worry about danger (see p.177).[19]

By dawn the main force was only a mile and a half from the enemy camp, and Labienus was waiting in position, but was out of contact with Caesar. The Helvetii, like many tribal armies somewhat careless in scouting, were completely oblivious to the presence of either force. At this point Considius galloped in to report that the hill was not in fact held by the Romans, but by the Gauls. He was absolutely positive about this, saying that he had clearly seen their weaponry, crests and insignia. The news meant that Labienus had either got lost and never reached his destination or that he had been defeated. In either case the Helvetii were obviously well prepared and waiting for them. Caesar immediately halted the column. He had four legions, two of which were most likely the raw *Eleventh* and *Twelfth*. His men were also tired after the night march, still doubtless fresh enough to attack surprised and scattered opponents encumbered by baggage and families, but not necessarily up to a long drawn-out pitched battle. To attack under these circumstances would have meant fighting at a serious numerical disadvantage on ground chosen by the enemy. He ordered the column to withdraw to a nearby ridge and there formed them into a battle line to await any attack. Time passed. The Helvetii roused themselves and set off to continue their journey, still completely unaware that the shadowing Roman army had now come so close and had divided. Labienus followed his orders to the letter, not engaging until he saw Caesar's men beginning their attack. In any case, there was little that he could have done with just two legions at his disposal. It was only late in the day that scouts from the main force established contact with Labienus' detachment and confirmed that they, and not the enemy, held the key position. In what was left of the day Caesar took the army after the Helvetii, setting camp that night 3 miles away from them.[20]

It had been an embarrassing failure, but could so easily have proved disastrous if the Helvetii had fully appreciated the situation and turned on either section of the Roman army. Labienus' men had been especially vulnerable on the hill. Caesar had learned that he could trust the judgement and sense of his senior legate, but not that of other officers, however great their reputation. It was a lesson in the risks inherent in complex operations and the role in warfare played by chance. Caesar makes no mention of whether or not he punished Considius for losing his head, but the publication of the *Commentaries* ensured that his shame was widely known. In his account Caesar passed the blame for the failure onto his subordinate. This was not entirely unreasonable, but his soldiers may not have seen it that way at the time. Caesar had given the orders, and it was he who had halted the main force on a false report and taken a very long time before checking its accuracy. During this period their comrades in the two legions with Labienus had been left very much out on a limb. The pursuit of the Helvetii continued, but the situation was not good. The wheat ration was due for issue in two days, but there were no supplies for this. On the following morning Caesar decided that things could not continue as they were and gave orders to abandon their cautious chase of the Helvetii for the moment. The army turned away and marched to Bibracte, some 18 miles away. He planned to replenish his supplies there and then move against the Helvetii once more. Given the latter's plodding progress, it should not prove too difficult to catch up with them again.[21]

With hindsight this proved the turning point in the campaign. Some warriors serving amongst Caesar's Gaulish allies quickly deserted and rode over to the enemy, reporting the Roman withdrawal. The Helvetii decided to pursue, presumably interpreting the move as a sign of weakness. Caesar also wondered if they hoped to cut him off from Bibracte and his supplies. The Roman rearguard was soon under attack. Caesar reinforced it with all of his cavalry and used them to cover the deployment of his army. Occupying a nearby hill, he placed the experienced *Seventh*, *Eighth*, *Ninth* and *Tenth* legions in the main line. If he followed his later practice, then the *Tenth* was probably in the place of honour on the right of the line. Each legion was deployed in the normal formation, the triple line (*triplex acies*) with four cohorts in the front line, and three each in the second and third. The legionaries laid down their packs – normally carried suspended from a staff that was then rested on the shoulder – so that they could fight unencumbered. Shields were removed from their protective leather covers to expose the insignia of each unit, and crests fixed to helmets. Behind them, further up the slope, he stationed the inexperienced *Eleventh* and *Twelfth* legions along with his auxiliary infantry. They were to guard the packs and the baggage train, and began to dig out a small trench and rampart to surround them, but it is very unlikely that there was time to construct a fully fledged marching camp of the type normally built by any Roman army at the end of a day's march. It was important for the soldiers in the battle line to know that their possessions were safe, and clearly Caesar was still reluctant to trust these inexperienced soldiers. Probably the four experienced legions formed a line covering most of the slope, but as with most of Caesar's battles it has proved impossible to locate the site of this encounter, so that we cannot talk about the topography with any certainty. Caesar does tell us that the slope ensured that the two legions and the auxiliaries were clearly visible to the enemy, covering the hillside in men and creating a strong impression of the Romans' numerical strength.

The deployment of the army took time – probably several hours – and was covered by the cavalry, but the Helvetii also needed a good deal of time to advance and prepare themselves for battle. They had been travelling for some weeks now, and had through necessity developed a degree of co-ordination, but even so it was a major task concentrating enough of their warriors in one place to overcome the Romans. With the fighting men came their families and dependants, along with the baggage, and the Helvetii formed the wagons into a rough laager behind their line. Gradually their army began to form up, but the fighting would begin before some contingents had arrived. Caesar does not supply any figure for the number of warriors he faced at the start of the battle, but the willingness of the Helvetii to attack would suggest that the two sides had at the very least a rough parity of numbers – that is unless the tribesmen were utterly disdainful of the Romans' fighting prowess. Long delays before a battle were common in this period, which inevitably must have been a nervous time as men had little to do save wait. Caesar decided that a grand gesture was called for and very openly dismounted and sent his own horse to the rear, along with those of all his senior officers, in order to 'make the danger equal for all, and remove the temptation of flight'. Catiline had done the same thing in 62 BC before the battle when his outnumbered followers had been cornered by an army loyal to the Senate. The gladiator Spartacus had gone a step further in his last battle, slitting the throat of the expensive horse he had captured from a Roman general in an earlier encounter. A general on foot was a lot less mobile and therefore could see less of the battle as it developed, so Caesar had sacrificed a number of practical advantages to encourage the men in this way. He would never again do this in any of his later battles, and it does suggest that he was aware that his legionaries did not yet know him that

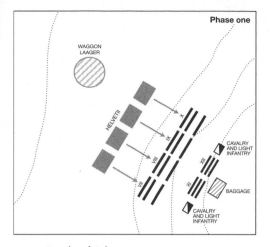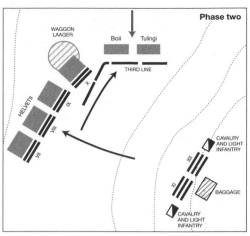

Battle of Bibracte

well, and that the campaign had not been going especially well in the last few days. Perhaps it was also an indication that he was not yet entirely sure of himself as a commander. For further encouragement he addressed the men, probably walking along and talking to each cohort in turn since it is unlikely that all four legions could have heard him at the same time.[22]

The battle began in the middle of the afternoon, when the Helvetii advanced up the slope against the Roman line. They came on in good order, keeping a close formation. Armies tried to intimidate their opponents before they reached them, frightening them with their battle cries, the noise of their trumpets and their ferocious appearance. It was not uncommon for one side to be so overawed that they would break and flee before ever a blow had been struck. This was one of the main reasons why it would have been risky to expose the recently raised legions to the pressure of battle. In this case, the experienced legionaries waited, their normal tactic in this period was to keep silent, intimidating the enemy by their apparent calmness. When the Helvetii came close – probably within 10–15 yards – the legions threw their *pila*, the heavy javelins punching through shields and in some cases even pinning two overlapping shields together. Some warriors were killed or wounded, others forced to drop their encumbered shields. The momentum had gone from the attack and the Romans followed up their advantage by cheering, drawing their swords and then charging into contact. They had the advantage of ground and the enthusiasm and impetus of the charge, but even so the Helvetii fought on for some time before they began to give way and retreated down into the plain. The Romans followed, but seem to have done so in an orderly manner and soon lost contact with the fugitives, who ran back to the high ground on the other side of the valley, about a mile away. However, at this point the Romans faced a new threat, as a fresh contingent of 15,000 warriors arrived on their open right flank. These were the Boii and the Tulingi, two allied peoples who had been further back in the Helvetian column. It is unlikely that this was a planned manoeuvre and that the first attack had been no more than a feint to draw the Romans down onto the level ground – it was probably just a happy coincidence for the Helvetii. A tribal army – even a Hellenistic army where the doctrine was to mass the infantry in a single dense line without significant reserves – would have been in serious trouble in this situation, in danger of its whole line being rolled up by the fresh enemy. In contrast the Roman military system emphasised the importance of a reserve, normally keeping at least two-thirds of their force back from the fighting line at the start of a battle. The third line of cohorts was peeled away and formed into a new line to face the Boii and Tulingi. The first and second lines dealt with the Helvetii, who had rallied at the appearance of their allies and returned to the fray. The *Eleventh* and *Twelfth* do not seem to have been brought up from the extra reserve Caesar had in this battle and appear to have remained mere observers of the action.[23]

The battle was hard-fought and continued until well after nightfall, but after the initial shock of the arrival of these new forces, the Romans made steady headway. The struggle for the wagon laager was especially bitter, as the warriors fought to defend their possessions and families. Caesar makes no mention in his account of what he did during the battle, it is simply 'the Romans' who wheeled and formed fighting lines facing in two directions. Presumably he was doing what every Roman commander should do, staying close behind the fighting line, encouraging the men and committing reserve troops as necessary. In the end the victory was complete, but the Roman losses were comparatively heavy and the army was to remain where it was for three days to look after the wounded and bury the dead. Numbers of prisoners had been taken, including both a son and daughter of Orgetorix, but Caesar says that 130,000 people escaped from the battle and fled north east towards the territory of the Lingones. In the circumstances it must have been hard for him to make an accurate count, but clearly sizeable numbers of the migrants survived the battle. Many may not have reached it at all, but those who had been involved had lost most of the baggage. Caesar did not pursue immediately. He had still not sorted out his supply situation, and the care he showed for his casualties was important in adding to the growing trust between army and commander. Instead he sent messages to the chieftains of the Lingones, ordering them not to aid the Helvetii, unless they wanted to be treated as enemies.

After three days he set out after the enemy, but was soon met by a delegation offering to surrender. Caesar instructed them to tell the tribesmen to halt and wait for him to reach them and give a decision. That they did so was an indication that they were not simply playing for time. When Caesar arrived he demanded and received hostages, as well as getting the Helvetii to return the slaves who had fled to or been taken by them during their migration. The warriors were also disarmed. On the first night some 6,000 men from one clan broke away from the camp, heading eastwards towards the Rhine. Caesar sent messengers to the communities in their path with the same stark warning as he had given to the Lingones. The fugitives were brought back and sold into slavery, being denied the terms that he extended to everyone else. The Helvetii and most of their allies were then ordered to return to their homelands and settle there once more. Instructions were sent to the Allobroges in his province to supply the returning tribes with grain until they had re-established themselves once more, rebuilding their burnt settlements and cultivating their farms again. After an appeal from the Aedui, Caesar allowed them to settle the Boii on lands within their tribal territory. Stability was restored to the lands surrounding Transalpine Gaul, but the cost in human lives had been very high. In conclusion, Caesar states that of the 368,000 people listed in the records captured from the Helvetii, only some 110,000 returned home; the 32,000 Boii – minus their casualties from the battle – settled in Gaul, while 6,000 fugitives were sold into slavery, leaving a massive deficit of 220,000. As always we cannot know how accurate these figures were, and presumably very large numbers of people had simply dispersed in the face of Roman attacks, just as the Tigurini had done at the Saône. Nevertheless, many – perhaps tens of thousands – must have been killed, but we should not let the modern horror at such huge loss of life blind us to the response of Caesar's Roman audience to such statistics. For them, a dangerous movement of hostile peoples had been stopped and their province, which was not far from Italy itself, secured for the future. In the *Commentaries* Caesar often makes use of the verb *parcere* which meant 'to pacify' and was used for the defeat of any people, anywhere, who had refused when challenged to submit to Roman authority. *Pax* or 'peace' was the outcome of a Roman victory. From the Roman perspective, peace had returned to the northern frontier.[24]

THE FRIEND OF THE ROMAN PEOPLE

By this time it was summer. Several months of the campaigning season remained, but there would not have been enough time to shift the forces back to the Balkan frontier and begin operations there. Caesar had already won a great victory, but was hungry for more and reluctant to stand idle even for a short time. He was soon presented with an opportunity for a further military adventure. Delegations had come in from most of the Gallic/Celtic tribes of central Gaul congratulating him on his defeat of the Helvetii. The praise may in part have been genuine, but it was obviously wise to establish good relations with any new power that had moved into the region. These envoys requested permission to summon a meeting of all the tribes at which they could meet him and present petitions. In another tearful scene, chieftains threw themselves at the proconsul's feet and, with the druid Diviciacus as their spokesman, begged Caesar to protect them from the German King Ariovistus. They claimed that the man who had been invited in to aid the Sequani had since then brought in and settled 120,000 of his people on their lands and taken hostages from all the tribes. They complained of his tyranny, calling him a 'wild, uncontrolled barbarian'. More Germans were said to be coming to join their war-leader and Caesar was asked 'to defend the whole of Gaul from the onslaught of Ariovistus'. Representatives from the Sequani silently supported the plea, Diviciacus answering Caesar's enquiry by saying that they were too afraid to speak lest word be carried to the Germans. Caesar then assured the gathered chieftains that he would take care of the matter and use his *auctoritas* to persuade Ariovistus to moderate his behaviour. Privately he took the matter very seriously, feeling that he must support the Aedui because of their long and loyal alliance with Rome. Apart from that, he also claims that he was concerned about the Germans getting into the habit of migrating across the Rhine, lest this happen too frequently and cause folk movements on the scale of the migrations of the Cimbri and Teutones.[25]

Envoys were sent to Ariovistus asking him to meet with Caesar at some point midway between them. The king declined, saying that Caesar must come to him if he wanted to talk, and also asking why the Roman felt he needed to intervene in this part of Gaul. In response Caesar sent a new message, reminding the king of the obligation he ought to feel because during his own consulship the Roman people had acknowledged him as 'king and friend'. This time the demands were clearly expressed. Ariovistus was not to bring any more Germans across the Rhine to settle in Gaul. Secondly, he must restore the hostages to the Aedui and refrain in future from raiding or threatening them. Compliance would ensure continued good relations with Rome, but refusal would force Caesar to take firm steps to safeguard the Aedui and other allies of the Republic. Ariovistus' reply showed a similar unwillingness to compromise. He was a conqueror and, just like the Romans, saw no reason to be dictated to by others in his treatment of the conquered. The Romans were free to run their provinces as they wished and he claimed the same right in the lands he and his warriors had taken. He had beaten the Aedui, and their hostages had nothing to fear from him as long as the tribe delivered their annual tribute to him. He and his warriors had never been defeated since they came to Gaul and feared no enemy. Having established Ariovistus' overweening pride to his audience, Caesar claims that within an hour of receiving this message, envoys came from the Aedui reporting that their lands had been raided by the Germans. In addition, the Treveri from further north sent word that huge numbers of Seubi – the Germanic people to which Ariovistus and his men belonged – were at the Rhine and trying to cross into Gaul. There were supposed to be one hundred clans making this attempt, a migration that would have dwarfed that of the Helvetii.[26]

Caesar decided to act, but this time made sure that his grain supply was secure before he began to move. He drove the army on at a quick pace, for they were no longer following the sluggish Helvetii, and after three days received a message informing him that Ariovistus and the German army were advancing on Vesontio (modern Besançon), the main town of the Sequani. Clearly by this time the tribe had broken with its former ally. As the tribal centre it was an important place, sited in a naturally strong position and with large food stores that would be very useful for any army. Not willing for this to fall into enemy hands Caesar drove his men on, force-marching both day and night with only brief rests until he reached the town, into which he put a garrison. With the race won, he gave the troops several days of rest to recover from their exertions, and also to allow his supplies to catch up. Discontent has always tended to flourish more when armies have time on their hands, rather than when they are busy. Rumours were rife in the town and:

> a panic spread after conversations with the Gauls and the traders, who said that the Germans were a race of huge stature, incredible courage and skill with weapons – they claimed that often when they met them they had not been able to sustain even their glance and keen expressions. Then very suddenly a great panic seized the entire army, dismaying the

minds and spirits of all ranks. The thing started with the military tribunes and prefects, and the rest of the men lacking military experience who had followed Caesar from the City in an effort to win his friendship: some put forward some excuse obliging them to depart, others asked permission to leave, and a few were shamed into staying . . . they were unable to conceal their depression, or at times hide their tears; they cowered in their tents to bemoan their fates, or gathered with friends to lament the common danger. Throughout the entire camp men started drawing up their wills. With these voices of despair, even men with long experience of campaigning, soldiers, centurions, and cavalry officers were affected.[27]

Some men claimed that they were more worried about the difficult terrain through which the army would have to pass in the next stage of the advance. Others said that they were nervous about the grain supply – a plausible enough concern in the light of the recent operations against the Helvetii. A few officers even declared that there would be an open mutiny and that the soldiers would not obey Caesar's order to advance. The episode provides another indication that the fanatical loyalty which Caesar's officers and soldiers displayed in later campaigns, especially during the Civil War, did not spring up instantly on Caesar's arrival in Gaul, but took time to grow. It is interesting that Caesar portrayed the tribunes and other officers as the source of the discontent, for these men were usually equestrians and often the sons of senators. This reinforces the view that these classes were not the sole, nor even necessarily the main target audience for the *Commentaries*. Dio claims that some of these men complained that the war against Ariovistus had not been authorised by the Senate, so that they were risking their lives purely because of Caesar's personal ambition.[28]

The proconsul summoned a consilium (a council or briefing). All of the centurions – some 360 men if all of these posts were filled in the six legions – were instructed to attend, along presumably with the other senior officers. It was time for Caesar the orator to use reason and charm his army as he had often in the past worked a crowd in the Forum. He began sternly, as befitted a general given imperium by the Senate and People of Rome, and told them off for daring to question the plans of their legally appointed commander. After giving them this shock and reminder of discipline, Caesar switched to argument. Their nervousness might well prove unnecessary, since there was every chance that Ariovistus would remember his obligation to Caesar because of his recognition by Rome in the previous year and see reason.

Even if fighting became necessary, Roman legions had met and defeated German warriors in the past, when Marius smashed the Cimbri and Teutones, and more recently when there were many Germans amongst the slave army of Spartacus. Ariovistus had beaten the Aedui and other Gauls by outwitting and surprising them, not in a fair fight. Such crude strategems would not work against a Roman army. Those who openly worried about the grain supply insulted him by doubting his care and competence, while ignoring the convoys already coming from allied tribes and the ripe harvest now visible in the fields. He was not worried by the claim that his soldiers would refuse an order to advance:

> . . . at any time when an army has not listened to its commander, either fortune has failed them or bad mistake been discovered . . .. My own integrity has been shown in my life, and my good luck in the war against the Helvetii. Therefore I intend to carry out what I had planned to postpone till a later date, and to break camp in the fourth watch of this coming night, so that I may see once and for all if duty and honour prevails in your hearts over fear. Anyway, even if no one else follows, I shall set out with just the Tenth Legion, for I have no doubt of its loyalty, and it will act as if it were my own guard.

Caesar had favoured this legion, and had the greatest confidence in its courage.[29]

The whole speech was a challenge to the centurions' pride in themselves and their units. Caesar's tone displayed disappointment in them, since only cowardice and lack of faith in his leadership could explain their threatened refusal to obey orders. The *Tenth* was flattered, and its tribunes immediately reported the legion's readiness to obey Caesar's every order and prove that his trust was not misplaced. The other units were each determined not to be outshone by any other legion, and their centurions asked the tribunes and senior officers to assure Caesar that there had never been any real question of disobedience.[30]

As he had promised, Caesar marched the army out of camp before dawn of the next day. He did change his plans in one way, which may suggest that he had seen some justification in a little of the criticism. Rather than continue as he had originally planned, through the hills, he sought advice from Diviciacus and took the column through open country. This meant a detour of 50 miles, but prevented a fresh outbreak of croaking amongst his officers. After a week, his scouts reported that the German army was only 24 miles away. Envoys soon arrived from Ariovistus, saying that he was now willing to have the face-to-face meeting that he had previously declined. In the *Commentaries* Caesar claims that he still hoped for a peaceful resolution of the problem, and this may not simply have been intended to emphasise his reasonableness to his audience. Many Roman commanders, Sulla included, had celebrated the occasions when, surrounded by the full pomp and ceremony of a Roman magistrate and surrounded by the serried ranks of the legions, they had confronted a foreign king and dictated terms to him. There was almost as much glory in such a deed as there was in defeating the enemy in battle, although the potential profits were less, with no prospect of plunder or slaves.[31]

Five days later the meeting took place on the neutral ground of a plain roughly equal in distance between the two camps. Only one large mound interrupted the flat land. The details of how this would take place had been hammered out in long negotiations during the preceding days. Ariovistus insisted that each of them should only have horsemen in his entourage. Not fully trusting his allied horsemen, Caesar borrowed their mounts and gave them to legionaries from the *Tenth* so that these provided his escort. Once again delighted to be singled out from the entire army, the soldiers joked that the proconsul was making them knights (*equites*), punning on the ancient role of the wealthy equestrian order. The two parties stopped 200 paces apart. In accordance with Ariovistus' wishes, each leader then rode forward with only ten men as escort. The language used was Gallic, which Ariovistus had learned during his time west of the Rhine. Caesar presumably used one of his usual interpreters. He began by reminding Ariovistus of the favour done to him by the Republic and the obligations that this implied. The Aedui were very long-standing allies of Rome, and the German's treatment of them was unacceptable and must stop. Caesar's demands were the same as before. No more Germans must be allowed across the Rhine into Gaul and the Aedui must have their hostages returned. Ariovistus' attitude had not changed. What he had won, he had won through right of conquest. Why was Caesar interfering in a place where no Roman army had ever ventured before? This was his 'province', just as Transalpine Gaul was Caesar's, and neither of them should interfere in the other man's territory. The German wondered whether 'despite Caesar's pretence of friendship, he had brought the army into Gaul to destroy him'. Until the Romans withdrew, Ariovistus would treat them as enemies. In the *Commentaries* he makes the barbed comment that if he killed Caesar, the news would be welcomed by 'many of the principal men and nobles' back in Rome. This may well have been true, but none of his opponents would have liked to be depicted as men so lacking in patriotism that they would be pleased by the defeat of a Roman army as long as it meant Caesar's death. Having made the threat, Ariovistus then offered to support Caesar in every future operation if he withdrew now.[32]

Caesar responded with more justification of the Roman position, but the parley broke up when some of the German warriors began throwing javelins or slinging stones at the mounted legionaries. He decided against fighting, since he did not wish to give the impression that the Romans had broken faith. After two days, Ariovistus sent word asking for another meeting, or alternatively for the Romans to send envoys to his camp. Reluctant to risk any of his senior officers on this mission, Caesar again showed his trust in Valerius Procillus by selecting him for the task. With him went Caius Mettius, a merchant who in the past had visited Ariovistus and received his hospitality. This time the welcome was less warm and both envoys were denounced as spies and thrown into chains by the Germans.[33]

Ariovistus had evidently decided on a military solution to the dispute. Yet he was an experienced war-leader who had welded his warriors into a more cohesive force than most tribal armies and he still acted cautiously. On the same day as he arrested the Roman envoys, he advanced to camp on high ground 6 miles from the Roman position. Probably remaining on high ground, he led his army out again on the following morning and marched past Caesar's camp to establish a new base 2 miles behind the Romans. This cut Caesar off from his supply lines to the allied tribes. For five days the proconsul ordered his army out of camp and formed a battle line. The Germans refused to come down and Caesar clearly felt it unwise to risk a direct attack on Ariovistus' camp, which suggests that it was in a strong position. There were skirmishes on these days, mostly between the cavalry, but no full-scale fighting developed. Ariovistus' horsemen worked closely with picked light infantry – who in later centuries were known to the Germans as the 'hundred' (centeni) – capable over short distances of keeping pace with the horses by grabbing onto their manes. The warriors on foot acted as a solid support, behind which the cavalry could retreat if worsted, and rest and re-form before advancing again. The tactics and the quality of the Germanic warriors usually gave them the edge over Gaulish cavalry.[34]

Caesar could not afford to remain where he was, for he was achieving nothing and each day his army consumed a significant part of the supplies he had with him. A direct attack was too risky, so instead he decided to reopen his supply lines. The army formed into three columns, each of which could be readily converted into a fighting line to make up the normal *triplex acies*. The baggage train and presumably some guards remained in the main camp, for Caesar only intended to create an outpost beyond the German position. The Romans marched past the German camp to a spot just under 1,000 yards away from it. Once there the legions faced towards the enemy. The German cavalry along with 16,000 infantry came out to oppose them. This was only a part of Ariovistus' foot, but it is unlikely that he was able to get more of them armed and ready for battle quickly enough to intervene. Caesar ordered the cohorts in the third line to begin laying out and constructing a new camp to accommodate two legions, while the first and second lines met any German attack. These probably took the form more of probes and feints rather than an all-out assault. If most of the six legions took part in this manoeuvre then two-thirds of their strength plus the cavalry and light troops would at the very least have matched the German numbers. After several hours of this, the camp defences were ready. Two legions were installed, while the rest of the army marched back in the same order to the main camp. The smaller fort would now make it easier to protect supply convoys coming from the allied tribes. The pressure on Caesar for a quick victory or an ignominious retreat was removed, and he could afford to wait for the moment and situation of his choice before engaging the enemy army.[35]

On the next day Caesar ordered the legions out of both camps to form up in the standard *triplex acies* facing the enemy. It was a gesture of confidence, intended to encourage his own men and impress the enemy, and he says that this was his normal practice during these days. Ariovistus declined the offer of battle and at noon the Roman commander sent his men back. Later in the afternoon the Germans did become aggressive, sending out troops to attack the smaller camp, but the troops there were able to repulse the onslaught. That evening Caesar personally questioned some of the prisoners who had been taken. These men claimed that Ariovistus was reluctant to risk a full-scale battle because the women who acted as diviners for the German army had declared that he would only win a victory if he waited until the full moon. Ceremonies and sacrifices were normal in most armies before battles, but Caesar, the *Pontifex Maximus*, makes no mention throughout the *Commentaries* of the rituals that were a very important aspect of the legions' routine. In this case, he decided to exploit the superstition of the enemy. On the next day he stripped the camps of all but the barest minimum of guards and formed the rest of the army into a *triplex acies*, with the cavalry probably on the wings. He then led the army straight up the slope against the Germans, going far closer to their camp than he had ever done on the previous days. This challenge was too bold

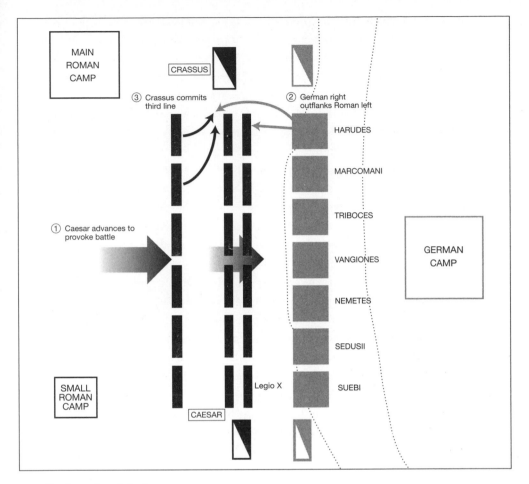

Battle against Ariovistus

to ignore without humiliation, and the risk that his warriors would become daunted by the enemy. Ariovistus led out his men, who formed in units according to their clans and tribes – mention is made of seven distinct contingents. Behind the line were the warriors' wives, perched on wagons and cheering on their men folk, begging them to protect them from slavery at the hands of the enemy.[36]

In this battle all six legions took their place in the battle line, so that Caesar clearly felt that the *Eleventh* and *Twelfth* now had sufficient experience of campaigning to cope with the stress of battle. Probably they were both sandwiched between more experienced units and it is very likely that a veteran legion was stationed on each flank. Caesar's five legates and his quaestor were each given command of a legion 'so that every man should have a witness of his courage'. He stationed himself on the right flank, where he thought the enemy line was weakest and most likely to be broken. The battle began suddenly, both sides charging into contact without the normal exchange of missiles. Caesar managed to break through the enemy left, but was too closely involved to keep much control of the other sectors of the battle. The German right began to drive back the Roman left, and it was only the prompt action of the young Publius Crassus, who as commander of the cavalry 'could move around more easily than the officers in the main line', which saved the day. Crassus ordered up the cohorts of the third line and they restored the situation. Soon afterwards the breakthrough on the far wing spread panic throughout the entire German army, which collapsed into flight. Caesar himself led his cavalry at the head of a pursuit that was both determined and utterly ruthless. One later source that probably refers to this battle claims that he deliberately gave an escape route to a group of Germans who were desperately resisting so that he could slaughter them more easily in flight. Ariovistus himself escaped, and from then on disappears from history. Two of his wives – one the sister of a Norican king – and one of his daughters were less fortunate and were killed amidst the general massacre. Another daughter was captured. Even some of those fugitives who escaped across the Rhine were then attacked by other tribes. The Seubi, who were supposed to have been waiting to join their kinsmen in Gaul, returned to their own homes. Much to Caesar's delight, the troops he was actually with came across Valerius Procillus and were able to rescue him from his captors. The proconsul claimed that the reunion gave him 'as much pleasure as the victory itself'. The emotion was surely genuine, though of course it also helped to confirm Caesar's reputation for loyalty to his friends. Procillus was doubtless even more relived, for he told them that the Germans had three times asked the diviners whether he should be burnt to death, but that thrice he had been saved by the lot. The other captured envoy, the trader Mettius, was also released unharmed.[37]

The campaigning season was at an end and Caesar had completed – in his own words – 'two very great wars in a single summer'. Neither had probably been anticipated by him before his arrival in the province, but he had seized the opportunities offered to him. For the moment at least his attention had switched to Gaul and would remain there in the immediate future. Caesar spent much of the winter in Cisalpine Gaul, carrying out the administrative and judicial tasks required of a Roman governor, and also keeping an eye on Rome. His army remained and went into winter quarters in the territory of the Sequani. Come the spring they would be ready for further operations deeper into Gaul.[38]

XI

'THE BRAVEST OF THE GAULISH PEOPLES': THE BELGAE, 57 BC

'They did not allow traders to come amongst them; they permitted no wine or any other luxuries to be imported, because they believed that these weakened the spirit and reduced courage.' – *Caesar*.[1]

'The whole race which is now called both Gallic and Galatic is war-mad . . . although not otherwise simple . . .. And therefore, if roused, they come together all at once for the struggle, both openly and without circumspection, so that for those who wish to defeat them by stratagem they become easy to deal with . . . .' – *Strabo, early first century AD*.[2]

During the winter months of 58–57 BC Caesar raised two more legions, the *Thirteenth* and *Fourteenth*. Once again he acted entirely on his own initiative and paid for the troops and their equipment with the funds he controlled as governor. Thus within twelve months he had doubled the size of the army allocated to him with his province. Centurions from the experienced legions were given steps in promotion and transferred to the new units. This made good military sense, providing the raw recruits with a leaven of veteran officers, and seems to have been Caesar's standard practice throughout his campaigns. The transfers created vacancies in the established legions, which must then have been filled by internal promotions or appointments from outside. In the *Commentaries* conspicuous gallantry is always given as the reason for advancing or rewarding centurions. Suetonius says that Caesar did not care about his men's 'lifestyle or wealth, but only their courage'. His tribunes and prefects, many of whom were appointed on the basis of recommendation or favour, had proved disappointing in the previous summer. We do not know whether the discontent at Vesontio resulted in any dismissals. Patronage was everywhere in Roman society, so that it is unlikely that it never played a role in Caesar's appointment of centurions, but it is clear that individual ability was his main concern. His centurions certainly came to believe that talent would always be rewarded. Caesar carefully cultivated them, learning their names, in much the same way that he and other senators took the trouble to greet passers-by by name in the Forum. The bond that was created between the proconsul and these officers was intensely personal. Centurions led from the front and suffered disproportionately high casualties as a result. This, combined with the continued expansion of Caesar's army, helped to ensure that there were always more posts to fill, and more brave junior officers to reward. By the end of the Gallic campaigns the vast majority of the centurions in his legions owed their initial appointment, promotion to senior grades, or both, to Caesar himself. This was an important part of the process whereby his legions became not simply the army in the province he happened to control, but Caesar's army.[3]

The winter months were also a time for training. Caesar was not a martinet in the old Roman tradition of stern commanders who flogged and executed their men to instil rigid discipline. He seems rarely to have employed either punishment, considering only desertion and mutiny as serious crimes. Off-duty and in the quiet months his men were allowed considerable leeway in their behaviour. Caesar is once supposed to have said that his men would fight as well even if they 'stank of perfume'. Marius had led his armies in the same way, and Caesar may deliberately have copied his famous relative, and perhaps felt that this was an appropriately *popularis* way of doing things. Yet for all their leniency in peaceful times, both Marius and Caesar had high standards of conduct for their legions during actual operations. Then it was a question of tight discipline, instant obedience and proficient manoeuvres, and to ensure that he received this Caesar trained his army hard. In this respect he conformed with the aristocratic ideal of a commander, for all the best generals were seen as men who carefully prepared their armies for battle through rigorous training. Caesar 'often stood his men to, even when there was no cause, and especially on festival days or when it was raining. Sometimes he would tell them to keep an eye on him, and then slip away suddenly by day or night, and lead them on an especially long march, designed to wear out those who failed to keep up.'[4] His personal example was vital in encouraging the soldiers to meet his standards. Caesar led the column on training marches and in the field, sometimes on horseback, but more often on foot, just like the ordinary legionaries. It was a gesture intended to show them that he was not expecting them to do anything he would not do himself. According to Plutarch the soldiers were astonished:

> that he should undergo toils beyond his body's apparent power of endurance . . . because he was of a spare habit, had soft and white skin, suffered from epileptic fits . . .. Nevertheless, he did not make his feeble health an excuse for soft living, but rather his military service a cure for his feeble health, since by wearisome journeys, simple diet, continuously sleeping in the open air, and enduring hardships he fought off his trouble and kept his body strong against its attacks. Most of his sleep, at least, he got in cars or litters, making his rest conduce to action, and in the day-time he would have himself conveyed to garrisons, cities, or camps, one slave who was accustomed to write from dictation as he travelled sitting by his side and one soldier standing behind him with a sword.[5]

When Caesar addressed his troops it was always as 'comrades' (*commilitones*), never 'men' or 'soldiers'. He and they were all good Romans, serving the Republic by fighting against its enemies, and also winning glory and plunder along the way, which he took care to share with them most generously. Already they had won two great victories. Mutual trust grew up gradually between the commander, his officers, and soldiers as they came to know and rely on each other. Pride in themselves and their units was also carefully fostered. Decorated weapons, some inlaid with silver or gold, were issued, most probably as rewards for valour, marking the recipients out as exceptional soldiers and making them feel special. The Roman military system had always sought to encourage boldness in its soldiers, but in Caesar's legions this ideal was taken to an extreme.[6]

Caesar spent much of the winter south of the Alps, so that presumably a good deal of training must have been supervised by his legates, tribunes and centurions. In the past he had championed the rights of the residents of Cisalpine Gaul, and during his time as governor he did his best to win the lasting support of the people of the area, especially the aristocracy. He employed many citizens of Gallic extraction on his staff, a good number of them aristocrats from the tribes of the Transalpine province. Apart from Valerius Procillus, who had played such a prominent role in the first campaigns, other men are mentioned later in the *Commentaries*. The father of the Gallic historian Pompeius Trogus also served on Caesar's staff, and was given responsibility for some of his letters. Caesar never mentions him, and it may be that he was one of a number of clerks who helped to cope with the proconsul's voluminous correspondence. Even while mounted and riding out to inspect the lines of his army, Caesar was said to have been able to dictate to two secretaries at a time. Letters went often to influential men in Rome, and on many occasions were reinforced by personal visits made by his agent Balbus. Much correspondence also went the other way, and Plutarch tells us that from the beginning many men travelled north to petition Caesar for favours such as appointments to his staff. Always eager to do favours and so place more men under obligation to him, he was almost always willing to grant any request. Yet in the main it still seems to have been the failures or those without good connection who approached him.[7]

Socially Caesar entertained and was entertained by the local aristocracy, many of whom had only possessed citizenship for a generation or so. Suetonius says that he regularly filled two dining halls, one with his officers and Greek members of his staff and the other for civilian citizens. On one occasion in Mediolanum (modern Milan), he dined at the house of one Valerius Meto, and the party was served with asparagus accidentally dressed in bitter myrrh rather than the normal olive oil. Caesar ate it without comment or change of expression, and rebuked his companions when they loudly complained. The patrician from one of Rome's oldest families was the perfect guest and as always a lively companion. Whether or not many of the local nobility were able to provide him with the witty, often philosophical or literary conversation that was so popular amongst Rome's elite is unknown. Even if they could not match the standards of sophisticated dinners at Rome, the pronounced literary interests of so many of his officers doubtless provided him with such diversions. Caesar was also friendly with the father of the poet Catullus, whose family came from the Po Valley. The son had gone to Rome, but after taking a few steps on a public career, had abandoned this and devoted himself to his verses. Many dealt with love, but not a few were bitter attacks on leading men of the day, including both Cato and Caesar. In one he styled Caesar a 'ravenous, shameless gambler', but another was even more scurrilous, alleging – amongst other things – a homosexual affair between the general and one of his prefects, Mamurra:[8]

> Well agreed are the abominable profligates, Mamurra the effeminate, and Caesar; no wonder either. Like stains, one from the city and one from Formiae, are deeply impressed on each, and will never be washed out. Diseased alike, very twins, both on one sofa, dilettante writers both, one as greedy in adultery as the other, rivals and partners in love. Well agreed are these abominable profligates.[9]

Caesar was outraged, but did not break his friendship with the poet's father, and when Catullus himself apologised, immediately invited him to dinner.[10]

No one seems to have actually believed that Caesar and Mamurra were lovers, but the latter was not a popular figure and attracted Catullus' spleen in other poems. After the stories about Nicomedes, Caesar remained sensitive about such things. However, the suggestion that the proconsul continued his womanising ways while in Gaul was widely – and certainly correctly – credited. Years later at his triumph Caesar's legionaries would sing about him frittering away the money he borrowed in Rome on his Gaulish women. In Tacitus' account of a rebellion in the Rhineland in AD 70, we read of one Gallic nobleman who claimed that he was descended from Caesar. The latter was supposed to have taken the man's great-grandmother as his mistress at some point during the campaigns in Gaul. It is difficult to know who Caesar's lovers were in these years, but probably most were from the aristocratic families inside his provinces and perhaps amongst the tribes elsewhere. Some, especially those with Roman citizenship, may have been educated and able to provide him with the witty and stimulating companionship that he had sought so often amongst the married women of Rome. In other cases it may simply have been a question of physical pleasure.[11]

THE BELGAE

Leaving his army to winter in the lands of the Sequani had shown that Caesar did not intend his intervention in the affairs of Gaul to be temporary. Even he admits that this caused disquiet amongst certain tribal leaders, who wondered whether they had truly gained from the expulsion of Ariovistus, if they were now to be dominated by a Roman proconsul. During the winter rumours and reports reached the proconsul south of the Alps that the Belgae, the tribes of northern Gaul, were even more disturbed and had formed a 'conspiracy' against Rome. They were encouraged by chieftains in some of the Gallic/Celtic peoples – men whom Caesar claims aspired to kingship – but judged that such revolutions would be harder to achieve in a region dominated by Rome. The Belgae also felt that once the Romans had secured control – 'pacified' is the word used in the *Commentaries* – of Celtic central Gaul, then the legions might soon march against them. In the light of subsequent events this was not an unreasonable concern, for Caesar was about to do precisely that. By taking his army outside Transalpine Gaul in the previous year, driving out first the Helvetii and then Ariovistus, he had shown that Rome was willing to intervene on behalf of its allies. In the past, the Roman province had maintained a ring of friendly states around its borders. Caesar had decided to push the Roman sphere of influence further north, claiming that this was necessary to prevent other forces from dominating the region, and ultimately threatening the security of the province. These motives were entirely appropriate for a Roman governor, and even if Caesar's actions interpreted his duty in an extremely aggressive way, he still remained within the boundaries of proper action for a magistrate of the Republic. Pompey had behaved in a similar fashion during his eastern campaigns, but his and Caesar's campaigns differed only in scale from the actions of many earlier Roman generals. Few of these men had subsequently been challenged because of their actions, and even fewer actually punished. In the *Commentaries* Caesar claims that the Belgae planned and began a pre-emptive attack to challenge Roman power. He was effectively acting in the same way. By the standards of the time, neither of them were acting unreasonably.[12]

Caesar uses the term Belgae or Belgians fairly vaguely to refer to all the peoples living to the north of the Celtic tribes. The area was much wider than modern Belgium, and included not only parts of Holland, but much of northern France. The 'true' Belgae appear to have been the tribes living in what is now the Pas de Calais and upper Normandy. Caesar considered all of the Belgae were Gauls, but also claims that many of them were descended from German settlers. As we have already seen, the distinction between Gaul and German was not always as clear as our ancient sources suggest but there may well have been some truth in this. At the end of the first century AD Tacitus also believed that the Nervii and Treveri were both Germanic. In Caesar's case his mention of the Germanic connection may well have been intended to make the Belgae seem more threatening, and therefore more deserving of Roman 'pacification'. He also takes care to report that one tribe boasted that they were the only people who had resisted the migrating Cimbri and Teutones, while another was descended from these great enemies of Rome. The Belgae were more warlike than the Celtic tribes, in part because they were further away from Roman influence. Ancient authors believed that access to the luxuries of civilisation softened a people, while a simple life preserved natural virtue and courage. The archaeological record confirms that Roman wine was far less common in northern Gaul than amongst those peoples who lay nearer the trade routes. The Nervii are supposed to have forbidden all imports, but elsewhere the tribal aristocracies did value wine, and possessing it even in small quantities helped to confirm their status.

Less is known about the walled towns of northern Gaul than the *oppida* of the Celtic tribes, but in general they seem to have been somewhat smaller and less developed. Some of the tribes still had kings, a few of whom were powerful, although aristocratic councils were more important in other tribes. Only a generation or so before, one monarch is supposed to have controlled much of the region and also part of Britain.[13]

Such political unity under a single strong leader no longer existed, but the Belgic tribes did show a willingness to join together to meet what they perceived as the threat posed by the Romans. During the winter they had exchanged hostages and agreed to form a combined army, to which each was to provide a set number of warriors. The whole force was to be led by Galba, King of the Suessiones, not by any right, but because the other leaders acknowledged his ability. Caesar began to concentrate his own forces before the campaigning season began, sending the two new legions under the command of the legate Quintus Pedius to join the rest of the army. The proconsul remained in Cisalpine Gaul, only travelling north to take charge when the spring was sufficiently advanced to provide forage for the army's animals. He immediately requested the allied tribes to inform him of events further north and received reports of the Belgic preparations. The Roman army marched north, the proconsul pushing on at his usual rapid pace, so that within two weeks they were approaching the Remi, the first of the tribes considered to be Belgae rather than Celts. Envoys arrived assuring him that they had never been hostile to Rome, immediately agreeing to Caesar's demands for hostages and supplies of grain. He questioned them about the numbers of warriors he was likely to face and was given a precise list of the tribal contingents. The Bellovaci had promised 60,000 men, the Suessiones and Nervii both 50,000, the Morini 25,000, the Atuatuci 19,000, the Atrebates 15,000, the Ambiani and Caleti each 10,000, while another six tribes altogether offered 50,000, producing a total of 289,000 warriors. These were the figures reported by the Remi and dutifully recorded by Caesar in the *Commentaries*. He never troubles to say whether or not he believed their estimates were accurate. The narrative of the campaign does suggest that the combined army was an exceptionally large and rather clumsy force, which may well have been significantly bigger than the Roman army. Caesar himself made sure that the full strength of the tribes was never united, by arranging with Diviciacus for the Aedui to attack the Bellovaci and keep their warriors busy defending their own lands.[14]

The Remi were closely related to the Suessiones, following the same customs and laws, and at times ruled by the same leaders. It is hard to know whether their readiness to join the Romans was a pragmatic acknowledgement of their inability to resist the sudden appearance of Caesar, or was based on rivalry with and fear of the other tribes. Certainly, the Remi were the first target of the Belgic coalition, whose army advanced to assault Bibrax, one of the Remi's main towns (probably modern Vieux-Laon). Caesar had advanced across the Aisne, which lay on the tribe's borders, and camped on the far bank. He left a detachment under the legate Sabinus on the other side of the river to build a fort protecting the bridge. Bibrax was about 8 miles away, and its leader – one of the chieftains who had led the delegation to Caesar – now sent word that he could not hold out much longer unless he received help. Guided by the men who had brought this message, the proconsul sent his Numidian, Cretan and Balearic light troops to slip into the town under cover of darkness. The method used by the Belgians for attacking a fortification was simple – a barrage of sling stones and other missiles pinned the defenders down, while other warriors advanced holding their shields over their heads and undermined the wall. The skilled archers and slingers sent by Caesar would have made this extremely difficult, and the Belgians abandoned the attempt, contenting themselves with ravaging the surrounding area, setting fire to the small villages and farms dotted about the countryside. They then moved to confront Caesar, camping 2 miles from the Roman position, with a valley between them. Caesar claims that the fires in the Belgians' sprawling encampment covered an area of some 8 miles.[15]

For days both sides then watched each other. There were cavalry skirmishes, by which Caesar gauged the quality of this new enemy and judged that his own men would be more than a match for them in most situations. His camp was on high ground with the River Aisne to the rear. On the slope in front he deployed his six legions with battle experience, leaving the two recently recruited formations to guard his camp – an echo of the deployment against the Helvetii. With no natural feature to protect the flanks, the legionaries dug a 400-pace (roughly 130 yards) ditch on each side, running back at right angles from the main line. Each ditch led up to a small fort, in which were emplaced light artillery pieces or scorpions, capable of firing heavy bolts with tremendous force and accuracy over distances far greater than any missile weapon the Belgians possessed. Sulla had once entrenched his position in much the same way to secure his flanks against an enemy army that was markedly superior in numbers. The Belgians would have to advance up the gentle slope before attacking the Roman position from the front, and the advantage of such a position had been clearly demonstrated the year before near Bibracte. To make matters worse for the Belgians, in the bottom of the valley between the two positions was a stream and an area of marsh. These were not impassable obstacles, but would have slowed an attack down and caused a line to fall into disorder. It was unlikely that the opposition would give the attacker the opportunity to stop and redress the line before continuing the advance.[16]

Caesar's position was a strong one and he could be confident of beating off even the heaviest of attacks. However, the Belgic host showed no sign of charging to its doom and was content to form up on the far side of the valley, waiting for the Romans to cross the boggy ground and fight at a disadvantage. This was always the risk for a commander who took up a very strong position, for if the advantages it gave were obvious, then there was little incentive for the enemy to engage. Both sides sent forward their cavalry, and the allied horsemen gained a slight advantage over the Belgian horse before Caesar withdrew them. Realising that a full-scale battle was not going to develop, the legions were ordered back to camp to rest. Reaching the same conclusion, the Belgic commanders sent a part of the army to ford the River Aisne and either threaten the Roman supply line by capturing the fort protecting the bridge, or draw Caesar off by ravaging the lands of his new-found allies, the Remi. The outpost at the bridge reported this new threat and Caesar responded by personally leading his cavalry, Numidians, and the other light troops back across to the far side of the river. They managed to catch the Belgic warriors when only a few had got across. The latter were surrounded and dealt with by the cavalry, while the missile troops shot down the other warriors as they waded through the water. After suffering heavy losses, the Belgians withdrew.

It was a difficult task to keep any tribal army in the field for any length of time, since their logistical arrangements tended to be extremely basic. Only a certain amount of food would have been carried by the warriors, or the wives and servants who in many tribes accompanied them to battle. In the summer months it was often possible to find food and forage from the countryside, but the quantities to be seized in this way were limited, and soon exhausted if the army remained in one place for any length of time. The Belgian army in 57 BC was exceptionally large, even if we must treat the figures given with some caution, and so the problems of supply were made considerably worse. The attack on Bibrax had failed, as had the attempt to cross the river and get behind the Romans. Caesar had shown himself willing to fight only if the Belgians put themselves at a severe disadvantage. He had doubtless told his men that the reluctance of the enemy to attack the Roman position showed that they were frightened. Galba and the Belgian chieftains could equally have assured their warriors that the Roman refusal to come down from their hilltop and trenches was proof that they feared the might of the tribes. The campaign had not been especially successful for them so far, but they had shown their numbers and confidence to this new enemy, and Caesar had not risked attacking their main force. It is possible that Galba and the other leaders felt that they had demonstrated their strength and that this might be enough to deter further invasion. There often seems to have been strong elements of display and gesture in inter-tribal warfare, so we do not necessarily need to follow Caesar and see the Belgians' next action in purely pragmatic terms. Yet the practical factors were undeniable, for the army had almost run out of food and could not stay where it was for much longer. In addition, news had arrived that the Aedui were advancing to the border with the Bellovaci in accordance with Caesar's arrangement with Diviciacus. At a council of the senior chieftains present with the army, the Belgians resolved to disperse and go home, each tribal contingent returning to its own lands, where they could easily be fed. Pledging themselves to come to the aid of any tribe that Caesar might attack over the coming months, the great army broke up. It did not do this in any ordered manner, individual leaders and groups simply packing up and walking off during the night.[17]

The Roman outposts reported the noisy departure of the Belgian army, but Caesar was suspicious that it might be a trap. The failure of the surprise attack against the Helvetii in the previous year may well have made him rather cautious about operations at night. At dawn he sent out patrols that confirmed that the enemy really were simply drifting away without any serious attempt to cover their retreat. The cavalry rode out under Pedius and Cotta, while Labienus followed them with three legions to provide close support. There was little resistance, and large numbers of Belgic warriors were killed and captured as they fled from the Roman pursuit. For the moment the great army had dispersed – it would take some time before the tribes were able concentrate their forces again. Caesar made sure that they did not have that time. On the following day he marched against the Suessiones, whose lands bordered on those of the Remi. By a forced march he reached one of their main towns at Noviodunum. (Like most of the other Belgic *oppida* mentioned by Caesar, its precise location is unknown, but it was most probably fairly near modern Soissons.) Believing from reports that the town had no defenders, Caesar sent his men straight into the attack. There were indeed few warriors to resist him, but the Romans had no ladders or other siege equipment and those few were able to repulse the attack. After this failure, Caesar made sure that the business was done properly and set the legionaries to making a ramp, siege towers and mantlets to take his men up to and over the wall. The town was not yet blockaded, and numbers of warriors from the dispersing army took refuge within it. Their morale was shaky, however, and the sight of the Roman siege machines caused dismay. The Suessiones surrendered, winning favourable terms because the Remi interceded on their behalf. They gave up hostages from their leading families, including two of King Galba's sons, and handed over quantities of weapons – perhaps a token amount as a symbol of disarmament.[18]

Caesar needed to move on while the advantage was still with him and now attacked the Bellovaci. These similarly put up little resistance and swiftly surrendered. This time it was Diviciacus of the Aedui who spoke for them, pleading long-standing friendship between their two tribes. The recent hostility of the Bellovaci was blamed on a few chieftains who saw the Aedui's alliance with Rome as slavery. These men had now fled to Britain and could no longer influence tribal policy. Caesar happily granted the pleas and accepted the surrender on similarly lenient terms, although he did demand and receive 600 hostages, which was clearly far more than normal. In part this was because he wanted to honour Diviciacus and the Aedui, but it was also important to weaken the coalition facing him by removing as many members as possible. The high total of hostages makes it likely that most of the Suessiones' aristocratic families sent someone to Caesar's camp and this was clearly intended to ensure that they did not risk renewing the war. Throughout the *Commentaries on the Gallic War* there are frequent references to hostages, but never once does Caesar say what happened to any who came from tribes that broke their treaties with him. It would be surprising if most of these were not executed on such occasions. After thus dealing with two powerful tribes individually, Caesar next attacked the smaller Ambiani, who swiftly capitulated. Well over a third of the force that it was claimed the Belgians had mustered earlier in the year had now been defeated and the odds were turning in Caesar's favour. However, the easy victories of the last days were over and resistance was hardening.[19]

THE BATTLE OF THE SAMBRE

Caesar now drove north-west against the Nervii, the largest tribe still willing to fight.

After three days the Roman column was about 10 miles away from the River Sambre, and captives revealed under interrogation that the tribal army was waiting on the far side. They had been joined by the Atrebates and Viromandui, and another tribe, the Atuatuci, were on their way. According to the Remi's estimates, the Nervii, Atrebates and Viromandui had contributed 75,000 men to the coalition army raised earlier in the summer, and Caesar gives the first tribe 10,000 more men in this battle. As we have seen, the reliability of theses figure is questionable, and their contingents had probably anyway been weakened by the earlier operations and further reduced by warriors who had not yet been able to join the army. Caesar's eight legions probably mustered somewhere in the region of 30–40,000 men, backed by several thousand cavalry and as many light troops. It seems likely that the Nervii and their allies had at the very least parity of numbers with Caesar's men, and probably a significant numerical advantage, although probably not as much as double the Roman numbers. The Belgians were determined to fight, and had evacuated their women, children and other non-combatants to places of sanctuary deep in inaccessible marshland. They also had information sent secretly by some of the Gauls and Belgians marching with Caesar as allies or hostages. These had reported that Caesar's normal order of march was for each legion to form up separately, guarding its own baggage train. This meant that the fighting troops were split up into eight main sections, with cumbersome lines of servants, carts and pack animals between them, which would have made it difficult to form a battle line.[20]

Such a formation made the Romans vulnerable, and the Nervii had picked their ground carefully. As usual there can be no certainty as to the precise location of the battle, but a site within a few miles of Maubeuge seems quite probable. It is possible that the tribe had repelled invaders at this spot before. They evidently knew where Caesar would cross the river, which makes it probable that he was following a well-trodden route, used by the tribes for the movement of trade as well as armies. Low hills rose on either side of the river, which at this time of year was only about 3 feet deep and easily forded. On the far bank, the valley side was open for about 200 paces, but was then heavily wooded, allowing the warriors to wait in concealment. On the side from which the Romans were approaching, the ground was broken by lines of thick, high hedges, made deliberately by the Nervii to hinder

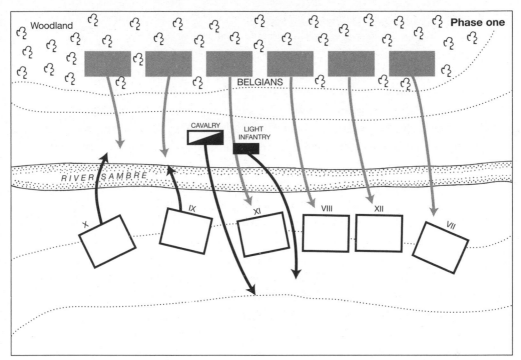

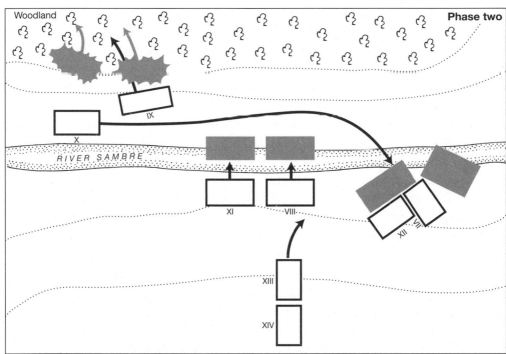

Battle of the Sambre

raids by enemy horsemen. These were an obstacle both to movement and visibility, and were intended to send a clear message to raiders that once they crossed this point their attack would be resisted by a tribe proud of its martial reputation. Now they intended to give Caesar a demonstration of this and would launch an all-out attack as soon as the baggage behind the leading legion came into view.[21]

The captives – presumably men brought in by the cavalry patrols and scouts that preceded the main army – had warned Caesar that the river crossing would be contested. As a result he changed the march formation, adopting what he claims was his standard deployment when there was a risk of encountering the enemy. After the screen of cavalry and light troops, the six experienced legions marched unencumbered by baggage, all of which was massed together and guarded by the two new legions who followed at the rear. On this particular day the *Tenth* was in the lead, followed by the *Ninth*, then the *Eleventh*, *Eighth*, *Twelfth* and *Seventh*. A party of centurions accompanied the forward scouting patrols and had the task of selecting and marking out the camp site for the night. The construction of a marching camp protected by a ditch and an earth wall formed from the spoil was standard practice for any Roman army in the field, and was the equivalent of modern infantrymen digging in at the end of a move. A camp took several hours to construct, but then offered security against sudden attack, and was laid out to a regular design, so that each unit knew its place. The centurions marked out a site on the hill on the near side of the river. When the main force began to arrive, the cavalry and light troops splashed through the water and formed a screen on the enemy-held bank. The bulk of the tribal army was hidden amongst the trees, but a few small groups darted forward and skirmished with the Romans. The Nervii had very few cavalrymen, and the auxiliaries easily held their own in the resulting combats, but took care not to pursue too far and enter the woods. As the legions arrived, they began the task of building the camp, packs were laid down, helmets, shields and *pila* piled, but it was normal for legionaries to keep their armour on while they dug. Each legate supervised the legion under his command, for Caesar had instructed them – probably as a permanent standing order – to remain with their men until the camp was complete. Small detachments of armed legionaries may well have been sent out as piquets, but there was no real effort to protect the labourers from a full-scale attack.

In the previous year Caesar had covered the construction of a camp close to Ariovistus' army by keeping the first and second lines of the legions in battle order facing the enemy, while the cohorts of the third line dug.

Napoleon and many other commentators have justifiably criticised him for not adopting a similar practice here. Caesar already knew that the enemy were massed somewhere across the river, and would have seen his cavalry and light troops skirmishing with them on the far bank. The Nervii and their allies were close and therefore an attack possible, but he may have judged it unlikely. The day was considerably advanced and the enemy had done no more than harass his outposts. Weeks before, when he had faced an even larger army, it had refused to attack across some difficult ground and the river felt like a secure barrier. Keeping a substantial part of his army under arms would slow the building of the camp – in 58 BC the cohorts of the third line had had to construct a camp for only two legions, not the entire army. Whether through a conscious decision or simple omission, perhaps brought on by complacency after the easy defeat of three tribes in the last weeks, Caesar took the risk of not protecting the legions as they worked. It nearly proved fatal.[22]

The Belgians displayed admirable discipline as they waited for the moment to attack. The leaders of the army – a Nervian chieftain named Boduognatus was in overall charge – had agreed that they would wait until the Roman baggage appeared. Even though this did not follow the leading legion as they had expected, the warriors remained calm and only when the concentrated train of the army came into view on the far side of the valley did they leave the cover of the woods and advance. The Romans' auxiliary cavalry and light troops could not hope to withstand a massed attack and quickly gave way. The Belgian line had been formed into tribal contingents under cover of the trees and surged quickly down the slope and across the river. Some of their order was lost in the process, and the hedges on the far shore probably encouraged the line to break up even further. For all that, they were still better prepared for battle than the Romans, who struggled to form any sort of a fighting line. The battles against the Helvetii and Ariovistus – and indeed most large encounters in this period – were carefully prepared and anticipated affairs, with hours spent carefully deploying the lines and encouraging the troops for the clash to come. This time it was different and: 'Caesar had to do everything at the same time: to raise the standard, which was the signal to stand to arms, to sound the trumpet call which recalled the soldiers from work, to bring back the men who had gone further afield in search of material for the rampart, to form the line of battle, to address the soldiers, and to give the signal for battle.'[23]

The proconsul could only be in one place at a time, and later paid tribute to his legates, who set about organising the troops nearest to them without waiting for instructions from him. Similarly the legionaries and centurions did not panic, but began to form up often in ad hoc units of whoever happened to be near at the time. A battle line began to coalesce surprisingly quickly, and even if it was less neat than was usual, and also less impressive – there was no time to take the leather covers off shields or to fix crests and plumes onto helmets – it was capable of putting up a resistance. It is questionable whether the army would have coped so well with such a crisis in the previous year, when army and commander were still unfamiliar with each other and had yet to build up the cohesion that came from training and the confidence derived from success. Caesar himself rode to each legion in turn, coming first to his favourite the *Tenth*, who were on the left of his ragged line. He gave them a few words of encouragement, telling them to remain steady and to remember their proven courage. The Belgians – mostly Atrebates on this flank – were now within 100 yards or so, and Caesar ordered the *Tenth* to charge, which they did with considerable effect. A volley of *pila* smashed into the enemy front ranks, halting the Atrebates. The slope at this point was mostly in the Romans' favour, and the enemy tired from their rapid charge, so that the *Tenth* and neighbouring *Ninth* soon drove them back down the slope. In the centre the *Eleventh* and *Eighth* were also able to hold their own, pushing the Viromandui to the river. The right and centre of the Belgian army was crumbling, and the *Tenth* and *Ninth* even crossed the Sambre to chase the enemy back up the far slope. However, the main weight of the Belgian attack, and the bulk of the Nervii led by Boduognatus himself, had fallen on the Roman right. It was hard for the Roman officers to see what was going on, since vision was so often restricted by the high hedges, but by instinct or clear realisation the proconsul had galloped to the spot:[24]

> After addressing *Legio X*, Caesar hurried to the right wing, where he saw his men hard pressed, and the standards [a shorthand term for the units' formations] of *Legio XII* clustered in one place and the soldiers so crowded together that it impeded their fighting. All the centurions in the fourth cohort had fallen, the *signifer* was dead and his standard captured; in the remaining cohorts nearly every centurion was either dead or wounded, including the *primus pilus* Sextus Julius Baculus, an exceptionally brave man, who was exhausted by his many serious wounds and could no longer stand; the other soldiers were tired and some in the rear, giving up the fight, were withdrawing out of missile range; the enemy were edging closer up the slope in front and pressing

hard on both flanks. He saw that the situation was critical and that there was no other reserve available, took a shield from a man in the rear ranks, – he had come without his own – advanced into the front line and called on the centurions by name, encouraged the soldiers, and ordered the line to advance and the units to extend, so that they could employ their swords more easily. His arrival brought hope to the soldiers and refreshed their spirits, every man wanting to do his best in the sight of his general even in such a desperate situation. The enemy's advance was delayed for a while.[25]

Roman generals normally led from close behind the fighting line, and were at risk from missiles or the attacks of bold individuals eager to win fame by killing the enemy commander. In this way they shared some of the risks of the soldiers in their armies, and this was an important element in bonding leader and led. This time Caesar went a step further, going right up into the front of the fighting line, and displaying the personal courage that was as fundamental an aspect of aristocratic *virtus* as the higher skills expected of a commander. This willingness to stand and fight, if necessary to die, with his men was the confirmation of the growing trust that had developed between Caesar and his troops. Once there he encouraged the men around him – the centurions as individuals, the ordinary legionaries as 'fellow-soldiers' and units – and he improved their deployment. There were a number of stories about Pompey fighting at the front of his men, striking down enemies with sword or spear in heroic fashion. This was how Alexander the Great had fought his battles, and Pompey revelled in comparisons between the two of them. Caesar was also said to be very skilled with his personal weapons, but there is no mention in his own account of his actually fighting. It may be that this was deliberate false modesty, intended to allow his audience to imagine for themselves the heroism of the proconsul, hinted at by the matter of fact comment about borrowing a shield. However, Caesar does not seem to have wanted to emphasise his personal prowess, instead concentrating on his role as a leader and commander. In the end his account acknowledges that the Sambre was a soldier's battle, ultimately won by the determination and discipline of the legionaries.

During a lull in the fighting Caesar redeployed the *Twelfth* and *Seventh* legions, wheeling them back so that they formed a rough square or circle and were able to defend against attacks from any direction. Such pauses in the fighting were common, contrary to the Hollywood image of frenzied battles in which every man rushed forward, intermingled with the enemy and fought individual duels, deciding the battle in a matter of minutes. Battles usually lasted for hours, but hand-to-hand fighting was physically and mentally exhausting and seems usually to have occurred in short furious bursts, before the lines separated by maybe just a few yards, drew breath and tried to build up enough enthusiasm to close again. When Caesar arrived the line had been disintegrating, men from the rear ranks slipping off to escape from danger. Many centurions were dead or wounded and collapse appeared imminent. His example – and doubtless that of the other officers there, for he encouraged the centurions and gave orders for a formation change through the tribunes – stabilised the situation for the moment, but the two legions were still under huge pressure and a collapse was probably only a matter of time.[26]

The Roman right flank held out, but the battle was won elsewhere. The two legions marching at the rear of the column to protect the baggage came into the view of those Belgians who had bypassed the Roman right and gone up the hill to attack the camp itself. The arrival of fresh Roman forces dismayed the Belgians and encouraged those Romans able to see them. Labienus was in charge of the victorious Roman left, and on his own initiative sent the *Tenth* back across the river again to aid the rest of the army. This legion, realising that things were not going well, hurried forward and struck the Nervii in the rear. The Roman right was now able to advance, and drive off the warriors facing it. In the meantime even the slaves accompanying the baggage had joined the rallied cavalry and light troops and repulsed the Belgians around the camp. The Nervii did not give way quickly, many fighting on for a long time. Caesar claims that some warriors even stood on the mounds of their own dead to keep on fighting. This was doubtless an exaggeration, but testified to the ferocity of a combat that he had seen from particularly close quarters. His claims for the number of casualties inflicted on the tribe – that only 500 warriors survived out of 60,000, and just three tribal leaders out of 600 – were clearly also greatly inflated, and are in fact disproved by his own comments in a later book of the *Commentaries*. Nevertheless, the losses were high, and the will of the Nervii and their allies to continue the struggle was utterly broken. Envoys came and surrendered to the proconsul, who ordered them to remain in future inside their own borders and not to attack anyone else. He also sent instructions to the neighbouring tribes not to raid the Nervii in their currently vulnerable state.[27]

MOPPING UP

The Atuatuci had not rendezvoused with the other tribes before the battle was fought. Learning of the defeat they returned to their homeland, but showed no inclination to submit to Rome and prepared for a desperate defence. Bringing the people in from other communities, they decided to occupy a single walled town that lay in a strong natural position on a craggy hilltop. Food supplies had been gathered to support them if Caesar attempted a blockade. The defenders were confident, and showed this by their willingness to sally out and attack the Roman army, which had arrived and camped outside the town. Caesar ordered the legions to build a ditch and rampart surrounding the hilltop, strengthening it with forts at short intervals to form a line of circumvallation. Altogether, it stretched for some 430 yards, which gives some indication of the comparatively small size of the stronghold. The forts probably contained light artillery of the sort used before by the Aisne, which soon deterred the defenders from venturing outside their walls. The Atuatuci could not get out, but at first they despised the ramp and siege tower that the Romans laboured to make. Caesar tells of how they mocked the 'pygmy Romans' and adds that the whole population of Gaul was disdainful of the smaller stature of the Italian legionaries. A siege tower was an unknown device, and there was dismay when the Romans began to wheel it up the ramp and towards the wall. Now in a state of despair, the defenders sent out delegates who offered to surrender and asked only that they be allowed to keep their weapons lest their neighbours decide to raid them. Caesar rejected this plea, saying that he would defend them as he would defend the Nervii, placing them under Rome's protection and ordering the nearby tribes to refrain from any acts of hostility. The defenders began to hurl down their weapons from the ramparts, creating a mound that eventually almost equalled the wall in height.[28]

Although the gates of the town were left open, only a small number of Caesar's troops were allowed inside. As night fell, he ordered even these to return to their camp, for he was not confident that their discipline would hold when they were out of view of their officers in the dark streets. Army pay was low, the career attractive only to the poor and the failures of society, and it is probable that most legions contained their share of petty criminals and others, who could readily get out of hand. Caesar was to repeat the same precaution on other occasions. He had the gates closed to protect the tribesmen who had surrendered themselves to Roman faith. However, some of these tribesmen either regretted or had never shared in the decision to surrender, and once night fell began to equip themselves with hidden arms and hastily improvised shields. In the small hours they charged out to attack what they judged to be the weakest part of Caesar's fortified line. The Romans were alert, and sentries lit the prepared fires, which were the agreed signal to stand the army to. Reinforcements moved to the threatened point and the attackers were greeted with a barrage of missiles. All were killed or driven back to the town. The next day Caesar held the entire population responsible for this breach of the peace. His men battered down the gates and arrested everyone inside. It is doubtful that there was any question of keeping the legionaries under tight discipline. Everyone inside – 53,000 men, women, and children according to Caesar – was bought at a single price by a company of merchants who would then sell them on as slaves. It would have been quite normal for the era if most of the women were raped by the soldiers before this occurred. A share of the purchase price would also have gone to all of the legionaries, with larger shares to the centurions and tribunes. The sale of war captives was one source of profit. Another was plunder, though this is rarely mentioned in the *Commentaries*. Caesar says that the Gauls had many sacred sites where gold and precious objects had been dedicated to the gods and left piled up in public view. All the tribes respected these sacred sites and no one dared to steal from them. According to Suetonius, Caesar was unimpressed by such taboos and never failed to loot them. The wealth he was gaining restored his own finances, but as ever his main interest in money was to use it to buy friends and popularity, both with his army and back in Italy.[29]

The defeat of the Belgic tribes was another massive victory, following on from those of the previous year. If the suggestion that a book of *Commentaries* was published each winter is correct, people in Rome were already aware of the humbling of the Helvetii and Ariovistus. Now news came to Rome of the fresh success and was greeted with great enthusiasm. As Caesar proudly reports, the Senate voted him a public thanksgiving of fifteen days, a longer period than that ever awarded to any general, including Pompey. This official celebration vindicated his actions, making it difficult for those enemies who tried to deny the legality of his appointment. Yet not everything at Rome was going as Caesar would have wished. Pompey may have been a little unhappy at the success and fame of his son-in-law, and Dio claims that he had began to talk about recalling Caesar before his five-year term of office had expired. The triumvirate seemed about to collapse. The next danger Caesar was to face would not come from foreign enemies.[30]

XII

POLITICS AND WAR:
THE CONFERENCE OF LUCA

'Pompey replied to him in vehement terms, and made an unsubtle hint in Crassus' direction, saying openly that he would be much better prepared to guard his own life than Africanus had been, who was murdered by C. Carbo.. . . Caius Cato is being supported by Crassus; Clodius is also being funded, and the pair encouraged by Crassus.' – *Cicero, 15 February 56 BC.*[1]

'I am in agreement with you, chosen fathers of the Senate . . . while you did not approve, then I was also not of one mind with him; yet now that his achievements have made you alter your opinion and feelings, then you see me not only sharing this view but praising it' – *Cicero, May 56 BC.*[2]

Caesar had already been away for two years, and the time had not passed quietly in Rome. His consulship had been controversial, but in many ways was mild in comparison with the turbulent months that followed, when orchestrated mob violence became a regular feature of public life. In politics few things last forever, and this was especially true in the Roman Republic. Individual senators gained or lost influence, broke with old allies and found new ones, occasionally made up old quarrels, but more often gained new ones, and discovered that it was now in their interest to alter their views on certain issues. In 59 BC Cicero had openly criticised the triumvirate, prompting them to make his personal enemy Clodius a plebian and open his path to the tribunate. Two years later, Caesar's public thanksgiving was awarded by a Senate voting on a motion that Cicero himself had proposed. In the intervening months the orator had been exiled – if not necessarily with Caesar's actual co-operation, then certainly with his acceptance – and some time later recalled, this time only after Caesar had acquiesced. Although of huge personal importance, and recorded in emotional detail in his published correspondence, Cicero's expulsion from Rome was a relatively minor episode in the political struggles of these years, when virtually nothing and no one seemed secure from attack. Caesar's role in most of this was as an observer, but a deeply interested one, since although he could not himself go to Rome he could be deeply affected by events there. At best he hoped to influence the key players in the political game, for he certainly could not control them. There was no inevitability about the course events took, or how they were eventually resolved. In the end, his position was strengthened, at least for the moment, but this might not have happened, and it was for a while quite possible that his work as consul would be undermined, and his extraordinary command in Gaul prematurely terminated. That this did not happen owed something to the skill with which he used his connections and influence, as well as his imagination. As great, or even greater a role, was played by luck, and in Rome as on the battlefield, the goddess Fortuna continued to smile on Caesar.

In 59 BC the two wealthiest and most influential men in Rome had joined together to achieve their immediate aims, using Caesar as their tool to overcome opposition that until then had proved too solid. Pompey had secured his Eastern Settlement and provided land for his veterans, while Crassus had renegotiated the tax-farmers' contracts. Both men were satisfied, as was Caesar with his land reform and military command, but only for the moment, and each of the triumvirs had further ambitions for the future. Ultimately, like all Roman politicians, their aims were personal and individual. It had suited each man's purpose to combine their efforts for a while, permitting a degree of success that none could have managed on his own. Yet it was not an alliance built on deep roots of shared ideology or commitment to a cause, and would last only so long as each man felt himself to be better off remaining loyal to the other two rather than splitting from them. Caesar's relations with both of the others were cordial, which is not to say that he or they would never contemplate turning against former allies. In spite of his recent successes in Gaul, he was still the junior partner and had most stake in a continued association with the other two, especially as they were still in Rome and he was not. Pompey and Crassus were never close since, in the end, they disliked each other intensely and the rivalry that had been such a feature of their lives was only ever just below the surface. Working together with a consul like Caesar as their agent, they had been able to get what they wanted, although not without a struggle. The consuls for 58 BC were favourably inclined towards the triumvirs, but neither man had Caesar's ability or drive. No one else at Rome could match Pompey's and

Crassus' wealth, fame and *auctoritas*, but these things gave a man influence more than power, and even in combination the two men could not permanently control every aspect of public life. Cato would not be muzzled, and he and other members of the 'good' (*boni*) or 'best' (*optimates*) men also had reputations, wealth and clients. So did many other ambitious men with aims of their own. How men felt towards the triumvirs as a group or as individuals was only one factor influencing their behaviour, and often it was a minor one. Office-holders, especially those able to preside over meetings of the Senate or assemblies, had the opportunity to act in a way always denied to other senators, no matter how eminent. In 70 BC Pompey and Crassus had restored full powers to the tribunes of the plebs. Now it was from this office most of all that challenges would come to their recent dominance.

THE 'PATRICIAN' TRIBUNE OF THE PLEBS

Pompey and Caesar – presumably with Crassus' approval – had arranged the transfer of Publius Clodius Pulcher from patrician to plebian status in 59 BC (see pp.176–7). It would be wrong then or later to see him as their man, just as it would be mistaken to view Caesar as Pompey's or Crassus' man. They had done him a favour and, by convention, he was expected to be grateful and willing to assist them in return, but by no stretch of the imagination could he be seen as under their control. In part this was simply because Roman politics was ultimately a question of individual success, but had even more to do with his fiercely independent character. No one else could ever really control Clodius, or for that matter Caesar, Pompey, Crassus, Cato, Cicero or any other leading senator. His family was one of the greatest patrician houses, which unlike the Julii had managed to remain at the heart of the Republic for generation after generation, producing a long succession of consuls and famous statesmen. The pride or arrogance of the Claudii was proverbial, reinforced by the tales of men like the Publius Claudius Pulcher who had led a Roman fleet to disaster during the First Punic War. Before the battle he had been annoyed when the sacred chickens had refused to eat up their meal in the approved manner, which would have demonstrated that the gods favoured the Romans and that their attack on the Carthaginian fleet would succeed. Publius had promptly picked the birds up and tossed them over the side of his flagship, declaring that 'if they would not eat, then they would drink'. A few years later his sister was frustrated by the crowds that slowed her litter as she was carried through the streets of Rome and loudly wished that her brother would go and drown some more of the poor. Though the Claudii were not always especially liked, they were always important. Although he might have officially become a plebian, Clodius remained in everyone's mind a Claudian and enjoyed the *auctoritas* of the name, and the solid support of clients and other connections built up by a great patrician house over the centuries.[3]

The Claudii promoted themselves just like any aristocratic family. Clodius' father died when he was young and the family was headed by his oldest brother Appius Claudius Pulcher, who was obsessed with maintaining their prestige. Simply because of their name the Claudii could not be ignored, but the flamboyance of this generation made them a powerful force in the public life of the city. There was also strength in numbers. Clodius had another brother, Caius, as well as three sisters, each of whom had been married off to a husband from a prominent family. One of the three was immortalised as the Lesbia of Catullus' poems, the lover with whom he shared a brief, passionate and adulterous affair, but whose subsequent rejection of him inspired some of his bitterest verses. Publius was the youngest of the six children, and perhaps the wildest, although all of them had a popular reputation both for unpredictable behaviour and for their scandalous sexual exploits. The Bona Dea scandal had shown Clodius' contempt for sacred tradition, but his subsequent exoneration had shown that he was a survivor, and a man to be reckoned with. Apart from his adulterous liaisons, it was widely rumoured that he had enjoyed incestuous relationships with each of his sisters. This was publicly stated by one of their husbands, Marcus Lucullus, when he finally divorced her. It may have been no more than malicious rumour, a number of other prominent Romans were accused of the same thing, but both at the time and since it was very difficult to be sure of anything with Clodius and his siblings. There was bad blood between him and the brothers Lucullus from the time Clodius had served on Lucius Lucullus' staff in Asia. It was perfectly normal for young aristocrats to gain military experience under the command of a relative or friend, but Clodius was never one to be bound by convention and chose to lead a mutiny against his brother-in-law. Shortly afterwards, he transferred to the staff of the husband of another sister, and seems to have managed to complete his service without falling out with this man.[4]

No one can have been too sure just what Clodius planned to do when his tribunate began in December 59 BC. It may be that he had not yet made up his mind whether or not to fulfil his threat, made some months before, to attack Caesar's legislation, but more probably this had been intended to let the triumvirs know that he could not be taken for granted. His chief aim was personal, to confirm his existing popularity amongst the population of Rome, and especially the less well-off citizens. To do this, his most important piece of legislation involved the wholesale reorganisation of the supply of State-subsidised grain to Italy, including the provision that citizens actually living in Rome would receive a regular dole of free corn. He also removed the ban imposed in 64 BC on the *collegia* – guilds or associations based on trade or regions within the city. Other reforms outlawed attempts to use unfavourable omens to block public business – a clear reference to Bibulus' recent activity, although the law was not retrospective so did not actually overrule his declarations – and restricted the freedom of the censors to expel men from the Senate. All four bills were passed in early January 58 BC. The free grain was very popular with the urban plebs, and Clodius used the *collegia* to help organise his supporters. Having done a deal with the two new consuls to assist them in securing lucrative provinces – both men were in debt and needed a profitable command – he now decided to flex his muscles.[5]

Cicero was the first target, and soon discovered that all the assurances he had had from Pompey, and subsequently even from Clodius himself, were hollow. The execution of the conspirators in 63 BC was the chief charge against him. The attack began in early 58 BC, while Caesar was still just outside Rome – he could no longer enter the city since he had assumed his provincial command – watching events and defending himself against the attacks of two of the new praetors. A public meeting was held in the Circus Flaminius, a stadium for chariot racing that lay outside the formal boundary of Rome, so that Caesar could be present. However, his support for Clodius was limited. Caesar repeated his arguments from the debate over the fate of the conspirators, saying again that he did not feel that it was right for them to have been executed. However, he also added that it would be wrong to make retrospective legislation formally outlawing past actions in order to prosecute Cicero. Around the same time he repeated his offer for the orator to become one of his legates and so secure himself from prosecution. It would have been a considerable coup for Caesar if Cicero had accepted, for it would have placed the orator under a strong obligation to him. It would also have removed a powerful and potentially hostile voice from Rome. Cicero declined the offer, as well as the chance of an extraordinary legateship from the Senate to travel abroad on public business. His initial confidence then began to waver, as he realised that he could not count on Pompey's support, nor on that of many leading senators whose loyalty he had expected.

Too many of the great men had some link or other with the Claudii and saw no reason to break with Clodius on behalf of a 'new man'. In the middle of March – roughly the same time that Caesar set out for Gaul – Cicero fled the city to go into voluntary exile, and soon passed into deep depression, blaming everyone else for his plight and lamenting his own momentary cowardice. Clodius had a bill passed formalising the expulsion and confiscating his property. His house was burned down by a mob of the tribune's supporters and a shrine to the goddess of liberty (*Libertas*) set up on the site. Clodius had given a demonstration of his power by removing a famous ex-consul, even if he was a rather boastful 'new man' without strong family connections. Cato was sidelined more subtly, as the tribune arranged for him to be sent to oversee the incorporation of Cyprus into Rome's empire. This wealthy kingdom had been annexed in part to pay for the new corn dole, and it was felt that the temptations open to the man appointed to oversee the business were so great that Rome's most famously moral citizen must be sent. Cato accepted the honour, which further augmented his stern reputation, even though he doubtless realised the true motives behind it. He also effectively admitted that it was right for a tribune of the people such as Clodius to interfere in foreign affairs rather than permitting the Senate its traditional control of this sphere.[6]

The Cyprus business was something of an insult to Pompey, for it altered some of the settlement that he had imposed on the East. A far greater humiliation came when Clodius arranged the escape of the son of the King of Armenia, held as a hostage in Pompey's household. The tribune also turned his gangs on the consul Gabinius, beating him up and smashing his fasces, simply because he had taken Pompey's side in the dispute. By the summer of 58 BC Clodius began openly questioning the validity of Caesar's legislation as consul, calling Bibulus as a witness in a public meeting to testify against his former colleague. It was a remarkable return to his position in April of the previous year, and cheerfully ignored the question mark this would then raise over his own plebian status and right to hold the office of tribune. In June Pompey encouraged the Senate to vote for the recall of Cicero, but the motion was vetoed. In August Clodius arranged for one of his slaves to let fall a dagger at a public meeting and under interrogation he claimed to have been sent to murder Pompey. The latter was a brave man on the battlefield but had a deep-rooted terror of assassination, which was perhaps unsurprising given the events he had witnessed in his youth. He retired to his house and stayed there for several months. Clodius lost some of his power when his term of office as tribune expired, and this encouraged a revival of efforts to recall Cicero. He still had his gangs of followers based on the *collegia*, and these were frequently used to threaten his opponents or break up meetings. Pompey replied by backing two of the new tribunes, Titus Annius Milo and Publius Sestius, who formed their own groups of thugs with which to combat Clodius' men. Both sides included many gladiators amongst their bands and at times there were large-scale battles with killed and wounded on both sides. These disturbances were more frequent, on a larger scale and far more violent than the struggles during Caesar's consulship. Pompey also toured Italy, visiting his many clients and urging them to come to Rome and support a law to recall Cicero. In the summer of 57 BC the Senate passed a decree to this effect, with only Clodius voting against the motion, and the decision was promptly ratified by the People.[7]

After some initial reluctance Caesar had followed Pompey's example and urged his clients by letter to support the move. From the start he had not especially desired Cicero's exile, although he had wanted to prevent the orator from continuing to lend his weight to the attacks on the legislation he had pushed through as consul. Now there was a chance to put Cicero under obligation to him by backing his cause, and Caesar characteristically seized on it. His initial hesitation – Publius Sestius travelled to his province at one point to convince him – may well have been intended to make sure that Cicero was aware of the debt that he would owe. Moving the vote of thanksgiving in the Senate and other public statements were proof that this had worked. There was an even greater debt to Pompey – though never quite enough to erase the memory of his failure to protect him in the first place – and Cicero had already had an opportunity of repaying some of this. Grain imports to Italy were erratic, and the new system of state-controlled supply set up by Clodius was not yet functioning well. He proposed a motion to give Pompey an extraordinary command to sort out the problem. In its eventual form the command was for five years, although there was an unsuccessful attempt by a tribune – probably with Pompey's tacit backing – to give him *imperium* throughout the empire, which was superior to every other governor, as well as control of substantial military and naval forces. Pompey had power again, and although this meant that he theoretically had to stay outside Rome the Senate was happy either to grant him a special dispensation from this rule or to meet outside the formal boundary of the city. Later disturbances in Egypt led to manoeuvring to secure him a further command to restore the situation there, but others were ambitious for this as well, and in the end it came to nothing.[8]

As 56 BC opened Pompey had a formal position, but so did Clodius once again for he had been elected aedile. He prosecuted Milo for political violence, but the latter was defended by Pompey and Cicero, and each side had brought along a mob of supporters to shout down and threaten their opponents. Cicero subsequently described the scene to his brother Quintus:

Pompey spoke, or at least tried to; but when he stood up, Clodius' gang began yelling, and he had to put up with this for the whole time he was speaking, getting interrupted not just by shouts, but jeers and insults. When he had finished – he showed great determination given the situation, never flinching, he said all that he meant to say, some of it even in silence coming from his force of character – but anyway when he stopped up sprang Clodius. He was greeted by yells from our supporters – we were pleased to return the compliment – and lost control of his spirit, voice and expression. This went on from the sixth hour, when Pompey finished speaking, to the eighth hour, with all sorts of abuse and foul verses about Clodius and Clodia. Enraged and white with anger he called out questions to his gang – and he was heard clearly above the shouting – who was it who starved the people? 'Pompey!' his cronies replied. Who wanted to go to Alexandria? 'Pompey!' they called. Who do YOU want to go? 'Crassus!' they replied. The latter was there, but without any goodwill towards Milo.[9]

The hostility between the two old rivals seemed to be brewing again, and Pompey told Cicero that he believed Crassus was supporting Clodius and Caius Cato, the youth who had accused him of dictatorship in 59 BC and was now tribune. He even claimed that Crassus was plotting to murder him, and once again relapsed into morbid fears and sent for extra bodyguards from his rural clients. Mistrustful of Crassus, there were indications that Pompey was also beginning to wonder whether or not he still needed Caesar. The problems of maintaining the grain supply did not yield to an easy or swift solution, and were made worse because the Treasury was seriously short of funds. Cato had not yet returned with the wealth of Cyprus to swell the coffers. Since 59 BC the Republic had lost a major source of revenue through the distribution of the public land in Campania. Cicero and others now advocated repealing Caesar's law to return this important source of income to the State. Cicero does not seem to have believed that Pompey was firmly opposed to such a move. Caesar's legislation was under threat, and so from different quarters was his command. A tribune seems to have proposed his immediate recall, while one of the favoured candidates for the consulship for 55 BC was openly eager to replace Caesar after his own year of office. This was Lucius Domitius Ahenobarbus, descendant of the man who had ridden on an elephant and helped to settle Transalpine Gaul, and his family connection to the region helped his case. It was not his first attack on Caesar, for he had been one of the praetors who in early 58 BC had questioned the validity of Caesar's acts as consul. Cicero described him as a man for whom the consulship was practically his birthright. This time Caesar was in some ways the victim of his own success, since it could be argued that the public thanksgiving he had received after his great victories showed that the war had been won, and therefore that there was no need for him to remain for the full five years of his command. Once again, Pompey was not believed to be wholly averse to this, while Crassus simply said nothing. His recent support for Clodius, which was widely perceived even if never open, had been a reminder that he was still powerful and that Pompey could not afford to ignore him. The latter had his new command, had just been voted a substantial budget by the Senate to fund his activities and seemed to be considering whether it was worthwhile maintaining the alliance. The triumvirate seemed on the point of crumbling.[10]

In later years what followed was seen as a fairly public summit meeting, where the triumvirs agreed to carve up the Roman world to their mutual advantage. Suetonius says that: 'Caesar made Pompey and Crassus come to Luca, a city in his province, where he persuaded them to seek a second consulship, thwart Domitius, and secure for him a five year extension to his provincial command.'[11] Appian and Plutarch talk of 200 senators trudging north to Luca with their entourages – he claims that no less than 120 lictors were counted – to wait outside while the three great men hammered out their deal. The story evidently grew with the telling, and the few accounts written nearer to the time suggest less organisation and much last-minute improvisation. Crassus became worried about Pompey's new strength sometime in the spring of 56 BC and hurried north to Ravenna, just inside Caesar's province, for a meeting about Cicero's fresh attempt to revive the question of the Campanian land. Pompey was due to leave Rome on 11 April, going first to Sardinia and then to Africa as part of his responsibilities for overseeing the corn supply. Cicero claims that he at least had no inkling of this, but before embarking on his official trip Pompey diverted to Luca, on the west coast of Cisalpine Gaul, to see Caesar. In Cicero's account the natural inference would be that Crassus was not present and that Caesar represented his interests, but this is by no means certain. The outcome of the meetings was, as the later sources maintained, a pact for Pompey and Crassus to stand for the consulship in 55 BC, and a five-year extension of Caesar's command. In this way, since after their consulship Pompey and Crassus could expect major provincial commands, all three men would have armies and formal *imperium* for the next few years.

The deal suggests that Caesar was less of a junior partner in the association than had been the case when the triumvirate was formed, and it is tempting to see him as the prime mover in arranging it. His personal charm was doubtless a major asset in calming the hostility and suspicion between Pompey and Crassus. Perhaps he devised the compromise, but the secret of this, just like the original alliance, was that each man realised that the association would be to his own personal advantage. As consuls, and then proconsuls with armies, Pompey and Crassus would have personal security and the ability to act. It also gave them the option of seeking new military adventures, something that seems now to have had particular appeal to Crassus, who was beginning to feel overshadowed by the martial achievements not just of Pompey, but also of Caesar. Pompey was also satisfied. More than either of the others he had appeared in recent months to have been drifting away, but in the end he would not have been as well off if the triumvirate had been broken. Even if he turned against Caesar, he would still not have become acceptable to many leading nobles in the Senate, and would have continued to face the criticism of Cato and the hostility of Clodius. It is significant that he had not accepted the suggestion of a friend some months before that he divorce Julia. Love may have been part of the reason, but it is also likely that he felt that for the moment a connection with Caesar remained a major asset. At its most basic level, it remained a useful thing to have his son-in-law in command of an army stationed in northern Italy, especially until he had troops of his own to command. In many ways all three triumvirs gained more from the agreement in 56 BC than their original association.[12]

It took time for the extent and full implication of the deal to be realised. Cicero seems to have been genuinely shocked, but quickly accepted the reality of the situation and came to terms with it. At the beginning of April he had won a personal victory over Clodius and his family when he successfully defended the young aristocrat Marcus Caelius Rufus. The latter was accused of orchestrating political violence, murder and the attempted murder of Clodius' sister Clodia. Cicero's speech was a skilful and highly vicious character assassination of the pair, raking up the old allegations of incest along with many other things, speaking of 'that woman's husband –

I'm sorry I mean her brother'. This personal revenge may well have made the subsequent renewal of the triumvirate easier to bear. Cicero's brother Quintus was one of Pompey's legates on the grain commission and was given a blunt reminder to pass on that Pompey and Caesar had not supported his recall to have him criticise either of them. Probably at the beginning of May, Cicero delivered a speech in the Senate arguing against the moves to remove Transalpine and Cisalpine Gaul from Caesar's control and send out a new governor. His praise of Caesar was fulsome, and, so he claimed, justified by the victories won in Gaul whatever their past differences:[13]

> Under the command of Caius Caesar, we have fought a war inside Gaul; in the past we have merely repelled attacks. Our generals always felt that these people needed to be driven back in by war . . .. Even Caius Marius himself whose divine and matchless courage protected the Roman people after dreadful disasters and casualties and who drove back hordes of Gauls who were flooding into Italy, did not attack them in their towns and lairs. . . . I see that Caius Caesar's thinking has been very different. For he did not feel it sufficient to fight only against those already in arms against the Roman people, but felt that all of Gaul should be brought under our dominion. Therefore he has, with stunning good fortune, smashed in battle the greatest and fiercest tribes of Germans and Helvetii, and terrified the other peoples, checked them and brought under our domination and power of the Roman people; our general, our soldiers, and the arms of the Roman people have now made their way through regions and nations which till now have not even been known by story or written account.[14]

Backed by Cicero's eloquence, and the combined weight of Pompey and Crassus, Caesar's command was confirmed and later extended. The Senate also voted to accept responsibility for funding the extra legions Caesar had recruited, not, as Cicero declared, because he lacked resources from his provinces, but because it was unseemly to appear stingy with such a distinguished servant of the Republic. Caesar was secure in his command, but it required rather more effort to ensure that Crassus and Pompey would be the consuls for 55 BC. Disturbances orchestrated by the tribune Caius Cato, and apparently backed by Clodius, prevented elections being held in the last months of 56 BC. Both men had evidently been persuaded to work with the renewed triumvirate. The decision was a pragmatic one, but Crassus may also have persuaded them, since he was widely believed to have been backing them in recent years. Pompey and Crassus had not declared their candidature until after the legal date, and the consul due to preside over the elections, Cnaeus Cornelius Lentulus Marcellinus, refused to exempt them from this rule. Therefore the elections were not held until January 55 BC, after Marcellinus had laid down his office, and so were conducted under a temporary official known as an *interrex*, who permitted them to stand. The other candidates had largely fallen away, but Ahenobarbus was never a man to back down and refused to give up his ambitions.

Crassus' son Publius had lately returned from Gaul, and brought with him a large number of soldiers given special leave to take part in the elections. Some were officers – centurions perhaps, and certainly tribunes and prefects – but others were probably just burly members of the rank and file. The election day was marked by huge violence in which Ahenobarbus was wounded and one of his attendants killed, before Crassus and Pompey were declared the victors. The triumvirate was once again firmly in control of Rome, although it had taken far more brute force than on the first occasion. Intimidation prevented Cato the Younger from winning the praetorship. At the election of the curule aediles the fighting was so widespread and brutal that even Pompey ended up spattered by someone else's blood. With Pompey and Crassus as consuls it would be difficult for anyone to attack them, but after their year of office was over things might change, especially if one or both set out for provincial commands. Clodius was still there and it was hard to judge what he would do in the future, while men like Ahenobarbus and Cato were even more bitterly opposed to the triumvirs than they had been in the past. In Rome power was never permanent, but for the moment the triumvirate were riding high.[15]

TO THE ATLANTIC

Although there was to be considerable military activity in Gaul in 56 BC, the operations were on a significantly smaller scale than in the previous years. With the Helvetii, Ariovistus and the Belgic confederation defeated, it was with some justification that Caesar felt that 'Gaul was at peace'. He did not have a major campaign planned for the summer, which meant that it was easier for him to loiter in Cisalpine Gaul until well into April and arrange matters at Luca. There was no obvious opponent left in Gaul and it may well be that he was once again considering diverting his attentions to the Balkans. In the following year he would lead an expedition to Britain, and it is highly likely that this possibility was already in his mind. Up until the meeting at Luca political concerns occupied most of his attention, and afterwards he had the security of an additional five years of command, which meant that he was not pressed for time and so could afford to let the year pass without a grand offensive. Detachments of his army under the command of legates had anyway been active in a number of operations that were too small in scale to require the commander and his main force. In the autumn of 57 BC the *Twelfth* Legion under the command of Sulpicius Galba had attempted to occupy the Great St Bernard Pass, so keeping this route over the Alps secure for military convoys and commerce. The attempt failed and Galba was forced to withdraw. Other parts of the army spent the winter deep in Gallia Comata. Publius Crassus with the *Seventh* Legion was in the west, amongst tribes who had submitted to him late in the previous summer. The tribal leaders had obeyed the standard Roman request for hostages and everything seemed calm.[16]

At some point in the spring or early summer of 56 BC the mood of these western tribes changed. Roman officers despatched to the tribal centres to arrange for grain to be supplied to the army were seized and a message sent to Crassus saying that they would only be released when their own hostages were returned. It may simply have been that the locals had not at first appreciated that the Romans expected to stay and make continued demands for food, and that realisation swiftly turned to resentment. The first tribe to act were the Veneti, living in what is now southern Brittany. They were a maritime people, deeply involved in trade along the Atlantic coast. Dio claims that they had heard rumours of Caesar's planned expedition to Britain and feared that this would disrupt their trade with the island, or throw open the markets there to competitors. To Caesar, and doubtless to his Roman audience, this was a rebellion, the tribes breaking the treaty that they had so recently accepted and taking his officers – several of whom were equestrians – as hostages. He gave orders for a fleet to be constructed on the Loire, before hurrying to the area. The rebellion had spread rapidly and he was afraid that other tribes might be tempted to join if they judged that the Romans were weak. This was because the Gauls as a race were 'inclined to revolution and could readily be stirred to war'. He also acknowledged that like all mankind, they 'deeply loved freedom and hated slavery'. Therefore he split his army into several independent columns. Labienus was left to watch over the Belgic tribes defeated in the previous year, while Crassus took twelve cohorts – probably the *Seventh* Legion reinforced with some additional troops – into Aquitania. A larger force of three legions under the command of Sabinus was sent to Normandy.[17]

Caesar himself led the remainder against the Veneti, striking at what he perceived to be the heart of the rebellion. The tribe was reluctant to form an army and face the legions in the open, so the Romans targeted their towns, many of which were built on coastal promontories. Although several of these were stormed, in each case the inhabitants escaped in ships, along with most of their possessions. The main strength of the tribe was its fleet, numbering some 280 ships according to Caesar, and only when the newly built Roman navy arrived was it possible to confront this. The Gallic vessels were big sailing ships, designed for trade more than war, but they still proved difficult propositions for the oared galleys that the Romans employed. The standard methods of naval fighting in the Mediterranean world were ramming and boarding. The first was ineffective against the thick timbered hulls of the Veneti's ships, while the second was made extremely difficult by their high sides. The Roman fleet was led by Decimus Brutus, and through ingenuity and good fortune it managed to destroy the enemy navy in a single encounter. Devices similar to those used in sieges were made to cut through and pull down the enemy sails and rigging, but it was a sudden drop in the wind that left the Veneti becalmed and vulnerable, for their ships had no oars. Caesar and the bulk of the army were mere spectators to the action, watching from the shoreline. Without their fleet, and unable to resist Roman assaults on their towns and villages, the Veneti had no choice but to surrender.

No tribe allied to Rome seems to have come forward to plead their case and Caesar decided that his punishment would be harsh. Their entire ruling council – probably numbering several hundred – were beheaded, and the rest of the population of the tribe sold as slaves. It is doubtful that the entire region was depopulated, and the sheer practicalities of rounding up large numbers of people make it unlikely that all were found and dealt with in this way. It may only have been those men of military age who had been captured or surrendered who were sold. Nevertheless, it was clearly an appalling blow to the Veneti, removing all of their leaders and elders, along with a substantial chunk of the rest of the tribe. This can only have caused massive social and political dislocation. Caesar justified this terrible punishment by claiming that it was necessary to show that representatives or ambassadors ought to be accorded proper respect. Some scholars have rightly pointed out that officers sent to collect grain would not normally be classed as ambassadors. Yet Caesar's attitude would have probably been shared by most contemporary Romans. His officers had been seized while visiting peoples who were supposed to be allied to Rome – he makes no mention of the men's fate and whether or not any or all of them were recovered. The severe punishment meted out to the Veneti was a warning that no Romans – particularly senior officers and equestrians – could be mistreated without risking appalling consequences. Taking hostages from the tribes was an important way for Caesar to retain their loyalty, which was something demanded both of the communities who welcomed Rome and those who were defeated. The attempt to overturn the system by taking Roman prisoners could not be allowed to succeed. Therefore the punishment of the Veneti was deliberately appalling as a warning to others. The Roman attitude to such brutal measures was entirely pragmatic. Cruelty for its own sake was condemned, but atrocities that brought practical advantage to Rome's position – and were inflicted on foreigners – were acceptable. An extreme example had been Crassus' mass crucifixion of Spartacus' followers in 71 BC. Whenever he felt that it was in his interest, Caesar was utterly ruthless.[18]

Labienus' presence had ensured that there was no attempt to renew the war in that area. Both Crassus and Sabinus won victories in Aquitania and Normandy respectively. At the end of the summer Caesar personally led a force against the Menapii and Morini who lived along the coast of what is now the Pas de Calais and Belgium. The attack was prompted because they had never sent envoys to Caesar and acknowledged his and Rome's power by seeking his friendship. Both tribes were believed to have contributed warriors to the great Belgic army that had taken the field in the previous year. They had no large towns and lived in scattered settlements. Even these were abandoned when the Romans advanced, and the population took their cattle, flocks and movable possessions and hid in the deep woodland and marshy areas of their country. It was difficult terrain for the Romans to operate in, and the legions had no fixed target to fight. They burned the villages and farms that they found, but this did not make the enemy give in. Then the legionaries began clearing areas of woodland and managed to capture some parties of the enemy along with their animals, but they also suffered losses in ambushes. It was a different type of warfare to the campaigns waged up to this point and little was achieved in the few weeks left of the campaigning season. As the weather closed in, Caesar withdrew leaving both tribes still undefeated. It was a failure, but not a major or irredeemable one. On balance the year had gone reasonably well, both in Gaul and especially with the resolution of affairs in Rome. Secure in his command, Caesar was free to plan major enterprises for the next summer. This was another reason for his harsh treatment of the Veneti. He may well already have selected Britain as his next target, but it is possible that he once again had pondered turning his attentions to the Illyricum frontier. Either way, he needed to ensure that warfare would not erupt in Gaul while he and the bulk of the army were elsewhere. The savage punishment of a single rebellious tribe was a reminder that Caesar's wrath was to be feared.[19]

XIII

'OVER THE WATERS':
THE BRITISH AND GERMAN
EXPEDITIONS, 55–54 BC

'On the 24th October letters came through from my brother Quintus and from Caesar, dated 25th September and sent from the nearest place on the coast of Britain. Britain is subdued, hostages have been handed over, no plunder, but a tribute of money imposed, and they are bringing the army back over from Britain.' – *Cicero, late October 54 BC.*[1]

'The divine Julius was the first of the Romans to cross to Britain with an army. He cowed the inhabitants by winning a battle and got control of the coast. Yet it is fair to say that he did no more than show the island to his descendants, but did not bequeath it to them.' – *Tacitus, c. AD 98.*[2]

In 56 BC the pace of operations in Gaul had slackened, but now Caesar was determined to regain the momentum of his first two years there. During the winter months he seems finally to have decided that Britain was to be his next target, if he had not in fact already done so. He claimed that this was a necessary task because the tribes of that island had sent military aid to the Gauls fighting against him. There were certainly close trading links between the coastal tribes of northern Gaul and the peoples on the other side of the Channel. In the past there may also have been political connections, but in his account of the defeat of the Veneti and other coastal tribes Caesar makes no mention of large-scale participation by the Britons. However, it was common amongst the tribes of northern Europe for individual warriors to seek employment with the famous chieftains of other tribes, and it may well be that some Britons had fought against Caesar's legions in this way. Ultimately, the suggestion that the British tribes were a military threat to Rome's interests in Gaul was no more than a pretext and Britain attracted

Caesar's attention for other reasons. There were rumours of rich natural resources, which offered the prospect of a lucrative war. Suetonius claims that Caesar's personal fondness for pearls was an additional incentive, for he believed – falsely as it turned out – that particularly fine examples were to be found on the British coasts. More important than the possibility of riches was the glory that always came to the man who was the first to lead a Roman army into previously unexplored countries. With Britain there was an added glamour because it lay across the sea, on the edge of the vast ocean that was believed to encircle the habitable lands of the globe. No Greek or Roman knew much about Britain and its peoples, and in the absence of facts wild stories of strange creatures and weird customs flourished, resembling in many ways the tales of the New World in the age of European exploration. A success in Britain was bound to grab the attention of Romans of all classes.[3]

TREACHERY AND MASSACRE

As usual Caesar spent the winter in Cisalpine Gaul, and he was still there when news reached him of a new migration. Two Germanic tribes, the Usipetes and the Tencteri, had left their homes east of the Rhine and crossed the river into Gaul. Caesar claims that 430,000 people were on the move, which on the same proportion as the Helvetii of one warrior to three women, children or other dependants, would give a total force of over 100,000 fighting men. As always we should be very cautious about accepting such a number as meaning anything more precise than that 'a substantial body of' people were on the move. Most probably, like the Helvetii, the tribes moved not in a single massive column, but in many parties spread over a wide area. Once again, the cause of the migration was warfare and raiding, but in this case the two tribes were fleeing from the regular depredations of their larger and more powerful neighbours, the Suebi. This broad group of related tribes seems to have formed a loose confederation and was consistently depicted by Caesar as more ferocious – and therefore more dangerous – even than the other Germanic peoples. He claims that the tribes maintained vast numbers of warriors, half of whom were available for war every year. German tribes took pride in the amount of land around their boundaries that they kept free from settlement as a sign of their martial power and as a deterrent to any raiders. The *Commentaries* repeat a rumour, which Caesar does not bother to confirm or deny, that on one side of their land no other people dared to live within 600 miles of the Suebi. Yet although unable to cope with the onslaught of their larger neighbours, the Usipetes and Tencteri remained warlike people, and were only briefly blocked by the Belgic Menapii, who held the river crossings against them. The Germans pretended to retire, marching eastwards for three days, but then sent their cavalry hastening back under cover of darkness to launch a surprise attack. The Menapii were fooled by the trick and dispersed, so that they were unable to mount any concerted resistance. Their boats were captured and used to ferry the migrants across the river. The two German tribes were able to subsist throughout the rest of the winter on the food they had seized from the Menapii, sheltering in the villages they had overrun.[4]

Caesar decided to rejoin the army earlier than usual. Before he arrived, the migrants had begun to move again, pushing south into the lands of the Eburones and Condrusi. The ensuing campaign very quickly became a source of controversy, with Caesar's actions being publicly attacked in the Senate by Cato, who accused him of serious misconduct. Therefore, even more than usual, the account presented in the *Commentaries* was intended to defend his every move and show that he had behaved reasonably and honourably, as well as with his accustomed calm efficiency. Yet even his sternest critic would have conceded that the arrival of the two German tribes threatened Roman interests. In the last three years Caesar had spread Roman power throughout Gaul. The region was not as yet formally annexed as a province and the tribes continued to govern themselves, but virtually all openly or tacitly acknowledged Rome's dominance. The Menapii were one of the few exceptions, and had yet to submit and give hostages to Caesar, but the Eburones and Condrusi had almost certainly done so in 57 BC. From the beginning the proconsul had emphasised his readiness to protect allied peoples from any enemy, making clear in each campaign both the advantages offered by alliance with Rome and the terrible punishment awaiting any who opposed its legions.

The migrants introduced a new and unstable element into the balance of power that had been created. There was no unoccupied land in Gaul for them to settle, and they had already demonstrated their willingness to use force against anyone who did not admit them. Individual tribes – or more probably chieftains within them – might choose to welcome the new arrivals, feeling that the numbers and reputation of these warriors would be a great asset to them as allies. Exactly the same motive had led some Gallic leaders to welcome Ariovistus, the Helvetii and Caesar himself. Such a course was now most attractive to those who had not done well since the area had been dominated by the Romans, and especially those recently defeated by the legions. There was the prospect of new rivalries and conflict within and between tribes, made worse by the possibility that the victors may eventually win through Germanic rather than Roman support. When Caesar had expelled Ariovistus from Gaul, he had publicly proclaimed his refusal to admit German tribes across the Rhine. As we have seen he clearly exaggerated the distinction between Gauls and Germans, and continually presented the latter as a potential threat to Rome. Yet if he exaggerated, he did not entirely invent either the differences between the peoples or the menace posed to Roman interests. The Romans had never welcomed the incursions of peoples into the regions around their frontiers.[5]

When Caesar reached his army in Gaul he received more information about the migrants. Presumably much of this, along with the earlier reports that had reached him south of the Alps, came from his legates left in command of the winter camps. These seem to have taken no direct action against the Germans. In part this was because campaigning was always difficult in the winter months, but more importantly legates were not expected to display too much initiative and it would have been inappropriate for them to have embarked on a major operation on their own. Caesar also received reports from allied tribes. A comment in a subsequent passage of the *Commentaries* suggests that it was his normal custom to stay in the houses of Gallic noblemen while he was travelling in Gaul. This was a useful way of showing how highly he valued their friendship, for hospitality played an important role in Gallic culture, but it also helped him to gauge their mood and views. As in Rome, many of the great affairs of a Roman magistrate were conducted at a very intimate level. Overall his various sources presented a worrying picture. Already some chieftains and tribes had approached the German migrants seeking alliance and making offers of land in return for their military aid. Caesar summoned the leaders of all the tribes to a council, where he arranged for them to supply the usual contingents of cavalry and grain supplies. He did not feel that it was useful to reveal that he knew some of the chieftains had been dealing with the Germans. If he could quickly defeat the two tribes, then such negotiations would not matter. The Roman army concentrated and marched north.[6]

When the column was within a few days march of the two German tribes, a deputation came from them. The envoys told of how they had been driven from their homes by the Suebi and asked Caesar to grant them land, or at least let them keep what they were able to seize by force. As usual, his account emphasised the barbarians' pride, making them declare that they were fully ready to fight if he refused them, since they feared no one apart from the

Suebi. The proconsul replied 'as seemed appropriate', but made it clear that he would not permit them to settle in Gaul. However, he offered to arrange for them to settle amongst the Ubii, another German tribe who lived on the east bank of the Rhine. They were also under pressure from the Suebi and had recently sent ambassadors to him requesting support. The envoys from the two tribes agreed to take this offer back to their people, and return to Caesar in three days' time with a decision. In the meantime they asked him to halt his advance. Caesar refused, suspicious that this was merely a ploy to gain time, for he knew that the bulk of the German cavalry was away on a plundering and foraging raid.[7]

The Romans pressed on, until they were within 12 miles of the main tribal encampment. This had probably taken three days, since Caesar was met by the same deputation returning as arranged. Once again they asked him to stop and wait, but the legions continued to advance. Caesar did grant their plea to send orders forward to his cavalry screen telling them not to engage any Germans they met. If they were attacked then the auxiliary and allied horse were to do no more than defend themselves. In addition, the Germans wanted permission to send envoys to the Ubii so that they could themselves negotiate a settlement. Once again they requested that he grant them three days for this to occur. Caesar remained sceptical of their motives, feeling that this was simply another pretext to gain time for the raiding party to return. This was not unreasonable, for even if the Germans were sincerely hoping for a peaceful settlement it was obviously in their interest to negotiate from a position of greater strength. Equally, if they intended to fight they would want to have these troops, who had spearheaded the attack on the Menapii and doubtless included some of their best warriors. In addition, if the raiders returned with food and forage this would make it easier for the tribes to maintain themselves during days of either negotiating or military manoeuvring.

Caesar made one modest concession, saying that he would only advance 4 miles during the day, moving to a position where his camp would have a convenient water supply. In the meantime fighting had already broken out between the cavalry of the two sides. The Germans had some 800 horsemen still guarding their encampment. Caesar had 5,000 cavalry, although if these were performing their duties as a patrolling and screening force properly, then they would not all have been concentrated in one place. Even so, the Gallic auxiliaries probably had a significant numerical advantage, and were mounted on larger horses than their opponents, which makes it all the more notable that the Germans quickly gained an advantage. In Caesar's account the Germans charged first, chasing away part of the Gallic cavalry, but were in turn met by their supports. Many of the Germans then dismounted to fight on foot – perhaps with the support of the picked infantrymen who regularly supported the horsemen of some Germanic tribes. The Gauls were routed and fled, spreading panic amongst a large part of the auxiliary and allied cavalry who galloped in terror back to the main force, which was probably several miles away. Caesar maintains that the Germans were the ones to break the truce with an unprovoked attack on his unsuspecting allies. Elsewhere he notes that the Germans did not ride with saddles and, despising horsemen like the Gauls who did so, were inclined to attack them on sight. The truth of what happened will never be known, and may have been unclear even at the time. Both the Gauls and the Germans were individualistic warriors who prized displays of conspicuous valour and skill. It was difficult for their leaders to impose any rigid discipline upon such men, and when large numbers of warriors from different tribes met, then there was always the potential for violence. Taunting could easily escalate into personal duels or massed fighting. Throughout the Gallic campaigns German warriors consistently defeated their Gallic counterparts, each success adding to their fierce reputation. In this case seventy-four of Caesar's Gallic allies were killed, one of the very rare occasions where he gives a specific figure for his own casualties. Amongst them was an aristocrat from Aquitania called Piso, whose grandfather had been the king of his tribe and was recognised by the Senate as a 'friend of the Roman people'. Piso turned back during the rout to rescue his brother, but as they escaped he was thrown from his horse, surrounded and cut down. His brother spurred back towards the enemy and was also killed.[8]

Caesar claims that the skirmish showed that the German tribes were acting treacherously, spinning out peace negotiations until they were strong enough to attack him. This may or may not have been true, but if it was, then provoking a fight at this stage was clearly not in their interest. Worried that rumours of the skirmish might be inflated into a major defeat and encourage unrest amongst the Gallic tribes, Caesar summoned his legates and quaestor and gave orders for an all-out attack on the following day. The next morning, as the legions prepared for battle, a large deputation arrived from the Germans. It included all of their main leaders and chieftains, who wanted to apologise for the fighting on the previous day and explain that they had not intended to break the truce in this way, but were still keen to negotiate. The *Commentaries* stress the 'treachery and dissimulation' of the German leaders, and in a rare moment of emotion say that 'Caesar rejoiced' because they had placed themselves into his hands. Forgetting his outrage at the detention of his own officers – and that was the key difference, for they had been Romans and his own men – he arrested the envoys. The legions marched out in three columns, which could readily be converted into the battle line of the *triplex acies*, and advanced the 8 miles to the German camp. The Usipetes and Tencteri were surprised and leaderless, so that what followed was more of a massacre than a battle:[9]

> When their terror was made clear by the confusion and chaos, our soldiers, enraged by the treachery of the previous day, surged into the camp. There, those who were able to take up arms quickly fought for a while amongst the wagons and baggage: All the rest, a mob of women and children . . . started to run in all directions; Caesar sent his cavalry to hunt them down.
>
> Hearing the clamour from their rear, and seeing their own people killed, the Germans threw down their arms, dropped their military standards, and fled from the camp; and when they reached the point where the Meuse and the Rhine join, they despaired of flight; many had already fallen, and the remainder jumped into the river, and drowned there, overcome by fear, fatigue or the current of the water.[10]

Caesar's army suffered no fatal casualties and only a small number of wounded in the one-sided fighting. He gives no figure for the German losses, but these were probably considerable, with many being killed or taken to be sold as slaves. Even more escaped, but at the cost of losing their possessions in their abandoned wagons. If, as seems likely, the two tribes were not all in a single encampment but in a number of parties spread over a fairly wide area, then the other groups may have got away more lightly. The only organised group of fugitives was the raiding band of cavalry, which recrossed the Rhine and took refuge amongst the Sugambri tribe. After the destruction and dispersal of their peoples the tribal leaders were granted their freedom, but chose to stay in the Roman camp rather than face possible retribution from the Gauls whose lands they had plundered.[11]

The Romans celebrated the easy victory that had freed them from 'the fear of such a great war'. The success reinforced the Roman dominance of Gaul created by Caesar's earlier campaigns. If he wanted to mount a British expedition this year, then the speed of the campaign left this possibility open. In practical respects the victory was good for Rome, but when news of this episode reached the city it was not well received by a number of senators. It is unlikely that the first report came from Caesar himself, and more probable that it reached Rome in letters written by men on his staff, or – directly or indirectly – from merchants with the army. Cato led the attack against Caesar, which focused not so much on the massacre itself, but on the belief that the proconsul had violated the truce by seizing ambassadors and attacking by surprise. The Romans set great store on their 'good faith' (*fides*), contrasting it with the – in their view – duplicity of other races. While their record was in fact scarcely unblemished, nevertheless they were aware that honouring treaties and other formal agreements had the practical advantage of helping future negotiations. At a more fundamental level, Rome's special relationship with the gods, which was demonstrated by its remarkable success in war, relied upon virtue and honouring sacred obligations or oaths. In the Senate: 'Cato urged them to surrender Caesar to those whom he had wronged, and not to turn upon themselves, or allow to fall upon their city, the pollution of his crime. "However," said he, "let us also sacrifice to the gods, because they do not turn the punishment for the general's folly and madness upon his soldiers, but spare the city."'[12]

On a handful of occasions in the past the Romans had formally handed over one of their magistrates to a foreign enemy in expiation of an injustice. The most recent case had occurred in 137 BC after the consul Caius Hostilius Mancinus had let his army be surrounded by Celtiberians outside their town of Numantia. Mancinus had saved the lives of his soldiers by surrendering. His army was allowed to go free, but the Romans were to accept a peace that favoured the Numantines. Subsequently the Senate refused to ratify the treaty, and ordered that Mancinus, as its guarantor, be clapped in irons and left outside the walls of Numantia. (The Celtiberians did not see this as much consolation and ignored him. Mancinus returned to Rome and, since he was a Roman aristocrat, commissioned a statue of himself naked and in chains. This was displayed prominently in his house to remind visitors of the time he had been willing to sacrifice himself for the good of the Republic.) Cato did not have a good case for comparing Caesar to men like Mancinus. In the past men had only been handed over to an enemy when the Romans were seeking reasons for recent defeats or wished to avoid an inconvenient treaty. Caesar had won victory after victory, and as long as he continued to do so it was unthinkable that the Senate would actually agree to Cato's demand, particularly while Pompey and Crassus were consuls. Yet there clearly was disquiet among the senators and it may well have been on this occasion that the Senate actually voted to send a commission to 'investigate the state of the Gallic provinces'.[13] As far as we know no such commission was ever actually sent. Cato's criticism had clearly stung Caesar, for he chose to send a letter defending his actions to a friend who read it out at a meeting of the Senate, 'and when it was read, with its abundant insults and denunciations of Cato, Cato rose to his feet and showed, not in anger or contentiousness, but as if from calculation and due preparation, that the accusations against him bore the marks of abuse and scoffing, and were childishness and vulgarity on Caesar's part'.[14] Cato was too good an actor not to be able to milk the situation to his advantage. Had Caesar been present then his oratory might well have been more persuasive, and at the very least he could have realised that he was losing the debate and changed tack. This was the weakness of his position in these years, for he could not take part in the meetings of the Senate or public gatherings at Rome. After his letter had been read out, Cato was able to plunge into a detailed attack of all of Caesar's actions. For the moment he, and those who shared his hostility to Caesar, could do no more than this, but their continued sniping showed no sign of going away and was always in the background, even when the Republic was formally celebrating the proconsul's achievements.[15]

News of the slaughter of the Tencteri and Usipetes would not have reached Rome for some time, so it is unlikely that these debates occurred until late in 55 BC. Immediately after his success, Caesar had decided to take his army across the Rhine in a display of force intended to deter any other German tribes from invading Gaul. The Ubii had already given him hostages and sought his protection from the Suebi, providing further justification for the expedition. The tribe now offered to supply him with boats to ferry the army over the river, but the proconsul felt that it was 'too risky, and beneath his own dignity and that of the Roman people' to employ such a method. Instead he set the legions to building a bridge, the design of which was described in loving detail in the *Commentaries*, for the Romans valued the engineering skills of their soldiers almost as much as their battlefield successes. In ten days the bridge was complete and strongly garrisoned forts set to protect both ends of it. The location of the bridge remains a mystery – as, in spite of Caesar's description, do some details of its construction. However, somewhere between modern Coblenz and Andernach seems likely.[16]

Once across the river, the legions found no one to fight. The Sugambri had already fled with their possessions into the deep forests, urged on by the horsemen of the two migrant tribes who had sought refuge amongst them. In a similar way the Suebi evacuated their settlements and sent their families and herds into woodland where they could best hide from the invader. Their warriors were told to muster at a well-known place in the centre of their lands, where their army would confront the Romans. Caesar had no particular wish to penetrate deep into their territory or to seek battle. For eighteen days he ravaged the land, burning farms and villages and harvesting or destroying their crops. Then he withdrew to the western bank of the Rhine, breaking down the bridge behind him. He had shown the Germans of the region that the Roman army was both willing and able to reach and attack their lands whenever it chose to do so. The fate of the Usipetes and Tencteri, and before that the defeat of Ariovistus, provided dire warning to any tribe who tried to settle in Gaul. The leaders of the Ubii were assured that Caesar would return to aid them if the Suebi moved against them once more. For the moment, the frontier of Gaul was secure.[17]

RECONNAISSANCE IN FORCE – THE FIRST EXPEDITION TO BRITAIN, 55 BC

It was now late in the summer, but Caesar was still determined to launch an attack on Britain. It could be little more than a raid, hastily prepared and with the expectation of returning to winter in Gaul. The fleet constructed to fight the Veneti, along with whatever ships had been captured in that campaign or could now be provided by his allies, were gathered on the coast in the territory of the Morini (modern Pas de Calais). Caesar himself marched with the legions from the Rhine to rendezvous with them, their arrival prompting the previously hostile Morini to decide that making peace with Rome was the prudent course for the moment. In addition to his oared warships the proconsul had just under 100 sailing ships to serve as transports. This was not an especially large total for the task in hand. Caesar decided to take the barest essentials when it came to baggage and very little food, since at that time of year he could expect to supply himself from the ripe crops in the fields. Two legions, the *Seventh* and *Tenth*, were squeezed into eighty transports. It seems likely that by this time these mustered no more than 4,000 men apiece, so that on average 100 would have been in each vessel. Some legionaries may instead have acted as rowers in the warships. A further eighteen transports were allocated to the cavalry, perhaps providing enough space for several hundred of these along with their mounts. His senior officers, plus their staffs and whatever possessions they considered to be essential, were transported in the cramped conditions of the war galleys. In comparison to the armies he had led in recent years, it was with this small force that Caesar set out to invade Britain. The bulk of the army remained in Gaul, sizeable columns being sent under its legates to subdue the Menapii,

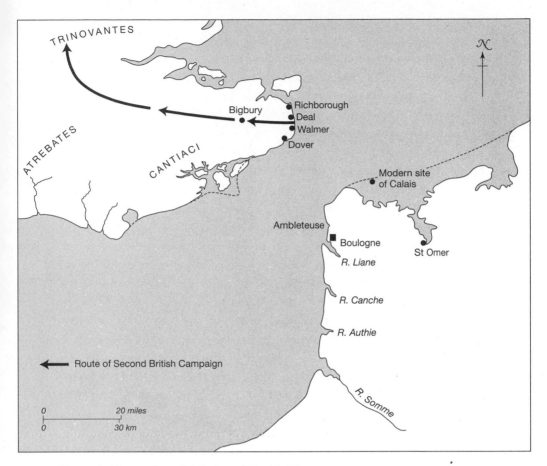

The probable coastline of Britain and Gaul in 55 BC

and those of the Morini who had not surrendered. An additional force acted as garrison to his embarkation port, which was most likely near the site of modern Boulogne – the land around what is now Calais does not yet seem to have been reclaimed from the sea. After all the preparations, the Roman fleet did not set sail until late August.[18]

During the weeks before setting out Caesar had tried to gather as much information about Britain and its inhabitants as possible, but had in fact discovered very little useful information. He interviewed traders who had travelled to the island, but they claimed to know little. Caesar was planning a landing in the south-eastern corner of Britain, while the principal trading ports at this time lay much further west, one of the most important being at Hengistbury Head. Therefore the merchants may genuinely have known little about his target, but it is more than likely that they were also reluctant to supply him with information at all. The trade to Britain seems to have been mainly in the hands of Gauls, with few Romans operating on these routes. Many of these men came from the coastal tribes of Gaul that had so recently been suppressed by Caesar. It would have been entirely reasonable for these men to resent Roman intervention in the island, fearing that this would open the market to Roman competitors. Having failed to learn anything very useful by this method, Caesar sent a warship on a reconnaissance voyage across the Channel. One of his officers, Caius Volusenus, was placed in charge of this. He returned after five days with a series of observations about the coastline, but since he had not risked a landing the detail contained within these must have been limited. The coastline of south-eastern England was very different at this period, with much of the lower lying land such as Romney Marshes still under the sea. Thanet was a genuine island, and the lagoons around the Wantsum Channel could have offered an extensive sheltered anchorage for the invaders. However, Volusenus does not seem to have discovered this. The news of the Roman intentions reached the British tribes and a number of leaders sent representatives to Caesar's camp on the Gaulish coast. These offered to accept alliance with Rome and the usual demand for hostages as surety. The proconsul decided to send his own envoy back with the deputations, and chose Commius, a Gallic chieftain whom he had made King of the Atrebates, for this task. Commius was believed to have influence and connections amongst the British tribes. In fact, these proved of questionable value, for on arrival in Britain he was almost immediately imprisoned. No report came back to Caesar of his mission. In a real sense Caesar was sailing into the unknown when he set out for Britain, but he was impatient to be off and achieve something more tangible and spectacular – and perhaps less controversial – before the year was out. When the winds turned in his favour he led the warships and the legions out of harbour.[19]

There were problems from the beginning. The cavalry had not yet embarked, and by the time that they had hastened to another port and gone aboard the eighteen transports allocated to them the weather had changed. Although he had spent some time with warships in the eastern Mediterranean, Caesar consistently underestimated the power and unpredictability of the sea, and especially the English Channel. The cavalry transports were unable to follow. The main convoy had left before dawn and the leading elements reached Britain – probably somewhere near modern Dover – by late morning. Volusenus may well have located the natural haven at Dover, and it is quite possible that Caesar had chosen this for his landing. However, at this point the beach was overlooked by high cliffs, at the top of which crowds of British warriors were waiting. Caesar waited at anchor until late afternoon, when most of his straggling convoy of ships had concentrated. His senior officers were rowed across to his flagship for a meeting and told that the nature of the operation required them to respond especially quickly to his signals. Once all the ships had caught up, they were to move 7 miles along the coast to a good landing spot that seems to have been located by Volusenus on his earlier patrol. The Britons shadowed the Roman fleet as it moved, but only their cavalry and chariots were able to keep pace with the ships and contest the landing. Volusenus' beach was probably near Deal or Walmer, and was wide and not dominated by high bluffs. Yet even so the Britons knew the ground and the tides and the Romans did not. Horsemen and chariots swooped in to attack the legionaries as they tried to disembark. The transport ships were not designed to land people or cargo directly onto a beach and ran aground while still in fairly deep water. The legionaries had to wade their way forward, encumbered by their bulky equipment. They were vulnerable to missiles, which they could not easily dodge or ward off with their shields, and arrived on the beach scattered in ones and twos and in little shape to mount an organised resistance. There is no evidence that the legionaries had been given any special training for this operation. Caesar comments that on this occasion his veteran troops failed to show their normal enthusiasm and aggression, but in the circumstances it was hard for the assault on the beach to generate any momentum.[20]

Caesar signalled to his warships, ordering their captains to head for the beach and run in as close as they could so that the crews on their decks could bombard the Britons with slings, bows and bolt-shooting artillery. This helped to relieve the pressure on the assaulting infantry, but even so they were making little progress:

And then, when our soldiers were still hanging back, mainly because of the depth of the water, the eagle-bearer of the *Tenth* offered up a quick prayer and then yelled out, 'Jump down, soldiers, unless you want to give up your eagle to the enemy; everyone will know that I at least did my duty to the Republic and my commander!' After saying this in a loud voice he jumped off the ship and began carrying the eagle-standard towards the enemy. Then our 'squaddies' called out to each other not to allow so terrible a disgrace [as to lose the standard of their legion] and leapt down from the transport. When those on the nearby ships saw them, they followed and began to close with the enemy.[21]

There was still heavy fighting, and the Romans' line was ragged as the legionaries formed up with the first officer or standard-bearer they met, just as they had done when surprised at the Sambre. As a rough fighting line developed, Caesar watched from the deck of his flagship and sent forward parties of men in rowing boats and his light scouting vessels to reinforce any group that became cut off. Although the Britons resisted fiercely, by their nature cavalry and chariots were not suited to defending a position and in the end they gave way. Their mobility ensured that most of them escaped. It is interesting that Caesar did not name the heroic eagle-bearer (*aquilifer*), although he does have a tendency to celebrate the collective exploits of the *Tenth* rather than the deeds of individuals from the legion. Presumably the man was not of sufficiently high social class to warrant a mention by name. The army would have known who he was, and although he does not mention it, it would have been expected that as a Roman general Caesar would have rewarded the man with promotion, a decoration and wealth.[22]

Caesar was ashore, but his army had no cavalry, limiting its capacity not only to pursue a defeated enemy, but also to scout and gather intelligence from the surrounding countryside. The legions constructed a camp as usual, probably just behind the beach. In the normal way the oared vessels were dragged ashore, while the transports sat at anchor offshore. Fortunately the successful landing in the face of determined resistance was enough to overawe the closest tribes, whose leaders sent to Caesar and willingly began to give the hostages he demanded. Caesar probably also demanded grain supplies. Commius was released by his captors and returned to Caesar. He brought with him some thirty of his retainers along with some Britons, all of whom were mounted and provided Caesar with at least a small force of horsemen. As the *Commentaries* put it 'by these things, peace was established'. However, there were some things beyond Caesar's control. Four days later the cavalry transports set out again from Gaul and came within site of Caesar's camp before a storm blew up and drove them away. The weather turned worse – as it often did and still does in the Channel at the end of summer – but the Romans had either not been warned as Caesar claims, or had not bothered to listen to the Gallic sailors who sailed these waters. The storm may also have been an especially bad one and the Roman fleet suffered terribly, with twelve ships dashed to pieces and most of the rest damaged to a greater or lesser extent. Lacking significant food supplies and for the moment cut off from the Continent, Caesar's army was placed in a very difficult position. The Britons quickly realised its vulnerability and decided to renew the war. The chieftains quietly slipped out of the Roman camp. Knowing that the legions lacked food, they decided to cut off the grain supply. The Romans would be starved into submission, or made to fight them at a disadvantage. If this first expedition could be utterly destroyed, then it was not unreasonable to think that the invaders would never return.[23]

While some men worked to repair as many ships as possible, each day parties of legionaries went out to harvest the wheat in the fields around the camp. As each area was used up, the parties had to go further afield and it was fairly obvious where the Romans would go next. The Britons prepared an ambush, hiding their forces in woodland bordering on the fields. After several days, foragers from the *Seventh* were suddenly attacked by a large force, again consisting mainly of chariots and cavalry. Chariots had long fallen out of use among the Gauls, but persisted in Britain and Ireland for several more centuries. They were expensive pieces of equipment, affordable only to the tribal aristocracy. The aristocratic warrior fought, while an unarmed charioteer controlled the team of two ponies. Social changes, along with increasing availability of large numbers of bigger cavalry mounts, probably explained the disappearance of chariots in Continental Europe. British chariots were fast and light, but they were not projectiles that rammed into the enemy – the remarkably persistent myth that scythes were fitted to their wheels is not based on a shred of reliable ancient evidence. Caesar gave a detailed description of chariot tactics, knowing that his audience would be fascinated by these exotic vehicles, so reminiscent of Homeric heroes:

This is how they fight from chariots – to start off with they drive all over the field and throw javelins, and so with the terrifying appearance of the horses and the roaring of the wheels they often shake the order of the enemy ranks; when they have charged forward between the troops of their own cavalry, they jump down from the chariot cars and fight on foot. In the meantime the chariot drivers withdraw gradually away from the fighting and wait in such a way that, if they [the warriors] are hard presssed by a host of foes, they may have an easy means of escape. Therefore in battle they combine the speed of cavalry and the steadiness of infantry, and by daily use and training they are so skilled that they are able to gallop their horses down the steepest of slopes and retain full control, to stop and to turn in an instant, to dash out along the yoke and then like lightning run back to the car.[24]

Chariots allowed an aristocratic warrior to look spectacular on the battlefield, were mobile missile platforms and let a warrior go forward to fight single combats on foot and then retire as necessary. They came from an older tradition of warfare, which celebrated the personal prowess and heroism of individual warriors. Yet, in combination with the British light cavalry and especially against an enemy entirely on foot, they were dangerous opponents. Some of the Roman foragers were cut down, the rest surrounded and exposed to the javelins thrown by opponents whom they could not easily catch. The outposts, stationed outside the Roman camp as part of the army's normal routine, reported that there was a large cloud of dust visible in the direction where the foragers had gone. It was far larger than would normally have been thrown up simply by the legionaries' feet. Caesar guessed what had happened and immediately led the outposts off to rescue his men. Before he left, he ordered two cohorts to relieve them in position outside the ramparts of the camp and the rest of the army to follow as soon as it was equipped and formed up. The expedition to Britain was small in scale compared with earlier campaigns, but even so it is striking that a proconsul commanding eight legions and many auxiliaries personally led a force of less than a thousand men into battle. The arrival of these cohorts was enough to check the Britons. Caesar formed up facing them for a while, but then led the foragers and his relief force back to the main camp. The Britons had won a small victory, and more importantly had prevented the Romans from gathering the grain. Encouraged by this success, they mustered their forces for an all-out attack on the Roman camp. Caesar formed up his legions, along with Commius' tiny troop of cavalry, on the plain outside the rampart to meet them. In massed fighting the legions were at their best and the Britons were quickly routed, although very few were caught by the pursuers. Caesar's men had to content themselves with torching the neighbouring farms and villages.[25]

The reverse was sufficient to persuade many British leaders once again to sue for peace. Caesar now demanded double the number of hostages, but said that the Britons must transport them to Gaul as he was no longer willing to delay his return there. Somehow all of the army was crammed into the surviving warships and the sixty-eight transports which had been restored to some sort of order. It was now near the September Equinox, but Caesar's luck held and in a patch of fair weather he set sail just after midnight. All of the ships made it back, though two transports were driven off course and landed on the coastline of the Morini. Seeing a good opportunity for plunder, the local warriors began to attack them, more and more gathering as the news spread. When reports of this reached Caesar the entire cavalry of the army was sent to their relief, and brought them off without the beleaguered men having suffered a single fatality. Next day Labienus took the weary legionaries of the *Seventh* and *Tenth* legions in a swift punitive expedition against the tribe. Unlike 56 BC the summer had been dry and this reduced the extent and difficulty of the marshes of the region. The Morini soon surrendered. The Menapii had also been defeated by the legions sent against them before Caesar had left for Britain.[26]

In most practical respects the first expedition to Britain had been a failure and, indeed, had narrowly missed becoming a disaster. It had not even contributed a great deal to Caesar's pool of intelligence concerning the tribes of the island, for he had been confined in a narrow stretch of country for the few weeks he had spent there. Some help came from the native chieftains who came as hostages or sought refuge in his camp, much as they had done at Gaul. It is unclear how many came across the Channel over the winter months, but at least one refugee prince does seem to have come to him, driven from his own tribe by his enemies. By 54 BC Caesar had a little more information, though scarcely enough to justify the effort required to gain it. Left until very late in the campaigning season, the preparations for the first raid were inadequate and the forces involved too small for the task. All of these were errors for which Caesar was responsible. In this sense the campaign was scarcely his greatest achievement, although as usual he showed his huge ability in getting himself and the army out of a series of difficult situations. Yet by the end of the year Caesar must have realised that, in propaganda terms, the British expedition was a fabulous success. Rome went wild when the news of this adventure arrived, thrilled at the idea that its legions had now crossed to that strange and mysterious isle. The Senate voted Caesar twenty days of public thanksgiving, five days more than he had been awarded at the end of 57 BC after three campaigns of genuine value. This formal recognition by the Republic of his achievements was the best possible answer to the attacks of Cato, which may possibly have been made at the same meeting. The year ended well, but Caesar was already resolved to return to Britain in the following summer. He remained curious about the place, and especially its rumoured wealth. The reaction back in Rome also made a second visit attractive – the scale of the celebrations may even have made it essential to live up to such acclaim.[27]

INVASION

The second expedition was more thoroughly prepared. Before the winter was over Caesar set the craftsmen in his legions to ship building. They were issued with a standard design for a broad, low-sided transport ship equipped with both sails and oars. In the following months 600 of these vessels were constructed, making use of ropes, tackle and other equipment provided by the Spanish provinces, which from the start of 54 BC were controlled by Pompey. An additional twenty-eight war galleys were also put together. As usual Caesar spent the winter in Cisalpine Gaul performing his administrative and judicial duties. When he was about to leave to rejoin the army he was diverted by news of raids into Illyricum. He hastened to the spot, raised local levies and pressured the tribe responsible into making peace. Travelling north he toured the army in its winter camps, praising the officers and men for their energy in construction. He gave instructions for the entire fleet to concentrate at Portus Itius (almost certainly modern Boulogne), ready for the crossing to Britain. Before the campaign could get under way, he was diverted again, this time by an internal dispute amongst the Treveri as rival chieftains struggled for pre-eminence. Caesar took four legions in light marching order and 800 cavalry to back the claims of his favoured candidate for power. His rival offered to surrender and promptly supplied the requested 200 hostages, including his son and other close relatives. For the moment Caesar was content, and had no wish to delay the attack on Britain any longer. He returned to the coast and set about final preparations. Since he planned to take a much larger force with him this time, he was eager to make sure that Gaul remained peaceful in his absence. Chieftains from all the tribes assembled at his camp, bringing with them the 4,000 cavalrymen that he had requested for the coming year. In this way the legions were provided with adequate numbers of good cavalrymen to support them. These warriors, and particularly the aristocrats who led them, were also in effect additional hostages for the good behaviour of their peoples.

Amongst them was a contingent of Aedui led by Dumnorix, the younger brother of Diviciacus the druid. In 58 BC Caesar had had good reason to be suspicious of the ambitions of this man and had kept him under observation. Recently he had heard from another Gallic aristocrat that Dumnorix had claimed at a meeting of the Aeduan council that the proconsul was planning to make him king of the Aedui. Reluctant though they were to subject themselves to the rule of a monarch, most of the other chieftains were equally nervous of showing dissension regarding any of Caesar's acts and did not bother to check whether or not there was any truth in the claim. Only half of the Gallic cavalry would accompany Caesar to Britain, but he had already decided that Dumnorix must certainly go, since he was a man 'craving revolution'. The chieftain tried a whole range of excuses, pleading ill health, fear of sea travel and finally a religious taboo preventing him from leaving Gaul. Caesar remained unmoved, so Dumnorix sought safety in numbers and tried to persuade other Gallic chieftains to join him in his refusal to go to Britain. He claimed that the Romans planned to kill them all once they had taken them away from their tribes and crossed to the island. A number of the other chieftains informed on him to the proconsul. There was ample time for plotting and gossip in the camp, as unfavourable winds delayed departure for the best part of a month. In the end Dumnorix and his warriors slipped out of camp and fled on the very day when the weather broke and embarkation began. Caesar was taken by surprise, but immediately sent a large part of his cavalry in pursuit. He was determined not to leave until the chieftain had been dealt with, even though he was impatient to start. His men were ordered to bring him back alive if possible, but to kill him if he resisted. Dumnorix did not lack courage, and challenged his attackers by yelling out that he was a 'free man from a free people'. Although none of his warriors stood with him, he chose to fight and was cut down. It was an openly brutal demonstration of Caesar's power and the inability even of one of Gaul's wealthiest aristocrats to stand against him. Diviciacus is not mentioned as taking an active part in events after 57 BC, and it is possible that he was no longer alive to plead for clemency. Yet in the end Dumnorix was simply inconvenient, and Caesar was impatient and so gave orders for the man's death.[28]

The second invasion force was much larger. Caesar took five legions – including the *Seventh* and *Tenth*, although the identity of the others is unknown – and half of the auxiliary and allied cavalry. His other three legions, along with the remaining 2,000 cavalry, were left under the command of Labienus. They were to secure the ports, ensure that if necessary grain convoys could be despatched to the army in Britain, and also to keep an eye on the tribes. The Roman fleet left harbour at sunset, but once again Caesar and his officers underestimated the power of the Channel. The wind dropped and the tides carried them off course. It had been a considerable achievement to construct so many vessels in such a short time, but this did not mean that all could be crewed by experienced sailors. The design of the new transports, while well suited to carrying men, horses and equipment and getting them onto a beach, was not ideal for coping with adverse weather. However, the provision of oars proved highly advantageous, especially when combined with the legionaries' willingness for heavy labour. Only by rowing did the Roman ships manage to make their designated landing beach. Caesar tells us that this was at the most suitable place, but its location is unclear. Some have speculated that he was now aware of the Wantsum Channel and used it, but this is not entirely convincing in the light of subsequent events. A more natural reading would suggest that it was at or fairly close to the beach chosen the year before. Wherever it was, the Britons had mustered to meet them but were daunted by the sight of hundreds of vessels coming towards them and retired. Most of the fleet was at the beach by noon. The Romans began landing, marking out and constructing a camp behind the beach as almost their first task. Patrols went out to find prisoners, who informed them of the withdrawal of the British army to a new position inland.[29]

Caesar decided on an immediate attack, and marched out under cover of darkness with forty cohorts and 1,700 cavalry. The remaining legionaries and horsemen were left at the camp under the command of Quintus Atrius. The Roman fleet lay mostly at anchor, Caesar confident that it would be safe lying off 'a calm, open shore'. Caesar's column made good progress, covering some 12 miles before dawn came and revealed the Britons waiting behind the line of a river – most probably the Stour near modern Canterbury. On wooded hills there was a walled enclosure – possibly the hillfort at Bigbury Wood – where the main tribal force waited. Small parties of cavalry, chariots and skirmishers periodically dashed forward from this shelter to hurl missiles at the Romans. Such tactics were doubtless effective enough in inter-tribal warfare, but posed few problems for veteran legions. Caesar attacked, his cavalry brushing aside the Britons and allowing the *Seventh* Legion to launch a direct assault on the hillfort. The legionaries formed the famous *testudo* or tortoise, overlapped shields held above their heads to create a roof able to stop all but the heaviest missiles. There was little need for the more complex engineering often employed by the Romans in sieges. A simple ramp was piled up against the wall and the enclosure stormed. There was only a short pursuit of the fleeing enemy. Caesar's men were tired after the Channel crossing, night march and battle, and he still wanted them to construct a marching camp in the proper way. The army halted for the night.[30]

On the following morning Caesar sent out three independent columns to seek the enemy. It was normal on such occasions to burn and plunder during the advance until the local leaders came to seek peace. Caesar clearly believed that there was no prospect of the Britons re-forming as a single main army so soon after their defeat, and therefore it was better to cover more ground with a number of flying columns. He does not seem to have accompanied any of these troops, but remained in the marching camp and was there when a messenger came in from Quintus Atrius. The news was bad, for a storm had blown up during the previous night and struck the anchored fleet causing a great deal of damage. Caesar recalled the three columns and rode back to inspect the damage, discovering that forty ships were smashed beyond repair. The craftsmen were called out from the ranks of the legions and sent back to the camp to work on the remainder. A message was also sent to Labienus in Gaul ordering him to set his legionaries to the task of building more ships. After ten days of intense labour the bulk of the ships with Caesar were once again in serviceable condition. Other soldiers worked to construct a ditch and rampart running from the camp onto the beach itself. All of the repaired ships were dragged ashore and beached inside the protection of this fortification. The root of Caesar's problem was that he had no harbour in which his ships could be sheltered and easily loaded and off-loaded. The Wantsum Channel around the Isle of Thanet would probably have given him most of what he needed, but the damage suffered in this storm makes it very unlikely that he used it. Perhaps the Romans remained unaware of it, or lacked the knowledge to find and navigate its entrance. Throughout history the weather has always posed huge problems to seaborne invasions – in 1944 the British, Americans and Canadians took their own artificial 'Mulberry' harbours to Normandy, but still suffered great disruption to the build-up after D-Day because of the heavy storms from 19–23 June. Although it is hard to see what he could have done to solve this problem, there is something cavalier in the way Caesar had done nothing to alter his plans in 54 BC in spite of the carnage wrought on his fleet by the storm in the previous year. The new fortification would serve to defend the ships from enemy attack, but offered little protection against the elements. Many commentators have criticised this failure to learn from experience. Most of such criticism has been justified, but, unless he had simply sent the ships back to the ports of Gaul and hoped that they would be able to return when needed, the only safe alternative was not to have launched the second expedition at all. Caesar was determined to do this, for reasons that were essentially political and personal. On both British expeditions his luck nearly failed him, but in each case he managed to escape.[31]

The pause gave the Britons time to recover. Several tribes, who in normal circumstances were hostile to each other, combined to face the common danger and appointed a war-leader named Cassivellaunus. Caesar tells us that he came from a tribe north of the Thames, but nothing else is known of him and we cannot be certain which tribe this was. When Caesar rejoined the main force at the inland camp and resumed his advance, his patrols were continually harassed by parties of chariots and horsemen. In close combat, especially between large formed bodies of troops, Caesar's legionaries and auxiliary cavalry consistently demonstrated their superiority, but in a number of skirmishes parties of his men were lured into ambushes and suffered badly. Cassivellaunus was encouraged and launched a big attack on the Romans when they halted at the end of the march to begin entrenching their camp. Caesar sent two cohorts up to reinforce his outposts, but it took more reinforcements to drive the Britons back. One of his tribunes was killed in the fighting. On the following day the British attacks were not pressed as hard, until Caesar sent one of his legates out with three legions on a foraging expedition. When most of the legionaries dispersed to set about their task, the British chariots and cavalry rushed in to exploit this weakness. However, the Romans quickly rallied, formed up and drove the enemy off. For a while the British tribes dispersed and resistance was light.[32]

Caesar decided to target Cassivellaunus' own homeland and marched towards the Thames. It is not clear where he crossed – probably somewhere in what is now central London – but his men forded the river and brushed aside the warriors defending the far bank. The British commander decided not to risk another open battle and resolved instead to harass the enemy, relying mainly on his chariot force. Caesar claims that there were 4,000 of these, but this seems likely to be an inflated figure – for instance it would mean 8,000 ponies. Herds were driven from the fields along the Romans' route of march and food supplies destroyed or hidden. The chariots were there to ambush the Roman foragers. Caesar's men began to suffer a steady trickle of losses in these skirmishes, until he was forced to keep men close to the main column at all times. Fortunately, as he had so often done in Gaul, Caesar was able to make use of a local ally. With the army was Mandubracius, a prince of the Trinovantes – a people living north of the Thames in East Anglia – who had been driven into exile after Cassivellaunus had killed his father. This tribe surrendered, asking Caesar to restore Mandubracius to the throne, and willingly handed over both hostages and food. Their example was soon followed by five other small tribes, whose names are not otherwise known to history. The fragile alliance between the British tribes was crumbling under the pressure of long-standing animosities. From these new allies Caesar discovered the location of Cassivellaunus' own stronghold, hidden amidst woods and marshes. Straightaway he marched the legions there and stormed the place, capturing considerable quantities of cattle. It was a major blow to the war-leader's prestige. At around the same time Cassivellaunus had arranged for the tribes of Kent to mount an attack on Atrius and the cohorts guarding the ships, but this was repulsed with heavy losses.[33]

Following these twin blows Cassivellaunus decided to seek peace. It was now nearly the end of September and the proconsul was eager to resolve matters and get back to Gaul. Negotiations were facilitated by Commius, who had once again accompanied Caesar. The British war-leader promised hostages and an annual tribute, and pledged not to attack Mandubracius and the Trinovantes. Waiting only for the hostages to be delivered, Caesar began to embark his army. However, even with all the repaired vessels he doubted that there was enough capacity to carry both the soldiers and the large numbers of hostages and slaves they had taken. The proconsul decided to make two crossings. The first went smoothly, but it proved impossible for the empty ships to return from the Gaulish side of the Channel. Similarly, none of the vessels built or found by Labienus were able to get to the army in Britain. After waiting for several days, Caesar decided that it was too risky to stay where he was. It was already September and the weather was likely to get worse, raising the prospect that he might be stranded in Britain with only part of his army. Cramming the troops into those vessels he had, they sailed overnight to reach Gaul by dawn. Caesar left Britain never to return. It would be almost a century before another Roman army would invade the island and turn it into a province.[34]

On both British expeditions Caesar avoided disaster, if only narrowly. It is normally assumed that the annual tribute promised by the British tribes was never paid or at least quickly lapsed. Trade between Britain and the Roman world steadily increased in the years after Caesar, shifting away from the old routes to the south-west and moving instead to the south-eastern corner that he had visited. The destruction of the Veneti probably contributed much to this shift, but it does also seem that more Roman merchants were able to reach Britain as the century progressed. Yet even the tribes who had submitted to Caesar could not in any meaningful way be described as now being part of Rome's empire – despite the occasional claims of Roman propagandists. Cicero noted the quick realisation in Rome that campaigns in Britain were not going to yield the eagerly anticipated profits. There was no silver, nor any hope of 'booty except for slaves; but I doubt we'll find any scribes or musicians amongst them' – in other words those likely to fetch a high price. Yet he remained excited by the whole business and wrote with enthusiasm about his brother's account of the expedition, for Quintus Cicero was now serving as one of Caesar's legates. Although influenced by this family involvement, his mood seems to have been fairly typical of many Romans. The expeditions to Britain brought Caesar huge and highly favourable public attention, excited by the novelty and tales of chariots and barbarians who painted their bodies blue with woad. The landings were undoubted propaganda successes, even if the actual results were negligible and the risks taken very high. Cato's attacks on him in 55 BC had shown the difficulty of dealing with opponents when he could not confront them face to face in the Senate or Forum. Yet no one could doubt that Caesar was making the most of his opportunity to win glory and make himself fabulously rich in the process. Even if the profits of the British expeditions were a little disappointing, the cumulative result of five years of successful campaigning had raised him from a debtor on the brink of ruin to one of the Republic's wealthiest men.[35]

XIV

REBELLION, DISASTER AND VENGEANCE

'And then, since he had not anticipated anything, Sabinus panicked, and rushed here and there deploying the cohorts, but even this he did timidly and in confusion – as is usually the case when a man is forced to decide everything in the heat of the action. In contrast Cotta, who had guessed that this might happen on the march and because of this had spoken against setting out, did everything to ensure the safety of the force – and in challenging and inspiring the legionaries he did the duty of a general, while in the fighting he played the part of a soldier.' – *Caesar*.[1]

While Caesar was in Britain in August 54 BC, his daughter Julia died in childbirth. The infant – a girl in some accounts and a boy in others – survived her by just a few days. For the Roman aristocracy, as indeed for most of humanity until the modern age, such deaths were all too common. Julia had become pregnant at least once before during her marriage, but had miscarried, shocked, it was said, by the sight of her husband coming back from the elections spattered in blood – someone else's blood as it turned out. Since we do not know her date of birth we cannot calculate Julia's age when she died, but at most she was in her mid twenties. Caesar's mother Aurelia also died in 54 BC. The cause is unknown, but she was by this time in her sixties, and had been a widow for three decades. In one year Caesar lost the two members of his family who were closest to him. It was his mother to whom he had declared that he would come home as *Pontifex Maximus* or not at all, and who had presided over the Bona Dea celebrations in his house. She was a formidable woman who had had a great influence on her only son, and had lived long enough to see some of his great successes. Now she was gone. The news of both deaths reached Caesar by letter. There is no evidence that he had seen either his mother or daughter in the four years since he had left

Rome. These were bitter personal blows, most especially the loss of his child. Cicero wrote an earnest letter of condolence to Caesar – he was devoted, perhaps excessively so, to his own daughter Tullia and heartbroken when she also died some years later. There was genuine grief and emotion and not mere political bonding on such occasions. Pompey, too, was deeply sorrowful at the death of his young wife. The couple had been very much in love in spite of the great difference in age and the political inspiration of their union. In recent years Pompey had often been criticised for spending too much time with his wife on his grand estates, enjoying himself when he ought to have been attending to the Republic's affairs. Plutarch claims that he had not even had any affairs while married to Julia.[2]

For all the real emotion of father and son-in-law at Julia's death, the concerns of public life were never far away for a senator. Pompey arranged to have her ashes interred in a tomb on one of his Alban estates near Rome, but after her public funeral in the city the great crowd of onlookers carried her remains onto the Campus Martius and buried her there. They were said to have been moved more by sympathy for Julia than particular fondness for either Caesar or Pompey, but as ever it is difficult to know whether this was genuinely spontaneous or orchestrated. A monument was subsequently erected and remained visible for centuries. Caesar announced that he would stage funeral games for her, although it would be a decade before these actually took place. Julia's death removed the closest bond between Pompey and Caesar. Over subsequent months Caesar searched around for another female relative to renew the marriage alliance. He proposed that Pompey should marry his great niece Octavia, while he should in turn marry Pompey's daughter Pompeia. This would have required Caesar, Octavia and Pompeia all to divorce their current spouses – Pompey's daughter was married to Sulla's son Faustus. Pompey turned the idea down, and showed no inclination to marry again for some time, perhaps because he wished to wait for a more advantageous situation. Political concerns were never wholly absent from the mind of a Roman senator, but it is quite possible that emotion also played a part in his decision. His love for Julia had been deep, and Pompey's grief was real and powerful.

Although the bond between Pompey and Caesar was weakened it was certainly not broken, and both men for the moment realised that it was to their advantage to remain in alliance. By 54 BC all three triumvirs were proconsuls and so unable to enter Rome itself without laying down their office. During their consulship in 55 BC Pompey and Crassus had arranged for the tribune Trebonius to pass a bill granting them each a five-year command in enlarged provinces much like the one Caesar had received in 59 BC. Pompey was given charge of the two Spanish provinces. There was the prospect for a campaign there, taking Roman rule right up to the north and the Atlantic coasts, but the fifty-one-year-old Pompey had no desire for a return to campaigning, especially while Julia was alive. He had already triumphed three times and believed that no other commander could hope to match his glory. Therefore he sent legates to govern the provinces and lead the legions there, while he himself remained in Italy, usually hovering just outside Rome in one of his comfortable villas. Pompey was still in charge of the grain supply, and this provided an excuse for his unorthodox conduct, for no Roman governor had ever acted in this way before.[3]

Crassus was in a different position. He had fought well for Sulla, but believed that he had not received full credit for his deeds. The defeat of Spartacus had been a major operation, during which he had shown his competence as a commander after a string of humiliating Roman defeats. Yet once it was over it was all too easy to forget the danger and dismiss the campaign as just fought against slaves. By 55 BC Crassus had decided that he wanted a major command in a foreign war and was allocated Syria. The current governor of that province completed a campaign in Egypt before Crassus could replace him, robbing him of one obvious chance for glory and profit. Instead he planned to conquer Parthia, the great kingdom lying beyond Armenia. Even by Roman standards, there was no good pretext for attacking the Parthians. Pompey in his eastern campaigns and Caesar in Gaul had pushed to the very limit their interpretation of what was in Rome's interests, but they had never quite gone beyond that to fight wars from purely personal motives. With Crassus it was blatantly obvious that his own ambition had little to do with the needs of the Republic. As word spread of his plans there were public protests from two of the tribunes. One went so far as to shadow Crassus' entourage as he left the city in November 55 BC, calling down terrible curses on his name for involving the Republic in a needless and unjust war. As Cicero dryly remarked, it was not an impressive beginning, and there was much that was incongruous about the expedition.

Crassus was in his late fifties, which was very elderly for a Roman field commander, and had not been on active service for sixteen years. In the past elderly men had been recalled to serve the Republic as generals, but normally only at times of crisis. This time there was no dire threat to Rome, and Crassus' conduct of the war seemed slow and uninspired. He spent most of 54 BC in Syria, levying taxes ostensibly to fund the planned invasion, but malicious tongues suggested that he was also lining his own pockets. The prospect of a lucrative campaign was clearly one of the main reasons why Crassus had wanted a command. There was also an element of balance, since if both Pompey and Caesar had provinces and legions to control then the third triumvir needed a command to match them if he was not to be placed at a severe disadvantage. Yet in most respects Crassus had already achieved his main objectives in life – prominence, two consulships, a huge fortune, massive influence and, as the Catilinarian debates had shown, virtual freedom from political attacks or prosecution – and it is hard to avoid the conclusion that rivalry with his political allies was his main reason for craving a military command. He and Pompey had been jealous of each other since they had both served Sulla, and Crassus had always resented the fame the other man had won. Now Caesar too was proving himself to be a great general, and Crassus, the oldest of the three triumvirs, does not seem to have wanted to be overshadowed.[4]

With all three triumvirs away from Rome from 54 BC onwards, they were all reliant to a great extent on agents acting on their behalf. They remained dominant, but as in the past could not control everything. Lucius Domitius Ahenobarbus made it to the consulship for 54 BC, and had Clodius' eldest brother Appius Claudius Pulcher as his colleague. At the same time Cato was one of the praetors. Both consuls complained that they were unable to make appointments even to such junior ranks as that of military tribune. Between them the triumvirs commanded over twenty legions, the overwhelming majority of the Roman army in existence at that time. Appius even travelled north to visit Caesar in Cisalpine Gaul in order to secure a tribune's commission for one of his clients. Pompey hovered close to Rome, and probably had little cause to miss regularly attending the Senate for he had never been a particularly gifted speaker. Crassus was less of a force when he was away from the city, since he was no longer able to keep himself in the public eye and do favours by appearing as an advocate. Caesar was already used to the problems of maintaining his interests in Rome while he was away from Italy. His agents, particularly Balbus, were active, and we get some glimpse of the flood of correspondence that went back and forth between Caesar's headquarters and the leading men of Rome from Cicero's letters. His brother Quintus had served as one of Pompey's legates supervising the grain supply to Rome, and then went to Gaul as one of Caesar's legates in 54 BC. This was a mark of the goodwill that his brother owed to both men for his recall. Cicero himself was reluctant to leave Rome, and was anyway more useful to the triumvirs there, and so Quintus was obliged to undertake this service for the good of the family. In his letters to his brother Cicero makes constant inquiries about Caesar's mood, and signs of favour towards them. He mentions sending poetry and other literary compositions to Caesar for his opinion. Much of this communication was not overtly political, but informally cemented the bonds between them. We know that Caesar wrote at least three letters to Cicero in Rome during the course of the second expedition to Britain.[5]

Several letters have also survived written by Cicero to one of his clients, Caius Trebatius Testa, who had been given a post on Caesar's staff at the orator's request. The young man would later become a famous jurist and was already committed to pursuing a career in law. We have the original letter of recommendation sent to Caesar, which brought the appointment about. The orator later told Quintus how Caesar 'expressed his thanks to me very politely and wittily. He says that in all his huge staff there was no one able to put together properly even a form of recognizance'. Trebatius was not given a military post – although Cicero did secure a commission as military tribune for another client – and was employed on administrative and legal duties. Even so, Trebatius was for a long time unenthusiastic about his new post and missed Rome intensely. By August 54 BC Cicero was writing to tell him that he had just heard from Caesar, who had written to him 'very politely' to say that he had not yet had much chance to get to know Trebatius, but assuring him that he would do so. Cicero informed his young client that he had spoken to the proconsul on his behalf asking for further favours. In this and other letters he expresses more than a little exasperation at the impatience and lack of initiative he perceived in his client. A man's own prestige was weakened if his recommendations proved inadequate, and although Caesar was probably willing to accept anyone so long as it strengthened the obligation that Cicero felt towards him, the orator was keen to play his part in the relationship. What is most striking is that both men were in contact and discussing the normal preoccupations of Roman senators even while Caesar was engaged in active campaigning. Most of the letters between Cicero and Caesar have failed to survive even though they were published. We can safely assume that Caesar was engaged in equally copious correspondence with many other senators.[6]

REBELLION

Although Caesar never neglected his political concerns, in the coming months he was to have little break from active service. On his return from Britain he had called the leaders of the Gaulish tribes to a meeting and then supervised the movement of his army into winter quarters. The harvest had been poor, and Caesar blamed this on an unusually dry summer, but it seems likely that the campaigns he had fought in the last years had also disrupted the agriculture of many regions. As a result his eight legions would camp separately and were dispersed over a very wide area. Most were amongst the Belgic tribes whose commitment to the new alliances with Rome remained uncertain. In other years he had set out for Cisalpine Gaul very quickly, but this time Caesar waited longer than usual, wanting to make sure that the army was securely placed before he left. Each legion was placed under the command of either a legate or his quaestor, who in this year was Crassus' eldest son Marcus. One of the new legates was the same Trebonius who as tribune in 55 BC had secured five-year commands for Pompey and Crassus and a similar extension for Caesar (see p.263). Each of these officers was instructed to send a report as soon as they were in position and their camp suitably fortified. We know that Quintus Cicero was allowed to choose the exact location of his legion's camp, and it may well be that other legates were given similar freedom of action. While this was underway, Caesar became aware of unrest in a number of tribes. The king he had imposed on the Carnutes was killed by other chieftains, prompting him to change his dispositions and move one legion from amongst the Belgae to winter amongst this tribe.[7]

Some chieftains had benefited from Caesar's arrival in Gaul, but for others it had meant seeing their rivals elevated. The summary killing of Dumnorix when he became inconvenient had shown such men that Caesar needed little provocation to dispose of anyone who did not behave as he wished. Yet Roman domination did not end the fierce competition for power between the aristocrats of a tribe, and if they were not doing well under Caesar, then successfully opposing him offered a path to fame and power. Before leaving for Britain in the summer of 54 BC, the proconsul had intervened in a dispute between rival leaders of the Treveri. The man who lost out to an opponent with Roman backing was Indutiomarus. At the time he had made his peace with Caesar, going to his camp and handing over 200 hostages. During the winter he saw an opportunity to strike at the Romans while their army was dispersed and vulnerable. Indutiomarus planned to raise all the Treveri who were loyal to him and attack the legion commanded by Labienus, which was camped on tribal lands. Yet he knew that the Treveri on their own could not defeat Caesar, and had spent time encouraging chieftains of neighbouring tribes who similarly resented Roman dominance to join him in the rebellion.

This was not a well co-ordinated revolt directed by a single leader, but a series of separate outbreaks occurring at roughly the same time and feeding off each other by dividing the Roman forces. It began not with the Treveri and Indutiomarus, but amongst the Eburones, who lived in what is now the Ardennes. The tribe appointed two war-leaders, Ambiorix and Catuvolcus, who then proceeded to inflict on Caesar's army one of the only three serious defeats it ever suffered.[8]

Fifteen cohorts were quartered amongst the Eburones at a place called Atuatuca (perhaps somewhere near modern Liège or Tongres, but its precise location is unknown). The force included the entire *Fourteenth* Legion, but it is not clear whether the remaining five cohorts were detached from other legions or independent units – Caesar was to raise at least twenty cohorts in Transalpine Gaul, where the recruits did not even have Latin status like those from the Transalpine province. Caesar mentions that some Spanish cavalry were with the legionaries, and there may have been other auxiliaries as well, so that the force probably numbered between 6,000 to 8,000 men. It was commanded by two of Caesar's legates, Cotta and Sabinus, both of whom had held independent commands in the past and proved reasonably competent, if uninspired. They had also worked together against the Menapii in 55 BC. Caesar does not say whether one of the men held overall authority, but his narrative implies that they were jointly in command. The first attack on their camp was repulsed without difficulty, but then Ambiorix came forward to parley and claimed to have been forced to go to war by his people. He told the Roman representatives that there was a conspiracy throughout Gaul for each tribe to attack the legions on this set day. In honour of favours he had received from Caesar in the past, he then offered to give the Romans free passage to march and join either of the other two legions that were camped within 50 miles. Late into the night, the legates argued over what they should do. Sabinus wanted to accept the offer, while Cotta said that they should not disobey Caesar's orders but remain in the camp, where they had plenty of food and could reasonably hope to hold out until relieved. In the end Sabinus prevailed, and at dawn on the next day the Roman force marched out. The Eburones knew the ground and were waiting in ambush where the track passed through a ravine. The Romans were surrounded and gradually whittled down. Cotta was wounded by a slingstone early on, but still kept on encouraging the men and trying to organise resistance. Sabinus despaired and was surrounded and killed while negotiating with Ambiorix. Cotta fell when the final charge swept over the rough circle of men he had formed into the last organised resistance. A handful of survivors straggled into the camp of Labienus over the coming days, but the fifteen cohorts had effectively been wiped out.[9]

In the *Commentaries* Caesar places all the blame for the disaster on Sabinus. Cotta is shown arguing sensibly and behaving as a Roman aristocrat should during a crisis. Neither man came from an especially influential family and therefore Caesar did not have to worry too much about upsetting powerful interests in the Senate. He claims to have reconstructed events from the stories of survivors and interrogation of prisoners captured in later actions. There is nothing inherently implausible about the version given in the *Commentaries*, which has similarities with other military disasters in other periods – Elphinstone and Macnaughten at Kabul during the First Afghan War spring to mind. It may genuinely have happened that way, but the narrative was obviously intended to soften the impact of the disaster and distance Caesar himself from blame. The account is very detailed, describing the debate between the commanders, and the confusion in the column when the ambush was sprung. Apart from Cotta's stirring but futile efforts to hold the men together, there are heroic cameos, such as the centurion who died trying to rescue his son, or the eagle-bearer – this time named, unlike the hero of the landing in Britain – who threw his standard to safety before he was killed himself. (The eagle was presumably captured anyway when the last survivors who had taken refuge inside the camp all committed suicide during the night.) Caesar tried to shift the blame onto his legate, but few if any of his contemporaries were fooled and all our sources see this as *his* defeat. As the proconsul with *imperium*, he was responsible for the entire army under his command – hence the conventional opening for any letter from a Roman governor to the Senate, 'I am well, and so is the army.' Both Sabinus and Cotta were his legates or 'representatives', chosen by him and acting under his orders. If they held joint command then it was Caesar's fault for permitting such an untidy situation to exist. Napoleon was later to comment that it was better to have one bad commander than two good ones with shared authority. Sabinus may have been disobeying Caesar's orders when he chose to march out of his camp, but even this suggests that the proconsul had either not made his intentions sufficiently clear or had failed to accustom his legates to strict obedience. Ultimately Caesar was responsible, and even if the mistakes had been made by his subordinates, the defeat was still his. A substantial part of his army had been destroyed by one of the least prestigious tribes of Gaul. It was the first time that such a thing had happened, and it challenged the illusion of Roman invincibility created by his constant success up to this point.[10]

The first sign of this came when Ambiorix and his retainers rode into the lands of their neighbours the Atuatuci, and then on to the lands of the Nervii. The vast majority of the Eburones had dispersed, carrying back their plunder to their homes in the manner of so many tribal or irregular armies throughout history. Yet the story of their success was enough to rouse the other tribes and persuaded the Nervii to strike against the legion wintering in their lands. This was commanded by Quintus Cicero, serving as a legate simply to confirm good relations between his brother and Caesar. Quintus did what was necessary for his family, but he was not the most enthusiastic of soldiers. In his letters home he complained of the rigours of life on campaign, and his mind does not seem to have been focused entirely on his duties. In the autumn of 54 BC, while moving his legion into its winter camp, he informed his brother that he had composed four tragedies in just sixteen days. However, when the Nervii suddenly attacked his camp, Quintus Cicero responded well. The Romans had no warning, for they had not yet received any word of the disaster, but although surprised they repulsed the first attack. The Nervii, backed by allied clans and numbers of Atuatuci and some Eburones, then settled down to besiege the camp. Overnight Cicero's men built 120 small turrets to strengthen the ramparts of their camp – the material for these had already been gathered into the camp, but evidently the fortifications were not yet completed. Now the work continued at a furious pace. A second all-out attack was repulsed on the following day. Whatever his personal inclinations and abilities, Quintus Cicero behaved as a Roman senator should, encouraging the men by day as they fought, and supervising them each night as they laboured to strengthen the defences further and to produce fresh supplies of missiles. His health was poor and eventually he was persuaded to retire to his tent by the soldiers. It is tempting to think that Cicero's officers were the real heart of the defence, and that at times he may have almost got in the way. Caesar wanted good relations with Quintus and especially with his older brother, and this ensured that he would be portrayed favourably in the *Commentaries*. Yet even if his skill and experience were limited, Quintus Cicero showed real courage, and did all that he could, coldly rejecting the offer of a truce to permit his men to march away to safety. The siege continued, the Belgians surrounding the fort with a ditch and wall, and constructing mantlets and other siege devices. Just a few years before such things had been unknown in Gaul, but the tribes had watched Caesar's men in action and learned from them. The Roman garrison was slowly worn down, many men being wounded, which meant that those who were fit had to shoulder more of the burden. They were heavily outnumbered

– Caesar reports that the Nervii had 60,000 men, quietly forgetting his claim of the massive casualties they had suffered in 57 BC – and must eventually have been overwhelmed if they were not relieved.[11]

Quintus Cicero had sent messengers to Caesar as soon as he had been attacked, but none of these men had been able to get through the Belgian lines. Several were brought back to within sight of the walls and executed in full view of the legionaries. The siege had lasted for more than a week before a man was able to get through. The messenger was a Gaul, a slave of a Gallic nobleman who had remained loyal to the Romans and had stayed with Cicero. The news reached Caesar in his camp at Samarobriva (modern Amiens) late in the evening. As well as reporting his own situation, Cicero's dispatch gave Caesar the first inkling of the destruction of Sabinus' and Cotta's men. Up to this point he had been completely oblivious of the rebellion, an indication of just how much his intelligence was reliant on friendly noblemen amongst the tribes. It was a dreadful shock, but Caesar realised that he must act swiftly. Quintus Cicero's garrison needed to be relieved as soon as possible if it was not to fall. A second victory would add even more momentum to the rebellion, encouraging more and more leaders and tribes to join. With him at Samarobriva he had only a single legion, guarding the main baggage train of the army with its records and pay chest, and also supplies of grain brought in from all over Gaul, as well as the hundreds of hostages he had taken since 58 BC. Cicero's client Trebatius was there along with many other administrative officials and clerks. Caesar could not move quickly with all these non-combatants and impedimenta, but neither could he leave them unprotected. Therefore his first order was to his quaestor, Marcus Crassus, who was camped with his legion no more than 25 Roman miles away. Crassus was ordered to march with all haste to Samarobriva, leaving his camp at midnight. This probably meant that he sent off his standing pickets first, the rest of the legion following as soon as it was ready to march. By mid morning on the next day the leading patrols of Crassus' legion – probably mounted men – reached Caesar and informed him that the main force was not far behind.[12]

Leaving his quaestor to guard Samarobriva and its precious contents, Caesar himself set out, covering 20 miles in that first day. He had managed to scrape together 400 auxiliary and allied cavalry to add to his one legion, and hoped to be joined by two more legions on the march. A messenger had gone to Caius Fabius, who was amongst the Morini, instructing him to march through the lands of the Atrebates to rendezvous with Caesar as he went through the same region. Another order was sent to Labienus, telling him to try to join the main force on the borders of the Nervii, but granting him considerable discretion to stay where he was if the local situation required it. Fabius was a little late, but still managed to join him. Labienus sent a despatch rider to report that he was unable to move, because the Treveri had gathered an army and were now camped just 3 miles from his position. He also confirmed the fate of Sabinus and Cotta, giving some of the details provided by the survivors who had reached him. Caesar concurred with his senior legate's reasoning, but was left with just two legions, both of which had been on campaign for some time and were markedly under strength. Even with his cavalry, he had little more than 7,000 men, but there was no prospect of gaining further reinforcements for a number of weeks. If he waited, then Cicero's camp might well fall and another legion be lost, a success that was bound to fuel the rebellion. He had marched with only light baggage and minimal supplies of food. It was well into the autumn and his men could not expect to find much food or fodder in the lands they passed through. The Romans needed to win quickly and could not afford a cautious, long drawn-out campaign of manoeuvre. Caesar pushed on to rescue the beleaguered garrison. The decision made strategic sense, and conformed to Roman military thinking, which always emphasised aggression, but it was certainly risky. Yet there was another, more personal motive that meant that Caesar had to keep going. His legionaries were in danger, and the trust that had grown up between army and commander was based at its most fundamental level on each keeping faith with the other. Caesar could not leave his men to die if there was any chance of saving them. He had already shown the depth of his feeling for the loss of the fifteen cohorts by swearing an oath not to shave or cut his hair until he had avenged them. This was a particularly significant gesture for the ever fastidious Caesar. Unshaven, the proconsul force marched his 7,000 men onwards.[13]

Patrols had brought in prisoners who confirmed that Cicero's men were still holding out. A Gallic cavalryman was persuaded to take a message through the lines. It was written in Greek characters, which it was believed the Belgians would not be able to read. Unable to get into the camp, he did as instructed and tied it to a spear, which he then hurled into the camp. For two days no one noticed the unusual attachment on the spear stuck into the side of one of the towers, before someone spotted it and took it to Cicero. The legate paraded his men and read out the contents, which informed them that Caesar was on the way. Confirmation came when they sighted columns of smoke rising in the distance – a sign that a Roman force was advancing, setting fire to 'enemy' farms and villages along its route in the normal way.

Belgian patrols reported the same thing, and the besieging army abandoned the siege to meet this new threat. Even if they did not have the 60,000 men reported by Caesar, they probably still outnumbered his small column by a big margin. Cicero, calling on the same Gaulish aristocrat as before to provide a man willing to slip through the enemy lines, wrote to Caesar informing him that the Belgic army was moving against him. The Gaul arrived in Caesar's camp at midnight, and the proconsul immediately told his men of its contents – Suetonius claims that he usually broke any bad news to them himself, telling the soldiers in a matter of fact way and so confidently that it showed they need not be worried. Sometimes he even exaggerated the danger. For all this he remained a careful commander. Up until now he had begun his marches before the night was over, but on the next day he waited until dawn before moving his column 4 miles. In this season the days in northern Europe are short. The Nervii and their allies were waiting for them on a ridge behind the line of a stream. Twice in 57 BC the Belgians had adopted a similar position, and it is quite possible that in each case they occupied sites on main routes into their land, which were often used in inter-tribal warfare.[14]

Caesar was heavily outnumbered and did not have enough food to engage in protracted manoeuvring. Attacking over a stream and uphill against the waiting enemy would have placed his men at a severe disadvantage and probably resulted in disaster. Therefore he needed to persuade the Belgians to give up their position and come and attack him. To this end he made his camp deliberately smaller even than was normal for a small force without baggage, making the streets that intersected the various units' tent-lines narrower than usual. He wanted the Nervii to despise his army, hoping to persuade them to attack him, but in case this did not work he sent out patrols to look for other routes across the stream, wondering whether he could outflank the enemy position. During the day the two armies stared at each other from opposite sides of the valley, and only the cavalry went forward to skirmish. At dawn on the next day the same thing happened, but Caesar ordered his auxiliaries to give way before the enemy. The Nervii had few horsemen and these did not have a good reputation, so it was doubtless especially encouraging when these chased Caesar's cavalry back to their camp. To add to the impression of fear, the Romans made the ramparts of this higher than usual, and blocked up each of the four gateways with a wall consisting of a single row of cut turf. The Nervii took the bait and came across the stream to the Roman side of the valley. Warily, they edged closer and closer to the enemy camp, lured on by deliberate displays of panic. The legionaries even abandoned the walls as if terrified of the approaching warriors. The Belgians sent forward heralds, proclaiming that any of Caesar's men who wished to desert could freely do so, but any that failed to come across by a set hour would be shown no mercy. After a while the Nervii came up to the ramparts, and some began to tear down the turf walls blocking the gates. Only then did Caesar order an attack. The column of troops that had been waiting behind each gateway now charged, easily pushing down the flimsy barrier. The Nervii panicked and fled, pursued by the legionaries and the cavalry that Caesar ordered out in support. Some were killed, others abandoned weapons and shields as they fled, but he recalled his men before very long, fearing that they might suffer if they followed the enemy too far and were ambushed in the nearby woods and marshes.[15]

With the enemy army dispersed, Caesar pressed on to relieve Cicero. He took care to praise his legate, and separately inspected and commended the officers and men of the garrison. Only one-tenth had escaped being wounded during the siege, although it seems likely that many of the injured were fit enough to perform duty. On the following day there was another parade, and this time the proconsul spoke of the defeat of Cotta and Sabinus, making the latter the scapegoat and encouraging the troops for the future. When news of the Roman victory reached the Treveri, their army withdrew from its position facing Labienus' camp. Caesar sent Fabius and his legion back to their camp amongst the Morini, and led Cicero and his own legion back to Samarobriva. He kept both of these units and Crassus' legion near the town throughout the winter to give himself a concentrated striking force in case of further rebellions. The proconsul stayed with them, the first time that he had not gone south of the Alps for this season. The situation in Gaul was simply too tense for him to leave. It is also likely that this was the only year when a book of *Commentaries* on the last campaign was not published. Most probably books five and six came out together in the winter of 53–52 BC. Caesar was simply too busy, and until he had stamped out all the embers of rebellion then it was doubtful that he wanted to send a narrative of an uncompleted conflict. The news had already reached Rome of hard fighting in Gaul by December 54 BC, when Cicero would write to Trebatius that he had heard that they had been having a 'hot time of it' lately.[16] Throughout the winter Caesar kept a close eye on the tribes: 'Now when they heard of Sabinus' death and defeat, nearly all the Gaulish tribes started to take thought of war, sending off ambassadors and delegations to every region to discover what the rest thought and where the war would begin, holding night-time meetings in remote spots.'[17]

In Amorica (roughly equivalent to modern Brittany) a force of tribesmen gathered near the camp of Lucius Roscius and the *Thirteenth* Legion, but subsequently dispersed. Another of Caesar's appointees, Cavarinus the king of the Senones, was attacked by his chieftains and only narrowly escaped with his life and made his way to Caesar at Samarobriva. The only real fighting of the remainder of the winter was done by Labienus. Indutiomarus had tried and failed to raise German allies but, nevertheless, once again brought an army of his fellow tribesmen against Labienus' camp. For days the Treveri formed up in battle order in the plain outside and challenged the Romans to battle. Labienus repeatedly declined, but then one day as the Treveri once again dispersed to go back to their own camp, he sent his allied cavalry out against them. The men were ordered to kill Indutiomarus and ignore everyone else. He was caught and his head brought back to the Legate. Without their leader, the warriors dispersed again.[18]

VASTATIO – PUNISHING THE TRIBES

Over the winter Caesar took care not simply to make good his losses, but to raise double the number of new troops so that the Gauls would come to believe that Roman resources of manpower were inexhaustible. Three new legions were recruited in Cisalpine Gaul, a new *Fourteenth* to replace the massacred unit, the *Fifteenth* and the *First*. Although raised in Caesar's province, the last of these had actually been intended to form part of Pompey's army in Spain and had taken an oath to him, hence its number came from another sequence. Not planning major campaigns of his own, Pompey agreed to 'loan' the new legion to Caesar 'for the good of the Republic and out of personal friendship'. Caesar now had ten legions, but the tribes in rebellion were also gathering their strength. Ambiorix was playing a key role in encouraging them, and had made formal alliance with the Treveri. In addition the Nervii, Atuatuci and Menapii were all in open war with Rome, while other tribes like the Senones and Carnutes had rejected leaders favourable to Caesar and were refusing to come in answer to his calls to council. Caesar decided that he must begin operations before the normal start of the campaigning season at the beginning of spring. He wanted to regain the initiative, which inevitably at the beginning of a revolt lay with the rebels. The Roman army would attack and would show that Rome was still strong in spite of a defeat, and that the consequences of opposing it were appalling. The tribes had no single leader, no capital and looked unlikely even to mass into a single field army. Nor would the defeat of one necessarily cause others to capitulate, and each had to be defeated in turn. Lacking these clear targets, Caesar would instead attack the homes and farms of the warriors. Houses would be burned, crops and herds consumed or destroyed, and people killed or enslaved. The Romans had a word for this activity, *vastatio*, which is the root of the word devastation, and even a verb *vastare* for the process. It was brutal in the extreme, but could be effective, terrifying the enemy into admitting defeat and coming to terms. Throughout history occupying forces have often turned to similar methods, but few have surpassed Caesar's legions in their ruthlessly efficient application.[19]

Before the winter was over Caesar concentrated four legions – presumably somewhere near Samarobriva – and attacked the Nervii. It always took time to muster a tribal army and the Nervii had little chance either to defend themselves or to flee. The surprise was all the greater because no large Gallic army could have operated at this season – in 57 BC the great Belgic army had even been forced to disperse when it ran out of food in the summer months. Only the organised supply system supporting the Roman army made this possible. Caesar's column captured large numbers of people, rounded up their herds and flocks, and torched the villages. Faced with this onslaught the Nervii quickly capitulated and supplied the Romans with hostages. Caesar withdrew his army, and sent messages to the tribes summoning them to a council at the beginning of spring. Once again the Senones and Carnutes failed to attend, as did the Treveri, who were now led by some of Indutiomarus' family. The council was to be held for the first time at Lutetia on the Seine, the main town of the Parisii, the people whose name is preserved in that of the modern capital of France. Before the council convened, Caesar took his legions against the Senones. Surprised before they could take refuge inside the walls of their town the tribe swiftly submitted. The Aedui spoke on their behalf and Caesar treated them relatively leniently. Partly this was because of his desire to show respect to Rome's old ally, but also because he wanted to get on with operations against the other rebellious tribes. One hundred hostages were handed over to his camp, but there was no mass enslavement of the population. Realising that they were most likely next on Caesar's list, soon afterwards the Carnutes sent envoys to him, accompanied by representatives from the Remi. The proconsul was again willing to accept their surrender. As was his usual practice, at the council he requested contingents of cavalry from the tribes. Privately he resolved to keep those supplied by the Senones with him, so that he could keep an eye on their commander, the chieftain Cavarinus.[20]

Central Gaul was now 'pacified' and the proconsul turned his attention to the north-east. Ambiorix was the most influential and charismatic of the leaders opposing him, but Caesar judged that he was unlikely to risk open battle. Therefore he decided to strip him of real or potential allies in the region. The army's baggage and supply train was sent to Labienus with an escort of two legions. Caesar himself took five legions with minimal stocks of food and heavy equipment and led them against the Menapii – at this point only one of the three new legions seems to have reached the main army. As usual, the Menapii avoided contact and relied on the inaccessibility of the forests and marshes of their land for protection. This time, however, the Romans were prepared. Caesar divided his force into three independent columns, each of which began clearing a route into tribal territory, constructing bridges and causeways as necessary. Such was the engineering skill of the legions that there were few places where they could not go if they were led with determination. Dismayed to realise that they were not as safe as they had believed, and seeing the smoke rising from their burning villages, the Menapii sent in envoys and surrendered. The main army moved on, leaving the Atrebatian chieftain Commius and his retinue of warriors behind to ensure that the Menapii did not repent of their decision. While this operation was underway, the Treveri had moved against Labienus. Showing all his accustomed skill, the latter had lured them into a bad position and then turned on them, allegedly telling his men to 'show the same courage they had often displayed for their general'. His three legions – his own legion having been reinforced by the two escorting the baggage just before the engagement – cut the Treveri to pieces. After this defeat the hostile chieftains fled across the Rhine, and power within the tribe was restored to Caesar's candidate Cingetorix.[21]

Indutiomarus and Ambiorix had both sought allies from the German tribes on the east bank of the Rhine. Neither had enjoyed much success, for according to Caesar the Germans were still intimidated by the fate of Ariovistus and the Usipetes and Tencteri, and only a few bands of warriors had come to their aid. Even so the proconsul now decided to cross the Rhine for a second time, both to deter the tribes from offering even such modest aid to his opponents in Gaul and to prevent Ambiorix from seeking refuge on the far side of the river. The Roman army marched to the Rhine and built a bridge only a short distance away from the one they had constructed and then destroyed in 55 BC. Caesar did not bother to describe the design in any detail, but noted that having performed the task once before, his legionaries completed it very quickly. Bridging the Rhine in 55 BC had been an exciting foray into unexplored country, but now it was simply a matter of routine. That was essentially the point of the operation, to make it absolutely clear that the river was no barrier to the Romans and that Caesar could attack the Germans in their homeland whenever he wanted. As on the first occasion there was no actual fighting. The Ubii quickly sent envoys telling Caesar that they had remained faithful to their alliance with Rome. The Suebi withdrew into their heartland, and Caesar was informed by the Ubii that they were massing their army to meet him if he invaded. He made arrangements to ensure that he had sufficient supplies, ordered the Ubii to hide their own food stores and herds so that the enemy could not try to make use of them, and then advanced. When they learned of this, the Suebi withdrew and decided to offer battle at a place much deeper within their country. It may well be that the size of Caesar's force had surprised them and that more time was needed to mass sufficient warriors to oppose him. Caesar decided not to march further away from the Rhine, claiming that it would be difficult to supply his army since the Germans were essentially pastoralists rather than farmers, making it difficult for him to live off the land. Archaeology has shown that Caesar's portrayal of the Germans is misleading, for there was a long tradition of agriculture in the region. Nevertheless, it may be that the population was less dense and the amount of wheat and barley produced smaller in comparison with much of Gaul. Supporting his army would probably have been possible, but certainly would have been considerably more difficult in a region where he did not have numbers of allies capable of providing for his needs from their own surplus. Meeting and defeating the Suebi was not essential for Caesar. He had put on another show of strength, and had made their army retreat from its first position. Both sides had a wary respect for the other's power and were unlikely to attack each other, especially while both Caesar and the Suebi had closer and weaker opponents to fight.[22]

Caesar exaggerated the importance of the Rhine as a boundary and the differences between Gauls and Germans, but did so to justify a clear strategy. For all his willingness since 58 BC to exploit opportunities for new conflicts, he was not pursuing some dream of endless conquest in the manner of Alexander the Great. He knew that he would only hold his command for a limited time, and eagerly anticipated his eventual return to Rome with the benefits his new-found glory and wealth would bring. Quite early on he decided to focus his attention on Gaul and to bring the whole region under Roman dominion. This was a task that he could reasonably hope to complete – his first thought was probably within the initial five years of his command, but certainly when this was extended in 55 BC. Conquering Germany was too big a project to add to this objective, and operations east of the Rhine were always a distraction, if a necessary one, to winning in Gaul. He may well have believed that he could manage to add Britain, or at least its south-eastern corner, to Gaul, but his initial thinking on this subject was based on a very vague concept of the island's geography. After the second expedition, Caesar never had the time, if indeed he still had the desire, to establish more permanent control. Any plans for significant operations in Illyricum were also abandoned as the years went by. Caesar concentrated on Gaul, and everything else was subordinate to this in strategic terms. The River Rhine offered a readily understandable boundary for an Italian audience, a boundary beyond which no one must be allowed to challenge Roman dominance of the new province of Gaul.[23]

After he returned to the west bank, Caesar broke down a wide section of his bridge and left a garrison to protect it. It was now late summer and the harvest was ripe, making it much easier for armies to rely on foraging. Caesar now turned to the Eburones and Ambiorix whose heartland lay in the forests of the Ardennes. The cavalry were sent ahead of the main army and ordered to light no fires at night lest their position be revealed by the light itself, or the reflection from clouds. Their sudden appearance surprised the enemy and they were able to take many prisoners. These revealed the whereabouts of Ambiorix, and the chieftain was nearly taken when the cavalry swooped down on a village. Most of his possessions, horses and plunder were found by the allied horsemen, but Ambiorix himself slipped away, and he and his followers hid themselves in the densest woods of the area. Catuvolcus – the man who had shared with him the glory of defeating Sabinus and Cotta – felt himself too old to hide in this way and hanged himself from a yew tree. (Caesar makes no comment, but it is tempting to see some element of ritual in this suicide, perhaps a king killing himself after a failure to avert the harm from his people.) Caesar moved the army to Atuatuca, the site of the disaster in the previous winter. Around this time he was also joined by the remaining two of the recently raised legions. He left his baggage there, protected by the new *Fourteenth* Legion under the command of Quintus Cicero, and divided the rest of his force into a number of flying columns to harass the enemy. Caesar himself led three legions towards the River Scheldt, Labienus took three more against the Menapii, and Trebonius with a force of equal size moved against the Aduatuci. Speed was of the essence and the columns marched with basic rations, for it was planned that all should return to Atuatuca after a week. None of the forces met serious resistance, but stragglers or small groups who separated from them were often ambushed. Caesar decided that his legionaries were too valuable to risk the steady drain of casualties likely to come from continuing to ravage the land himself. Instead he issued a decree throughout Gaul, granting permission for anyone who chose to plunder the Eburones and their allies. Many warriors welcomed the call, and there were soon many parties of Gauls enthusiastically plundering the tribe.[24]

Before Caesar returned to Atuatuca, Cicero's camp came under attack from a band of Germans. These had originally crossed into Gaul to share in the despoiling of the Eburones, but then decided that the Roman baggage train was too tempting a target to miss. The attack was repulsed, but not before a couple of cohorts caught outside the camp had been badly cut up. In the *Commentaries* Cicero was lightly admonished for disobeying Caesar's orders and permitting troops to go too far outside the camp, but the criticism is gentle in the extreme, since he did not desire to alienate either the legate or his brother. It was an embarrassing reverse, especially since it occurred so close to the site of the previous winter's disaster, but still a minor one. For the rest of the year Caesar continued to hunt Ambiorix, but never quite caught up with him. It was a grim business, as more and more Gallic allies arrived to share in the spoils:

> Every village, every house that anyone could see was put to the torch; captured cattle were everywhere rounded up; the wheat was not only consumed by soldiers and animals, but squashed flat by the heavy rain common at that time of year, so that if anybody managed to hide themselves in the meantime, it seemed that they were bound to starve once the army left.[25]

Caesar spent most of 53 BC on campaign, beginning before winter was over and continuing into the early autumn, but did not fight a single battle. The only significant action was fought and won in his absence by Labienus. During the year the Romans had spread destruction and terror – mainly terror, for the armies only destroyed what was in their path – over a wide area. North-eastern Gaul suffered badly, and it is striking that there is a huge drop in the quantities of gold and other precious metals found in sites in this area after Caesar's time in Gaul. Overall the archaeological record shows a marked decline in the quality and quantity of material culture, and suggests that the region did not recover for at least a generation. The danger with such a policy of intimidation was that it sowed the seeds of future resentment, but Caesar decided that the memory of Sabinus' defeat could only be eradicated by extreme ruthlessness. It is not recorded at which point he decided that his vow of vengeance for his lost soldiers was fulfilled and he had his slaves shave him and cut his hair. At the end of the campaigning season he withdrew the army and summoned the leaders of Gaul to another council, this time at Durocortorum (modern Reims), one of the chief towns of the Remi. Earlier in the year he had been content to let the matter of the disturbances amongst the Senones and Carnutes pass. Now he investigated the affair, and decided that the prominent Senonian aristocrat Acco was the man behind the affair. Caesar resolved to impose a harsher penalty than was 'his normal custom' and had Acco publicly flogged and then executed. This action shocked the tribal leaders even more than the killing of Dumnorix and was to have deep consequences. It may have been a carefully considered decision on Caesar's part, but it is also likely that a desire to depart for Cisalpine Gaul made him especially impatient. The fact that one of his own appointees had been killed and another driven out by rivals also encouraged particular harshness, for Caesar always stressed his loyalty to and care for his 'friends', whether Roman or foreign. Whatever his thinking, Caesar gave the order, dividing his army so that two legions wintered in a position to watch the Treveri, two more observed the Lingones and the remaining six were concentrated near one of the main towns of the Senones.[26]

After spending the last year and a half north of the Alps, there was doubtless much that needed his attention in Cisalpine Gaul and Illyricum. It was probably during these months that he wrote and released books Five and Six of the *Commentaries on the Gallic War*, covering 54 and 53 BC. Book Five carefully presented the defeat of Cotta and Sabinus, not only contrasting the behaviour of the two legates, but then following this with the more inspiring tale of Quintus Cicero's successful defence of his camp and the heroism of his centurions and soldiers. Book Six included long digressions discussing Gallic and Germanic culture, padding out an account of punitive expeditions that involved little actual fighting and did not make the most dramatic reading. Some of the details appear to have been lifted from existing ethnographic works and it is tempting to see this as an indication of especially rapid composition. He repeats a number of bizarre stories, for instance of an animal called an elk, which lived deep in the forests of Germany and had no knees so slept leaning against a tree. Hunters were supposed to catch these animals by sawing almost completely through the trunk of a tree, so that when the elk leaned on it to go sleep, tree and animal both fell over.

Perhaps the only sculpture surviving from Caesar's lifetime, this bust from Tusculum in Turin may well be the most accurate representation of Caesar in middle age, showing his receding hairline. (W&N Archive)

This portrait of Caesar made from green slate was found in Egypt and probably dates to the first century AD. Like many later portraits some features are exaggerated. (AAA Collection)

Although recognisably the same man, the various busts of Caesar show slightly different features. Most, like this one, were made after his death. (Vatican Museums)

This bust shows the extent to which Caesar's features became stylised in later portraiture. The strong lines and firm jaw are intended to show massive strength of character. Note the full head of hair. (W&N)

Pompey the Great's career began at a young age and was as spectacular as it was unorthodox. This portrait shows him in middle age, by which time he was keen to appear very respectable. (W&N)

Crassus built up an immensely strong position through clever use of his wealth and dedicated trading in favours. However, he lacked charm and never received the adulation given to Pompey or Caesar. (Bridgeman)

Cicero's career was based on his brilliant oratory, and his copious writings provide our most detailed window into this period. Personally Cicero liked Caesar, but was very unsure of him politically. (Bridgeman)

Left: Cato's political prominence owed much to his conscious emulation of his famously stern ancestor, Cato the Censor, as well as to judicious use of family connections. He loathed Caesar, both for his politics and as a man, and this antipathy cannot have been helped by the long-term affair between Caesar and Servilia. (W&N)

Overleaf: Most of the remains visible in the Roman Forum date to after Caesar's time. In the foreground is the Basilica Julia, begun by Caesar and dedicated in 46 BC, but subsequently rebuilt several times. To the rear, the three columns mark the Temple of Castor and Pollux, rebuilt during the reign of Augustus. On the right in the distance is the slope of the Palatine hill. (W&N)

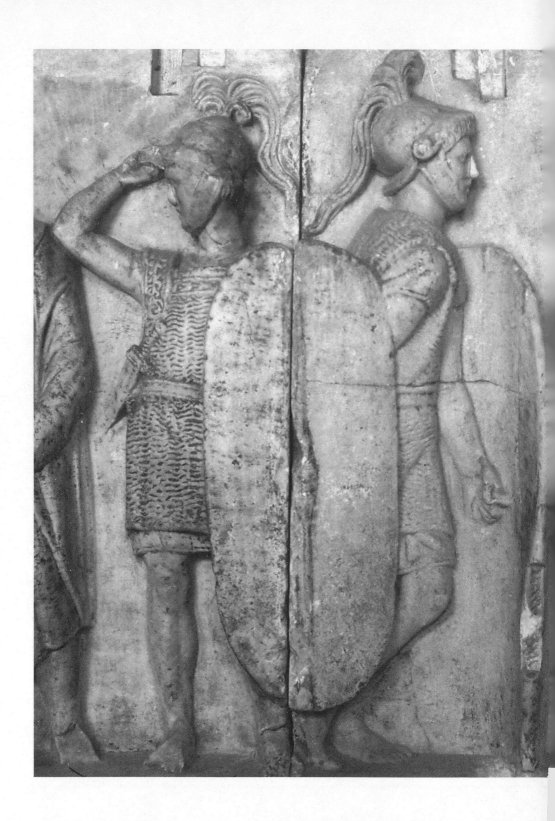

One of the few detailed depictions of Roman soldiers from the first century BC, *the Domitius Ahenobarbus monument may show something close to the uniform worn by Caesar's legionaries: Montefortino helmets, oval shields, and ring mail body armour. (AAA Collection)*

This relief from the legionary fortress in Mainz dates to at least a century after Caesar's death and shows a more classic image of the Roman legionary. It is possible that some of the types of equipment shown here were already in use in Caesar's day. (AAA Collection)

This chariot was reconstructed for a BBC television documentary and is based on an example excavated at Wetwang in Yorkshire. British chariots were used as mobile missile platforms and also allowed warriors to advance and withdraw quickly, before jumping out to fight on foot. (Robert Hurford)

This nineteenth-century model of Caesar's siege lines at Alesia is based on the account in the Commentaries and the excavations carried out under Napoleon III. It gives a good indication of the formidable obstacles facing the besieged Gauls. (Bridgeman)

Right: *This aerial photograph shows the hilltop on which the town of Alesia lay. Since the nineteenth century archaeological excavation has largely confirmed Caesar's account of this critical siege. (W&N)*

This silver denarius minted in 48 BC by Caesar's supporters carries on its reverse side a depiction of a British war chariot. (Bridgeman)

This coin showing the head of Vercingetorix was minted by his tribe, the Arverni. It is based on a Greek original, making it an uncertain guide to his actual appearance. (Bridgeman)

This silver coin was minted by the city of Ascalon in 50–49 BC and shows the head of Cleopatra wearing a royal diadem. (British Museum)

Left: The huge reliefs from the Temple of Hathor at Dendera depict Cleopatra and her son Caesarion, on the right, making an offering to the gods shown on the left. (AAA Collection)

This bust has been widely accepted as showing Cleopatra, although it is impossible to be certain. It was probably made long after her death and so may not be an accurate representation of her features. (bpk/Staatliche Museen zu Berlin)

Coin showing Mark Antony from the period of the second triumvirate, formed in 43 BC. Antony was strong and powerfully built, and this image hints at the force of the man. (W&N)

This coin, minted during Caesar's dictatorship, shows him wearing the wreath of a triumphant general. He was the first Roman to be depicted on a coin during his lifetime. (W&N)

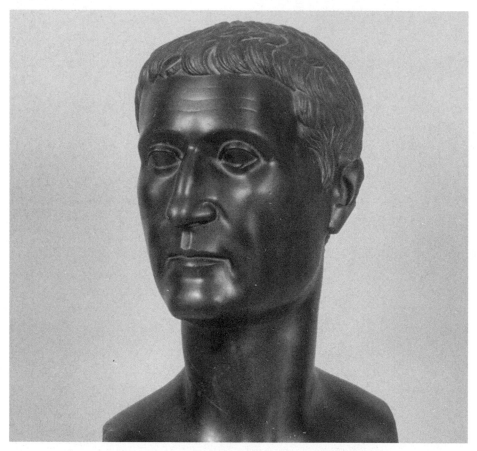

This bust has been identified as Mark Antony and does share many features with the head depicted on coins. Antony was distantly related to Caesar, and seems always to have been faithful to him, but their relationship was not always close. Antony made a poor job of running Rome in Caesar's absence. (National Trust/Kingston Lacy)

This bust has been identified as Marcus Junius Brutus, one of the main leaders of the assassins who killed Caesar. Caesar and Brutus' mother Servilia were lovers and there were persistent but unfounded rumours that Caesar was his real father. (W&N)

This imperial statue shows an idealised Caesar. From Augustus onwards the emperors were highly selective in which aspects of Caesar's career were to be celebrated. Both Cato and Brutus continued to be widely admired amongst senators during the principate. (W&N)

The Greeks and Romans had great difficulty obtaining accurate information about distant lands, but it is very hard to believe that a man as intelligent and well educated as Caesar took such absurd tales seriously. It is very tempting to see this as a rare note of humour in the otherwise calm reportage of the *Commentaries*, but difficult to know whether or not his audience would have recognised it as such.[27]

Much had happened since Caesar was last south of the Alps and the public life of Rome had continued to be turbulent, but the most important event for him had occurred far out on the eastern edge of the Roman world. Late in 54 BC Crassus had been joined by his dashing son Publius and a contingent of 1,000 cavalry he had brought with him from Gaul. Father and son had then begun their long anticipated invasion of Parthia, although little was achieved before the campaigning season was spent. In the spring of 53 BC they resumed the offensive. With a force centred around seven legions, they were confident, for in the past Lucullus and Pompey had demonstrated how easy it was for the Romans to smash far larger Asian armies. The Parthians were equally sure of themselves, again used to beating their neighbours without difficulty, and it came as something of a shock to both sides to realise that this new enemy was very different from anything they had met before. In spite of their allied cavalry and light infantry, the Roman army was still essentially an infantry force. In contrast the Parthians relied on their two types of cavalry – the heavy lance-wielding cataphracts where both horse and man was protected by armour, and the fast-moving horse archers armed with powerful composite bows. When the two sides clashed for the first time at Carrhae the cavalry army proved superior, although not by as big a margin as is often claimed. Publius Crassus was lured away from the main force and he and all his men killed, but the battle ended in a tactical stalemate, neither side able to break the other. The Romans had certainly suffered heavier casualties and were a long way from home. Crassus had shown flashes of his old military skill during the battle, but in the night after the battle his spirit and that of his army broke. They retreated, something that was never likely to be easy when the Romans were on foot and the Parthians mounted. In the pursuit the Roman army was virtually destroyed. Crassus was killed while negotiating with the enemy, and his head sent back to the Parthian king. It was a humiliating disaster, which dwarfed in scale the loss of fifteen cohorts in the Ardennes just a few months before. The first of the triumvirs had gone, and the death of one of Rome's richest and most influential men inevitably caused a deep shift in the political balance in the Republic.

By coincidence the Parthian campaign also brought fame to Crassus' quaestor, who managed to lead a force of survivors back to Syria and repulse Parthian raids on the province. His name was Caius Cassius Longinus, and nine years later he would be one of the two leaders of Caesar's assassins.[28]

XV

THE MAN AND THE HOUR: VERCINGETORIX AND THE GREAT REVOLT, 52 BC

'The chieftains of Gaul called councils in remote spots deep in the forests and bemoaned the death of Acco; they realised that the same fate could well befall any of them; they pitied the common plight of Gaul; by pledges and gifts they encouraged men to start the war and risk their own life in the cause of the liberty of Gaul.' – *Caesar*[1]

Successful imperial powers have always relied as much – or even more – on diplomacy and political settlement as on military force. Armies could and can smash formal opposition, and were and are capable of curbing guerrilla warfare, although they may not be able to destroy it. Yet if military actions were not to be constantly repeated, then a settlement needed to be reached which was acceptable to enough of the occupied peoples, and in particular those with power and influence. This principle was as true for men like Wellesley in British India or Bugeard in French North Africa as it was for Caesar in Gaul. All of them were gifted soldiers who won great battlefield victories, but each realised that this was not enough without effective diplomacy and competent administration. For senators, the intimate connection between war and politics in the Roman Republic helped to prepare them for this aspect of their role as a provincial governor. It was also important that Roman expansion outside Italy was not a question of eradicating the indigenous population and replacing them with Roman colonists, or even of imposing a Roman elite who would exploit a subject population. For all the massacres and mass enslavements that accompanied Roman imperialism, the province of Gaul that Caesar created would be lived in by the tribes who were there when he had arrived. In most day-to-day affairs they would be ruled by leaders drawn from the existing aristocracy.

315

A permanent conquest relied on persuading the tribes and their leaders that it was more in their interest to accept Roman rule than to oppose it.[2]

From the beginning Caesar understood this and embedded his campaigns firmly within a political context. His initial interventions in Gaul all came in response to appeals from allied tribes. Invaders were expelled, but Gaulish opponents were treated far less harshly than German enemies, and following a defeat became Roman allies deserving of his protection. Caesar met with the tribal leaders frequently – there was invariably at least one council every year, and usually two or more. He paid close attention to the balance of power within each tribe, and tried to gain some idea of the character and inclinations of individual leaders. Certain men were favoured, strengthening their position within the tribes to provide leaders who were indebted to Caesar. One of these was Diviciacus, who virtually became the leader of the Aedui for a few years, and was also able to place other tribes in his debt by seeking favours for them from the proconsul. Commius, the man who acted as Caesar's envoy in Britain, was made king of his own tribe the Atrebates and was also given overlordship of the Menapii. It would be wrong simply to dismiss such men as mere quislings, no more than tools of the Roman imperialists. Each had ambitions of his own. The arrival of Caesar's legions in Gaul could not be ignored. The alternative powers – the Helvetii, Ariovistus and the German migrants – had all been driven out and could no longer be used to counterbalance the Romans. Winning Caesar's favour offered chieftains great advantages, and as far as they were concerned they were using him just as much as he was using them. The proconsul's influence was considerable, but he could not control the internal politics of the tribes, as was shown by the rejection of the kings he had raised up amongst the Senones and Carnutes. The Gaulish aristocracy was not changed in any fundamental way by Caesar's arrival and chieftains still competed for power. Alliance with Rome brought advantages, but these were not necessarily overwhelming, and there were other sources of prestige and wealth. The position of king was a precarious one in most tribes, so that even if Caesar elevated a man to the monarchy there was no certainty that he would be able to remain there.[3]

Caesar's understanding and manipulation of tribal politics was generally good, but over the winter of 53–52 BC, his policy failed badly. There were a number of reasons for this failure, but at its root was the growing sense of the extent to which his presence had changed things. This was especially true of the Celtic/Gallic peoples of central and southern Gaul, one of the three broad groups into which the *Commentaries* divided 'the whole of

Gaul'. These tribes had not yet fought against Caesar to any meaningful degree, although it was in their lands that the campaigns against the Helvetii and Ariovistus had been waged. Dominating the trade routes with the Roman world, tribes like the Aedui, Sequani and Arverni were wealthier and more politically sophisticated than the peoples to the north. They had aided Caesar, and he in turn had favoured the tribes and leaders most sympathetic to him and had fought – or so at least he claimed – on their behalf against the Helvetii and Ariovistus. Now, over the course of the next year, virtually all of them would turn against him. This was not simply a question of rebellion by those who had not received the proconsul's favour and had watched as their rivals were elevated above them. The rebels eventually included many chieftains who had done rather well under Roman dominion. That was at the heart of this new mood, the realisation that Caesar and his legions were in Gaul to stay, and would not be returning to the confines of the Transalpine province after a few swift campaigns. Rome now expected her power to be acknowledged on a permanent basis throughout Gaul. The ally had become the conqueror without ever facing serious resistance from the Celtic peoples.

Some of Caesar's own actions had brutally exposed this new reality. The summary killing of Dumnorix and the flogging and beheading of Acco – probably especially humiliating because the head had a great importance in Gallic religion – showed that the proconsul had no qualms about disposing of leaders accused of plotting against him. It was shocking to see great chieftains disposed of in this way, and suggested that no one was entirely safe. With hindsight Caesar's actions could be viewed as misjudged, but it is not easy to see how either situation could have been handled more effectively. Ultimately, the execution of Acco was the spark that ignited rebellion, but the rising probably would have happened at some point. Throughout the *Commentaries* Caesar openly acknowledged that many of his opponents were fighting for their freedom, which Rome's best interests required him to take from them. A large part of the Gaulish aristocracy decided that continued Roman domination would mean their losing more than they would gain. The Romans spoke of peace as the product of victory, but peace in a real sense was imposed on the tribes as a result of Caesar's campaigns. Yet warfare had long played a central role in Gaulish culture and society, and chieftains were first and foremost war-leaders, whose power was shown by the number of warriors in their retinue. Tribes were no longer as free to fight each other and martial glory could now only be won fighting as allies of the Roman army. Powerful chieftains knew that seizing kingship amongst their own people would invite swift retribution if the Roman governor did not approve. It was also harder to create a network of friends, allies and clients within the leadership of other tribes. The world had changed, and the leaders of the tribes now found that they lacked full liberty to govern themselves in the traditional way. Even if Caesar only occasionally interfered in the tribes' day-to-day affairs, it was still evident that he could. Political liberty had been curbed by a supposed ally, and along with it had gone the freedom to raid and behead your neighbours, or to seize power by force within your own tribe. Chieftains were judged by the size of their retinues, but such followings of warriors were hard to support without regular warfare and raiding. Throughout Gaul resentment was widespread and during the winter months there were secret meetings where rebellion was discussed and planned. Many took place in the territory of the Carnutes, perhaps because these contained cult sites sacred to all of Gaul. The leaders could not exchange hostages to cement their new alliances, since this would probably have come to the attention of the Romans. Instead they symbolically stacked their standards together and took oaths.[4]

Growing resentment of the Roman presence in Gaul spurred the plotters on, but they also sensed an opportunity. Caesar had gone south to Cisalpine Gaul and they knew from experience that his legates were unlikely to act aggressively until he returned in the spring. There was even the hope that he would not be able to come back at all, for rumours spread of chaos at Rome. The stories were not invented, for after Crassus and Pompey had left to take up their commands the public life of the city had been turbulent. Bribery on a scale that was staggering even by the standards of the Republic had been uncovered in the consular elections for 53 BC, and after repeated disruptions these had still not been held when the year began. Clodius was standing for the praetorship for 52 BC, promising electoral reform that would benefit freedmen, and many of these swelled the ranks of the gangs who used force to back his campaign. Against them his old enemy Milo, who was seeking the consulship himself, ranged his own band of thugs and gladiators, and the ensuing violence made it impossible to hold elections once again, so another year opened without consuls or senior magistrates to guide the Republic. On 18 January 52 BC, the rival gangs encountered each other on the Appian Way just outside Rome, and in the ensuing fighting Clodius was killed. The next day his supporters carried his body into the Senate House, built a pyre there and cremated him, burning the building down in the process. Not for the first time there was talk of making Pompey dictator to restore order by force. A levy of all male citizens of military age and living in Italy was also decreed in case emergency forces would be needed. Caesar duly performed this in Cisalpine Gaul, and naturally watched events in Rome with a keen interest. A chance remark from a letter written over two years later, tells us that Cicero travelled up to Ravenna in the Cisalpine province for a meeting with Caesar. The orator was doubtless not the only visitor, and it may have been around this time that Caesar put forward his proposals for renewing the marriage bond with Pompey. The Gauls were wrong to believe that the troubles in Rome would prevent Caesar from returning, but they were certainly right to guess that they would not be the main focus of his attention during these months. If his legates in Gaul gained any inkling of the planned rebellion, then they ignored or disbelieved the reports. The outbreak came as a complete surprise to the Romans.[5]

The Carnutes had pledged themselves to launch the first strike. Two of their chieftains led their warriors to the town of Cenabum (modern Orléans) and massacred the Roman traders who were living there. Also killed was an equestrian who had been given charge of the grain supply by Caesar. News of the massacre spread rapidly, the *Commentaries* claiming that it was known 160 miles away by midnight. The next to take up arms was a young Arvernian aristocrat named Vercingetorix. His father had for a while dominated much of Gaul, but had been killed by the tribe when he tried to make himself their king. Vercingetorix was known to Caesar and seems to have been one of those young aristocrats whom the proconsul had tried to win over. Past friendship was now set aside and he began raising an army, but was forcibly expelled from the Arverni's main town of Gergovia (probably a few miles from modern Clermont) by his uncle and other leading men of the tribe. Not disheartened, he recruited more men – Caesar says vagrants and outcasts, but they may actually have been warriors who simply lacked a chieftain to support them. With this new strength he returned, forced his opponents out of Gergovia and was proclaimed king by his men. Virtually all the tribes to the west as far as the Atlantic coast rapidly joined him, their chieftains acknowledging him as their war-leader. From the beginning his attitude was markedly different to most Gaulish commanders, and he tried to impose discipline on his army and organise its supply. Caesar claims that disobedience was punished by death or mutilation.[6]

Vercingetorix was soon ready to attack, targeting tribes allied to Rome. While another chieftain took one force against the Remi, he led his main army against the Bituriges, who lived to the north of his own people. The Bituriges were dependants of the Aedui and immediately appealed to them for protection. They in turn consulted Caesar's legates, who advised the

Aedui to send an army to help the Bituriges. It is striking that the Roman officers did not themselves act, and suggests that they did not yet appreciate the scale of the uprising. With the exception of Labienus, Caesar's legates appear to have been men of modest talent, and he did not encourage too much initiative on their behalf. It was still winter, making operations difficult – though not impossible, as Caesar had shown a year before. Revolts are at their weakest when they begin, while many prospective recruits are waiting to see whether or not it seems likely to succeed. Normally Roman commanders tried to strike as soon as possible at the first sign of rebellion, but in this case the reaction was half-hearted. The Aedui were similarly tentative in their response. Their army reached the Loire, marking the border between their own lands and the Bituriges. There they halted for a few days, before withdrawing, claiming that their dependants were in league with Vercingetorix and planned to attack them as soon as they crossed. Caesar says that even after the rebellion he was not sure whether the leaders of the Aeduan force actually believed this, or were already plotting treachery. After they had retreated the Bituriges openly joined the rebellion.[7]

Perhaps by this stage Caesar's officers were beginning to realise that something big was occurring, and their report on this episode was enough to convince him of the need to rejoin the army. The situation in Rome had stabilised by this time, Pompey having been made sole consul rather than dictator, and having brought troops into the city to restore order by force. Caesar crossed the Alps to Transalpine Gaul. By this time more tribes had joined Vercingetorix and the rebels – some willingly and others through coercion. The revolt was gaining momentum. Tribes loyal to Rome or her close allies were being systematically attacked, and most were switching sides. Caesar was in one of the worst possible situations for any general, separated from his army by hundreds of miles at a time when an enemy was in the field against him. If he ordered the army to march to join him, then it might encounter the enemy's main force on the journey and have to fight without him. That could mean defeat, or at best a victory where the credit went to Labienus or one of the other legates. There were also great risks if he went to the legions, since his escort would be small and with so many tribes defecting to the rebels he would not know which chieftains could be trusted. It is doubtful that he took long reaching his decision. For Caesar danger to himself was preferable to risk to his army. Even after six years of victories, he knew that one bad defeat would be all the ammunition needed by his domestic enemies to destroy his reputation. He also knew that it would be quicker for himself, his attendants and probably some staff, and his escort of 400 German cavalrymen, to hasten to the army than for the legions to march to him. Yet before he could set out, there were threats to the Transalpine province itself. A number of tribes living on the borders had gone over to the rebels, and now a rebel force had invaded the province and was moving against the colony of Narbo.[8]

COUNTER ATTACK

Caesar rushed to the town and organised its defence. There were no legions in the province, but there were a number of locally raised cohorts as well as drafts of new recruits he had brought from Cisalpine Gaul. He probably also had cavalry from the tribes of the province. Some of these he stationed in a defensive line to protect against attacks and soon forced the raiders to withdraw, but he ordered the bulk to concentrate in the lands of one of the Gaulish tribes living in the province, the Helvii. From there he led this improvised and largely inexperienced force over the Pass of the Cevennes and down to attack the Arverni. Surprise was complete, for it was still winter and even the locals assumed that the road would be closed by snow. Caesar's men toiled to clear a path through 6 foot drifts, and then pushed on to reach Arvernian territory. Once there Caesar sent his cavalry out in small detachments, ordering them to range over a wide area, burning and killing. The damage they inflicted was probably slight, but the attack gave the impression of the beginning of an all-out invasion. Messengers went to Vercingetorix who was camped with his main army about 100 miles north amongst the Bituriges. The Gaulish leader started his army marching south to reassure his own people. After two days of raiding the surrounding country, Caesar left Decimus Junius Brutus in charge, telling him to continue sending the cavalry on marauding expeditions. The proconsul announced that he needed to return to the province to raise more levies and allied cavalry, but that he would return in three days. He seems to have been confident that this news would swiftly reach the enemy, for after recrossing the mountains he rode quickly to Vienna (not the modern Austrian capital but Vienne in the Rhône Valley). Earlier he had arranged for a force of cavalry to be waiting there for him. Without halting even for one night, he took this force on, riding hard through the lands of the Aedui, until he reached the two legions wintering amongst the Lingones to the north. Once there he halted, but sent despatch riders to the other legions and ordered them to concentrate at Agedincum (probably near modern Sens). It had been a bold ride through potentially hostile territory. (Suetonius tells a story of Caesar disguising himself as a Gaul to reach his army during a rebellion, which, if true, may refer to this incident.) The commander and his army were reunited. Now it was a question of seizing back the initiative.[9]

Vercingetorix had been wrong-footed by the raid over the Cevennes and it had taken him several days to realise that this was only a feint. Then he returned to his plan of moving against the tribes still loyal to Rome. He came north again and attacked the Boii, who had accompanied the Helvetii in 58 BC and been permitted to settle on their lands at the request of the Aedui. The Gaulish army besieged one of their main towns at a place called Gorgobina. It was still winter and it would be difficult to supply the legions if they took the field, since there had been no time to prepare for operations and to gather food and transport animals. Yet if Caesar delayed the Boii might be forced to capitulate and join the rebellion. Vercingetorix would then be free to attack other tribes and clans allied to the Aedui, demonstrating to all that even the Aedui, the people closest to Rome, were unable to protect their friends. If this happened, then there was little incentive for any tribe to remain loyal to Rome. Rather than accept such a 'shameful humiliation', Caesar sent envoys to the Boii telling them that he and the army were coming to their relief. The Aedui were instructed to gather sufficient grain supplies for the army's need. Then, leaving two legions to guard his baggage train at Agedincum, he led the remaining eight to help the Boii. Only weak cavalry forces accompanied the column, for Caesar had not had a chance to raise the usual levy of allied contingents from the tribes. The Romans also had little food, which meant that they could not afford to remain in the field for very long unless they were able to find a new source of supply. It was a gamble, but it was better than sitting idly by and watching the revolt gain strength and momentum. Inactivity would be seen as weakness, but putting on a bold front and counter-attacking was likely to make wavering tribes and chieftains pause, at least for the moment.[10]

After a day Caesar reached Vellaunodunum, one of the walled towns of the Senones. The legions began to besiege the place and on the third day the inhabitants surrendered, promising to hand over their weapons, 600 hostages and – most important of all for the army's immediate needs – pack animals. Moving on the Romans came swiftly to Cenabum, the place where the rebellion had begun with the massacre of the Roman merchants. Caesar reached it in only two days, surprising the townsfolk who had not yet finished their preparations to resist a siege. It was late when the legions arrived, so the proconsul decided to postpone his assault until the following morning.

Yet he also ordered two legions to stand to arms during the night, in case the townsfolk chose to flee across to the far bank of the Loire. The guess proved correct, and at about midnight the Roman scouts reported that crowds of people were heading from the town for the bridge over the river. There was no significant resistance when he sent his two legions into the town, while congestion at the bridge prevented many of the people from escaping captivity. Caesar ordered the town to be sacked and then burned down, and presumably had most of the prisoners sold as slaves. Then he crossed the Loire and advanced against the Bituriges. The Romans had regained the initiative, forcing Vercingetorix to respond to their actions and not vice versa. The latter had already abandoned his attack on the Boii and hurried back to protect the Bituriges. The Gaulish army arrived just as the Romans were accepting the surrender of the town of Noviodunum, and prompted the townsfolk to renew the fight, chasing out the centurions and small groups of soldiers who had entered their walls. A cavalry combat took place in the fields outside the town, and the Romans eventually won this when Caesar threw in his band of 400 Germans. This minor success, as well as the fact that the Romans were close outside their walls and the bulk of the Gaulish army still some way away, prompted the people of Noviodunum to change their minds for a second time, and they surrendered again, handing over the men responsible for breaking the truce. Caesar resumed his advance, heading for Avaricum (modern Bourges), one of the most important and certainly the best defended town of the Bituriges. Having regained the initiative, it was vital to keep it and give the enemy no chance to recover.[11]

From the beginning Vercingetorix was sceptical about his ability to defeat the legions in battle, and the speed with which the Romans had taken three towns had only confirmed his respect for their fighting power and siegecraft. Instead he planned to shadow the enemy, ambushing small detachments but not risking a massed encounter. He wanted to deprive the Romans of supplies, and to do this he told his followers that they must be utterly ruthless: '. . . private possessions must be disregarded, villages and houses put to the torch in all areas as far afield as the enemy foragers were likely to range from their main route of march'.[12] Even entire towns that could not be protected from the enemy were to be destroyed, to prevent the legions from capturing the food stores within them. The Bituriges set fire to twenty of the main settlements in response to this order. Vercingetorix argued that terrible though this was, the alternative was death for the warriors and enslavement for their families. His strategy was considerably more sophisticated than that employed by Caesar's earlier opponents, and Vercingetorix must clearly have possessed considerable charisma and force of personality to persuade his followers of the necessity of such uncompromising measures. It was remarkable just how much the tribes were willing to sacrifice, but unsurprising that they occasionally balked at the prospect. After pleas from all the leaders of the Bituriges, Avaricum itself was not destroyed. Vercingetorix grudgingly made an exception of the town, although he lacked their conviction that its natural and man-made defences rendered it impregnable.[13]

Avaricum was certainly a more daunting prospect than the towns taken so easily in the past weeks. Surrounded by river or marshes on most sides there was only one practical route for an assault, and it was next to impossible to create a solid blockade. Caesar's army camped at the foot of this slope and began to build a ramp that would allow them to reach the wall. The legionaries also made mantlets and sheds to shelter the workers as they got nearer to the enemy, and two siege towers to climb the ramp when it was finished. Caesar's eight legions were most likely under strength, so that he had perhaps 25,000–30,000 men, along with a few thousand auxiliaries and many more slaves and camp followers. It was very difficult to feed such a force while it was moving. When it settled down to besiege Avaricum the task became almost impossible. Foraging was unproductive and dangerous, since Vercingetorix was camped no more than 16 miles away and shadowed every detachment the Romans sent out, cutting up any group that became exposed. The proconsul sent repeated messages to the Aedui and Boii asking them to send him convoys of provisions, but very little arrived. The Aedui showed no enthusiasm for this task, although – perhaps in part because – they had been one of his main sources of supply since 58 BC. The Boii were still grateful for his support, but were too small a people to have much of a grain surplus available. The scorched earth tactics of Vercingetorix were beginning to bite. At one point the Romans completely exhausted their stocks of grain, but fortunately the foragers had brought in enough cattle for these to be slaughtered and a meat ration supplied. Caesar praised his men for their fortitude in keeping on working while receiving only a meagre and monotonous issue of food. (The persistent myth that Roman legionaries were vegetarian is based on a misunderstanding of this and a couple of other passages. Normally they ate a balanced diet of meat, grain and vegetables. What was exceptional in this case was that they were receiving only meat, not that they were eating it at all.)[14]

In spite of the shortages, and the watching menace of the main Gaulish army – for Vercingetorix kept in close communication with the defenders of the town – the legionaries kept toiling at the siege works. Caesar toured the lines as they laboured, inspecting the work and encouraging the men. On several occasions he offered to abandon the siege and withdraw if they felt that the task was beyond them. It was a clever way of exploiting the legionaries' pride in themselves and their units, as no one wanted to be seen as the first to quit. The men implored him to let them finish the job, rather than suffering the shame of giving up. The memory of the massacre of the Romans at Cenabum was still strong and provoked widespread anger. Caesar tells us that the soldiers requested their officers to emphasise to him their determination to continue and their absolute faith in their ultimate victory. By this time the ramp was getting bigger, so that the siege towers could move close to the walls, though not yet close enough for the rams mounted in them to begin creating a breach.

It was not only the Romans who were facing supply problems, and there were serious shortages in the Gaulish camp. In part this was simply because of the season and the need to remain in one place, but it also highlights the lack of logistic organisation in tribal armies. Vercingetorix was a better commander than most Gaulish leaders, and his army more flexible and better prepared than the average tribal force, but it still lagged a long way behind the Roman army in these respects. The progress of the siege may also have made him feel that he needed a fresh victory to encourage his men. The Gaulish army moved a little closer to the town. He then led out his cavalry and light infantry in person, hoping to mount an ambush on the Roman foragers. Caesar found out about this, either from his patrols, from prisoners or from deserters, and took the bulk of his army out to threaten the Gaulish camp. The enemy formed up to meet him, but were in too strong a position for him to attack without suffering heavy losses. The legionaries were keen for battle – encouraged by their own record of success and brimming over with the frustration caused by hard work and short rations. Caesar told them that he would not suffer casualties needlessly, for 'their lives were more important than his own needs'. The Romans watched the enemy for a while and then marched back to camp. The threat had been enough to cause Vercingetorix to change his plans and return to his main force. Caesar had made it clear that he could not press too closely if he was unwilling to fight. For a while there was dissension in the Gaulish army, some even claiming that Vercingetorix was in league with the Romans and wished to be made king of all Gaul with Caesar's aid. It is more than likely that the two men had met, and fairly probable that Vercingetorix had even received some favours from Caesar during his cultivation of the Arvernian aristocracy.

Eventually he calmed them, bringing out captive Roman slaves and claiming that they were legionaries. The men had been coached to tell a plaintive story of the hardships and shortages in the Roman camp. Having convinced the men of the wisdom of his plan, he and the other chieftains selected 10,000 warriors and sent them to reinforce Avaricum.[15]

Sieges were tests of ingenuity as much as sheer determination. Some of Avaricum's importance came from the iron mines in the area and as a result skilled miners were available to try to undermine the Roman ramp. Other men worked to run up wooden towers strengthening the wall, and kept adding to these as the Romans increased the height of their own works. As the defender or attacker gained an advantage, so the other tried to devise a countermeasure to rob them of it. Yet in the end the Romans had greater engineering skill and, in spite of frequent sallies aimed at setting light to it, after twenty-five days the ramp was virtually complete. All in all it measured 330 feet wide and 80 feet high and had almost reached the town wall, so that soon the battering rams in the towers would be in range. That night the defenders set light to the timber supports in their mine, hoping either to collapse the whole ramp or to set fire to it. In the small hours Roman sentries spotted smoke coming from the wooden ramp. Almost immediately a shout went up from the wall and two groups of defenders charged out of separate gates carrying torches and incendiary material as well as weapons. According to Caesar's standing orders, two legions were on piquet duty throughout the hours of darkness. More Roman troops were sent in to support them as the furious combat swayed back and forth. Some of the legionaries fought off the enemy, while others dragged the siege towers back to safety, although they were not able to save some of the mantlets and shelters further up the ramp. It was a desperate struggle, and in the *Commentaries* Caesar makes one of those rare mentions of a minor incident that he witnessed. A Gaulish warrior stood near one of the town gates and kept hurling lumps of pitch and tallow at the Roman works. He was killed by the bolt from a scorpion – one of the Romans' light artillery pieces that shot its projectile with great accuracy and appalling force. As soon as he fell, another took his place, then another and another, as each was struck down by a bolt from the same ballista. Caesar was clearly impressed by their courage, something that the *Commentaries* never tried to deny the Gauls, even if Caesar tended to depict it as somehow not quite as good as the disciplined bravery of the legions.[16]

After bitter fighting the defenders were driven back inside their walls, having failed to inflict enough damage to seriously impede the Romans. A day later they willingly obeyed Vercingetorix when he urged them to escape from the town. Under cover of darkness the warriors tried to sneak out of the town and make their way through the marshes to the main army. The attempt failed when their abandoned families realised what was happening and raised such loud cries that it was feared the Romans would discover their purpose. On the following day – the twenty-seventh of the siege – the legionaries completed the ramp. It was raining heavily and Caesar decided on an immediate assault, judging that the defenders were likely to be off their guard. Orders for the storming were issued, and the necessary preparations made, the attacking troops forming up under cover of the sheds and shelters of the siege works to conceal the Roman purpose. Roman generals were always keen to encourage individual boldness, and the proconsul promised great prizes to the first men over the wall. At a signal the men suddenly erupted from cover and charged forwards, overcoming the surprised defenders and quickly seizing the rampart. A few parties of Gauls formed up in such open spaces as the market place, but their nerve cracked when they saw the Romans swarming around the walls. Throughout history troops who have stormed a fortified position have often been inclined to run amok once inside. Sieges have always been difficult and dangerous operations, the actual assault even more hazardous, and it was often hard for men who had endured both to switch off once they were inside, especially since in the narrow streets they were no longer under the close gaze of their officers. When a town was stormed it was normal for anyone who showed even the slightest resistance to be killed, while women were raped. This time the mood of the soldiers was more ferocious even than was usual on such occasions. Caesar says that the legionaries: 'Remembering the massacre at Cenabum and the labours of the siege, did not spare the elderly, the women and the infants. In the end from the whole number, about 40,000 people, little more than 800 who had fled the town at the first shout escaped to join Vercingetorix.'[17]

About a century earlier Polybius had described how the Romans sometimes deliberately massacred the inhabitants of a captured town, killing even the animals they found there, so that this would inspire terror and persuade future enemies to surrender and render an assault unnecessary. There is no reason why Caesar should not have told us if he had ordered the slaughter of Avaricum's population as a warning to others. He was candid about other massacres or mass executions, and no Roman reader was likely to be too upset about the fate of foreign enemies. It does seem that it was sheer rage on the part of the legionaries, frustrated and weary after a difficult siege in cold weather and with very poor provisions, that led to the slaughter. Killing the inhabitants – and even if it was perhaps not quite as total as

Caesar implies, the death toll must have been substantial – was not really in their interest on a pragmatic basis, since every defender killed was one fewer to be sold as a slave for the profit of all. Having said that, Caesar does not seem to have made any effort to restrain his men, although it is highly questionable whether he would have been able to do so even if he had tried.[18]

SETBACK AT GERGOVIA

Caesar rested his army for several days after the sack of Avaricum. Large stores of grain and other provisions were discovered inside the town, greatly easing the supply situation. Spring was also beginning, making foraging more practical. The two legions left to guard the baggage train were brought up to join the main force. Caesar was eager to resume the offensive to make it harder for Vercingetorix to wrest back the initiative, but he now received an appeal from the Aedui that he could not afford to ignore. Two men were both claiming to have been elected to the tribe's supreme magistracy, the post of Vergobret. Dissension amongst the chieftains of his largest and most important ally was obviously dangerous at a time of rebellion, for it would be all too likely that one side or the other would seek support from Vercingetorix. Therefore Caesar hastened south to meet with the rivals – the Vergobret was forbidden to leave tribal territory in his year of office, so this restriction, as well as the reluctance to offend an ally at this time, meant that he could not make them come to him. The proconsul decided which man was the rightful magistrate, having discovered that tribal law effectively barred his opponent. He then asked that the tribe supply him with as many cavalry as they could as well as 10,000 infantry to be used to defend his supply lines. Hurrying back to the army, Caesar decided to divide into two columns. Labienus was to take four legions and move north against the Senones and Parisii, while he took the remaining six southwards and attacked the Arverni. It was clearly dangerous to divide his resources in this way, but given the reluctance of the rebels to risk a pitched battle, he must have judged that the risk was acceptable. The rebels had no single capital or even a united army, the defeat of which would convince them to surrender. For all the charisma of Vercingetorix, he still led many fiercely independent tribes and each of these would need to be suppressed. If an area in rebellion was left unmolested, then this would only cause the rebels to grow in confidence and in numbers, and make it likely that more neighbouring peoples would be encouraged or coerced into joining.[19]

The short lull had given Vercingetorix time to recover from the loss of Avaricum. In some ways the defeat strengthened his own prestige, since he had spoken against defending the town from the beginning and had only reluctantly been persuaded to relent. His plan remained much the same, to harass rather than confront Caesar and his army, and to try to win over more chieftains and tribes to his cause. As the Romans marched along the line of the River Allier, Vercingetorix kept pace with them on the opposite bank, sending men out to break down all the bridges and to guard all the spots where a new one might be built. Caesar needed to cross if he was to threaten Gergovia, the town where Vercingetorix had first declared himself as the leader of the Arverni, but at this time of the year the river could not be forded by an army. That day the Roman column camped in wooded country close to one of the destroyed bridges. When the army marched out the next day, Caesar and two legions stayed behind under cover of the trees. The other four legions 'opened out some of their cohorts, so that the number of units looked the same'. The Gauls suspected nothing as the Roman column marched on and eventually built its camp in the same way that it had done on all the other days. They in turn moved on, ready to deny all the crossing places further down to the enemy. However, late in the day, by the time he thought that the main force would have halted, Caesar brought out his two legions and set them to constructing a bridge. Once that was complete they went across and began work on the ditch and wall of a camp. Messengers went to the main force recalling them. By the time that Vercingetorix discovered what had happened, it was too late to do anything about it. He headed away from the river, eager to put more distance between himself and Caesar since he had no wish to stay too close. His plan was still to avoid battle. Caesar followed him and in five days reached Gergovia.[20]

The proconsul rode forward to inspect the enemy position and soon realised that it was a strong one. The town itself stood on a hill, and on the rolling high ground around it Vercingetorix had camped his army, each tribal contingent having been allocated a position to hold. Direct assault looked impractical and would certainly be costly. The enemy might be starved into submission, but the Romans could not hope to mount an effective blockade until they had secured their own stocks of food. A convoy from the Aedui was on its way but had yet to reach the army. As Caesar waited he mounted a night attack to capture one of the Gaulish outposts, giving him a position from which to threaten the enemy's water supply and access to forage. A smaller camp occupied by two legions was built on this spot and connected to the main camp by a route enclosed by a deep ditch on either side. Both sides settled down to watch their opponents warily, sending out their cavalry and light infantry to skirmish, but neither willing to risk a full-scale battle. Vercingetorix held daily meetings for his chieftains and for the moment continued to impose an unusually high standard of discipline for a tribal army.[21]

The loyalty of the Aedui was beginning to waver. Convictolitavis – the man whose claim to the post of Vergobret Caesar had upheld – was in secret contact with representatives from the Arverni and had accepted gifts from them. At his instigation a chieftain called Litaviccus, who commanded the 10,000 warriors escorting the food convoy to Caesar's legions, resolved to turn against his Roman allies. Halting the convoy when he was 30 miles from Gergovia, he announced to his men that the Aeduan cavalry serving with Caesar had all been executed by the Romans on a charge of negotiating with the enemy. Their only choice was to join Vercingetorix and so save themselves from a similar fate. Like the Arvernian chieftain, Litaviccus was said to have produced men who claimed to be survivors of this massacre and told a dreadful story of Roman treachery. The ruse worked and the Aedui swiftly turned on the Romans accompanying the column, torturing them to death and plundering the food they were escorting. When news of this reached the Aeduan chieftains leading the cavalry with Caesar's army, one of them went straight to the proconsul to report what he had learned. Caesar immediately led out four legions in marching order, urging the troops on until they managed to cover 25 miles and had come within sight of Litaviccus' men. The proconsul sent the Aeduan cavalry on ahead, telling them to show themselves to their fellow tribesmen and so expose the lies of Litaviccus. The warriors of the escort promptly surrendered, while Litaviccus and his retainers fled and made their way to join Vercingetorix. Giving his legionaries only three hours rest Caesar force marched the weary men back to the positions outside Gergovia. On the way they met despatch riders sent by Fabius, the legate left in charge of the two legions outside the town. He reported that they had come under heavy attack throughout the day and, with two legions having to cover positions built for six, had barely managed to hold their own, aided by the power of their artillery. Caesar quickened the pace and managed to bring his force back to the camps before dawn. Their presence was enough to deter Vercingetorix from another direct assault on the Roman positions.[22]

Caesar had sent messengers to reassure the Aedui, but riders sent by Litaviccus arrived first and prompted Convictolitavis to raise his people against Rome. At the town of Cabillonum, a military tribune and some Roman merchants were persuaded to leave and then set upon by a mob. As more and more Gaulish warriors arrived to share in the spoils, Caesar's messengers arrived, informing them that their cavalry contingent and the 10,000 infantry were all now in Caesar's camp – and thus not only still loyal to him, but effectively in his power. The Aeduan leaders officially repented of their actions, blaming the common folk of the tribe. For the moment Caesar was content merely to remind them of his past favours and urge them to renewed loyalty, but privately he knew that the alliance with Rome hung by the slightest of threads. His position was no longer good. Although he had regained the initiative for a while by launching an offensive, now he was stuck outside Gergovia without the resources to drive off Vercingetorix and his army or to take the town. Staying where he was would achieve nothing, but withdrawing would mean a huge loss of face. Since he had raided the Arverni from Transalpine Gaul months before, he had kept on attacking and advancing almost without pause. In practical terms this had forced Vercingetorix to react to him, but even more important was the impression it created of absolute confidence in Rome's overwhelming might and the inevitability of her ultimate victory. It did not matter if the impression was largely a façade, it was still powerful in the minds of those who were as yet undecided on whether or not to join the rebellion. Once Caesar stopped advancing and began to retreat, then the illusion of Roman invincibility would be shattered. Withdrawal in the face of the enemy was always a dangerous operation, and in this case it would be seen as an admission of failure and was very likely to convince uncommitted tribes that the rebellion was going to succeed. However, it would allow him to regroup and add Labienus' four legions to his force – with ten legions he would probably have had sufficient strength to win at Gergovia. Caesar chose the lesser evil and decided to withdraw, but hoped first to win a minor victory and so make his pulling out seem less of a retreat.[23]

While inspecting the smaller fort the proconsul noticed that one of the hills, which had been strongly occupied by the Gauls on previous days, was now virtually empty. Interrogating some of the many deserters who had come into the Roman lines, he was told that Vercingetorix had become very worried that the Romans might take one of the other hilltops and so had drawn off most of his men to fortify it. Caesar saw the opportunity and began to feed the enemy's insecurity. That night cavalry patrols were sent out to look at the hill Vercingetorix was busy fortifying. The horsemen were told to make more noise than usual, just to ensure that the Gauls were aware of their presence. On the following morning he mounted large numbers of the army's slaves on pack horses and mules, gave them helmets to wear and, putting a few genuine cavalrymen around them to make the deception more convincing, sent the whole mass off towards the same spot by a roundabout route. Later on a legion followed them, but halted in some dead ground and then took cover in a patch of woodland. As the Gauls' attention was drawn towards the place where they expected and feared attack, Caesar saw their forces shift to meet it. Then he quietly moved his legions to the smaller camp, telling them to keep their shields covered and have their crests out of sight. They moved not as organised cohorts but as dribs and drabs, strolling along without any impression of purpose. Caesar briefed the legates put in charge of each legion, explaining what he wanted them to do and emphasised that they must 'keep their troops under control, and not let their enthusiasm for battle or hope of plunder carry them too far forward'.[24]

At a given signal the legions attacked up the slope, while the Aedui went up the opposite side of the same spur. Each group made its way as best it could, but the ridge was broken by re-entrants and it was often difficult for one group to see the others. There were very few defenders and the legionaries easily scrambled over a 6-foot wall of piled stones that the Gauls had built halfway up the hill. The obstacle did not delay the Romans for long, but it must have caused some disorder in the formations, and this was made worse as they charged through the Gallic camps that were dotted around the slope. The king of one tribe who had not long before defected to Vercingetorix was surprised in his tent and was still only half dressed when he managed to gallop away. Caesar was with the *Tenth* and, when he decided that the attack had done enough damage, halted the legion and ordered the trumpeters to sound the recall. The sound did not carry well. Some officers heard it and tried to get the legionaries to obey, but most of the men kept on going. They surged up through the camps against the wall of the town itself. In the past they had overwhelmed and destroyed far more numerous opponents in surprise attacks, and perhaps memories of these successes spurred them on. For a while it looked as if Gergovia might actually fall, for there were very few defenders at this spot and the inhabitants panicked:

Married women hurled down clothing and silver from the wall and, baring their breasts, stretched out their hands to beg the Romans to spare them, and not massacre women and children as they had done at Avaricum. Some of the women even lowered themselves by hand from the wall and gave themselves to the soldiers. Lucius Fabius, a centurion of *Eighth*, who was known to have announced to his unit that he was inspired by the rewards at Avaricum, and would not permit anyone to climb the wall before him, got three of his legionaries to lift him up so that he could climb on top of the wall. He then pulled each of them up onto the rampart.[25]

By this time the Gauls working on the fortifications beyond the far side of the town heard the noise of the Roman attack and realised that they had been duped. Vercingetorix also started to get messengers bringing pleas for help from the townsfolk. He sent his cavalry back to meet the Roman attack and the warriors on foot followed. As they arrived thoughts of surrender were banished from the minds of the townsfolk and the women on the walls now started to implore their menfolk to save them. The Roman attack had run out of steam, the men being tired and disordered and unprepared to meet fresh opponents. Many panicked when the Aedui suddenly appeared on their flank, mistaking them for hostile Gauls and failing in the heat of the action to notice that they had their right shoulders bared – the accepted sign of a Gallic ally in Caesar's army. The elation of success soon turned sour:

> At the same time the centurion Lucius Fabius and those who had climbed the wall with him were surrounded, killed and flung from the rampart. Marcus Petronius, another centurion from the same legion, who had tried to hack through the gate, was being overwhelmed by numbers and was now in a desperate situation. Wounded many times, he called out to the men of his unit who had followed him: 'Since I cannot save both myself and you, whom I led into danger through my own lust for glory, I can at least manage to save your lives. When you get the opportunity, look after yourselves.' Straightaway he charged forward into the midst of the enemy, killed two of them and forced the rest back from the gate a short distance. His men tried to come to his aid, but he said, 'There is no hope of you saving my life, for my life's blood and strength are draining away. So escape whilst you have a chance and make your way back to the legion.' So before long he fell fighting and saved his men.[26]

Caesar could do little more than cover the retreat, using the *Tenth* and quickly ordering up the cohorts of the *Thirteenth* that had been left behind to guard the small camp. In this way the Gauls were prevented from pursuing too far, but even so casualties were very high. Around 700 soldiers and no less than 46 centurions had been killed. Centurions led from the front and normally suffered a disproportionately high casualty rate, especially if things went wrong. On the day after the defeat, Caesar paraded the legions and spoke to them, praising their bravery but sternly reprimanding their lack of discipline. In conclusion he assured them that they had only lost because of the difficult ground, the enemy defences and their failure to obey orders – the fighting power of the Gauls had had little to do with it. To ram the message home, for the next two days he selected a good position – probably on a ridge – and deployed in battle order, challenging Vercingetorix to come out and fight. When the Gaulish leader was understandably reluctant to risk a battle with the ground in the enemy's favour, Caesar was able to assure his men that the enemy were still frightened of them. On the following day he marched away, moving towards the lands of the Aedui and not the way he had come. The Romans reached the Allier in three days, rebuilt another of the destroyed bridges and crossed. The Gaulish army made no serious attempt to stop them. Caesar had already decided that he must accept the bad impression created by a withdrawal. His attempt to lessen this by a token success had ended in failure. Word of this soon spread and over the next weeks more tribes openly joined the revolt. The Aedui were amongst the first. The leaders of the cavalry serving with Caesar asked permission to go home. He granted the request, since even though he no longer trusted them he did not want to make the situation worse by holding them against their will, so feeding fresh stories of Roman 'treachery'.

Shortly afterwards the Aedui in the town of Noviodunum slaughtered the small Roman garrison and the Roman traders who were there. This was a doubly serious blow, for the town contained not only huge grain depots gathered to support the army but also the main baggage train, with its records and the hostages taken from the various tribes. Judging that they could not defend the position, the Aedui burned the town, carrying off or spoiling all the grain. Then they used the hostages to begin negotiations with the other tribes. Vercingetorix and chieftains from all over the country were summoned to Bibracte. There the Aedui tried but failed to have one of their own men appointed to replace the Arvernian as overall commander. Rather sullenly, they agreed to obey him for the common good. Now almost all the Celtic or Gallic tribes were ranged against Caesar, and most of the Belgic peoples had joined as well. Vercingetorix was determined to persist with his strategy of avoiding battle, instead harassing the Romans and preventing them from getting food for their men and forage for their animals. Roman military slang called this style of fighting 'kicking the enemy in the stomach'. Keeping the same number of infantry that he already had with him, Vercingetorix asked the tribes to supply more cavalry to increase his force to 15,000 riders. To divide the Romans' effort, he arranged for the Aedui and other tribes to launch fresh attacks on Transalpine Gaul, hoping that the peoples there – notably the Allobroges, who had rebelled only a decade before – would join the rebellion.[27]

Hearing of the defection of the Aedui, Caesar pressed northwards in an effort to join up with Labienus' command. By forced marches he reached the Loire unexpectedly and managed to ford the river even though it was running high with melted winter snows. Cavalrymen formed a chain upstream of the legionaries as they waded chest deep through the water, carrying their equipment in the shields raised over their heads. A few days later he was met by Labienus, who was fresh from a victory near Lutetia (Paris). The Roman field army was now once again concentrated, and its ten legions probably mustered somewhere in the region of 35,000–40,000 men, supported by some auxiliaries. Unable to get many horsemen from his dwindling supply of Gaulish allies, Caesar sent across the Rhine to the German tribes for cavalry and their supporting light infantry. When these arrived Caesar replaced their small German ponies with better mounts taken from his tribunes and other equestrian officers, as well as wealthier veteran soldiers who had been recalled to the colours. The attacks on Transalpine Gaul were worrying and he led the army through the borders of the Lingones into the territory of the Sequani so that he could be nearer to the province. In the event the attacks were dealt with by the levies from the province and the tribes themselves, all under the command of his distant cousin Lucius Julius Caesar, a member of the other branch of the family who had been consul in 64 BC and was currently serving as a legate. Yet the initiative had for the moment passed back to Vercingetorix and the Gaulish leader now resolved to press the Romans more closely. With his great force of cavalry he would attack the legions on the march, while they were encumbered with their baggage. Either the enemy would have to leave their train and press on with the march or stop to protect it and so be slowed to a snail's pace, making the problems of supply even worse. Spontaneously the warriors took an oath not to 'go back under roof, or see their parents, children or wives' unless they had ridden twice through the Roman column. On the following day the Gaulish cavalry attacked in three groups – one striking the head of the column and the others threatening the flanks. Caesar's cavalry were heavily outnumbered but he likewise divided them into three groups and moved up infantry as close support whenever they were hard pressed. The legionaries could not catch the enemy horsemen, but they provided a solid block for their own horsemen to rally behind and re-form. In the end the Germans won the combat on the right, routing the warriors facing them and causing the rest to withdraw.

The Romans pursued, two legions staying behind to protect the baggage train while the remaining eight followed closely behind the cavalry. Gaulish casualties were heavy. Caesar noted with considerable satisfaction the capture of a number of notable Aeduans, including two chieftains who had fought under him earlier in the year, as well as the man whose claim to the post of Vergobret he had rejected. He does not mention their fate.[28]

CLIMAX – THE SIEGE OF ALESIA

The fortune of the campaign had swung once again. Vercingetorix had misjudged the situation, believing that Caesar was retreating and that he needed to be harried mercilessly if the Romans were not simply to return in the future in greater strength. In fact Caesar and his men were far from beaten, and rapidly switched back to the offensive now that the Gaulish army was close and provided them with a clear target. Vercingetorix retired to camp outside Alesia (modern Mont Auxois in the hills of Côte d'Or), a hilltop town of the Mandubii. A day later Caesar camped facing the town and went out to reconnoitre the position. The town lay on a long hill with steep slopes. To the west was a wide, open plain, but on the other three sides there was high ground, intersected by a number of valleys. Together these hills and ridges were roughly crescent shaped. A stream ran to the north and south of the central hill of Alesia. Direct assault would be risky and involve heavy casualties whether or not it succeeded, since Vercingetorix and his men would have the advantage of ground. Caesar claims that he now had 80,000 infantry in addition to his cavalry, but as usual it is hard to know how reliable this figure is. Napoleon was sceptical and doubted that the Gauls can have outnumbered the Romans at all. Even if this is correct, a direct assault was an unattractive option, but in other respects the situation was very different to that at Gergovia. Now Caesar had his full army and, looking at the lie of the land, he was confident that they could enclose and blockade Alesia and the Gaulish army.[29]

The Romans began to work on a monumental set of siegeworks, with a rampart stretching for 11 miles and including twenty-three fortlets as well as larger camps in which the soldiers would rest. The Gauls did not let this go unmolested and sent their cavalry down to attack. They were met by the auxiliary and allied cavalry, but it was not until Caesar committed his reserve of German horsemen and formed up some of the legionaries in support that the Gauls were driven back. Reconciling himself to enduring a siege,

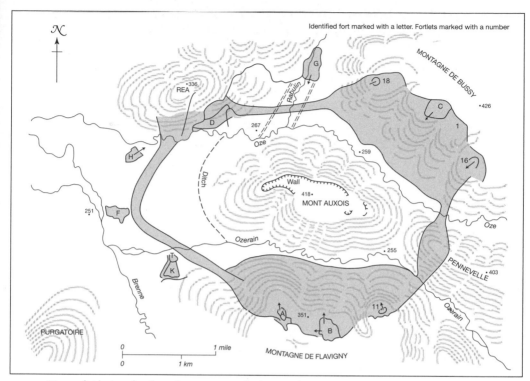

Siege of Alesia: plan based on recent and nineteenth century excavations. Not all of the area has been fully excavated, given the vast size of the site.

Vercingetorix sent his cavalry away before the blockade was closed, telling them to return to their tribes and raise a relief army. The fate of Gaul would be decided at Alesia, for Caesar would be pinned there just as surely as he had bottled up Vercingetorix. Stocks of grain in Alesia were taken under central control to be doled out as a fair ration, while the cattle were distributed to individuals to look after them until they were slaughtered. The Gauls settled down to wait for rescue and the final clash with Caesar. The Romans toiled on to complete their line of circumvallation, completely surrounding the hill. The site was located and excavated under the aegis of Napoleon III, who had a personal passion for this episode of France's history. More recently, modern techniques and further work has added to a picture that in all important respects strikingly conforms to the description given in the *Commentaries* – the dimensions of the actual trenches are not always as regular as Caesar suggests, but since these were so extensive this is unsurprising.

In the west where the plain was open, the Romans dug a straight-sided ditch some 20 feet in width, which ran from one stream to the other. This was intended as an obstacle to delay any attack and give warning of its approach. Four hundred paces (*c*. 130 yards) further back was the main defence line. This consisted of a double ditch, the inner one flooded wherever this was possible, and behind this a 12-foot high rampart strengthened with high towers at 80-foot intervals. In front of the ditches were a series of obstacles and traps to which the legionaries gave macabre nicknames. The stakes with ends that had been sharpened and fire hardened were 'marker-stones' (*cippi*), those hidden in circular pits covered in foliage were lilies (*lilia*), from their shape, while the caltrops and spikes half buried were spurs (*stimuli*). Such traps might cause an attacker some casualties, especially if he came under cover of darkness, but their main function was to slow a charge down and rob it of momentum, as men were forced to walk past them somewhat gingerly. The defences were strong enough so that even a small number of men could hold the lines under all but the heaviest assault, so that much of the army would be free to forage and to continue building. As soon as this line was complete, the proconsul set his men to building another, even longer line – a line of contravallation – facing outwards to defend against the relief army that was bound to come. It was vital to hunt out as much grain and round up as many farm animals as possible before it arrived, and Caesar instructed his men to gather sufficient to supply the entire army for thirty days. The labour and effort involved in these tasks had been massive, but Caesar now had his whole army and his ablest senior officers. In addition to the legates, who included Quintus Cicero and Caius Trebonius, he also had young Decimus Brutus and his new quaestor Marcus Antonius – Shakespeare's Mark Antony. The Romans worked and the Gauls in Alesia watched them, occasionally launching harassing raids but unwilling to chance a major encounter until outside aid arrived. Both sides were waiting for the storm to break.[30]

It took time for the tribes to mass a relief force. The chieftains met and agreed on the numbers of warriors to be supplied by each people. Caesar gives a long list of the contingents requested from each tribe and claims that the army eventually mustered 8,000 cavalry and 250,000 infantry. His information may have been incorrect, and he may deliberately have inflated the figure, but it is worth noting that the numbers are in keeping with those he gives throughout the *Commentaries* for tribal forces, although that may mean no more than that he was consistent in his exaggeration. Nevertheless, even if he exaggerated, the circumstances of such a big coalition, aware that it was fighting the critical battle, would make it likely that this was one of the largest Gaulish armies ever to take the field. Caesar says that the tribes did not call out everyone who could bear arms, since they judged that such a host would be too vast, making it clumsy to control and almost impossible to feed. Even so we would guess that many men who would normally only have fought in defence of their own lands were included in the army, whether willingly or at the command of their chieftains. Four leaders were appointed. One was Commius, the king of the Atrebates, and two of the others were the chieftains who had commanded Caesar's Aeduan cavalry at the beginning of the year. The other was Vercassivellaunus, a cousin of Vercingetorix, the only one who does not seem to have served with Caesar's army at some stage in the past. The army gathered slowly and then moved slowly, as was inevitable with such a big force. The men surrounded at Alesia grew nervous as aid failed to arrive and decided on desperate measures. The people of the town itself – the women, children and the elderly who could not fight effectively – were driven out so that these 'useless' mouths would no longer consume provisions needed by the warriors. Vercingetorix may have assumed that the Romans would permit them to pass through their lines to safety. If so, then he was disappointed. Caesar strengthened the sentries on the rampart and would admit no one. He may have feared that the passage of so many refugees could shield an attack by the warriors, or have been reluctant to let them go into an area where his army was still foraging and use up resources that he needed for his army. Perhaps he just felt that the Gauls would be forced to take the civilians back and so make his blockade more quickly effective. They did not. At this stage of the campaign each commander was able to match the other's cold ruthlessness. The townsfolk's pleas were ignored and they were left to starve to death between the lines. Caesar may have felt that the sight would demoralise the Gauls. It certainly made the final clash an even grimmer affair.[31]

The relief army finally arrived and camped on high ground, probably to the south-west, little more than a mile from the outward facing line of contravallation. On the following day the army massed, with the cavalry in advance on the plain and the vast crowds of infantry on the slopes behind, showing their great numbers to the enemy and their beleaguered friends. In response Vercingetorix brought his warriors out of the town and their camp. They moved forward and filled in a section of the wide trench Caesar's men had dug in advance of their lines. There they waited, ready to attack in concert with the relief army. The legions were ready, men deployed on both of the siege lines to meet attack from each direction. As a gesture of confidence, Caesar sent his cavalry out from the lines to engage the horsemen of the relief force. A whirling fight developed and lasted throughout the afternoon, and seemed for a long time to have been going the Gauls' way, when once again Caesar's German cavalry charged and won the day for the Romans. The Gauls did not commit their infantry, and the armies returned to their camps as darkness fell. The next day was spent in preparation, the Gaulish warriors working to make ladders and gathering ropes to climb the Roman rampart and preparing fascines – bundles of sticks to fill the enemy ditches. The relief army attacked at midnight, raising a great cheer to let Vercingetorix know what was happening – with the Romans between them the two Gaulish armies had no means of direct communication. The Arvernian ordered trumpets to be sounded as a signal for his own warriors to attack, targeting the corresponding stretch of the line of circumvallation. However, it took them a long time to organise, and then even more time to fill in more stretches of the Roman ditch. In the end they were too late to help their comrades. Fighting was bitter but eventually Mark Antony and the legate Trebonius, who were in charge of this section of the lines, moved up reserves and repulsed both attacks. The defences constructed with so much labour by Caesar's men had proved their worth.[32]

Before launching another assault the four leaders of the relief army took more care to scout and to speak to locals who knew the ground. They decided that the vulnerable spot was a Roman camp on the slopes of a hill that formed the north-western tip of the crescent-shaped high ground surrounding the town. The Romans had been unable to include the hill within their lines, since this would have massively increased the already huge task of building the lines. Only two legions occupied the camp, but Commius and his fellow chieftains resolved to send almost a quarter of their infantry, some 60,000 picked warriors, against the position. Vercassivellaunus took his men out at night, leading them to the reverse slope of the hill where they could wait out of sight of the enemy. Diversionary attacks would be launched elsewhere before the real assault began at noon. Vercingetorix saw some of the preparations and, although he did not know the details of the plan, resolved to give what aid he could by launching an all-out attack on the inner lines. At midday Vercassivellaunus and his men spilled over the brow of the hill and poured down the slope against the vulnerable camp. Attacked in so many places simultaneously, the Roman defenders were spread thinly and came under great pressure. The lines were very extensive, but Caesar went to a position from which he could see most of the action and began ordering reserves up to reinforce threatened sectors. Even so, he was especially reliant on his senior officers to keep him informed and to take the initiative where there was not time to consult him. Vercassivellaunus steadily began to make headway against the camp on the hillside, so Caesar sent Labienus – his best subordinate – with six cohorts to reinforce the men there. The senior legate was told to use his judgement, giving up the position and getting the garrison out if he felt that it could not be held.

Caesar now moved, knowing that it was not enough simply to observe and direct. He went to the men and encouraged them as they fought, telling them that this day would decide the whole war. Vercingetorix and his warriors had been repulsed in their first attacks against the weakest sections of the line of circumvallation. Now they switched to assaulting several spots that were better protected by the slopes, but only thinly guarded by the Romans. At one point they got over the rampart and used grappling irons and ropes to pull over one of the Roman towers. Caesar sent Decimus Brutus to the spot with some troops, but he could not hold the enemy back. More cohorts led by the legate Caius Fabius were despatched to support them and the gap in the line was plugged. The crisis over, Caesar galloped off to see how Labienus was coping at the fort on the hillside. He did not go alone, but hastily gathered four cohorts from one of the nearby fortlets. Most of the army's cavalry was also uncommitted and he split these into two, keeping one force with him and sending the other outside the line of contravallation to come round and take Vercassivellaunus' men in the flank. By this time Labienus' men had lost control of the fort's rampart, but the legate had managed to find fourteen cohorts to add to the six he had brought and the two-legion garrison. With this formidable force he had patched together a fighting line inside and near the fort and sent messengers to Caesar letting him know what was happening. Everything was set for the crisis of the siege and the campaign – in many ways, at least as far as the *Commentaries* were concerned, the culminating point of Caesar's campaigns since 58 BC. In his account the skilful actions of Labienus and the other legates are noted, but the focus at the end is on the author himself. His:

> . . . arrival was known through the colour of his cloak, which he always wore in battle as a distinguishing mark; and the troops of cavalry and the cohorts which he had ordered to follow him were also visible, because from the higher parts of the hill these downward slopes and dips could be seen. Then the enemy joined battle: both sides cheered, and the cry was taken up by a shout from the men within the fortifications and rampart. Our troops threw their *pila* and got to work with their swords. Suddenly [the Gauls] spotted the cavalry behind them; other cohorts approached. The enemy turned around and were caught as they fled by the cavalry; and a great slaughter ensued. . .

74 captured war standards were carried to Caesar; very few of this vast host escaped unscathed to their camp.[33]

The Roman counter-attack tipped the balance irrevocably in their favour. The attempt to break into Caesar's lines ended in bloody repulse. Vercingetorix and his men had also been unable to break out and withdrew when they saw the utter failure of the relief army's efforts. Although the fortunes of the day may not have turned quite as quickly or simply as Caesar suggests, the decisive nature of his victory is unquestionable. The heart went out of the rebellion. Vercingetorix and his men were now very short of food and saw no prospect of escape. The relief force had made two great attacks and failed in both. Such an enormous tribal army could not hope to supply itself in the field for very long and there was no prospect of mounting a successful assault before they had to disperse.[34]

The next day Vercingetorix summoned his chieftains to a council. He suggested that they surrender, saying that he was willing to hand himself over to the Romans. None of the council seem to have demurred. Envoys went to Caesar, who demanded that they hand over weapons and that their leaders surrender. In the *Commentaries* the act of capitulation is briefly described. According to Plutarch and Dio, Vercingetorix put on his finest armour and rode out of the town on his best warhorse. Approaching Caesar on the tribunal where he sat on his magistrate's chair, the Arvernian chieftain rode once around his adversary, dismounted, lay down his weapons and sat down at his feet waiting to be taken away. The *Commentaries* could not allow their hero to be upstaged in this way.[35]

Virtually all the tribes involved in the rebellion capitulated. In many ways Caesar's final victory was all the greater because so many peoples had joined. The Celtic/Gallic tribes had finally tested the military strength of the legions and been utterly defeated. Virtually all of them now accepted the reality of conquest. Caesar was generous to the captives from the Aedui and Arverni, and probably also those from their dependent tribes. These men were not sold into slavery, although Vercingetorix was held as a captive until the celebration of Caesar's triumph, when he was ritually strangled in the traditional Roman way. However, there were plenty of other captives who could be sold and the profits shared amongst the army. The Aedui and Arverni were important peoples whom Caesar would prefer as more or less willing allies, hence his leniency. He had won military victory, but knew that creating an enduring peace was now a question of politics and gentle diplomacy. In the case of both tribes, it seems to have worked.[36]

XVI

'ALL GAUL IS CONQUERED'

'Regarding Caesar, there are lots of rumours whispered about him, none of them very good. According to one his cavalry have been wiped out – but that one is certainly a fiction in my view; another says that the *Seventh* legion has been badly mauled, and that Caesar himself is surrounded in the territory of the Bellovaci and is cut off from the rest of his army. However nothing is actually known so far, and even these unconfirmed stories are not circulating widely, but told as an open secret amongst a clique – you know who they are; Anyway, Domitius [Ahenobarbus] puts his hand over his mouth before he speaks.' – *Marcus Caelius Rufus writing to Cicero, c. 26 May 51 BC.*[1]

Throughout his time in Gaul, Caesar took great pains to remind Rome of his existence and to celebrate his achievements. The *Commentaries* were a major part of this effort, but they were not his only literary output during these years. Early in 54 BC, while travelling north from Cisalpine Gaul to rejoin his army, he produced a two-volume work *On Analogy (De Analogia)*. The title was Greek, but the book analysed Latin grammar and argued for accuracy and simplicity in speech and writing, in contrast to the fashion for using archaic forms of words and complicated expressions. It was dedicated to Cicero, and paid tribute to him as Rome's greatest orator and 'virtually the creator of eloquence', but followed this by saying that it was also a good thing to consider everyday speech. No more than a few fragments of the book have survived, but to have written such a detailed and authoritative study at a time when his mind was occupied with the affairs of Gaul and preparations for his second British expedition was an indication of both Caesar's intellect and his restless energy. In comparison with the *Commentaries*, it was aimed at a narrower audience, though one that included the many senators and equestrians obsessed with literature. Caesar the author was a figure whom many found less controversial than Caesar the *popularis* politician. The praise of Cicero was unforced and had much to do with his new, closer relationship with Caesar resulting from his return from exile. The orator sent drafts of his own works to Caesar and the two men discussed these in a way that cemented the political friendship between them.[2]

Literature was important to Rome's elite, but other means were necessary to reach much of the wider population. There was a long tradition of distinguished men, and especially successful generals, building monuments in Rome as physical memorials to their achievements. In 55 BC during his second consulship Pompey commemorated his unprecedentedly great victories with a grander monument than anyone else had ever built, formally opening his great theatre complex. It was the first permanent stone theatre ever to be built in the city and Dio still considered it to be one of Rome's most spectacular features almost three centuries later. Some ten thousand people were able sit on its stone seats – the sensible and well prepared took along cushions when they attended a performance. It stood on the Campus Martius, towering high above a row of temples dedicated by other victorious commanders over the centuries. No less than five shrines were actually built into the structure, the main one to Venus Victrix (Venus the victorious), and others to the deities personifying such virtues as Honour (*Honos*), Courage (*Virtus*), and Good Fortune (*Felicitas*). Attached to the semi-circular theatre was a portico, which itself covered an area of some 585 feet by 440 feet, and everything about the structures from design to materials testified to the vast expense of the whole project.

The same was true of the lavish festivities that marked the opening of the complex. There were musical performances and displays of gymnastics, as well as chariot racing and beast fights in the nearby Circus Flaminius. Five hundred lions were killed in five days, while at one point heavily armoured hunters were matched against about twenty elephants. The beasts made an effort to escape from the arena, frightening the crowd as they tried to smash through the iron railings, until they were driven back. Fear soon turned to sympathy, and the people began to feel sorry for the animals and angry against Pompey for ordering their slaughter. For all that the Romans craved violent displays in the circus, simply spending huge amounts of money on a show did not necessarily mean that the crowd would enjoy it and so feel gratitude to the man who had provided it. Privately, Cicero also felt that the sheer scale of Pompey's theatre and portico were excessive. Other conservative senators muttered that it was a mistake to give the theatre – that most Greek of institutions – a permanent home in the city. In the past most of the audience for any performance had stood, and they feared that giving them seats would just encourage more citizens to waste their days as idle spectators.[3]

Caesar had his own plans to leave his mark on the city, and in 54 BC work began on a large extension to the north side of the Forum and on the Basilica Julia, which would border onto his new development. Not content with this, he followed Pompey's example and looked towards the Campus Martius, where the *saepta* used for voting was to be replaced by a permanent marble-decorated structure. The scale was immense, with a colonnade a mile long running along the side. In another open sign of their new political relationship, Cicero helped Caesar's agent Oppius in planning and arranging the projects. The enormous price – Cicero says that merely purchasing the land needed for the Forum extension cost 60 million sestertii, while Suetonius gives the figure as 100 million – of these grand structures was paid from the profits of conquest in Gaul. When completed these projects would provide a bigger and more spectacular Forum as a centre to the city, with more space for public business and private commerce, and create a far grander environment for voting in the Campus Martius. In the short term work on the buildings provided paid employment for many poorer citizens in the city, as well as profitable contracts to companies supplying materials.

The same was true of the gladiatorial games Caesar announced in honour of his daughter. This was the first time that such contests would be staged to mark the death of a woman, an extension of his earlier staging of public funerals for his aunt Julia and first wife Cornelia. Large numbers of gladiators were collected for the occasion, Caesar having arranged to save the lives of men defeated in earlier appearances in the arena. These had then been trained, not in a gladiatorial school as was usual, but in the households of senators and equestrians known to be skilled in armed combat. Suetonius tells us that Caesar wrote from Gaul to these men, asking them to take great care in the training. By 49 BC he owned at least 5,000 of these fighters, many of them in gladiatorial schools at Capua. A natural showman, Caesar was determined that the games would be something special. The same was true of the public feasts that formed the other main part of his daughter's memorial. Some of the food was prepared in his own household by his own cooks, but much was bought from the expensive shops for which Rome was famous. Traders benefited and the crowd was indulged, hopefully adding to the number of citizens who thought well of Caesar. Although Julia's memorial games and feasts would not actually be celebrated for several years, the preparations for them were very public and the events eagerly anticipated.[4]

For all Caesar's efforts to remain in the public eye, there were times when it must have been difficult for anyone at Rome to pay much heed to what was going on away from the city. In the closing years of the decade, it almost seemed as if the institutions of the Republic were irreparably broken. Electoral bribery was rampant. In the campaign for the consulship for 53 BC two of the candidates had joined together and offered 10 million sestertii for the vote of the *centuria praerogativa*, the century of the First Class chosen to open the voting in the *Comitia Centuriata*, while a further 3 million would go to the consuls of 54 BC who would preside over the elections. Caesar and Pompey were both indirectly involved in the scandal, and were none too pleased at its disclosure. However, it was not until the summer of 53 BC that elections were actually held, with the proconsul Pompey supervising them at the Senate's request. The candidates for the following year were similarly corrupt, and the situation made worse by the violence between the gangs of Milo and Clodius, which culminated in the latter's murder (see p.318). Senators' attendants had been killed in political riots in recent memory and a number of leading men injured. It was far worse for a famous man, who was not only a former magistrate but currently a candidate for office, to die by violence. The cold-blooded nature of the killing added to the widespread shock at the crime. Clodius had been wounded in the initial clash and had then taken refuge in a tavern. Milo had deliberately sent men to drag his old enemy outside and finish him off.

The disturbances that followed, as Clodius' family and supporters vented their grief in destruction, suggested that the Republic was relapsing into anarchy – almost in a literal sense, since the Greek word originally meant that disturbances had prevented the election of archons, the senior magistrates of Athens. The Senate met and passed its ultimate decree, calling upon Pompey to do what was necessary to protect the State. As a body it had no police force or troops to control such a situation. Pompey had the *imperium* of a proconsul and soldiers to command. There was some doubt over what title and power to offer him and once again talk of dictatorship. Others suggested recalling Caesar so that he could hold the consulship with Pompey until the crisis was over, and all ten tribunes of the plebs supported this proposal. Caesar wrote to thank them, but asked them to withdraw the bill since he was needed in Gaul. In the end Bibulus – the same Bibulus who had been Caesar's colleague in 59 BC and had no love for either him or Pompey – proposed that Pompey be made sole consul for the year. Cato backed the motion and it was passed comfortably, since Pompey's opponents realised that he offered the best chance of restoring order to the city. Yet they deliberately avoided the word dictator, and wished to make clear that he was not being invested with permanent supreme power of the sort Sulla had taken, but that this was simply a temporary measure to cope with the crisis.[5]

Pompey's third consulship was anomalous in so many ways, not least that he had no colleague, violating the most fundamental principle of this magistracy. He had also not been elected by the people but was simply appointed. Normally a consul had only his lictors to clear a path for him through the streets, but Pompey brought armed soldiers into the city to police its streets. When Milo was put on trial the court was surrounded by the consul's troops, who prevented his followers from disturbing the proceedings. The court and its procedures were specially created by Pompey to deal with the recent electoral abuses and political violence. Juries were drawn from a pool of names selected by the consul. Milo's guilt was clear and, although this was not always a decisive factor in Roman trials, in this case the mood of the court and the watching crowd was extremely hostile. Cicero had agreed to defend Milo, for he felt a bond with the man who had been the bitterest opponent of his own enemy, Clodius. However, his courage failed him when he stood up to speak and was exposed to the barracking and hatred of the crowd and he did not deliver his speech. Milo went into exile in Massilia in Transalpine Gaul. Rather tactlessly, Cicero subsequently sent him the manuscript of the speech that he had meant to deliver. His former client replied sarcastically that he was glad that it had not been delivered, since otherwise he would never have had the chance to sample the fine fish of Massilia. Clodius' supporters were jubilant at the outcome, but several of his leading associates soon found themselves on trial and condemned in the following months. Pompey was taking his role seriously and made a real attempt to control the violence and bribery that had come to pervade public life. Unlike earlier uses of the *senatus consultum ultimum*, in 52 BC there were no summary executions and everything was done through the courts, although these were the special courts created for the occasion and operating under new regulations.[6]

Electoral bribery had become chronic, especially in the campaigns for the consulship. Pompey passed a new law imposing even harsher penalties for electoral malpractice. However, the sums involved were enormous and many candidates relied on being given a wealthy province after their year of office. Their creditors could then be paid from money squeezed from the unfortunate provincials and from bribes given by the companies of *publicani*, who wished no interference in their own exploitation of the people. The consequences were bad for the provinces, but most senators were more concerned with the impact on elections. To break this circle Pompey introduced a law imposing a five-year delay between the consulship and a man going out to his province, on the basis that creditors would be much less inclined to wait so long for repayment of debts. This inevitably created a shortage of provincial governors, and therefore it was necessary in the short term to make use of former magistrates who had chosen not to take a command after their year of office. Cicero was one of these, and in 51 BC found himself appointed proconsul of Cilicia, a task for which he had little enthusiasm. At the same time Bibulus was despatched to govern Syria. Pompey's measures do seem to have substantially reduced the levels of bribery and corruption in the consular elections for 51, 50 and 49 BC. Cato stood for the office for 51 BC, proclaiming that he would do nothing at all to win the favour of the electorate. While he was widely admired, he was never particularly popular and such an approach was eccentric in the extreme, and certainly not traditional. It came as little surprise that he lost by a big margin. Pompey is unlikely to have been enthusiastic about Cato's candidature, but he could not control the outcome and the elections in these three years showed the strength of the old established families. The victors were three patricians and three members of one of the most distinguished plebian lines. The brothers Marcus and Caius Claudius Marcellus won the consulship in 51 and 49 BC respectively, while their cousin Caius was consul in 50 BC. The latter was married to Caesar's great niece Octavia – the same one he had recently offered to Pompey as a prospective wife. Whether or not he knew about this, Marcellus preferred to align himself with his cousins, who were deeply hostile to Caesar.[7]

Pompey's third consulship was another important step in his highly successful, but utterly unorthodox, career. Once again he had been singled out by the Republic as the only man who could deal with a crisis, with even his personal enemies accepting the necessity of employing him. In the past it had been Lepidus, then Sertorius, the pirates, Mithridates and the grain supply, and now it was political violence in the city. As usual, he performed the task well, but he would not have been a Roman senator if he had not also taken the opportunity for gaining personal advantages. He made sure that he was granted an extension of five years to his command of the two Spanish provinces, ensuring that he would keep his *imperium* and his legions even after his year as consul was complete. Early in 52 BC Milo and two of the remaining three candidates for the consulship were condemned and sent into exile. The last man, Quintus Caecilius Metellus Pius Scipio Nasica, had one of the most distinguished family lines in Rome, as was indicated by his enormously long name. Born a patrician Scipio – the family that had produced the man who had beaten Hannibal in the Second Punic War and the one who destroyed Carthage in the Third War – he had subsequently been adopted into a branch of the Metelli, one of the most distinguished plebian families. Metellus Scipio thus combined great wealth with enormous family connections and hugely prestigious ancestors. His own abilities were extremely limited, but he did have a pretty daughter, Cornelia, who had been married to Crassus' dashing son Publius and had been widowed since Carrhae. Pompey decided to marry for the fourth time and found that his approach was welcomed by Metellus Scipio. The charges faced by the latter were quietly dropped and the wedding took place. Like Julia, Pompey's new bride was young enough to be his daughter, indeed almost his granddaughter, but the marriage again proved a happy and successful one. Cornelia was intelligent, sophisticated and charming, as well as physically attractive. Pompey had always revelled in adoration and willingly responded to a wife who gave every sign of being in love with him. He was fifty-four, but for a man who had been so successful at such a young age and was proud of his personal fitness and enjoyed having his good looks praised, coping with late middle age may not have been easy. It is tempting to suggest that taking two much younger wives helped him to feel rejuvenated. Politically the connection was also a very good one, allying the maverick general with some of the families at the very heart of the Republic's elite. Cornelia's father also profited, not only by escaping prosecution but also being named as Pompey's consular colleague in August.[8]

Caesar may well have been disappointed at his former son-in-law's decision to seek a marriage alliance elsewhere. With hindsight we know that just two and a half years later the two men would be fighting against each other, but there is little evidence at the time of any great breach opening up between the two surviving triumvirs. He had not wanted to return to become Pompey's colleague, since apart from the rebellion he had not yet completed the settlement of his new conquests. Caesar was beginning to think of the future and had already made it clear that he hoped to go straight from his command in Gaul to a second consulship. He did not wish to spend an interval as a private citizen, when he would be liable to prosecution, most probably relating to his year as consul. Some of Pompey's actions in 52 BC seemed to conflict with this aim. The delay imposed on consuls going out to their province indirectly threatened Caesar's position. Until now, the provinces that would be allocated to new consuls had to be named before the elections, so that there would be plenty of warning – some eighteen months or so – if the current governor was going to be replaced. With the new system an ex-consul could, in theory, be instantly appointed to any province, including Caesar's and especially Transalpine Gaul, which had been granted to him by the Senate and not through popular vote. This was unsettling, but it was reasonable to suppose that Pompey and Caesar's other friends in Rome could prevent this from happening, in spite of the efforts of men like Domitius Ahenobarbus.

Of more concern was a law passed by Pompey that outlawed the practice of candidates standing for the consulship *in absentia*, that is without actually being present in the city. This meant that Caesar would have to lay down his *imperium* and therefore become subject to prosecution if he wanted to stand for a second term as consul. Earlier in the year he had persuaded the tribunes, who had wanted to recall him to become Pompey's colleague, to bring in a bill specifically granting him the right to stand for election without being present. Caesar's associates in the Senate were quick to remind Pompey that this earlier law seemed now to be contradicted by his own legislation. The inscribed bronze tablet bearing the text of the new law had already been deposited in the Republic's records, but Pompey wrote an additional clause with his own hand and ordered that this be attached to the main law. Obviously such an addition was of questionable legal validity. The apparent slight to Caesar may well have been unintentional, or it may be that Pompey just wished to remind his ally that he could not be taken for granted. Both of them were allies for as long as it seemed beneficial. For the moment neither would gain from a split. The alliance may have been weaker by the end of 52 BC than it had been in earlier years, but it still held. When news arrived of the defeat of Vercingetorix, Caesar was voted another twenty-day public thanksgiving. Pompey was still willing to celebrate the deeds of his ally, but also took care to commemorate his own achievements, dedicating a temple to Victory (*Victoria*).[9]

THE END IN GAUL

'The whole of Gaul was conquered . . .' wrote Hirtius as he opened the narrative of the book that he added to complete Caesar's *Commentaries on the Gallic War*. Yet his own account soon makes it clear that this was not quite true. Many of the rebellious tribes capitulated after the surrender of Vercingetorix at Alesia, but a few remained recalcitrant. On 31 December

52 BC Caesar left Bibracte and took the *Eleventh* and *Thirteenth* legions out of winter quarters and led them on a punitive expedition against the Bituriges. The Romans attacked suddenly and the proconsul ordered his men not to set fire to farms and villages in the normal way, so there were no plumes of smoke to warn the tribe of their approach. Thousands of prisoners were taken as the Gauls were unable to mount any organised resistance. Their lands had been campaigned over by the rival armies in the previous summer, when they had willingly obeyed Vercingetorix's order to burn their towns and food stores, and the Bituriges were in no position to fight and soon surrendered. They were encouraged by the generous terms Caesar had granted to other rebel tribes, and he was eager to extend his clemency to them. In these circumstances there were no slaves or plunder to distribute to the soldiers, so the proconsul gave them a bounty of 200 sestertii per man, and 2,000 to each centurion, to reward them for their good conduct on a winter campaign. Two and a half weeks later he took the *Sixth* and *Fourteenth* legions on a similar operation to punish the Carnutes. The Gauls fled from their homes and for a while Caesar billeted many of his men in the houses of the town of Cenabum, scene of the massacre in the previous year. Raiding parties of infantry and cavalry were sent out on a regular basis to maraud around the surrounding countryside. Living in hiding and exposed to the winter weather, the Carnutes soon ran short of food and suffered badly. Many of them fled to take refuge with other tribes.[10]

Leaving Trebonius in charge at Cenabum, he called out the *Seventh*, *Eighth* and *Ninth* legions from their winter quarters, ordered the *Eleventh* to join them and moved against the Bellovaci. This tribe had a high reputation for courage and had not sent many warriors to join the great army that had tried to relieve Alesia. Only a couple of thousand men went at the special request of Commius, who was well connected within the tribe. The rest preferred to fight the Romans on their own and in their own way. Early in 51 BC the Bellovaci massed a strong army, led by Correus with the assistance of Commius, who had refused to give himself up after Alesia. From prisoners Caesar learned that the enemy planned to attack him if he was accompanied by no more than three legions, but would otherwise observe and wait for a better opportunity. He tried to conceal his fourth legion behind the army's baggage train, hoping to lure the Bellovaci into battle and win a quick victory. The Gauls refused to be drawn and the two armies camped facing each other across a valley. Neither side was prepared to attack uphill against the enemy and place themselves at a disadvantage, but for added security Caesar had his legionaries fortify the position more strongly than was usual for a marching camp. There were frequent skirmishes – both sides were using German troops, for Commius had managed to persuade 500 of these to join the Bellovaci – and on one occasion the Gauls ambushed and cut up a foraging party of the Remi who were fighting as Roman allies. Caesar decided that his forces were inadequate for the task and summoned the *Sixth*, *Thirteenth* and *Fourteenth* legions to join him. The campaign was proving a lot tougher than he had anticipated, and as news of this reached Rome wild rumours circulated about serious defeats. When the enemy scouts reported their approach the Bellovaci decided to withdraw, successively disengaging under cover of a burning barrier of straw bales and dried wood that they had secretly prepared for the occasion. After this they relied on ambush rather than direct confrontation, keeping their main army some distance back. Over the next days they inflicted a number of small reverses on the Romans. Intelligence plays a huge role in such operations and Caesar sensed an opportunity when he learned from the interrogation of a prisoner that Correus, with 6,000 infantry and 1,000 cavalry, was lying in wait for one of his foraging parties. Forewarned, the auxiliary cavalry were able to hold the ambushers off until the legions hurried up to support them. Most of the Gauls fled, but Correus himself refused either to escape or to surrender and was killed with javelins. Caesar took the legions on, moving against the main enemy camp that his scouts believed was some 8 miles away.

Correus' death and the arrival of fugitives from his defeat prompted the Bellovaci to send peace envoys to Caesar. These men attempted to place all the blame for the rebellion on the dead chieftain. The proconsul informed them that he doubted that one man had been entirely responsible but was anyway content to accept their surrender and not impose further punishments on them. The Bellovaci gave him hostages. Impressed by his leniency, a number of other tribes capitulated over the next weeks. There was some truth to what Caesar had said about the influence of a single chief, but he certainly realised the importance of charismatic leaders in keeping a rebellion going. Soon afterwards he led another punitive expedition against the Eburones, since their chieftain Ambiorix was still at large. Commius also escaped from the defeat of the Bellovaci and he and his retinue were hunted by the Romans. At one point Labienus feigned a willingness to negotiate with the Atrebatian king in the hope of murdering him but Commius escaped with just a wound. Later he was nearly caught by another Roman patrol and declared that he was willing to make peace, so long as he never had to come into the presence of another Roman. Caesar's response to this is not reported, but in the end Commius fled across the sea to Britain, making himself king of one of the tribes on the south coast and founding a dynasty.[11]

There was one final major rebellion, this time amongst the tribes of the South West, and centring around the walled hill town of Uxellodunum in modern Dordogne. One of the two main leaders was Lucterius, the man who on Vercingetorix's orders had raided Transalpine Gaul early in 52 BC. Much of the fighting was done by Caesar's legates, but the proconsul himself arrived to complete the business, on his way accepting the surrender of the Carnutes after they handed over to him for punishment the main leader of the rebellion. According to Hirtius, Caesar was forced to execute the man because his soldiers were still outraged by the massacre at Cenabum. The rebels were surrounded in the town and using his legionaries' engineering skill, he managed to cut off the Gauls' water supply. When the defenders came out to surrender, Caesar decided to make an example of them 'since his mildness was already well known' as Hirtius puts it. Each of the warriors had his hands cut off and was then set free to live on as a warning to others. Some modern scholars are inclined to see Hirtius' comment as more relevant to the Civil War than Caesar's campaigns in Gaul, but this is to see things with a modern eye. Earlier in the book Hirtius has already given examples of Caesar not imposing harsh terms after rebellious tribes had surrendered, and noted that this encouraged others to give in. After military victory Caesar was keen to win a political peace by persuading leading men throughout Gaul of the advantages of loyalty to Rome. There was proof of the effectiveness of this policy soon afterwards when Lucterius, who had escaped capture at Uxellodunum, was handed over to the Romans by another Arvernian chieftain. Hirtius described Caesar's activity in the winter of 51–50 BC: 'Caesar had one main aim, keeping the tribes friendly, and giving them neither the opportunity nor cause for war. . . . And so, by dealing with the tribes honourably, by granting rich bounties to the chieftains, and by not imposing burdens, he made their state of subjection tolerable, and easily kept the peace in a Gaul weary after so many military defeats.'[12] Although he may have misread the situation in the build-up to the great rebellion in 52 BC, Caesar seems now to have handled the diplomacy very well. The next summer passed peacefully. At the beginning of 49 BC he would leave Gaul, eventually taking the greater part of his troops with him. However, there would be no great rebellion as soon as the Roman yoke slackened its grip. The Bellovaci would rise again in 46 BC and have to be suppressed, but otherwise Gaul remained peaceful for the next decade.[13]

❖

Caesar spent nine years in Gaul, extending Roman rule to the Rhine in the east, the English Channel in the north and the Atlantic coast in the west. The area would remain part of Rome's empire for the best part of five centuries. During most of that time it would have internal peace – broken by a few rebellions in the first generation or so after conquest, then only by occasional Roman civil wars and, especially in the later years, periodic barbarian raids – and enjoyed widespread prosperity. The aristocracy earned Roman citizenship and within a century of Caesar's death the descendants of men who had fought against him would take their place in Rome's Senate. As the population, or at least the wealthier classes, were granted the benefits of glass in their windows, running water, sewers, bath-houses and central heating, Gaulish culture was modified and influenced by Roman ideas and concepts to become what is today known as Gallo-Roman culture. Latin became commonly used, especially in the towns and cities and amongst the aristocracy. Literacy and the idea of written records spread. The druidic priesthood was suppressed and practices such as head-hunting and human sacrifice stopped, but many other aspects of Gaulish religion continued, even if gods and goddesses were sometimes given new Roman names. In time the old religions would be challenged by the spread of Christianity, at first as a secret cult, but from Constantine onwards as the official religion of the Roman Empire. The new faith was just one of many ideas and concepts that reached Gaul because it had become part of the wider Roman world in which it was much easier and safer for people to travel. Rome's impact on Gaul and its peoples was profound and proved tenacious, far more so than in Britain where most traces of Roman culture vanished within a generation or two of its ceasing to be a province.

This was the history that Gaul would have as a result of Caesar's campaigns. We cannot know what would have happened if these had not occurred – if, for instance, he had embarked upon a Balkan war instead. More than two thousand years have passed and the number of possibilities for what might have happened are truly vast. It is highly probable that the Romans would at some point have conquered Gaul, although perhaps not with the speed and intensity that Caesar brought to his campaigns. Given the relatively limited possibilities for Roman expansion in the middle of the first century BC, it is equally likely that this would have happened fairly soon. Roman rule brought to Gaul and other provinces many advantages. At a most basic level it is not unreasonable to say that more people were better off living under the Roman Empire than they were before it came or after it failed. The faults of Roman society – and there were many – were often shared by other cultures including the Gauls. Slavery is an obvious example. The violent entertainments of the arena, which came alongside literature, art and drama as part of Rome's influence, were less usual. Caesar was not responsible for Roman imperialism or for Roman culture, although he was certainly an enthusiastic agent of the Republic's expansion. His conquest of Gaul was not a fulfilment of a long-term aim or ambition, in any sense other than that he had long craved the chance to win glory. It was chance and opportunity that led to him focusing his attention on Gaul.

The benefits of Roman rule are arguable but the grim nature of Roman conquest is not. Plutarch claims that one million Gauls were killed during Caesar's campaigns, and the same number were captured and, in most cases, sold as slaves. Pliny, adding in the casualties inflicted by Caesar's legions on the enemy in the Civil War, says that his men killed 1,192,000 opponents in battle, although he did not feel that such an achievement added to his glory. Velleius Paterculus says that 400,000 enemies were killed in the Gallic campaigns and 'still more captured'. It is hard to know the basis for any of these numbers. The figures given for enemy casualties in the *Commentaries on the Gallic War* do not add up to such a great total, while Caesar's account of the Civil War often did not mention such things. It is questionable that numbers for losses amongst the Gaulish tribes were known with precision, although it may just have been possible to calculate from records the number of prisoners taken and sold into slavery. Probably these numbers are exaggerated, but still give some indication of the appalling human cost of Caesar's victories. The impact of these campaigns on Gaul cannot have been anything but massive. Certain areas were devastated and would not recover for decades. In 50 BC Caesar set the annual revenue from his new Gallic province at 40 million sestertii – less than he had paid for the land needed for his forum project. This amount probably reflected the cost of eight years of intensive campaigning. We can only imagine the social dislocation caused by, for instance, Caesar's execution of the entire ruling council of the Veneti. Caesar was entirely pragmatic – effectively amoral – in his use of clemency or massacre and atrocity. During the course of the conquest of Gaul his soldiers did some terrible things, sometimes by order, as when they massacred the Usipetes and Tencteri, and occasionally spontaneously, as when they slaughtered women and children at Avaricum. Other Roman armies under other commanders had done similar things in the past, and would continue to do so in the future. Indeed atrocities as bad, or even worse, were committed by virtually all armies of the ancient world. This is not to justify what Caesar did, merely to place it into context. Warfare in antiquity was generally an extremely cruel business.[14]

Caesar had worked for years for the opportunity of high command and when he was given it in 58 BC he seized the chance with both hands, exploiting every opportunity for conflict and conquest. In the campaigns that followed he proved himself to be a general of genius, ranking amongst the finest Rome had ever produced. His command style was typically Roman, controlling a battle from close behind the fighting line, ordering up reserves and encouraging the men while observing their conduct. His strategy was aggressive, seizing and maintaining the initiative, and never doubting his ultimate success regardless of the odds ranged against him. Again this was the Roman way of warfare, and much that might seem rash to a modern observer would not have been seen in this way by other senators. Of contemporary commanders only Pompey might match his achievements and skill, for although Lucullus had been a great tactician he lacked Caesar's ability as a leader. Both men were similarly aggressive in their campaigns. None of this had come instantly – Caesar had faltered at times in his early campaigns, and it took prolonged service and continued success before his legions were won over by his charm, generosity and competence. There were mistakes and failures, notably the haphazard nature of the British expeditions, the loss of Cotta and Sabinus' men and the defeat at Gergovia, but Caesar convinced his men that under his command they would always win through in the end. In eight years of intensive operations success after success reinforced the legionaries' certainty. By 50 BC he had created an army that was utterly devoted to him. Caesar had won huge glory and made himself fabulously rich, allowing him to spend freely in his efforts to win more support in Rome itself. It now remained to be seen whether this was enough to allow him to return to Rome and stand alongside Pompey as the Republic's greatest citizens.[15]

PART THREE

❖

CIVIL WAR AND DICTATORSHIP
49–44 BC

XVII

THE ROAD TO
THE RUBICON

'Then, catching up with his cohorts at the river Rubicon, the point at which his province ended, he paused for a moment, and understanding what a huge thing he was planning, he turned and spoke to the men with him. "Even now we could turn back; but once we cross that tiny bridge, then everything will depend on armed force."' – *Suetonius, late first century AD.*[1]

'All this has made him [Caesar] so powerful, that the only hope of standing up to him rests on one citizen [Pompey]. I really wish that the latter had not given him so much power in the first place, rather than waiting till he was strong before fighting him.' – *Cicero, 9 December 50 BC.*[2]

Gaul had provided Caesar with glory and wealth. By 50 BC there was no serious fighting and there was every indication that the series of devastating defeats inflicted on each rebellion had combined with the careful diplomatic efforts of the proconsul to create a stable new province for the Republic. The willingness of the vast majority of the tribal leaders to accept Roman rule was not just a question of personal loyalty to Caesar. His murder six years later did not provoke fresh outbreaks of unrest in Gaul. Like any other successful Roman commander he had reaped great personal benefits from his victories, but this should not obscure the gains his conquests had brought to Rome. Formally, the Republic now had a new source of revenue, although this had to balanced against the costs of garrisoning the province. Transalpine Gaul and the important land routes to Spain were secured, while Italy itself was now much better shielded from invasion by northern tribes following in the footsteps of the Cimbri and Teutones. There was no imminent threat to Italy from this direction, and such strategic concerns were not foremost in

Caesar's mind when he initiated his campaigns. Yet they were no less real for all that and it was undeniable that in this respect the conquest of Gaul was beneficial to Rome. However, throughout history expansion has tended to benefit individuals far more than states, and this was certainly true of Roman imperialism. Trade with Gaul was important before Caesar's arrival, but his campaigns helped to open up new markets – for instance in Britain – to Roman merchants and allowed them to operate in very favourable conditions in the new province of Gaul. Fortunes were made even more rapidly by Caesar's senior officers and staff, who shared in his generous distributions of plunder and slaves. He was also not one to hoard his own new-found wealth, but spent lavishly on his building projects and planned entertainments, and at a more personal level offered interest free loans or even gifts of money to men he wished to cultivate. Many Romans who had never been anywhere near Gaul gained from its conquest.

There were benefits to the Republic – and even more to individuals – from the victories in Gaul, but all were dwarfed by the immediate and irrevocable change these brought to Caesar's personal fortune and status. By 50 BC he was wealthier, had a more extensive network of friends and clients, and could boast of greater and more glorious achievements than any other senator except for Pompey. For several years he had made it clear that he intended to seek a second consulship on his return to Rome. His electoral success was virtually guaranteed, for he had always been popular with the voters and now had even more money with which to court their favour. Long established law, restated by Sulla during his dictatorship, decreed that a ten-year interval should elapse between consulships. This had been set aside in Pompey's case in 52 BC, just one of many unorthodox steps in his career, but the law remained in force and Caesar had no desire or need for preferential treatment in this respect. He planned to put his name forward as a candidate for election in the autumn of 49 BC, to assume the consulship in January 48 BC, ten years after he had laid down the office at the end of his first term as consul. The controversies of that year still dogged him, and Caesar knew that he would be prosecuted as soon as he became a private citizen. For that reason he wished to go straight from his proconsular command into the second consulship. The law put forward by all ten tribunes of 52 BC – admittedly in at least one case after some initial reluctance – had granted him permission to become a candidate without actually entering the city in the normal way. Pompey and Crassus had done the same thing in 71 BC, waiting with their armies outside Rome and only crossing the formal boundary of the city when they actually assumed the consulship. Once he had become consul – ideally with a sympathetic colleague, perhaps even one of his own former legates such as Labienus – Caesar would be in a position to present new legislation, rewarding his veteran soldiers with land and confirming his settlement of Gaul. Other bills could have been tailored to add to his popularity with various sections of society. Back in the heart of public life, he would have had a year in which either to win over his political enemies or, at the very least, make himself so strong that they would not risk attacking him in the courts. We do not know what he planned after that, and it is more than possible that he had no clear idea himself at this stage and intended to await events. A fresh provincial command would have been one option, perhaps against the Parthians to avenge the stain of Crassus' disastrous defeat at Carrhae. Alternatively, he may have hoped for some appointment similar to Pompey's, allowing him to hold *imperium* and control legions while hovering just outside Rome.[3]

In the event, nothing worked out as Caesar had planned. Instead of coming back home to a second consulship, a Gallic triumph, games honouring his daughter and general acknowledgement as Pompey's equal as the two foremost men in the Republic, he returned as a rebel. His opponents held very different ideas about the manner in which he should return, and so increasingly did Pompey. There were attempts at negotiation, many offers of compromise, but in the end it proved impossible to find a settlement that all were willing and able to accept. Stubbornness, pride and suspicion on all sides, as well as deep personal enmities in a few cases, all contributed to this impasse. So did misplaced optimism, leading to the belief that opponents would back down. Some had seen the possibility of civil war for more than a year before it actually broke out, but very few of the key participants actually wanted it. Most, including Caesar and Pompey, were gradually and reluctantly drawn into a situation in which they decided that they no longer had any other acceptable alternative. It would be very hard to say when war finally became inevitable. The Civil War was not fought over great issues or between conflicting ideologies, but was about personal position and *dignitas* – most of all that of Caesar. In later years, especially for men living under the rule of Rome's emperors, some were inclined to see Caesar as aiming at revolution and monarchy from his early youth. No contemporary evidence supports such claims, while his actions certainly give no hint of such plans. A peaceful return to take up a pre-eminent position within the Republic, his prestige, influence and *auctoritas* acknowledged by all other senators, even those who disliked him, was what Caesar craved. Having to resort to armed force to protect his position was a sign of political failure, for Pompey as much as for Caesar.[4]

THE BREAKDOWN OF AN ALLIANCE

The pressure on Caesar had built up gradually. When Cato had condemned his actions against the Usipetes and Tencteri in 55 BC, there had been no realistic prospect that the Senate would act upon his proposal and actually hand the proconsul over to the Germans. The triumvirate had been renewed at Luca and between them Pompey, Crassus and Caesar – especially the first two because they were actually in Rome – were too strong to oppose. Domitius Ahenobarbus could only be denied the consulship for a year, but his ambition to replace Caesar in the Gallic command was blocked without too much difficulty. The death of Julia weakened the bond between Caesar and Pompey. That of Crassus fundamentally shifted the balance of Roman public life, since so many leading men had been under obligation to him for past loans or favours. His surviving son Marcus was neither old enough nor able enough to step into his father's shoes at the centre of this network of clients and political friends. Some of these men now attached themselves to Pompey and some to Caesar, but the bonds could not instantly become as strong as the ones to Crassus, who had devoted much effort over many years to expanding his political capital as much as his financial wealth. Many of the strongest critics of Caesar had also in the past been hostile to Pompey, which made his appointment as sole consul in 52 BC on the motion of Bibulus backed by Cato all the more striking. Cato did stress his continued personal independence, bluntly telling Pompey that he would advise him for the good of the Republic but that this did not imply any personal friendship between them. This no doubt contributed to his failure to gain the consulship. However, for the moment at least, Pompey, through his new marriage and willingness to restore order to the State, had become more acceptable to many of the leading men in the Senate. These liked to be known as the 'good men' (*boni*) – or sometimes the 'best' (*optimates*) – and came predominantly from very well-established families. In 52 BC they willingly supported Pompey as a means of dealing with the violence that was disrupting public life, especially since, apart from Milo, virtually all the casualties from the trials in the new court were partisans of Clodius. Cato had even said that Milo ought to be acquitted as one who had deserved well of the Republic for disposing of his dangerous rival.[5]

In 51 BC Marcus Claudius Marcellus was consul and began a concerted attack on Caesar, who was his personal enemy. The ultimate source of this hostility is obscure, though a major factor was doubtless the resentment of the virtual monopoly of grand and important commands held by the triumvirate. Under normal circumstances, such opportunities for serving the Republic and winning glory ought to have gone to men from the great aristocratic families – men like Marcellus himself, his brother and cousin. Pompey was too strong to attack at present, but Caesar appeared to be vulnerable. Marcellus openly declared his intention of having Caesar recalled from his command, arguing that his great victory over Vercingetorix, which the Republic had marked with a public thanksgiving, showed that the war in Gaul was now over. This justification was necessary, since in 55 BC Crassus' and Pompey's law had granted Caesar a new five-year command in Gaul. Marcellus also argued that Pompey's more recent law concerning provincial commands superseded the tribunes' law granting Caesar the privilege of becoming a candidate for his second consulship without actually returning to the city. As early as March Pompey expressed his disapproval of the consul's intentions. Apart from his ties with Caesar, it was deeply insulting to have his own law challenged in this way, especially since clauses in the law itself had forbidden alteration of it by subsequent meetings of the Senate or Assembly. He made it clear that he would never support any move to have Caesar recalled before his legal term as proconsul had expired.

In July questions were asked in the Senate about the legion that Pompey had 'loaned' to Caesar after the defeat of Cotta and Sabinus, and he was urged to take it back under his direct command. Grudgingly Pompey declared that he would do so, but refused to be coerced and set no date for recalling his troops. Marcellus kept up the pressure and, after a postponement, managed to ensure that the Senate would debate the matter of Caesar's province on 1 September. The Senate met outside the formal boundary of the city, so that Pompey could once again be present. He again stated his view that it would not be proper for the Senate to rule on this question at the moment. His father-in-law Metellus Scipio did put forward a motion for the issue to be raised again on 30 March 50 BC, and it seems unlikely that Pompey disapproved of this. In fact Marcellus was able to secure a fuller debate much earlier than this on 29 September. Once again Pompey was present. Marcellus put forward a motion very similar to that of Scipio decreeing that the Senate should address the issue of the 'consular provinces' on or after 1 March. This was approved. Further measures, one to bar any tribune from vetoing the decision of that debate, and another to begin the process of discharging any of Caesar's soldiers who had served for their full legal term – which at this period was most probably sixteen years – or had other grounds for honourable discharge were debated. Both of these proposals were vetoed by two or more tribunes, as was another dealing with appointments to propraetorian provincial commands that would also have affected the number of men waiting for commands when Caesar's term expired.[6]

Marcellus had not won outright, but neither had he altogether lost. Caesar was still formally acknowledged as rightful governor of his three provinces when the consul laid down his office at the end of the year. Earlier in the year he had shown a sign of his frustration with working solely through the proper channels in the Senate. In 59 BC as part of his agrarian legislation Caesar had established a colony at Novum Comum in Cisalpine Gaul north of the River Po. Throughout his time in Gaul, he had also treated the Transpadanes as citizens even though they as yet had only Latin status. Marcellus ordered a former magistrate of the colony to be flogged, a punishment from which citizens were exempt, telling the man to go back to Caesar and 'show him his stripes'. It was a crass act, which disgusted Cicero when he heard about it, and indicates just how bitterly Marcellus loathed Caesar. Even if he had not secured the proconsul's recall, Marcellus had raised serious questions over his future. Some of Pompey's comments during and after the debate on 29 September certainly encouraged Caesar's opponents. He stated that he could not countenance the removal of Caesar from his command until 1 March 50 BC, but that after that his attitude would be different, which rather suggests that he believed that the command granted to Caesar by his own and Crassus' law would expire on that date. Asked what his attitude would be if a tribune vetoed the Senate's decision at that point, Pompey's answer implied little closeness with his ally and former father-in-law. He said that it did not matter whether Caesar opposed the Senate himself or via the agency of a tribune – either by implication would be wrong. Cicero was not in Rome at the time – having gone reluctantly to govern Cilicia as a result of the new regulations introduced in 52 BC. Fortunately one of his correspondents – the same Caelius Rufus he had successfully defended in 56 BC and who was now aedile – sent him a detailed account, which mentions one last question put to Pompey: '"What if," someone else said, "he wants to be consul and still retain his army?" To this Pompey responded mildly, "What if my son wants to attack me with a stick?" These words have made people suspect that Pompey is having a row with Caesar.'[7]

The question of precisely when Caesar's provincial command expired has long been a source of academic debate and seems unlikely ever to be finally resolved. Clearly some obvious significance must have been attached to 1 March 50 BC for Pompey to select this as the date after which it would be proper to consider a replacement. This tends to suggest that the law passed in 55 BC granting Caesar an extension of his command had come into force in February of that year. Therefore the five years granted to Caesar began then and expired on the first day of March 50 BC, known to the Romans as the Kalends of March. From that point, a new governor could be appointed by the Senate and Caesar's command would end as soon as this replacement arrived. Caesar clearly interpreted the law differently and may have preferred to see it as having granted him an extension of his original five-year command, the new period not commencing until the first was complete. However, he does not seem to have made any formal announcement as to when he believed his command should legally end. It is perfectly possible that the original law was imprecise, for it was likely to have been prepared in considerable haste and at a time when the alliance between the triumvirate was strong. The situation was further complicated by the bill passed by all ten tribunes, granting Caesar the right to stand for election without having to present himself in person as a candidate. He took this to mean that he should not be replaced in Gaul until the elections had occurred, a period of some eighteen months if his term ended in March 50, and he intended to wait till the consular elections in the autumn of 49 BC.[8]

Domitius Ahenobarbus had wished to take over the command in Gaul for some time and since his praetorship had also attacked Caesar's consulship. Cato was equally vocal in his criticism and repeatedly stated his intention of prosecuting Caesar for the events of 59 BC, and had even taken an oath to that effect. More recently he had taken to declaring that Caesar would stand trial just as Milo had done, with armed soldiers surrounding the court. Bibulus had also lost none of his resentment, though for the moment, just like Cicero, he found himself despatched as provincial governor, in his case to Syria. Marcellus, his brother and cousin were all equally hostile, and Metellus Scipio was at best unfriendly. All were united in their desire to prevent Caesar from returning to a second consulship and avoiding trial. Yet for all their bitter hatred, none of this would really have mattered if Pompey had decided to give his full support to Caesar, since this would surely have allowed the latter to secure everything he wanted. Pompey had proconsular *imperium* and a formed army in Spain. Without him there was no force with which to threaten Caesar, still less to fight him if it came to open conflict. Caesar's opponents could achieve nothing without Pompey's support, as the failure of Marcellus to recall him from Gaul in 51 BC clearly demonstrated. Equally, Caesar would struggle to remain in his command and return to Rome as he wished without Pompey's backing, or at least, neutrality. As was so often the case, what Pompey was thinking was not clear to anyone else. Caelius already suspected a rift between the two remaining triumvirs in the autumn of 51 BC. Pompey's position was extremely strong and, in the end, his greatest concern was how to profit from and maintain this dominance. His old ally Caesar needed his help to get what he wanted. So did Caesar's opponents, to whom Pompey had become closer in the last few years. If Caesar came back with all the wealth and glory of his Gaulish victories then he would become Pompey's equal and perhaps, in time and given his greater political skill, eventually his superior. Yet if Caesar was disposed of altogether, as Cato, Domitius, the Marcelli and their allies wanted, then they would have less need of Pompey, and he might easily find himself reduced to the comparative political impotence that had been his fate when he returned from the east in 62 BC. For the moment Pompey held the advantage, showing both Caesar and his opponents that they needed him, but that neither could take his aid for granted.[9]

The new year seemed to augur well for Caesar's enemies. Another Marcellus was consul, after being acquitted on a charge of electoral bribery, with Lucius Aemilius Lepidus Paullus as his colleague. The latter was the son of the Lepidus who had rebelled in 78 BC, only to be suppressed by Pompey. In spite of this, he was not believed to be especially well disposed towards Caesar either, and was anyway currently more concerned with his efforts to rebuild in grander fashion the Basilica Fulvia et Aemilia, a great monument to an earlier member of his family. One of the new tribunes was Curio the Younger, who in 59 BC had been one of the few men to criticise the triumvirate publicly. Cicero's lively correspondent Caelius was close to the tribune at this time. Both were prominent members of a generation of young Romans notorious for their wild lifestyle, which, combined with their grand ambitions, often placed them into debt. Mark Antony was another of this group of reckless youths, and Curio is said to have first introduced him to the pleasures of mistresses, drinking and a flamboyantly luxurious lifestyle. The consequence of this was that Antony was soon massively in debt, and Curio's father banned him from their house lest his own son proved too willing to pay his friend's way. More recently Curio had spent a huge sum on staging spectacular funeral games in honour of the Elder Curio, who died in 53 BC. He even constructed a wooden amphitheatre that revolved and could be divided into two semi-circular theatres for individual theatrical performances. A little later he had married Clodius' widow, the forthright and forceful Fulvia. These young men – they were still 'adolescents' in the Roman understanding of the term – were talented, but did not seem at all stable to the older generation.

Caelius was convinced that Curio planned an all-out attack on Caesar, but one of his first acts as tribune was to propose a new programme of distributing land to the poor. The hostility of the consuls effectively blocked this and instead he put forward bills for a new grain dole to citizens in Rome, and a five-year programme of road building in Italy. At the same time he began to make it clear at public meetings that he supported Caesar's cause. Later there was talk of Caesar buying his support by paying off his massive debts with gold from the spoils of Gaul. Velleius Paterculus mentions rumours of a bribe of 2.5 million denarii, while Valerius Maximus talks of the staggering sum of 15 million. Gossip doubtless inflated the figure, but in one sense Caesar was doing for Curio effectively what Crassus had once done for him, covering his staggering debts in order to gain a useful political ally. There was also talk of Paullus benefiting on the scale of 9 million denarii, helping him to complete his building plans. Both men were ambitious Roman aristocrats and looked to their own advantage when they switched to supporting Caesar. For the moment they had been persuaded that it was in their interest to support him. Curio was probably frustrated by the blocking of his bills, which gave him no incentive to aid the leading men in the Senate.[10]

The profits of his victories had allowed Caesar to win useful friends amongst the magistrates. When Marcellus duly raised the question of Caesar's command on 1 March 50 BC his colleague did not support him, but the real counter-attack was led by Curio, who focused most of his attention on Pompey's position. If Caesar was to be replaced in his Gallic command, then the tribune argued that it would only be fair, as well as safe for the Republic, if Pompey simultaneously gave up his extraordinary command of the Spanish provinces. He had already voiced this proposal at public meetings to the approval of the crowd. Caesar certainly approved of the tactic and may well have suggested it in the first place. The Spanish command had been renewed in 52 BC and still had several years left to run, so there were no legal grounds for this proposal, but it was a reminder of Pompey's unprecedented position. It placed him and Caesar on the same level, suggesting that either both or neither should enjoy the honours voted to them by the Roman people. More personally, it was clearly intended to show Pompey that it was to his advantage to maintain the alliance with Caesar, since his own position might not in reality be as strong as he thought. Adding this element to the debate raised the stakes, but took back some of the initiative from Caesar's opponents. They were at first stunned, and for several months there was deadlock, with Curio vetoing any attempt by the Senate to act against Caesar. In April, Caelius wrote again to Cicero:

> As for the situation of the Republic, all contention is focused on a single cause, namely the provinces. At the moment Pompey seems to be backing the Senate in demanding that Caesar leave his province by the Ides [13th] of November. Curio is utterly determined to prevent this – he has abandoned all his other projects. Our 'friends' (you know them well!) are afraid of pushing the issue to crisis point. This is the scene – the whole thing – Pompey, just as if he was not attacking Caesar, but making a fair settlement for him, blames Curio for making trouble. At the same time he is absolutely against Caesar becoming consul before giving up his province and army. He is getting a rough ride from Curio, and his entire third consulship is attacked. You mark my words, if they try to crush Curio with all their might, Caesar will come to the rescue; if instead, as seems most likely, they are too frightened to risk it, then Caesar will stay as long as he wants.[11]

It is not clear why Pompey chose 13 November as the new date for the end of Caesar's command. It was not much of a concession, since he would still have had the best part of a year to wait before the consular elections in the autumn of 49 BC. It might have been acceptable to Caesar if he wanted to stand for the consulship in the elections at the end of 50 BC, but he does not seem to have made any attempt to secure exemption from law decreeing a ten-year interval between consulships. In any case, given the circumstances he may have decided that this was unlikely to succeed. By June, Caelius was reporting that Marcellus suggested negotiating with the tribunes, but the Senate voted against any such compromise. Curio continued to insist that Caesar's command should not be discussed independently and that he must be treated in the same way as Pompey. A year before there had been talk of Pompey going out to Spain – now some suggested that either he or Caesar should go to deal with the Parthians. Cicero was very nervous that the latter might launch an all-out invasion of Rome's eastern provinces before he could give up his own post as governor of Cilicia – knowing that once an attack occurred it would be dishonourable for him to leave. That summer the Senate decided to take one legion from Pompey's and another from Caesar's armies and send the troops out to bolster Rome's forces on the Parthian border. Pompey decided to send the one that he had loaned to Caesar in 54 BC, and which had been campaigning with him ever since. Effectively this meant that Caesar lost two legions, but before he sent the men on their way he gave each soldier a bounty of 250 denarii, a sum amounting to more than one year's pay. The whole affair seemed even more suspicious when the two units marched back to Italy and then remained there, no one making any effort to send them overseas. A young member of the Claudian family had collected the troops from Gaul and returned claiming that Caesar's entire army was disaffected. It was just what Pompey wanted to believe.

Soon afterwards Pompey fell ill, suffering from a recurring fever that may possibly have been malaria. Apparently spontaneously, people throughout Italy began praying and making offerings for the return to health of the man who had performed such great services to the Republic. When he recovered the celebrations were ecstatic, crowds greeting him all along his route as he went from Naples back to the outskirts of Rome. Pompey had always thrived on adoration, whether from his wives, his soldiers or the people, and was deeply moved. More dangerously he interpreted this enthusiasm as a clear sign of widespread devotion to his cause. While still ill he had sent word to the Senate that he was willing to resign his command, assuring them that Caesar would do the same. Curio responded by saying that that would be fine, as long as Pompey laid down his post first. By August Caelius was speaking to Cicero of the prospect of civil war. 'If neither of the two sets off on a Parthian war, then I can see great discord ahead, which will be decided by cold steel and brute force. They are both well prepared in spirit and with armies.'[12]

Yet there was little enthusiasm for conflict beyond the immediate partisans, as was shown when the Senate debated the issue on 1 December. Curio again proposed that both Caesar and Pompey should give up their commands simultaneously. The consul Marcellus split this into two and presented separate motions to the House. The first, that Caesar should resign, was passed by a big majority, but the second asking Pompey to do the same was defeated by a similarly large margin. When Curio responded by asking the Senate to divide on the motion that both men should resign, the result was highly revealing. Only twenty-two senators voted against this, but no fewer than 370 backed it. The 'back bench' pedarii had lived up to their name and voted with their feet, even though most of the great names had been with the twenty-two. Marcellus dismissed the meeting, declaring 'If that is what you want, be Caesar's slaves!', and the votes were ignored. It had not been a victory for Caesar, since a clear majority had wanted him to lay down his provinces and his army, while supporting Pompey's claim to retain his command. Yet in the end what it had shown was that nearly the entire Senate wanted peace above all else. They were certainly not committed to Caesar's cause, but nor were they eager to risk civil war on behalf of Pompey, still less of Cato, Domitius and their associates. By this time Cicero had come back to Italy from his province and his view was similar. He felt that Caesar's demands were outrageously excessive, but even so preferred to grant them rather than allow the Republic to tear itself apart. He, like many others, remembered the dark days of the struggle between Sulla and the Marians and had no wish to see such ghastly strife repeated. In his view there was still the chance for compromise and a peaceful settlement. Perhaps there was, but the mood of the main participants in the dispute had hardened to the point where war was becoming more and more likely.[13]

A hard core of distinguished senators loathed Caesar, many of them for personal as well as political reasons. Much of this hatred was not entirely rational. There were memories of his *popularis* behaviour as aedile and praetor, and even worse his turbulent consulship. To Cato and his associates Caesar was the Catiline who had never quite allowed his villainy to become so open. They saw the effect of his charm on others – on other men's wives as often as on the crowd in the Forum – but felt that they had seen past it, which only made it all the more frustrating that others had not. It can never have helped that Cato's half-sister had been one of Caesar's most ardent lovers. Cato, his son-in-law Bibulus and brother-in-law Domitius Ahenobarbus had stood up to Caesar in the past and had had their moments of success. More often they had simply pushed Caesar into going further, and time after time he had got away with it, riding roughshod over them in 59 BC. They despised Caesar as a man, which made his obviously exceptional talent in public life and as an army commander all the more galling. Appius Claudius, older brother of Clodius, who had co-operated with Caesar much of the time, was obsessed with maintaining the dignity of his ancient patrician heritage. One of his daughters was married to Servilia's son and Cato's nephew Brutus, and another to Pompey's eldest son. Opposition did not just come from Cato's extended family, for families like the Marcelli and Lentuli did not like to see their current resurgence of electoral success overshadowed. For Metellus Scipio there was concern both to live up to his famous ancestors – both real and adopted – and eagerness to exploit the advantages offered by his marriage tie to Pompey.

Ultimately, no Roman senator liked to see another man excelling him in glory and influence. It was not so much what Caesar had done that provoked their hostility – most would have happily praised the same deeds, especially his victories in Gaul, if only they had been performed by someone else, or better yet by several other men so that no one individual gained too much glory. Men from established families were raised to believe that they deserved to guide the Republic, but Caesar's eminence robbed them of much of this role. Now there was a chance to end his career – preferably in court, and a court that shared their view of the accused and the need to be rid of him, but if not, by armed force. Pompey's aid made this possible and so, for the moment, he was useful enough for his own anomalous position to be ignored. In the future then it might be possible to discard him or at least reduce his dominance. Since he first hinted that he was not firmly committed to backing Caesar's demands, Pompey had encouraged his opponents. Cato at least does seem to have hoped to avoid civil war, and once it began made some effort to moderate the vehemence with which it was fought. His expectation was that Caesar could be forced to submit. The attitude of his allies was less clear. Some of them clearly hoped to profit from war. Cicero was surprised and rather disgusted by the militancy he saw in many of these men. He could also see no sense in fighting Caesar after years of allowing him to become so powerful.[14]

Pompey's attitude was different. Even at the end he would have been content for Caesar to return to public life so long as it was in a way that made it clear that he was not Pompey's equal, still less his superior. This desire had hardened as the months had gone by, and Curio had made such efforts to place the two men on the same level. Crassus he had been able to accept as an equal, for he was several years his senior and had fought for Sulla. Perhaps as importantly, Pompey had always been confident that his own charisma and spectacular military exploits – three triumphs compared with Crassus' mere ovation – gave him a comfortable advantage over his rival. Caesar was younger by just six years, but more importantly he had done nothing when Pompey had formed and led his own armies to victory, and in this respect his career was decades behind. He found it easier to like Caesar than Crassus, but perhaps in part that was because he did not see him as a competitor, at least at first. Even after Caesar's successes in Gaul, Germany and Britain, Pompey still viewed him as a junior ally. After all he had won triumphs on three continents – Asia, Africa and Europe – and defeated many different opponents, some of them Roman, in the process and not just barbarian tribes. 'What if my son wants to attack me with a stick?' – the comment implied not just the ease of dealing with such a threat, but how absurdly unlikely it was that it would even happen. Pompey did not want civil war, but had little doubt that he could win it if the worst came to the worst and it occurred. Around this time he would begin to boast that he had only to stamp his foot and armies would spring up from the soil of Italy. In the end Caesar must realise that he needed to respect Pompey, accept his terms for coming back, and trust to his friendship for protection in the courts. Curio's attack on his own position made him all the less inclined to grant too many concessions to the proconsul in Gaul. Caesar would have to see sense, but he could still be very useful to Pompey, who was aware that Cato and his allies had no great love for him either.

Caesar claimed later that he had to fight a civil war in order to defend his *dignitas* – his reputation. In his view the laws of his consulship had been necessary and effective, especially the land laws. Since then he had served the Republic well, defending its interests and its allies, and making Roman power respected in regions that had never before seen a legion. For these achievements the Senate had awarded him no less than three public thanksgivings of unprecedented length. Now his command was to be prematurely curtailed – at least in his view – while the law put forward by all ten tribunes in 52 BC as an expression of the will of the Roman people was being set aside both in detail and in spirit. His enemies, ignoring all his successes, were boasting of attacking and condemning him because of his consulship almost a decade ago. The great men of the Republic were not taken to court. Pompey had not been prosecuted since his youth, before he had raised his own legions. No one had ever dared to bring Crassus to trial. Simply having to defend himself would have been a great blow to Caesar's pride and *auctoritas*. There was also the very real danger that he might be condemned, especially if the court was controlled by enemies. As consul his behaviour had been controversial at the very least, although innocence or guilt was seldom the decisive factor in Roman trials. Milo's fate offered a warning, as did that of Gabinius, the man who as tribune in 67 BC had secured Pompey the command against the pirates, and as consul in 58 BC with Caesar's father-in-law Calpurnius Piso had helped to secure the triumvirate's position. After that he had gone to govern Syria and, largely on his own initiative, had taken his army into Egypt to restore the deposed Ptolemy XII, a highly profitable enterprise. Yet he was a deeply unpopular man and, in spite of his money and the support of Pompey, he was eventually condemned when he returned to Rome in 53 BC, going into exile.

Caesar could easily have suffered a similar fate, but at the very least would have been politically damaged, when any hint of vulnerability would attract further prosecutions. He would therefore be taking a great risk if he placed his trust in Pompey's protection and gave up his command. Even if he chose to support Caesar, Pompey might not have been able to save him. In any case, Cicero's exile had demonstrated that Pompey was not always reliable. Had Caesar given up his command he could have retained his *imperium* and the command of some detachments of troops and remained just outside Rome, on the reasonable basis of waiting to celebrate the triumph that must surely be awarded for his victories in Gaul. Until he entered the city and so laid down his *imperium* he would remain exempt from prosecution. Yet there was no guarantee that if he did this he would still be permitted to become a consular candidate in accordance with the tribunician law. While still in command of three provinces and an army of ten legions, his bargaining position was strong. After well over a year of attacks on his position, he was very reluctant to sacrifice this. He knew that his enemies were determined to destroy him. Pompey's attitude was never easy to read. By the close of 50 BC Caesar felt himself backed into a corner, reluctant to place too much faith on his old ally.[15]

A century later the poet Lucan would write that 'Caesar could not accept a superior, nor Pompey an equal.' For him, the Civil War was virtually inevitable after Julia's death severed the close bond between them, while Crassus' loss in Parthia removed from each the fear that he could end up fighting alone against the other two. It was a fairly common view in the ancient world and contains more than a grain of truth. Yet this tends to imply an inevitability about the Civil War, and this should not be pushed too far. Even in the last months before the war broke out, neither Caesar nor Pompey seems to have believed that the other would not back down, or at least offer acceptable terms. The long dispute had eroded their trust in each other, however, and this made compromise far harder. They had raised the stakes, which added to their nervousness about making a mistake at the last minute. The outcome of the autumn's elections further increased the tension. The third Marcellus would become consul in the new year, with a colleague from another noble family. They had beaten Servius Sulpicius Galba, who had served competently as Caesar's legate for most of the Gallic campaigns, one of the few patricians to serve with him for any length of time. Appius Claudius and Caesar's father-in-law Calpurnius Piso became censors. The former began to purge the Senate of men he considered to be unfit, something that was generally seen as ironic given his own dubious reputation, and his targets were mostly men believed to be associated with Caesar. Sallust, the future historian, was expelled at this time and soon joined Caesar. An attack on Curio was thwarted by Piso and the consul Paullus, but still resulted in a brawl in the Senate during which the tribune tore the censor's robe. There was also a vacancy in the priestly college of augurs and Domitius

Ahenobarbus was enraged to be beaten in the race for this by Mark Antony, who was also elected tribune for the coming year. Most of Caesar's opponents were united only in their hatred of him, so it would be a mistake to see their actions as co-ordinated. Yet there was a sense that the proconsul of Gaul was vulnerable, and this encouraged their hostility and so helped to make him even more suspicious and nervous. The mood on both sides was scarcely conducive to compromise.[16]

Mark Antony would play a major role in what followed and it is worth pausing to consider this flamboyant character. He had already proved himself to be a courageous and skilful soldier, leading Gabinius' cavalry during the operations in Judaea and Egypt. In 52 BC he was Caesar's quaestor and had served in the campaign against Vercingetorix, as well as the rebellions of the following year. The two men were distant relations, for Antony's mother was a Julia, although from the other branch of the family. Her brother was the Lucius Julius Caesar who was consul in 64 BC. In the familiar Roman way, Antony's father and grandfather were both also named Marcus Antonius. His grandfather was one of the leading orators of his day, but was killed in the purge that accompanied Marius' return to Rome in 87 BC. His father was given a special command to deal with the pirate problem in 74 BC but could not call on the resources later lavished on Pompey and was defeated, dying shortly afterwards. Antony was only nine at the time. His mother soon remarried, and the boy spent much of his formative years in the house of his step-father Lentulus, one of the Catilinarian conspirators executed on Cicero's orders in 63 BC. This may well have given little cause for Antony to like the orator, but there is no evidence that the bitter feud between the two men developed until much later. After Caesar's death, Cicero's rhetoric – especially his famous *Philippics*, a series of virulent speeches modelled on those originally delivered by the famous orator Demosthenes warning the Athenians of the threat posed by Alexander the Great's father, King Philip II of Macedon – would do much to blacken Antony's name. Yet in spite of the exaggeration and bias, other sources suggest that Antony had genuinely provided plenty of material with which Cicero could work. As already noted, tradition maintained that it was Curio who had first introduced Antony to wild parties, wine and women (see p.365). Whether or not this was true, there is no doubt that Antony took immediately to all such things with enormous enthusiasm and almost no self-restraint. There was a great passion in the man that seemed always ready to boil over, and which gave force and massive determination to all that he did. His oratory, his soldiering – as well as his drunkenness and womanizing – all seem to have had a power behind them that came from his personality more than skill or training. A big, burly man, it was said that he liked to be compared with Hercules, just as Pompey had enjoyed references to himself as a new Alexander. As tribune, Antony's strident character would make him hard to ignore, and even harder for Caesar's opponents to browbeat. Yet for more subtle negotiation Caesar would need to rely more on men like Balbus, the equestrian from Spain who privately acted as his agent. Antony was unlikely to give anyone the impression that the proconsul was keen for compromise and did not plan a radical second term as consul.[17]

'THE DIE IS CAST'

Rumour and misinformation also played their part in the growing crisis. In October the story circulated that Caesar had concentrated four legions in Cisalpine Gaul, which was taken as an indication that he was preparing for war. In fact he had only one legion in the province, the *Thirteenth*, which he claimed was there to secure the border areas against barbarian raiding. In early December, shortly after the disgusted Marcellus had dismissed a Senate for wanting to disarm both men and avoid conflict, another report came to Rome claiming that Caesar had already massed his army and invaded Italy. The story was false, but the consul probably did not know this and now urged the Senate to act. Helped no doubt by Curio, but also by the reluctance of the overwhelming majority to plunge into war, the House refused. Accompanied by the consuls elect, but not by his own colleague, Marcellus went to Pompey and presented him with a sword and called on him to protect the Republic. He was given command of the two legions recalled from Gaul ostensibly for the projected war against Parthia and instructed to raise more troops. None of this was legal, since the Senate had not approved the action or granted emergency powers. Pompey told them that he would accept their charge and fight, if this proved necessary. He began trying to recruit troops, but no aggressive moves were made. In part this was because the troops were not ready to fight, but the discovery that the rumour was untrue must have played a part.

Public business went on at Rome almost as if nothing had happened. Caesar had not in fact started a war, so his opponents were determined that they would not take the blame for beginning a conflict. Marcellus and Pompey may still have been more interested in making a gesture, sending a message to the senators of their confidence and to Caesar of their determination to fight if he provoked them. They may well have still hoped that he would back down. Caesar was at a major disadvantage because he could not leave his province to negotiate in person and had to rely instead on letters or representatives. Curio tried to persuade the Senate to pass a decree condemning Pompey's recruitment drive and instructing good citizens to ignore the call to arms. This failed, and since the tribuncian year began and ended earlier than the normal political cycle, his term of office ended and he left to consult with Caesar. What Caesar's men did not do was as eagerly scrutinised as what they actually did and said. On 6 December Caesar's trusted subordinate Hirtius arrived in the city, but left after just a few hours. He did not visit Pompey, and did not wait around for the meeting with Metellus Scipio which had been arranged for the following morning. Pompey told Cicero that he interpreted this as a sign that the breach with Caesar was now irreparable. However, although he and others were now expecting war, they still did not wish to initiate it.[18]

On 1 January the new consuls took up their office. Lentulus, who was hugely in debt, and according to Caesar boasted that he wanted to be a second Sulla, proved far more extreme than Marcellus. However, Mark Antony was now tribune and, along with one of his colleagues Quintus Cassius Longinus, was fulfilling Curio's role. It was only through the persistence of these men that a letter from Caesar was allowed to be read out in the Senate, although the consuls prevented a debate on it. In the letter the proconsul recounted his great achievements on the Republic's behalf and returned to the demand that he should only be forced to lay down his command if Pompey did the same, appearing to threaten war if the latter refused. Cicero, who had just arrived back on the outskirts of Rome, described it as a 'fierce and threatening letter'. A vote was taken on a motion proposed by Metellus Scipio, stating that Caesar must lay down his command by a set day or be considered a public enemy. It was passed, but promptly vetoed by Antony and Cassius. In private, Caesar's tone was more conciliatory and he seems to have written or sent representatives to many leading figures including Cato. He offered to give up Transalpine Gaul and all save two of his legions, so long as he was permitted to retain the rest of his command and make use of the privilege granted to him by the tribunes in 52 BC. This would have balanced the forces under Pompey's command in Italy but seriously impeded his capacity to fight an aggressive war. Cicero became involved in the negotiations, for he believed everything should be done to prevent conflict and felt that the overwhelming majority of senators agreed with him. He spoke to Caesar's opponents and friends, and the latter agreed to a further concession, allowing him to keep just Cisalpine Gaul and a single legion. It was still not enough. Cato declared that he could not agree to anything presented in private rather than before the whole Senate, but ultimately neither he nor any of his closest allies were willing to accept anything that would allow Caesar an unhindered path to his second consulship. Even in late December Cicero had felt that Pompey had reached the point of actively wanting war. The sources are contradictory, but he probably rejected the first proposal. The second – just one legion and Cisalpine Gaul – satisfied him, but he found that he was overruled by Cato, Metellus Scipio and the rest. Overall it was hard for anyone to be too trusting in the atmosphere of suspicion and hate. Nor did the distance help. Caesar away in Gaul at the head of a veteran army was a fairly sinister figure even to moderates. His charm had no opportunity to work at such a long range.[19]

Senatorial meetings were becoming deadlocked, with Antony and Cassius vetoing the repeated motions attacking Caesar that were presented by the consuls. The situation was difficult, but even so Antony's temperament probably did not help. He was a man who always struggled to contain his passions. Years later Cicero would speak of him 'vomiting his words in the usual way' when delivering a speech. A few weeks earlier the tribune had delivered a particularly vitriolic performance in the Senate, attacking Pompey's whole career and threatening armed conflict. Afterwards, Pompey had commented 'What do you reckon Caesar himself will be like, if he gets to control the Republic, if now his weak and worthless quaestor acts like this?' Following one of the Senate's meetings, Pompey summoned all of the senators to his house outside the city's boundary, seeking to reassure them of his steadfast support and willingness to fight if necessary. Caesar's father-in-law Piso asked that he and one of the praetors be permitted six days to travel up to Cisalpine Gaul and talk directly to Caesar before the Senate did anything else. Other voices suggested an even larger deputation. Lentulus, Cato and Metellus Scipio all spoke against this, and these ideas went no further. Instead, on 7 January 49 BC the Senate passed the *senatus consultum ultimum*, calling on 'the consuls, praetors and tribunes, and all the proconsuls near the city to ensure that the Republic comes to no harm'. There was no specific mention of Caesar – whereas the reference to proconsuls was obviously intended to place Pompey at the centre of things – but its target was obvious to all. Caesar claimed that Lentulus, Pompey, Cato and Scipio, along with many of his other opponents, were now all determined on war. Some of them may have been, but for others this may have represented the final raising of the stakes, making it utterly clear to Caesar that he could not get his way save by fighting and so must back down. The Senate's ultimate decree suspended normal law and was not subject to veto. Lentulus warned Antony and Cassius that he could not guarantee their safety if they remained in Rome. Along with Curio, who had returned probably carrying Caesar's letter read out on 1 January, the two tribunes disguised themselves as slaves and were smuggled out of the city in a hired wagon.[20]

The precise chronology of what happened over the next few days cannot be firmly established. Caesar had been in Cisalpine Gaul for some time, arriving first – or so he claimed – to canvass for Mark Antony in his bid to be elected augur and then, since this had already succeeded by the time he arrived, in his campaign for the tribunate. Lately he had stayed in Ravenna, close to the border of his province. With him he had the *Thirteenth* Legion and some 300 cavalry. Several of our sources state that the legion was at near enough full strength, with 5,000 men, but it is questionable whether they had any reliable information about this. It is more likely that it was somewhat under strength. Since the early autumn Caesar had redeployed his army, placing some legions ready to block any threat from Pompey's army in Spain, while the equivalent of three or four more were ready to move to join him south of the Alps. However, he had studiously avoided concentrating a field army lest his opponents use this as proof that he was seeking war. Pompey, with his vast military experience, seems to have been convinced that Caesar was not ready for an invasion of Italy. On the road from Ravenna to Ariminum (modern Rimini) the boundary between the province and Italy itself was marked by the Rubicon, a small river that to this day has not been positively identified. Caesar heard quickly of the attacks on him in the Senate at the beginning of January, of the passing of the ultimate decree and the subsequent flight of the tribunes. The news may have reached him before the fugitives. In any case he decided to act.

The *Commentaries* skim over what happened next, not mentioning the Rubicon at all, but later sources provide a more detailed version. Caesar spent the day in Ravenna, calmly going about his normal business as if nothing unusual was about to happen. It was probably 10 January, though yet again certainty is impossible regarding this crucial episode in the history of the ancient world. He had already despatched some centurions and legionaries in civilian clothes and with concealed weapons to seize control of Ariminum. The proconsul spent some hours watching gladiators practising and inspecting plans for a training school that he wanted to build. As night fell he bathed and went to dinner, first greeting the numerous guests invited to join him. Much earlier than usual he excused himself and left, asking them to stay and await his return. A few of his senior officers and attendants had been warned of this and met him outside. One was Asinius Pollio, who would later write a history of the Civil War, which was used as a source by Plutarch and probably Suetonius as well. Orders were also issued to the *Thirteenth* and the cavalry to follow him as soon as they were ready. He and several of his officers travelled in a hired carriage – Suetonius claims that it was drawn by a team of mules borrowed from a nearby baker's shop. Then they set off into the night down the road to Ariminum. According to Suetonius an element of farce entered the proceedings when Caesar and his carriage got lost in the darkness and blundered around until dawn, when they found a guide who set them on the right path. Plutarch and Appian make no mention of this, and both state that he was already at Ariminum as dawn broke. Therefore at some stage early on the 11th he overtook the marching cohorts and came to the River Rubicon. Before he crossed the bridge, he is said to have stopped, spending some time in silent thought before beginning to talk to his officers, Pollio amongst them. He is supposed to have spoken of the cost to himself if he did not take this step, and the price the whole Roman world would pay if he did so. Suetonius claims a supernatural being appeared, played first upon a flute and then, grabbing a trumpet from one of the military musicians, sounded a blast and strode across the river, encouraging the troops to follow. It seems unlikely that Pollio was the source of this tall tale. He did presumably repeat Caesar's final words as he decided to cross, although even here we have several slightly different versions. Plutarch maintains that he spoke in Greek, quoting a line from the poet Menander, 'Let the die be thrown!' (*aneristho kubos*). Suetonius gives the more familiar Latin expression 'The die is cast' (*iacta alea est*).[21]

The gambler's phrase was appropriate, for he was embarking on a civil war when little more than a tenth of his forces were with him. Even when all his troops were concentrated, he would still be overmatched in resources by his enemies. Although with hindsight we know that Caesar prevailed, this was by no means certain – perhaps not even likely – at the time. He chose to fight because as far as he was concerned all the alternatives were worse. The Republic had become dominated by a faction who ignored the normal rule of law and particularly refused to acknowledge the traditional powers and rights of the tribunate. Yet Caesar was quite open that it was first and foremost because this faction of men had attacked him that he now moved against them. The Roman world was being plunged into chaos and bloodshed because one man was as determined to protect his *dignitas* as others were to destroy it. Over the preceding eighteen months the stakes had been raised in turn by both sides. Attitudes had tended to harden, suspicions had grown, and trust declined too far to give compromise a real chance. The Civil War that began in January 49 BC could not have happened without the bitter, almost obsessive hatred felt towards Caesar by men like Cato, Domitius Ahenobarbus and the others, which made them determined to prevent his return to public life as a consul. Even this would not have mattered if Pompey had not seen an opportunity to demonstrate his supremacy and show these men, as well as Caesar, that they needed to placate him. Finally, the struggle would not have begun had Caesar not placed such a high value on his prestige and position. His life up to this point had demonstrated his willingness to take risks if there was a chance of a valuable prize. Only rarely – as when he was dismissed from his praetorship – had he been willing to back down, and even then it had only been because this was clearly his sole means of continuing his career. In 49 BC that option had largely been closed to him, or at least been surrounded by risks that appeared greater even than those of fighting. The ethos of the Roman aristocracy celebrated determination and especially admired the generals who would not concede defeat. Yet for all the dubious legality of his opponents' actions, in the end only one thing mattered. North of the Rubicon Caesar held rightful *imperium* and south of the river he did not. As soon as he crossed Caesar was undoubtedly a rebel, whatever the reasons that had driven him to this act. In this sense his enemies won a victory and could more readily claim to be fighting for the legitimate Republic. They were determined now to crush him by force, just as Catiline and, before him, Lepidus had been suppressed. Resorting to his army was a mark of Caesar's failure to get what he wanted by political means. The die had been rolled, but so far no one knew what number it would show when it came to rest.

XVIII

BLITZKRIEG: ITALY AND SPAIN, WINTER–AUTUMN, 49 BC

'I ask, what is going on? What is happening? As for me I am in the dark. Someone says, "We hold Cingulum – we have lost Ancona; Labienus has deserted from Caesar." Are we talking about a general of the Roman People or about Hannibal.. . . He claims that he is doing all this to protect his dignity. How can there be any dignity where there is no honesty?' – *Cicero, c. 17–22 January 49 BC.*[1]

'Let us see if in this way we can willingly win the support of all and gain a permanent victory, since through their cruelty others have been unable to escape hatred or make their victory lasting – save for Lucius Sulla, and I do not intend to imitate him. This is a new way of conquest, we grow strong through pity and generosity.' – *Caesar, early March 49 BC.*[2]

At the beginning of the Civil War Caesar paraded the *Thirteenth* Legion and addressed the men. In his own account he tells us that he spoke of the injustices done to him by his enemies, and of how his old friend and ally Pompey, now jealous of his achievements, had been lured away to join them. Most of all the proconsul laid before the legionaries the contempt shown for the hallowed rights of the tribunes of the people, ignoring their right of veto – something that not even Sulla had done. He did not dispute the Senate's right to pass the *senatus consultum ultimum*, but denied that it had been necessary, and also made clear that it had never been used in similar circumstances, but only when Rome itself was under direct threat. Other sources tell us that to underline his point Caesar brought Antony and Cassius before the troops. They were still wearing the disguises in which they had fled from Rome, and the sight is said to have deeply moved the soldiers, first to pity and then to anger against the men who had trampled on the college of magistrates first created to protect the ordinary citizens. By the time Caesar had finished, the legionaries were yelling out that they were ready to avenge the wrongs done both to him and to the tribunes. It is not clear whether this parade occurred in Ravenna or in Ariminum after crossing the Rubicon. What mattered most was the reaction of the troops. The *Thirteenth* had been formed by Caesar seven years earlier and had served with him ever since. The soldiers trusted him to bring them victory as he had always done in the past. They remembered his generosity with spoils, with praise and decorations. At some point he almost doubled the basic annual salary of a legionary, from 125 to 225 denarii. Many of the *Thirteenth* were probably from north of the Po, men officially with Latin status, but whom he had treated as full citizens. Their officers, both the half-dozen or so tribunes and the sixty centurions, all owed their commissions and subsequent promotions to him. Some may originally have been recommended to him by Pompey – all of these were allowed to leave unharmed and with all their possessions, if their conscience told them to honour their earlier loyalty. We are not told how many men chose to take advantage of this. All ranks – not just in the *Thirteenth* but throughout the entire army – had gained much from Caesar and could expect even more in the future, particularly plots of land for discharged veterans. A Senate dominated by Caesar's opponents was unlikely to be generous in this regard. In this pragmatic sense the army in Gaul had a vested interest in Caesar's victory, now that it had come to civil war. They knew and trusted their commander after serving together for so long, whereas few knew his opponents to any degree.

The loyalty of Caesar's army throughout the Civil War – and indeed even after his death – was truly remarkable, but is all too easily taken for granted. Much of it was clearly the result of the bond between the general and his officers and men, which grew up during the campaigns in Gaul, as he carefully cultivated and rewarded them. Yet it would be wrong to see this as the whole story, or to deny that politics played any part at all. The officers in particular may have had fairly detailed knowledge of what had gone on in Rome. It seems reasonable to say that most of Caesar's army came to believe that he – and by extension they – had been treated shabbily by a group of senators whose own behaviour made it difficult to see them as the legitimate leaders of the Republic. For many Romans – wealthy and humble alike – there was a strong sentimental attachment to the tribunate. A sense of what was right, along with old loyalty and self-interest combined to ensure that Caesar's army had no hesitation about fighting other Romans to set things right.[3]

The choice of which side to join does not seem to have required much thought for the overwhelming majority of Caesar's troops, but for most Romans it was very difficult. Only a small number of people were deeply committed by the time hostilities opened. Even some of those who might have appeared fervent partisans now took a step back. One was Caius Claudius Marcellus, who as consul in 50 BC had presented the sword to Pompey and called on him to defend the Republic. Now that civil war had come, he chose to remain neutral, perhaps thinking of his marriage to Caesar's niece. Calpurnius Piso could not be expected to side against his son-in-law, but did not play an active part in the war, especially in the early months. Family ties and longstanding bonds of friendship played a major role in determining allegiance for many men, but in the small world of the Roman elite many men had links with the leaders on both sides and faced a very difficult decision. Most did not feel a strong commitment to either side, but memories of the struggle between Sulla and the Marians suggested that refusing to take part would not guarantee a man's safety. Brutus, Servilia's son, had studiously avoided ever speaking to Pompey, as he had executed Brutus's father in 78 BC during Lepidus' rebellion. Now he decided that his mother's long-time lover was in the wrong and declared himself willing to serve under the command of his father's killer. In part this was a matter of principle, but with his family connections there can have been little real doubt about his decision. He had been raised in Cato's house and shared his uncle's love of philosophy, while his wife was one of Appius Claudius' daughters.[4]

There was one major defection from Caesar's army when Labienus left him in the middle of January. His senior legate had served with him in Gaul from the very beginning and had proved himself to be by far the most gifted of his senior officers. Compared to the other legates, Labienus was granted a more prominent place in the *Commentaries*. Scholars have put forward the conjecture that Labienus held the praetorship before coming to Gaul, perhaps in 60 BC, but there is absolutely no evidence for this. If this is correct, then he would have been at least fifty years old by the time of the Civil War and thus had been eligible for the consulship for a considerable time. On Caesar's behalf he had effectively postponed his own career for the duration of the campaigns in Gaul. As a legate he won some glory, although the lion's share of this went always to the proconsul. Several of his independent operations, especially those against the rebellious tribes in 54–53 and 52 BC, would certainly have won him a triumph had Labienus been a provincial governor himself, instead of a subordinate. He had also become very rich during these campaigns, for Caesar was far more generous with money than he was with glory. Cicero bemoaned the new-found wealth of Labienus. He may also have attracted the scorn of Catullus, if the theory is true that he was the *Mentula* – dick or dickhead – attacked in his poems. It is more than possible that Caesar intended further reward and hoped to have Labienus as his consular colleague in 48 BC. There seem to have been rumours about the senior legate's loyalties as early as the summer of 50 BC, but Caesar had chosen to show his confidence in his subordinate by sending him to Cisalpine Gaul, near to Italy and therefore also nearer to hostile influences. In the event the gesture failed and Labienus went to join Caesar's enemies. He may in fact have simply returned to an earlier loyalty, since he came from Picenum, a region dominated by Pompey's family. Past service with Pompey has been conjectured, as well as support in his career. All of this is plausible enough, but personal dissatisfaction may have been just as important. Successful generals have throughout history tended to display supreme self-confidence, often combined with a readiness to denigrate the skill of others, and jealousy of other men's fame – Napoleon's marshals and the Allied senior commanders in the Second World War spring to mind, but many examples could be found. Labienus had given a large chunk of his best years to Caesar and seems to have felt that this had not been sufficiently recognised. On several occasions during the campaigns he may well have felt that it was his ability and deeds, and not Caesar's, which had won the day. Our sources give the impression that he had an abrasive character and was by no means a likeable man. Resentment at having always to come second to another man, and the conviction that his real worth had not been recognised, may well have contributed to his decision. He may also have judged that Caesar was likely to lose the war, especially once the proconsul was deprived of his own talent. Hearing that Labienus had defected, Caesar decided on another gesture and gave instructions that all of his baggage should be sent after him.[5]

The prospect of gain and personal advantage from picking the right side were evidently important for many men faced with the prospect of war. As early as August 50 BC Cicero's correspondent Caelius Rufus had expressed his own cynical view:

You won't forget of course, that in a domestic squabble, carried on constitutionally and without resort to armed conflict, then men ought to espouse the more honourable cause; however, when it's a war and the military camp, espouse the stronger, and hold the side to be best which is strongest. In all this strife I can see that Pompey will be backed by the Senate and the 'lawyers' – all those with plenty of fear and little hope will join Caesar, whose army is incomparably better.[6]

True to his word, Caelius joined the side with the better army rather than the one championed by most distinguished men and with the better cause. Not everyone agreed with his judgement on the balance of power. Caesar had ten legions, all veterans of the campaigns in Gaul, along with the equivalent of two more in the twenty-two independent cohorts raised in Transalpine Gaul, and auxiliaries and allies from Gaul and Germany. Losses to battle, accident and disease make it unlikely that any of the legions – especially the ones with longest service – had anything like their paper strength of soldiers. A generous estimate would give Caesar something like 45,000 legionaries at the beginning of 49 BC, but the figure could as easily have been as low as 30,000–35,000. Man for man these soldiers were better than any of the troops available to the enemy. There were the two legions that had been taken from Caesar and were now camped in southern Italy. One of these, the *First*, had on its formation taken an oath to Pompey, but the other – originally the *Fifteenth*, now renumbered the *Third* – had been raised by and for Caesar. Both units had served for three campaigns in Gaul. Pompey swiftly realised that the optimistic reports of their disaffection with their old commander were little more than a fantasy. For the moment at least, he did not feel confident enough to lead these men into battle against their former comrades and general. He did have seven fully formed and trained legions in the Spanish provinces, but these had little or no experience of actual warfare and so lacked the confidence Caesar's men possessed after years of victory. Even more importantly they were far away, unable to play a part in the initial stages of the conflict. In the long term Pompey and his allies could call on far greater resources of manpower, money, animals and equipment than Caesar. A flood of recruits in all parts of Italy was confidently predicted, and with the consuls on their side they had access to the wealth of the State. Overseas, Pompey had clients and connections in Spain, North Africa and throughout the East, all of whom could be called upon to supply soldiers and contribute financially to the cause. It would take time to mobilise all these resources, to raise an army or armies, equip them and provide logistic support, as well as turning raw recruits into soldiers. One of the reasons why Pompey and his allies had adopted such an inflexible line in the months building up to the war was their absolute confidence that they possessed the military might to crush Caesar. On balance this was probably a fair assessment, as long as their opponent gave them time to prepare.

THE ITALIAN CAMPAIGN, JANUARY TO MARCH

The news that Caesar had crossed the Rubicon stunned his opponents. January was a difficult time to keep an army supplied in the field. In spite of earlier rumours, they may well have known that the bulk of his forces were still north of the Alps. It was probably also an indication that, even after passing the *senatus consultum ultimum* and beginning to mobilise, many of them really did expect him to back down in the face of their unity and obvious strength. Perhaps there was an assumption that he would wait for the campaigning season and carefully mass his forces before acting, maybe even remain on the defensive in the hope of continued negotiation. In the days following 7 January the Senate had convened on several occasions outside the boundary of the city, so that Pompey could reassure the senators. His father-in-law Metellus Scipio was given command of Syria, while Domitius Ahenobarbus was to go to Transalpine Gaul as proconsul. Caesar notes in the *Commentaries* that they did not deign to ratify all these appointments with a vote in the Popular Assembly in the usual way. However, both men did perform the normal ceremonies for a magistrate setting out for a command, and then rushed off to their provinces, as did the propraetors appointed to other commands. One of the latter was given Cisalpine Gaul. Caesar's opponents had openly decided to make use of force against him, but they were not yet ready. Levies were underway, arms and equipment were being gathered, but by no stretch of the imagination could Italy have been described as prepared to meet an invasion. Caesar was not ready either, in the sense that he would surely have liked to have a stronger force at his immediate disposal before acting. He had sent orders to several other formations instructing them to move to join him, but they would not all arrive for some time. His opponents were still unprepared, and waiting would only give them a chance to grow stronger. Never one to delay unless this would bring him clear advantage, Caesar advanced with only the *Thirteenth*.[7]

Ariminum, already infiltrated by his men, did not resist him. For a while he remained there but sent Antony with five cohorts to occupy Arretium (modern Arrezo), despatching three more to Pisaurum, Fanum (modern Fano) and Ancona respectively. There was no fighting. News of the crossing of the Rubicon seems to have reached Rome on about 17 January. Pompey and his leading allies promptly left the city, for Pompey quickly realised that at present he simply did not have the forces to stop Caesar. This meant that Rome had been abandoned by all senior magistrates and so the public life

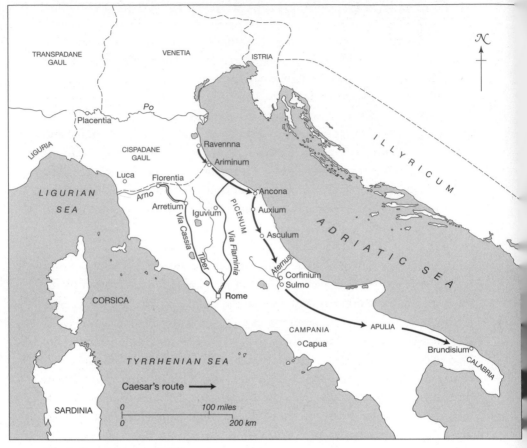

The Italian campaign 49 BC

of the Republic for the moment ceased to be conducted in the proper way. Many uncommitted senators went with them, remembering the bloody entries into Rome made by Marius and Sulla. Others simply left Rome and went to their country houses, planning to keep a low profile. Around this time a number of unofficial envoys came to Caesar at Ariminum. One was Lucius Julius Caesar, son of the former consul who had served as his legate for a number of years. He brought a message from Pompey, assuring Caesar that his actions were not motivated by personal hostility, but were dictated by his duty to the Republic. His old ally urged Caesar to lay down his command voluntarily and prevent civil war. A similar request was brought by the praetor Lucius Roscius. Caesar replied by stating that all he wished was to exercise the rights legally granted to him by the Roman people. His enemies had been raising troops for some time. If they wanted peace then

Pompey should go to his province, then both of them could lay down their commands and disband their armies – along with all the other troops in Italy – at the same time. Not for the last time he also asked Pompey to come and meet him in person. By 23 January Lucius Caesar the Younger reached Pompey, who was now at Teanum in Apulia. According to Cicero writing two days later, Caesar's:

> terms were accepted with the proviso that he must at once withdraw all his garrisons from the towns which he had occupied outside his province. Once that was done, they replied that we should return to the city and settle the matter in the Senate. I hope at present that it will be possible for us to have peace. For one leader regrets his rash folly and the other his lack of forces.[8]

Letters were sent to Caesar informing him of the offer – as he himself put it, that he should 'go back to Gaul, abandon Ariminum and disband his forces'. To him this was an 'unfair deal'. No date was given for Pompey's departure to his provinces or his laying the command down and giving up his armies. It was obvious that he was effectively being asked to give up the military advantage he had gained by his sudden invasion. His opponents wanted him to withdraw and then trust to their giving his demands a sympathetic hearing in future meetings of the Senate. There was no reason for Caesar to believe that things would go better for him than they had in the debates of the last eighteen months. Pompey and his allies did not trust Caesar enough to stop raising troops in expectation that he would accept their terms. In return Caeser did not trust them sufficiently to take the first step towards peace and go back to his province. Caesar does seem to have been especially frustrated by Pompey's reluctance to agree to a face-to-face conference. In the past the two men had got on well and he seems to have been confident that he could reach a genuine agreement with his former son-in-law. Pompey may have been unsure about whether or not he could resist Caesar's persuasiveness. For a man with a morbid fear of assassination and memories of an earlier and very brutal civil war, it is possible that he was reluctant to risk such a meeting. Yet in the end it was probably more a question of his relationship with Cato and his other new allies. Their alliance was recent, his friendship with Caesar older and of longer duration. Whatever he felt himself, Pompey knew that these men simply would not believe in his good faith and constancy if he privately met Caesar. Cato had already urged the Senate to appoint Pompey as supreme commander until the crisis was over and the rebellious proconsul defeated. This was rejected by the consuls and ex-consuls who were too proud to be commanded by anyone else. Jealousy and suspicion between allies was as much a hindrance to a negotiated settlement as mistrust between enemies.[9]

Caesar resumed his advance. A report reached him that Iguvium was held by a garrison of five cohorts under the command of the propraetor Quintus Minucius Thermus, but that the townsfolk favoured him. The two cohorts with him at Ariminum were added to the one stationed in Pisarum and sent under Curio to the town. Thermus retreated, his raw recruits deserted and went home, and Curio's men were welcomed at Iguvium. Trusting in local goodwill, Caesar pushed on to Auxinum and had soon overrun Picenum, supposedly the heartland of Pompey's family. There was one small skirmish in which a few prisoners were taken, but the general population was displaying no enthusiasm for rising up against Caesar and his men. The cause against Caesar had little popular appeal and his army was not plundering or doing anything else that might have created hostility. A few of the Pompeian soldiers even chose to join him. Many communities also remembered the gifts Caesar had distributed to them from the profits of Gaul – he took particular satisfaction in reporting that even the town of Cingulum, which had been especially favoured by Labienus, now willingly opened its gates to him.[10]

By this time it was February and Caesar had reunited the detachments of the *Thirteenth* and been joined by the *Twelfth*. At Asculum another Pompeian garrison fled before him, and it was not until he reached Corfinium that he encountered any serious opposition. In command there was Domitius Ahenobarbus, who had not yet managed to get anywhere near his province. Together with his subordinates he had managed to muster a force of more than thirty cohorts, but these were entirely raw recruits. Pompey had not wanted Ahenobarbus to defend the town, as he had no doubt of the inevitable outcome when such inexperienced troops came up against Caesar's veterans. He was himself much further south in Apulia with the *First* and *Third* legions, as well as a number of recent levies. However, he had no power to issue orders to Ahenobarbus and could do no more than send letters urging him to abandon the town and join him. Domitius Ahenobarbus was not a man to change his mind too readily and wrote replies imploring Pompey to come to him. There were no similar divisions over strategy for Caesar. He closed on Corfinium, driving off some enemy cohorts which attempted to break down the bridge outside the town. Soon afterwards Antony was sent with a quarter of the army to Sulmo in response to an appeal from the town.

In another bloodless victory the Pompeian commander was captured, taken to Caesar and promptly allowed to go free. In the meantime the Caesarean army gathered food in preparation for the siege of Corfinium. After three days it received a major boost to its strength when it was joined by the *Eighth* Legion and the twenty-two cohorts raised from Transalpine Gaul and trained and equipped as legionaries. The troops were set to building a line of circumvallation strengthened by forts to surround the town.

Before the blockade was complete, Domitius Ahenobarbus received a final letter from Pompey making it clear that he had no intention of marching to relieve Corfinium. Deciding now that the town's prospects were not good, he publicly announced that help was on its way, while privately planning his own escape. However, his increasingly furtive manner soon revealed the truth to his legionaries. A council was organised consisting of the tribunes, along with the centurions – almost two hundred of these if the thirty-three cohorts were at full strength – and representatives of the ordinary soldiers to debate the matter. Some of the troops were Marsi, who had a close tie to their commander through his family's estates in the region. At first they were staunchly loyal, even threatening to use force against the other legionaries, but their mood changed when they became convinced that their leader planned to abscond. Ahenobarbus was placed under arrest by his own men, who immediately sent envoys to surrender themselves and the town to Caesar. This was welcome news, since although he had little doubt of the outcome of the siege it would clearly pin him down for several weeks. Instead the matter had been resolved in only seven days. However, he was reluctant to enter the walls immediately, for night was falling and he did not trust his legionaries not to misbehave once they got into the dark streets of the town. So far his army had not plundered or laid waste the lands they passed through, as they had so often done in the past. Instead he had the troops stand to arms in the lines around Corfinium throughout the night to prevent any fugitives from slipping out. Near dawn one of the senior Pompeians, Publius Cornelius Lentulus Spinther, who had been consul in 57 BC, surrendered himself and was soon followed by the remaining senior officers.

Caesar's portrait of Ahenobarbus is scarcely flattering, but our other sources were even less kind. It was claimed that he had decided to commit suicide and demanded that his physician supply him with poison. However, when he heard that Caesar was not executing his important prisoners, he immediately repented of his rashness and was delighted to be informed by his doctor that he had only taken a harmless draught. Domitius Ahenobarbus then went out to surrender to the man whose bitter opponent he had been for at least a decade. Altogether there were fifty senators and equestrians amongst the Pompeians who surrendered, probably on 21 February. Caesar had them brought before him, repeated the charges that he had been unfairly and illegally treated and forced into war, reminding some of them of personal favours he had done them in the past. After that, all were allowed to go free. Caesar had already followed the same policy earlier in the campaign, but never up to this point had so many or so distinguished a group received the benefit of his clemency. Ahenobarbus had brought 6 million sestertii of public money with him to provide pay for his troops. This was handed over to Caesar by the town's magistrates, but he ordered that it be sent back to his enemy, lest it be thought that 'he was more restrained in dealing with men's lives, than their wealth'. The surrendered soldiers were asked to take an oath to him. Soon, these legions would go under Curio's command to fight for Caesar in Sicily and Africa.[11]

The clemency of Corfinium became famous, and his moderation formed a central part of Caesar's propaganda campaign. Everyone had expected him to behave like Sulla or Marius – or even, though few would dare to say it, like the Pompey who had earned the nickname of the 'young butcher'. Instead his soldiers were kept under tight discipline, did not plunder and only fought when they were themselves resisted. Even his bitterest enemies were allowed to go free, although both Lentulus and Ahenobarbus went straight off to fight against him again. The overwhelming majority of people in Italy were apathetic to the issues about which the Civil War was being waged. Amongst the wider population both Pompey and Caesar were highly respected and seen as great servants of the Republic. If Caesar's legions had come marauding and slaughtering their way through Italy, then this might well have turned more of the population against him. His policy of clemency made practical sense. Armies failed to spring from the soil of Italy as Pompey had promised just a few months before. One senator acidly suggested that maybe it was about time the great man started stamping his foot. Very early on Pompey had decided that Rome was indefensible. At some point he reached the further conclusion that Caesar could not be beaten in Italy with two veteran, but possibly unreliable, legions, supported by the rawest of recruits. Instead he planned to shift the war away, taking his forces across the sea to Greece where they could be trained and a massive army gathered with the support of the eastern provinces. It was not a popular decision with other senators, and for this reason, as well as wanting to conceal his intentions from Caesar, he at first kept the idea to himself. The stand at

Corfinium wasted the equivalent of three legions, but Pompey managed to concentrate the remainder of his forces at Brundisium (modern Brindisi). Merchant vessels were requisitioned and the process of shipping men and equipment over the Adriatic begun. It was a long and complex task, but Pompey had always excelled at organisation on a massive scale and set about the task with all his accustomed skill.[12]

Caesar arrived outside Brundisium on 9 March. He had six legions, the veteran *Eighth*, *Twelfth* and *Thirteenth*, along with some new recruits and presumably the cohorts from Transalpine Gaul, some of whom were soon to be formally converted into a legion, the *Fifth Alaudae* – the name meant the 'Larks', probably from its distinctive feathered crest or shield design. Pompey had only a rearguard of two legions awaiting shipment. Caesar set his men to building booms to close off the narrow entrance to the harbour. The defenders put their own engineering skills to good use to prevent this. There were further attempts at negotiation, but none came to anything. Pompey once again refused Caesar's plea for a personal meeting. Then, when they were at last ready, the Pompeians evacuated the town during the night of 17 March. Pompey escaped with virtually all his men, apart from two ships that ran aground on the boom built by Caesar's men. The townsfolk – at last able to express their resentment against the Pompeians according to Caesar, but doubtless also through a keenness to avoid rough treatment at the hands of the legionaries – pointed out the traps built by the enemy to cause casualties amongst Caesar's men. Pompey had got away with a substantial force, around which he could in time build a great army. Then, when he was ready he could invade Italy from Greece just as Sulla had done so successfully. As Pompey so often declared, 'Sulla did it, why shouldn't I?'[13]

ROME

For the moment Caesar could not follow. The Pompeians had gathered up and taken most of the merchant ships from the region, and it would take a long time to collect and bring vessels from elsewhere. Caesar was not inclined to wait, sitting on the defensive and handing the initiative back to his opponents. It was now spring, the opening of the proper campaigning season when armies found it easier to operate. The bulk of his own army – some seven legions along with numerous allies and auxiliaries – was still north of the Alps. Pompey's best legions were in the Spanish Peninsula, cut off from their commander and led by his legates. At the moment they were still passive but it was unlikely that this would last forever, especially if Caesar massed all his forces and prepared for a seaborne invasion of Greece. He did not need a fleet of ships to reach Spain, neither would the enemy forces there have much difficulty marching on Gaul or Italy. In contrast it would take many months for Pompey to form and train an army, so that there was no real prospect of his trying to invade Italy from Greece during 49 BC. Yet Pompey was not inactive and he and his allies planned to cut off the food supplies going to Italy from the provinces. Defeating the armies in Spain would deprive Pompey of his best troops and weaken him, even if it would not be the decisive encounter of the war. It was beneficial and, most important of all, it was possible. Without hesitation Caesar decided to attack the Pompeians in Spain. He joked that he was going to fight 'an army without a general', and that then he would deal with 'a general without an army' when he went to confront Pompey in Greece. In the meantime Curio would go to secure Sicily and ensure that it continued to ship its surplus crops to Italy. Another force went to take Sardinia.[14]

Caesar had military control of all of Italy, for not a single walled town or city resisted him. He was eager to hasten to Spain since time was not on his side, and as every month passed Pompey would only continue to grow stronger. Most of the magistrates had gone with his opponents, as had some distinguished senators. Many more remained in Italy but had yet to commit themselves to either side. Caesar wanted the Senate to meet and hoped to give every impression that the organs of the State continued to function even at this time of crisis. His enemies claimed that they represented the true Republic. Caesar wanted to challenge this and show that the State continued to function in Rome, where it was supposed to be, and so to make clear that his cause was legitimate, that he did not fight against the Republic, but against a faction that had usurped power. As a result he wanted as many senators as possible to attend the meeting that was called for 1 April. Cicero was still in Italy, and in a series of letters Caesar's associates tried to persuade him to attend. The orator had worked hard to avoid the situation developing into war in the first place and had been dismayed by the militant enthusiasm he had seen in others. When war began, he was appalled by the speed with which Rome was abandoned, and then even more disgusted when he realised that Pompey planned to evacuate Italy altogether. Cicero felt an old and deep loyalty to Pompey as a man, and from the beginning his instinct and judgement had dictated that whatever happened, he must in the end be on the same side. Pompey had often disappointed him, not always giving him the praise he wanted, forming the alliance with Crassus and Caesar and, most of all, abandoning him to his fate when Clodius had forced Cicero into exile. Nevertheless, the deep affection remained, along with the hope that the great man would one day live up to what the orator believed was his full potential to be a force for good within the Republic. Yet since his return from exile Pompey and others had encouraged him to develop a friendship with Caesar. Apart from the warm correspondence, the involvement in Caesar's building plans and Quintus' service in Gaul, Cicero himself had received a major loan from Caesar. In the months leading up to the war this had greatly exercised him, as he had no wish to be seen as having been bought by Caesar, still less of fighting against him in order to avoid the debt.[15]

Cicero had not welcomed his posting as governor of Cilicia, but had taken care to perform his duties well. In a campaign against the tribes of Mount Amanus he – or in truth his more experienced legates – had won a minor victory. Though scarcely a military man, the orator was desperately eager to be awarded a triumph for this success. In 50 BC the Senate had voted him a public thanksgiving, a common preliminary to the greater honour. Cato had opposed the motion and later primly informed Cicero that this was because he felt it would be better to honour him for his good and honest administration, since this was of far more worth to the Republic. Curio had at first also been hostile. Days of thanksgiving prevented public business from being conducted and he may have been worried that Caesar's opponents would seek to gain advantage through manipulating the calendar in this way. However, Caesar swiftly instructed the tribune to back the claim and in the end the motion passed easily. Salt was rubbed into the wound when Cato successfully put forward a vote awarding twenty days of thanksgiving to Bibulus, who had campaigned in the same mountains as Cicero, which bordered Cilicia and his own province of Syria. Cato's son-in-law had achieved little and had in fact suffered at least one serious defeat. Granting him an honour at all was questionable, but one of this length was absurd, yet presumably it was felt that he should be granted a number of days surpassing those ever given to Pompey and only equalled by Caesar. Cicero accepted the hypocrisy necessary for success in politics. His predecessor in Cilicia had been Appius Claudius, who had plundered the province for his own gain. Privately Cicero described his actions as those of a 'wild beast', but he was invariably scrupulously polite, even warm, in his dealings with Claudius himself. Nevertheless Cato's actions left a bitter taste. Caesar wrote to Cicero after the vote congratulating him, doubtless encouraging his hopes for a triumph, and crowing over his old adversary's double standards.[16]

Cicero was in a difficult position when the Civil War began. He had not yet laid down his proconsular *imperium* for he could not do this until he celebrated his longed for triumph. Therefore he was still attended by lictors and had the right to command troops. Much as he disapproved of the attitude and behaviour of Pompey, Cato, Domitius Ahenobarbus and their associates, he did not feel that he could side against such men or fail to support the legally elected consuls of the year. He was given the task of raising troops, but soon gave this up as impractical and played no active part in the campaign. Caesar's crossing of the Rubicon he thought an appalling crime, but his attitude softened a little when he heard of the clement treatment of the captured Pompeians. Cicero wrote to commend him, especially in the case of Lentulus, who had supported him in 63 BC. Cut off from Pompey at Brundisium – admittedly Cicero made no great effort to reach him since he hated his strategy of leaving Italy – he waited events at one of his country villas. In early March, probably before Brundisium fell, Caesar had written a brief letter to the orator, urging him to:

> have no doubt that I have many times been grateful to you, and look forward to having even more reason to be grateful to you in the future. This is no more than you deserve. First, though, I implore you, since I expect that I shall swiftly come to Rome, that I may see you there, and draw on your counsel, goodwill, dignity, and assistance of every kind. I will close as I began. Please excuse my haste and the brevity of this letter.[17]

Cicero responded on 19 March, writing to ask exactly what Caesar meant by his 'goodwill' and 'assistance'. He repeated his willingness to work for peace, as long as this protected 'our mutual friend Pompey', for the Republic would benefit most if the two men were reconciled. On the 26th Caesar wrote again, thanking Cicero for commending his clemency, and noted that 'there was nothing further from my nature than cruelty'. Again Caesar urged him to come to Rome, this time saying that he wanted his 'counsel and resources'. Another incentive was the presence with the Caesarean army of the orator's son-in-law Publius Cornelius Dolabella, and Caesar assured the orator of the favour in which the young man was held. Two days later the two men met at Formiae. Cicero was determined not to be used and staunchly resisted the pressure to come to Rome:

He kept saying that my refusal was a condemnation of him, which would make others less likely to come, if I did not go. After a lot of talk, [Caesar said] 'Well come then, and talk about peace.' 'As a free agent?' I asked. He said, 'Should I tell you what to say!' 'In that case,' I said, 'I will argue that the Senate cannot approve your taking an army to Spain or transporting one to Greece. And more than that,' I went on, 'I shall deplore Cnaeus' [i.e. Pompey's] fate.' So then he said, 'I really do not want you to say that.' 'That's what I thought, but I do not want to go there, because I will either have to say that and more besides, about which I cannot hold my tongue, if I am present, or else I cannot go.'

Caesar urged Cicero to think the matter over. The latter was convinced that Caesar had no great love for him at present, but felt that he had regained some self-respect. There was a definite hint of menace when Caesar concluded by saying brusquely that if Cicero would not advise him, he would seek guidance from others. The commander's officers were a motley crew in the orator's opinion, making the threat seem more ominous.[18]

The Senate met on the appointed day, summoned by the tribunes Antony and Cassius, and convened outside the formal boundary of the city so that the proconsul Caesar could attend. In itself this was proper, although subsequently Cicero at least was unwilling to accept it as a proper meeting rather than an informal gathering. The turnout was poor, and most notable of all was the absence of distinguished men. Even so Caesar used this as a public opportunity to repeat his grievances – that all he had wanted was the right to exercise privileges granted to him legitimately by the tribunes, but that Pompey's attitude had changed over time. It was the bitter hatred of his personal enemies who had forced him to war. More practically Caesar requested that senatorial envoys be sent to negotiate with Pompey and effect a reconciliation. Caesar declared his own ambition was to display the same gifts in 'justice and equity' as he displayed in action. The motion was approved, but no one was willing to go. Always a *popularis*, Caesar did not confine his attentions to the Senate. Antony summoned the *Concilium Plebis* to vote on a number of measures. Before the meeting Caesar addressed a gathering of the people, again explaining his actions and blaming his opponents for the war. He assured them that the city would continue to receive the grain it needed, and even promised to give every citizen a gift of 300 sestertii. As in the Senate, the reception seems to have been muted. The memories of the vicious reprisals inflicted by Marius and Sulla still lingered and the way the war would develop was unclear. In the *Commentaries* Caesar claims that Pompey had threatened to treat even those who stayed in Italy as if they had sided with Caesar. In the end, most people of all classes felt no strong attachment to either side, wanted to be neutral and simply hoped to survive the Civil War unscathed. Some were convinced by Caesar's words and attitude, but most remained wary. The only open resistance to Caesar came from one of the tribunes, Lucius Caecilius Metellus, who began by hindering him in the Senate.[19]

The main confrontation came when Caesar decided to make use of the State Treasury. The conquest of Gaul had made him wealthy, but he had never been one to hoard his money and had spent freely to win the loyalty of his army and men like Curio and Aemilius Paullus. He was now faced with the cost of supporting a truly enormous war effort. In just a few months he had added three new legions and numbers of recruits to the ten legions, independent cohorts and auxiliaries that he had controlled at the start of the year. In time additional forces would be raised. All of these men had to be paid – it was especially unwise to give any cause for discontent to soldiers who had once served with the enemy. More than that these armies needed to be equipped and fed. In Gaul Caesar had relied heavily on allied communities to supply him with food, but the conditions of civil war were different. Not all provincial and allied communities would side with him, but it was important to avoid treating those who did not too harshly, for in the end he must hope to win them over to his cause. Where necessary Caesar would have to pay for a good deal of his armies' requirements. Crassus had boasted that only a man who could raise an army from his own resources could truly call himself rich. Caesar was rich, but he was now being called upon to fund a conflict on a massive scale, and no individual possessed that much money.

However, when he went to the Treasury – or perhaps sent men, since this would otherwise have meant crossing the boundary of the city – Metellus stood in front of the doors and imposed his veto. The Treasury was housed in the Temple of Saturn in the Forum. The consuls had left the door locked and barred, taking the key with them, but the soldiers ignored the tribune and chopped it down with axes. In Plutarch's version blacksmiths had to be summoned to perform this task, and there was a confrontation between Caesar and Metellus outside the building. As the tribune repeatedly tried to halt the work, Caesar's temper flared up and he threatened to kill him. As Metellus at last backed down, Caesar declared that it was harder for a man of his natural clemency to make such a threat than it would be for him actually to do the deed. The man who had proclaimed that he was championing the rights of the tribunes in January was now as ready as his opponents had been to override and threaten one of these magistrates. He had never hidden the fact that his greatest aim was to protect his own *dignitas*. Now that war had come the only way to do that was to win, and in order to win he needed cash. The money was taken – 15,000 gold bars, 30,000 silver bars and no less than 30 million sestertii. In addition, Caesar took a special fund kept over the centuries in case there was a repeat of the Gallic attack on Rome in 390 BC. Caesar announced that there was no longer any need of this since he had permanently dealt with the threat from the Gauls. Even so, he made no mention of any of this in the *Commentaries*, merely noting that Metellus, spurred on by his enemies, was generally obstructive.[20]

Caesar had returned to Rome for the first time in nine years. At most, he stayed for a couple of weeks and then pressed on to join the army massing for the Spanish campaign. Mark Antony was left in charge of Italy. From Cicero's correspondence we know that men like Curio, Caelius and Dolabella were all confident that the campaign in Spain would be both swift and successful. Sardinia and Sicily were soon taken without meeting any serious resistance. Caesar had won a victory in the Italian campaign, but it was a hollow one in the sense that Pompey and his army had escaped. The war would go on and was already widening. In time it would spread to virtually all the lands around the Mediterranean. Caesar's enemies were still powerful and would grow stronger. In Italy people were relieved that he had not turned out to be a Sulla, but few had so far been turned into his enthusiastic supporters.[21]

THE ILERDA CAMPAIGN, APRIL TO AUGUST, 49 BC

Caesar described the Pompeians in Spain as an army without a general. Three legates commanded the seven Pompeian legions in the Spanish Peninsula, but they did not prove an effective team. One, Marcus Terentius Varro, was widely respected as a scholar and during his lifetime wrote a long list of books on an exceptionally broad range of subjects. He had a long political association with Pompey, having in 70 BC written a manual for him on the procedures of the Senate. He had served as his legate before and in 49 BC had charge of Further Spain, but seems to have had only modest military ability. During the campaign his army did not join the main Pompeian force and played no significant role. Most of the fighting was done by the remaining five legions under the command of Marcus Petreius and Lucius Afranius. Petreius was the more experienced of the two. He had been in effective control of the army that defeated Catiline in 63 BC. According to Sallust he had already served for thirty years at that time. It is possible that he was the son of one of Marius' senior centurions. By the time of the Civil War he must have been about sixty and, although a very experienced campaigner, had mainly acted as someone else's subordinate. Afranius was the consul for 60 BC, better known as a dancer than for any other talents. He had taken part in several of Pompey's campaigns and so had some military experience, but had never held an independent command. As an ex-consul he was senior to Petreius, but it is unclear whether he took charge or the two men acted as if they had joint authority. In addition to their five legions they had substantial auxiliary forces, including some 10,000 cavalry and eighty cohorts of Spanish infantry. The latter were predominantly heavy infantry (*scutati*), but also included units of light infantrymen (*caetrati*) armed with javelins and small circular shields.[22]

Caesar sent orders for his legate Caius Fabius to take the three legions in the west of the Transalpine province at Narbo and secure the passes of the Pyrenees. Once this was done, Fabius pushed on to close with Afranius and Petreius who had concentrated near the town of Ilerda (modern Lérida). Messengers went to three other legions instructing them to march and join Fabius, along with 5,000 auxiliary infantry and 6,000 allied and auxiliary cavalry. Caesar himself followed, but paused en route outside Massilia. This ancient Greek colony was one of Rome's oldest allies. As proconsul of Gaul he had taken care to honour and favour the community, but the place also had a strong connection with Pompey dating back to the war against Sertorius. Now the city closed its gates to Caesar's men and refused to let him enter. The Massilian magistrates claimed that they did not understand the intricacies of Roman politics, but felt that they could not side with either Caesar or Pompey against the other. This plea of neutrality soon rang a little hollow when they let Domitius Ahenobarbus sail into their harbour with a force raised from his own household and slaves. The latter's family connections with the region may also have encouraged them to welcome him. Unabashed by his recent surrender and release, Domitius Ahenobarbus had finally reached the province he had craved for so many years. The Massiliotes immediately gave him command of the defence and readied themselves to face a siege. Caesar moved three legions to the town and placed them under the command of Caius Trebonius. In support was a squadron of warships under the command of Decimus Brutus, the same man who had led the fleet against the Veneti. After moving them into place and beginning the siege, Caesar left his subordinates to the task and pressed on, escorted by a personal bodyguard of 900 German auxiliary horsemen. It was a busy time, with plans having to be made and appropriate orders despatched. The loss of Massilia to the enemy was a blow, for it was a major port and its facilities and merchant fleet would have been a great asset in supplying the army fighting in Spain. Yet time was not on Caesar's side and he could not afford to wait. However, in spite of the pressures of command he still found time to write letters to prominent men. Cicero received one from him that had been written just a few days before he reached Massilia. In it Caesar urged the orator against any rash act such as joining Pompey.[23]

By the time Caesar joined Fabius in June, the six legions were already concentrated in one force along with most of the allies and auxiliaries. The units were probably the *Sixth*, *Seventh*, *Ninth*, *Tenth*, *Eleventh* and *Fourteenth*. In numbers the enemy may – or may not, since we do not know the strengths of individual units on either side – have had a slight numerical advantage. Spirit and experience were very much in Caesar's favour. In spite of the money taken from the Treasury it remained a struggle to meet all the costs of fighting the war. Therefore, 'at this time he borrowed money from the military tribunes and centurions; and distributed the cash to the soldiers. By doing this he achieved two things at once, since he took a security for the loyalty of the centurions and won the enthusiasm of the legionaries with his largess.' Caesar's army was confident, but the enemy had taken up a strong defensive position. Their main camp was situated on the same ridge as the town of Ilerda itself. A smaller force controlled the bridge over the River Sicoris (modern Segre), which separated the two armies. Before Caesar arrived Fabius had constructed two bridges some 4 miles apart and crossed over to the enemy-held west bank. With two substantial armies sitting in position close to each other over the following days and weeks supply soon became a problem, and both sides regularly sent foraging expeditions to the east side of the river as food and forage became increasingly difficult to obtain. Two of Fabius' legions were out on such an expedition when the bridge they had crossed suddenly collapsed. Fortunately, a relief force crossing by the more distant remaining bridge was able to reach them before they were too badly handled by four legions and a strong force of cavalry sent by Afranius to attack them.[24]

Caesar arrived two days after the skirmish. The broken bridge was almost repaired and under his orders the work was completed during the night. That same day he carried out a thorough reconnaissance, looking particularly at the terrain. The next morning he led out the entire army, save for six cohorts left behind to protect the camp and the bridge, and advanced to form up in battle order at the bottom of the slope in front of the Pompeian camp. Afranius and Petreius responded to this challenge, but deployed their line no more than halfway down the slope, not too far from the rampart of his own camp. In the manner typical of warfare in this period, the two armies then stared at each other for some time, neither wishing to go forward any further and force a battle. Caesar was reluctant to risk fighting with the ground in the enemy's favour. At some point in the day he claims to have learnt – presumably from prisoners or deserters – that it was Afranius' caution that was holding the enemy back. He decided to establish a new camp on the spot, but as on similar occasions in the past was careful to make sure that his troops did not become vulnerable to attack by the nearby enemy during the construction. The legions were formed in the normal *triplex acies*, so Caesar withdrew the cohorts of the third line and set them to digging a 15-foot wide ditch. As an added precaution they did not construct a rampart, since this would have been too visible. Even without its protection, such a wide ditch would seriously obstruct an enemy charge. By the evening it was ready, and Caesar withdrew the rest of the army behind the line of the ditch. During the night he kept the men under arms, but the enemy made no hostile move. On the following day three legions formed up for battle facing the enemy, while the remaining units, sending parties out to fetch the necessary material for a rampart, in the meantime dug ditches leading back at right angles from the first to create a greater semblance of a camp. The covering force easily repelled enemy harassing attacks and the work was completed. The next day ramparts were finally added behind the ditches.[25]

Caesar next attempted to occupy a hillock that dominated the ground between the Pompeian camp and the town of Ilerda. He took three legions with him and sent the leading elements of one of them to seize the hill. Afranius had observed the column marching out and his own men were able to beat them in the race to get there first, driving back Caesar's men as they tried to scramble up the slope. The *Commentaries* lay some of the blame for this failure on the enemy fighting in the same style as the Spanish tribes, moving at speed and caring little about their formation. While this may well be true – Caesar notes that troops stationed in one place for a long time tend to be influenced by local fighting styles – it may also have been intended to depict his enemy as less Roman than his own men. It was harder to excite an audience by a description of fighting against fellow countrymen than against the wild tribes of Gaul. The fighting went on for much of the day, as each side fed in reserves. The position was narrow and no more than three cohorts could fit into the space and form a fighting line. Losses were heavy on both sides, but after five hours men of the *Ninth* Legion had enough energy left to charge sword in hand and close one last time with the enemy. The Pompeians gave way for long enough to allow Caesar's men to withdraw. Caesar lost seventy dead, including a senior centurion of the *Fourteenth* Legion and some 600 wounded, while the enemy suffered around 200 casualties including one *primus pilus* and four other centurions. Both sides believed that they had won, but the basic truth was that Caesar had failed to capture the position he had attacked.[26]

The weather then took a hand, heavy rain causing the river to flood and wash away both of Fabius' bridges. For the moment Caesar and the army were cut off from the supplies brought by allies as well as reinforcement. One party of Gauls coming to join Caesar was attacked by a large enemy raiding force and took some losses before it was able to pull back to a defensive position. All attempts to repair the bridges at first failed and the basic ration had to be cut to a level that could not long be sustained without the soldiers' health suffering badly. After some days the legionaries were set to making simple leather-covered, timber-framed boats of the type they had seen in Britain. Under cover of darkness these were carried in carts to a spot 22 Roman miles away and a small camp was built behind a hill next to the river. Later a legion was sent there and, after sending detachments across to the far bank, was able to build a new bridge in just two days. The Gauls, along with the supply convoy they were escorting, were then able to use the bridge and join the main army. For the moment the crisis was over, but Caesar was no nearer to defeating the enemy. There were encouraging signs when a number of Spanish communities, sensing that the odds were shifting in his favour, sent envoys promising to defect to him. All were asked to supply him with the wheat he so desperately needed. The new bridge was a vital lifeline, but the distance did not make it convenient for all purposes. Caesar's legionaries now dug canals to channel the water of the Sicoris and so create a crude ford. By this time the two Pompeian legates felt that they were too exposed, for the enemy cavalry had grown in numbers and confidence and was making their own foraging difficult. They decided to withdraw to the region occupied by the Celtiberians who were especially well disposed towards Pompey.[27]

They prepared carefully, ordering ships and barges to be gathered all along the River Ebro and brought to the town of Octogesa, some 30 miles from their camp. The craft were used to create a pontoon-style bridge over the wide Ebro. The work did not go unnoticed by Caesar's scouting patrols, and by coincidence the project was completed on the same day as the improvised ford in the Sicoris was felt to be usable. Afranius and Petreius had a route across the biggest obstacle in their path. They knew that once over the Ebro they would be free from immediate pursuit, at least for a few days. However, they also knew that they first needed to get the army as far as Octogesa. Two of their legions crossed the Sicoris by the bridge outside the town and camped on the eastern bank. During the night the rest of the Pompeian army, save for two cohorts left to garrison Ilerda, marched across to join up with the two legions and the entire force then set off towards the Ebro. Caesar's outposts reported the movement, and Caesar sent out cavalry to harass and slow down the enemy column. When the sun rose he could see from the high ground near his camp that the Pompeian rearguard was hard pressed by his own horsemen and was having to stop and form up repeatedly to drive the pursuers back. The legionaries knew what was happening and via the tribunes and centurions urged Caesar to let them risk the man-made ford and go across the river to fight. Encouraged by their enthusiasm, he led out five legions, leaving the remaining unit to guard the camp. The cavalry formed a screen above and below the crossing point, and the troops managed to wade through without suffering any losses. In spite of their later start, the advance guard came up with the Pompeian rearguard by late afternoon. Both armies deployed facing each other, but the Pompeians had no wish to fight and remained on high ground, while Caesar's men were tired. Both armies camped for the night. Ahead of the Pompeians was a line of hills and the two legates planned another night march in order to reach the pass through these before the enemy. The plan failed when it was revealed to Caesar by some prisoners. Though it was still dark he ordered the trumpet call to be sounded that would raise his men. Hearing this, and realising that surprise was lost, the Pompeians went back to camp.[28]

The next day both sides sent out small reconnaissance patrols to investigate the routes through the hills and confirm the presence of a pass some 5 miles away. Whoever gained possession of this would be able to deny the route to the enemy. The night march having failed, the Pompeians decided to move at dawn. Their camp was between Caesar and the pass, but they were encumbered by a baggage train, whereas the Caesareans had only basic equipment and minimal rations. Caesar set out before dawn, surprising his enemies by heading off in a different direction. Relief turned to dismay as his column slowly began to swing to the right and head round towards the pass. The Pompeians set out and the two sides raced to get there first. Caesar's men had a more difficult route, but had started earlier and were more lightly burdened. His cavalry also continued to harass the enemy

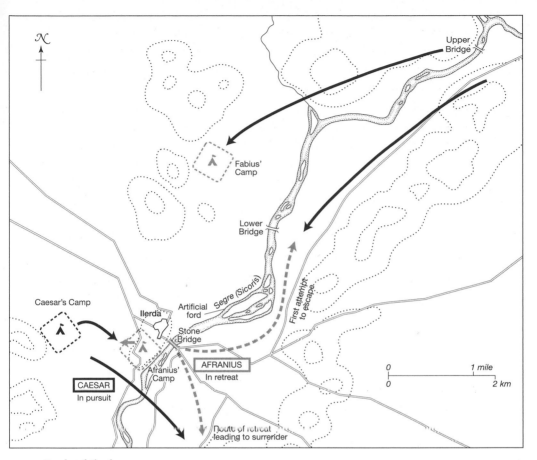

Battle of Ilerda

column and slow it down. The Caesareans won the contest, and Afranius and Petreius halted their despondent troops. The officers and men in Caesar's army were all keen for battle with the enemy at such a disadvantage of position and morale, and pressed him to give the order to attack. Caesar refused, believing that the enemy, cut off from all supplies, would have to surrender anyway. He saw no need to waste the lives of any of his soldiers, or even of the citizens fighting for the enemy. This provoked some muttering from his veterans and half-hearted talk of not fighting whenever he finally did give the order.

Over the next days the two sides began building lines of fortification, the Pompeians to secure a water supply and Caesar to hem them in and deny them this. During the work large numbers of men on both sides began to fraternise with the enemy, seeking out relatives, friends and neighbours.

403

Some Pompeian officers were already speaking of capitulation, and Afranius' own son sent a friend to treat with Caesar. His father's will to go on seems to have collapsed, but Petreius was still determined and led out his bodyguard of Spanish cavalry and light infantry to massacre every Caesarean soldier they found mingling with their own troops. Some managed to fight their way out, while others were hidden by Pompeian troops and allowed to slip away during the night. Caesar let all the enemy troops in his own lines either go freely or stay as they wished. Petreius begged his soldiers to remain loyal and took an oath never 'to desert or betray the army and its officers, or to think of personal safety before the common good'. He cajoled Afranius into taking the same oath, followed by the senior and then the more junior officers, and finally the ordinary soldiers.[29]

The Pompeians made one last attempt to break out of the encirclement. Caesar followed, continually harrying the retreating column. The enemy was again hemmed in, this time in an even worse position with no water supply at all. Caesar still wished to avoid battle and both sides again set to building lines of fortifications. An attempt by the Pompeians to recross the Sicoris was blocked and with their forage almost exhausted Afranius sought peace terms from Caesar. The latter berated the enemy generals for needlessly wasting lives. Nevertheless, as at Corfininium and throughout the war so far, all of them were allowed to go free. Their army was disbanded, Caesar carefully supervising the process. By this time in Further Spain, the remaining legate Varro had been so encouraged by Afranius' earlier, highly optimistic reports, that he decided to prove himself a keen agent of Pompey and the cause. He held levies and massed supplies. After the surrender at Ilerda was complete Caesar headed towards the Further province. Varro's confidence had by this time ebbed as news reached him of Caesar's success and it became apparent that the population of his province was generally well disposed to the victor. His troops deserting him, he swiftly sent word to Caesar and surrendered. All of Spain was now under Caesar's control. Although there were difficult moments, his expectation of rapid success had proved to be justified. By the end of the summer the resistance at Massilia also ended. This time Domitius Ahenobarbus managed to escape by ship shortly before the city surrendered and so was not captured for a second time. He would fight against Caesar again. So would Afranius and Petreius, who like him were ready to accept their enemy's mercy, but did not hate him any the less for it. Nor was there any sign that Pompey and his more senior allies were any more eager for peace other than through victory. The war would go on.[30]

XIX

MACEDONIA,
NOVEMBER 49–AUGUST 48 BC

'Look at Cnaeus Pompey's position, when neither the glory of his name or past deeds, nor even his client kings and states, of which he has so often boasted, can keep him safe, and even the chance of an honourable escape, which even the humblest possess, is denied him; chased out of Italy, Spain lost, his experienced army captured, and now on top of it all blockaded, something which I do not think has ever happened to another general [imperator].' – *Publius Cornelius Dolabella, writing to Cicero from Caesar's camp outside Dyrrachium, May–June 48 BC.*[1]

'But fortune, which has great power in all matters and most of all in war, causes great shifts in human affairs with just a little disturbance.' – *Caesar.*[2]

Caesar left Quintus Cassius Longinus in command in Spain. It was an unusual post for a tribune of the plebs, but these were exceptional times, and Cassius had already served in Spain during his quaestorship so had some experience of the region and its peoples. The choice was not to prove a happy one. Caesar welcomed any man who came to him, rewarding loyalty with honours, office and wealth – he once said that he would faithfully reward even a bandit if the man had done him a service. Cicero and others were scornful of the band of dissolute wastrels who had flocked to join Caesar. They saw them as people who had squandered their own inheritance and now expected to govern the Republic. Suetonius claims that in the years before 49 BC, Caesar often jokingly told such men that they needed a civil war. Certainly there were many desperate men for whom Caesar's victory offered a last chance of wealth and success in public life, but it would be a mistake to take the sweeping judgements of Cicero and Pompeian propaganda at face value. It is true that Caesar's legates and senior subordinates during the Civil War were, with a few exceptions, not notable for their great ability or good character. Several made serious misjudgements. However, the competence and honesty of many of the senior Pompeians were equally questionable, even if these possessed more distinguished names. A high proportion of the ex-consuls in Pompey's camp had faced charges of electoral bribery in the past. Caesar had the advantage of being able to issue orders and did not have to deal with wilfully independent men like Domitius Ahenobarbus. However, it was certainly the case that things tended to go better when Caesar was present. Trebonius and Decimus Brutus had handled the siege of Massilia efficiently. Curio had secured Sicily without fighting, for Cato, sent by the Pompeians to command the island, had no significant forces at his disposal and had seen no point in wasting any lives in a hopeless defence. After this success Curio took legions to North Africa in the summer of 49 BC. At first he did well, routing a strong Pompeian force, but he was then lured into an ambush by the Numidian army of King Juba. Curio died fighting along with many of his soldiers. Others were slaughtered as they fled or surrendered only to be executed on the king's orders. Only a handful escaped, including Asinius Pollio, and it may well have been Caesar's flattering portrayal of Curio that made Pollio later question the reliability of some passages in the *Commentaries*. A smaller defeat was suffered by Mark Antony's younger brother, Lucius, who surrendered in Illyricum along with fifteen cohorts.[3]

News of these setbacks reached Caesar as he returned from Spain. They were unfortunate, but the initiative still lay with him and he was determined to confront Pompey and the main enemy army as soon as possible. Perhaps more worrying was a mutiny that broke out amongst his legions when they had camped at Placentia (modern Piacenza) in northern Italy. The trouble began amongst the *Ninth*, who had fought well for Caesar in Spain, and like many mutinies throughout history had a range of causes, with festering grievances coming to the surface during a period of rest and inactivity. With the war far from decided their general needed them, and many legionaries must have guessed that this placed them in a strong position to bargain for favours. Some of the men had now served their full term and wanted to be discharged. More complained that they had not yet received the bounty of 500 denarii that he had promised them at Brundisium earlier in the year. There was also resentment that the mildness and clemency with which he was waging war was delaying their victory and – and this was probably most important – depriving them of plunder. Caesar was still at Massilia when he received a report of the mutiny, but at once hastened to the spot and confronted the mutineers. The proconsul's tone was stern and unrelenting as he explained that such a great conflict could not be hurried. He then announced that he intended to decimate the *Ninth*, an ancient punishment that involved selecting by lot one out of every ten men to be beaten to death by his comrades. The remainder of the legion would be dishonourably discharged from the army. The veteran soldiers were dismayed and their officers began to beg their stern commander for mercy. Caesar knew how to work a crowd and gradually gave ground, finally saying that only 120 ringleaders would need to draw lots to choose twelve men to be executed. The selection is supposed to have been rigged to ensure that the names of the main troublemakers were drawn. However, Appian claims that one man who had not even been in the camp during the mutiny was included in the twelve. As soon as Caesar discovered this, he released the soldier and replaced him with the centurion who had tried to arrange the death of an innocent man in this way. It was the first time since 58 BC that Caesar had faced any serious disobedience on the part of his soldiers, but the outbreak was quickly suppressed. The *Ninth* would fight with great distinction for Caesar in the forthcoming campaign, as would his other troops. The *Commentaries* make no mention of the whole affair.[4]

Since he had slipped away from the enemy at Brundisium in March, Pompey had been exercising all his organisational skill to create the army with which he would win final victory. At the same time he used his connections in the region – nearly every community and certainly all major rulers were amongst his clients – to mobilise the manpower and resources of the eastern Mediterranean, to provide his soldiers with pay, food and equipment, and to supplement their numbers with allies and auxiliaries. He had nine legions, a mixture of the troops he had brought with him and newly levied units from the citizens settled or resident in Greece and Asia. Metellus Scipio had gone to Syria and would in time bring two legions that had been stationed on the border with Parthia. Frantic diplomatic activity had ensured that the latter would not threaten the province, but it is hard to know whether our sources are correct to claim that serious attempts were made to seek military aid from the Parthians. Pompey certainly did make extensive use of foreign troops and amassed a particularly strong force of cavalry. The raw material of a great army was there and as the months went by Pompey dedicated himself to training the inexperienced soldiers. He was fifty-seven, and until the Civil War began had not served in the field for more than thirteen years, but everyone is said to have been impressed with his energy. Their commander trained with the men, going through the drills with legionary equipment or mounting a horse and demonstrating to the cavalry how they were to fight. Plutarch says that he could throw a javelin further, more accurately and with greater force than many a younger man. Inspired by his example, a strong and effective army began to take shape. As the year went on, the Pompeians grew steadily more powerful.[5]

During Caesar's absence there had also been a slow trickle of senators leaving Italy and deciding to end their neutrality and join the Pompeians. Some went because they judged that Pompey would win and wished to join the victors. For others it was a matter of conscience or persuasion by family and friends. It was a strange feature of the Civil War that letters continued to be exchanged freely and men remained in regular contact with correspondents on both sides. The most distinguished of those who decided at this stage to play a more active role in the conflict was Cicero, who had sailed to Greece after much soul searching. He still felt the Civil War unnecessary and hated Pompey's plan of abandoning Rome and Italy. Caesar's clemency had cheered him, although he was not sure how long this would last and whether Caesar would prove himself as cruel as Cinna had been in the eighties BC as soon as his dominance was secure. Curio had paid him a visit on his way to invade Sicily and done little to assuage his fears. The tribune had openly said that he thought Caesar's moderation was purely a matter of policy, which conflicted with his naturally cruel disposition. In time the veil would be drawn aside and his true nature revealed. These were somewhat strange words from an ally, but Curio had never been one to restrain his speech. However, he did not know Caesar well, having only joined him a year before, so his judgement may be questioned. Latter events would show that Caesar did not abandon his merciful treatment of his enemies and never attempted to rule by fear. Throughout his life it is hard to see any real trace of cruelty. He could be utterly ruthless if he felt that this was advantageous, and had a coldly furious temper, but was never cruel simply for the sake of cruelty. Cicero was unsure about how Caesar would behave in the long run. His feelings about Pompey were similar and he judged that whoever won the Civil War would then be effectively a dictator, possessing royal power or *regnum*. Yet always there remained his deep attachment to Pompey and his respect for the distinguished men who fought alongside him. In each case it was often more respect for the sort of men he felt they ought to have been, rather than necessarily the ones they actually were, but it was no less strong for that. He also hated inactivity, but did not feel willing to join in the politics of a Republic controlled by Caesar. In spite of letters from his friends and family in Caesar's camp, and from Caesar himself, Cicero eventually decided that he must stand with the Pompeians. His brother Quintus, in spite of his years as Caesar's legate in Gaul, did the same.[6]

There were defections, but the bulk of the Senate still remained neutral, and Caesar continued to maintain at least a façade of normal public life at Rome. He wished now to become consul for 48 BC, but there was no existing consul to preside over elections. A praetor was available, but a praetor had never supervised the appointment of new consuls, and when Caesar proposed this it was rejected by the college of augurs. Instead the praetor Marcus Lepidus appointed Caesar dictator so that he could hold the elections. There was a single precedent for this, dating back to the darkest days of the Second Punic War. Caesar returned to Rome, summoned the *Comitia Centuriata* and was duly made consul for the following year with Publius Servilius Vatia Isauricus as his colleague. It was unorthodox, though strictly speaking legal, although it is perfectly possible that there were no other candidates in the elections then held. Caesar would be consul again in 48 BC, the proper ten years after his first consulship. His colleague was the son of the man under whom he had served in Asia during the seventies BC, and was very much a member of the established elite, married to a niece of Cato. It was another indication of how complex and confusing loyalties were during the Civil War.

Elections were also held for the other magistracies – Caelius Rufus became praetor – and then afterwards Caesar used his powers as dictator to pass a series of laws. One recalled from exile all of those condemned by Pompey's extraordinary courts in 52 BC. Milo was specifically excluded, so that in the main those benefiting from this were men associated with Clodius. Caesar also recalled men such as Sallust, who had been expelled by Appius Claudius during his censorship, as well as Gabinius, the Syrian governor who had restored Ptolemy to the Egyptian throne. Both would fight for him during the war. Full political rights were also finally restored to the children of the victims of Sulla's proscriptions. Such measures were mainly intended to confirm the loyalty of his supporters and win him new ones. Of more general concern was the problem of debt, as the value of property had in some cases plummeted since the war began. There was pressure for an abolition of debt, especially from those – many of whom had joined him – who owed huge sums of money. The cry of 'new tablets' (*novae tabulae*) – meaning rubbing out all account books and starting from scratch – had been a frequent one in recent decades, and a major rallying call of Catiline's rebels. Many feared that Caesar, well known as a *popularis* and a frequent debtor himself –

would seek support in the same way. However, the dictator refused to employ such a drastic measure and instead sought a compromise. Assessors were appointed to value all property at its pre-war value, and debtors were then made to give this to their creditors in payment. An old regulation was also revived which stipulated that no one was supposed to have more than 15,000 denarii in hard cash. The aim was to deter hoarding, which was bound to have an impact on the economic life of Rome and Italy. Such a measure was inevitably difficult to enforce.[7]

THE GREAT CLASH

After just eleven days Caesar resigned the dictatorship and left Rome. He did not wait for January to take up his consulship in the normal way, but hastened to Brundisium where he had ordered his army to concentrate. Despite the best efforts of his officers during the last six months, there was still a serious shortage of transport vessels. Caesar had twelve legions – probably some 25,000–30,000 effectives, for they had suffered casualties, and many stragglers and convalescents had been left behind on the march back from Spain – in or near Brundisium, but there were only enough ships to transport 15,000 infantry and 500 cavalry. Even these troops would have to travel with the barest minimum of baggage, while the low proportion of horsemen was simply a reflection of the much greater space required by their mounts. It was obvious that more than one crossing would need to be made, but there was a great risk that the troops landed first would be overwhelmed by the enemy. Even the initial voyage would be dangerous, for the Pompeians had amassed a very large fleet of some 500 warships and many smaller vessels used for scouting. The bulk of this was under the command of Bibulus and was stationed in ports along the eastern Adriatic shore to intercept any invasion force. Caesar had only twelve war galleys, certainly not enough to protect the transport ships if they were caught by the enemy navy, and every trip needed to ferry his army across the Adriatic faced this serious threat. Caesar understood these factors, but also knew that they were unlikely to change in the immediate future. He was eager to strike at the heart of the enemy, knowing that waiting would only give Pompey time to grow stronger and better prepared. Bad weather delayed him for some weeks and it was not until 4 January 48 BC that he set sail. Twelve months earlier no one had expected him to attack in the winter months when armies normally rested. The same was true this time. Pompey's legions were dispersed in winter quarters and Bibulus' fleet was not ready. Caesar was able to cross and disembark at Paeleste on the coast of Epirus without any opposition. This was done quickly and the ships sent back to Brundisium on the same night, but by this time the enemy had realised what was happening and managed to catch a few vessels. Caesar claims that Bibulus was so enraged that he ordered these ships to be burned along with their crews. The vast majority of the transports got back safely, but it was clear that the next convoy would face a warned and waiting enemy.[8]

For the moment Caesar was cut off from reinforcements and supply convoys. He had seven legions, each with an average strength of about 2,140 men, as well as the 500 cavalry, but there had been no room to carry significant quantities of food and they would need to rely on obtaining this locally. The Roman calendar was currently running weeks ahead of the natural seasons, so in reality it was late autumn, and he would need to find some way of keeping the army concentrated and fed during the coming winter months while still operating against the enemy. On the night after the landing Caesar marched against Oricum, which quickly surrendered when the townsfolk turned against the small Pompeian garrison. The *Commentaries* report that they were unwilling to fight against a man holding legal *imperium* on behalf of the Roman people. A rational calculation that the Pompeians were unlikely to win this encounter may also have contributed to their decision. With much of the population of Italy not strongly committed to either side, it was unsurprising that there was little trace of any stronger sentiment in most of the provinces. The garrison commander, Lucius Manlius Torquatus, was as usual spared by Caesar and chose to remain with him. After this success Caesar pushed on to Apollonia, and once again the population refused to fight against him, forcing the Pompeians to flee. Most of Epirus soon followed the example of these towns and went over to Caesar. He had secured a base in Greece and for the moment the towns were able to keep his army supplied. Some food stores gathered by the enemy had been captured, although one convoy of grain ships anchored near Oricum was scuttled by the Pompeians sailing as escort. Pompey's main supply depot was at the great trading port of Dyrrachium (modern Durazzo in Albania), further north along the coast. Caesar made a drive to capture this great prize, but by this time the enemy was beginning to react. Pompey ordered his legions to concentrate, force-marched the men to Dyrrachium and arrived before Caesar, who promptly withdrew. The enemy had nine legions, each much closer to their proper strength, and must have outnumbered Caesar by more than two to one. Yet the morale of the

Pompeians seems to have been shaken by the unexpected enemy landing and their initial successes. Labienus made a public profession of his faith in Pompey, taking an oath never to desert him and to share his fortune. He was followed by the tribunes and centurions, and finally all of the legionaries collectively made the same vow.[9]

Caesar retired to Epirus. Although he controlled the ports of Apollonia and Oricum, Bibulus' fleet was now very active, imposing a tight blockade. One convoy carrying reinforcements of legionaries and cavalry was forced to turn back to Brundisium, and lost a single ship. Bibulus had all the men on board executed, regardless of their rank. Perhaps he hoped that such a display of brutality would help to deter further attempts to get through to Caesar, but his deep-seated hatred of his former colleague as aedile, praetor and consul doubtless fed his anger. Personal sorrow probably also played a part, for his two eldest sons had recently been murdered in Egypt. Bibulus fought with a dreadful savagery, but was not unique in this. From the beginning of the war few of the Pompeians had shown any inclination to compete with Caesar in displays of clemency and moderation. If anything, his policy, with its obvious implication of his personal superiority, seemed only to increase their rage and stir them to further atrocities. Cicero had been shocked by the attitudes he encountered in Pompey's camp. Most of the leading Pompeians declared that men who had remained neutral were almost as bad as Caesar's active partisans, and there was talk of widespread punishment when they finally led the army back to Italy.[10]

Caesar camped near the River Apsus, not far from Apollonia. Pompey's larger army took up a position on the opposite bank but showed no inclination to attack and force a battle. There was another attempt at negotiation, initiated when Caesar sent back one of Pompey's officers, whom he had captured for the second time. He suggested that both he and his opponent take an oath to dismiss their armies within three days – a seemingly fair if probably impractical measure – and then rely on the Senate and People to arbitrate in their dispute. No response came from Pompey at first, but Caesar was content to wait, in the hope that more of his troops would be able to join him from Italy. In the meantime he put pressure on Bibulus' fleet by denying them landing places on the coast. War galleys had very large crews for their size, since they relied on the strength of many rowers for their speed and manoeuvrability. There was little space for carrying food and fresh water, and even less space for the rowers to move around or rest, since their combined body weight acted as ballast to keep the ship stable. Therefore, it was necessary to land at regular intervals – at the barest minimum every third day – so that they could resupply and allow the rowers and crew to recover. Ancient fleets acted best when they had bases nearby or when closely supported by land forces. Caesar's men controlled the harbours and watched the coast, attacking any ships that tried to land, forcing Bibulus' men to return to their bases on the island of Corcyra more regularly than they would wish. Added to the severe winter weather, imposing the blockade became a great strain for the Pompeian fleet. Bibulus asked for a truce, but sent his senior subordinate Lucius Scribonius Libo to the talks, excusing his own absence by saying that his personal animosity towards Caesar and his natural hot temper was likely to hinder agreement. Libo's daughter was married to Pompey's younger son Sextus, again showing the close family links between many of the leading Pompeians. Caesar went to the meeting, but was disappointed when Libo simply asked for a truce, during which the Pompeian ships would be free to land as they wished, and promised only to refer anything else to Pompey for his consideration. Caesar replied by stating that he would only permit such a truce if the enemy ended their blockade. He asked Libo to give safe conduct to envoys he would send to Pompey. Neither request was granted and, as the *Commentaries* put it, 'when Caesar understood that his entire speech was framed with a view to the present danger and the shortage of supplies, and that he offered no hope or serious offer of peace, he returned to his plans for continuing the war'.[11]

Bibulus succumbed to disease and fatigue soon afterwards. No one was appointed to replace him as overall commander of the fleet, but still the Pompeians maintained the blockade in spite of the difficulties. At the Apsus, the rival armies continued to stare at each other from the opposite banks. There were more negotiatons. At one point Vatinius went to the river bank and called out to the enemy outposts until finally he was told that an officer would come for a meeting the next day. This occurred, but was interrupted by the angry intervention of Labienus and ended in a shower of missiles. Caesar's former legate shouted out afterwards that they could, 'Stop all talk of peace terms; there was no possibility of peace until Caesar's head was brought to them!' Shortly before this Pompey himself is supposed to have said that he would not even consider peace if it looked as if he was holding on to life through 'Caesar's generosity'. The stand-off continued and Caesar grew increasingly desperate as the weeks and months went by without any reinforcement from Italy. Several sources claim that he grew suspicious of the determination and loyalty of his subordinates in Italy. Deciding that only his own presence could impart the necessary energy, he decided to go to Brundisium in person. He did so in disguise, pretending to be one of his own slaves who were often employed as messengers, aboard a small merchant ship anchored near the mouth of the River Aous. As the craft headed down river to the sea the crew had to struggle against a strong wind blowing in from the sea. After a while, the sailors decided to give up the attempt and turn back, but Caesar suddenly threw back his cloak and told them not to be afraid because they carried 'Caesar and Caesar's good fortune'. The rowers and helmsman redoubled their efforts, trying to force the craft out to sea, but in the end were forced to give up. It is extremely questionable whether a general should have left his army in such circumstances, even if this was to fetch reinforcements, and it was probably for this reason that no mention of the incident is made in the *Commentaries*. However, Plutarch claims that when his legionaries discovered what had happened, they did not feel abandoned, but merely offended that their commander did not feel confident in winning with them alone. As he returned to camp the men are supposed to have clustered around him, imploring him to have more faith in them. It was a mark of the incredible bond and trust between general and soldiers that had grown up since the early days in Gaul.[12]

DYRRACHIUM

Eventually, on 10 April, Mark Antony was finally able to bring the bulk of the troops across from Brundisium to Greece, landing near Lissus in the north with four legions and 800 cavalry. Pompey was too slow to prevent the two Caesarean forces from joining together. Caesar now had a more powerful army at his disposal. He was still outnumbered, especially in cavalry, but could rely on the better quality of his veteran legionaries to counterbalance this. However, the arrival of more troops increased the problems of supply, especially if the army was forced to remain in one place for any length of time. A number of large detachments were sent away from the main army to protect his allies in Thessaly and Macedonia. With the remainder Caesar offered battle to Pompey, who refused to be drawn. He remained convinced that the Caesareans could be worn down by depriving them of food. Caesar was aware of the danger and decided to try once again to capture Pompey's main supply base at Dyrrachium. This time he managed to get there before the enemy, although not quickly enough to capture the town and its supplies. Instead he pitched camp between Dyrrachium and the Pompeian army, which took up position on a hill called Petra, overlooking a natural harbour. With ready access to the sea, Pompey was able to keep in easy communication with the town itself and his forces elsewhere. He sent orders instructing grain convoys to be brought directly to the army from as far afield as Asia. Caesar's camp was on high ground inland and his troops would have to rely on gathering food and forage from the surrounding lands. He decided to construct a line of fortifications on the hills, both to protect his own foraging parties and to hinder those sent out by the Pompeians, who had far more cavalry mounts and supply animals and so even greater requirements than his own forces. In addition 'he wished to reduce Pompey's prestige (*auctoritas*) amongst foreign nations, when the story spread around the world that he was besieged by Caesar and was afraid to fight a battle'. Pompey could not afford to withdraw and allow Caesar to capture Dyrrachium and its depots. Therefore, he set his own men to constructing a fortified line facing Caesar. Skirmishes were fought to secure key points along the high ground, and in one instance a detachment of the *Ninth* had to be ordered to retire from a position where it was too exposed to enemy archers and slingers. At one point the legion turned around and, led by Mark Antony, charged and routed their pursuers to demonstrate that they were not retiring because they had been defeated, but through choice. When completed, the Pompeian line was 15 Roman miles long and strengthened by twenty-four forts. Caesar was on the outside, and inevitably his line had to be larger, especially since he hoped to hem the enemy in completely, and his siegeworks eventually stretched for some 17 miles.[13]

Caesar's men were short of food, for it was still winter by the natural seasons even if by the calendar it was well into spring. Livestock was reasonably plentiful, so that meat was usually available and came to form a greater than usual proportion of the diet. Grain was hard to come by and often the men had to be content with barley – usually reserved for animal feed – rather than wheat. Even this could not always be found and sometimes they had to make do with the root of a plant called charax, which could be mixed with milk and baked into a sort of loaf. When Pompey saw some of these loaves his rueful comment was that they were fighting beasts rather than men. Caesar's men had good access to water supplies, but he ordered them to divert or dam the streams that flowed through their lines into the enemy position. The Pompeians had plenty of food, since supplies were constantly coming in by sea, but began to run short of water. Pompey ordered them to dig new wells, but this was only partially successful. A very large number of men were concentrated in a small area within their siege lines and apart from the soldiers and servants there were many animals. Priority for fodder and water was given to cavalry mounts, and large numbers of baggage and pack animals started to die or were deliberately killed. In the crowded camps disease – perhaps typhus, but the descriptions in our sources are somewhat vague – also broke out. Both sides were suffering, for this was effectively a siege carried out on an enormous scale, but now that they were committed neither commander wished to back down, and the enemy's problems only encouraged them to persist. Caesar felt that his own confidence was shared by his soldiers. At times they threw loaves of charax into the enemy lines to taunt them with this sign of their determination. As the weeks went by and the crops in the fields started to ripen there was further encouragement with the prospect of plentiful grain. Caesar anyway claims that some of his sentries were overheard saying that they would eat the bark from trees before letting Pompey escape.[14]

The building of the fortified lines went on, Caesar still hoping to complete his encirclement so that Pompey would be forced either to escape by sea, to break through Caesar's lines or to watch his army wither. Skirmishes and raids continued. The Pompeian archers and slingers took to shooting at or near the fires visible in Caesar's lines. In response the soldiers sat or slept away from the flames, preferring to be concealed and cold rather than warm but at risk. Pompey then launched a series of major attacks on a number of sections of Caesar's fortifications, testing their strength and probing for weak spots. One attempt to capture a key hill was repelled when Publius Cornelius Sulla – the dictator's nephew, for his son Faustus Sulla was with the Pompeians – brought up two legions to reinforce the threatened fort. The Pompeians were routed, but Sulla chose not to counter-attack and exploit the situation. Caesar approved his caution as appropriate for a legate, since such decisions were the prerogative of the commander-in-chief. The *Commentaries* proudly reported the bravery of Caesar's legionaries. In one sector three cohorts of the *Ninth* held off an entire legion supported by large numbers of allied archers and slingers. After a day of bitter fighting virtually every one of the defenders was wounded, although clearly a good number were still able and willing to fight. Most of the wounds were caused by missiles – 30,000 arrows are said to have been picked up within the fort after the last attacks had been beaten off. Four out of the six centurions in one cohort were hit in the face and lost an eye. The shield of one centurion, a man named Scaeva, had been hit by no less than 120 missiles. Other sources tell us that he was one of the men hit in the eye, but in spite of this wound and others to the thigh and shoulder, kept fighting. At one point he feigned

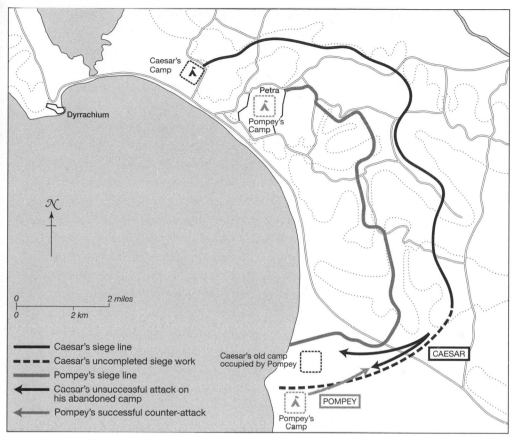

The lines at Dyrrachium

a willingness to surrender and then, when the enemy rushed forward, killed one and lopped the arm off another. Scaeva and his men then stood their ground, their defiance so intimidating the Pompeians that none dared to advance against them. Scaeva may have served with Caesar for many years, possibly having been with him during his time as propraetor in Spain as well as the years in Gaul. Their commander now rewarded the entire cohort lavishly, doubling their pay, awarding decorations to many of them, issuing them with new clothes and – at the time this may have been the most valued, although we should never doubt the importance of pride for good soldiers – an extra grain ration. Scaeva was promoted to *primus pilus*, the senior centurion of the legion, and given a bounty of 200,000 sestertii. It was not his last service to Caesar, and in later years he seems to have become an equestrian and for a while led a unit of auxiliary cavalry that took his own name – the *ala Scaevae*.[15]

417

The attacks had been repulsed, but it was difficult for Caesar with fewer troops to hold a longer line than the enemy. The *Commentaries* claim that the Pompeians suffered around 2,000 casualties, including a number of centurions, one of whom was the son of a former praetor. In contrast Caesar lost only twenty dead, although even he implies that the number of wounded was substantial. It is questionable how soon Scaeva and many of his men would have been able to return to duty. After this burst of fighting Pompey's men spent several days working hard to strengthen vulnerable parts of the line of fortification, raising the rampart to a height of 15 feet. Caesar countered by leading his army out for battle each morning and deploying in a line just out of catapult range of the enemy fortifications. Pompey felt that it would have lowered his own prestige and the confidence of his men if he did not respond, but formed his legions with the rear line of cohorts of the *triplex acies* only just in front of his rampart. He had no desire to fight, feeling that it was better to starve the enemy into submission. A battle was more likely to favour Caesar's veterans than his own inexperienced legionaries, especially in the rough ground between the lines where it would have been difficult to exploit his superiority in cavalry. Caesar refused to give the order for an attack. The slope favoured the Pompeians, who would have had the additional benefit of support from missiles thrown or shot from the rampart behind them. Caesar contented himself with the knowledge that his soldiers would see this as a reluctance on the part of the Pompeians to face them on anything like equal terms. For the moment Caesar seems to have despaired of successfully negotiating with Pompey, but he made an indirect approach by sending an envoy with a personal letter to Metellus Scipio, who had arrived in Macedonia with the legions from Syria. In the meantime, to add to the pressure on Pompey, Caesar's legionaries extended their fortifications to block the two approaches to Dyrrachium itself. Pompey had sent a force of cavalry by sea to land near the town. Around the same time he may have made an attempt to capture the town with a surprise night attack, possibly after a traitor had offered to admit his men. The attempt failed, but the additional fortifications made it even harder for Pompey's cavalry to find sufficient fodder and after a few days they were taken by ship back to his main position within his own fortifications. By this time the horses were being fed mainly on leaves and reeds, since not enough proper feed could be brought by ships from Corcyra or even further afield.[16]

Pompey realised that his own army was suffering as much, perhaps even more than the enemy, and decided that he needed to seize back the initiative once again. An opportunity came with the desertion of two Gaulish noblemen, the brothers Roucillus and Egus. They were the sons of one of the main chieftains of the Allobroges from Transalpine Gaul and had served with Caesar for many years, leading a contingent of tribal cavalry with some distinction. Characteristically he had rewarded their loyalty well, making them senators, probably within their own tribe, although some have preferred to take the more natural reading of this passage to suggest that he had actually enrolled them in the Senate at Rome. It is certainly probable that the men were citizens. However, more recently the brothers had taken to siphoning off much of their men's pay and also sending in false returns of the number of warriors they had to claim extra money and rations. In the end their own troopers went and complained to Caesar, who delayed making a formal decision, but privately spoke to them and warned them to stop these corrupt practices. The brothers realised that they had become unpopular and feared punishment in the future, so soon began to plan their escape. They borrowed substantial sums of money – the rumour was that they wished to make recompense to their men – and started buying up horses. A plan to murder the overall commander of Caesar's cavalry was abandoned as impractical, so Roucillus and Egus then simply rode over to the enemy lines. With them went their household warriors, whose oaths of loyalty ensured that they must always follow their chieftains. Pompey was pleased, for up until this point no one had deserted from Caesar's army during the entire campaign. He had them paraded around his lines and shown to the troops as a sign that the enemy must be weakening when two distinguished men chose to abandon them. Even more usefully the brothers had held senior positions and so were well acquainted with Caesar's lines of fortification and the routine of his army.[17]

Armed with this information, Pompey prepared for another major attack that was intended to break through Caesar's lines and end the blockade. During the day his legionaries made wicker coverings for their helmets. These reduced the chance of the bronze glinting and so revealing their position when it caught the light, but also added further protection, taking some of the force out of a missile. This was especially important for stones flung from a sling or thrown by hand, which could concuss a man even without penetrating his helmet. The point chosen for the attack was the southernmost sector of Caesar's lines where these came closest to the sea. Knowing that these were vulnerable, he had ordered the construction of an additional line behind the first, but work on this and on a wall at right angles to join the two together had not yet finished. Archers and light infantry, along with equipment for filling the enemy ditch and scaling the wall, were sent to the spot in boats. At midnight Pompey himself led out the main force of sixty cohorts. The attack began just before dawn and fell heavily on the *Ninth*, which was on duty in this sector. The Pompeians' helmet covers proved very effective against flung stones, while the incomplete fortifications allowed the lines to be outflanked and quickly infiltrated. The two cohorts on the spot were driven off, and other units sent up in support failed to stem the rout and were quickly put to flight themselves. All save one of the centurions of the legion's first cohort were killed and the eagle standard was only saved when its bearer flung it over the rampart of the nearest fort. It was not until Mark Antony brought up twelve cohorts from further along the line that the situation began to stabilise. Messages – many through a system of smoke signals that had been arranged to allow communication between the different forts in the line – summoned more reserves, accompanied now by Caesar himself. The fort was held, but the Pompeians controlled the positions closest to the sea and were building a camp there. They had punched a hole in Caesar's line and would now be able to forage more freely over a wide area.[18]

Caesar built a new camp for a strong force facing the one built by Pompey's men. In this area was another fort about half a mile from Pompey's main camp. It had originally been built by the *Ninth*, but was subsequently abandoned when the layout of this sector of the fortifications was changed. Later, the site had then been occupied and modified by the enemy, but these had also left after a few days. Now, Caesar's scouts reported that a Pompeian force, roughly equivalent to a legion in size, was moving towards this position. Later patrols confirmed that the old fort now housed a legion. Caesar felt that his opponent had left this unit exposed and sensed an opportunity to win a local victory that would help to balance the recent enemy success. He left two cohorts to guard his own lines and took the rest of the immediately available troops – some thirty-three cohorts, although these included the *Ninth*, which was still shaken and had lost many centurions – on a march that took them to the fort by a roundabout route. The deception was successful and Pompey was unaware of the threat until Caesar's men had actually begun their attack. After a stiff fight the fort was stormed, the legionaries hacking apart the barrier of stakes that blocked its main gateway. However, things then started to go badly wrong. Although Caesar's men were past the outer wall of the fort, there was another smaller enclosure within this and the garrison managed to cling on within this protection. Meanwhile, the cohorts of the right wing were unfamiliar with this stretch of the line and got lost, following a rampart that led away from their objective when they mistook this for one of the walls of the fort. Although puzzled that they had not encountered a gateway, the units kept going, and were followed by Caesar's cavalry. By this time Pompey had responded, launching an immediate counter-attack with the five legions working to fortify his new camp, their approach inspiring the survivors of the garrison to renewed enthusiasm. A large body of Pompeian cavalry also headed towards Caesar's right wing, and the Caesarean horsemen dissolved into panic, fearing that their line of retreat back to their own lines would be cut off. The situation was confused, the panic quickly infectious. The right wing crumbled first, but as men saw this happening the rest of the attacking force also began to flee. Some men were trapped in the ditches around the camp as the cohorts dissolved into a mob and each man tried to force his way past his comrades. As the *Commentaries* put it, 'everywhere there was chaos, terror and flight, so much so that when Caesar took hold of the standards carried by fleeing men and ordered them to stop, some spurred their horses past him without stopping and fled, while others in their fear even dropped their standards, and not a single one halted.' This time Caesar was unable to steady the line as he had done at the Sambre and on many other occasions. The accounts from other sources report an even less heroic incident, claiming that one of the fleeing men actually tried to stab Caesar with the spike at the butt end of his standard. The commander was only saved because one of his bodyguards was faster and sliced off the man's arm with his sword.[19]

The attack had ended in costly failure, Caesar losing 960 soldiers, 32 tribunes and centurions, and a number of other senior officers. The Pompeians captured 32 standards as marks of their success, along with a number of prisoners. However, Pompey contented himself with repulsing the attack and made no attempt to assault Caesar's lines. This was widely felt to have been a mistake, since his men were elated at a time when the Caesareans were badly demoralised. Caesar himself declared that the enemy 'would have won today, if only they were commanded by a winner'. In the aftermath Labienus asked to be given charge of the captured legionaries and, mockingly calling them 'comrades', had them all executed in clear sight of the enemy lines. On the next day Caesar paraded his men and spoke to them, just as he had done after Gergovia. He reminded them of that earlier defeat and how that had been followed by their great victory. He encouraged them with just how much they had achieved, confining a bigger enemy army for so long, and urged them to make up for yesterday's failure by fighting all the harder in the next encounter. His reprimands were mild, as were his punishments, contenting himself with demoting a number of the standard-bearers. The soldiers greeted his appeal with enthusiasm and some of his officers even urged him to risk a battle. Caesar was less confident that his men had recovered sufficiently from the defeat, and may also have realised that there was no reason why Pompey should accept his challenge. It was clear now that the attempt to blockade the Pompeians had failed. The enemy had captured one end of his encircling line of fortifications and he did not have the resources to construct a new, inevitably longer line to box them in once more. Pompey's army could now supplement the supplies brought by sea with those foraged locally. Caesar knew that he had failed in his objective, but as he had told his men was determined to make sure that the campaign still ended in victory. He decided to withdraw, marching away from the sea where it was so easy for his enemy to resupply. During the night he sent one legion to escort his baggage train and large numbers of wounded men to Apollonia. An hour or two before dawn he set out with the rest of the army, apart from two legions who formed the rearguard and remained in the lines. These men sounded the normal trumpet calls that woke the army to a new day. The Pompeians were deceived, and the rearguard was able to follow and rejoin the main force. Pompey sent his cavalry in pursuit, but these were held off by Caesar's outnumbered horsemen closely supported by 400 legionaries marching in battle order. After a few skirmishes the two armies broke contact, as Pompey did not chose to follow Caesar straightaway.[20]

PHARSALUS, 9 AUGUST, 48 BC

As Caesar's army marched away from the enemy it moved into regions that had not yet been visited by foraging parties from either army. By this time it was summer and the new grain crops had ripened sufficiently to be harvested by the hungry soldiers. Caesar was also rejoined by some of the detached troops, which helped to replace some of his losses. However, as news spread of his defeat at Dyrrachium, some communities decided that it would be a mistake to aid a leader who looked likely to lose the war. At Gomphi the city's magistrates closed the gates and refused to admit his men. Caesar refused to tolerate this challenge. His army stormed the town, which was then sacked, the drunken soldiers killing, raping and plundering at will. The magistrates committed suicide. When the army moved away on the following day, some sources claim that its progress was more of a drunken revel than a disciplined march. Curiously, it was also claimed that the debauch greatly improved the health of many of the men who had suffered during the food shortages and heavy labour in the lines outside Dyrrachium. It was the first time since the start of the Civil War that Caesar had permitted his men to mistreat the population of a captured town, and was clearly a deliberate display of ruthlessness. Fear of suffering the same fate as Gomphi ensured that other cities and towns in the region all welcomed Caesar's army.[21]

Dyrrachium was undoubtedly a victory for the Pompeians and a mood of elation spread throughout their camp, for this was the first time since the beginning of the Civil War that Caesar had suffered a reverse. Most confident of all were the senior officers, who now felt that only decisive action was necessary to end the war. Afranius urged Pompey to use his naval power to take the army back to Italy, so that they could reoccupy Rome and take from Caesar any pretence that he represented the true Republic. Others, particularly men like Domitius Ahenobarbus, argued that Caesar was now at their mercy and should be brought to battle and crushed as soon as possible. Pompey remained more cautious and still had great respect for the fighting power of Caesar's veterans. He had always planned to return to Italy at some point, but with Caesar still at large, he was nervous that it might seem as if he had been forced into another evacuation by sea. More importantly this would leave his father-in-law Scipio, who with his Syrian legions had still not yet reached the main army, at the mercy of Caesar's larger army. Pompey preferred to stay in Greece, but still believed that fighting a battle was both unwise and, at least at the moment, unnecessary. Better to shadow the enemy and wear them down by depriving them of supplies.

This caution was not popular with his more distinguished allies. Ahenobarbus took to calling him Agammemnon – the King of Mycenae who had led the Greeks in the ten-year struggle at Troy – or 'King of Kings' and accusing him of prolonging the war to maintain his own supremacy. If Cicero, who had a deep affection for Pompey, openly spoke of the Civil War being a question of whether Pompey or Caesar would hold supreme power, then it is unsurprising that others were even more suspicious of his motives. With victory now eagerly expected in the near future, many men were looking to secure for themselves a generous share in the spoils. Some sent agents to Rome to buy them a grander house closer to the Forum – especially one that was owned by one of Caesar's partisans. Domitius Ahenobarbus, Metellus Scipio and Lentulus Spinther were already bickering over who would succeed Caesar as *Pontifex Maximus*. Many of the leading Pompeians had themselves benefited from Sulla's victory decades before, and now hoped to escape their debts and thrust themselves even further into the forefront of public life. Cicero found the mood of the camp sickening, and later made a grim pun on Cato and his associates' name for themselves – the 'good men' or *boni*

– by saying that there was 'nothing good about them, apart from their cause'. He doubtless exempted Cato himself from this judgement, but the latter was not with the army, having been left in command of the garrison protecting Dyrrachium. Malicious rumour said that Pompey had given Cato this task so that he would be unable to influence events when Caesar was defeated. There was much in-fighting between the various leaders as well as their suspicion of Pompey. Afranius was accused of betraying the army during the Spanish campaign. Others squabbled over who should be permitted to stand for election in the next year. Domitius Ahenobarbus was more concerned with punishing not only Caesar's supporters, but also those who had remained neutral in Italy. Pompey had never enjoyed the same unquestioned authority with which Caesar directed his own war effort.

In the days after Dyrrachium, the mood amongst the senior officers in the Pompeian camp became a volatile mixture of overconfidence and pride, greed and ambition, jealousy and mutual suspicion. The pressure on Pompey to provoke a final encounter with the enemy grew. He had never coped well in the face of hostility and, like every other participant in the war, was concerned for his own position when peace returned. Since his third consulship he had drawn closer to the established elite of the senate, and now had to be careful not to alienate these men. After Dyrrachium Pompey was less decisive and more readily influenced by the advice of others. Beginning to place too much trust in his own legions, Cicero said that after this success Pompey 'was no longer a general'.[22]

Pompey waited until Scipio had joined him before advancing into Thessaly and closing with the enemy. It was early August and for a number of days the two armies manoeuvred close to each other in the familiar style of warfare in this period. Caesar felt that his men were now in both better health and spirit than they had been at the start of the retreat, and formed them up to offer battle. Pompey declined, which does show that he had certainly not been pressured to the point where he was determined to fight under any circumstances. He remained enough of a general to wait for a better opportunity on more favourable ground. The cavalry of the two armies skirmished, and once again Caesar's outnumbered horsemen were able to hold their own with the aid of picked infantrymen providing them with close support. The Pompeians were camped on a hill and Pompey deployed them on the slope in front of this, inviting Caesar to attack at a disadvantage. The supply situation had greatly improved, but even so Caesar was reluctant to keep his army in one locality for too long unless there was good reason for this. After several days of this stand-off, on the morning of 9 August he gave the order to strike the camp and march away, hoping to find a better opportunity for battle elsewhere. As this was underway, he was surprised to observe the Pompeian army advance down off the slope and onto the open plain. With part of his own column already formed up for the march, Caesar gave the order to halt, declaring that, 'We must postpone our march and think instead of battle, as we have always craved; let us ready our spirits for the struggle; we will not readily get another opportunity.' The legionaries set down their packs and moved out with only their armour and weapons. The greatest battle of the war, fought by armies commanded by the ablest generals of the age, was about to occur and inevitably sources recounted the great omens that foreshadowed this massive shift in fortune. Appian tells us that Caesar spent the night performing sacrifices to Mars and his ancestor Venus, vowing to build the goddess a temple in Rome if he prevailed. As usual his own account makes no mention of such concerns and deals with more practical matters, although as is so often the case, there is not enough detail for us to locate the battlefield with absolute certainly.[23]

The plain of Pharsalus was wide and open, bounded on one side by the River Enipeus. Pompey deployed his army with his right flank resting on the river. A small force of 600 cavalry were on this flank, probably with the support of some light infantry and allied troops. Next to them was the main force, eleven legions deployed in the usual *triplex acies*. The best legions were divided between the flanks and the centre – the *First* and *Third*, the two that had once fought for Caesar, now held the left of the line. Each cohort was formed ten ranks deep, a much thicker formation than was usual. Deep formations made it harder for the men in the front rank to flee and so helped to keep inexperienced soldiers in the battle line as they struggled to cope with the stress of combat. The chief disadvantage was that only a small proportion of the men in such a formation were able to fight, and it would have been difficult for the men in the rear ranks even to throw their *pila* effectively. Altogether Pompey had 110 cohorts, making up a total of some 45,000 legionaries according to the *Commentaries*, although some other sources made the figure smaller by several thousand. The right wing was placed under the command of Afranius (or Lentulus in Appian's version), while Metellus Scipio had charge of the centre and Domitius Ahenobarbus the left wing. The legions were ordered to stand their ground rather than advance to meet the enemy – their task in the battle was essentially to pin and occupy the enemy foot. Pompey expected to win the battle with his cavalry, some 6,400 of which were massed on the left flank under the direct command of Labienus. They were supported by thousands of light

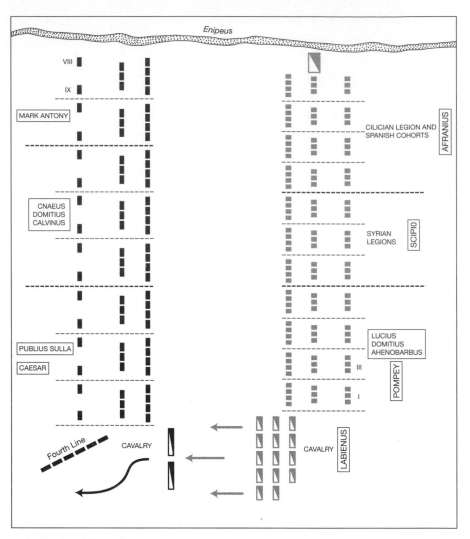

The Battle of Pharsalus

infantrymen, but it was the horsemen who were expected to overwhelm Caesar's outnumbered cavalry and then attack the flank and rear of his legions. It was a simple plan, but reasonable enough, exploiting their advantage in numbers and especially the great superiority in cavalry that would have room to manoeuvre on the open plain. Its main disadvantage was that there was no thought for what might happen if the cavalry attack failed. Yet Pompey was confident that it would not and that his own legions would be able to resist Caesar's men for long enough to allow the mounted troops to roll up the enemy line. Labienus harangued the army after Pompey had

426

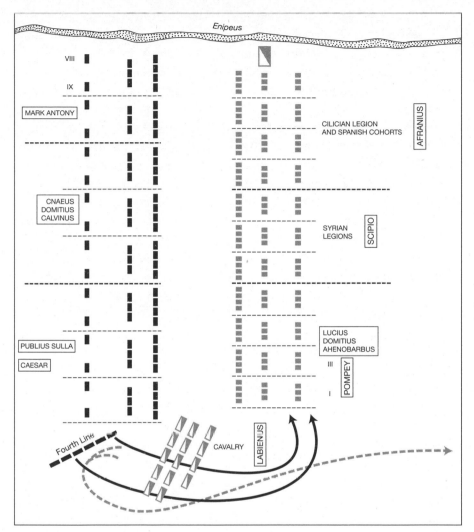

The Battle of Pharsalus

encouraged them, assuring his listeners that there were hardly any of the tough veterans of Gaul left in the ranks of Caesar's army.[24]

Caesar formed his army up with the river on his left. He had eighty cohorts, but these were much smaller than those in Pompey's legions and amounted to no more than 22,000 men. Both sides left some additional forces to guard their camps – seven cohorts in Caesar's case. The legions formed up in three lines just like their opponents, but of necessity the cohorts were in shallower formations, perhaps some four, five or six ranks deep. Also like their opponents, the flanks were entrusted to the best units. The

Tenth was on the right of the line, in the place of greatest honour, while the left was held by a combined formation of the *Ninth*, which had suffered particularly heavy casualties at Dyrrachium, supported by the *Eighth*. Mark Antony was given charge of the left wing, Cnaeus Domitius Calvinus had the centre and Publius Sulla the right. The last appointment was in some respects nominal, since Caesar himself took station with the *Tenth* and remained with the right wing throughout the battle, having guessed rightly that the key tactical moves would occur in this sector. He had only 1,000 cavalry and seems to have stationed all of them next to the *Tenth* to face the mass of enemy horsemen on their left. Pompey's plan was obvious, since such a great force of cavalry was clearly not intended to act defensively. To counter it Caesar took six cohorts from the third line of his army and brought them into a position behind his own right wing to form a short fourth line set back at an oblique angle. Shielded from view by the troopers ahead of them, and doubtless also masked by the clouds of dust inevitably thrown up by so many men and horses moving on the plain, the enemy commanders failed to notice this redeployment.[25]

It must have taken hours for the two armies to move into their positions, their front lines probably less than a mile apart. Battles have always been confusing, those in a civil war doubly so, and to reduce the chance of mistaking friend for enemy and vice versa, each side issued a password. Caesar took the name of his divine ancestor in the form that associated her with military success – 'Venus, the Bringer of Victory' – while the Pompeians used 'Hercules the Unconquered' as their sign. Some of the later sources spoke of a time of hesitation, when the two sides balked at the prospect of slaughtering fellow citizens, but this is most likely mere romantic invention. Both armies seem to have been confident. Caesar was encouraged by the spirit of his men as he rode along the lines, talking to them and checking that the units were in their appointed place. He does claim to have recounted to them once again the wrongs done to him and all the efforts he had made to arrange a peaceful settlement. He had gone all along the line and was with the *Tenth* when he gave the signal for the advance. As the trumpets blared out, close to him was Crastinus, a retired *primus pilus* of the legion, who called out,

'Follow me, my old comrades, and give your general true service. Only this battle remains; when it's over he will regain his dignity and we our freedom.' At the same moment he turned to Caesar and said, 'Today, general, I shall earn your gratitude whether I live or die.' After saying this he charged forward from the right wing, and about 120 handpicked soldiers from the same century – all serving as volunteers – followed him.[26]

Caesar's infantry advanced in good order, keeping to a steady pace to preserve their formation. When they came closer to the enemy, the front line of cohorts charged forward ready to throw their *pila* when they came within effective range of about 15 yards. The normal tactic was to keep silent, save for the orders and encouragement of the centurions and other officers, and only to raise a cheer when they flung their heavy javelins and ran forward to close with the enemy. This time the Pompeians stayed rooted to the spot, not advancing to meet them. The centurions had judged the moment to order the charge on the assumption that the enemy would also come forward. Now they realised at the last minute that this was not going to happen, and that there was the danger they would launch their volley of *pila* too soon and have lost formation by the time they reached the enemy. In a frightening display of their discipline, Caesar's veterans halted, calmly redressed their ranks and then came on again in good order. At the right moment they then accelerated for a second time, hurled their *pila*, raised a shout and charged sword in hand at the Pompeian line. Caesar felt that Pompey's order for his troops to remain stationary was a mistake, since it denied them the enthusiasm of the charge. However, helped no doubt by their numbers and deep formation, the enemy legionaries for a while managed to resist the charge and heavy fighting developed all along the line.

Pompey did not need his legionaries to beat the enemy, merely to keep them occupied and allow the cavalry attack time to succeed. As the battle began Labienus led his men forward against the massively outnumbered Caesarean horse. The latter gave ground, perhaps deliberately retiring to draw the enemy onwards. Over 6,000 cavalry were concentrated in a small area. They were a mixed bag of many different races, inexperienced and led mainly by enthusiastic but equally raw, young aristocrats. Pompey's cavalry had had few opportunities to operate en masse in the campaign so far. Their horses can only have been in a poor state after the hardships endured at Dyrrachium, which may well have meant that the charge occurred at no faster rate than a trot. In the beginning such a large body of cavalrymen should have been divided into several lines and care taken to make sure that reserves were kept back to exploit any success or give support as required. However, as the cavalry advanced and drove back Caesar's horsemen this good order seems to have vanished, as the riders and mounts both became carried away by the exhilarating sense of power derived from the close presence of so many others. Labienus and his officers lost control, and instead of an ordered body the force seems to have degenerated into a great disordered mass. At this point Caesar gave the order for the six cohorts in his fourth line to attack. The legionaries came forward, infantry attacking horsemen in a way that has been rare throughout history. They kept their *pila* in their hands and used them as thrusting spears. Labienus' men had lost order and momentum. It may well be that they had halted, perhaps because he was trying to regain control before moving against the flank of Caesar's infantry. Whatever the cause, the result was a rout in which the entire mob of cavalry stampeded to the rear and played no further part in the battle. Their supporting light infantrymen fled or were cut down.

Caesar kept his fourth line under tight control. Rather than pursuing too far, they swung round to strike the left flank of the Pompeian infantry. All along the rest of the front, the cohorts of Caesar's first and second line were already heavily engaged – these two lines usually worked closely together. They had made some headway and more progress was made as the enemy line was turned. Now Caesar gave the order for his final reserves, the fresh cohorts of the third line, to advance into the fighting line. The Pompeians gave more ground, and then their line collapsed and degenerated into flight. Caesar kept some troops in hand and led them on to storm the enemy camp. He and his officers exhorted the men to spare fellow citizens whenever possible, but it is claimed that they also told them to massacre the enemy auxiliaries to make it clear that their mercy was a special favour. Caesar claims that 15,000 enemy were killed and 24,000 captured along with the eagles of nine legions and 180 other standards. Asinius Pollio gave the lower figure of 6,000 for the Pompeian dead, which may well be more accurate. Domitius Ahenobarbus was killed in the fighting, but most of the other leading Pompeians escaped. Servilia's son Brutus soon joined the prisoners, and Caesar is alleged to have sent men out looking for him and been delighted when he was found to be still alive. His own losses had been comparatively small considering the scale of his victory, amounting to 200 men and 30 centurions – the latter tended to suffer disproportionately high casualties because of the aggressive leadership expected of them. Crastinus was amongst the dead, killed by a sword thrust that went through his mouth and came out of the back of his neck. This was only after he had performed great heroics. Appian tells us that Caesar gave him an honoured burial and even decorated him, which was unusual since the Romans did not normally give posthumous decorations. Caesar himself tells us that he and his men were disgusted by the lavishness of the enemy camp and the arrogance shown by the tents and shelters already decorated with symbols of victory. Asinius Pollio recorded the more revealing comment made as Caesar looked across the field strewn with enemy dead. 'They wanted it; even after all my great deeds I, Caius Caesar, would have been condemned, if I had not sought support from my army.'[27]

Even allowing for hostile sources, Pompey had not done well at Pharsalus and had little impact on the course of the battle after it had begun. Soon after the cavalry attack failed, he returned to camp. A little later, as he saw the signs of collapse, he took off his general's insignia and fled. It might not have made any difference if he had remained with his soldiers, but it was very poor behaviour for a Roman commander, who was never supposed to admit defeat and, even if things went badly, should try to get as much of his army away in as good order as possible. A battle might be lost, but the general's task was to make sure that the war would eventually be won. At Pharsalus Pompey despaired, perhaps because for most of the campaign he had wished to avoid fighting such a pitched battle at all. He made no real effort to re-form an army in Greece, but with his advisors soon thought of fleeing overseas. There were rumours that he even considered seeking refuge and aid from the Parthians, but in the end Pompey chose to go to Egypt, where the throne was being fought over by the children of King Ptolemy. Egypt had supplied him with military aid in the recent campaign and was wealthy, so may well have seemed a likely base for rebuilding his fortune. Along with his wife Cornelia, some officers and attendants, Pompey sailed into Alexandria. Openly, the young king – or rather his advisors since the boy was only in his early teens – sent messages of welcome. Pompey got into a boat sent out from the shore. On board were several Egyptians, but also two Roman officers who had served with him years before, and then subsequently been part of Gabinius' army, remaining in Egypt after the restoration of Ptolemy. As his wife and friends watched from the deck of the ship, these officers stabbed Pompey to death. Thus ended Pompey the Great, a man who had celebrated three triumphs and been consul three times. He was just one day short of his fifty-ninth birthday. His head was cut off and kept to present to Caesar in the hope of gaining the goodwill of the victor, but the rest of the body was left on the beach until one of his own freedmen came and buried it.[28]

XX

CLEOPATRA, EGYPT
AND THE EAST,
AUTUMN 48–SUMMER 47 BC

'Caesar also had affairs with queens . . . most of all with Cleopatra, with whom he often feasted until first light, and he would have sailed through Egypt on her royal barge almost to Aethiopia, if his army had not refused to follow him.' – *Suetonius, late first/early second century AD.*[1]

'Cleopatra . . . was a woman of surpassing beauty, and at that time, when she was in the prime of her youth, she was most striking; she also possessed a most charming voice and a knowledge of how to make herself agreeable to every one. Being brilliant to look upon and to listen to, with power to subjugate every one, even a love-sated man already past his prime, she thought that it would be in keeping with her role to meet Caesar, and she reposed in her beauty all her claims to the throne.' – *Dio, early third century AD.*[2]

Caesar followed up his success at Pharsalus with his usual vigorous pursuit and arrived in Alexandria just three days after Pompey's murder. It was important to complete the victory by preventing the enemy from regrouping. Pompey's skill, reputation and huge array of clients made him still the most dangerous opponent even after his defeat, and Caesar had focused his main attention on hunting down his former father-in-law. He travelled quickly, taking with him only a small force. At one point he came across a far larger squadron of enemy warships, but such was his confidence that he simply demanded – and promptly received – their surrender. Caesar paused for a few days on the coast of Asia, settling the province and arranging for the communities, especially those that had strongly supported the Pompeians, to supply him with the money and food he needed to support his ever-growing armies. At this point news arrived that Pompey was on his way to Egypt and Caesar immediately resumed the hunt, taking with him some 4,000 troops and reaching Alexandria at the beginning of October. Almost immediately he learned of Pompey's death, and soon afterwards the latter's signet ring and head were presented to him by envoys of the young king. Caesar wept when he saw the first and would not look at the second. His disgust and sorrow may well have been genuine, for from the beginning he had taken great pride in his clemency and willingness to pardon his enemies. Whether Pompey would have accepted this is another matter, having earlier in the year declared that he had no intention of living on indebted to 'Caesar's generosity'. A cynical observer might say that it was very convenient for Caesar to be able to transfer to foreign assassins the guilt for killing one of the greatest heroes in the history of the Republic. Yet in the past there does seem to have been some genuine affection between the two men as well as political association. Even when they came to see each other as rivals, it is extremely unlikely that Caesar ever wanted to kill Pompey. His aim was to be acknowledged by everyone, including Pompey himself, as Pompey's equal – and perhaps in time as his superior. A dead Pompey was far less satisfying.[3]

Nevertheless, the murder made it clear that the local authorities were keen to please the newcomers, and Caesar decided to land with his troops. With him were the *Sixth* Legion, reduced by constant campaigning to under 1,000 men, and one of Pompey's old formations that had now been renumbered the *Twenty-Seventh* and mustered some 2,200 legionaries. Supporting these were some 800 auxiliary cavalry, at least some of whom were Gauls and others Germans. It is possible that this was the bodyguard unit that had accompanied Caesar in the recent campaigns. It was not an especially strong force, but Caesar did not expect to face serious opposition. He disembarked and marched to take up residence in one of the palaces in the royal quarter of the city. As consul, he was preceded by twelve lictors carrying the fasces which symbolised his *imperium* as a Roman magistrate. The sight provoked a hostile reaction from the royal troops in the city and from many of the Alexandrians. The Romans were jeered and over the next few days a number of legionaries caught alone in the streets were attacked and killed by mobs. Caesar had stumbled into the middle of Egypt's own civil war and would soon be besieged and fighting for his life, completely out of touch with events in the rest of the Mediterranean. Before describing what became known as the Alexandrian War, it is worth pausing to consider Egypt in the fading years of the Ptolemaic dynasty.[4]

PTOLEMAIC EGYPT AND ITS QUEEN

Alexander the Great had taken Egypt from the Persians in 331 BC, founding Alexandria that same year – one of a number of cities bearing his name, although in time it outstripped all the others. When he died his massive empire was torn apart by his generals as they struggled to carve out kingdoms of their own. One of the most successful was Ptolemy, son of Lagus, who became Ptolemy I *Soter,* or 'saviour', and took Alexandria in Egypt as his capital, even managing to divert Alexander's funeral cortege so that the body of the great conqueror was interred in the city. The dynasty Ptolemy founded would rule for almost three centuries, controlling an empire that at times included not just Egypt, but also Cyrenaica, Palestine, Cyprus, and parts of Asia Minor. Its extent varied, outlying territories being lost to rebellion or the renewed vigour of the other great successor kingdoms of Antigonid Macedonia and the Seleucid Empire. The balance of power between the three rivals fluctuated over the years, but by 48 BC both of the others had gone. Macedonia had become a Roman province in 146 BC, while Pompey had deposed the last Seleucid king in 64 BC and taken Syria under Roman rule. The Macedonians and Seleucids had chosen to fight Rome and had lost. In contrast the Ptolemies formed an alliance with the Roman Republic even before it began to extend its power into the region. The kingdom survived, but it gained few benefits from Roman expansion and during the second century BC this was a contributory factor in its steady decline. As important were the almost unending dynastic struggles within the royal family. Ptolemy II had married his sister, inaugurating a tradition of incestuous marriages – brother to sister, nephew to aunt and uncle to niece – which persisted to the end of the dynasty. Such unions, broken only by occasional marriages to foreign, usually Seleucid princesses, prevented the aristocratic families from gaining claims to the throne. The price was to make the pattern of succession very unclear. Factions grew up surrounding different members of the royal family, all eager to advance them to become king or queen and so gain influence as their advisor. Civil wars were frequent, and over time it became more and more common for Rome to act as arbiter, formal recognition by the Romans helping greatly to legitimise a monarch's rule. The kingdom's independence was gradually eroded.

Egypt remained very wealthy. In part this was through trade, Alexandria being one of the greatest ports in the ancient world, but more than anything else it rested on agriculture. Every year the Nile flooded – as it still did until the construction of the Aswan dam. When the water receded the farmers were able to sow their seeds in fields rendered very fertile by the moisture. The scale of the annual inundation varied and, as in the Book of Genesis, there could be years of famine as well as years of plenty, but in general the harvest produced a substantial surplus. Many centuries before the unrivalled fertility of the Nile valley had allowed the civilisation of ancient Egypt to flourish and create its awesome monuments. More recently it had made the region an attractive conquest for the Persians and after them the Macedonians. The power of the Ptolemies was always based firmly on Egypt. Through a sophisticated bureaucratic machine, much of it inherited from the earlier periods, they were able to exploit this productivity. An important component within the system was the temples – many of which preserved the worship and rites of the old Egyptian religion and were little influenced by imported Hellenic ideas. The temples were major landowners, but also centres for industry and craft, and had privileged status, exempting them from most taxation. Roman visitors to Egypt were amazed by the fertility and wealth of the country, as much as they claimed to have been shocked by the intrigue and opulence of the royal court. By the first century BC Egypt seemed to offer the prospect of massive wealth to a number of ambitious Romans.[5]

The career of Cleopatra's father illustrates both the instability of Egyptian politics and its ever more blatant dependence on Rome. He was Ptolemy XII, illegitimate son of Ptolemy IX and (most probably) one of his concubines. His father had become king in 116 BC when his mother chose him as joint ruler and husband, but was later rejected in favour of another brother, the massively obese Ptolemy X. He eventually returned to oust them both by force and remained on the throne until his death at the end of 81 BC. Ptolemy IX was succeeded by his nephew Ptolemy XI, who was taken as husband and consort by his stepmother, promptly murdered her and was himself in turn assassinated soon afterwards. Ptolemy XII was then recognised as King of Egypt by Sulla. He styled himself the 'New Dionysus' (Neos Dionysus), but was often known less flatteringly as Auletes or the 'flute player' – some would argue that oboe player would probably be a better translation, but the other version is more commonly used. In 75 BC rival claimants to the throne had gone to Rome to lobby the Senate, but eventually left without achieving anything.

Yet the wealth of Egypt remained a great temptation to ambitious Romans. A decade later Crassus hoped to use his censorship to annex Egypt as a province, probably on the basis that Ptolemy X had bequeathed it to Rome in his will, a copy of which had been sent to the city. As noted earlier, Caesar was credited with similar plans (see p.114–5). Neither man succeeded, but as consul in 59 BC Caesar did share with Pompey the staggering 6,000

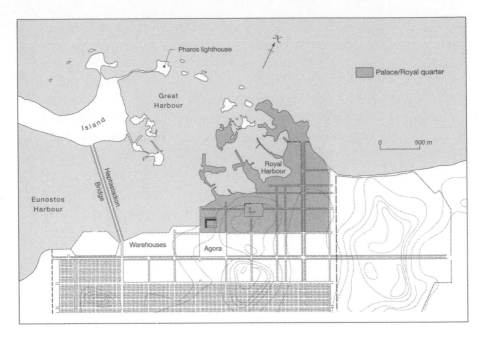

Alexandria

talent bribe that Ptolemy XII promised as payment for having him formally acknowledged as 'friend and ally' of the Roman people. Collecting this sum proved difficult and probably contributed to the uprising that forced him to flee from Egypt in the following year. He went to Rome in the hope of winning the support that would restore him to power, and it is just possible that he took his eleven-year-old daughter Cleopatra with him. The issue became a fiercely contested one, since many craved the chance of a campaign in Egypt and the rewards likely from a grateful king. In 57 BC the consul Publius Lentulus Spinther – the same man who later surrendered to Caesar at Corfinium – was given the task of restoring Ptolemy to the throne, but political opponents managed to 'discover' an oracle that was interpreted as meaning that he would not be allowed an army for this task. Eventually, in 55 BC, Gabinius took it upon himself to do this, inspired by Auletes' promise of 10,000 talents. In the event the bulk of the money could not be found, and Gabinius returned to trial and condemnation at Rome, before reviving his fortunes by joining Caesar in 49 BC.[6]

After his expulsion in 58 BC, Ptolemy's daughter Berenice IV had been made ruler, at first with her sister the elder Cleopatra VI as co-ruler, but following the latter's death she married a son of Mithridates of Pontus, a connection that only increased the pressure on Rome to act. On his return

Auletes had Berenice killed, but his efforts to raise the money owed to Gabinius and other Roman creditors were generally unsuccessful. He remained deeply unpopular, but even greater hatred grew up for the Romans who had backed him and who now wished to exploit the country so shamelessly. Alexandria in particular witnessed frequent rioting and attacks on Romans. In 51 BC Auletes finally died, leaving the throne jointly to his third daughter, the seventeen-year-old Cleopatra VII, and his elder son, the ten-year-old Ptolemy XIII. He had already sent a copy of his will to be kept at Rome, a measure that made clear his acknowledgement of the Republic's power. Brother and sister were promptly married in the usual way. In spite of her youth, Cleopatra was evidently already a forceful character, and decrees issued at the beginning of her reign make no mention of Ptolemy. The boy was not old enough to assert himself, but his ministers and advisors, led by the eunuch Pothinus and the army commander Achillas, soon began to oppose his older sister. Alexandria had been turbulent for some time. A series of poor harvests added to the discontent of the wider population – the Nile was at its lowest recorded level in 48 BC. In 49 BC Pompey sent his son Cnaeus to Egypt to secure support for the forces he was gathering in Macedonia. Cleopatra welcomed him – much later there were rumours of an affair, but this may well be no more than gossip or propaganda – and sent a contingent of the soldiers left behind by Gabinius along with fifty ships. This compliance with the Romans was sensible, given their power and the debt of her father to Pompey, but it may well have been unpopular. Controlling much of the army, and with a good deal of support from the Alexandrians, the regents were able to drive Cleopatra from the country. The queen took refuge in Arabia and Palestine, and was supported by the city of Ascalon – one of the former Philistine cities from the Old Testament period, which in recent centuries had usually been under Ptolemaic control. By the summer of 48 BC she had gathered an army and had returned to reclaim the throne. This force and those loyal to her brother were warily shadowing each other from opposite sides of the Nile Delta when Pompey, and then Caesar, arrived in Egypt.[7]

Cleopatra is one of a handful of figures from the ancient world whose name still commands instant recognition, but it must be emphasised that we know far less about her early life and her liaison with Caesar than might be supposed. More is known of her later life and subsequent affair with Mark Antony, although even then most of our sources were written long after her death and are tainted by the propaganda inspired by Augustus, against whom the couple had fought and lost. Yet the queen has fascinated generation after generation, and over the centuries she has been often portrayed in art, literature, drama and, more recently, cinema and television, all of which have freely embellished the ancient sources. It is difficult for anyone looking at the period to step back entirely from these popular images of Cleopatra, but it is useful to begin with what can more confidently be said. When Caesar arrived in Egypt Cleopatra was nearly twenty-one years old and had been queen for almost four years. She was highly intelligent and extremely well educated in the Greek tradition. Later, she would be credited with writing books on a very broad range of subjects, from cosmetics and hairdressing to scientific and philosophical subjects. Cleopatra was a noted linguist, who it was claimed rarely needed an interpreter when conversing with the leaders of the neighbouring countries. The Ptolemies were a Macedonian dynasty who had imposed themselves by force on Egypt, but they had found it expedient in the past to present themselves to their native subjects as true successors to the pharaohs. Cleopatra was not the first to support the traditional cults of the land, but she does seem to have taken an especially close interest in the details of ceremonies. Later in her life she would style herself as the New Isis, choosing an Egyptian goddess – though admittedly one whose cult had spread to much of the Mediterranean world – rather than a Greek deity after her father's example. Plutarch tells us that she was the first of the Ptolemies who was able to speak the Egyptian language. All of this made sound political sense, for a monarch aware that challenges to her rule were likely needed as broad a base of support as possible, and the temples played a vital economic as well as spiritual role in the country's life. Ptolemaic Egypt was internally divided and was faced with the overwhelming power of Rome. This could not be ignored, but might be placated. No ruler could ever be secure, and it is in this context that we must place Cleopatra's undoubted ruthlessness. By this stage, it was unlikely that any of the Ptolemies could be anything else.[8]

Some of the most frequently asked questions about Cleopatra are what did she look like, and was she really beautiful? It is unlikely that we will ever be able to answer either of these with any real certainty. On coins her image is rather severe, probably because it was intended to project an image of power and authority, rather than a flattering portrait of her features. In some cases corrosion has rather emphasised the long, curved nose and pointed chin. Some coins minted at Ascalon show a more youthful and slightly softer featured woman. Over the centuries many portrait busts have been identified as Cleopatra, but few of these are now generally accepted as such. Depictions of her in the traditional Egyptian style, for instance in temple reliefs, followed a different set of conventions, but are equally unhelpful for showing us Cleopatra's true appearance. The coins and busts invariably show her hair tied back in a bun – a style that academic convention rather unflatteringly describes as melon shaped – and wearing the diadem of a Hellenistic monarch. She does appear to have had high cheekbones, but her most powerful feature was her nose, high at the bridge, rather long and probably somewhat hooked – hawk-like would doubtless be the term used by a romantic novelist. Dio tells us that she was exceptionally beautiful. A passage from Plutarch is sometimes mistakenly understood to contradict this, for he says that it was not so much her beauty that first struck an onlooker but her charm, personality and the gently musical tones of her voice. Thus he did not deny her beauty, but rather said there were other reasons for the powerful impact she had on men. Beauty proverbially is in the eye of the beholder, and different generations have had very different ideals of its perfection. It is not difficult to think of famous film stars who have captivated audiences and clearly possessed huge sex appeal without being unusually pretty. A person's liveliness and animation have always been very difficult for a sculptor to capture, while such things are extremely unlikely to be conveyed by a coin portrait.

On balance it seems reasonable to say that Cleopatra was an extremely attractive woman, and would probably have been seen as such had she lived in any generation. To her good looks she added intelligence, sophistication, wit, vivacity and enormous charm. Add in the glamour of being a queen, along with her real political importance, and it is not difficult to understand how she captivated two of the greatest Romans of the age. The colour of her hair and her complexion are unknown. There is a tradition popular in some circles that she was black, but there is not a shred of evidence to support this. The Ptolemies were Macedonians, although there was some Greek and, through marriages to Seleucids, also a little Persian blood in their recorded family line. We do not know the identity of Cleopatra's grandmother. There is also a little doubt over her mother, although most accept that it was Auletes's full sister, which would then increase the significance of the grandmother even further. The accepted conjecture is that the latter was a concubine, which makes it possible that she was not of Macedonian stock, but perhaps an Egyptian or from even further afield. Therefore it is not absolutely impossible that there was some more specifically African blood in Cleopatra, but there is no actual evidence to support this. Equally, it is not absolutely impossible that she was a blonde, since some Macedonians had fair hair (which is again a rather subjective term), but equally none of our sources claim this. This uncertainty will continue to allow different people to imagine very different Cleopatras.[9]

Alexandria was a young city compared with Rome. It was probably smaller – one estimate puts its population at something like half a million people – but still vastly bigger than any other city in the Greco-Roman world with the exception of Syrian Antioch. It was certainly more splendid than Rome, its deliberate foundation ensuring that it had been laid out neatly in the best traditions of Hellenistic architecture. The two main roads, which lay at right angles to each other, may well have been as much as 100 feet wide. The harbour was enormous, and on the island at its edge lay the massive Pharos lighthouse, one of the Wonders of the World. Facing the sea was the royal quarter, which consisted of numerous lavish palaces, since there was apparently a tradition of each new ruler building his or her own complex. This region of the city is now largely underwater, but in recent years archaeologists have begun a programme of investigation that has already revealed a good deal. One surprise was the number of ancient Egyptian monuments that had been moved and brought to decorate the city. Clearly many of the Ptolemies wished to emphasise the great antiquity of the country that they had come to rule. However, Alexandria was founded by a Macedonian king and most of its original colonists had been Macedonians or Greeks. Since then the population had become more mixed and the city contained the largest Jewish community outside Judaea itself. It was also a bustling port, and trade in spices, ivories and other luxuries from India seems to have increased during Cleopatra's lifetime. However, for all this coming and going of peoples, in cultural terms Alexandria remained overtly Greek and had become one of the greatest centres of learning in the Hellenic world. Its Library was massive, filled not only with books, but also with curiosities and scientific wonders – a model able to move by steam power is mentioned in one source – and the Ptolemies had a long tradition of encouraging philosophers to come to the city to study and teach.[10]

THE ALEXANDRIAN WAR

There is no evidence that Caesar had ever visited either Alexandria or Egypt before he landed there in October 48 BC. He does seem to have been surprised by the hostility provoked by the sight of his lictors and the swagger with which he and his legionaries processed through the city. For the moment the weather prevented him from leaving and moving on, and he decided to keep himself busy. A great part of the money promised to him by Auletes over a decade before had never been paid, and Caesar announced that he intended to collect 10 million denarii of this debt. The victory at Pharsalus had only increased his already massive financial commitments, for he now had to provide for the tens of thousands of Pompeian soldiers who had surrendered to him. Around the same time he also announced that as the man who had secured recognition for Ptolemy Auletes, he would now arbitrate in the succession dispute. Pothinus the eunuch, acting as regent for Ptolemy XIII (who was still no more than thirteen or fourteen) made no public protest, but secretly sent orders summoning Achillas and the army to the city. The *Commentaries* claim that Achillas had 20,000 men, consisting mainly of a mix of Gabinius' former soldiers, who had remained behind and taken local wives, and mercenaries, many of whom were runaway slaves from the Roman provinces. Caesar was seriously outnumbered and soon found himself blockaded in the walled palace compound and a number of other buildings that he had occupied in the royal quarter. At first there was an uneasy truce, but soon Achillas launched an all-out attack. In repulsing one assault Caesar's legionaries set light to some buildings and the fire got out of hand, according to some sources spreading to the Library, although it is unlikely that this caused serious damage to its books and it remained a centre of learning for several centuries afterwards. Most of the population of the city supported the royal army or was neutral, and there was much talk of the need to stand up to the Romans if Egypt was not simply to be absorbed. Caesar sent messengers summoning aid and reinforcements, but it would be some time before any could arrive and it is clear that he was in serious danger of defeat and death.[11]

At the beginning both Ptolemy XIII and his sister Arsinoe were within Caesar's lines along with many of their attendants, including Pothinus. The latter was deliberately insulting, feeding the Romans poor food in rough vessels and brusquely telling them that all the gold and silverware was going to pay Caesar the money he demanded. At this point Cleopatra made her startling appearance on the scene, smuggling herself into the palace at dusk. She came with only a single member of her household, Apollodorus of Rhodes, who rowed her across the harbour in a small skiff. He then carried her into Caesar's presence, not rolled up in a carpet in the best Hollywood tradition, but inside a laundry bag. The bag was untied and the queen revealed, perhaps standing up as it dropped down – it is hard to resist the analogy of a dancer appearing from a cake. Dio claims that the queen had learnt of Caesar's womanising reputation and had dressed herself carefully to excite both his pity for the loss of her throne and his passion as a well-known rake. The two became lovers, and around this time Caesar decreed that the terms of Auletes' will were clear and that Cleopatra and her brother should rule jointly. The boy was unimpressed and probably already aware that his sister was closer to the Roman consul than he could ever be. He spoke to a crowd of Alexandrians, who responded by rioting. Tension within the palace compound grew and there were rumours of plots to assassinate Caesar. In the past he had never been a heavy drinker, but now he took to staying with his officers after dinner and drinking well into the night. It was claimed that he did this for protection. One of Caesar's personal slaves overheard Pothinus plotting and a watch was set on the eunuch, who was soon proved to be in communication with the besiegers and was promptly executed. At some point Arsinoe escaped and joined the Egyptian army, who promptly proclaimed her queen. With her former tutor, the eunuch Ganymede, she arranged the murder of Achillas and took control of the troops. The two men most responsible for killing Pompey had both suffered a similar fate within a short space of time.[12]

The siege continued with renewed intensity. At one stage the besiegers contaminated the water supply to the area held by Caesar's men, forcing the latter to order his legionaries to dig for wells. A third legion, the *Thirty-Seventh,* formed from surrendered Pompeians, managed to reach him by sea, bringing with it a convoy of supplies as well as artillery and other equipment. It was vital for Caesar to maintain his access to the harbour exits, since if he became cut off from the sea then it would be very difficult for any more aid to reach him. A series of small-scale naval battles were fought in and around the harbour between the small squadron of warships that had accompanied Caesar and an Egyptian navy hastily put together from the boats that policed the Nile and warships that had been discovered half-forgotten in the old royal shipyards. Beams were taken from the ceilings of great buildings to be turned into oars. In most of these encounters Caesar's vessels gained the advantage and this encouraged him to launch an attack to secure all of Pharos island, named after the lighthouse that stood on it. This was connected to the mainland by a bridge almost a mile in length. Caesar already controlled a small section of the island, but he now launched an attack, landing ten cohorts by boats, while other warships made a diversionary attack on the far side of the island. On the next day a second attack was sent to secure the approach to the bridge. This began well, but ended in chaos when a party of sailors who had disembarked from their ships were panicked by an enemy counter-attack. The confusion spread and soon even the legionaries were fleeing for their lives, swarming aboard the closest boats in their desperation to escape. Caesar managed to keep some of the men fighting for a while, but soon realised that this small band would be overwhelmed and so joined the retreat. His own craft was swamped by panic-stricken soldiers so that it was impossible for the crew to push away from the shore. Seeing what was going to happen, the consul took off his cuirass and general's cloak and dived into the sea. Then, holding his left hand above the water to preserve some important documents he was carrying, he calmly swam to safety. Suetonius maintains that he also managed to carry his famous cloak with him, but elsewhere it is claimed that the enemy captured and subsequently paraded this trophy. By this time the boat he had left had foundered, but he was able to send other vessels back to save a few of the trapped men. It was the most serious defeat of the whole campaign and cost him some 800 casualties, just under half of which were legionaries and the remainder sailors. However, his men's morale remained high and they continued to repulse any attacks on their positions.[13]

Soon afterwards – it was probably by this time late January or early February 47 BC – a deputation came from the Alexandrians asking Caesar to release Ptolemy to them, claiming that they were weary of the despotism of Arsinoe and Ganymede. Caesar agreed, but first urged the boy to stop the attacks, which were not in the interest of his people, and remember his loyalty towards Caesar and Rome. The boy burst into tears and begged Caesar not to send him away, prompting the consul to say that if he truly felt that way then he should swiftly end the war and return. Once outside the Roman positions, Ptolemy cheerfully joined his sister and began inciting his soldiers to redouble their efforts to destroy the invaders. According to the author of the *Alexandrian War*, 'a lot of Caesar's legates, friends, centurions, and soldiers were delighted by this, because Caesar's excessive kindness had been made absurd by the deceit of a boy'. Yet personally he doubted that Caesar had been naive, and in his account each of the parties felt that they were tricking the other in this episode. The renewed assaults against the Roman position made no headway, and things were beginning to turn in Caesar's favour, for a relief army had come overland from Syria under the command of Mithridates of Pergamum. It was a force of allies rather than Romans, and included a contingent of 3,000 Jews contributed by the High Priest Hyrcanus II and led by Antipater, the father of Herod the Great, as well as various Syrians and Arabs. The involvement of Hyrcanus encouraged the Jewish population of Alexandria to become far more sympathetic to Caesar. Mithridates stormed the town of Pelusium, and news of this success prompted Ptolemy and the other leaders to shift the bulk of their forces eastwards to try and stop the enemy before they had completed crossing the waterways of the Delta. A messenger from Mithridates reached Caesar at about the same time. Taking some of his troops he sailed round the coast and was able to join up with the relief army before it came into contact with the Egyptians' main force. In the ensuing battle Ptolemy's army was utterly routed. He fled down the river, but was drowned when his boat was swamped by fugitives and capsized – an episode reminiscent of Caesar's narrow escape some weeks earlier.[14]

The war was over and now it was a question of settling Egypt. Arsinoe was a prisoner and would march in Caesar's triumph before being permitted to live on as an exile. She would later be killed on the orders of Mark Antony, almost certainly with the encouragement of her older sister. Cleopatra now took her remaining brother, Ptolemy XIV, as co-ruler, although it was obvious that real power lay with her. In the early negotiations Caesar had granted Arsinoe and this same younger brother joint rule of Cyprus, which was a major concession given that it had recently been turned into a Roman province. This may have been a reflection of his military weakness at that stage, or perhaps was an attack on Cato, who had overseen the process. However, Cyprus was again included in the realm granted to Cleopatra and her brother. It is not entirely clear whether Caesar was able to secure the money he had demanded on arrival in Alexandria, but probable that he did so. The *Alexandrian War* implies that he left Egypt soon after the victory, but it is clear that this is incorrect and that he remained there for some time – perhaps as much as three months. He and Cleopatra took a cruise along the Nile in her luxurious royal barge. Appian claims that 400 vessels and most of the army accompanied them, which suggests that it was not entirely a pleasure cruise. Part of the purpose may well have been to parade through the country the newly confirmed ruler and the Roman might that supported her. The political dimension was rarely far from the mind of Caesar, or indeed of Cleopatra, but in itself it does not quite explain the episode. The situation in Egypt no longer truly required Caesar's personal attention and there were many other issues that ought to have concerned him more. He had now been away from Rome for well over a year, and for the months of the siege itself he had been virtually cut off from events in the world outside Alexandria. Suetonius claims that Caesar would happily have kept on going ever further south along the Nile, had the army – probably most of all the senior officers – not refused to follow him. There is an echo in this story of the mutiny that brought Alexander the Great's conquests to an end, but this does not necessarily mean that it was an invention.[15]

None of the theories put forward to explain this trip have been entirely adequate, and in the end it is very hard to avoid the conclusion that Caesar simply wanted a rest. He had been almost constantly on campaign for over a decade, and since crossing the Rubicon had enjoyed no significant break from his labours. For all his restless energy, it is difficult to believe that he was not tired, and perhaps somewhat empty. In his view he had been forced to fight a civil war he had not wanted, and since Pharsalus and the death of Pompey his world had changed forever. His greatest rival, a man who had only been his enemy for a short time, had gone and there was no one now in the Roman world against whom he could compete. Fatigue and perhaps also depression, as much as fear of plots, might also explain the late-night drinking parties that had begun in the months at Alexandria. His fifty-third birthday was approaching in July 47 BC, while his hairline was rapidly receding, something that upset a man who had always been very conscious of his appearance. Looked at in this context, the attractions of a life of luxury and ease cruising along the Nile at a steady pace and not rushing on to the next task become more obvious. Added to these there was Cleopatra as companion and lover. She was young, which was surely especially attractive if Caesar was beginning to feel old age encroaching, and she was also clever, witty and well educated. As well as sexual pleasure, there was the joy of the affair, of conversation both frivolous and learned, and of simply being with a sophisticated woman. Many of these things he had enjoyed in the past with the aristocratic ladies of Rome, but Cleopatra added the glamour of royalty, the charm of Greek culture and probably some sense of Egypt's exotic past. In many ways she was much like him, perhaps more his equal than many of his other mistresses. It was a heady mix, and from a personal perspective the Nile cruise was probably just what Caesar needed. Spending time with a Hellenistic monarch may even have revived memories of his first travels abroad. There is no reason to disbelieve sources that state that he was in love, although his past and future record make it clear that this never meant that he felt any obligation to be loyal to one particular lover. Cleopatra's attitude can only be guessed. She owed her throne to Caesar, and had doubtless seen enough of Rome's influence over the destiny of Egypt to know that it was wise to gain the favour of the most powerful Roman alive. Yet she may also have genuinely been in love. Caesar was much older, but he possessed the great attraction of wielding great power, added to the personal charm that had captivated so many women in the past. Some sources, and particularly the imagination of later generations, have tended to depict the court of the Ptolemies as rife with sexual intrigue and excess, and portray the queen as highly knowledgeable and experienced in all the sensual arts. Yet we really know so little about her early life that it is hard to confirm or deny any of this. It is equally possible, perhaps even rather more likely, that the affair with Caesar was her first romantic experience and that she was a virgin when she met him.[16]

In the end news of a crisis in Asia persuaded Caesar to leave Egypt. There was surely an element of political thinking in his association with the queen, but in the long run his prolonged stay in Egypt was to cause him considerable problems. Three legions remained behind to ensure that Cleopatra was secure and also to prevent any surviving Pompeians from trying to occupy the country and make use of its wealth and resources. By this time he had received enough information to force him to accept that the Civil War was not yet over and that more campaigns would be needed. Interestingly he chose an officer named Rufio, who was the son of one of his freedmen, to command the three legions. It would later be the policy of Rome's emperors to have an equestrian as governor of Egypt, and to forbid any senator even to visit the country without express permission. Caesar's choice of a man who was not a senatorial legate has often been seen as foreshadowing this, but alternatively he may have thought this more tactful to the sensibilities of the Alexandrians. A senatorial legate could well have been seen as effectively a governor rather than simply the commander of troops of an ally eager to support the monarch. The legions were probably not the only thing that Caesar left behind, for by the time that he set out for Asia the sources suggest that Cleopatra was pregnant.[17]

THE QUICKEST VICTORY – ZELA, 2 AUGUST 47 BC

Caesar was now aware that the Civil War would go on, but the news that finally dragged him from Egypt concerned a foreign threat. King Pharnaces of Bosporus was a son of Mithridates of Pontus, but had managed to change sides and ally with Rome early enough not to share in his father's defeat. In his Eastern Settlement, Pompey had left him monarch of just a small part of his father's domains. Pharnaces saw the Civil War as a grand opportunity to reclaim the lost territories, and in a rapid offensive had soon overrun Cappadocia, Armenia, Eastern Pontus and Lesser Colchis. He was particularly cruel in his victory, ordering the castration of any captured Roman. The majority of these prisoners were probably civilians, since the whole region had been stripped of troops by the Pompeians, and there was little serious opposition until Caesar's legate Cnaeus Domitius Calvinus moved against him in December 48 BC. His army was a motley collection of

Roman and foreign legions, most of whom had originally been raised by the Pompeians and all lacking in experience. Some fought well, but two legions raised from his subjects by the Galatian king and organised and equipped in the Roman manner fled after very little fighting. Its line broken in the centre, Calvinus' army was swiftly routed.[18]

Caesar does not seem to have left Egypt until the summer – the actual timing remains disputed. On his way to Asia he paused at Antioch in Syria and Tarsus in Cilicia. We know that Hyrcanus the high priest and Antipater were both rewarded for their part in the Egyptian campaign. Still hard pressed for the money to meet his ever-growing expenses, he also levied money from many communities in the region, and especially those who had supported Pompey. There was bad news of political squabbles and misbehaviour amongst his subordinates in Italy, but even so Caesar pushed on into Cappadocia to confront Pharnaces. His prestige would have suffered badly if a foreign enemy had been allowed to go unpunished. He had brought the veteran, although badly depleted, *Sixth* Legion with him from Egypt. To this he added one legion of Galatians and two others that had also shared in Calvinus' defeat. Pharnaces sent envoys to Caesar, seeking a peace that would allow him to keep his conquests, and reminding him that the king had refused to send aid to Pompey. They presented the Roman commander with a golden wreath as a mark of his victory. Caesar offered no concessions, reminding the ambassadors of the mutilation and torture of captured Romans. He demanded that Pharnaces should immediately withdraw from Pontus, return the spoils taken from the Romans and release his prisoners. The Roman army continued to advance and came up against the enemy forces near the hilltop town of Zela. Expecting the usual gradual build-up to a battle, Caesar was surprised when Pharnaces launched an all-out attack as the Romans were entrenching their camp on high ground. Such an assault was against the military wisdom of the age, but at first the surprise caused some confusion. Yet Caesar and his men quickly recovered, put together a fighting line, and drove the enemy back down the hill. The veterans of the *Sixth* broke through on the right and soon the entire enemy army dissolved into rout. Pharnaces escaped, but was killed by a rival when he returned to his kingdom. The whole campaign was decided in just a few weeks, and Caesar imposed a settlement on the region. The speed of his success was summed up in a letter to one of his agents at Rome with a laconic tag later displayed on placards carried in his triumph: VENI, VIDI, VICI –'I came, I saw, I conquered.' At the time he also mocked Pompey, commenting on how lucky generals were who made their name fighting against such fragile foes.[19]

XXI

AFRICA,
SEPTEMBER 47–JUNE 46 BC

'No one reports that Caesar has left Alexandria, and it is known that no one at all has left there since 15th March, and that he has sent no letters since 13th December.' – *Cicero, 14 June 47 BC.*[1]

'"For if," said he [*Cato*], "I were willing to be saved by grace of Caesar, I ought to go to him in person and see him alone; but I am unwilling to be under obligation to the tyrant for his illegal acts. And he acts illegally in saving, as if their master, those over whom he has no right at all to be their lord."' – *Plutarch, early second century AD.*[2]

Caesar reached Italy near the end of September. It was twenty months since he had left to begin the Macedonian campaign and more than a year since his victory at Pharsalus. For most of 48 BC he remained in regular contact with his deputies and other prominent men, although according to Dio he sent no official despatch back to Rome to report Pompey's defeat, feeling that this would have been in poor taste. During the Alexandrian campaign his normal flood of correspondence ceased altogether. At first this was due to the blockade imposed by the enemy, but even when this had been broken he remained silent for some time. In June 47 BC Cicero wrote that nothing had been heard from Caesar for six months. It was uncharacteristic behaviour and adds to the impression that fatigue had taken its toll on him. There is no doubt that the lengthy stay in Egypt caused Caesar great problems, giving his enemies time to regroup and creating a dangerous mood of uncertainty in Rome and Italy. Caesar's supporters had little to unite them apart from their loyalty to him, which was often reliant mainly on gratitude for past favours and lively expectation of more in the future. As the Macedonian campaign went on, few could be sure who would win, for they were aware of the odds against Caesar.

Cicero's lively correspondent Caelius Rufus had quite cynically joined the side with the better army at the start of the Civil War. Caesar rewarded him with a praetorship in 48 BC, but Caelius was annoyed when the most senior post of urban praetor was given to someone else, the Legate Trebonius who had taken Massilia the year before. Disaffected, Caelius tried to rally support for himself by declaring plans to abolish all existing debts. This was a radical measure intended to appeal to those who felt that Caesar's moderate law had not gone far enough. With a gang of followers he led riots against both Trebonius and Caesar's consular colleague Servilius. The Senate promptly passed the *senatus consultum ultimum* and, in spite of vetoes by two tribunes, the consul diverted a draft of soldiers on their way to Brundisium and brought them into Rome. Caelius was driven from the city. For a while he hoped to join up with Milo, who had returned to Italy from his exile in Massilia in spite of Caesar's refusal to pardon him. Now he tried to raise rebellion in Pompey's name, backing the man who had ensured that he went into exile in the first place. He did not make much headway and was soon defeated and killed before Caelius could reach him. The praetor met a similar fate shortly afterwards. The use of the *senatus consultum ultimum* was ironic, though it should be said that Caesar had never challenged its validity, merely the appropriateness of its use against him.[3]

In October 48 BC Caesar was appointed dictator again, but unlike the first time this was not simply to permit him to oversee elections. No consuls or other magistrates apart from the tribunes of the plebs were elected for the following year. Probably this was because Caesar was unable to return and did not wish to delegate the task of overseeing the elections to anyone else. The dictatorship traditionally lasted for only six months. Sulla had ignored this and held the office until he chose to lay it down. While Caesar did not wish to be seen to be aping the author of the proscriptions, he needed official power. The consul Servilius named him dictator for a year, thereby imposing some limit on his power, even if this was to last for double the normal term. A dictator had a subordinate rather than a colleague and this officer was titled the Master of Horse (*Magister Equitum*) – when originally created it had been considered important for the dictator to stay with the heavy infantry of the legions and so his deputy was given the task of leading the aristocratic cavalry. Mark Antony was named as Caesar's Master of Horse. For a while the priestly college of augurs, of which Antony himself was a member, protested that it was improper for a Master of Horse to remain in the post for more than six months, but this rather bizarre objection was soon withdrawn. Antony returned to Italy after Pharsalus and was effectively the supreme authority there from January 47 BC until Caesar's return in the autumn. He was a gifted subordinate, but his behaviour became less and less restrained during these months when he was largely left to his own devices. He feasted often, both lavishly and very publicly. His drinking was on a staggering scale – later in life he wrote a book on the subject, which seems to have contained many boasts about his prowess – and he is supposed to have conducted much public business while only partly sober or at the very least suffering from a hangover. On at least one occasion he had to interrupt a meeting in the Forum in order to vomit in sight of all. At times he processed around the country in a great caravan, riding himself in a Gallic – presumably British – chariot, followed by carriages containing a famous actress who was currently his mistress, while another carried his mother. The whole column was incongruously preceded by his lictors. Apart from dressing up as Hercules, some sources even claim that he experimented with a chariot pulled by a team of lions. Apart from this mistress, he had a number of scandalously public affairs with senators' wives. Mark Antony revelled in power, and his conduct was scarcely likely to convince moderate opinion that Caesar's victory would bring anything other than tyranny in the long run.[4]

Antony did not deal well with the problems that confronted him in 47 BC, which were considerable and all directly or indirectly caused by Caesar's long absence. The reports of Pompey's death were not generally believed until his signet ring was sent back to Rome and displayed. Many Pompeians had surrendered at Pharsalus, and others in the weeks that followed. Cicero had not been at the battle, but immediately decided that the war was lost. He turned down the offer of supreme command made to him by Cato, who then had to restrain Pompey's son Cnaeus from killing the orator on the spot. Cicero returned to Italy, but was informed by Antony that he could not be pardoned and allowed to return to Rome without specific instructions from Caesar. Yet for months there was no word from Caesar, and indeed no assurance that he would prevail and survive the war in Egypt. In the meantime Cato had taken the garrison of Dyrrachium by sea to Cyrenaica, and then overland to the province of Africa, where he joined up with Metellus Scipio, Labienus, Afranius, Petreius and many other die-hard Pompeians, all determined to continue the war. They were backed by the Numidian King Juba – the man whose beard Caesar had once pulled during a court case and who more recently had played the key role in the defeat of Curio. As time passed their strength grew, and by the summer there were fears that they might be able to attack Sicily or Sardinia, and even Italy itself. It was a nervous time for men like Cicero, who began to wonder if they had surrendered too soon and remembered the bitter hostility of many leading Pompeians even to those who had remained neutral. All the orator hoped for was a return to some semblance of normal public life, and his nervousness fuelled his anger at Caesar for not finishing the war off more quickly.

Caesar's veteran troops were equally frustrated, for most of the experienced legions, including the *Ninth* and *Tenth*, had been sent back to Italy after Pharsalus. There they waited, with little to do for month after month except think of their grievances. There were still time-expired soldiers wishing for discharge, and all recalled the promises of bounties and land grants that Caesar had made to them during the last few years. Led by some of their centurions and tribunes the legions were soon in a mutinous state and stoned the officers sent to restore order. Antony himself was forced to go to the camp, but failed to resolve the situation and restore order. While he was away from Rome, there was trouble instigated by some of the tribunes of the plebs. One of these was Cicero's son-in-law Dolabella, who now renewed Caelius' cry of the abolition of debt. There was rioting in the Forum once more as a number of men scented the chance to carve out a stronger personal position at this time of uncertainty. Eventually Antony returned with some troops who had not joined the mutiny and used force to restore order, backed by a Senate that had once again passed its ultimate decree. He did this efficiently, but this action only reinforced the perception of a regime based solely on military might. His dislike of Dolabella was intense and reciprocated. It doubtless did not help that Antony believed that the tribune was having an affair with his wife, whom he divorced soon afterwards.[5]

MUTINEERS, DEBTORS AND FORMER ENEMIES

Caesar met Cicero on his way from Brundisium and the nervous orator was relieved and gratified by the warmth of his greeting, which was followed by an immediate pardon and encouragement to return to Rome. In the dictator's absence he had been awarded the right to deal with his enemies as he saw fit, granting some formal legitimacy to what he had been doing since the start of the Civil War. Similarly, he was awarded the power to declare peace and war, and also to preside over – indeed virtually control – elections to all the senior magistracies. Although Caesar did not get back to Rome until the beginning of October, he decided to make use of this last right and appoint magistrates for the remaining weeks of the year. As consuls he chose Quintus Fufius Calenus and Publius Vatinius – the man who as tribune in 59 BC had secured him the Gallic command. Both men had served as his legates. The other magistracies, as well as a number of priesthoods made vacant by the casualties of the last few years, similarly went to his supporters. It is doubtful that the new magistrates had much time to do anything, but there were many men to reward for their loyalty and Caesar did not wish to lose any of his reputation for generosity. For the next year he created ten praetors instead of the usual eight. For the moment he chose not to continue as dictator and was instead elected consul for the third time – another of the honours voted by the Senate during his absence was the right to hold the supreme magistracy for five consecutive years. As colleague he chose Marcus Aemilius Lepidus, a man who seems to have been more notable for his loyalty and reliability than any great talent or imagination. It is tempting to see the choice as an indication that Mark Antony had fallen from favour following his behaviour in the last year. There may be some truth in this, but it should be noted that Caesar had other men to reward and may have been reluctant to seem to mark out any one individual as a permanent second-in-command.[6]

The mutiny in the army had not been calmed by news of Caesar's return to Italy, for the resentment had had too long to fester. He sent Sallust – the future historian and recently made praetor for the following year – to confront the troops, but he was attacked by a mob and barely escaped with his life. The mutineers began to march from their camp in Campania towards Rome itself. By this time the tribunes and centurions who were the ringleaders seem to have aimed at gaining some concessions and promises of even greater rewards in future. They were aware that Caesar was soon to go to Africa to confront the Pompeians and felt that his need for his best soldiers would make him more pliant. It seems doubtful that the bulk of the troops, and indeed most of their officers, had any such clear aims, but simply a strong, if unfocused, sense of grievance. Caesar made some preparations to defend Rome if the worst came to the worst, but outwardly remained calm and, in spite of the advice of some of his staff, went in person to meet the legions. The latter had camped on the outskirts of Rome, when without warning Caesar quietly rode into their lines and climbed up onto the podium that was usually constructed near the headquarters. As news of his arrival spread the soldiers clustered around to hear what he had to say. He asked them what they wanted and they replied, recounting their long and difficult service and reminding him of the promises he had made to them over the years. Finally they demanded that they all be discharged, which seems to have been intended to remind him that he wanted them for his new campaign, but could not take their loyalty for granted. Caesar's reply began calmly, which made it all the more shocking. In the past the soldiers had always been his 'comrades', but now he addressed them as 'citizens' (*Quirites*), and told these mere civilians that he willingly released them from service since that was what they wanted. The soldiers were stunned by this casual dismissal and their commander's gentle reassurance that he would in time give them all the rewards that he had promised.

Just as on campaign, Caesar had seized back the initiative and now it was his soldiers who struggled to regain their confidence and determination. Men began calling out that they volunteered for further service with him, and then one of the leaders of the mutiny repeated this request more formally. Caesar declined the offer, but then repeated his promise to assign land and the promised gifts of money to all of them – by this time it seems he had adopted a tone of gentle reproach, as though he was saddened that his own men had doubted the truth of his promises. Perhaps at this point he turned to leave, making the mutineers even more desperate as they begged him to take them back and lead them to Africa, assuring him that they would win the war for him without any need for other troops. Now Caesar relented, but in a complete reversal of his speech at Vesontio in 58 BC, he said that he would take all of them except for the *Tenth* Legion. He reminded the veterans of the *Tenth* of all his past favours, and said that for their ingratitude he would now discharge them, but that each man would still get all that he had been promised after his victory in Africa. Their immense pride in their unit challenged, and their devotion to their old commander reignited, the legionaries of the *Tenth* begged Caesar to decimate them as long as he took them back. Gradually, and with feigned reluctance, he allowed himself to be persuaded and announced that this time there would be no executions. However, he had made a note of the tribunes and centurions who had provoked the outbreak and is said to have arranged for most of them to be placed in the most exposed and dangerous positions during the coming campaign.[7]

Caesar had emphasised to his soldiers that he would not follow Sulla's example of seizing land throughout Italy to give to his veterans. Instead he would provide for them from publicly owned or publicly purchased land. This, and the continuing cost of the war, added to his already massive financial burden, and much of his effort during the autumn of 47 BC was devoted to meeting these costs. He took loans – supposedly voluntary, but no community was likely to risk disappointing him – from the towns of Italy and clearly had no intention of repaying them, at least in the short term. After the defeat of Pompey he had often been sent crowns and wreaths of gold or silver by the inhabitants of the eastern provinces, both as a sign of victory and a donation to his expenses. The same gesture was now encouraged in Italy. The activities of Caelius and Dolabella had made it clear that there was still much discontent amongst the many debtors. Caesar now relented a little, copying one of the latter's laws by setting a relatively low limit on the rent due to landlords for the current year. However, he still refused to abolish all existing debts, saying now that he could not consider this since he had recently taken out so many loans himself and therefore would be the chief beneficiary. Some property owned by leading Pompeians who were either dead or still fighting against him was auctioned off. Antony bought Pompey's great house in Rome, anticipating that he would have to pay only a fraction of its worth. Sulla had allowed many of his partisans – Crassus, Pompey and Lucullus chief amongst them – to acquire valuable estates and houses in this way, and clearly many of Caesar's men expected to benefit in a similar fashion. If so, then they were rudely disappointed, for Caesar insisted that the full value, assessed at pre-war market rates, must be paid for everything. In part this was doubtless to lessen comparison with Sulla, but at root it was simply a reflection of the massive financial burden he faced. Only a few people got bargains. One was Servilia, his long-time lover. Caesar clearly still had a deep affection for her, although we have no idea whether or not their relationship remained a physical one. Around about this time he also had an affair with one of her daughters, Tertia or 'Third', without this seeming to weaken the bond between them. The gossip even claimed that she had arranged the liaison. In addition she was the mother of Brutus, one of the most distinguished – and certainly one of the most widely respected – of the Pompeians to defect to Caesar after Pharsalus. Servilia was now able to purchase some valuable estates at a fraction of their true price. Cicero joked that people did not realise how much of a bargain this really was, for there was a 'Third' taken off the price.[8]

THE AFRICAN CAMPAIGN

Caesar remained in Rome for only as long as was essential to restore order and prepare for an attack on the Pompeians in Africa. Troops and supplies were ordered to concentrate at the port of Lilybaeum in Sicily, where the invasion force was being prepared. There were still serious shortages of ships, especially transport ships, and once again it would prove impossible to carry the entire army in one go. It was also now winter, which meant bad weather and all the problems of supply familiar to the Macedonian campaign. The diviners who accompanied the army declared that the omens were unfavourable for launching a campaign in the near future, but Caesar had never been too concerned about such things and ignored them. He was impatient to set off, hoping that defeat of the enemy in Africa would finally bring the war to an end. When he arrived at Lilybaeum on 17 December 47 BC, he had his own tent pitched almost on the beach itself, as a gesture to convey his sense of urgency, warning his men to be ready to move 'at any day or hour'. The apparent lethargy of Egypt had long gone and his familiar energy returned, perhaps sharpened with an even greater edge of impatience. Caesar had brought only a single legion with him, but during the next week five more arrived. Only one was a veteran unit, the *Fifth Alaudae,* which he had raised in Transalpine Gaul and given citizenship. The other five legions – the *Twenty-Fifth*, *Twenty-Sixth*, *Twenty-Eighth*, *Twenty-Ninth* and *Thirtieth* – had all been raised during the war, and most likely all contained many men who had originally been levied by the Pompeians.

As it arrived each unit was embarked and crammed into the waiting transport ships. Strict orders were issued that no one was to take any baggage or equipment that was not absolutely essential. The legions were accompanied by 2,000 cavalrymen and their mounts, but there was little room to carry substantial supplies of food and fodder, or for the pack and draught animals to transport them after the landing. Caesar trusted that he would be able to obtain all of these things in sufficient quantities once he arrived in Africa. On 25 December he set sail, but the operation was not well planned. In the past, it had been his custom to issue sealed orders that would be opened at a set time and provided such essential details as where to land on the hostile shore. This time he had insufficient information to know where the army could land and simply trusted that a suitable spot would be discovered once the fleet arrived off the coast of Africa. Strong winds added to the confusion and the convoys of ships became scattered, straggling along individually or in small groups. Only a small fraction of the fleet was with Caesar when he sighted land on 28 December. For a while he sailed parallel to the coast, looking for a good landing spot and also hoping that more ships would catch up with him. He eventually landed near the enemy-held port of Hadrumentum. He had only 3,500 legionaries and 150 cavalry with him. It is said that when he disembarked he stumbled and fell on the beach, but those around him were able to laugh off the bad omen when he grabbed two handfuls of shingle and declared, 'I have hold of you, Africa!'[9]

The forces arrayed against him were considerable. Before leaving Sicily reports had reached him claiming that Scipio led no less than ten legions – doubtless under strength and inexperienced, but the same was true of a large part of his own army – backed by a strong cavalry force, as well as the troops of King Juba, which now included four 'legions', organised, trained and equipped in Roman style. The Numidians were famous for their numerous light cavalry and infantry skirmishers – the horsemen having an especially high reputation – and Juba fielded very many of these. There were also no less than 120 war elephants, which were something of a rarity by this period. Elephants were frightening, but were dangerous to both sides as they were liable to panic and stampede through friendly troops. Later in the campaign Metellus Scipio took some care to try and train his animals to cope with the chaos and noise of battle. Caesar was hugely outnumbered, and would remain so even when over the following days he was joined by most of the rest of his ships. This was not achieved without considerable effort, officers being despatched with small squadrons of warships to hunt for the scattered parts of the convoy. At one point Caesar himself had secretly left the army to look for the lost ships, but they appeared before he was actually under way. Yet, as in Macedonia in 48 BC, he did enjoy the great advantage of surprise, for once again the enemy had not expected him to move so soon and to arrive in winter. Their forces were widely dispersed and it would take them some time to gather in sufficient numbers to overwhelm him. In the meantime he sent his fleet back to Sicily with orders to return as soon as possible with more troops, but the Pompeians still possessed a strong navy and as in the earlier campaign there was no guarantee that later convoys would reach him. For the moment his main priority was to secure sufficient supplies to support his forces in the meantime. He could not go too far afield in his search for these, since not only would the enemy seek to hinder him, but it was vital that he stay near the coast if there was to be any chance of reinforcement. The Pompeians had already gathered up much of the available food. In addition, the widespread conscription of local farm labourers to serve in their forces had seriously disrupted the agriculture of the region. In the opening weeks of the campaign Caesar's main concern was supply, and orders were despatched to other provinces, including Sardinia, to gather supplies of grain and send them to him with all urgency.[10]

Soon after landing an unsuccessful attempt was made to persuade the garrison commander at Hadrumentum to surrender. Caesar was in no position to begin a siege and so moved on, establishing his main base at

Ruspina. On 1 January 46 BC he reached the town of Leptis, which welcomed him. As at Corfinium he took the precaution of posting guards to prevent any of his men from entering the town and looting it. Six cohorts were left to garrison the town when he returned next day to Ruspina. On 4 January he decided to mount a large-scale foraging expedition, taking out thirty cohorts. Just 3 miles out from the camp an enemy force was spotted, so Caesar sent orders to bring up the small force of 400 cavalry and 150 archers, which were all that were then available. In person he went out with a patrol to reconnoitre, leaving the column of legionaries to follow. The Pompeian force was led by Labienus and included 8,000 Numidian cavalry, 1,600 Gaulish and German horsemen, as well as numerous infantry. However, he had formed them in a dense line, far closer together than horsemen would normally deploy, and from a distance Caesar mistook them for a conventional battle line of close order infantry. Acting on this mistaken premise, he brought up his troops and formed them into a single line of cohorts. It was rare for the Romans to deploy in this way, for normally at least a second line was employed, but the legionaries were badly outnumbered and he decided that it was better to match the length of the enemy line rather than risk being outflanked. His small force of cavalry – many had not yet disembarked – were divided between his wings and his few archers sent out to skirmish in front of the line. He was ready, but did not choose to attack the enemy line, since he had no wish to provoke a fight unless it was necessary. Suddenly Labienus began to move and ordered his cavalry to extend on both flanks. Numidian light infantrymen swarmed forward from the main line as Caesar's legionaries advanced to meet it. So far in the campaign there had only been some small-scale actions and this was the first time that the Caesareans encountered the characteristic tactics of the local troops. Sheer weight of numbers forced their cavalry back, but in the centre the legionaries struggled to cope with an enemy that fled before they could come to grips, but quickly rallied and came back, all the while harassing them with a hail of javelins. They were especially vulnerable to missiles aimed at their unshielded right side. It was dangerous to pursue too far, for the agile enemy could easily overwhelm any individuals or small group that became separated from support. Caesar sent orders along the line that no one was to go more than four paces away from the main line occupied by his cohort.[11]

The pressure was great, with probably more wounds being inflicted than fatalities. Caesar's men found themselves surrounded and unable to strike back at an enemy who slowly whittled them down. Most of the legionaries were inexperienced and nervousness spread throughout the army. Caesar as usual took care to remain calm and to encourage them. It was probably during this action that he had more success dealing with a standard-bearer who was about to flee. Caesar grabbed the man, physically turned him around, and said, 'Look, that's where the enemy are!' As he strove to steady his wavering men, Labienus was haranguing them from just behind the enemy front line. The author of the *African War* describes how:

Labienus was riding about bare headed in the front line, urging on his own men, and sometimes calling out to Caesar's legionaries: 'What are you up to, you raw recruit? Really ferocious aren't you? Are you another of those taken in by "his" fine words. He's taken you into a tough spot. I feel really sorry for you.' Then one of our soldiers said, 'I'm no recruit, Labienus, but a veteran of the *Tenth* Legion.' 'I don't see the insignia of the *Tenth*,' said Labienus. Then the soldier retorted, 'You will soon know what sort of man I am.' At the same moment he pulled off his helmet, so that the other would recognise him, and threw his *pilum* with all his might, aimed square at Labienus, struck deep into the chest of his horse, and said, 'That will show you, Labienus, that it's a soldier of the *Tenth* attacking you.'[12]

Yet overall there were few veterans with the force, and the many recruits were struggling to cope with the pressure. As at the Sambre more than a decade before, the nervous troops were tending to bunch together, restricting their own ability to fight and making themselves a better target. Caesar ordered the line to extend, and then had alternate cohorts face about, so that half now confronted the cavalry that had surrounded his rear, and the rest the infantry and skirmishers to the front. Once this was done, the cohorts charged simultaneously, hurling a concentrated volley of *pila*. It was enough to drive the enemy back for a while, and Caesar quickly halted the pursuit and began to withdraw back to his camp. Around the same time the enemy was reinforced by Petreius who brought with him 1,600 more cavalry and a large number of infantry. Their enthusiasm revived, the Pompeians began to harry Caesar's men as they retreated. After only a short distance he was once again forced to turn into battle order and face them. Caesar's legionaries were tired, and the mounts of his cavalry – not fully recovered from the voyage and now wearied by prolonged manoeuvring and in some cases wounds – were close to exhaustion. Yet most of the enemy were also far from fresh as it was nearing the end of a long day of fighting. Caesar urged his men to make one last effort and then, waiting for the enemy pressure to slacken a little, he launched one last determined counter-attack and drove them back over and past some high ground. Petreius was wounded and Labienus may well have been carried from the field after falling from his wounded horse, so it is possible that the enemy for a while lacked their most aggressive and experienced leaders. Whatever the precise cause, this success was enough to permit Caesar to withdraw the rest of the way unmolested. The action outside Ruspina – it is sometimes described as a battle – was without doubt a defeat for Caesar, who had been prevented from his aim of gathering the supplies that his army required. Yet the outcome could have been far worse, and he had managed to fight his way to safety. On balance it was a setback, but certainly not a decisive one. Curio's army had been destroyed by an enemy fighting in much the same style and Caesar had managed to escape the same fate.[13]

In the aftermath Caesar heavily fortified the camp at Ruspina and took sailors from the fleet to serve as light infantry on land, while craftsmen in the army were set to manufacturing sling bullets and javelins of various sorts. More despatches went off ordering grain and other supplies to be gathered and brought to him. In the meantime some soldiers were very imaginative in finding substitutes for the things so desperately needed. Some of the veterans gathered seaweed, which was washed in fresh water, dried and then fed to the horses, keeping them alive if not in the best of health or condition. Metellus Scipio had brought his forces to support the Pompeians, and the combined army camped 3 miles away from Caesar's position. King Juba was also on his way to join them, but was forced to turn back when his lands came under attack from the forces of his rival, Bocchus of Mauretania, whose troops were led by a Roman mercenary, Publius Sittius. The latter had fled to Africa after being implicated in Catiline's rising. Caesar had not arranged for Bocchus to open a second front in this way, and it was extremely fortuitous that he and Sittius acted so effectively on their own initiative. It was obviously attractive for the king to ally with the enemy of his own great enemy Juba, for the support of the Pompeians had increased the latter's power. Caesar made great use of this in his propaganda, announcing that the Pompeians were behaving shamefully for Roman senators in allowing themselves to side with and serve under a foreign monarch. In the *African War* it is claimed that when the enemy forces finally did combine, Metellus Scipio stopped wearing his general's cloak because it displeased Juba. It was also claimed that the Pompeians had alienated most of the province by their brutal rule. As the word spread that Caesar himself, and not simply one of his legates, had come to the region, there were a few defections from local communities. Some are said to have remembered their obligation to his uncle Marius, whose name still provoked great loyalty in the region sixty years after his victory in Numidia. There was a steady stream of deserters coming across from the Pompeian lines, but none of Caesar's soldiers went over to the enemy. From the beginning of the campaign the Pompeians regularly executed prisoners, although in one case this was after the centurion in charge had refused to change sides and join them. Neither side made any serious attempt to end the war by negotiation. The Pompeians still fighting loathed Caesar bitterly. In turn he despised them. When the rumour had spread that the family of the Scipiones would always be victorious in Africa, Caesar attached to his staff an obscure member of the line named Scipio Salvito or Salutio, who was generally felt to be worthless in every respect save for his famous name.[14]

Outside Ruspina the two armies continually probed and skirmished with each other, the Pompeians frequently attempting to ambush any enemy detachments that strayed too far from Caesar's camp. Metellus Scipio often deployed in battle order just outside his camp, and when after several days Caesar made no move to match this, he ordered them to advance closer to the enemy. Even then he was not confident enough to launch an all-out attack. Caesar sent orders to withdraw any patrols or foraging parties that might find themselves exposed, and told his outlying pickets to pull back only if pressed. All this was done with great nonchalance, for he did not bother to go up onto the rampart of the camp and observe the enemy, but was content to remain in his headquarters tent, calmly receiving reports and issuing appropriate orders, 'so remarkable was his expertise in and knowledge of warfare'. His estimation of his opponent's caution proved accurate, for Scipio did not launch an attack, deterred by the formidable defences of the camp, the ramparts and towers well manned and mounting artillery. In addition the Pompeians found the enemy inactivity unnerving and worried that Caesar was trying to lure them into a trap. However, Scipio was able to encourage his men by claiming that Caesar was afraid to fight them. Shortly afterwards a convoy arrived from Sicily, bringing the *Thirteenth* and *Fourteenth* legions, along with 800 Gaulish cavalry and 1,000 light infantrymen. In addition to these experienced troops the ships also carried enough grain to relieve Caesar's immediate concerns over food. Defections and desertions from the enemy continued, and on the night of 25 January, Caesar suddenly moved onto the offensive, leading out his main force from the camp. At first they marched away from the enemy, back past the town of Ruspina, but then they swung round and moved to seize a line of hills, occupation of which threatened the lines of the Pompeians. There was some fighting to secure these, and the next day a larger cavalry combat, which Caesar's men won. Most of Labeinus' Numidians escaped, but their retreat exposed the German and Gallic warriors serving with him and many of these were killed. The sight of the fleeing horsemen demoralised the rest of the army. The next day Caesar advanced on the town of Uzitta, the main water source for the Pompeians at this time. Metellus Scipio responded by advancing in battle order to confront him, but neither side chose to press the issue and force a battle.[15]

THE BATTLE OF THAPSUS, 6 APRIL 46 BC

Metellus Scipio had also been reinforced by this time, for Juba had left one of his officers and a strong force to contain Sittius and had brought three of his 'legions', 800 heavy cavalry and large numbers of Numidian horsemen and light infantry to join up with the Pompeians. Rumours of the king's arrival had spread throughout Caesar's camp, with the numbers and formidable fighting power of his men growing with each telling of the tale. Suetonius tells us that Caesar decided to address the men, in a matter of fact way, saying:

> Let me tell you that in a couple of days the king will be here with ten legions, 30,000 horsemen, 100,000 skirmishers, plus 300 elephants. Right then, some of you can now stop asking questions or guessing and can believe me, because I know all about it. If not, then you can be sure that I will order them put on some old hulk of a ship and blown away to whichever land the wind takes them.

The tone was similar to Vesontio, with a combination of utter self-confidence and mild annoyance that their faith in him and their respect for discipline had wavered. It may also have helped that he exaggerated the numbers of royal troops, so that when the real size of the enemy reinforcement became known it probably came as a relief. There followed a period of manoeuvring around Uzitta. Both sides contested some high ground between their positions, but an attempt by Labienus to ambush Caesar's vanguard failed because of the poor discipline of some of his troops who refused to wait patiently for the enemy to arrive. The Caesareans easily routed them and constructed a camp on the hill. When the main force withdrew back to camp at dusk, the Pompeians launched a sudden cavalry attack, but this was beaten off. Skirmishing continued, and Caesar's men began work on lines of fortification designed both to restrict the enemy's freedom of movement and to threaten the town.

Shortly afterwards news arrived that another convoy of reinforcements had been sighted approaching Ruspina. There was a delay of several days, because they mistook some Caesarean warships waiting to escort them for an enemy force, but eventually the confusion was sorted out and the *Ninth* and *Tenth* legions disembarked. Remembering the latter's role in the mutiny in Italy, Caesar saw the opportunity of making an example of some of the ringleaders. One of these, the tribune Avienus, had selfishly insisted on filling an entire ship with his personal household and baggage – an especially crass act when space was needed for fighting men and vital supplies. He was now dismissed from the service and sent home in disgrace, along with another tribune and several centurions who had been guilty of similar misbehaviour. Each man was permitted only one slave to accompany him. Caesar now had ten legions, half of which were veteran formations. There were more desertions to him, and he was able to persuade some Gaetulian leaders to rebel against King Juba, who was then forced to detach some more of his troops to oppose them.[16]

The fortifications facing Uzitta were now complete, but although a few days later both sides formed up in battle order with their front lines little more than a quarter of a mile apart, neither chose to force the issue. There was a skirmish between the cavalry and light troops, in which the Pompeians gained the advantage. The armies continued to face each other outside the town and Caesar set his men to extending the lines of fortification. A third convoy of reinforcements was now reported to be approaching Africa, but this time the Pompeians had warning of its approach and captured or destroyed some of Caesar's warships, which had been sent to escort the transports on the last part of their journey. Hearing of this Caesar left the army at Uzitta and galloped with all haste the 6 miles to the coast at Leptis. Taking charge of one of his own naval squadrons he chased down and defeated the enemy warships. Although this is not made clear, the original rumour may have been false and the *Seventh* and *Eighth* legions may not have reached Caesar before the campaign was decided.

Securing enough food for the army continued to be a great problem. Learning that it was the local custom to bury food stores, Caesar led out two legions on an expedition to find as many of these hidden sites as possible. He had also learned from deserters that Labenius was planning an ambush, so over the course of a few days he sent out other parties to hunt for food along the same routes, in order to make Labenius complacent. Then one morning before dawn he sent out three veteran legions supported by cavalry to hunt down the ambushers. The enemy was checked, but the supply problem had not eased. The successive reinforcements had greatly strengthened Caesar's army, but had also inevitably added to the number of mouths needing to be fed. He had been unable to force the Pompeians to fight a battle in circumstances of his choosing, and there was no immediate prospect of taking Uzitta and depriving the enemy of their main water supply. Caesar decided that there was nothing to be gained by remaining where he was. Having set fire to their own camp, his army marched away in the early hours of the morning, halting near the town of Aggar, where he sent out numerous foraging parties who managed to bring in considerable quantities of grain – though mostly barley rather than wheat – and other types of food.[17]

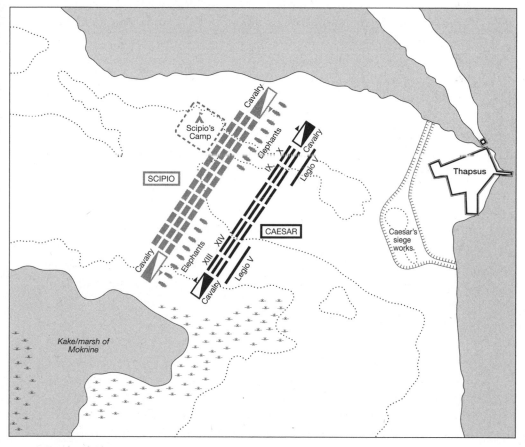

Battle of Thapsus

An attempt was then made to surprise an enemy foraging party – the Pompeians were also finding it difficult to feed such a large concentration of troops – but Caesar withdrew when he saw that enemy reinforcements were already approaching. As Caesar's army continued its march it was constantly harassed by Numidian horse, so that it was often necessary to halt and repulse them. These attacks were wearying and seriously impeded the march. At one point the column was only able to cover 100 paces (about 33 yards) in four hours. Caesar withdrew most of his cavalry behind his infantry, and found that the legions were able to make steadier progress since the enemy cavalry would always withdraw when they came too close. He pressed on, but even so only managed to reach a suitable camp site after night had fallen. Over the following days he gave thought to training his men and developing new drills to cope with this style of fighting. In spite of his withdrawal, towns were still defecting to him, although in one case Juba learned of this and had stormed the place and massacred the inhabitants before Caesar could send a garrison. On 21 March Caesar's army carried out a *lustratio*, the ceremony of ritual purification that the army performed each year, which the author of the *African War* chose to mention, unlike Caesar himself in the *Commentaries*. The day after this he offered battle, but this was declined, so he continued on his march.

As part of his new standing orders Caesar instructed each legion to keep 300 men moving in battle order ready to act as close support for the cavalry, and these troops helped to fend off the Numidian horsemen who pursued them. He reached the town of Sarsura and stormed it, capturing considerable stocks of grain that had been gathered there by the enemy. Scipio made no effort to hinder him. The next enemy-held town was too strong to be taken without a formal siege, so Caesar swung back and camped again near Aggar, winning a cavalry action in spite of the fact that his men were heavily outnumbered. Again he offered battle, but the Pompeians refused to come down from the high ground they occupied and Caesar was not willing to place his men at a disadvantage by attacking them in this position. On 4 April he once again set out in the early hours and was able to cover the 16 miles that brought him to the coastal town of Thapsus and began to besiege it. Scipio followed and divided his force between two camps some 8 miles from the town. With the sea on one side and a large salt water lagoon on another, the two main approaches to the town were narrow. Anticipating the enemy, Caesar had already placed a fort to block the most obvious route. Thwarted, Scipio led his men on a wide night march around the lake to approach the town from the other side, using a narrow spit of land no more than a mile and a half wide. He arrived on the morning of 6 April. Juba and Afranius seem to have remained in camp with their forces to keep Caesar boxed in.[18]

Caesar left two legions of recruits in his siege lines and led out the rest to form in normal *triplex acies* battle order facing Scipio. He placed veteran formations supported by archers and slingers on the flanks – the *Tenth* and *Ninth* on the right and the *Thirteenth* and *Fourteenth* on the left. As added protection, especially against the enemy war elephants, he divided the *Fifth Alaudae* into two and used them to make an additional fourth line of five cohorts behind each of his wings. Three of the less experienced legions – we are not told which ones – formed the centre. The cavalry were as usual on the wings, although in this narrow spit of land there was little room to manoeuvre. This was a greater restriction on the Pompeians whose horsemen were more numerous, although presumably the bulk of the Numidians had remained with Juba. In a rather unusual move, Caesar gave instructions for some of his warships to use the channel to threaten the rear of the enemy army once the battle had begun. Our sources give few details for the Pompeian deployment, nor any reliable figure for the number of troops with Scipio, as opposed to those left behind with Juba and Afranius. Probably the deployment was conventional, with the cavalry on the wings, legions in three lines and the elephants in advance, presumably massed on each flank. It was a good opportunity for Caesar. The Pompeians had divided their forces, and chosen to take station on terrain that would only permit a simple head-to-head encounter in which his more experienced troops were likely to prevail. His legionaries were keen to attack and confident of victory. Most of his officers urged him to give the signal to advance straightaway. Caesar could see their enthusiasm as he went along the line to urge them on. Even so, the author of the *African War* tells us that:

> Caesar was doubtful, resisting their eagerness and enthusiasm, yelling out that he did not approve of fighting by a reckless onslaught, and holding back the line again and again, when suddenly on the right wing a *tubicen* [trumpeter], without orders from Caesar, but encouraged by the soldiers, began to sound his instrument. This was repeated by all the cohorts, the line began to advance against the enemy, although the centurions placed themselves in front and vainly tried to restrain the soldiers by force and stop them attacking without orders from the general.

When Caesar perceived that it was impossible to restrain the soldiers' roused spirits, he gave the watchword 'Good Luck' [*Felicitas*], and spurred his horse at the enemy front ranks.[19]

The confidence of the army proved justified, for the Pompeians failed to cope with this sudden attack and were quickly routed. Plutarch presents another version of the story in which he claimed that as the battle was about to begin Caesar felt an epileptic fit coming on and had to be taken away to shelter, hence the confused start to the advance. There are very few stories of specific epileptic attacks suffered by Caesar, and this is the only one that claims that his epilepsy interfered with his ability to command.[20]

The elephants attacking Caesar's right flank were panicked by the hail of missiles from his skirmishers and stampeded back through their own lines. The whole Pompeian left wing soon collapsed and all attempts at rallying the army failed in the face of a ferocious pursuit. Caesar's legionaries were in a grim mood and killed more freely than they had done after Pharsalus. They wanted the war over and had no wish to see men being pardoned and let free to fight them again. Caesar himself had already ordered the execution of one Pompeian whom he had pardoned during the surrender in Spain in 49 BC, but who had now been captured for a second time. This was his normal policy, forgiving a man once but killing him if he had chosen to continue fighting in spite of this pardon. At Thapsus his soldiers had no concern for such distinctions and many Pompeians died as they tried to surrender. The legionaries even cut down several of Caesar's own officers when they tried to stop the killing. By the end of the day 10,000 Pompeians had been killed for little more than fifty casualties on Caesar's side. The main enemy leaders escaped, but most would die in the following weeks. Afranius and Sulla's son Faustus were captured by Sittius and handed over to Caesar, who then had them executed, in response to the clamour of his soldiers. A few other prisoners were executed but in some cases – for instance, that of Lucius Caesar, the son of his cousin and legate – it is unclear whether he ordered the deaths or whether the decision was taken by his subordinates. Petreius and King Juba arranged a somewhat bizarre suicide pact, fighting a duel to the death. The versions of the outcome vary from source to source, but the most likely seems to have been that the Roman killed the Numidian, and then with the help of a slave ran himself through. Metellus Scipio escaped by sea, but killed himself when his ships were intercepted by a pursuing Caesarean squadron. Of the few who escaped, Labienus managed to make his way to Spain where he joined up with Pompey's sons Cnaeus and Sextus.[21]

Cato was in command of the city of Utica throughout the African campaign and so had not been present at the defeat. Indeed it is striking how minor a role he played in the military operations in the entire Civil War. Fugitives soon brought news of the disaster and word that Caesar's men would soon arrive. Cato consulted with the Romans in the city, three hundred of whom he had formed into a council, but realised that whatever their resolve there was little prospect of continuing to fight. The choice then became either to flee, to surrender or to commit suicide. After dinner, which since Pharsalus he had refused to eat reclining in the proper manner and so had taken sitting down, he retired to his chamber. (It was not the first such gesture he had made, for he is supposed to have refused to be shaved or have his hair cut once the Civil War began.) He complained when he noticed that his son and servants had removed his sword, and insisted that they return it, but then went back to his reading. His choice of work was significant, Plato's *Phaedo*, a discussion of the immortality of the soul, but throughout his life he had pursued the study of philosophy. Finally, without warning, he stopped reading, took up his sword and stabbed himself in the stomach. The wound was bad, but not immediately mortal, and once they heard the commotion his son and slaves rushed to him. A doctor was brought and Cato's wound cleaned and bound up. However, he had never lacked determination or courage, and once they had gone the forty-eight-year-old tore open the stitches and began ripping out his own entrails. He was dead before they could restrain him. When Caesar heard the news he said that he bitterly begrudged the opportunity of pardoning his most determined opponent, but to a great extent Cato had acted out of a desire to avoid his enemy's mercy.

Less than three and a half years after crossing the Rubicon most of the leading men who had forced Caesar to take that step were dead, and of the survivors nearly all had given up the fight. The bloodshed was not quite over, for a year later there would be another campaign in Spain, fought with even greater savagery. When the Civil War began his opponents had been wrong to think that Caesar would not fight, and then mistaken to believe that the greater resources under their control meant that their victory was assured. Against the odds, Caesar had won the Civil War and it now remained to be seen whether or not he could win the peace and create a lasting settlement. That was the priority, but first, as in Asia, he had to settle the region. As usual communities that had supported the Pompeians were subject to punitive fines, while those who had supported him were rewarded. It was probably around this time that he had an affair with Eunoe, the wife of the Moorish King Bogudes. It was not until June that he left Africa, almost five and a half months after he had landed.[22]

XXII

DICTATOR, 46–44 BC

'It is always the same at the end of civil wars, and it is not just the wishes of the victor which are carried through, for he also needs to humour those who have helped him to win.' – *Cicero, December 48 BC.*[1]

'As victor Caesar returned to the city and, in a way that almost exceeded human belief, pardoned all those who had carried arms against him.' – *Velleius Paterculus, early first century* AD.[2]

Caesar reached Rome near the end of July 46 BC. The Senate had already voted him the staggering total of forty days of public thanksgiving for his latest victory – tactfully considered to be over King Juba and not his Roman allies. This was double the number awarded even for the defeat of Vercingetorix. Fourteen years earlier Caesar had given up the right to celebrate a triumph in his quest for the consulship. Now, after weeks of frantic preparation, he celebrated no less than four triumphs, over Gaul, Egypt and the Nile, Asia, and King Juba and Africa. In his long career Pompey had triumphed three times, and it is likely that most were aware that Caesar was now also commemorating victories won on the continents of Europe, Africa and Asia, just as his great rival had done. The celebrations began on 21 September, but were not held on consecutive days and so lasted until 2 October. The scale was lavish, with parades of prisoners, including Vercingetorix, the infant son of Juba, and Cleopatra's sister Arsinoe. The latter is said to have inspired pity in the crowd and she and the boy were spared the fate of the Gaulish war leader, who was ritually strangled at the end of the Gallic triumph in the traditional way. Tradition – certainly recent tradition – was altered in a number of special privileges granted to Caesar. One of the most conspicuous was the right to be preceded by no fewer than seventy-two lictors. A consul was normally attended by a dozen of these men and a dictator by twenty-four, and the number seems to have been intended to show that Caesar had held the latter office three times – six times the number who normally attended a consul and treble the amount given to a dictator. In addition, following precedents found only in the distant past of the Republic, Caesar rode in a chariot pulled by a team of white horses. However, if Suetonius and Dio are to be believed, early on in the first triumph – the one over Gaul – the axle on his chariot broke and he had to finish the procession in a hastily summoned replacement. Perhaps in expiation of this bad omen, at the end of the ceremony Caesar climbed on his knees up the steps of the Temple of Jupiter on the Capitol. Pliny tells us that Caesar always uttered a magical formula before setting out anywhere in a chariot because of some earlier accident, but clearly this did not have the desired effect on this occasion.[3]

In each of the processions were carts carrying the spoils taken from the enemy, usually weapons and armour as well as silver, gold and other precious objects. Others mounted placards carrying slogans – including the famous *Veni, Vidi, Vici* – or lists of achievements. It has often been suggested that Pliny's figure of 1,192,000 enemies killed by Caesar during his campaigns was derived from adding up the numbers of enemy casualties proclaimed during his triumphs. Quantifying victory had always been important for the competitive aristocracy of Rome. Another tradition was to show paintings of notable scenes from the campaigns, and Caesar's triumphs included many of these. Officially he was celebrating the defeat of foreign enemies of the Republic, and there was no mention or depiction of Pompey and Pharsalus. There were said to be pictures of Metellus Scipio stabbing himself to death and Cato tearing open his own wound. The sight provoked groans from the crowd, and has sometimes been seen as crass exultation over the defeat of his enemies that contrasted with his usual emphasis on clemency. Yet the sources do not suggest that the sight encouraged hostility to Caesar, and the reminders of the waste of life and horror of the Civil War were certainly encouragement to accept the new regime simply to avoid further conflict. The soldiers who marched in the procession wearing their decorations and finest equipment certainly had no qualms about causing offence. Long-standing tradition gave them licence to sing not just about their own deeds in the war, but to chant bawdy rhymes at the expense of their commander, for on a day of triumph normal military discipline was relaxed. Caesar's veterans sang of his mistresses in Gaul, claiming that he had squandered on them the funds granted to him by the Republic, and warned the Romans to 'lock up their wives' because they brought with them the 'bald adulterer'. They joked about how wrongdoing normally brought punishment, but that instead

Caesar had made himself master of Rome through defying the Senate. Another verse recalled the old gossip about his time in Bithynia:

> Caesar subdued Gaul – but Nicomedes subdued Caesar:
> Behold now Caesar triumphs, who has conquered Gaul –
> Nicomedes does not triumph, although he conquered Caesar.[4]

This was the only slur that annoyed Caesar and soon afterwards he took a public oath denying that there was any truth in the allegation. Dio says that this only made him look ridiculous.[5]

In the days between the triumphal processions there were great feasts open to all, with no fewer than 22,000 tables laid out with the finest foods and wines. At nightfall after the final banquet, Caesar walked home in a procession whose progress was illuminated by twenty elephants that carried great torches. There were also theatrical performances, and at one of these he insisted that the famous equestrian playwright Decimus Laberius actually perform on stage. The latter resented this, but obeyed and had the satisfaction when he uttered the line 'He whom many fear, must therefore fear many' of seeing the audience all turn to face Caesar. After the performance Laberius was rewarded with 500,000 sestertii and a gold ring to signify restoration to the equestrian status that he had been forced to forfeit by appearing on stage – acting was not considered a proper activity for a wealthy citizen. Apart from the drama, there were sporting and athletic competitions, and – since Caesar finally celebrated the funeral games to Julia he had promised years before – gladiatorial fights. Chariots raced in the Circus, while special temporary venues were constructed for the athletics on the Campus Martius and some of the gladiatorial fights in the Forum. However, the scale of these was so massive that a few combats were staged elsewhere. Five days were devoted to beast fights, in which 400 lions were killed, as were a number of giraffes, animals never seen in Rome before. Apart from the usual matched pairs of gladiators, there was a battle between two armies each composed of 500 men on foot, 30 cavalry and 20 elephants. Another version claims that the twenty elephants and their riders fought each other separately. In addition there was a naval battle fought in a specially flooded lake dug on the right bank of the Tiber. All of these celebrations were intended to be bigger and more spectacular than anything Rome had ever seen before.

The city was packed with hordes of people who had come to see the celebrations. Many lived in tents pitched wherever there was open space, and Suetonius claims that a number of people, including two senators, were crushed to death in the crowds that thronged the great events. The cost was staggering, not simply for staging the entertainments and processions, but also through the more direct largesse that accompanied them. At the end of the triumphs Caesar gave 5,000 denarii to each of his soldiers – more than a legionary would earn even if he served a full sixteen-year term in the army. Centurions each got 10,000, while the tribunes and prefects, most of whom were equestrians, received 20,000 apiece. In each case this was probably more than he had promised the men during the Civil War. Yet he also now chose to extend his generosity to the civilian population and especially the poorer inhabitants of Rome, each of whom was given 100 denarii, as well as gifts of wheat and olive oil. Some of the soldiers were angered by this gesture, which they saw as an unnecessary sharing of the wealth that they had earned. Doubtless drink and the atmosphere of holiday also contributed to this discontent, which led to an outbreak of rioting. Caesar had not been willing to back down in the face of mutiny and was no more inclined to do so now. He had one of the rioters led off and executed. Two more were ceremonially beheaded by the college of pontiffs and the *Flamen Martialis* (the priest of Mars). The ritual, whose precise meaning escapes us, took place on the Campus Martius, but the two heads were taken into the Forum and displayed near the Regia. Order was restored and the period of celebration was overwhelmingly successful. Caesar had always been a good showman and had given thought not only to the displays but also to the comfort of the crowds. At several performances silk awnings were erected to provide shade for the audience.[6]

REWARDS AND SETTLEMENTS

In general the crowd had delighted in Caesar's triumphs, celebrations and games, although Dio claims that some people were shocked by the scale of the bloodshed during the gladiatorial fights. The dictator's habit of reading letters and dictating to his secretaries while watching these shows was disliked by the people, but gave indication of the sheer amount of business that required his attention. Caesar had not fought the Civil War in order to reform the Republic, and in spite of what Cicero and others later claimed, there is no evidence that he had been aiming at supreme rule for much of his life. He had wanted a second consulship and doubtless had planned a programme of legislation for his twelve-month term of office. Instead, he

471

had – at least in his own mind – been forced to fight the Civil War, and his victory brought him far greater power. His third consulship in 46 BC was followed by a fourth and fifth term in 45 and 44 BC respectively, and for most of this period he was also dictator and had a number of additional rights granted to him by the Senate. He was not in Rome for the entire time, since the last campaign of the Civil War took him to Spain in November 46 BC and he did not return to Italy until the following summer. This makes the sheer scale and scope of his legislation and reforms all the more astonishing. Caesar was constantly at work and, though his assistants such as Oppius and Balbus clearly undertook a good deal of the detailed work of framing laws, the basic concepts seem always to have been his. Given the comparatively short time period it is unsurprising that some projects were never actually begun, while many more were uncompleted at his death. It is also not always easy to establish what precisely he did do, and even harder to discern his intentions. His assassination was followed by renewed civil war between his partisans and assassins, during which it was clearly in each sides' interest to put forward radically different claims of his long-term aims.

To add to the confusion, the civil wars would finally be ended when Caesar's adopted son Octavian – later named Augustus – became Rome's first emperor. Following the adoption his name was formally Caius Julius Caesar Octavianus. This meant that whether Caesar himself or his adopted son passed a law or founded a colony, each would be known as a *lex Julia* or *colonia Julia* respectively. Therefore, if only the name is preserved without any indication of date, it is often impossible to know which of the two was responsible. It is especially confusing since it is known that in some cases Augustus implemented a design of Caesar's, whereas on other issues his thinking was very different. Detailed discussion of each possible measure introduced by Caesar would require immense space and take us too far from our main purpose. Instead what follows is an overview, concentrating on the more generally accepted acts.[7]

It is obvious that Caesar wielded immense power, but there has been little consensus amongst scholars about his overall aims. Some would like to see him as a visionary who discerned the problems facing the Republic, realised that its system of government could simply no longer cope with the changed circumstances of empire, and understood that a form of monarchy was the only answer. His plans included not only political change but a radical shift in the relationship between Rome and the rest of Italy, and of both to the provinces. A comment in a letter to Metellus Scipio in 48 BC, that Caesar wanted only 'tranquillity for Italy, peace for the provinces, and security for

[Roman] power' has sometimes been taken as a clear programme. Critics of this view would instead see it as a vague slogan employed in the midst of civil war. For them Caesar was not a radical reformer or visionary, but a deeply conservative aristocrat who won power in a quest for personal glory and status within the Republic. Motivated by such traditional ambitions, he had little idea of what to do once he took control of Rome. In this view his numerous reforms dealing with such a wide range of different issues were the sign not of a coherent programme, but of the total absence of any broader design. Caesar tinkered with so many things simply because he did not know what to do and instead just kept himself busy, mistaking activity for achievement. Both views are extreme, and most scholars have more reasonably adopted a position somewhere between the two, but before returning to this question it will be useful to review the evidence.[8]

Caesar did not take over a Republic that was functioning effectively. The Civil War had disrupted the entire Roman world, but even before that the institutions of the State had been struggling for many years to cope with turbulent and often violent political struggles. Respect for tradition – and the extent to which Caesar himself felt this need not concern us too much, since he was aware of its importance to others – had to be balanced against the practical importance of providing effective government as soon as possible. There was also always the central importance of dealing with individuals, both those who had fought for him and deserved reward and those who had opposed him, and who now required either generosity to win them over or stern judgement. In the autumn of 46 BC Caesar began the colonisation programme to provide farms for his veteran soldiers. His intention was to employ public land or properties confiscated from dead or incorrigible Pompeians, but where this was insufficient land was to be bought at a fair rate. As he had told the mutineers, Caesar was anxious to avoid the upheaval and hardship caused when Sulla gave land to his troops. At first it seems that only the men who had served their full term of service were discharged – we do not know what proportion of the army this was – and the remainder were to wait until they were demobilised at the proper time. The focus was mainly on Italy, but there were also veterans settled in North Africa and in Transalpine Gaul, where, for instance, the colony at Narbo seems to have been expanded. In the same way that he had given money to the people of Rome as well as the soldiers to commemorate his triumphs, Caesar now also included civilians in his colonisation programme. A number of colonies were created in the provinces, and even more planned as part of a programme that would see the resettling of 80,000 people. Caius

Gracchus' plan of a colony on the site of Carthage was revived, and another new settlement was set down at Corinth, which like Carthage had been destroyed by the Romans in 146 BC. In some cases the selection of locations was intended to punish communities that had sided against him in the war, but even so this was not intended to be especially harsh. The whole programme of colonisation required immense effort, surveyors going out to all the regions under consideration, and correct ownership of land being investigated before lots were marked out and the process of allocating them to individuals begun. At every stage Caesar and his staff appear to have been open to pleas from interested parties. Cicero successfully secured an exemption for the community of Buthrotum in Epirus on behalf of his friend Atticus, who owned an estate and had interests there. As far as possible the intention was to satisfy the discharged veterans and civilian settlers without causing too much hardship to the regions where the colonies were set down – especially when these had influential friends.

There was a great tradition of distribution of land to citizens by *popularis* politicians, stretching back far beyond the Gracchi. Caesar's agrarian law had been the cornerstone of his legislative programme in 59 BC, and now with greater freedom of action he had resumed his activity on a far greater scale. He rewarded his soldiers, and also removed a potentially volatile section of Rome's population and gave them the means to support themselves and their families. Politically he gained from this, and placed very many people in his debt, but at the same time it greatly increased the number of affluent citizens. There is no reason to doubt that Caesar – and indeed many contemporaries – did not feel that the programme of colonisation was good for the State as well as in his own interest. In 59 BC even Cato had felt that the only thing wrong with Caesar's agrarian law was the man who presented it. Yet the scale of these projects was enormous and could not be rushed. Only a small part of his plans in this respect were complete by Caesar's death. Ambitious plans to drain the Pomptine marshes and so provide a fresh supply of good farmland do not seem to have moved beyond the theoretical stage, but do suggest plans for further distributions and so a major attempt to provide livelihoods for more poor citizens. Another project that does not seem to have been started was the plan to alter the course of the Tiber, improving river access and protecting parts of the city vulnerable to flooding.⁹

Army officers, especially tribunes and centurions, also benefited from the land distribution. Caesar's more distinguished followers were rewarded with high office, and this resulted in a number of alterations to the traditional pattern of magistracies. In 47 BC he had increased the number of praetors from eight to ten. In the autumn of the following year there was insufficient time between returning from Africa and going to Spain for most elections to be held. Therefore, when he returned from Spain in October 45 BC he promptly had fourteen praetors and forty quaestors elected for what remained of the year, with sixteen praetors and another forty quaestors to take up office on 1 January 44 BC. At the same time he resigned his own consulship for 45 BC, which he had held without a colleague, just like Pompey in the opening months of 52 BC. His legates Fabius and Trebonius were duly elected replacement or suffect consuls for the rest of the year. Although the Senate had granted him the right to appoint magistrates, Caesar contented himself with sending recommendations to be read aloud at the relevant voting assembly – 'Caesar the dictator to [*the name of the tribe*]. I commend to you such and such to hold the dignity of office by your vote.' These seem always to have been successful, and it may well be that no rivals bothered to put their names forward. To some extent this preserved the proper formalities, but Caesar's obvious desire to grant to numerous followers the dignity and status of the high magistracies acted against this. When Fabius Maximus went to watch a play and was announced as consul, the audience is said to have yelled out, 'He is no consul!' He died on the morning of his last day in office. Caesar received the news while presiding over a meeting of the Tribal Assembly, which was going to elect quaestors for the next year. Instead, he had the people reconvene as the *Comitia Centuriata* and vote for a new consul. Just after midday another of his legates from Gaul was chosen, Caius Caninius Rebilus, whose spell as consul therefore lasted no more than a few hours. A few days later Cicero joked that 'in the consulship of Caninius nobody ate lunch. However, nothing bad occurred while he was consul – for his vigilance was so incredible that throughout his entire consulship he never went to sleep.' At the time he is supposed to have urged everyone to rush and congratulate Caninius before his office expired. Privately he thought the affair more a matter for tears than wit.[10]

Caesar's replacement consuls can rarely have had time to achieve much during their term of office, even supposing that they were granted any freedom of action and not simply expected to put through his legislation. Yet they gained the dignity and symbols of the office. Caesar actually granted ten former praetors consular status without ever holding the senior magistracy, for he had many followers to reward and limited time. Resigning and appointing replacements in this way was not illegal, but was unprecedented and scarcely added to the dignity of the office. In a similar way the dramatic increase in the numbers of other posts inevitably devalued these to some extent, but in this case there was more practical justification. Sulla had fixed the number of praetors at eight because this was adequate to provide enough governors for the provinces then controlled by the Republic. Since his day, Rome's empire had increased markedly by conquest and annexation and there was a real need for more magistrates to administrate the new provinces. Men elected to the quaestorship were automatically enrolled as senators, so that the House would be augmented by at least forty new members each year. Caesar was also granted the power to create new senators, and to grant patrician status as he felt necessary.

Even before the disruption and losses of the Civil War the censorship had failed to function properly in practice, often because of squabbles between the colleagues holding the post. Thus the ranks of the Senate were depleted. Caesar appointed hundreds of new senators, compensating for the losses and then expanding the House dramatically. Sulla had doubled the Senate in size to around 600, but by the time of Caesar's death there were somewhere between 800–900 members. A few of these were men who had been expelled from its ranks in previous years, or whose families had been barred from public life because of their Marian sympathies. Most of the new members were from established equestrian families, including many who came from the local aristocracies of Italy, but they may also have included a few former centurions. There were also a few from citizen families outside Italy, including a number of Gauls from the Cisalpine, and probably also Transalpine, provinces. There were jokes at the time of the 'barbarians' taking off their trousers to put on a toga, and someone daubed up a slogan in the Forum proclaiming that it would be a good deed not to tell any of the new senators the way to the Senate House. It is unlikely that any of the 'foreigners' added to the Senate were not fluent in Latin, well educated and in cultural respects little different from genuinely Roman aristocrats.[11]

A few of the appointments may have been unsuitable – as we have seen, Caesar is supposed often to have said that he would reward even criminals if they had helped him. A number of the men he appointed to provincial commands were subsequently charged with and condemned for corruption and extortion. One was the future historian Sallust, who had been left behind to govern Africa after Thapsus. In his writing he protested his innocence and it is just possible that he was more naive than corrupt. Another loyal follower with an established reputation for cruelty was refused a province by Caesar, who instead let him have a gift of money. Yet in general Caesar's new senators were probably little different from other members of the House. Corruption, pettiness, incompetence and many other vices had all in the past been displayed frequently by the scions of many of the oldest and noblest families of Rome. A more serious charge might be that in enlarging the Senate in this way Caesar made it too big to function effectively as a forum for debate. This is certainly possible, but there was so much business to conduct that only a small proportion was actually debated in the House during these last years of Caesar's life. More often matters were decided by Caesar and his advisors behind closed doors, who then issued a decree as if produced by the Senate, even including an invented list of attendees at the meeting. Cicero was surprised to receive a number of letters from rulers or communities in the provinces thanking him for voting to grant their petitions, since in most cases he had not even heard of them before and had certainly not taken part in any meeting to discuss the matter. So many things needed attention that there was simply not time to deal with them in the proper way, although it is interesting that Caesar ensured that his decisions were presented in the correct traditional form, especially to distant communities who would have no idea that this was a sham. Oppius and Balbus were his two main assistants in such work and both remained outside the Senate during his lifetime. Although the manner in which it was conducted was unprecedented and unconstitutional, it is notable that even his critics did not claim that Caesar and his associates generally did not make good and sensible administrative decisions.[12]

Cicero was one of a large number of former Pompeians who had been pardoned by Caesar and now sat in the Senate – at least when it actually met – alongside his partisans. At first he resolved to take no part in debates, devoting his energies to writing instead of public life. Servilia's son Brutus was another such man, although he chose to be more active and was sent by Caesar to govern Cisalpine Gaul, probably as propraetor although he had not yet held the magistracy. His brother-in-law Cassius also accepted a post as legate around this time. Other Pompeians had ceased to fight, but had not formally surrendered themselves to Caesar for judgement and could not return to Italy without his permission, so waited in exile, hoping that family and friends would be able to persuade him to be lenient. It was rumoured that he took some pleasure in responding slowly in the case of his most vitriolic opponents, feeling that the nervousness this engendered was some small payment for the trouble they had caused him. One of these was Marcus Claudius Marcellus, the consul for 51 BC, who had begun the concerted attack on Caesar's position and flogged the magistrate from Novum Comum (see p.363). He had not taken much active part in the Civil War that his actions had helped to precipitate, but still refused to write to

Caesar directly. Instead his case was raised by Caesar's father-in-law Piso, backed by Marcellus' cousin, the consul for 50 BC and the husband of Caesar's great-niece, as well as the other senators present at the meeting. Caesar granted their request, prompting Cicero to break his silence and launch into a speech of praise for the man who preferred to place the '*auctoritas* of the Senate and the dignity of the Republic before personal wrongs and suspicion'. Not long afterwards he made another speech – this time in the Forum rather than in the Senate – urging the recall of Quintus Ligarius. Plutarch says that before he began Caesar openly declared that Ligarius was an enemy who did not deserve mercy, but that, although his mind was already made up, he would still listen to Cicero for the sheer pleasure of hearing his oratory. In the event the speech moved him to tears and prompted an immediate pardon. Gradually a trickle of Pompeians, some of them very distinguished, returned to Rome and some at least to public life. Marcellus was not amongst them, for he was murdered by one of his household in a domestic dispute before he was able to enjoy his pardon. In addition a growing number of men who had remained neutral were persuaded to take office under Caesar, such as the noted jurist Sergius Sulpicius Rufus, who went out as governor to Greece. Cicero continued to be active publicly and for a while at least was optimistic, advising Caesar to do more to restore the Republic to a proper condition.[13]

TIDYING UP

Caesar's programme of colonisation removed a significant part of Rome's population, but he was also very concerned to improve and regulate the living conditions of those who remained. He looked closely at the system for giving out free grain to citizens and judged that it was subject to abuse and badly run. A new calculation of those eligible to receive this was made, based on a survey of the city's population conducted on a street-by-street basis, and making use of information provided by landlords for those living in their tenements. The overall number of recipients was reduced from 320,000 to 150,000 names. The new figure was fixed and arrangements made for the praetors to add new names when the deaths of recipients created vacancies on the lists. Some of those taken from the list are likely to have found work and a wage in Caesar's continuing and massive building projects focused around the *saepta* on the Campus Martius and his new Forum complex. Apart from his lavish shows and games, Caesar also found other ways to benefit Rome and seems likely to have been influenced by what he had seen in Hellenistic cities, most of all Alexandria. He granted citizenship to any doctor or teacher willing to come and work in Rome. In direct emulation of the famous Library at Alexandria, he gave orders for the creation of a similar centre of learning at Rome, placing Terentius Varro, the famous scholar – and former Pompeian commander in Spain – in charge of the task of gathering the works of Latin and Greek literature. Another plan involved the thorough codification of Roman law, but this may not have even begun and was not actually achieved for several centuries.[14]

One of Caesar's most lasting projects was the reorganisation of the calendar, and again this showed Hellenistic influence with the Alexandrian astronomer Sosigenes playing a leading role in the calculations. Rome's existing calendar consisted of 355 days, was based originally on the lunar cycle and needed constant modification. The college of pontiffs – of which Caesar was the most senior – were charged with adding extra or intercalary months at their discretion in an effort to keep the official year at least vaguely connected to the seasons of the natural year. It was a confusing system and one open to political manipulation, for instance, extending the year of office of an associate. During his time as proconsul of Cilicia, Cicero had been very nervous that someone would do this and thus postpone the date on which he could leave and return to Rome. By the time of the Civil War the calendar was running some three months ahead of the actual seasons. Caesar's system was far more logical and was intended to function without any need for annual changes. One intercalary month of about three weeks had already been inserted into 46 BC at the end of February. Two more were now added between November and December so that the year eventually consisted of 445 days. This was to allow the new calendar to begin on 1 January 45 BC at what was thought to be the proper time in the solar cycle. The Julian calendar had months that varied in length but added up to a total of 365 days. Every fourth year a single day, rather than an entire month, was added after 23 February. It does not seem to have been given its own number. This system remains in use with the Orthodox churches, but in the sixteenth century it was slightly modified under the auspices of Pope Gregory XIII and this Gregorian calendar is the one followed today. Caesar's reform was practical and removed confusion and the possibility for political abuse. It also added ten days to the year, each of which was considered to be *fas* or a day on which public business, such as summoning the Senate or the Assemblies, could be conducted. Even so there is some sign that the change – or more accurately the fact that Caesar imposed it – was resented. When someone mentioned to Cicero that the constellation of Lyra was due to rise on the next day, he remarked snidely that obviously it did so in accordance with official command.[15]

Caesar was certainly concerned with regulation, much of it well within Roman tradition. In the past many sumptuary laws had been passed with the aim of restricting excessive luxury amongst Rome's elite. Caesar brought in one of his own, forbidding the use of litters and the wearing of purple clothes or pearls, save by certain named individuals or groups on specific days. Various exotic and expensive foods were banned and men set around the Forum to watch what the shops were selling. There were even stories of soldiers breaking into houses and confiscating forbidden foods from the dinner table. In the long run his law had as little impact as earlier legislation. The purpose behind it was in part political, to deny potential rivals – or at least potentially disruptive politicians – the chance to display their wealth or win support through lavish entertainment. There may also have been a desire that the merchants in the city should devote more effort to providing essential goods rather than the exotic. Even Caesar does not seem to have had much hope that the rules would be obeyed as soon as his back was turned. Perhaps there was also a desire for a return to traditional frugality, so often praised, if rarely emulated, by the Romans, although if this was the case then it was more than a little ironic that it came from Caesar, the noted collector of pearls and fine art. Dio also claims that he wished to encourage the birth rate by offering incentives for families with three or more children. Yet his restrictions were not simply felt by those well enough off to want luxuries. The *collegia*, the guilds of particular trades or regions of the city that men like Clodius had turned into political gangs, were now banned. The only exceptions to the law were legitimate associations – the synagogue meetings of Rome's Jewish population were expressly given an exemption. Roman citizens between the ages of twenty and forty were forbidden to spend more than three consecutive years abroad, unless serving as a soldier or in another official capacity. Particular attention was paid to senators' sons, who were barred from going abroad at all other than on the staff of a governor or with the army. The aim of such laws is unclear, although presumably the restriction on young aristocrats may have been intended to stop them joining armed opponents and so compromising the rest of the family. Other bills were far more practical, dealing with keeping the streets of Rome clean and the administration and infrastructure of the city in good working order. There was a *popularis* tone to many of Caesar's measures, but the reforms themselves were not extreme. He tried to improve the lot of many different sections of society and there was a clear effort not to indulge any one group at the expense of others.[16]

It was not simply Rome that concerned Caesar. Probably with memories of Spartacus' rebellion, he passed a law that stipulated that at least one-third of the workforce on the great ranching estates of southern Italy must be free rather than servile labour. It has sometimes been suggested that he laid down a template for the constitutions of the towns or *municipia* of Italy, although this question is fiercely debated. He may have taken an interest in such things, and it does seem that much of his legislation was intended to apply also in Italy and the provinces. Much of his time during the campaigns fought around the Mediterranean had been spent in settling disputes and confirming or modifying the regulations covering communities and monarchs in the provinces. As we have seen, raising funds was a major concern on such occasions, but he was also eager to leave behind stable and peaceful regions, if only because discontent could readily lead to rebellions that would aid his Roman enemies. Early in his career he had made a name in prosecutions against corrupt provincial governors, and during his first consulship had passed a law regulating the behaviour of these magistrates. As dictator he added further restrictions, one of the most significant of which was to set their term of office at no more than two years for a proconsul and just twelve months for a propraetor. Dio felt that this was intended to prevent anyone else from following his own example, but even critics saw the measure as sensible.[17]

THE SPANISH CAMPAIGN, AUTUMN 46–SPRING 45 BC

An unwise appointment as governor precipitated the last major episode of the Civil War. Quintus Cassius Longinus had served in Spain as quaestor and was left to govern the Further Spain province after the defeat of Afranius and Petreius. Through a combination of greed and his own unpleasant temperament, he managed to make himself loathed by provincials and his own troops alike. This led to rebellion and mutiny, with many openly declaring their defection to the Pompeians. Cassius survived one assassination attempt, but subsequently decided to flee and was eventually drowned when the ship carrying him and his plunder foundered. Before this Caesar had heard of his misbehaviour and assigned a replacement, but the damage had already been done. Pompey's sons Cnaeus and Sextus soon arrived in Spain to rally support in this region that had so many connections with their father. After Thapsus, Labienus and other refugees joined them. Caesar at first felt the problem was a minor one and hoped that his legates could deal with the Pompeians without requiring him to go to Spain in person. By the end of November 46 BC he judged that this was not sufficient and set out to take charge. As noted earlier, no senior magistrates had been elected and instead he left Rome in the charge of Lepidus as Master of Horse, aided by eight appointed prefects, although much of the day-to-day decision making was in the hands of Oppius and Balbus. In less than four weeks – Suetonius says twenty-four days, but several other sources say twenty-seven – he reached the theatre of operations in Further Spain. To keep himself occupied he not only conducted his normal business from the carriage, but also composed a poem entitled *The Journey* (*Iter*). Cnaeus lacked his father's talent as a soldier, but he was an extremely determined individual who now found himself at the head of an army consisting of thirteen legions as well as numerous auxiliaries. After Caesar left for Spain there was concern that even after all his victories he might be defeated, for he could muster only eight legions, just two of which – the *Fifth Alaudae* and the *Tenth* minus its time-expired men – were considered veteran. Amongst the former Pompeians who had come to terms with Caesar there was also much nervousness, for Cnaeus was known to be an irascible man. In January 45 BC Cassius – the brother-in-law of Brutus and future conspirator – wrote to Cicero and expressed his concern:

> Now to return to matters affecting the Republic, report what's happening in Spain. I am really worried by this, and would rather stick with the old clement master than have a new and cruel one. You know how fatuous Cnaeus is; you know how he mistakes cruelty for courage, and how he thinks we always mock him. I am afraid he'll repay our wit with the sword in peasant fashion.[18]

An account of the campaign known as the *Spanish War* was written by one of Caesar's officers, but is by far the least satisfactory of the books added to his *Commentaries*. Many of the details of these operations elude us and a brief summary will suffice. When Caesar reached Spain he learned that the enemy had been besieging the town of Ulia for some months, and that this was the only important community in the immediate area that had remained loyal to him. To relieve the pressure on the town, he immediately marched against Corduba, the capital of the province. It was defended by Sextus Pompeius, and his pleas for help soon drew his older brother and the main army away from Ulia. Cnaeus shadowed and harassed Caesar's army as he settled down to a winter siege of Corduba, but he refused to be drawn into a pitched battle. Conditions were difficult and from the very beginning the campaign was fought with extreme savagery by both sides. Deciding that the city was too strong to take and that no useful purpose was served by staying where he was, Caesar withdrew and instead besieged the smaller town of Ategua. Pompey followed, but still declined to fight a battle. Considerable progress was made in the siegeworks and it soon became clear that a substantial part of the population wished to surrender. Subsequently, the commander of the Pompeian garrison had all those suspected of this brought up to the walls and slaughtered along with their families. Even so Cnaeus was unable to aid them and eventually the garrison surrendered on 19 February 45 BC. Defections of provincial communities to Caesar were now becoming common, as were desertions from the Pompeian legions. Cnaeus responded with executions of suspects. Near the end of the month Caesar's men captured four enemy scouts and crucified three of them because they were slaves. The remaining man, a legionary, was beheaded as befitted a citizen. As Pompeius retreated Caesar followed, and approached the town of Urso (modern Osuna). The enemy camped near the town of Munda some 6 miles away.[19]

On the morning of 17 March, Cnaeus led his men out of camp and deployed in battle order on the ridge outside Munda. Caesar judged that this was the chance to fight the battle that he had desired since the beginning of the campaign and ordered his own army to take positions on the plain in front of the enemy. He expected the Pompeians to come down and fight on level ground, since they were showing every sign of confidence. However, Cnaeus kept his men on the slope, but Caesar decided to attack anyway, in spite of the disadvantage his troops would face. Numbers were probably also against them, although it is doubtful that all thirteen of the Pompeian legions were present in full strength, given losses earlier in the campaign and the need to detach troops as garrisons. Caesar did have significantly more cavalry than the enemy, but the ground was not immediately favourable for its use. Caesar trusted to his luck, ability and the bravery of his troops, who as at Thapsus expressed their frustration at any delay. As usual the *Tenth* was on the right, the *Fifth* and *Third* – possibly the unit that had served him in Gaul and then been taken over by Pompey – on the left flank, with five more legions forming the centre. Caesar gave the order to advance, but the enemy did not match the movement until the last minute when they launched a counter-attack. The fighting was bitter and for a while seemed

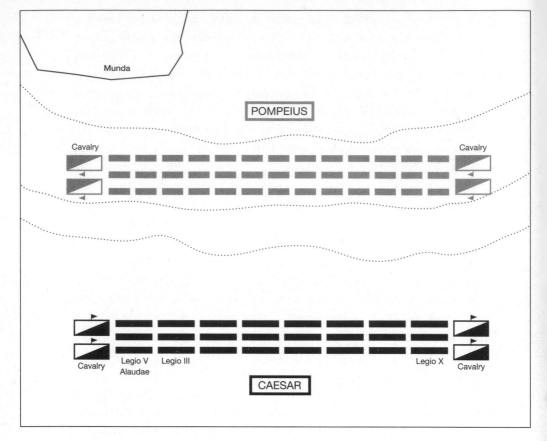

Battle of Munda

to be going Cnaeus' way. At one point some of the Caesareans began to waver and there was a danger that his line might collapse. As at the Sambre years before, Caesar was a match for the crisis and rushed to the spot. He is said to have advanced to within 10 paces of the enemy line. At first he was alone, dodging the missiles or catching them in his shield, but he was then joined by the nearest officers, and finally by the legionaries. The tale is not included in the *Spanish War*, and doubtless grew in the telling, but gives some indication of the desperate struggle at Munda. According to Plutarch Caesar later said that he had often fought for victory, but that this was the first time he had fought for his very life. The *Tenth* were the first to break through, punching a hole in the enemy left and exploiting it in spite of their small numbers. Cnaeus ordered Labienus to take a legion and plug the gap, but Caesar's cavalry were already enveloping the Pompeians' other flank. As they struggled to meet this crisis the whole army swiftly collapsed into flight. The toughness of the fighting was shown by the fact that Caesar lost around 1,000 men, more than at Pharsalus, and a high proportion from an army that is unlikely to have numbered much more than 25,000–30,000. Pompeian casualties are said to have numbered over 33,000, although this was probably an exaggeration. Caesar's legionaries erected a grisly trophy topped with severed heads outside Munda, which resisted siege for some time. Labienus was killed in the battle. Cnaeus Pompeius was wounded, but escaped only to be caught some weeks later. He was beheaded and the head sent to Caesar. Sextus escaped in command of a small squadron of ships, but for the foreseeable future he was in no position to pose any significant threat. Although a few Pompeians still kept on fighting, the Civil War was effectively over.[20]

News of the victory reached Rome about a month later, and prompted the Senate to decree fifty days of thanksgiving. Caesar was also granted the title of 'Liberator', and a Temple of Liberty was to be set up. In addition he was given the title *Imperator* permanently – in the past a general had only been hailed in this way by his soldiers immediately after a victory. He remained in Spain for some time, mopping up the last strongholds that remained loyal to the Pompeians and also resettling the province. However, he still found time for his usual flood of correspondence, and we know that near the end of April he wrote to Cicero to offer condolences at the death of his beloved daughter Tullia. Cicero was an important public figure whose political friendship Caesar greatly desired to encourage, but in this case it may have been more than just a question of formality since he knew what it meant to lose a daughter. Cicero was far fonder of Tullia than of either his wife or son, and he never truly recovered from the loss. In Spain, Caesar was busy re-forming a number of towns as colonies, which included existing inhabitants as well as parties of discharged veterans or other settlers. He was eager to reward the loyalty of both soldiers and civilians, provincials and citizens. During his return journey he paused for several weeks in Transalpine Gaul, carrying out similar administrative tasks and looking at the progress of veteran settlement at Narbo and Arelate (Arles). The Gaulish towns of the province were granted Latin status, which meant that their magistrates automatically received full Roman citizenship after their term of office. Mark Antony met him in Gaul and the rift between the two was clearly healed.

Caesar did not return to Italy until late in the summer, and then seems to have remained outside Rome until he celebrated another triumph at the beginning of October. This time there was no doubt that he was commemorating a victory over a Roman foe. In an unprecedented act he also permitted two of his legates, Quintus Pedius and the Fabius whom he would shortly make consul for the remainder of the year, to celebrate triumphs for the Spanish campaign. None of this was popular with critics in the Senate. During his own triumph Caesar was annoyed when the tribune Pontius Aquila, alone of the college of ten, refused to stand as he passed. Aquila was a former Pompeian who had suffered the confiscation of some of his property, but had evidently been permitted to pursue a public career. The sight so angered Caesar that he lost his temper and called out mockingly, 'Come on, Tribune Aquila, take the Republic back from me!' Unwilling to let the matter drop easily, for the next few days he is said to have not made a promise to anyone without adding the sarcastic caveat, 'That is, as long as Pontius Aquila lets me.'[21]

Caesar's honours were now exceptional. He was made dictator for ten years and all magistrates were formally subordinate to him. To this he added the consulship, for as much of each year as he chose to retain it. Soon this was extended to the formal right to hold the office for ten years. According to Dio he was also given the powers and rights of a tribune of the plebs, although this is not mentioned in other sources. In addition, he controlled the entire Roman army, as well as the Republic's Treasury. The honours accepted by him – which Dio tells us represented a small fraction of those awarded him by a sycophantic Senate, being merely the ones he chose to take – were staggering. At formal meetings in the Senate or Forum he sat on a special chair of office between the two consuls. An ivory statue of him was included with the statues of the gods and carried in a special carriage at the ceremonies opening the games. There was also a statue of him set up on the Capitol near those of the kings, and one in the Temple of Quirinus, another name for Rome's mythical founder Romulus. This amused Cicero, since there was a story that Romulus had been torn to pieces by senators and he joked that he was happier to see Caesar with Quirinus than with Salus, the personification of good health and safety. By this time he had become less optimistic than he had been a year before when Caesar had pardoned Marcellus and other leading opponents. It was clear that Caesar held supreme power and showed no sign of returning complete freedom of action to the Senate. Most key decisions were made privately, by men like Oppius and Balbus when the dictator himself was absent. It was not that the decisions themselves were bad, but what bothered him was how and by whom they were taken. For a senator, especially one who had held high office and was used to a prominent role in its debates, important matters should only ever be dealt with in the proper manner by the Senate. The Senate should in turn be guided by its best and most distinguished members, composed primarily of the established aristocracy, joined – so he had always desired – by a handful of talented new men like himself. That was the tradition, and Caesar's position was a clear violation of this senatorial ideal.[22]

Many senators were willing to tolerate Caesar's exceptional power as long as the crisis and the threat of renewed civil war remained, but as soon as this was removed were desperate for a return to normality and the prominence of their own class. Brutus met Caesar as the latter passed through Cisalpine Gaul on his way back to Italy and felt that he 'was going over to the good men' – one of those expressions like 'best men', which always meant those allied and of like mind to the speaker. Cicero thought the view absurdly naive. It is probable that Caesar had at the same meeting promised Brutus the praetorship for 44 BC and the consulship as soon as he was old enough in 41 BC, which may have contributed to his enthusiasm. Brutus had always shown great respect for his uncle Cato, but this had grown markedly since his uncle had chosen to die rather than accept clemency like his nephew. He divorced his wife, who was a daughter of Appius Claudius – the man himself had died of natural causes early on in the Macedonian campaign – and instead married Cato's daughter Porcia. Marriage between cousins was not that uncommon amongst Rome's elite. Porcia was the widow of Bibulus and thus had an even greater association with Caesar's most bitter opponents. In 46 BC Brutus wrote a book entitled *Cato*, which was a fiercely eulogistic work in praise of his uncle. Cicero claimed it was sloppily researched and was annoyed that Cato's role in the debate over the Catilinarian rebels was exaggerated and his own part played down. Nevertheless, at Brutus' urging, Cicero was persuaded to write his own *Cato*, which focused on the latter's personal virtue and steadfastness rather than his political career, for he was eager not to cause Caesar too much offence. This was also easier in other respects, since in the past Cicero had often doubted Cato's judgement in public life. He was subsequently delighted when he was shown a letter from Caesar in which the latter declared that through studying Cicero's book he had improved his own literary style. In contrast he said that reading Brutus' *Cato* made him feel like a better writer himself.[23]

Within months of his suicide, one of Caesar's bitterest opponents was being held up as the ideal of aristocratic virtue in books which were openly circulated and widely praised. One was written by an ex-consul who was acknowledged as Rome's foremost living orator, and the other by Brutus, widely believed to be the foremost of the up and coming men of his generation. When Sulla was dictator no-one would have dared to praise one of his enemies in this way. Yet from the beginning Caesar had declared that he would not emulate Sulla, and did not deviate from this now. When the books were released he found time to read them, but was too busy with the campaign against Cnaeus Pompeius to do anything about it. Instead he ordered Hirtius to collect material and produce his own book criticising Cato. After defeating the Pompeians, Caesar then used this as a basis for writing his own Anticato. The work has not survived, but it was clearly highly abusive. It claimed that when Cato cremated his half brother he had adorned the body in fine clothes and precious metals, but subsequently had the ashes sieved to retrieve the melted gold. This may have been simple invention, but Cato's lifestyle had been highly eccentric and did offer much material for Caesar to work with. One of the oddest episodes of his life was his decision to divorce the wife who had given him a number of children, so that his friend the famous orator Hortensius could marry her and have offspring of his own. Hortensius was fabulously wealthy, and when he died a little later, Cato remarried the widow, and thus resumed what had always been a successful marriage and at the same time brought a lot of property and money into the family. Such behaviour was at best strange, or – as Caesar averred – deeply cynical.

It is tempting to see flashes of personal anger in the Anticato, although it is worth remembering that political invective at Rome was often wildly exaggerated and frequently vulgar. Cato had hated Caesar bitterly, had frustrated him in a number of their public encounters and, finally, had played a major part in causing the Civil War. 'They wanted this' – Caesar's comment at Pharsalus could most of all be applied to Cato, the man whose implacable hostility had, he felt, forced him to cross the Rubicon, to fight and to kill so many fellow citizens and tear the Roman world apart. From his point of view there was reason enough to loathe Cato, or if not the man himself, then what he felt the man had made him do. Perhaps there was an emotional element adding to the invective of the Anticato, but the most significant part of the whole episode was that Caesar contented himself with simply writing this response. He did not in any way withdraw his friendship from either Cicero or Brutus, but sought instead to persuade educated Romans not to idolise Cato. In this he failed, for as an ideal of stern virtue and unflinching constancy Cato was much easier to revere than he had been as a living, active politician.[24]

Caesar's regime was not repressive and, for all his flashes of temper and jibes at the dead Cato, or the living Pontius Aquila, it did not become any more harsh after Munda. Yet discontent remained widespread. Cicero wrote a draft letter of advice on how to reform and restore the Republic, but took care to show it to Oppius and Balbus before sending it to Caesar. They suggested so many alterations that he felt unable to complete the task. When he heard of Brutus' optimism about Caesar's intention to join the good men, with black humour he wondered how this would be achieved 'unless he hangs himself'. The Civil War was over, problems long neglected were being addressed so that large numbers of people were better off than they had been for a long time. Rome itself now enjoyed a peace and stability that had rarely been its lot for more than a decade. Yet the scars of the war were deep. So many had died – especially amongst the famous names of the Senate – and some of those who lived had to cope with the consequences of their decisions during those turbulent years. Caesar had employed clemency and political skill to win over the neutrals and his defeated opponents, but ultimately his position had been gained through military force. In a way the situation had much in common with the creation of a settlement in conquered Gaul. Caesar had to persuade his fellow citizens, especially the aristocratic elite, that tolerating his dominance was preferable to opposing it. This was the final test.[25]

XXIII

THE IDES OF MARCH

'Caesar gave the impression to some of his friends that he did not wish to live any longer, and took no precautions due to his failing health. . ... Some also say that he declared that it was more important for the Republic than himself to go on living; for he had already ample glory and power; however, if anything happened to him, there would be no peace for the State, which would relapse into civil war of a much worse kind.' – *Suetonius, early second century* AD.[1]

'I have lived long enough for either nature or glory.' – *Caesar, 46* BC.[2]

At the beginning of 44 BC Caesar was fifty-six. It would be surprising if the effort of so many years on campaign had not taken some toll on his system, and Suetonius speaks of failing health. However, there is no good evidence to suggest that his epilepsy had grown worse and certainly his great energy does not seem to have declined. By Roman standards he was well past the prime of life, but there was no particular reason why he should not have lived on for another fifteen or twenty years, and perhaps even longer. Caesar did not expect to die in March 44 BC and the men who killed him were obviously not confident that nature would do their work for them in the near future. The dictator's death was sudden and unanticipated by all but the conspirators. Therefore, to look at Caesar and the regime he created is inevitably to examine something that was incomplete and still developing. Augustus would hold supreme power for over four decades and the system he created had time to evolve very gradually. It is ultimately impossible to know what Caesar planned to do and how successful this might have been. Rumours – often very wild ones – about his intentions were rife during his lifetime and after his death even more confusion was added by the energetic propaganda campaigns maintained by the opposing sides during the ensuing civil wars. It is especially unfortunate that Cicero's letters for the first three months of 44 BC were never published, leaving no contemporary literary evidence from this vital period.

Inevitably some doubt must remain over many of Caesar's long-term aims, but one thing that is clear is that he expected to be away from Rome and Italy for at least three years. The conspirators struck when they did because they knew that the dictator was to leave the city in a few days time to set out for fresh campaigns. This time his opponents would be foreign and so the glory won by their defeat unambiguous. First he would strike against the Dacians under their King Burebista, fighting the Balkan war which he had probably anticipated in 58 BC. He may well have hoped to complete this campaign by the end of the year. After that he would move against the Parthians, for Crassus' defeat at Carrhae was still unavenged. More recently the Parthians had again invaded Syria and given support to a renegade Pompeian who was intent on reviving the Civil War. The Parthian war was envisaged on a massive scale, for Caesar had given orders for sixteen legions supported by 10,000 cavalry to be massed. A planned canal through the isthmus of Corinth, although also expected to foster trade, seems to have been intended to help maintain supply lines to the theatre of operations. Plutarch tells us that a Greek architect had been appointed to this project, but it seems unlikely to have progressed beyond the theoretical stage before it was abandoned on Caesar's death. It appears that the defeat of Parthia was widely considered to be desirable – there had, of course, been speculation that either Pompey or Caesar should be sent there in the build-up to the Civil War. Caesar is said to have planned to begin cautiously, learning as much about the enemy and their way of fighting as possible before launching an attack in earnest. It is not clear whether he planned to conquer Parthia or merely inflict a serious defeat on its king, which would force him to accept peace on Roman terms. There were fantastic stories that he planned to return by a wide circuit, marching around the Caspian Sea through what would become southern Russia and conquering the German tribes on his way back to Gaul, but this conflicts with the otherwise methodical tone of the planning. It is also obvious that this would inevitably have taken longer than three years. It is possible that the idea of an eastern war was made more attractive to Caesar by its associations with Alexander the Great, but there is simply no good evidence to suggest that he had become prey to such megalomaniac dreams. It is obviously impossible to say whether or not his Parthian campaign would have succeeded. Caesar's past military achievements suggest that it would, as long as his energy and skill – not to mention his good fortune – had not altogether abandoned him. Yet the Parthians were formidable opponents and gave Mark Antony a severe mauling when he attacked them six years later. Augustus preferred diplomacy, backed by threat of force, to open warfare and achieved a satisfactory peace on his eastern frontier. His success – and the failure of later emperors to win a complete victory over Parthia – does not necessarily mean that Caesar's planned operation was doomed to failure.[3]

Caesar did not stay in Rome all the time in the months following his triumph, but wherever he was he remained very busy. In December 45 BC he was on the coast of Campania, accompanied by a large staff that included Balbus and an escort, so that altogether he had some 2,000 men with him. He stopped for a night at a villa near to Cicero's outside Puteoli and the latter wrote a detailed account of the dinner he gave on 19 December. It is interesting that he thought it necessary to borrow guards – probably gladiators – from a neighbour, for he seems to have been suspicious that otherwise his house might be looted by the soldiers camped outside. In the morning Caesar remained in the neighbour's villa until:

> the seventh hour [*i.e.* early afternoon], admitting no one; I understand he was busy at his accounts with Balbus. Later he walked along the shore. After the eighth hour he bathed. Then he listened to the matter of Mamurra without altering his expression [it is unknown what this was, but a likely speculation is that the latter had breached the sumptuary law]. He was rubbed down, and had dinner. He was taking a course of emetics. And so he ate and drank freely and without concern – the dinner was grand and well presented, and not merely that, but 'well cooked, and properly seasoned, and if you ask, all went well.'

At the same time his followers, including slaves and freedmen, were entertained, the most senior in some style. At the main dinner 'there was no talk of the affairs of state, and plenty of discussion of literature. To answer your question, he was happy and enjoyed it.' For all the success of the dinner Cicero ruefully declared that Caesar was not the sort of visitor you would encourage to pop in again, although obviously he felt that he was in no position not to invite Caesar when he was nearby. In the last months of his life Caesar seems always to have been busy, but remained an easy and charming companion at the dinner table. Yet he was not always as accessible as he might have liked. At some point in 44 BC Cicero went to visit him at his house in Rome and was kept waiting for some time before being ushered into his presence. Later he recalled Caesar saying, 'Can I have any doubt that I am deeply loathed, when Marcus Cicero has to sit and wait and cannot simply come to see me as he wishes. If ever there is an easy mannered man then it is he. Yet I have no doubt that he hates me.'

Caesar was prone to flashes of temper, but in the same way that the evidence does not support the view that his health was rapidly declining, there is no reason to believe that his character had changed profoundly. He was occupied with a vast amount of work, the load added to because of his plan to set off on campaign in the near future, and so gave the impression of being in a hurry. As a person Cicero and most other senators still found him pleasant, and his behaviour was moderate and inclined to be generous. It was not so much Caesar the man they hated, but the position that he had acquired and what it meant for the Republic. In late 45 and early 44 BC this position was still being defined, and at the same time as his power and status developed, attitudes towards it were changing. This brings us back to the fundamental question of what Caesar intended for the long term.[4]

KING, GOD OR CAESAR?

There is no doubt that by late 45 BC Caius Julius Caesar was effectively a monarch, in the literal sense that he enjoyed far greater power than any other person, group or institution within the Roman Republic. He had gained this position through victory in the Civil War, but his specific powers had been awarded him by the Senate and People. Traditionally a dictator had been limited to a six-month term of office. Sulla, in similar circumstances to Caesar, had held greater power without any time limit, resigning and retiring to private life only when he chose. Caesar thought him a political illiterate for doing this. He was already consul and dictator for ten years, a time period far longer than anything imagined in the traditions of Rome's constitution. Early in 44 BC this would be extended to a permanent dictatorship (*dictator perpetuo*). In addition he was awarded the censorship – whose powers he had anyway effectively been employing– for the rest of his life. Many of his honours were more symbolic. He was named 'Father of his Country' (*parens patriae*), although he was not the first to be addressed in this way for Cicero had been proclaimed as such after the exposure of the Catilinarian conspiracy. Caesar was also to be permitted to perform the only ritual more prestigious than the triumph, the right to dedicate the 'highest spoils' (*spolia opima*), an honour that was properly won by a commander who killed the enemy leader in personal combat. There is no evidence that he actually had time to celebrate this rite. Another exceptional award was permission to sit with the tribunes of the people at the theatre. On other formal occasions his chair was already placed between the consuls – when he was not actually holding the magistracy himself – but now his ivory chair of office was replaced with one decorated with gold. His birthday became a public festival and the month itself was renamed Julius. He was also the first Roman to be depicted on coinage minted during his lifetime. His head only appeared on some coins, and it was left to Augustus to make this practice universal. (Hence in the Gospels Jesus could ask whose head was on a silver coin, knowing that all carried a depiction of an emperor.)[5]

Caesar's honours clearly belonged to a tradition of celebrating the achievements of other famous Roman aristocrats, like Scipio Africanus the Elder and the Younger, Marius and Sulla, and most of all Pompey. Yet in his case everything was taken much further and the sheer scale and number of privileges awarded to one man was unprecedented. The inclusion of his statue in the procession of those of the gods at the opening ceremonies of the games, and the placing of more statues in and around the temples on the Capitol, suggested a status that was somewhat more than human. When news had reached Rome of the victory at Thapsus, a statue of Caesar had been set up showing him standing on a globe, with an inscription on the pedestal reading 'To the Unconquered God', but he ordered this erased after his return. However, in late 45 and early 44 BC this impression was reinforced when Caesar was given further honours. His house was to be given a pediment or high-pointed front supported by pillars, just like those on the great temples. A Julian college of priests was created and associated with the colleges that oversaw the ancient festival of the Lupercalia. This was taken further when it was decided to dedicate a temple to Caesar and his clemency – or perhaps strictly Caesar's clemency for the sources are unclear. The cult was to be the charge of a new priest or *flamen*, resembling the ancient post of *Flamen Dialis* or priest of Jupiter, and Mark Antony was named as the first of these. Dio goes so far as to claim that Caesar was now to be worshipped as Jupiter Julius, but there is no other evidence for such a specific identification with Rome's most important divinity. After Pharsalus, Caesar had already been formally referred to as a god in the honours and decrees of Hellenistic communities in the provinces. There was nothing new about this – other Roman commanders in the last century and a half had been honoured in much the same way. There was a long tradition of divine kingship in the East and a tendency to extend this to powerful Romans who appeared in the region. Yet in the past no one had attempted to extend these ideas to Rome.[6]

After his death Caesar was declared a god – the Divine Julius (*divus Julius*) – and his adopted son would style himself the son of a god. However, Augustus himself was not deified in Rome until after his death and this remained the pattern with his successors. The process became effectively automatic, so that the Emperor Vespasian's last words are supposed to have been a macabre joke – 'I think I am becoming a god.' Only megalomaniac emperors were ever declared living gods, and the knowledge of this later pattern has added to the dispute over whether or not Caesar accepted such status. Roman religion was complex and polytheistic, with a huge number of different gods and goddesses, some far greater than others, as well as a great variety of demi-gods and heroes. Legends, both Greek and Roman, told of humans who had become divine – Hercules/Herakles being probably the most famous. Caesar's family boasted of their descent from Venus and other aristocrats claimed that their line went back to other deities. The clear division between God and human, maintained in the monotheistic tradition more familiar to the modern mind, was much less simple for the Romans. In a speech delivered just a few weeks after Caesar's death, Cicero referred to Antony and his appointment as Caesar's *flamen*, so we can be confident that this was announced, although it is unlikely that he had actually been inaugurated. This does mean that it is very hard to argue against the view that Caesar was declared at least semi-divine during his lifetime, and perhaps was said to be a god. However, the cult does not seem to have received great prominence, if indeed there was time for it to be properly set up, and it is best to think of Caesar as at most a minor addition to Rome's pantheon. Dio presents this episode as one purely of politics, with a sycophantic Senate praising the dictator. It is notable that he follows it by reporting that Caesar was also given the right to be buried inside the city – Roman custom dictated that burials should take place outside the formal boundary of Rome. The decree was to be inscribed in golden letters on a silver tablet and to be placed beneath the statue of Capitoline Jupiter. Dio says that this was intended as a clear reminder to the dictator that he was mortal.[7]

Apart from his formal powers Caesar stood out in many ways. His family claimed descent from the kings of Alba Longa, a city that no longer existed since the Romans had absorbed it early on in their history. On formal occasions he now took to wearing what he claimed was the costume of these monarchs, notably calf-length boots in red leather. The reddish-purple tunic and toga of a triumphing general, which he now wore at festivals and formal meetings, also had regal associations. To this he added a laurel wreath – an honour that he is said to have especially relished because of his growing baldness – and in 44 BC this seems to have been replaced with a gold version. His formal power was massive, and his informal control even greater and sometimes blatant. Probably in late 46 BC Cleopatra, her brother-husband Ptolemy and their court arrived in Rome. They were accommodated in one of Caesar's houses on the far bank of the Tiber and remained there till after his death. It is not known whose idea the visit was, but it does seem unlikely that she would have travelled to Italy and remained so long if Caesar had been opposed to the idea. Cleopatra owed her throne to her Roman lover, and may well have felt safer near him and away from Egypt, hoping that time would help the more hostile elements in Alexandria and elsewhere to grow used to her rule. She may also have felt that there were political advantages and concessions that could only be won from Caesar himself. Perhaps the news of his affair with Queen Eunoe during the African campaign caused her concern that his support for her might prove fickle. From his point of view, it was obvious that Egypt and its rich grain harvests would play an important part in the supply effort required by his projected war against Parthia. Political concerns were rarely far from the mind of either Caesar or Cleopatra, but her arrival less than a year after he had left Egypt, and the length of her subsequent stay, strongly suggest that he wanted her with him and there is no reason to doubt that they resumed their affair. Cleopatra certainly continued to stand high in his affections. The Temple of Venus Genetrix was the centrepiece of his new Forum. Caesar had a gold statue of the Queen made and placed next to that of the goddess. Appian says it was still there in his day, over a century and a half later. Caesar was still married to Calpurnia and Plutarch's account suggests that the couple continued to sleep together. It seems inconceivable that she was not aware of his infidelities, or that the Egyptian Queen living across the river was his mistress. During her time in Rome Cleopatra was often visited by distinguished Romans, eager perhaps for a gift, for a favour concerning one of their clients with business in her realm, or maybe in the hope that she would influence Caesar on their behalf. Cicero seems to have been disappointed and complained of the queen's arrogance, but the main point is that he had visited in the first place.[8]

At least one of the honours voted to Caesar was expressly to be handed on to his son and grandson, but as yet he had no son, or at least not a legitimate child. His only daughter was dead and her baby, if indeed it was a boy, had not survived her by more than a few days. When Cleopatra gave birth she named her son Caesarion, apparently with Caesar's permission. His year of birth is not absolutely established, but sometime late in 46 BC seems most likely. Although it is probable that the infant came with her to Rome, Caesarion is not mentioned by any sources written before Caesar's death. This has sometimes led to the suggestion that he was not the dictator's son, but a child produced only when Antony and Cleopatra wanted to diminish the prominence gained by Octavian as Caesar's heir. One argument in favour of this view is the simple fact that Caesar, for all his three marriages and frequent affairs, had not fathered another child since Julia, who had been conceived decades earlier. The claim of at least one Gaulish aristocrat over a century later to be descended from Caesar may or may not have had any basis in fact. However, it is worth remembering that Caesar's marriage to Pompeia ended in divorce and may well have been unhappy, while for the vast majority of the years he was married to Calpurnia he was away on active service. It was not usual for wives to accompany or visit provincial governors in the Republic and so their chances of having a child were severely limited. It does seem unlikely that Antony and Cleopatra could produce a child that had never been heard of during Caesar's lifetime and have expected his claim to be accepted, so it seems probable that the boy was already in Rome before March 44 BC. Whether or not Caesar was actually his father is impossible to say with absolute certainty and would require far more intimate knowledge of the queen's life than we possess. The majority of the ancient sources who comment on the matter seem to have accepted that Caesarion was the dictator's child, but then these authors all wrote considerably later. Suetonius does mention that after Caesar's death his long-time assistant and confidant Caius Oppius wrote a book to refute this claim.[9]

On balance, a better case can be made for assuming that Caesar was (or perhaps at least believed that he was) the father of Caesarion, but he was illegitimate, not a Roman citizen and only an infant. The boy was not even mentioned in a will drawn up by the dictator in the last months of his life. The most prominent position was given to the grandson of his sister, the eighteen-year-old Caius Octavius, in whom he had taken some interest in recent years. It seems likely that Caesar discerned some of the great talent in the youth who would become in time Emperor Augustus. His father and namesake had held the praetorship, but had died in 59 BC. Aged only twelve, Octavius had delivered the oration at the funeral of Caesar's daughter. In 47 BC Caesar had admitted him to the college of pontiffs, taking up the vacancy caused by Domitius Ahenobarbus' death at Pharsalus. This was an exceptional honour for one so young. Octavius was to have accompanied him on campaign in Spain, but due to ill health only joined the dictator when the fighting was over. In the will Octavius was his main heir and was formally adopted as Caesar's son, but it would be unwise to exaggerate his importance before the Ides of March. He was still very young, the son of a new man, and his public role was minor. Mark Antony and Dolabella were much more prominent as Caesar's favourites. After Antony had met Caesar in Gaul in 45 BC, he rode with the dictator for the rest of the journey, while Octavius travelled in a second carriage alongside Decimus Brutus. Mark Antony was to be Caesar's colleague as consul in 44 BC, but his continuing feud with Dolabella threatened to disrupt the dictator's plan to resign in his favour when he left Rome. The provision for Octavius' adoption in the will does not seem to have been widely known. It seems extremely unlikely that, had the dictator suddenly died of natural causes, the youth would have been able to inherit anything more than his fortune and property. He was not marked out as successor to Caesar's powers and honours, and politically other men seemed much closer to the dictator. Both Antony and Dolabella were in fact technically too young to hold the consulship, but they were well established in public life.[10]

The Gracchi had been suspected of craving royal rule (*regnum*) – there was a rumour that Tiberius had been sent a diadem by an Asian king. Since the expulsion of the last king and the creation of the Republic, the Roman aristocracy maintained a deep hatred of monarchy and it was a common aspect of political invective to accuse rivals of seeking kingship. The powers of the dictatorship were effectively monarchical, and to these Caesar had added other rights, so that in practice he ruled as a monarch. He also dressed like the kings of Alba Longa. In the Hellenistic world rulers were both kings and gods, so that some have chosen to see the divine or semi-divine honours voted to him as steps towards establishing a formal monarchy after this model. In the first months of 44 BC the question of whether or not Caesar should take the name of king was brought firmly into the public eye. On 26 January he celebrated the traditional Latin festival on the Alban Hill outside Rome, and the Senate had granted him special permission to celebrate an ovation – the lesser form of triumph – and ride back into Rome accompanied by a grand procession. During the parade some of the crowd hailed him as king. *Rex* was the Latin for king, but it was also a family name, Marcius Rex, and Caesar turned it into a joke by replying that he was 'Not King, but Caesar.' A few days before two of the tribunes, Caius Epidius Marullus and Lucius Caesetius Flavus, had ordered the removal of a royal diadem or headband from one of his statues in the Forum. Now the same pair ordered the arrest of the man who had first raised the shout. Caesar was annoyed, suspecting that the two tribunes were trying to cause him trouble and deliberately raising the spectre of monarchy to blacken his name. He protested at their action and they responded by issuing a statement that he was preventing the tribunes of the people from carrying out their lawful function. Summoning the Senate, Caesar condemned the men, saying that they had placed him in the impossible position of either accepting an insult or acting harshly against his true nature. Someone seems to have suggested the death penalty, but he did not want this, and was content to have them removed from office following a motion put forward by another tribune. Caesar asked Flavus' father to disinherit his son, who had two more gifted brothers, but when he refused to do this the dictator let the matter drop. Once again the man who had talked of tribunes' rights when he went to war had ridden over opposition from tribunes, although his punishment was far milder than that Sulla had been wont to dispense.[11]

On 15 February 44 BC Rome celebrated the Lupercalia, an ancient festival whose main associations were with fertility. As part of the rituals the Lupercal priests, naked save for loincloths made of hide, ran through the streets, flicking passers-by with goatskin whips. It was considered lucky to be touched in this way, especially for women hoping to conceive or for those already pregnant who hoped for an easy and successful delivery. The thirty-nine-year-old consul Antony was the leader of these runners, since he was head of the Julian college of priests. Caesar watched, clad in his wreath, the purple robes of a triumphing general, the long-sleeved tunic and high boots of the Alban kings, sitting on his gilded chair of office. Antony ran up to him and presented him with a royal diadem, urging him to take it and become king. At the sight the crowd went silent. When Caesar refused they cheered and, when Antony repeated the offer and the dictator again declined, the acclamation grew even louder. Caesar ordered the diadem to be sent to the Temple of Jupiter on the Capitol, because Rome had only one king. It was – and is – very hard to believe that this episode was not carefully staged, although to what extent Antony added his own touches to the performance is impossible to say. Cynics then and subsequently said that Caesar wanted to accept the crown, and would have done so if only the watching crowd had seemed more enthusiastic. If so, then this was a very clumsy way of going about this, and it should be noted that his earlier honours were all proposed first in the Senate. More probably he wanted the glory of refusing such an offer and perhaps also hoped to put an end to the talk encouraged by the episode of the tribunes. In this he did not succeed, for a rumour soon began to circulate that an oracle had been discovered that revealed that the Parthians could only be defeated by a king. As an augur Cicero later stated that the story was false and no such oracle existed, but many seem to have believed it, which does give some indication of the mood of the times. From this story grew another claiming that it would be proposed in the Senate that Caesar become king everywhere save in Italy. Caesar already had *regnum*, in the sense of absolute supremacy, and none of the contemporary evidence suggests that he also wanted the name of king. Indeed, even most of the later accounts do not claim that this was true, merely that it was rumoured. He had seen Hellenistic monarchy in his youth in Bithynia, and more recently in the far greater kingdom of Egypt, but there is no good evidence that he wished to impose something similar on Rome, perhaps encouraged by the influence of Cleopatra. His position within the Republic was personal, and as yet he had no real successor to inherit the kingship.[12]

THE CONSPIRACY

Some sixty senators eventually joined together in the plot to assassinate Caesar. There had been rumours of similar conspiracies for several years, but nothing had come of them. Until early 44 BC Caesar had been protected by a bodyguard of Spanish auxiliaries, but he very publicly dismissed them after the Senate had taken an oath of loyalty to him and had also offered to form a new guard composed of senators and equestrians. Similar bodies had been raised at times of crisis – Cicero had been attended by armed equestrians in 63 BC – but in this case it was never formed. The motives of the conspirators were many and varied, but underlying everything was a sense that to have one man possessing as much permanent power as Caesar was incompatible with a free Republic. The State should be led by elected magistrates holding office for a limited term and guided by a Senate whose debates were open and dominated by the most distinguished former magistrates. Under Caesar many decisions were made behind closed doors by the dictator and his close advisors, and even though they were often good ones, this was not the way the Republic was supposed to work. Tradition permitted the suspension of the normal way of doing things during a crisis, but only for a short time until the danger was over. Sulla's rise had been far more savage than Caesar's, but he had eventually resigned the dictatorship. Caesar was clearly not intending to emulate him and the grant of perpetual dictatorship emphasised the permanence of his power. The Republic had changed and it was not so much what Caesar was doing as the way he was doing it that bred discontent amongst the aristocracy. Caesar did make considerable efforts to maintain at least a façade of the traditional constitution. His magistrates were elected following his recommendation and not appointed. The Senate continued to meet and debate, and it was in the House that most of the honours awarded to him were first proposed. In addition, the courts continued to function in the traditional way and Caesar gained the reputation for a strict application of the law. On one occasion he annulled the marriage of a former praetor, who had married his wife only a day after she had been divorced by her previous husband. Juries were now composed solely of senators and equestrians, for he removed the third group, the *tribunii aerarii*, from which Sulla had decreed that a third of jurors should be drawn.[13]

Caesar, although usually charming and mannered, had always been prone to impatience and bursts of temper. For the last fourteen years he had spent the majority of his time in supreme command of an army, never in the company of anyone possessing equal authority. He had constantly been required to exert himself, planning campaigns and leading the army in the field, administering his provinces and, from 49 BC onwards, also an area that grew in size to encompass all of Rome's empire. In addition, he had found that matters often went badly unless he was present to supervise in person. During these years he had taken very little rest and there was no opportunity to do so in the last months of his life. Caesar continued to be very busy and it is more than likely that, long accustomed to command, he became less patient with the often ponderous and inefficient conventions of public life, especially since many had now become more than a little hollow. Late in 45 or early in 44 BC the Senate met to vote him many of the honours mentioned already. He was absent, since it was felt better to preserve the illusion that the debate was entirely free. At the end of the meeting the entire body of senators, led by the consul Antony – or Fabius and Trebonius if it occurred in 45 BC – then trooped out to inform Caesar of their decision. They found him sitting on his ceremonial chair conducting business, either near the Rostra or outside the Temple of Venus in his own partially constructed Forum. Caesar did not get to his feet to greet them when they arrived to offer him the new honours. This created a bad feeling, since it seemed that he was contemptuous of the consuls and the dignity of the senatorial order. Technically, as dictator, he was senior to a consul and so was quite at liberty to remain seated, but many senators took offence. It was rumoured that he had begun to rise, but had been stopped by Balbus who thought that it was unfitting for him to show such respect to inferiors. Another source claims that Caesar later explained the incident by claiming to have felt an epileptic attack coming on and was afraid to disgrace himself in public, since these often made him dizzy and caused his bowels to open. This had not actually occurred, and we are told that he walked back to his house without any difficulty once his business was complete. His actual reply to the senators was moderate, for he declined a number of the honours voted to him as excessive and only accepted a minority. A handful of senators, one of whom was Cassius, had actually spoken or voted against the new powers and honours in the Senate itself, but as usual no direct action was taken against such men. However, now – or perhaps in subsequent days – many of those senators who had supported the motions came to resent Caesar's failure to treat them with sufficient respect and the incident was blown out of all proportion. It is notable that no one seems to have been concerned that Caesar had failed to stand when approached by the consul Antony on the Lupercalia.[14]

Most of Caesar's closest associates also disliked the fact that the Republic was now effectively controlled by one man. This was true even of many who continued to declare themselves utterly loyal to him after his murder. Yet for all this general disquiet, it is striking how far most senators went about their business adapting to the new situation. All had obligations to their clients and, since many favours or concessions ultimately depended on Caesar, they went to the dictator – or to friends who were believed to be able to influence him – to gain these. This aspect of senatorial life went on, even if politically there was little freedom. The assassination plot was eventually large, but still involved only some 7 per cent of the Senate. The majority of the conspirators had been Caesareans during the Civil War and a few had held high rank. Caius Trebonius had served for most of the years in Gaul as a legate and had presided over the siege of Massilia during the Civil War. He had been rewarded with a suffect consulship in 45 BC after Caesar's return from Spain. Decimus Junius Brutus, the son of the Sempronia who was said to have been so heavily involved in Catiline's conspiracy, had also served with distinction in Gaul. Caesar had a great fondness for him and had named him consul for 42 BC. He was also listed amongst the secondary heirs in the dictator's will. Servius Sulpicius Galba was another legate from the Gallic Wars, but he had failed at the consular elections for 49 BC, probably because of his association with Caesar, and seems to have borne him a grudge as a result. Another disappointed man was Lucius Minucius Basilus, whom Caesar had refused a provincial command probably because of justified suspicion over his character. To a greater or lesser extent all of these men had done well as a result of choosing the winning side in the Civil War, as had many of the more obscure conspirators. Yet evidently some felt that they ought to have done even better, and all had now decided that they would prefer to continue their careers in a Republic without Caesar. In some cases they had arrived at this decision some time ago. Almost a year earlier Trebonius had sounded out Mark Antony about joining the conspiracy. This was at the time when the breach between the latter and Caesar still seemed very wide. Even so he declined and remained loyal, but he did not betray the confidence and perhaps expected that the plot would come to nothing in the end.[15]

Although there were many of Caesar's long-term supporters in the conspiracy, the two men who became its principal leaders were both former Pompeians. Brutus had surrendered after Pharsalus and his influence with Caesar helped to persuade the victor to welcome Cassius as well. In 44 BC both men were praetors and Brutus had already been marked down for the consulship. According to Plutarch, Cassius was secretly bitter because Caesar had given the prestigious post of urban praetor to Brutus. The dictator is supposed to have said that Cassius had the better case, but that his own fondness for Servilia's son meant that the prize should go to him instead. Other sources mention an older grudge against Caesar, who is said to have confiscated some animals Cassius had gathered with a view to putting on games. The latter certainly seems to have lost his enthusiasm for the man he had described as the 'old clement master' now that the threat of the brutal Cnaeus Pompey had been removed. Cassius was married to one of Brutus' three sisters, the Junia Tertia, whom gossips claimed had had an affair with Caesar. There may have been no truth in the story and certainly none of the sources attribute such a personal motive as jealousy to him. Even with Brutus, though he can scarcely have been unaware of the talk about and the actual affair between his mother and Caesar, there is little suggestion that this played any significant part in his actions. He does seem to have been one of the last to join the conspiracy, spurred on by anonymous pamphlets and slogans painted on walls asking whether Brutus was asleep. Rome's last king had been deposed and expelled by a Brutus, and the family boasted of descent from this man, although even amongst the Romans there was considerable doubt over the veracity of this claim. A keen student of philosophy, especially Stoicism with its emphasis on stern duty, he was well aware of the praise given to tyranicides in Hellenistic literature. Family pride also encouraged him to act, reinforced by his growing adulation of his uncle Cato. Porcia appears to have been a forceful, if rather unstable, woman – several sources report the tale that she deliberately stabbed herself in the thigh to prove that she could cope with pain and so was worthy to be taken into her husband's confidence. It would be surprising if guilt did not play a part. His hero Cato had gone on fighting long after he had surrendered. By the time his uncle was tearing apart his own wound at Utica, Brutus was governing Cisalpine Gaul on Caesar's behalf. There was every indication that he would continue to do well under the dictatorship. Caesar once commented that 'Whatever Brutus wants, he wants badly', and his character does seem to have been somewhat obsessive. Once he decided to join the conspirators his determination to follow the act through was unshakeable. The influence of his uncle and wife, and the burden of living up to his own and his family's reputation, all pushed him on, but in the end he was moved to act because he felt that it was inappropriate for a free Republic to contain one man with so much power. Whatever his other personal motives, the same belief was foremost in Cassius' mind.[16]

The conspirators spoke of liberty, and believed that this could only be restored by removing Caesar. Most, perhaps all, felt that they were acting for the good of the entire Republic. With Caesar dead the normal institutions of the State ought to function properly again and Rome could be guided by the Senate and freely elected magistrates. To show that this was their sole aim they decided that they would kill the dictator but no one else, including his fellow consul and close associate Antony. Brutus is said to have persuaded them to accept this, against the advice of some of the more pragmatic conspirators. Of the whole group, he had the greatest reputation, at least amongst Rome's elite. Yet although these men believed that they were doing what was right for the Republic, they would not have been Roman aristocrats if they did not also crave the fame and glory that they felt would be attached to such a deed. It should also be noted that the conspirators, especially the most distinguished of them like Cassius, Marcus and Decimus Brutus, Trebonius and Galba, were bound to do very well politically if the venture succeeded. They were men likely to be foremost amongst those senators who would guide the restored Republic, especially since it was scarcely likely that those who had remained staunchly loyal to Caesar would prosper after his death. Both Marcus and Decimus Brutus gave up certain consulships, but could confidently predict that they would win the magistracy by election. The disappointed among them could expect to win the offices and postings they craved. Liberty and the cry of a return to the Republic also meant a return to the dominance of few well-established families, and the opportunity to bribe the electorate and make fortunes by exploiting the inhabitants of the provinces. Brutus was widely respected and in much of his life seems to have justified Shakespeare's phrase the 'noblest Roman of them all'. However, on one occasion it is known that he had ordered his agents to extort by any means possible 48 per cent interest from a community in Crete that had unwisely taken a loan from him at four times the legal rate. The Republic that the conspirators believed in was one that maintained the privilege of the senatorial elite. Faith in the system was no longer so deeply entrenched amongst the rest of society as they supposed.

THE ASSASSINATION

The conspirators resolved to act quickly, since they knew that Caesar planned to leave Rome on 18 March and would not return for years. They were probably also encouraged by the hostility he had encountered due to his treatment of Flavus and Marullus, and also the controversy over the episode of the Lupercalia. Cicero later claimed that Antony was Caesar's true killer because he had raised the spectre of kingship on that day. Then came the false rumour of the prophecy and wild tales that Caesar planned to move the capital of the empire to Alexandria or even Troy. It was also claimed that one of the tribunes, Helvius Cinna, had told friends that he planned to propose a bill granting to Caesar the right to marry as many women as he liked with a view to producing a son and heir. This story may not have spread until after the murder, since Cinna was lynched in the aftermath of Caesar's funeral and was not able to deny it. Anyway good gossip has always tended to be passed on even when people do not actually believe it. Aware that the dictator was about to leave Rome, the conspirators decided to strike on 15 March when Caesar was expected to attend a meeting of the Senate, for it was felt that he would be less on his guard and easier to approach on such an occasion. Reports and rumours of plots certainly reached the dictator, but these were vague and as often implicated men like Antony and Dolabella as any of the real conspirators. Caesar dismissed them all, although he is said to have stated that he was far more inclined to suspect the lean Cassius with his serious nature than the wild-living Antony and Dolabella. On another occasion he is supposed to have declared that Brutus had enough sense not to be impatient for his death.[17]

Caesar was a rational man and judged that Rome needed him, because without him it would simply relapse into civil war. He was dictator and he was effectively a monarch, but he was not a cruel one and used his powers for the general good. The Republic had peace, and was better run than it had been for decades, even if things were not being done in the traditional way. This last point mattered little to a man who had declared the Republic no more than an empty name, but perhaps he did not realise how much the old ideal meant to others, or simply felt that the benefits of his rule must overcome any nostalgia for the past. Despite repeated requests from his close associates, Caesar refused to re-form his bodyguard or take other precautions for his safety, replying that he did not wish to live in fear or permanently under close guard. Perhaps the weariness of years of hard effort, combined with the prospect of unending labour governing the Republic and its provinces, made him less inclined to worry. For him the nature of public life had changed and now consisted almost entirely of dutiful effort, for all the men with whom he had once competed for supremacy – Crassus and Pompey most of all, but also Catulus, Cato and even Bibulus and their generation – had gone. There was no question that he had won, that he was the first man in the Republic, whose glory and achievements outstripped all of Rome's other great men, both past and present. Now he could only seriously compete with himself. Yet Caesar had always taken duty seriously and continued to throw himself and all his great energy into service of Rome. The planned wars against the Dacians and Parthians would certainly have brought him more glory – and clean glory since the enemy was foreign – but few even of his critics would not have felt that the conflicts themselves were against enemies who deserved to be humbled by Rome. Caesar may have been tired, and perhaps he found his victory a little hollow. He probably did not fear death, but that is not to say that he courted it. If his new regime was to succeed then it could not permanently be maintained by fear, but needed to rest on the acceptance that it was better than the alternatives. Showing that he was unafraid of his own class, both his allies and former enemies, demonstrated his own confidence. He knew he was disliked for his dominance, but hoped that this would be tolerated, and so he trusted to the good fortune that had in the past helped to win so many victories, to his own ability and just rule, and to the pragmatism of others. Three years spent on campaign and new victories would hopefully help Rome's elite get used to his rule – perhaps it would also remind them that Caesar was a better master than some of his subordinates. We do not know whether on his return he would have developed his position further, and possibly begun to mark out a successor to his powers. He is supposed to have intended to employ Octavius as his Master of Horse for at least one year of the campaign, but another man was also named so there was certainly as yet no final indication of succession. This is impossible to say and it could well be that he had not yet devised any specific plans. In the winter of 53–52 BC Caesar had badly misjudged the mood of the Gaulish aristocracy. Now he had done the same in Rome.[18]

Our sources are filled with prodigies warning of the death of Rome's most powerful man. One of the most famous claims that on the night of 14 March Calpurnia suffered a nightmare in which she is variously claimed to have seen either the pediment of the house collapsing or that she was holding his murdered body in her arms. Then the morning sacrifices on the 15th were repeated several times, but the omens were always unfavourable. Caesar is supposed to have been surprised because his wife was not normally given to superstition and eventually Calpurnia persuaded him to remain at home. He sent word to inform the Senate that ill health prevented him from leaving his house to perform any public business. It is possible that there was some truth in this and that he was unwell. Antony was to have carried the message to the Senate, but before he left Decimus Brutus arrived – it was normal for friends to greet an important senator early in the morning so there was nothing unusual in that. Both men had dined on the previous night at the house of Lepidus, where after the meal the question of what was the best death is supposed to have been raised. Caesar had been taking little part in the discussion, but quickly looked up to say that the answer was an end that was sudden and unexpected. On the following morning Brutus was able to convince Caesar to reverse his decision. Plutarch says that he mocked the warnings of the soothsayers and lured Caesar with the claim that the Senate was going to offer him kingship outside Italy, but this is probably a later invention. There were plenty of reasons why Caesar should wish to attend the Senate when he was due to leave the city in three days. Whatever the details, eventually the dictator got into a litter and was carried through the Forum to where the Senate was meeting in one of the temples that formed part of Pompey's theatre complex. A few months before Caesar had won praise for ordering the restoration of the public statues of and monuments to Sulla and Pompey, and so a statue of his former son-in-law would look on during the debate. After he left his house, a slave arrived claiming to have vital news for the dictator. The man was given permission to stay and await his return.[19]

It was late morning by the time Caesar arrived and the time had passed nervously for the conspirators, prey to fears that their plot had been exposed. Apart from Decimus Brutus, the conspirators had gathered early using the pretext that Cassius' son was formally becoming a man by publicly assuming the *toga virilis*. Then they went to the temple and waited outside for Caesar's arrival. Their daggers were concealed within the cases in which senators habitually kept their long stylus pens. In Pompey's theatre itself was a troop of gladiators owned by Decimus Brutus, who were armed and ready, but had reason to be there since it was to be the venue for some fights to be staged in the near future. One man greeted Brutus and Cassius in a rather cryptic manner, which they first interpreted as a sign that someone had given them away. Their tension increased when the same man went up to the dictator as he arrived and spoke to him for some time, but they soon realised that he was presenting a petition. En route Caesar had been handed a scroll by the Greek teacher Artemidorus, who had spent time in Brutus' household and seems to have known of the conspiracy. Through choice or lack of opportunity the dictator did not read it. None of the sources suggest that he was in any way suspicious and he cheerfully called out to a soothsayer, who had previously warned him to fear the Ides of March, in an exchange so familiar from Shakespeare – 'The Ides of March are Come.' 'Aye, Caesar, but not gone.' The conspirators greeted him as he stepped down from the litter. Trebonius – or in Plutarch's version Decimus Brutus – took Antony aside and kept him talking while Caesar and the remainder went in. They were aware that Caesar's fellow consul was both loyal and a burly individual, and would normally have sat beside the dictator, close enough to aid him. The senators already inside the hall rose when Caesar entered. The dictator then went to his golden chair, which presumably was next to Antony's curule chair since he was the only consul apart from Caesar.[20]

Before the meeting could formally begin the conspirators clustered around the dictator. Lucius Tillius Cimber, who had served under Caesar in the past, asked for the recall of his brother, who presumably had been an ardent Pompeian. The others pressed round to implore Caesar to grant the plea, touching and kissing his hands. Publius Servilius Casca Longus moved round to stand behind Caesar's chair. The dictator refused to be moved by the pleas, replying calmly to refute their arguments. Suddenly Cimber grabbed Caesar's toga and pulled it down from his shoulder. This was the agreed signal and Casca now drew his dagger and stabbed, but in his nervousness only managed to graze the dictator's shoulder or neck. Caesar turned and seems to have said something like, 'Bloody Casca, what are you playing at!' In some accounts he grabbed Casca's arms and tried to wrench his dagger away, although in Suetonius' version he used his own pen as a weapon and stabbed his assailant. Casca – Plutarch says specifically using Greek and not the Latin Caesar had employed – called out to his brother for help. The other conspirators stabbed and slashed at Caesar. Several, including Brutus, were accidentally wounded by the others in the confused mêlée that developed around the dictator. Only two senators tried to help Caesar, but they could not break through to him. The dictator struggled with them to the end, trying to fight or force his way out. Marcus Brutus stabbed him once in the groin, and some claimed that when he saw Servilia's son he stopped struggling and spoke one last time, saying 'You too, my son' – sadly there is no direct evidence for Shakespeare's version of *et tu Brute*. Then the dictator covered his head with his toga and collapsed, falling next to the pedestal of Pompey's statue. There were twenty-three wounds on his body.[21]

The attack had been so sudden and unexpected that the hundreds of watching senators had first been too shocked to react. When the deed was done and the conspirators stood, their clothes dishevelled, some wounded and all spattered with blood, Brutus called on Cicero, who had not been privy to the secret, to take the lead. Even as he did so panic spread throughout the hall and all of the other senators, including the famous orator, fled away as fast as they could. This was not quite the reception they had wanted, but still full of the success of their enterprise, the conspirators trooped out and walked up to the Capitol, carrying on a pole one of the caps that a freed slave traditionally wore, symbolising the liberty they had brought to the State. Antony for the moment was in hiding, and a little later three of Caesar's slaves dared to enter the hall, lifted the body and put it in his litter, then carried it back to his house. For a while all of Rome was stunned and an uneasy truce developed. Cicero eventually went to the Capitol and congratulated the assassins, but when Brutus and Cassius went down and spoke from the Rostra in the Forum, the crowd that gathered showed no sign of enthusiasm. Antony was alive, as was Lepidus, who held command of the troops camped just outside the city. For a while they seemed conciliatory, Antony met the conspirators privately and then on the next day in the Senate. The House passed a motion to recognise all of Caesar's acts and appointments, since too many people, including a number of the conspirators, had benefited from these to desire their repeal.

In the mood of reconciliation, the Senate voted to give Caesar a public funeral, which was held in the Forum on 18 March. Antony ordered a herald to read out the text of the honours so recently voted to the dictator by the Senate and the oath taken by every senator to preserve his life, and then gave a short speech – Shakespeare's famous version probably gives the best modern reflection of the power of Roman oratory. He also read out Caesar's will, which included the gift of extensive gardens near the Tiber to the people of Rome, and an additional award of 300 sestertii (75 denarii) to each citizen. His purple robe, rent and bloodstained from his wounds, was put on display, and some sources also claim that there was a wax effigy of Caesar showing his injuries. A large crowd had gathered – Cicero later dismissed them as the rabble of the city, but this was no more than conventional abuse of opponents, and it seems to have consisted of a broad range of different groups. A group of magistrates and former magistrates began to lift the byre on which the body was laid, for it was intended to carry it to a spot next to his daughter's tomb on the Campus Martius and cremate it there. The angry crowd would have none of this. Just as their hero Clodius had been burnt in the Senate House, so Caesar would also be cremated inside the city, in the Forum at its very heart. The seats and benches used by the magistrates and the courts were smashed and used to feed the fire. The mood was hysterical. The actors hired to dress in the triumphal and magisterial regalia of Caesar and his ancestors now tore these off, ripped them into pieces and tossed them into the flames. His veteran soldiers threw their weapons and armour into the blaze, while women added their finest jewellery. Occasionally crowds had protested against Caesar, but this had always been over a specific grievance. Their affection for him, as a man who throughout his career had consistently advocated measures for the benefit of the wider population and not simply the narrow elite, had never seriously wavered. In 49 BC the vast bulk of the wider population of Italy had not been inclined to take up arms against Caesar. Then and now they had found it much harder than his senatorial opponents to see Caesar as an enemy of the Republic, a term that anyway meant different things to different people. After the funeral came rioting and attacks on the houses of the conspirators and those who had supported them. The dictator's loyal supporter Helvius Cinna was murdered by a mob who mistook him for one Cornelius Cinna, who was a prominent critic of Caesar. It was not just Roman citizens who lamented Caesar. At the funeral, and for a number of nights afterwards, Suetonius tells us that there were many foreigners joining in the lamentation after the fashion of their culture. Especially prominent were members of Rome's Jewish population.[22]

A few weeks after the assassination one of Caesar's still loyal associates gloomily concluded that if Caesar 'with all his genius could not find a way out, then who will find a way?' The same man's predictions of immediate rebellion as soon as the news reached Gaul proved utterly unfounded, but he was correct in assuming that civil war would soon erupt again. Antony chose to fight against the conspirators. Octavius, now, since the will, formally adopted and thus named Caius Julius Caesar Octavianus, would show truly remarkable initiative and confidence for a youth of eighteen, rallying Caesar's veterans to his cause and making himself an important figure who, no one could afford to ignore. First he fought for the Senate against Antony, and then, guessing rightly that they would discard him as soon as victory was secured, he joined with Antony and Lepidus to form the Second Triumvirate. In its brutality the ensuing war kept no hint of Caesar's clemency and resembled more the struggle between Marius, Cinna and Sulla. Within three years virtually all of the conspirators had been defeated and were dead, often by their own hands. The senatorial and equestrian orders were purged by proscriptions on a larger scale even than Sulla had enforced. In time Lepidus was marginalised and left to live out his life as an obscure exile, while Antony and Octavian fought for supremacy. The latter was only thirty-two when the defeated Antony and Cleopatra killed themselves and left him unchallenged ruler of the Roman world. Rome became a monarchy once again, although the hated name of king was not employed, and this time the change proved permanent. Octavian became Augustus and showed more skill in veiling his power than his adopted father had done. This was part of the reason for his success, but his ruthlessness in disposing of enemies and the fatigue of a population that had endured over a decade more years of bloodshed helped to convince Rome's elite that it was better to accept his rule than return to civil war.[23]

EPILOGUE

'Blood and destruction shall be so in use, and dreadful objects so familiar'
– Shakespeare, *Julius Caesar,* Act III Scene 1.

Caesar was born into a Republic already prone to sudden outbreaks of savage political violence. The scale of the bloodshed grew worse during his life and his own murder was just one episode in an extremely turbulent period of Rome's history. Caesar's death was gruesome and spectacular, but very few of the men who have figured prominently in his story died of natural causes. The women fared rather better, although Cleopatra was an exception in this respect as in so many other ways. Saturninus' followers were massacred when Caesar was a baby, the Social War erupted when he was a child, followed by the civil war that raged as he matured into a man. Between them Sulla and his enemies caused losses to the Roman elite on a scale not seen since the darkest days of the war with Hannibal. It did not stop there. Lepidus soon rebelled in Italy and was swiftly suppressed, while Sertorius waged war with grim efficiency in Spain and was only defeated after years of struggle. Later there was Catiline, then Clodius and Milo, and many lesser figures willing to employ violence in pursuit of their ambitions, even before Caesar crossed the Rubicon. All the time foreign wars remained common, while the staggering initial successes of Spartacus awoke deep fears in a society so dependent on slave labour. However, far more senators and equestrians fell in disputes between Romans, and the bloodletting was probably even greater when Antony and Octavian first hunted down the conspirators and then turned against each other.

Caesar lived in a brutal and dangerous era. This should be an obvious truth, but it is sometimes easy to forget because it was also an extremely civilised age. Caesar's own *Commentaries*, Cicero's vast output of letters, speeches and philosophical treatises, along with Sallust's histories and the poetry of Catullus, represent some of the greatest works of Latin literature. Combined with the later sources they also ensure that these years are better known that any other period of the Roman Republic's history. Indeed, it is extremely difficult today to avoid looking at the earlier periods of the Republic through the prism of the first century BC, and especially the copious

512

writings and ideas of Cicero. The wealth of detailed information for these years, the day-to-day gossip or detailed discussions of elections and debates – once again so much of all this comes from Cicero – can lend an air of normality and stability that is deeply misleading. Roman public life in the first century BC was anything but stable. Violence was not ever present, but it was always a possibility, lurking just beneath the surface. The constraints that had restricted competition between earlier generations of senators no longer functioned as well. In most years the round of public life proceeded properly enough, with meetings of the Senate and Assemblies occurring, courts convening and dispensing verdicts, magistrates going about their business, and elections being held. Sometimes jurors were bribed or otherwise persuaded to change their view, or the voters manipulated, but on the whole the life of the *res publica* continued in a way that was acceptable, if not ideal. Rioting, orchestrated violence, murder – and still more open warfare – remained occasional exceptions that interrupted this pattern. The Republican system was remarkably resilient and sprang back into something like overt normality after each crisis. Yet none of these things was now unimaginable, as they had been to generations before the Gracchi. Men like Marius, Cinna and Sulla had shown that supreme power could be seized by force, while the early career of Pompey demonstrated that an able commander with his own army could force his way into the forefront of public life in a way never possible before.

Caesar's generation had essentially the same ambitions as the senators of earlier periods, craving high office, wealth and glory to enhance their own and their families' position. From the second century BC onwards, the profits of empire meant that there was ever more money around, and spending on monuments, entertainments, and other means of buying fame and popularity grew at a staggering rate. By the first century BC it cost far more to have a successful public career. Like many others, Caesar plunged himself into debt in pursuit of his career, trusting to future success to meet the demands of his creditors. Had he failed at any stage, then his ruin would have been complete and irrevocable – hence his comment to his mother on the day of the election to the post of *Pontifex Maximus*, that he would return as a winner or not at all (see p.125). Caesar kept on winning, but other men were not so lucky and failed, losing everything. Some succeeded for a while, until their rivals were able to secure their public condemnation in the courts or elsewhere. In 63 BC Cicero executed the former consul Lentulus, who had already been expelled from the Senate and had had to start his career afresh. Just a few years later the orator was himself forced into exile by Clodius and only the changing balance of politics allowed his subsequent recall. The risks of public life were greater than they had ever been before and very few men could ever feel entirely secure from attack. Those who failed swelled the ranks of the desperate, willing to join any enterprise led by a man promising to restore their funds and prospects. Many such men joined Catiline and died. Others rallied to Caesar in 49 BC and prospered, so long as they survived the Civil War. The violence of the times ensured that failure might not simply bring political and financial ruin, but death. Yet the new dangers of public life were set against the far fewer limits on success. It was possible, at least for a few men, to bend or break the rules and conventions supposed to regulate office-holding, and it was also possible to gain unprecedentedly large and long provincial commands. So many men had prospered by fighting for Sulla to make it clear that fortune and position could be won in civil war. Caesar's opponents in the Civil War presented themselves as the defenders of a traditional Republic, but the majority had done rather well out of Sulla's victory.

The combination of high risks and the potential for almost limitless success fuelled both ambition and fear amongst Caesar's generation. All had seen some men rise spectacularly high and others fall to ruin or death. Most men had neither the inclination nor favourable opportunity to advance their career through intimidation or open violence, but no one could ever be sure that his rivals would not choose such methods. Senators were very ready to believe rumours of revolution or assassination plots. Once civil war actually broke out even remaining neutral was not always a safe option as the proscriptions had shown. The higher a man rose and the greater the risks he took, the harder his fall was likely to be, and the more he worried that his enemies would turn savagely on any sign of weakness. The overweening ambition of so many of the famous figures in the Late Republic is obvious, but it is all too easy to forget the nervous climate in which they lived and struggled for power. Each success made it harder for a man to turn back and the only real safety lay in more successes. Caesar has gone down in history as the man who crossed the Rubicon, plunging the Roman world into chaos in a gamble whereby he would either win or lose all. It is a mistake to see him as all that different from his opponents or most of the other prominent Romans of the first century BC. It is equally unwise to see the key players in this and other crises as acting only on rational considerations. All were gamblers in their way, and all certainly were afraid of the consequences of defeat and reluctant to trust personal enemies. The spectre of military dictatorship and the proscriptions was always there, as was the memory of other less well-organised massacres and executions. Nor was there much within the mentality of the Roman elite to encourage compromise. Young aristocrats were raised to aspire to *virtus*, an important part of which was the absolute resolution never to give in even in the face of defeat. In foreign wars this had served the Republic well, baffling Pyrrhus and Hannibal, neither of whom could understand why the Romans would not give in when they were obviously beaten. In the age of civil wars it made sure that these internal conflicts were waged with relentless ruthlessness. Once the struggle began the men on both sides knew that they must win or die. It was exceptionally rare for Roman aristocrats to commit suicide when defeated in a foreign war, for it was their job to rally the troops and rebuild their strength until they were ready to fight with greater success. In civil wars the ordinary soldiers could usually expect mercy, but the leaders could not, and so killed themselves in great numbers, whether in despair or defiance.

Caesar tried to change this. In 49 BC he feared falling into the hands of his rivals, just as they were terrified of his returning at the head of an army. In each case the fears may have been ungrounded, but that did not make them less real. Once the war began Caesar paraded his clemency, sparing defeated enemies and in time allowing them to resume their careers. This was calculated policy, intended to win over the uncertain and deter the enemy from fighting to the death, but that does not reduce the contrast with his opponents or earlier victors. After he had won, the pardoned Pompeians were allowed back into public life and some treated very well indeed. Once again he clearly felt that this was more likely to persuade them and others to accept his dictatorship. Regardless of his motives, there was a generosity about Caesar's behaviour that was matched by no other Roman who came to power in similar circumstances. In the same way, while his lifelong backing for popular causes was intended to win support, at the same time he did implement a number of measures that were in the interest of a wide part of the population.

Caesar was determined to rise to the top. Shakespeare's Mark Antony said of Caesar that 'ambition should be made of sterner stuff'. In truth there can rarely have been a sterner or more determined ambition than Caesar's. At times he was utterly ruthless, although this was far more marked in Gaul than in the Civil War. He seems to have had few scruples and was coldly pragmatic in his willingness to order atrocities. Yet he was never wantonly cruel and used victory for a wider good as well as his own. Ultimately we return to the essential ambiguity of Caesar and his career with which we began. He was an exceptionally talented individual, but he was also a product of his age. Roman politics in the Late Republic was precarious, with increasingly few restraints on behaviour. The Republican system relied heavily on precedent and convention, but these were breaking down, not helped by the readiness with which the authorities employed the *senatus consultum ultimum* with its temporary suspension of law. The rules of the political game had changed and it would have been difficult, perhaps impossible, to return to the old system. Caesar's ambition, talent, determination and his much vaunted good fortune led him on as he rose to supremacy, and prevented him from ever giving up or backing down. Had he been born in another, less troubled age, his reputation might easily have been far less controversial. He could have been another Scipio Africanus, winning unambiguous glory by saving Rome from defeat by a foreign foe. (Perhaps then he would have ended like Africanus, bitter and disappointed living in self-imposed exile after being forced out of public life.) For all his faults, Caesar was undoubtedly a patriot and a very able man. Instead, Caesar fought and won the Civil War, became dictator and was stabbed to death by conspirators. Whatever the rights and wrongs of his actions, it is hard to imagine that in any way his life could have been more dramatic.

'ALWAYS I AM CAESAR' – CAESAR THROUGH THE AGES

Caesar the general has been widely admired down the ages. His *Commentaries* were rediscovered and began to be published again in the late fifteenth century. In the coming centuries as more organised states began to develop increasingly sophisticated professional armies, military thinkers often turned to Caesar's writing for inspiration. Perceptions of the Greek and Roman art of war had a profound influence on the theory and practice of European warfare in the sixteenth and seventeenth centuries. Until comparatively recently the *Commentaries,* along with other ancient texts, continued to play a significant part in the education of officers in Western countries. Napoleon often claimed to have been inspired by Caesar and even during his exile on St Helena produced a critique of the latter's campaigns. His emulation of the Romans was obviously not just confined to generalship, for he modelled himself on such great men in his own rise to consul and then emperor in a French Republic that had from the beginning drawn much inspiration from Republican Rome. Much of the iconography and language of Napoleon's empire was overtly Roman, and drew particular inspiration from Caesar and his heirs. Later, Napoleon III sponsored the first major archaeological programme examining the sites associated with Caesar's conquest of Gaul. Admiration for Caesar combined with a romanticism for the Gauls – children in French schools are still taught to think of these Iron Age tribes as 'their ancestors'. In the nineteenth century the association was strengthened because the great rival and potential enemy was Prussia, later Germany, mirroring Caesar's depiction of Gaulish peoples separated by the Rhine from hostile Germans.

As a military leader Caesar has been widely admired, though sometimes with some critical reservations, but attitudes to him as a statesman have been far more mixed from the very beginning. Octavian rose to power as Caesar's heir, rallying his veterans and supporters to avenge the dictator's murder. After Caesar's deification, he styled himself 'son of the divine Julius'. He did not emulate his adopted father's clemency and, whilst he could not also match the latter's military skill, he was an extremely gifted political operator. When the civil wars were over and his rule unchallenged Octavian-Augustus also shielded the reality of his supremacy from the public gaze in a way very different to Caesar. His divine father was now less useful and appears little in the propaganda of the new regime. Authors such as Livy seem to have been very uncertain about how to view Caesar and his deeds, and certainly did not eulogise him. Given that many of his contemporaries had struggled to make up their mind about Caesar this is perhaps unsurprising. It is likely that Asinius Pollio's lost history was at the very least not entirely uncritical of Caesar. Under Augustus and his successors, Cato, and to some extent Brutus and Cassius, were more often the objects of praise, idealised as noble defenders of the Republic. During the reign of Nero the poet Lucan produced his epic *Pharsalia* about the struggle between Pompey and Caesar, and the latter is most definitely not the hero of the piece. Yet nor is he quite an undoubted villain and at times comes across more as some mysterious elemental force than anything entirely human. Later in the century Suetonius began his biographies of the first twelve rulers of Rome with Caesar. Of the twelve men Augustus was clearly held up as closest to the ideal ruler, but in some ways the biography of Caesar stands apart from the rest, since although dictator he was not an emperor or *princeps* in the style created by his adopted son. Suetonius does criticise Caesar, but also reports in detail his many achievements. In many ways the uncertainty about Caesar and how to judge him began with the Romans, who admired his great conquests, but deplored other aspects of his life and career and continued to revere some of his opponents.

This uncertainty continued and has allowed many different Caesars to be depicted over the centuries. The most famous is probably the Caesar of Shakespeare's *Julius Caesar*. Despite its title, the focus is far more on Marcus Brutus, and Caesar appears relatively briefly before being murdered early on in the third act. Shakespeare's Caesar has few obvious traces of greatness, being somewhat pompous, boastful and readily flattered, but is certainly no tyrant. A greater sense of his power and dominance comes from the attitudes of the other characters, both before and, in many respects, after his death. Shakespeare was not the first playwright to take Caesar as a subject, and he was certainly not the last, many, including Voltaire, writing plays or operas looking at some or all of his life. The assassination has probably attracted most attention due to its inherent drama, and after that the affair with Cleopatra with all the hints of the exotic East and eroticism. However, the latter aspect is wholly absent from Shaw's *Caesar and Cleopatra*. This is a gentler, more obviously benevolent Caesar, and his relationship with the queen – made to be a 'child' of sixteen rather than the woman she actually was in 48 BC – is essentially avuncular. More recently there have been a number of cinematic portrayals of Caesar, of which probably the most memorable comes from Rex Harrison's performance in *Cleopatra* (1963).[1] His Caesar has more of the man of action about him, with the quiet but firm authority of a proven leader. He also has something of the quick intelligence and, in that actor's practised and precise delivery, a strong hint of the powerful orator. The relationship with Cleopatra – Elizabeth Taylor looking very beautiful, even if, for all we know, little or nothing like the actual queen – perhaps has more of politics than passion about it. Television has also had a go, with the film *Julius Caesar* (2002) starring Jeremy Sisto in the title role. This presented another largely sympathetic Caesar, but faced the massive problem of compressing his life's story into a little more than two and a half hours. Crassus is not mentioned at all, and matters of chronology are left extremely vague, with Cato already in the Senate at the time of Sulla's dictatorship, but it did try to give a broader view than simply Egypt and the Ides of March.

Caesar did a lot in his life, and the period in which he lived was very eventful and well documented, so that such attempts to cover all of his career have been almost as rare in novels as on celluloid. In recent years the largest and most detailed version has come from Colleen McCullough's *Masters of Rome* series, the six novels of which tend to weigh in around the 700–800 page mark. These are detailed, racy accounts that begin with Marius and Sulla and go through to the aftermath of Caesar's assassination. The author did her research well on these and sticks closely to the real events. Inevitably, given the scale of the books and the interest in the personal lives of the protagonists, the vacuums left by the many gaps in our evidence have been filled by invention. The novelist does not possess the historian's luxury of being able to state that we simply do not know something. Rather lighter – in sheer physical size if nothing else – is Conn Iggulden's *Emperor* series, adventure stories in which Caesar is the hero. These are fast paced with the emphasis on action, and with these priorities the author plays rather fast and loose with the facts. Both McCullough and especially Iggulden present Caesar in a favourable light, although still showing his ruthless streak. Alan Massie's *Caesar* is a much more critical and more serious novel. Its main character and narrator is Decimus Brutus and to a great extent it is a subversion of Shakespeare, with Marcus Brutus as a pompous fool rather than noble hero. Caesar is a great man, but his cynicism and ambition are far more to the fore. Caesar also appears in a number of Steven Saylor's *Roma sub rosa* mystery novels, and these also present him as a less admirable figure, more selfish destroyer of the Republic than hero. That the Republic in these stories is flawed and tottering does not reduce his responsibility for speeding its end.

Historical facts are only one concern to dramatists, scriptwriters and novelists alike, and have to be balanced against the demands of storytelling. Some have been far more faithful than others, but it would be unreasonable for an historian to criticise too much any deviations from the recorded fact (which itself is problematic at times) in works of fiction. Between them they have presented many different views of Caesar, but then it should also be noted that over the last two centuries serious historians have depicted his character, aims and importance in very different ways. In this book I have attempted to look at the evidence we have and to try and reconstruct his life. There are some things we do not know and are unlikely ever to know. The aim has been to treat each episode in his life without assuming the inevitability of subsequent events. Some aspects of his character, for instance his emotions in public and private life, his beliefs and particularly his ambitions in his final years, remain mysterious. They can be guessed at, but not known, and each person will inevitably shape their own Caesar, in admiration or condemnation – often perhaps a mixture of both. Over two thousand years later his story still fascinates. One thing is certain – these will most certainly not be the last words written about Caius Julius Caesar.

CHRONOLOGY

753 BC	Traditional date for foundation of Rome by Romulus.
509	Expulsion of Rome's last king, Tarquinius Superbus.
201	Rome wins the Second Punic War with Carthage.
146	Third Punic War ends with destruction of Carthage.
133	Tribunate and death of Tiberius Sempronius Gracchus.
123–122	Tribunates and death of Caius Sempronius Gracchus.
c.112	Birth of Crassus.
106	Birth of Pompey.
105	Cimbri and Teutones destroy a large Roman army at Arausio.
102–101	Marius defeats the Cimbri and Teutones.
c.100	Birth of Julius Caesar.
91–88	The Social War, the last great rebellion by Rome's Italian allies. The *socii* are defeated only after a hard struggle.
88	Sulla marches on Rome when Marius takes the command against Mithridates from him.
86	Death of Marius.
c.85	Death of Caesar's father.
84	Caesar marries Cornelia.
82–79	Dictatorship of Sulla.
81	Caesar refuses Sulla's order to divorce Cornelia and goes on the run. He is subsequently pardoned following appeals from his mother's relatives.
80–78	Caesar undergoes military service in Asia and wins the *corona civica* at Mytilene.
77	Caesar appears in the courts at Rome, unsuccessfully prosecuting Cnaeus Cornelius Dolabella.
76	Caesar unsuccessfully prosecutes Caius Antonius.
75	Caesar travels to Rhodes to study and is captured and ransomed by pirates.
74	On his own initiative Caesar goes to Asia, raises local troops and defeats an invasion or raid led by one of King Mithridates' commanders.

73	Caesar returns to Rome and is admitted to the college of pontiffs.
73–70	Rebellion of slaves led by Spartacus.
72 or 71	Caesar elected as military tribune and probably serves against Spartacus.
69	Caesar elected to the quaestorship and serves in Further Spain. Death of his aunt Julia and wife Cornelia, both of whom are given public funerals.
67	*Lex Gabinia:* Pompey given extraordinary command to clear the Mediterranean of pirates, and succeeds in a brief, but highly organised campaign. Caesar spoke in favour of the law. Around this time he married Pompeia.
66	*Lex Manilia:* Pompey given extraordinary command to complete the war with Mithridates. Caesar also supported this bill.
65	Caesar is curule aedile with Bibulus, who complains about being outshone. He also gives gladiatorial games in honour of his father.
64	Caesar placed in charge of one of the extraordinary courts required to deal with Cato's investigations into debts to the Republic left unpaid by Sulla's supporters.
63	Caesar appointed judge in prosecution of Rabirius. Conspiracy of Catiline. Caesar elected *Pontifex Maximus*.
62	Caesar is praetor. He supports the tribune Metellus Nepos and temporarily resigns after the latter has fled. Bona Dea scandal leads him to divorce Pompeia.
61–60	Caesar sent to govern Further Spain. He reforms administration and leads a highly aggressive punitive campaign. On his return to Rome he gives up the prospect of a triumph to stand for election for the consulship.
59	Caesar's consulship and the formation of the First Triumvirate between Caesar, Pompey and Crassus. Determined obstruction by his colleague Bibulus and supporters including Cato produces repeated disorders. Caesar forces through his legislation, but leaves himself vulnerable to future prosecution. Pompey marries Caesar's daughter Julia. Caesar marries Calpurnia.
58	Caesar takes command of his province and defeats the migrating Helvetii at Bibracte. Then he defeats the Germanic King Ariovistus.

57   Caesar defeats the Belgic tribes, winning the battle of the
           Sambre.

55   Caesar bridges the Rhine for the first time and leads an
           expedition to Britain.

54   Second and larger invasion of Britain. Death of Julia and her
           infant child. Death of Caesar's mother Aurelia.

54–3   First major Gallic rebellion against Caesar, leads to defeat and
           death of Cotta and Sabinus. Caesar bridges the Rhine a second
           time.

53   Crassus defeated and killed by Parthians under Surenas at
           Carrhae.

52   Second major Gallic rebellion led by Vercingetorix. Caesar
           storms Avaricum, is defeated at Gergovia, but besieges Alesia
           and forces the Gaulish rebels to surrender. Clodius murdered
           outside Rome. Pompey appointed sole consul and allowed to
           bring troops into the city to restore order.

51   Caesar fights a number of campaigns in Gaul, culminating in
           the siege of Uxellodunum.

51–50   Growing pressure to terminate Caesar's command.

49–45   The Civil War starts when Caesar crosses the Rubicon. He
           overruns Italy quickly. Afterwards he defeats the Pompeians in
           Spain.

48   Caesar is briefly dictator and consul for the second time. He
           crosses to Greece and is checked at Dyrrachium, but defeats
           Pompey at Pharsalus. Pompey flees to Egypt and is murdered.
           Caesar pursues to Egypt and intervenes in the power struggle to
           place Cleopatra on the throne.

48–47   The Alexandrian War. Caesar has an affair with Cleopatra.

47   Caesar leads a swift campaign to defeat Pharnaces, King of the
           Bosporus, at Zela.

46   Caesar is consul for the third time, but early in the year takes an
           expedition to Africa. Caesar suffers a near defeat at the hands
           of Labienus at Ruspina in North Africa, but finally defeats
           Pompeian army at Thapsus. Suicide of Cato. Caesar is given the
           dictatorship for ten years.

45   Caesar's fourth consulship. He wins final victory at Munda in
           Spain. He is granted the dictatorship for life.

44	Assassination of Caesar a few days before he planned to set out for a series of campaigns against the Dacians and Parthians. Caesar deified.
44–42	Caesar's assassination provokes a further cycle of civil war between the conspirators and Caesar's supporters led by Mark Antony, later joined by Octavian, Caesar's nephew and adopted son.
42	Brutus and Cassius defeated in twin battles of Philippi.
31	Antony defeated by Octavian in naval battle at Actium. Octavian becomes effectively the sole ruler of the Roman Empire.
30	Suicide of Antony and Cleopatra.

GLOSSARY

Aedile: The aediles were magistrates responsible for aspects of the day-to-day life of the city of Rome, including the staging of a number of annual festivals. Usually held between the quaestorship and the praetorship, there were fewer aediles than praetors and the post was not a compulsory part of the **cursus honorum**.

Aquilifer: The standard-bearer who carried the legion's standard (aquila), a silver, or gilded statuette of an eagle mounted on a staff.

Auctoritas: The prestige and influence of a Roman senator. *Auctoritas* was greatly boosted by military achievements.

Auxilia (auxiliaries): The non-citizen soldiers recruited into the army during the Late Republic were known generally as auxiliaries or supporting troops.

Ballista: A two-armed torsion catapult capable of firing bolts or stones with considerable accuracy. These were built in various sizes and most often used in sieges.

Bona Dea: Annual festival to the 'Good Goddess', the rituals were celebrated exclusively by women and held in the house of an elected magistrate. In 62 BC the rites were performed in Caesar's house and were the subject of scandal.

Cataphract: Heavily armoured cavalryman often riding an armoured horse. These formed an important component of the Parthian army.

Centurion: Important grade of officers in the Roman army for most of its history, centurions originally commanded a century of eighty men. The most senior centurion of a legion was the *primus pilus*, a post of enormous status held only for a single year.

Century (centuria): The basic sub-unit of the Roman army, the century was commanded by a centurion and usually consisted of eighty men.

Cohort (cohors): The basic tactical unit of the legion, consising of six centuries of eighty soldiers with a total strength of 480.

Comitia Centuriata: The Assembly of the Roman people that elected the most senior magistrates, including the consuls and praetors. It was divided into 193 voting groups of centuries, membership of which was based on property registered in the census. The wealthier members of society had a highly disproportionate influence on the outcome. Its structure was believed to be based on the organisation of the early Roman army.

Comitia Tributa: The Assembly of the entire Roman people, including both patricians and plebians. It was divided into thirty-five voting tribes, membership of which was based on ancestry. It had power to legislate and was presided over by a consul, praetor or curule aedile. It also elected men to a number of posts including the quaestorship and curule aedileship.

Commilito (pl. commilitones): Comrade. This familiar form of address was often employed by a Roman general when speaking to his troops, especially at times of civil war.

Concilium Plebis: The Assembly of the Roman plebs, whether meeting to legislate or elect certain magistrates such as the tribunes of the plebs. Patricians were not allowed to take part or attend. The people voted in thirty-five tribes, membership of which was based on ancestry. This assembly was presided over by the tribunes of the plebs.

Consul: The year's two consuls were the senior elected magistrates of the Roman Republic and held command in important campaigns. Sometimes the Senate extended their power after their year of office, in which case they were known as proconsuls.

Curia: The Curia (Senate House) building stood on the north side of the Forum Romanum and had traditionally been built by one of the kings. Sulla restored it, but it was burnt down during the funeral of Clodius. As dictator Caesar began work on a new curia. Even when the building was in good condition, on some occasions the Senate could be summoned to meet in other buildings for specific debates.

Cursus honorum: The term given to the career pattern regulating public life. Existing legislation dealing with age and other qualifications for elected magistracies was restated and reinforced by Sulla during his dictatorship.

Dictator: In times of extreme crisis a dictator was appointed for a six-month period during which he exercised supreme civil and military power. Later victors in civil wars, such as Sulla and Julius Caesar, used the title as a basis for more permanent power.

Equites (sing. Eques): The 'knights' were the group with the highest property qualification registered by the census. From the time of the Gracchi they were given a more formal public role as jurors in the courts, an issue that became extremely contentious.

Fasces (sing. Fascis): An ornamental bundle of rods some 5 feet long, in the middle of which was an axe. They were carried by **lictors** and were the most visible symbols of a magistrate's power and status.

Flamen Dialis: An ancient priesthood of Jupiter, the holder of which was subject to a great number of strict taboos. Effectively, the *Flamen Dialis* and his wife, the *Flaminica*, were considered to be permanently taking part in ritual observance, and so had to be kept free from any form of pollution. The young Caesar was selected for the post, but may never have been actually installed.

Forum Romanum: The political and economic heart of the city of Rome that lay between the Capitoline, Palatine, Quirinal and Velian hills. Public meetings were often held either around the **Rostra**, or at the eastern end of the Forum. The **Concilium Plebis** and **Comitia Tributa** also usually met in the Forum to legislate.

Gladius: A Latin word meaning sword, gladius is conventionally used to describe the *gladius hispaniensis*, the Spanish sword that was the standard Roman sidearm until well into the third century AD. Made from high-quality steel, this weapon could be used for cutting, but was primarily intended for thrusting.

Imperium: The power of military command held by magistrates and pro-magistrates during their term of office.

Legatus (pl. **Legati**)**:** A subordinate officer who held delegated **imperium** rather than exercising power in his own right. *Legati* were chosen by a magistrate rather than elected.

Legion (Legio): Originally a term meaning levy, the legions became the main unit of the Roman army for much of its history. In Caesar's day the theoretical strength of a legion was around 4,800–5,000 men. The effective strength of a legion on campaign, however, was often much lower.

Lictor: The official attendants of a magistrate who carried the **fasces,** which symbolised his right to dispense justice and inflict capital and corporal punishment. Twelve lictors attended a consul, while a dictator was normally given twenty-four.

Magister Equitum: Second-in-command to the Republican **dictator**, the Master of Horse traditionally commanded the cavalry, since the dictator was forbidden to ride a horse.

Maniple (manipulus): The basic tactical unit of the legion until it was replaced by the cohort, the maniple consisted of two centuries. It still seems to have had some role in administration and army routine – and perhaps also drill – in Caesar's day.

Nomenclator: A specially trained slave whose task was to whisper the names of approaching citizens permitting his master to greet them in a familiar way. Such a slave normally accompanied a canvassing politician.

Ovatio (ovation): A lesser form of the triumph, in an ovation the general rode through the city on horseback rather than in a chariot.

Pilum (pl. pila): The heavy javelin that was the standard equipment of the Roman legionary for much of Rome's history. Its narrow head was designed to punch through an enemy's shield, the long thin shank then giving it the reach to hit the man behind it.

Pontifex Maximus: The head of the college of fifteen pontiffs, one of three major priesthoods monopolised by the Roman aristocracy. The pontiffs regulated the timing of many state festivals and events. The Pontifex Maximus was more chairman than leader, but the post was highly prestigious.

Praetor: Praetors were annually elected magistrates who under the Republic governed the less important provinces and fought Rome's smaller wars.

Prefect (praefectus): An equestrian officer with a range of duties, including the command of units of allied or auxiliary troops.

Quaestor: Magistrates whose duties were primarily financial, quaestors acted as deputies to consular governors and often held subordinate military commands.

Rostra: The speaker's platform in the Forum from which politicians addressed public gatherings.

Saepta: The voting area on the Campus Martius where the various assemblies met to hold elections.

Scorpion: The light bolt-shooting ballista employed by the Roman army both in the field and in sieges. They possessed a long range, as well as great accuracy and the ability to penetrate any form of armour.

Signifer: The standard-bearer who carried the standard (*signum*) of the century.

Spolia opima: The highest honour that a triumphing general could claim was the right to dedicate *spolia opima* in the Temple of Jupiter Optimus Maximus on the Capitol. The right could only gained by killing the enemy general in single combat and was celebrated on only a handful of occasions.

Subura: The valley between the Viminal and Esquiline hills was notorious for its narrow streets and slum housing. Caesar lived in this region until he became **Pontifex Maximus**.

Testudo: The famous tortoise formation in which Roman legionaries overlapped their long shield to provide protection to the front, sides and overhead. It was most often used during assaults on fortifications.

Tribuni aerarii: The group registered below the equestrian order in the census. Relatively little is known about them.

Tribunus militum (military tribune): Six military tribunes were elected or appointed to each legion, one pair of these men holding command at any one time.

Tribune of the plebs: Although holding a political office without direct military responsibilities, the ten tribunes of the plebs elected each year were able to legislate on any issue. During the later years of the Republic many ambitious generals, such as Marius and Pompey, enlisted the aid of tribunes to secure important commands for themselves.

Triumph: The great celebration granted by the Senate to a successful general took the form of a procession along the Sacra Via, the ceremonial main road of Rome, displaying the spoils and captives of his victory and culminated in the ritual execution of the captured enemy leader. The commander rode in a chariot, dressed like the statues of Jupiter, a slave holding a laurel wreath of victory over his head. The slave was supposed to whisper to the general, reminding him that he was mortal.

Vexillum: A square flag mounted crossways on a pole, the *vexillum* was used to mark a general's position and was also the standard carried by a detachment of troops. A general's *vexillum* seems usually to have been red.

BIBLIOGRAPHY OF WORKS CITED

BOOKS

Adcock, F., *The Roman Art of War under the Republic* (1940).

Astin, A., *Cato the Censor* (1978).

Austin, N., & Rankov, B., *Exploratio: Military and Political Intelligence in the Roman World*(1995).

Badian, E., *Roman Imperialism in the Late Republic* (1968).

Badian, E., *Publicans and Sinners* (1972).

Bishop, M., & Coulston, J., *Roman Military Equipment* (1993).

Brunt, P., *Social Conflicts in the Roman Republic* (1971a).

Brunt, P., *Italian Manpower, 225 BC – AD 14* (1971b).

Calwell, C., *Small Wars* (1906).

Connolly, P., *Greece and Rome at War* (1981).

Cornell, T., *The Beginnings of Rome* (1995).

Cunliffe, B., *Greeks, Romans and Barbarians: Spheres of Interaction* (1988).

Davies, R., *Service in the Roman Army* (1989).

Delbrück, H., *History of the Art of War*, Volume 1: *Warfare in Antiquity* (trans. J. Renfroe) (1975).

Derks, T., *Gods, Temples and Ritual Practices: The Transformation of Religious Ideas and Values in Roman Gaul* (1998).

Dyson, S., *The Creation of the Roman Frontier* (1985).

Epstein, D., *Personal Enmity in Roman Politics 218–43 BC* (1978).

Erdkamp, P., *Hunger and Sword: Warfare and Food Supply in Roman Republican Wars 264–30 BC* (1998).

Evans, R., *Gaius Marius: A Political Biography* (1994).

Feugère, M. (ed.), (1997), *L' Équipment Militaire et L'Armement de la République, Journal of Roman Military Equipment Studies 8*.

Fuller, Major General J., *Julius Caesar: Man, Soldier and Tyrant* (1965).

Gabba, E., *The Roman Republic, the Army and the Allies* (trans. P. Cuff) (1976).

Gelzer, M., *Caesar* (trans. P. Needham) (1968).

Goldsworthy, A., *The Roman Army at War, 100 BC – AD 200* (1996).

Goldsworthy, A., *In the Name of Rome* (2003).

Goudineau, C., *César et la Gaule* (1995).

Grainge, G., *The Roman Invasions of Britain* (2005).

Grant, M., *Cleopatra* (1972).

Green, M., *Dictionary of Celtic Myth and Legend* (1992).

Greenhalgh, P., *Pompey: The Roman Alexander* (1980).

Grimal, P., *Love in Ancient Rome* (trans. A. Train) (1986).

Gruen, E., *The Last Generation of the Roman Republic* (1974).

Gwynn, A., *Roman Education: From Cicero to Quintilian* (1926).

Hardy, E., *The Catilinarian Conspiracy in its Context: A Re-study of the Evidence* (1924).

Harmand, J., *L'armée et le soldat à Rome de 107 à 50 avant nôtre ère* (1967a).

Harmand, J., *Une Campagne Césarienne: Alésia* (1967b).

Harris, W., *War and Imperialism in Republican Rome, 327–70 BC* (1979).

Holmes, T. Rice, *Ancient Britain and the Invasions of Julius Caesar* (1907).

Holmes, T. Rice, *Caesar's Conquest of Gaul* (1911).

Holmes, T. Rice, *The Roman Republic,* Volume 3 (1923).

Holmes, T. Rice, *The Roman Republic,* Volume 1 (1928).

Hopkins, K., *Conquerors and Slaves* (1978).

Keaveney, A., *Sulla: The Last Republican* (1982).

Keaveney, A., *Lucullus: A Life* (1992).

Keppie, L., *The Making of the Roman Army* (1984).

Labisch, A., *Frumentum Commeatusque. Die Nahrungsmittelversongung der Heere Caesars* (1975).

Le Bohec, Y., *The Imperial Roman Army* (1994).

Le Gall, J., *La Bataille D'Alésia* (2000).

Lintott, A., *Imperium Romanum: Politics and Administration* (1993).

Lintott, A., *The Constitution of the Roman Republic* (1999).

Marrou, H., *A History of Education in Antiquity* (1956).

Maxfield, V., *The Military Decorations of the Roman Army* (1981).

Meier, C., *Caesar* (trans. D. McLintock) (1996).

Millar, F., *The Crowd in Rome in the Late Republic* (1998).

Mitchell, T., *Cicero: The Ascending Years* (1979).

Mitchell, T., *Cicero: The Senior Statesman* (1991).

Morrison, J., & Coates, J., *Greek and Roman Oared Warships* (1996).

Mouritsen, H., *Plebs and Politics in the Late Roman Republic* (2001).

Parker, H., *The Roman Legions* (1957).

Porch, D., *Wars of Empire* (2000).

Price, S., *Rituals and Power: The Roman Imperial Cult in Asia Minor* (1984).

Rawson, B. (ed.), *The Family in Ancient Rome* (1986).

Rawson, B. (ed.), *Marriage, Divorce and Children in Ancient Rome* (1991).

Rawson, B., *Children and Childhood in Roman Italy* (2003).

Rice, E., *Cleopatra* (1999).

Rickman, G., *The Corn Supply of Ancient Rome* (1979).

Rosenstein, N., *Imperatores Victi* (1993).

Roth, J., *The Logistics of the Roman Army at War, 264 BC – AD 235* (1999).

Roymans, N., *Tribal Societies in Northern Gaul: an anthropological perspective, Cingula* 12 (1990).

Saddington, D., *The Development of the Roman Auxiliary Forces from Caesar to Vespasian* (1982).

Saller, R., *Personal Patronage in the Early Empire* (1982).

Seager, R., *Pompey the Great* (2002).

Sherwin-White, A., *The Roman Citizenship* (1973).

Spaul, J., *ALA 2* (1994).

Stockton, D., *Cicero* (1971).

Stockton, D., *The Gracchi* (1979).

Syme, R., *The Roman Revolution* (1939).

Taylor, L. Ross, *Party Politics in the Age of Caesar* (1949).

Taylor, L. Ross, *Roman Voting Assemblies: From the Hannibalic War to the Dictatorship of Caesar* (1966).

Todd, M., *The Northern Barbarians* (1987).

Todd, M., *The Early Germans* (1992).

Todd, M., *Roman Britain,* 3rd edn. (1999).

Treggiari, S., *Roman Marriage: Iusti Coniuges from the Time of Cicero to the Time of Ulpian* (1991).

Tyrrell, W., *A Legal and Historical Commentary to Cicero's Oratio Pro Rabirio Perduellionis* (1978).

Walbank, F., *A Historical Commentary on Polybius,* Volume 1 (1970).

Walker, S., & Higgs, P. (eds.), *Cleopatra of Egypt: From History to Myth* (2001).

Walker, S., & Ashton, S. (eds.), *Cleopatra Reassessed* (2003).

Ward, A., *Marcus Crassus and the Late Roman Republic* (1977).

Watson, G., *The Roman Soldier* (1969).

Webster, G., *The Roman Invasion of Britain,* rev. edn. (1993).

Weinstock, S., *Divus Julius* (1971).

Welch K., & Powell, A. (eds.), *Julius Caesar as Artful Reporter: The War Commentaries as Political Instruments* (1998).

Wells, C., *The German Policy of Augustus* (1972).

Wells, P., *The Barbarians Speak: How the Conquered Peoples Shaped the Roman Empire* (1999).

Yavetz, Z., *Julius Caesar and his Public Image* (1983).

ARTICLES

Bradley, K. (1986), 'Wet-nursing at Rome: A Study in Social Relations', in B. Rawson (ed.), *The Family in Ancient Rome*, pp. 201–229.

Braund, D. (1996), 'River Frontiers in the Environmental Psychology of the Roman World', in Kennedy, D. (ed.), *The Roman Army in the East, Journal of Roman Archaeology Supplementary Series 18*, pp. 43–47.

Carson, R. (1957), 'Caesar and the Monarchy', *Greece and Rome* 4, pp. 46–53.

Collins, J. (1955), 'Caesar and the Corruption of Power', *Historia* 4, pp. 445–465.

Cuff, P. (1958), 'The Terminal Date of Caesar's Gallic Command', *Historia* 7, pp. 445–471.

Hansen, M. (1993), 'The Battle Exhortation in Ancient Historiography: Fact or Fiction', *Historia* 42, pp. 161–180.

Lintott, A. (1990), 'Electoral Bribery in the Roman Republic', *Journal of Roman Studies* 80, pp. 1–16.

Rankov, B. (1996), 'The Second Punic War at Sea' in Cornell, T., Rankov, B., & Sabin, P. (eds.), *The Second Punic War: A Reappraisal*, pp. 49–57.

Rawson, E. (1975), 'Caesar's Heritage: Hellenistic Kings and their Roman Equals', *Journal of Roman Studies* 65, pp. 148–159.

Rawson, E. (1976), 'The Ciceronian Aristocracy and its Properties', in Finley, M. (ed.), *Studies in Roman Property*, pp. 85–102.

Roymans, N. (1983), 'The North Belgic Tribes in the First Century BC' in Brandt, R., & Slofstra, J. (eds.), *Roman and Native in the Low Countries, British Archaeological Reports 184*, pp. 43–69.

Salmon, E. (1935), 'Catiline, Crassus, and Caesar', *American Journal of Philology* 56, pp. 302–316.

Salway, B. (1994), 'What's in a Name? A Survey of Roman Onomastic Practice from 700 BC – AD 700', *Journal of Roman Studies* 84, pp. 124–145.

Stockton, D. (1975), '*Quis iustius induit arma*', *Historia* 24, pp. 222–259.

Syme, R. (1938), 'The Allegiance of Labienus', *Journal of Roman Studies* 28, pp. 424–440.

Taylor, L. Ross (1941), 'Caesar's Early Career', *Classical Philology* 36, pp. 113–132.

Taylor, L. Ross (1957), 'The Rise of Julius Caesar', *Greece and Rome* 4, pp. 10–18.

Taylor, L. Ross (1968), 'The Dating of Major Legislation and Elections in Caesar's First Consulship', *Historia* 17, pp. 173–193.

Tchernia, A. (1983), 'Italian Wine in Gaul at the End of the Republic', in Garnsey, P., Hopkins, K., & Whittaker, C. (eds.), *Trade in the Ancient Economy*, pp. 87–104.

Treggiari, S. (1991), 'Divorce Roman Style: How Easy and Frequent was it?' in B. Rawson (ed.), *Marriage, Divorce and Children in Ancient Rome*, pp. 131–146.

Tyrrell, W. (1972) 'Labienus' Departure from Caesar in January 49 BC', *Historia* 21, pp. 424–440.

Yakobson, A. (1992), 'Petitio et Largitio: Popular Participation in the Centuriate Assembly of the Late Republic', *Journal of Roman Studies* 82, pp. 32–52.

ABBREVIATIONS

Ampelius, *lib. mem* = Lucius Ampelius, *Liber memorialis.*

Appian, BC = Appian, *Civil Wars.*

Appian, *Bell. Hisp.* = Appian, *Spanish Wars.*

Broughton, *MRR* 2 = Broughton, T., & Patterson, M., *The Magistrates of the Roman Republic,* Volume 2 (1951).

Caesar, *BC* = Caesar, *The Civil Wars.*

Caesar, *BG* = Caesar, *The Gallic Wars.*

*CAH*² IX = Crook, J., Lintott, A., & E. Rawson (eds.), *The Cambridge Ancient History* 2nd edn, Volume IX: *The Last Age of the Roman Republic, 146–43* BC (1994).

Cicero, *ad Att.* = Cicero, *Letters to Atticus.*

Cicero, *ad Fam.* = Cicero, *Letters to his friends.*

Cicero, *ad Quintum Fratrem* = Cicero, *Letters to his Brother Quintus.*

Cicero, *Cat.* = Cicero, *Catilinarian Orations.*

Cicero, *de Sen.* = Cicero, *de Senectute.*

Cicero, *Verr.* = Cicero, *Verrine Orations.*

CIL = *Corpus Inscriptionum Latinarum.*

Comp. Nic. = Fragment of Nicolaus of Damascus, *History.*

de vir. Ill. = the anonymous *de viris illustribus.*

Dio = Cassius Dio, *Roman History.*

Gellius, *NA* = Aulus Gellius, *Attic Nights.*

ILLRP = Degrassi, A. (ed.) (1963–1965), *Inscriptiones Latinae Liberae Rei Republicae.*

ILS = Dessau, H. (1892–1916), *Incriptiones Latinae Selectae.*

JRS = *Journal of Roman Studies.*

Justin = Justinus, *Epitome.*

Livy, *Pers.* = Livy, *Periochae*

Pliny the Elder, *NH* = Pliny the Elder, *Natural History.*

Pliny the Younger, *Epistulae* = Pliny the Younger, *Letters.*

Quintilian = Quintilian, *Training in Oratory.*

Sallust, *Bell. Cat.* = Sallust, *The Catilinarian War.*

Serv. = Servius.

Strabo, *Geog.* = Strabo, *Geography.*

Valerius Maximus = Valerius Maximus, *Memorable Doings and Sayings.*

Velleius Paterculus = Velleius Paterculus, *Roman History.*

NOTES

Introduction

1 M. Booth, *The Doctor, the Detective and Arthur Conan Doyle* (1997) p.204.

I Caesar's World

1 Velleius Paterculus, *History of Rome* 2. 1. 1 (Loeb translation by F. Shipley (1924), pp. 47–49).
2 Suetonius, *Caesar* 77.
3 Polybius, 6. 11. 1–18. 8, 43. 1–57. 9 for his description and analysis of the Roman Republic, with F. Walbank, *A Historical Commentary on Polybius*, 1 (1970), pp. 663–746. A detailed recent discussion of the topic can be found in A. Lintott, *The Constitution of the Roman Republic* (1999).
4 For a description of these campaigns see A. Goldsworthy, *In the Name of Rome* (2003), pp. 126–136.
5 For Saturninus and Glaucia see Appian, *BC* 1. 28–33, Plutarch, *Marius* 28–30.
6 Suetonius, *Caesar* 77.
7 Valerius Maximus 3. 7. 8.
8 On population and the problems of calculating it with precision see N. Purcell, 'The City of Rome and the *Plebs Urbana* in the Late Republic', in *CAH²* IX, pp. 644–688, esp. 648–656, and also K. Hopkins, *Conquerors and Slaves* (1978), pp. 96–98. On the importance of the Forum as the physical setting for Roman public life see F. Millar, *The Crowd in Rome in the Late Republic* (1998), esp. pp. 13–48.
9 Some of the most influential discussions of Roman imperialism include E. Badian, *Roman Imperialism in the Late Republic* (1968), W. Harris, *War and Imperialism in Republican Rome, 327–70 BC* (1979), and Hopkins (1978), esp. 1–98.
10 See E. Badian, *Publicans and Sinners* (1972).
11 See in particular Hopkins (1978), *passim*.
12 For the careers of the Gracchi see D. Stockton, *The Gracchi* (1979). The principal sources are Plutarch, *Tiberius Gracchus* and *Caius Gracchus*, and Appian, *BC* 1. 8–27; for the story of Caius' head see Plutarch, *Caius Gracchus* 17.
13 For a detailed account of Marius' career see R. Evans, *Gaius Marius: A Political Biography* (1994).

II Caesar's childhood

1 Velleius Paterculus 2. 41. 1.

2 Suetonius, *Caesar* 1. 3.

3 For a general survey of the significance of Roman names see B. Salway, 'What's in a Name? A Survey of Roman Onomastic Practice from 700 BC – AD 700', *JRS* 84 (1994), pp. 124–145, esp. 124–131.

4 For stories about the origin of the name see *Historia Augusta*, *Aelius Verus* 2; for a discussion of Caesar's family see M. Gelzer, *Caesar* (1968), p. 19, C. Meier, *Caesar* (1996), pp. 51–55, and E. Gruen, *The Last Generation of the Roman Republic* (1974), pp. 75–76.

5 Suetonius *Caesar* 6. 1; for uncertainty over Aeneas and his son see Livy 1. 3.

6 Plutarch, *Tiberius Gracchus* 1.

7 *Historia Augusta*, *Aelius Verus* 2.

8 B. Rawson, *Children and Childhood in Roman Italy* (2003), esp. pp. 99–113; on the ancients' knowledge of Caesarean section see p. 99 with references. See also the collection of papers in B. Rawson (ed.), *Marriage, Divorce and Children in Ancient Rome* (1991).

9 Plutarch, *Cato the Elder* 20. 3. For a more detailed discussion of this topic see K. Bradley, 'Wet-nursing at Rome: A Study in Social Relations', in B. Rawson, *The Family in Ancient Rome* (1986), pp. 201–229.

10 Tacitus, *Dialogues* 28. 6 (Loeb translation by Sir W. Peterson, revised M. Winterbottom (1970), p. 307).

11 Plutarch, *Coriolanus* 33–36, Livy 2. 40.

12 See H. Marrou, *A History of Education in Antiquity* (1956), pp. 229–291, A. Gwynn, *Roman Education: From Cicero to Guintilian* (1926), esp. 1–32; Cicero, *de Re Publica* 4. 3.

13 Cicero, *Orator* 120.

14 There is a useful discussion of the client system in R. Saller, *Personal Patronage in the Early Empire* (1982); for boys accompanying fathers as they went about their business see Gellius, *NA* 1. 23. 4, Pliny, *Epistulae* 8. 14. 4–5, and on importance of father's influence from the age of seven see Quintilian 2. 2. 4, and comments in Marrou (1956), pp. 231–233.

15 Rawson (2003), pp. 153–157; Suetonius, *Grammaticis et rhetoribus* 7 for Gnipho; Suetonius *Caesar* 56. 7 for Caesar's early works.

16 Cicero, *Brutus* 305, Suetonius, *Caesar* 55. 2.

17 Plutarch, *Caesar* 17, Suetonius, *Caesar* 57, 61.

18 Plutarch, *Marius* 30, 32.

19 On the question of the allies see E. Gabba, *The Roman Republic, the Army and the Allies* (trans. P. Cuff) (1976), P. Brunt, *Social Conflicts in the Roman Republic* (1971), pp. 101–104, A. Sherwin-White, *The Roman Citizenship* (1973), pp. 119–149.

20 The fullest ancient account of the war is Appian, *BC* 1. 34–53, but see also Velleius Paterculus 2. 13. 117. 3; for a modern survey see E. Gabba, 'Rome and Italy: The Social War', in *CAH2* (1994), pp. 104–128.

21 Appian, *BC* 1. 4046, Plutarch, *Marius* 33, *Sulla* 6.

22 For Sulla's career see A. Keaveney, *Sulla: The Last Republican* (1982), 1–63.

23 Plutarch, *Marius* 34–35, *Sulla* 7–8, Appian *BC* 1. 55–57, and Keaveney (1982), pp. 56–77.
24 Plutarch, *Sulla* 9–10, *Marius* 35–40, Appian, *BC* 1. 57–59.
25 Appian, *BC* 1. 63–75; Plutarch, *Marius* 41–46, *Sulla* 22, *Pompey* 3, Velleius Paterculus 2. 20. 1–23.3, and also R. Seager, *Pompey* (2002), pp. 25–29.

III The First Dictator

1 Plutarch, *Sulla* 31 (translation by R. Waterfield in *Plutarch: Roman Lives* (1999), p. 210).
2 For the importance of the Liberalia festival see Ovid, *Fasti* 3. 771–788; on the sacrifice to Iuventus see Dionysius of Halicarnassus 4. 15. 5; on the ceremonies associated with adopting the *toga virilis* in general see B. Rawson, *Children and Childhood in Roman Italy* (2003), pp. 142–144.
3 Suetonius, *Caesar* 1.1; for the sudden death of Caesar's father see Pliny, *Natural History* 7. 181; on assuming the *toga virilis* see H. Marrou, *A History of Education in Antiquity* (1956), p. 233, A. Gwynn, *Roman Education: From Cicero to Quintilian* (1926), 16, and B. Rawson, 'The Roman Family', in B. Rawson (ed.), *The Family in Ancient Rome* (1986), pp. 1–57, 41.
4 For restrictions on the *Flamen Dialis* see Gellius, *NA* 10. 15.
5 Velleius Paterculus, 2. 22. 2, Appian, *BC* 1. 74. On Merula and Caesar's nomination for the flaminate see L. Ross Taylor, 'Caesar's Early Career', in *Classical Philology* 36 (1941), pp. 113–132, esp. pp. 114–116.
6 For *confarreatio* see S. Treggiari, *Roman Marriage: Iusti Coniuges from the Time of Cicero to the Time of Ulpian* (1991), 21–24; on the name and connection with *far* see *Gaius* 1. 112, Pliny, *NH* 18. 10, Festus 78L; for the rituals see Servius, *Ad G.* 1. 31.
7 Velleius Paterculus 2. 22. 2 claims that Caesar was made *Flamen Dialis*, but Suetonius explicitly says that he was only 'nominated' (*destinatus*), Suetonius, *Caesar* 1. 1. See M. Gelzer, *Caesar* (1968), pp. 19–21, and Taylor (1941), pp. 115–116. Tacitus, *Annals* 3. 58 and Dio 54. 36. 1 both state expressly that Merula was the last *Flamen Dialis*.
8 For a useful discussion of these years see *CAH²* IX (1994), pp. 173–187; on the behaviour of Cicero and his mentors during these years see T. Mitchell, *Cicero: The Ascending Years* (1979), pp. 81–92.
9 Appian, *BC* 1. 76–77.
10 Plutarch, *Sulla* 2 for his appearance, failure to win the praetorship 5, and for the epitaph 38; in general see A. Keaveney, *Sulla: The Last Republican* (1982). For the single testicle see Arrius Menander Bk. 1 *On Military Affairs*. Keaveney (1982), p. 11 argues that the story was probably derived from a bawdy song invented by his soldiers.
11 On Sulla's good fortune see Keaveney (1982), pp. 40–41.
12 Appian, *BC* 1. 78–80, Plutarch, *Pompey* 5.
13 For the Civil War see Keaveney (1982), pp. 129–147.
14 Plutarch, *Sulla* 27–32, Appian, *BC* 1. 81–96.
15 Plutarch, *Sulla* 31.

16 On the proscriptions see Keaveney (1982), pp. 148–168, Appian, *BC* 1. 95, Velleius Paterculus 2. 28. 3–4, and Plutarch, *Sulla* 31, which includes the anecdote about the Alban estate.

17 Keaveney (1982), pp. 160–203. For the execution of Ofella see Plutarch, *Sulla* 33.

18 Taylor (1941), p. 116.

19 See Suetonius, *Caesar* 1. 1–3, Plutarch, *Caesar* 1, and also L. Ross Taylor, 'The Rise of Julius Caesar', *Greece and Rome* 4 (1957), pp. 10–18, esp. 11–12, and Taylor (1941), p. 116.

20 Suetonius, *Caesar* 74.

21 Suetonius, *Caesar* 1.

22 Plutarch, *Sulla* 1. 104, Suetonius, *Caesar* 77.

23 Keaveney (1982), pp. 204–213.

IV The Young Caesar

1 Cicero, *Brutus* 290 (Loeb translation by G. Hendrickson (1939), p. 253).

2 For Suetonius' description of Caesar see *Caesar* 45. 1; Plutarch's comments are in *Caesar* 17; Caesar's peculiar dress and Sulla's comments are in Suetonius, *Caesar* 45. 3.

3 Suetonius, *Caesar* 45. 2.

4 For Cicero's house see Velleius Paterculus 2. 14, and E. Rawson, 'The Ciceronian Aristocracy and its properties', in M. I. Finley (ed.), *Studies in Roman Property* (1976), pp. 85–102, esp. 86; for the synagogue in the Subura, see *Corpus Inscriptionum Judaicarum* 2. 380.

5 Velleius Paterculus 2. 14. 3.

6 Suetonius, *Caesar* 46–47.

7 Suetonius, *Caesar* 2.

8 See L. Ross Taylor, 'The rise of Julius Caesar', *Greece and Rome* 4 (1957), pp. 10–18, and M. Gelzer, *Caesar* (1968), p. 22. On the *corona civica* see Gellius, *NA* 5. 6. 13–14, Pliny, *NH* 16. 12–13, and discussion in V. Maxfield, *The Military Decorations of the Roman Army* (1981), pp.70–74, 119–120.

9 Suetonius, *Caesar* 2 and 49. 1–4, 52. 3.

10 Plutarch, *Marius* 13–14, Polybius 6. 37; on Cato as censor see Plutarch, *Cato the Elder* 17.

11 Suetonius, *Caesar* 22 and 49. 1–4.

12 For Caesar's public oath see Dio 43. 20. 4; Catullus 54, cf. Suetonius, *Caesar* 73.

13 For Cato see Plutarch, *Cato the Elder* 24; Plutarch, *Crassus* 5; for the Germans see Caesar, *BG* 6. 21. For a survey of Roman attitudes see P. Grimal, *Love in Ancient Rome* (trans. A. Train) (1986).

14 Suetonius, *Caesar* 3.

15 Catullus 10; Cicero, *Verr.* 1. 40.

16 Cicero, *Brutus* 317.

17 See Suetonius, *Caesar* 4. 1, 55, Velleius Paterculus 2. 93. 3, and Gelzer (1968), pp. 22–3; on provincial administration in general see A. Lintott's *Imperium Romanum: Politics and Administration* (1993); for Caesar's high-pitched delivery see Suetonius, *Caesar* 55. 2.

18 Plutarch, *Caesar* 4.

19 Cicero, *Brutus* 316.

20 For the pirate problem see Appian, *Mithridatic Wars* 91–93, Plutarch, *Pompey* 24–5; on Caesar's captivity see Suetonius, *Caesar* 4. 2, Plutarch, *Caesar* 2.

21 Plutarch, *Caesar* 2 (Loeb translation by B. Perrin (1919), p. 445, slightly amended).

22 For the pirates' throats being cut see Suetonius, *Caesar* 74.

23 Suetonius, *Caesar* 4. 2.

24 L. Ross Taylor, 'Caesar's Early Career', *Classical Philology* 36 (1941), pp. 113–132, esp. p.117–118.

25 For the journey back to Rome see Velleius Paterculus 2. 93. 2; for the trial see E. Gruen, *The Last Generation of the Roman Republic* (1974), p. 528; for Cicero's comment see Suetonius, *Caesar* 49. 3.

26 Taylor (1941), pp. 120-122; for the Slave War see Plutarch, *Crassus* 8-11, Appian, *BC* 1. 116-121.

27 For Crassus and Sulla see Plutarch, *Crassus* 6.

28 Suetonius, *Caesar* 5.

V Candidate

1 Plutarch, *Caesar* 5.

2 For the birth of Julia see M. Gelzer, *Caesar* (1968), p. 21, C. Meier, *Caesar* (1996), p. 105, and P. Grimal, *Love in Ancient Rome* (1986), p. 222.

3 Grimal (1986), pp. 112–115.

4 For the story of Praecia and Lucullus see Plutarch, *Lucullus* 6. 2–4; on Cethegus' influence see Cicero, *Brutus* 178; for the story of Pompey, Geminius and Flora see Plutarch, *Pompey* 2.

5 For Cytheris see Cicero, *ad Fam.* 9. 26; Cicero *ad Att.* 10. 10; Servius, on E10; *de vir. Ill.* 82. 2. Cicero's distaste became public in the *Philippics* 2. 58, 69, 77.

6 Suetonius, *Caesar* 47, 50. 1–52.

7 Suetonius, *Caesar* 50. 2, Plutarch, *Caesar* 46, 62, *Brutus* 5, Cicero, *ad Att.* 15. 11; see also R. Syme, *The Roman Revolution* (1939), pp. 23–24, 116; on Lucullus' divorce of Servilia's sister Servilia see Plutarch, *Lucullus* 38.

8 Grimal (1986), pp. 226–237, S. Treggiari, *Roman Marriage* (1991), esp. pp. 105–106, 232–238, 253–261, 264, 270–275, and 299–319.

9 Sallust, *Bell Cat.* 25.

10 Plutarch, *Pompey* 55 (translation by R. Waterfield in *Plutarch: Roman Lives* (1999), p. 273).

11 For a survey of Sertorius' career see A. Goldsworthy, *In the Name of Rome* (2003), pp. 137–151.

12 For Sulla's legislation see A. Keaveney, *Sulla: The Last Republican* (1982), pp.169–189.

13 For the 'young executioner' see Valerius Maximus 6. 2. 8; for the killing of Brutus' father see Plutarch, *Brutus* 4; for Pompey's early career see R. Seager, *Pompey the Great* (2002), pp. 20–39.

14 On the impact of military failure on a man's career see N. Rosenstein, *Imperatores Victi* (1993), *passim*.

15   For Pompey and the censors see Plutarch, *Pompey* 22; for Crassus' feasting see
     Plutarch, *Crassus* 2. 2, 12. 3; *Comp. Nic.* Crassus 1. 4; A. Ward, *Marcus Crassus
     and the Late Roman Republic* (1977), pp. 101–2.

16   Suetonius, *Caesar* 5, Gellius, *NA* 13. 3. 5; on suggestions that he played a wider
     role in the events of 70 BC see the discussion in Ward (1977), pp. 105–111.

17   For discussions of elections see L. Ross Taylor, *Party Politics in the Age of Caesar*
     (1949), esp. pp. 50–75, and *Roman Voting Assemblies: From the Hannibalic War
     to the Dictatorship of Caesar* (1966), esp. pp. 78–106, A. Lintott, 'Electoral
     Bribery in the Roman Republic', *JRS* 80 (1990), pp. 1–16, F. Millar, *The Crowd in
     Rome in the Late Republic* (1998), H. Mouritsen, *Plebs and Politics in the Late
     Roman Republic* (2001), esp. pp. 63–89, A. Yakobson, 'Petitio et Largitio: Popular
     Participation in the Centuriate Assembly of the Late Republic', *JRS* 82 (1992), pp.
     32–52; inscriptions on tombs, see *ILS* 8205–8207.

18   See Taylor (1966), pp. 78–83, A. Lintott, *The Constitution of the Roman
     Republic* (1999), pp. 43–49.

19   On the quaestorship see Lintott (1999), pp. 133–137; for the suggestion that
     winners of the *corona civica* were enrolled in the Senate see L. Ross Taylor, 'The
     Rise of Caesar', *Greece and Rome* 4 (1957), pp. 10–18, esp. 12–13.

20   Polybius, 6. 54. 1–2.

21   Suetonius, *Caesar* 6. 1, Plutarch, *Caesar* 5; for Cicero's public and private attitude
     to Marius see the discussion in T. Mitchell, *Cicero: The Ascending Years* (1979),
     pp. 45–51.

22   *Spanish War* 42, Suetonius, *Caesar* 7. 1–2, Velleius Paterculus 2. 43. 4, and
     comments in Gelzer (1968), p. 32; for his reaction to bust of Alexander and his
     disturbing dream see Plutarch, *Caesar* 11, Suetonius, *Caesar* 7. 1–2, and Dio 37.
     52. 2; for Cicero's arrival back from his own quaestorship see *pro Planco* 64–66.

23   Suetonius, *Caesar* 8.

24   Suetonius, *Caesar* 6. 2, Plutarch, *Caesar* 5; for discussion of marriage ceremony
     see S. Treggiari, *Roman Marriage* (1991), pp. 161–180.

25   Dio 36. 20. 1–36, Plutarch, *Pompey* 25–26; for a detailed discussion of the
     introduction of the *Lex Gabinia* see P. Greenhalgh, *Pompey: The Roman
     Alexander* (1980), pp. 72–90.

26   On Caesar's support for the *Lex Gabinia* see Plutarch, *Pompey* 25, and also T.
     Rice Holmes, *The Roman Republic*, 1 (1928), pp. 170–173; for the campaign
     against the pirates see Appian, *Mithridatic Wars* 91–93, Plutarch, *Pompey* 26–28.

27   For Lucullus' career see A. Keaveney, *Lucullus: A Life* (1992), esp. 75–128 for his
     campaigns in the east; on his replacement see Plutarch, *Pompey* 30–31, *Lucullus*
     36.

28   Dio 36. 43. 2–3 for Caesar's support; *pro Lege Manilia*, Cicero's speech in favour
     of the *Lex Manilia* has survived.

29   Plutarch, *Caesar* 5–6, Suetonius, *Caesar* 10–11, Velleius Paterculus 2. 43. 4; on the
     aedileship see Lintott (1999), pp. 129–133; on Caesar's career see Gelzer (1968),
     pp. 37–39, L. Ross Taylor, 'Caesar's Early Career', *Classical Philology* 36 (1941),
     pp. 113–132, esp. 125– 131, and (1957), pp. 14–15.

30   Suetonius, *Caesar* 10. 1.

31   Dio 37. 8. 1–2, Pliny, *NH* 33. 53.

32   Plutarch, *Caesar* 5.

33 Plutarch, *Caesar* 6, Suetonius, *Caesar* 11, Velleius Paterculus 2. 43. 3–4, and see also R. Evans, *Gaius Marius: A Political Biography* (1994), p. 4, who suggests that the monuments are unlikely to have been the originals but copies.

VI Conspiracy

1 Sallust, *Bell. Cat.* 12. 1–2.
2 Dio 36. 44. 3–5, Cicero, *pro Sulla* 14–17, Sallust, *Bell. Cat.* 18.
3 See Suetonius, *Caesar* 9, Sallust, *Bell. Cat.* 17–19. For discussions of the 'First Catilinarian conspiracy' see E. Salmon, 'Catiline, Crassus, and Caesar', *American Journal of Philology* 56 (1935), pp. 302–316, esp. 302–306; E. Hardy, *The Catilinarian Conspiracy in its Context: A Re-study of the Evidence* (1924), pp. 12–20; T. Rice Holmes, *The Roman Republic*, 1 (1928), pp. 234–235; D. Stockton, *Cicero* (1971), pp. 77–78; and M. Gelzer, *Caesar* (1968), pp. 38–39.
4 On the struggle between Crassus and Pompey see A. Ward, *Marcus Crassus and the Late Roman Republic* (1977), pp. 128–168; Rice Holmes (1928), pp. 221–283, esp. 242–249. For imperial views of Pompey's return see Velleius Paterculus 2. 40. 2–3, Plutarch, *Pompey* 43, Dio 37. 20. 5–6
5 See Plutarch, *Crassus* 2–3, and Ward (1977), pp. 46–57; for the Licinia incident see Plutarch, *Crassus* 1, with sceptical comments in Ward (1977), 74–75.
6 Cicero, *Brutus* 233.
7 Plutarch, *Crassus* 3, Cicero, *de Officiis* 1. 25, Sallust, *Bell. Cat.*48.5–7. For 'Straw on his horns' and possible pun see Ward (1977), pp. 78.
8 Plutarch, *Crassus* 13, Suetonius, *Caesar* 11, Dio 37. 9. 3–4; Ward (1977), pp. 128–135, Gelzer (1968), pp. 39–41.
9 Plutarch, *Cato the Younger* 16–18, Suetonius, *Caesar* 11, Dio 37. 10. 1–3.
10 Suetonius, *Caesar* 74. On Catiline see Asconius 84C; on Ofella see Plutarch, *Sulla* 33
11 Sallust, *Bell. Cat.*5, 14–17, Plutarch, *Cicero* 10, Ward (1977), p. 136, 145, Rice Holmes (1928), p. 241, Stockton (1971), p. 79–81, 97, 100.
12 For Cato the Elder see Plutarch, *Cato the Elder*, and A. Astin, *Cato the Censor* (1978). On Cato see Plutarch, *Cato the Younger*, esp. 1, 5–7, 9, 24–25.
13 See Stockton (1971), esp. 71–81, E. Rawson, *Cicero* (1975), T. Mitchell, *Cicero: The Ascending Years* (1979), esp. p. 93 ff. The inscription that mentions a Lucius Sergius, normally identified as Catiline, on Pompeius Strabo's staff is *ILS* 8888/*ILLRP* 515.
14 For an excellent survey of these years see T. Wiseman, 'The Senate and the Populares, 69–60 BC', in *CAH*² IX (1994), pp. 327–367; on the Rullan land bill see Gelzer (1968), pp. 42–45, Stockton (1971), pp. 84–91, Rice Holmes (1928), pp. 242–249, Ward (1977), pp. 152–162.
15 For Piso see Sallust, *Bell. Cat.* 49. 2, Cicero, *pro Flacco* 98; for Juba see Suetonius, *Caesar* 71.
16 For Honours to Pompey see Dio 37. 21. 4. For a discussion of Labienus' origins see R. Syme, 'The Allegiance of Labienus', *JRS* 28 (1938), pp. 424–440.
17 For The *perduellio* see trial Dio 37. 26. 1–28. 4, Suetonius, *Caesar* 12, Cicero, *Pro Rabirio perduellionis*, with W. Tyrrell, *A Legal and Historical Commentary to Cicero's Oratio Pro Rabirio Perduellionis* (1978); the anonymous, *de viribus illustribus* contains the claim that Rabirius paraded Saturninus' head.

18 See L. Ross Taylor, *Roman Voting Assemblies: From the Hannibalic War to the Dictatorship of Caesar* (1966), p. 16.

19 For the election to *Pontifex Maximus* see Suetonius, *Caesar* 13, Plutarch, *Caesar* 7, Dio 37. 37. 1–3, Velleius Paterculus 2. 43. 3.

20 For a useful discussion of the Regia and its history see T. Cornell, *The Beginnings of Rome* (1995), pp. 239–241.

21 Sallust, *Bell. Cat.* 23–24, Cicero, *pro Murena* 51–58, Dio 37. 29. 1–30. 1, Plutarch, *Cato the Younger* 21. 2–6.

22 Sallust, *Bell. Cat.* 22. 1–4, 26. 1–31. 3.

23 Sallust, *Bell. Cat.* 31. 4–48. 2, Rice Holmes (1928), pp. 259–272, Stockton (1971), pp. 84–109.

VII Scandal

1 Cicero, *In Catilinam* 3. 1–2 (Loeb translation by C. MacDonald (1977), p. 101).

2 Quote on canvassing with Catiline, Cicero, *ad Att.* 1. 2.

3 Cicero, *In Catilinam* 2. 22 (Loeb translation by C. MacDonald (1977), p. 91).

4 Plutarch, *Caesar* 4. 4 (Loeb translation by B. Perrin (1919), p. 451).

5 Sallust, *Bell. Cat.* 48. 5.

6 Sallust, *Bell. Cat.* 48. 9; Plutarch, *Crassus* 13.

7 Cicero, *pro Murena*, and Plutarch, *Cato the Younger* 21. 3–6.

8 Sallust, *Bell. Cat.* 49. 1–4, Plutarch, *Crassus* 13, and *Cicero* 20. See also D. Stockton, *Cicero* (1971), pp. 18–19.

9 Sallust, *Bell. Cat.* 44–47, Plutarch, *Cicero* 19, Dio 37. 34. 1–4, Appian, *BC* 2. 4–5.

10 On the debate in general see Sallust, *Bell. Cat.* 50. 3–53. 1; For Catiline's last appearance in the Senate see Cicero, *Cat.*1. 16.

11 For Appius Claudius Caecus see Cicero, *de Sen.*16, *Brutus* 61.

12 Sallust, *Bell. Cat.* 51. 1–3.

13 Sallust, *Bell. Cat.* 51. 33.

14 Sallust, *Bell. Cat.* 51. 20.

15 For Caesar's speech see Sallust, *Bell. Cat.* 51.

16 For discussion of Caesar's view see Gelzer (1968), pp. 50–52, and C. Meier, *Caesar* (1996), pp. 170–172.

17 See Plutarch, *Cicero* 20–21, *Caesar* 7–8, Suetonius, *Caesar* 14, and Appian, *BC* 2. 5.

18 Cicero, *Cat.* 4. 3 (Loeb translation by C. MacDonald (1977), p. 137).

19 On Caesar see Cicero, *Cat.* 4. 9–10, for Crassus, 4. 10, for scenes of horror, 4. 12.

20 Sallust, *Bell. Cat.* 52. 12.

21 Sallust, *Bell. Cat.* 52. 17–18, 24–25.

22 Plutarch, *Brutus* 5 and *Cato the Younger* 24. 1–2; For Cicero's reaction to Brutus' version of the debate see Cicero, *ad Att.* 12. 21. 1.

23 Sallust, *Bell. Cat.* 55. 1–6, Plutarch, *Cicero* 22 and *Caesar* 8, Dio 37. 36. 1–4, Ampelius, *lib. mem.* 31; Sallust placed the threat to Caesar earlier see *Bell. Cat.* 49. 4.

24 Cicero, *ad Fam.* 5. 2. 7–8.

25 Suetonius, *Caesar* 15, Dio 37. 44. 1–3.

26 Dio 37. 43. 1–4, Plutarch, *Cato the Younger* 26. 1–29. 2.

27 Suetonius, *Caesar* 16.

28 On Catiline's death see Sallust, *Bell. Cat.* 60. 7, 61. 4; on the informers see
    Suetonius, *Caesar* 17.

29 Plutarch, *Caesar* 9–10.

30 Cicero, *ad Att.* 1. 12. 3, 1. 13. 3, Suetonius, *Caesar* 74. 2, Plutarch, *Caesar* 10. For
    divorce in general see S. Treggiari, *Roman Marriage* (1991), pp. 435–482 and
    'Divorce Roman Style: How Easy and Frequent Was It?' in B. Rawson (ed.),
    Marriage, Divorce and Children in Ancient Rome (1991), pp. 131–146.

31 See Cicero, *ad Att.* 1. 13. 3, and Catulus in Cicero, *ad Att.* 1. 16, Dio 37. 50. 3–4.

32 Plutarch, *Caesar* 11, Suetonius, *Caesar* 18, Cicero, *Pro Balbo* 28.

33 See Suetonius, *Caesar* 18, Appian, *Bell. Hisp.* 102, Plutarch, *Caesar* 12, Dio 37.
    52. 1–53. 4. For a discussion of the situation in Spain and Caesar's operations see
    S. Dyson, *The Creation of the Roman Frontier* (1985), pp. 235–236.

34 *Spanish War* 42. 2–3, Cicero, *pro Balbo* 19, 23, 28, 63 and 43; for the hint at
    human sacrifice see Strabo, *Geog.* 3. 5. 3 and Rice Holmes *The Roman Republic*,
    1 (1928), pp. 302–8.

35 Plutarch, *Caesar* 11.

VIII Consul

1   Sallust, *Bell. Cat.* 54. 4.

2   Cicero, *ad Att.* 2. 5.

3   Pliny, *NH* 7. 97, Plutarch, *Pompey* 45, Dio 37. 21. 1–4, Appian, *Mithridatic Wars*,
    116–117.

4   For the eastern wars see P. Greenhalgh, *Pompey: The Roman Alexander* (1980),
    and A. Goldsworthy, *In the Name of Rome* (2003), ch. 7, esp. pp. 164–179.

5   Plutarch, *Pompey* 42–46, *Cato the Younger* 30, Velleius Paterculus 2. 40. 3; R.
    Seager, *Pompey the Great* (2002), pp. 75–76; on Crassus see Plutarch, *Pompey* 43,
    and A. Ward, *Marcus Crassus and the Late Roman Republic* (1977), pp. 193–199.

6   Cicero, *ad Att.* 1. 13; see also *ad Att.* 1. 14 on Crassus.

7   Cicero, *ad Att.* 1. 13, 12; Seager (2002), pp. 77–79.

8   Cicero, *ad Att.* 1. 12, Plutarch, *Pompey* 42, *Cato the Younger* 30. 1–5, Suetonius,
    Caesar 50. 1; for Cicero's efforts to placate Metellus Celer in 62 BC see Cicero, *ad
    Fam.* 5. 1, 2.

9   Dio 37. 49. 1–4, Plutarch, *Pompey* 44, *Cato the Younger* 30. 5, Cicero, *ad Att.* 1.
    18, 19.

10 Cicero, *ad Att.* 2. 1.

11 Horace, *Odes* 2. 1. 1; for a perceptive overview of these years see P. Wiseman,
    'The Senate and the *Populares*, 69–60 BC', in *CAH²* IX (1994), pp. 327–367, esp.
    pp. 358–367.

12 Cicero, *ad Att.* 2. 1, and 1. 17 for December 61 talk of alliance between Caesar
    and Lucceius. See M. Gelzer, *Caesar* (1968), p. 60, fn. 1, plausibly interpreting
    Suetonius' words literally to indicate that Caesar divorced Pompeia by letter.

13 Appian, *BC* 2. 8, Plutarch, *Cato the Younger* 31. 2–3, Dio 37. 54. 1–2.

14 Suetonius, *Caesar* 19. 2; for the suggestion that this was a means of keeping the consuls in reserve see Seager (2002), p. 84; on personal hatreds and enemies see D. Epstein, *Personal Enmity in Roman Politics 218–43 BC* (1978).

15 See L. Ross Taylor, *Roman Voting Assemblies:From the Hannibalic War to the Dictatorship of Caesar* (1966), esp. pp. 84–106.

16 See Taylor (1966), pp. 54–55, H. Mouritsen, *Plebs and Party Politics in the Late Roman Republic* (2001), pp. 27–32; on the population of Rome at this time see N. Purcell, 'The City of Rome and the *plebs urbana* in the Late Republic', in *CAH2* IX (1994), pp.644–688.

17 Suetonius, *Caesar* 19. 1; Cicero, *ad Att.* 1. 1; on the importance of the Italian vote see L. Ross Taylor, *Party Politics in the Age of Caesar* (1949), pp. 57–59.

18 Cicero, *ad Att.* 2. 3.

19 Suetonius, *Caesar* 19.

20 Suetonius, *Caesar* 19. 2, Dio 37. 56–58, Appian, *BC* 2. 9; see also Seager (2002), pp. 82–85, Ward (1977), pp. 210–216, Gelzer (1968), pp. 67–69, C. Meier, *Caesar* (1996), pp. 182–189.

21 Plutarch, *Caesar* 13, *Pompey* 47; on oaths see Livy, *Pers.* 103, Appian, *BC* 2. 9, and Pliny, *Epistulae* 10. 96; for a case of two enemies each canvassing for the same candidate see Cicero, *ad Att.* 2. 1.

22 Suetonius, *Caesar* 20. 1, cf. Plutarch, *Cato the Younger* 23. 3.

23 Dio 38. 1. 1–7, Suetonius, *Caesar* 20. 1; on the chronology of this year see L. Ross Taylor, 'The Dating of Major Legislation and Elections in Caesar's First Consulship', *Historia* 17 (1968), pp. 173–193; see also Gelzer (1968), pp. 71–74, Meier (1996), pp. 207–213, Seager (2002), pp. 86–87; on the five 'inner' commissioners see Cicero, *ad Att.* 2. 7.

24 Dio 38. 2. 1–3. 3 Suetonius, *Caesar* 20. 4 gives a slightly different version apparently dating Cato's arrest to later in the year. Plutarch, *Cato the Younger* 33. 1–2 also places this incident later; on Petreius' military experience see Sallust, *Bell. Cat.* 59. 6.

25 Dio 38. 4. 1–3.

26 Dio 38. 4. 4–5. 5, Plutarch, *Pompey* 47; for the date of the vote see Taylor (1968), pp. 179–181.

27 Dio 38. 6. 1–3, Plutarch, *Cato the Younger* 32. 2; see Taylor (1969), p. 179 on Bibulus' intentions.

28 Dio 38. 6. 4–7. 2 , Appian, *BC* 2. 11, Plutarch, *Cato the Younger* 32. 2–6, Suetonius, *Caesar* 20. 1.

29 Suetonius, *Caesar* 20. 2, Dio 38. 8. 2; see also Taylor (1968), pp. 177–179.

30 Suetonius, *Caesar* 20. 3–4, 54. 3, Dio 38. 7. 4–6, Cicero, *In Vatinium* 29, 38; see Gelzer (1968), pp. 75–6, Seager (2002), p. 88; for some sense of Vatinius' character see his letters to Cicero, *ad Fam.* 5. 9, 10 and 10A; on Caesar's law regulating governors see T. Rice Holmes, *The Roman Republic*, 1 (1928), p. 319, and Cicero, *pro Sestio* 64, 135, *In Pisonem* 16, 37, *In Vatinium* 12, 29, *ad Att.* 5. 10. 2.

31 Suetonius, *Caesar* 21, 50. 1–2, and on his fondness for pearls 47, Plutarch, *Pompey* 47–48, *Caesar* 14, Dio 38. 9. 1.

32 Dio 38. 7. 3, Suetonius, *Caesar* 20. 3, Cicero, *ad Att.* 2. 15, 16, 17 and 18.

33 Dio 38. 12. 1–3, Cicero, *de Domo* 41, *ad Att.* 8. 3, *de provinciis consularibus* 42, Suetonius, *Caesar* 20. 4, Plutarch, *Caesar* 14; see also Gelzer (1968), pp. 76–78.

34 Cicero, *ad Att.* 2. 9.

35 Cicero, *ad Att.* 2. 16 and 17; on C. Cato see *ad Quintum Fratrem* 1. 2. 5.

36 Cicero, *ad Att.* 2. 19.

37 Cicero, *ad Att.* 2. 21, 22 and 23.

38 Cicero, *ad Att.* 2. 24.

39 Cicero, *ad Att.* 2. 24, *In Vatinium* 24–26, *pro Sestio* 132, Dio 38. 9. 2–10. 1, Suetonius, *Caesar* 20. 5, Appian, BC 2. 12–13, Plutarch, *Lucullus* 42. 7–8; for Caesar as the prime mover behind these events see Rice Holmes (1928), pp. 323–324 and Gelzer (1968), pp. 90–92, Meier (1996), p. 221; for Clodius see Seager (2002), pp. 98–99; for Pompey's involvement see Ward (1977), pp. 236–241, Gruen, *The Last Generation of the Roman Republic* (1974), pp. 95–96; for a more complex interpretation and the suggestion that there may actually have been a plot see D. Stockton, *Cicero* (1971), pp. 183–186.

40 Suetonius, *Caesar* 23, 73, *Scholia Bobiensia* on Cicero, *pro Sestio* 40 and *In Vatinium* 15.

41 Suetonius, *Caesar* 22. 2 (Loeb translation); on Cicero's fears of civil war see *ad Att.* 2. 20, 21 and 22.

IX Gaul

1 Pliny, *NH* 7. 92.

2 Hirtius from his preface to *BG* 8.

3 Pliny, *NH* 7. 92, Appian, *BC* 2. 150.

4 For Theophanes see Cicero, *pro Archia* 24; for Caesar's earlier works see Suetonius, *Caesar* 56. 5–7; for the *Commentaries* in general see the collection of papers in K. Welch & A. Powell (eds.), *Julius Caesar as Artful Reporter: The War Commentaries as Political Instruments* (1998).

5 Cicero, *Brutus* 262.

6 'An orator should avoid a . . .', see Gellius, *NA* 1. 10. 4; see also L. Hall, 'Ratio and Romanitas in the Bellum Gallicum', in Welch & Powell (1998), pp. 11–43, esp. p. 23.

7 For the dating of the *Commentaries* see M. Gelzer, *Caesar* (1968), pp. 170–172, C. Meier, *Caesar* (1996), pp. 254–264; for the arguments in favour of annual publication see Welch & Powell (1998), and especially the article by P. Wiseman, 'The Publication of the *De Bello Gallico*', pp. 1–9, and also T. Rice Holmes, *Caesar's Conquest of Gaul* (1911), pp. 202–209 see also Hirtius, *BG* 8 preface and Suetonius, *Caesar* 56. 3–4.

8 Cicero, *de Finibus* 5. 52; see also Wiseman (1998), esp. pp. 4–7.

9 Suetonius, *Caesar* 56. 4.

10 Cicero, *de provinciis consularibus* 3. 5, *ad Quintum Fratrem* 2. 14–16, 3. 1–9.

11 On Labienus see R. Syme, 'The Allegiance of Labienus', *JRS* 28 (1938), pp. 113–128, esp. p. 120 and W. Tyrrell, 'Labienus' Departure from Caesar in January 49 BC', *Historia* 21 (1972), pp. 424–440.

12 On Cotta's book see Cicero, *ad Att.* 13. 44. 3, cf. Athenaeus 273b and Hall, (1998), pp. 11–43, esp. p. 25; on the identity of Caesar's legates see Broughton, *MRR* 2, pp. 197–199.

13 Caesar, *BG* 1. 39; Cicero, *ad Att.* 2. 18. 3, 19. 5, *de provinciis consularibus* 41; E. Gruen, *The Last Generation of the Roman Republic* (1974), pp. 112–116.

14 For Caesar's legions see H. Parker, *The Roman Legions* (1957), pp. 47–71, esp. 55–56. On the army in this period see F. Adcock, *The Roman Art of War under the Republic* (1940), P. Brunt, *Italian Manpower, 225* BC – AD *14* (1971), P. Connolly, *Greece and Rome at War* (1981), M. Feugère (ed.), *L'Équipment Militaire et L'Armement de la République. JRMES* 8 (1997), E. Gabba, *The Roman Republic, the Army and the Allies* (1976), L. Keppie, *The Making of the Roman Army* (1984), Y. Le Bohec, *The Imperial Roman Army* (1994), J. Harmand, *L'armée et le soldat à Rome de 107 à 50 avant nôtre ère* (1967).

15 For an introduction to this question with further references see A. Goldsworthy. *The Roman Army at War, 100* BC – AD *200* (1996), pp. 31–32.

16 For equipment see Goldsworthy (1996), pp. 83–84, 209–219, M. Bishop & J. Coulston, *Roman Military Equipment* (1993), Connolly, (1981), and Feugère, (1997).

17 See D. Saddington, *The Development of the Roman Auxiliary Forces from Caesar to Vespasian* (1982); Caesar, *BC* 1. 39 for numbers of auxiliary cavalry and infantry.

18 For a discussion of this see C. Goudineau, *César et la Gaule* (1995), pp. 130–148.

19 Caesar, *BG* 1. 1, 6. 11–20; for a good survey of Gallic society see N. Roymans, *Tribal Societies in Northern Gaul: An Anthropological Perspective, Cingula* 12 (1990), esp. pp. 17–47, and B. Cunliffe, *Greeks, Romans and Barbarians: Spheres of Interaction* (1988), esp. pp. 38–58 and 80–105.

20 See M. Todd, *The Northern Barbarians* (1987), pp. 11–13, *The Early Germans* (1992), pp. 8–13, C. M. Wells, *The German Policy of Augustus* (1972), pp. 14–31, and most recently the useful survey in P. Wells, *The Barbarians Speak: How the Conquered Peoples Shaped the Roman Empire* (1999).

21 For Domitius Ahenobarbus see Suetonius, *Nero* 2; on exchanging a slave for an amphora see Diodorus Siculus 5. 26. 3–4; on the relations between Gauls and Romans and the history of Transalpine Gaul see S. Dyson, *The Creation of the Roman Frontier* (1985), pp.126–173; on the wine trade see Cunliffe (1988), 59–105, esp. p. 74, and Roymans (1990), pp. 147–167 and A. Tchernia, 'Italian Wine in Gaul at the End of the Republic', in P. Garnsey, K. Hopkins & C. Whittaker (eds.), *Trade in the Ancient Economy* (1983), pp. 87–104.

22 Wells (1999), pp.49–78, Cunliffe (1988), pp. 48–49, 86–87, 96–97, 132–134, Dyson (1985), pp. 137–139, 154, and C. Goudineau (1995), pp. 141–143.

23 On human sacrifice at Rome see Pliny, *NH* 30. 12–13; on head-hunting see Polybius 3. 67, Livy 10. 26, 23. 24, Diodorus Siculus 5. 29. 2–5, M. Green, *Dictionary of Celtic Myth and Legend* (1992), pp. 116–118; on human sacrifice in Germany see Todd (1992), pp. 112–115.

24 Strabo, *Geog.* 4. 4. 5 (Loeb translation by H. Jones (1923), p. 247).

25 Caesar, *BG* 6. 15, cf. Strabo, *Geog.* 4. 4. 2; on Ribemont-sur-Ancre see T. Derks, *Gods, Temples and Ritual Practices: The Transformation of Religious Ideas and Values in Roman Gaul* (1998), p. 48, 234–5.

26 Caesar, *BG* 1. 18, 31–33; see also Dyson (1985), pp. 169–170, Cunliffe (1988), p. 94, 118.

27 For a more detailed discussion of Gallic armies see Goldsworthy (1996), pp. 53–60.

28 Dyson (1985), pp. 168–171; Caesar, *BG* 1. 36, 40, 44, Cicero, *ad Att*. 1. 19, 20.

X Migrants and Mercenaries: The first campaigns, 58 BC

1 Cicero, *ad Att*. 1. 19.

2 Caesar, *BG* 1. 6–7, Plutarch, *Caesar* 17.

3 Caesar, *BG* 1. 2.

4 Caesar, *BG* 1. 2–3, 18, cf. C. Goudineau, *César et la Gaule* (1995), 136–137.

5 Caesar, *BG* 1. 4, Pliny, *NH* 2. 170 records the meeting between Roman ambassadors and a Suebian king, who was probably Ariovistus; see also S. Dyson, *The Creation of the Roman Frontier* (1985), pp. 169–170. 172, B. Cunliffe, *Greeks, Romans and Barbarians: Spheres of Interaction* (1988), pp. 114–117.

6 For a discussion see T. Rice Holmes, *Caesar's Conquest of Gaul* (1911) pp. 218–224, and H. Delbrück, *History of the Art of War*, Volume 1: *Warfare in Antiquity* (1975), pp. 459–478.

7 Caesar, *BG* 6. 11; on the desire for allied tribes around provincial frontiers see Dyson (1985), pp. 170–173.

8 Caesar, *BG* 1. 5–6; for the focus on the Balkans, see Goudineau (1995), pp. 130–148; for Helvetii's numbers and size of columns see Holmes (1911), pp. 239–240, Delbrück (1975), pp. 460–463.

9 Caesar, *BG* 1. 7–8, cf Appian, *Mithridatic Wars* 99, Plutarch, *Crassus* 10.

10 Caesar, *BG* 1. 8.

11 Caesar, *BG* 1. 10.

12 Caesar, *BG* 1. 10–11, Cicero, *de provinciis consularibus* 28, Suetonius, *Caesar* 24; L. Keppie, *The Making of the Roman Army* (1984), p. 98.

13 Caesar, *BG* 1. 11, 16; on the logistics of the Roman army, including discussions of the number of slaves and camp followers see P. Erdkamp, *Hunger and Sword: Warfare and Food Supply in Roman Republican Wars 264–30 BC* (1998), J. Roth, *The Logistics of the Roman Army at War, 264 BC–AD 235* (1999), A. Labisch, *Frumentum Commeatusque. Die Nahrungsmittelversongung der Heere Caesars* (1975), and A. Goldsworthy, *The Roman Army at War, 100 BC – AD 200* (1996), pp. 287–296.

14 Caesar, *BG* 1. 12.

15 Caesar, *BG* 1. 13.

16 Caesar, *BG* 1. 13–14.

17 Caesar, *BG* 1. 15–16.

18 Caesar, *BG* 1. 16–20, cf. Goudineau (1995), p. 138.

19 See Arrian, *Alexander* 3. 10. 1–4 on the danger and difficulties of night attacks.

20 Caesar, *BG* 1. 21–22; for a discussion of this operation see Goldsworthy (1996), pp. 128–130.

21 Caesar, *BG* 1. 23.

22 Sallust, *Bell. Cat.* 59, Plutarch, *Crassus* 11. 6; for a discussion of the commander's role before and during battle see Goldsworthy (1996), pp. 131–163; on pre-battle

speeches see M. Hansen, 'The Battle Exhortation in Ancient Historiography: Fact or Fiction', *Historia* 42 (1993), pp. 161–180.

23 For the battle see Caesar, *BG* 1. 24–26; for discussion of the nature of battles in this period see Goldsworthy (1996), pp. 171–247.
24 Caesar, *BG* 26–29.
25 Caesar, *BG* 1. 30–33.
26 Caesar, *BG* 1. 34–37.
27 Caesar, *BG* 1. 39.
28 Dio 38. 35. 2.
29 Caesar, *BG* 1. 40.
30 Caesar, *BG* 1. 39–41.
31 Caesar, *BG* 1. 41, cf. Plutarch, *Sulla* 5 for the fame he derived from being the first Roman magistrate to receive a Parthian envoy.
32 Caesar, *BG* 1. 42–46.
33 Caesar, *BG* 1. 46–47.
34 Caesar, *BG* 1. 48, cf. Tacitus, *Germania* 6; for a discussion of Germanic armies see Goldsworthy (1996), pp. 42–53.
35 Caesar, *BG* 1. 49.
36 For the encouragement offered by German women to their warrior husbands see Tacitus, *Germania* 7–8.
37 Caesar, *BG* 1. 51–54; See Frontinus, *Strategemata* 2. 6. 3 on letting the Germans escape.
38 Caesar, *BG* 1. 54.

XI 'The Bravest of the Gaulish Peoples': The Belgae, 57 BC

1 Caesar, *BG* 2. 15.
2 Strabo, *Geog.* 4. 4. 2 (Loeb translation by H. Jones (1923), p. 237).
3 For promotions of centurions for gallantry see Caesar, *BG* 6. 40; Suetonius, *Caesar* 65. 1; on centurions' command style and heavy casualties see A. Goldsworthy, *The Roman Army at War, 100 BC – AD 200* (1996), pp. 257–8, cf. Caesar, *BG* 7. 51, *BC* 3. 99; also on the competition to show conspicuous valour and win promotion or reward see *BG* 5. 44, 7. 47, 50, *BC* 3. 91.
4 On sudden marches and relaxed discipline see Suetonius, *Caesar* 65, 67; for a discussion of Marius' style of command see A. Goldsworthy, *In the Name of Rome* (2003), pp. 113–136 (or 2004 edn, pp. 127–153).
5 Plutarch, *Caesar* 17 (Loeb translation by B. Perrin (1919), p. 483).
6 See Suetonius, *Caesar* 67. 2 for *commilitones* and inlaid weapons; see also Polybius 6. 39 and Goldsworthy (1996), pp. 264–282 on individual boldness.
7 On Pompeius Trogus see Justin, 43. 5. 12; for Caesar dictating letters while on horseback see Plutarch, *Caesar* 17; on receiving petitioners while in Cisalpine Gaul for the winter, Plutarch, *Caesar* 20.
8 On Valerius Meto see Plutarch, *Caesar* 17; for dining arrangements see Suetonius, *Caesar* 48; Catullus, 29.
9 Catullus, 57 (Loeb translation by F. Cornish (1988), pp. 67–69).
10 Suetonius, *Caesar* 73.

11 Suetonius, *Caesar* 51; Tacitus, *Histories* 4. 55; for other poems attacking Mamurra see Catullus, 41, 43.

12 Caesar, *BG* 2. 1; for a summary of Pompey's campaigns see Goldsworthy (2003), pp. 169–179 (or 2004 edn, pp. 190–201).

13 See N. Roymans, *Tribal Societies in Northern Gaul: An Anthropological Perspective, Cingula 12* (1990), pp. 11–15, cf. Tacitus, *Germania* 28, Caesar, *BG* 2. 4, 15, 5. 12; on resistance to Cimbri see *BG* 2. 4, and descent from them of the Atuatuci, 2. 29.

14 Caesar, *BG* 2. 2–5; on numbers see T. Rice Holmes, *Caesar's Conquest of Gaul* (1911), p. 71, and L. Rawlings, 'Caesar's Portrayal of Gauls as Warriors', in K. Welch & A. Powell, *Julius Caesar as Artful Reporter: The War Commentaries as Political Instruments* (1998), pp. 171–192, esp. 175, and fn. 13. For an extremely critical view of Caesar's numbers see H. Delbrück, *History of the Art of War, Volume 1: Warfare in Antiquity* (1975), pp.488–494. Delbrück believed that barbarians were markedly superior fighters to civilised Romans, and as a result consistently reduces the size of their forces, while inflating the numbers in Caesar's army.

15 Caesar, *BG* 2. 5–7.

16 For Sulla's use of trenches to protect his flanks see Frontinus, *Strategemata* 2. 3. 17.

17 Caesar, *BG* 2. 8–11.

18 Caesar, *BG* 2. 11–13.

19 Caesar, *BG* 2. 13–15.

20 Caesar, *BG* 2. 16–18, cf. 28 on the strength of the Nervii at the battle.

21 For the possible significance of the site see Rawlings (1998), pp. 176–177; for the suggestion of Maubeuge see Rice Holmes (1911), p. 76.

22 Caesar, *BG* 2. 19; cf. Rice Holmes (1911), p. 77 for Napoleon's comments; on marching camps see Goldsworthy (1996), pp.111–113.

23 Caesar, *BG* 2. 20; on delays before battle see Goldsworthy (1996), pp. 143–145.

24 Caesar, *BG* 2. 20–24.

25 Caesar, *BG* 2. 25.

26 See Goldsworthy (1996), pp. 154–163, esp. 160–161, and (2003), pp. 155, 176, 195 (or 2004 edn, pp. 175, 198, 219); on the nature of combat see Goldsworthy (1996), pp. 191–227.

27 Caesar, *BG* 2. 27–28.

28 Caesar, *BG* 2. 29–32.

29 Caesar, *BG* 2. 33; on his reluctance to let soldiers loose in a town during the hours of darkness see *BC* 1. 21, 2. 12, *African War* 3; on ritual offerings see *BG* 6. 17, Suetonius, *Caesar* 54. 2.

30 Caesar, *BG* 2. 35, Dio 39. 25. 1–2, cf. M. Gelzer, *Caesar* (1968), pp. 116–118.

XII Politics and War: The Conference of Luca

1 Cicero, *ad Quintum Fratrem* 2. 3. 3–4.

2 Cicero, *de provinciis consularibus* 25.

3 Publius and Claudia in the First Punic War see Livy, *Pers.* 19, Cicero, *de natura deorum* 2. 7, Florus 1. 19. 29, Suetonius, *Tiberius* 2. 3, Gellius, *NA* 10. 6.

4   Plutarch, *Lucullus* 34, 38, Cicero, *pro Milone* 73; for a discussion of the family's position see E. Gruen, *The Last Generation of the Roman Republic* (1974), pp. 97–100; on the identity of Lesbia see Apuleius, *Apologia* 10.

5   Dio 38. 12–13, see also M. Gelzer, *Caesar* (1968), pp. 96–99, G. Rickman, *The Corn Supply of Ancient Rome* (1979), pp. 104–119.

6   Plutarch, *Cicero* 30–32, *Cato the Younger* 34–40, see also D. Stockton, *Cicero* (1971), pp. 167–193, R. Seager, *Pompey the Great* (2002), pp. 101–103.

7   Plutarch, *Cicero* 33–34, Seager (2002), 103–109.

8   Cicero, *pro Sestio* 71, *de provinciis consularibus* 43, *In Pisonem* 80, *ad Fam.* 1. 9. 9; on Pompey and the Egyptian command see especially Cicero, *ad Fam.* 1. 1–9; see also Seager (2002), pp. 107–109, Gelzer (1968), pp. 117–119.

9   Cicero, *ad Quintum Fratrem* 2. 3. 2.

10   For Ahenobarbus see Cicero, *ad Att.* 4. 8b; for the Campanian land see Cicero, *ad Quintum Fratrem* 2. 1. 1, 6. 1, *ad Fam.* 1. 9. 8.

11   Suetonius, *Caesar* 24. 1.

12   Appian, *BC* 2. 17, Plutarch, *Pompey* 50, *Caesar* 21, *Crassus* 14; see also Gelzer (1968), pp.120–124, Seager (2002), pp. 110–119, C. Meier *Caesar* (1996), pp. 270–273, A. Ward, *Marcus Crassus and the Late Roman Republic* (1977), pp. 262–288.

13   Cicero, *ad Fam.* 1. 9. 8–10, *ad Quintum Fratrem* 2. 7. 2; for the accusation of incest between Clodia and her brother see *pro Caelio* 32.

14   Cicero, *de provinciis consularibus* 32–33.

15   Plutarch, *Crassus* 15, *Pompey* 51–52, *Cato the Younger* 41–42, Dio 39. 27. 1–32. 3; Seager (2002), pp. 120–122.

16   For 'All Gaul at peace' see Caesar, *BG* 3. 7, for Galba in the Alps see 3. 1–6, for Crassus see 2. 34, 3. 7.

17   Caesar, *BG* 3. 8–11.

18   Caesar, *BG* 3. 11–16; cf. Gelzer (2002), p. 126, and Meier (1996), pp. 274–275 pointing out that Caesar's officers were not ambassadors.

19   For Sabinus see Caesar, *BG* 3. 17–19; for Crassus see 3. 20–26, for Caesar and the Morini see 3. 27–28.

13 'Over the Waters': The British and German Expeditions, 55–54 BC

1   Cicero, *ad Att.* 4. 18.

2   Tacitus, *Agricola* 13.

3   Caesar, *BG* 4. 20, Suetonius, *Caesar* 47, Plutarch, *Caesar* 23.

4   Caesar, *BG* 4. 1–4, Plutarch, *Caesar* 22; for a detailed discussion of the incident see A. Powell, 'Julius Caesar and the Presentation of Massacre', in K. Welch & A. Powell (eds.), *Julius Caesar as Artful Reporter: The War Commentaries as Political Instruments* (1998), pp. 111–137.

5   See Powell (1998), esp. pp. 124–129; on Roman resistance to peoples moving into frontier zones see S. Dyson, *The Creation of the Roman Frontier* (1985), esp. pp. 172–173.

6   Caesar, *BG* 4. 5–7; in 52 BC he referred to his reluctance to trust his security to the tribal leaders, see *BG* 7. 6.

7   Caesar, *BG* 4. 7–9.

8   Caesar, *BG* 4. 11–12; cf. 4. 2 on German scorn for saddles; on small size of German horses see 7. 65, Tacitus, *Germania* 6.

9   Caesar, *BG* 4. 13–14.

10   Caesar, *BG* 4. 14–15.

11   Caesar, *BG* 4. 14–16.

12   Plutarch, *Cato the Younger* 51. 1–2 (Loeb translation).

13   Suetonius, *Caesar* 24. 3, and M. Gelzer, *Caesar* (1968), pp. 130–132, C. Meier, *Caesar* (1996), pp. 282–284.

14   Plutarch, *Cato the Younger* 51. 2 (Loeb Translation).

15   On Cato's attack see Powell (1998), pp. 123, 127–128, Gelzer (1968), pp. 131–132.

16   Caesar, *BG* 4. 16–18, cf. T. Rice Holmes, *Caesar's Conquest of Gaul* (1911), p. 100.

17   Caesar, *BG* 4. 18–19.

18   Caesar, *BG* 4. 20, 22. For general accounts of Caesar's expeditions and their place within the wider context of the later Roman conquest of Britain see G. Webster, *The Roman Invasion of Britain,* rev. edn (1993), pp. 43–40, and M. Todd, *Roman Britain,* 3rd edn. (1999), pp. 4–22. The most detailed treatment remains T. Rice Holmes, *Ancient Britain and the Invasions of Julius Caesar* (1907). See also the excellent recent analysis by G. Grainge, *The Roman Invasions of Britain* (2005), esp. pp. 83–109. It is not possible in a study of this nature to enter into the vigorous debates over many of the details of Caesar's expeditions.

19   Caesar, *BG* 4. 20–21; see the comments in N. Austin & B. Rankov, *Exploratio: Military and Political Intelligence in the Roman World* (1995), p. 13, who are critical of Caesar's failure to discover more information and cite Polybius 3. 48 in support. On the ports of Britain and trade with Europe see B. Cunliffe, *Greeks, Romans and Barbarians* (1988), pp. 145–149; on the coastline see the survey in Grainge (2005), pp. 17–42, 105–107.

20   Caesar, *BG* 4. 23–24; on the possible choice of Dover for the landing see Grainge (2005), pp. 101–105.

21   Caesar, *BG* 4. 25.

22   Caesar, *BG* 4. 25–26.

23   Caesar, *BG* 4. 27–30; for ' . . . peace was established', see 4. 28; see also Grainge (2005), pp. 107–109.

24   Caesar, *BG* 4. 33.

25   Caesar, *BG* 4. 32–35.

26   Caesar, *BG* 4. 36–38.

27   Caesar, *BG* 4 . 38, Dio 39. 53. 1–2.

28   Caesar, *BG* 5. 1–7.

29   Caesar, *BG* 5. 5, 8.

30   Caesar, *BG* 5. 9.

31   Caesar, *BG* 5. 10–11; see also Grainge (2005), p. 105–106.

32   Caesar, *BG* 5. 11, 15–16.

33   Caesar, *BG* 5. 17–22.

34   Caesar, *BG* 5. 22–23. In AD 16 part of a Roman army travelling by sea off
       Germany was blown off course and landed in Britain. The soldiers brought back
       wild tales of its inhabitants, see Tacitus, *Annals* 2. 24.
35   Cicero, *ad Att*. 4. 17; on excitement from receipt of his brother Quintus' account
       of operations in Britain see *ad Quintum Fratrem* 2. 16. 4.

XIV Rebellion, Disaster and Vengeance

1   Caesar, *BG* 5. 33.
2   Plutarch, *Pompey* 53, Suetonius, *Caesar* 26. 1, Vellieus Paterculus 2. 47. 2, Dio 39.
       64.
3   Plutarch, *Caesar* 23; on Trebonius' law see Velleius Paterculus 2. 46. 2, Plutarch,
       Crassus 15, Dio 39. 33. 2; on Pompey's position at this period see R. Seager,
       Pompey the Great (2002), pp. 120–132, esp. 123–124.
4   Plutarch, *Crassus* 15–16, Dio 39. 39. 5–7, Cicero, *ad Att*. 4. 13. 2, and A. Ward,
       Marcus Crassus and the Late Roman Republic (1977), pp. 243–253, 262–288.
5   Cicero, *ad Quintum Fratrem* 2. 15a. 3; for letters to Cicero from Caesar during
       the British campaign see Cicero, *ad Quintum Fratrem* 3. 1. 17 and 25, *ad Att*. 4.
       18. 5; on Quintus as Caesar's legate see M. Gelzer, *Caesar* (1968), pp. 138–139.
6   For letter of recommendation to Caesar see Cicero, *ad Fam*. 7. 5, letters to
       Trebatius, *ad Fam*. 7. 6–19, Cicero, *ad Quintum Fratrem* 2. 15a. 3 for quote; see
       also Gelzer (1968), pp. 138–139.
7   Caesar, *BG* 5. 24–25; Cicero, *ad Att*. 4. 19.
8   Caesar, *BG* 5. 26.
9   Caesar, *BG* 5. 26–37.
10   For a discussion see A. Powell, 'Julius Caesar and the Presentation of Massacre',
       in K. Welch & A. Powell (eds.), *Julius Caesar as Artful Reporter: The War
       Commentaries as Political Instruments* (1998), pp. 111–137, esp. 116–121, &
       Gelzer (1968), p. 143; for it seen as Caesar's defeat see Suetonius, *Caesar* 25. 2,
       Plutarch, *Caesar* 24, Appian, *BC* 2. 150; for a consideration of this campaign
       within the framework of Roman strategy see A. Goldsworthy, *The Roman Army
       at War, 100 BC – AD 200* (1996), pp. 79–84, 90–95.
11   Caesar, *BG* 5. 38–45, 52; on four tragedies in sixteen days see Cicero, *ad Quintum
       Fratrem* 3. 5/6. 8.
12   Caesar, *BG* 5. 46–47; on the presence of Trebatius see Cicero, *ad Fam*. 7. 16, 11,
       12.
13   Caesar, *BG* 5. 47–48, Suetonius, *Caesar* 67. 2.
14   Caesar, *BG* 5. 48–49, Suetonius, *Caesar* 66.
15   Caesar, *BG* 5. 49–51.
16   Cicero, *ad Fam*. 7. 10. 2.
17   Caesar, *BG* 5. 53.
18   Caesar, *BG* 5. 52–58.
19   Caesar, *BG* 6. 1–2; on plundering see J. Roth, *The Logistics of the Roman Army
       at War, 264 BC–AD 235* (1999), pp. 305–309; on legionary numbers see L. Keppie,
       The Making of the Roman Army (1984), p. 87.
20   Caesar, *BG* 6. 3–4.

21 Caesar, *BG* 6. 5–8.

22 Caesar, *BG* 6. 9–10, 29.

23 For a wide discussion of the importance of rivers see D. Braund, 'River Frontiers in the Environmental Psychology of the Roman World', in D. Kennedy (ed.), *The Roman Army in the East, JRA Supplementary Series 18* (1996), pp. 43–47.

24 Caesar, *BG* 6. 29–34, on the death of Catuvolcus see 6. 31.

25 Caesar, *BG* 6. 43.

26 Caesar, *BG* 6. 35–44; on the impact of Caesar's campaigns on the region see N. Roymans, *Tribal Societies in Northern Gaul: An Anthropological Perspective, Cingula 12* (1990), pp. 136–144 and 'The North Belgic Tribes in the First Century BC' in R. Brandt & J. Slofstra (eds.), *Roman and Native in the Low Countries, BAR 184* (1983), pp. 43–69.

27 On date of release see P. Wiseman, 'The Publication of the *De Bello Gallico*', in Welch & Powell (1998), pp. 1–9, esp. 5–6; on the elk see Caesar, *BG* 6. 27.

28 The main accounts of Carrhae are Plutarch, *Crassus* 17–33 and Dio 40. 12–30.

XV The Man and the Hour: Vercingetorix and the Great Revolt, 52 BC

1 Caesar, *BG* 7. 1.

2 For a classic study of fighting 'colonial' wars between a regular army on one side and irregular forces on the other see C. Calwell, *Small Wars* (1906); a readily accessible introduction to the topic is D. Porch, *Wars of Empire* (2000).

3 On elevation of Commius see Caesar, *BG* 7. 76.

4 For reaction to death of Acco see Caesar, *BG, 7.* 1–2; importance of a retinue, *BG* 1. 18, 6. 15; annual meeting of druids in land of Carnutes, *BG* 6. 13; for Caesar's attitude to the Gauls see J. Barlow, 'Noble Gauls and their other,' and L. Rawlings, 'Caesar's Portrayal of the Gauls as Warriors,' both in K. Welch & A. Powell (eds.), *Julius Caesar as Artful Reporter: the War Commentaries as Political Instruments* (1998), pp. 139–170, and 171–192 respectively.

5 For the events of these months in Rome see M. Gelzer, *Caesar* (1968), pp. 145–152, C. Meier, *Caesar* (1996), pp. 297–301, and R. Seager, *Pompey the Great* (2002), pp. 126–135; Cicero in Ravenna, *ad Att.* 7. 1. 4; on the role of legates see K. Welch, 'Caesar and his Officers in the Gallic War Commentaries', in Welch & Powell (1998), pp. 85–103.

6 Caesar, *BG* 7. 4; on friendly relations between Vercingetorix and Caesar see Dio 40. 41. 1, 3.

7 Caesar, *BG* 7. 5; on rebellions see A. Goldsworthy, *The Roman Army at War, 100 BC–AD 200* (1996), pp. 79–95, esp. 90–95.

8 Caesar, *BG* 7. 6–7; for 400 German cavalry see 7. 13.

9 Caesar, *BG* 7. 7–9; Suetonius, *Caesar* 58. 1 for story of dressing as a Gaul.

10 Caesar, *BG* 7. 10; on initiative see Goldsworthy (1996), pp. 90–92, 94–95, 99–100, 114–115, and Calwell (1906), pp. 71–83.

11 Caesar, *BG* 7. 11–13.

12 Caesar, *BG* 7. 14.

13 Caesar, *BG* 7. 14–15.

14 Caesar, *BG* 7. 16–17; for the types of food eaten by Roman soldiers see R. Davies, 'The Roman Military Diet', in R. Davies, *Service in the Roman Army* (1989), pp. 187–206.

15 Caesar, *BG* 7. 18–21; on the problems of supplying tribal armies see Goldsworthy (1996), pp. 56–60.

16 Caesar, *BG* 7. 22–25; cf. Rawlings (1998), pp. 171–192.

17 Caesar, *BG* 7. 28.

18 Caesar, *BG* 7. 26–28; Polybius 10. 15. 4–6, cf. W. Harris, *War and Imperialism in Republican Rome 327–70 BC* (1979), pp. 51–53.

19 Caesar, *BG* 7. 32–34.

20 Caesar, *BG* 7. 28–31, 35.

21 Caesar, *BG* 7. 36.

22 Caesar, *BG* 7. 37–41.

23 Caesar, *BG* 7. 42–44.

24 Caesar, *BG* 7. 45.

25 Caesar, *BG* 7. 47.

26 Caesar, *BG* 7. 50.

27 For the account of Gergovia see Caesar, *BG* 7. 44–54, and see also the comments on the style of this passage in A. Powell, 'Julius Caesar and the Presentation of Massacre', in Welch & Powell, (1998), pp. 111–137, esp. 122–123; for 'kicking the enemy in the stomach' see Plutarch, *Lucullus* 9. 1.

28 Caesar, *BG* 7. 55–56, 63–67; for Labienus' operations see 7. 57–62.

29 Caesar, *BG* 7. 68–69; on this campaign see J. Harmand, *Une Campagne Césarienne: Alésia* (1967), J. Le Gall, *La Bataille D'Alésia* (2000), and H. Delbrück, *History of the Art of War,* Volume 1: *Warfare in Antiquity* (1975), pp. 495–507, mentioning Napoleon's comments on p. 501.

30 Caesar, *BG* 7. 69, 72–73, and comments in Le Gall (2000), pp. 64–77.

31 Caesar, *BG* 7. 70–71, 75–78; for a discussion of the size of the relief army see Le Gall (2000), pp. 82–84.

32 Caesar, *BG* 7. 79–81.

33 Caesar, *BG* 7. 88.

34 For the account of the final battle see Caesar, *BG* 7. 82–88.

35 Caesar, *BG* 7. 89, Plutarch, *Caesar* 27. 5, Dio 40. 41. 1–3.

36 Caesar, *BG* 7. 89–90.

XVI 'All Gaul is Conquered'

1 Cicero. a*d Fam*. 8. 1. 4

2 Suetonius, *Caesar* 56. 5, Cicero, *Brutus* 252–255, ad *Quintum Fratrem* 2. 16. 5, 3. 9. 6–7.

3 On the opening of Pompey's theatre see Dio 39. 38. 1–6, Pliny, *NH* 7. 34, 8. 21–22, Plutarch, *Pompey* 52–53. 1; for criticism of Pompey see Cicero, *de Officiis* 2. 60, and of others, Tacitus, *Annals* 14. 20; the number of elephants was variously reported as seventeen, eighteen and twenty.

4 Cicero, *ad Att*. 4. 17. 7, Suetonius, *Caesar* 26. 2, Pliny, *NH* 36. 103; for gladiators in school at Capua see Caesar, *BC* 1. 14, and on the importance of games see Z.

Yavetz, *Julius Caesar and His Public Image* (1983), pp. 165–168.

5   See Dio 40. 48. 1–52. 4, Plutarch, *Pompey* 54–55, and also R. Seager, *Pompey the Great* (2002), pp. 130–135, M. Gelzer, *Caesar* (1968), pp. 148–152.

6   Plutarch, *Cicero* 35, Dio 40. 54. 1–4, E. Gruen, *The Last Generation of the Roman Republic* (1974), pp. 338–342.

7   Seager (2002), pp. 137–139, Gruen (1974), pp. 150–159.

8   Plutarch, *Pompey* 55. 1–2, *Cato the Younger* 49–50, Dio 40. 56. 3–58. 4, Suetonius, *Caesar* 28. 3; Seager (2002), pp. 131–132, Gruen (1974), pp. 154, 454.

9   Caesar, *BC* 1. 32, Suetonius, *Caesar* 26. 1, Appian, *BC* 2. 25, Dio 40. 51. 2, and Gelzer (1968), pp. 146–148, Seager (2002), pp. 137–139.

10 Caesar, *BG* 8. 1–5.

11 For the campaign against the Bellovaci see Caesar, *BG* 8. 6–23; Commius, 8. 23, 47–48; Ambiorix, 8. 25.

12 Caesar, *BG* 8. 49.

13 On Uxellodunum see Caesar, *BG* 8. 26–44, and comments on executions in A. Powell, 'Julius Caesar and the Presentation of Massacre', in K. Welch & A. Powell (eds.), *Julius Caesar as Artful Reporter: The War Commentaries as Political Instruments* (1998), pp. 111–137, esp. 129–132; Carnutes, 8. 38; for rebellion of Bellovaci in 46 BC see Livy *Pers.* 114.

14 On casualties see Plutarch, *Caesar* 15, Pliny, *NH* 7. 92, Velleius Paterculus 2. 47. 1, and see comments in C. Goudineau, *César et la Gaule* (1995), pp. 308–311.

15 For a discussion of Caesar as a general see A. Goldsworthy, 'Instinctive Genius: The depiction of Caesar the General', in K. Welch & A. Powell (1998), pp. 193–219.

XVII The Road to the Rubicon

1   Suetonius, *Caesar* 31. 2.

2   Cicero, *ad Att.* 7. 3.

3   On the struggle to get the ten tribunes to pass the law see Cicero, *ad Fam.* 6. 6. 5, and *ad Att.* 7. 3. 4, 8. 3. 3.

4   On Caesar's alleged ambition see Suetonius, *Caesar* 9, Plutarch, *Caesar* 4, 6, 28, Cicero, *Philippics* 5. 49.

5   For Cato and Pompey see Plutarch, *Cato the Younger* 48. 1–2, *Pompey* 54; Cato and Milo see Asconius on Cicero, *pro Milonem* 95, pp. 53–54, Velleius Paterculus 2. 47. 4, Cicero, *ad Fam.* 15. 4. 12.

6   Suetonius, *Caesar* 28. 2–3, Appian, *BC* 2. 25, Dio 40. 59. 1–4; on debate over the legion see Cicero, *ad Fam.* 8. 4. 4; for the debate on 29 September see 8. 8. 4–9; for a general discussion see M. Gelzer, *Caesar* (1968), pp. 175–178, R. Seager, *Pompey the Great* (2002), pp. 140–143, J. Leach, *Pompey* (1978), pp. 150–172, esp. 161.

7   For the flogging of the magistrate see Suetonius, *Caesar* 28. 3, Appian, *BC* 2. 26, Plutarch, *Caesar* 29, Cicero, *ad Att.* 5. 11. 2; see Caelius' quote from Cicero, *ad Fam.* 8. 8. 9.

8   Discussions of the terminal date of Caesar's command see Seager (2002), pp. 191–193, T. Mitchell, *Cicero: The Senior Statesman* (1991), pp. 237–239, P. Cuff,

'The Terminal Date of Caesar's Gallic Command', *Historia* 7 (1958), pp. 445–471, D. Stockton, '*Quis iustius induit arma*', *Historia* 24 (1975), pp. 222–259, and in general E. Gruen, *The Last Generation of the Roman Republic* (1974), pp. 460–497.

9   Suetonius, *Caesar* 30. 3; for a discussion of Pompey's attitude see Seager (2002), pp. 138–147.

10   On buying Curio and Paullus see Suetonius, *Caesar* 29. 1, Plutarch, *Caesar* 29, *Pompey* 58, Dio 40. 60. 2–3, Appian, *BC* 2. 26, Valerius Maximus 9. 1. 6, Velleius Paterculus 2. 48. 4; on revolving theatres see Pliny, *NH* 36. 177; on Caelius' belief in Curio's planned opposition to Caesar see Cicero, *ad Fam*. 8. 8. 10, moderated at 8. 10. 4.

11   Quotation from Cicero, *ad Fam*. 8. 11. 3; for the earlier debate see Velleius Paterculus 2. 48. 2–3, Plutarch, *Pompey* 57, *Caesar* 30, *Cato the Younger* 51, and Dio 40. 62. 3; for discussion see Seager (2002), p. 144, and Gelzer (1968), pp. 178–181.

12   Quotation from Cicero, *ad Fam*. 8. 14. 4; more generally see Cicero, *ad Fam*. 8. 13. 2, 8. 14, Appian, *BC* 2. 27–30, Plutarch, *Caesar* 29, Dio 40. 60, 1–66. 5.

13   Appian, *BC* 2. 28, with a slightly different version in Plutarch, *Pompey* 58, cf. Dio 60. 64. 1–4; on Cicero's attitude see Mitchell (1991), pp. 243–248.

14   Cicero, *ad Att*. 7. 3. 4–5, 7. 4. 3, 7. 5. 5, 7. 6. 2, 7. 7. 5–6, *ad Fam*. 8. 14. 3; Mitchell (1991) pp. 232–248.

15   For Caesar's attitude see especially Suetonius, *Caesar* 30. 2–5; on Gabinius see Seager (2002), pp. 128–130.

16   Lucan, *Pharsalia* 1. 25–26, and in general 1. 98–157; on censorship of Appius Claudius see Dio 40. 57. 2–3, 63. 2–64. 1.

17   Plutarch, *Antony* 2–5.

18   For Hirtius see Cicero, *ad Att*. 7. 4; Plutarch, *Pompey* 59, Caesar, *BG* 8. 52. 3, Dio 40. 64. 3–4, Appian, *BC* 2. 31.

19   Caesar, *BC* 1. 1–5, Plutarch, *Pompey* 59, *Caesar* 31, Suetonius, *Caesar* 29. 2, Appian, *BC* 2. 32; on Cicero's involvement in negotiations see *ad Fam*. 16. 11. 2, *ad Att*. 8. 11d.

20   Caesar, *BC* 1. 5, Dio 41. 1. 1–3. 4, Appian, *BC* 2. 32–33, Cicero, *ad Att*. 7. 8, *ad Fam*. 16. 11. 3; on Antony vomiting his words see *ad Fam*. 12. 2.

21   Suetonius, *Caesar* 31–32, Plutarch, *Caesar* 32, Appian, *BC* 2. 35.

XVIII Blitzkrieg: Italy and Spain, Winter–Autumn, 49 BC

1   Cicero, *ad Att*. 7. 11.

2   Cicero, *ad Att*. 9. 7C.

3   Caesar, *BC* 1. 7-8, Appian, *BC* 2. 33, Suetonius, *Caesar* 33, Dio 41. 4. 1; on the centurions recommended by Pompey see Suetonius, *Caesar* 75. 1; on soldiers' pay see Suetonius, *Caesar* 26. 3, and discussion of pay in G. Watson, *The Roman Soldier* (1969), pp. 89–92.

4   For Marcellus in R. Syme, *Roman Revolution* (1939), p. 62; Brutus see Plutarch, *Brutus* 4.

5   See Caesar, *BG* 8. 52, Cicero, *ad Att*. 7. 7. 6, 7. 12. 5, 7. 13. 1, *ad Fam*. 16. 12. 4, Dio 41. 4. 2–4, and R. Syme, 'The Allegiance of Labienus,' *JRS* 28 (1938), pp. 113-125, & W. Tyrell, 'Labienus' Departure from Caesar in January 49 BC', *Historia* 21 (1972), pp. 424–440.

6   Cicero, *ad Fam*. 8. 14. 3.

7   Caesar, *BC* 1. 6, Cicero, *ad Fam*. 16. 12. 3.

8   Cicero, *ad Att*. 7. 14.

9   Caesar, *BC* 1. 8–11, Dio 41. 5. 1–10. 2, Appian, *BC* 2. 36–37, Plutarch, *Caesar* 33–34, *Pompey* 60–61, *Cato the Younger* 52.

10 Caesar, *BC* 1. 12–15.

11 Caesar, *BC* 1. 16–23 and quote from 1. 23, cf. Dio 41. 2–11. 3; for the letters between Domitius and Pompey see Cicero, *ad Att*. 8. 11A, 12B, 12C, 12D.

12 Plutarch, *Pompey* 57, 60.

13 Caesar, *BC* 1. 24–29, Dio 41. 12. 1–3, Appian, *BC* 2. 38–40; for surveys of the beginning of the Civil War see M. Gelzer, *Caesar* (1968), pp. 192–204, C. Meier, *Caesar* (1996), pp. 364–387, and R. Seager, *Pompey the Great* (2002), pp. 152–161.

14 Caesar, *BC* 1. 29–31, Cicero, *ad Att*. 7. 11. 3, 9. 1. 3, 11. 3, Appian, *BC* 2. 37; Suetonius, *Caesar* 34. 2 for the quote.

15 T. Mitchell, *Cicero: The Senior Statesman* (1991), pp.243–266.

16 Cicero, *ad Fam*. 2. 15, 8. 11. 2, *ad Att*. 7. 1. 7, 2. 5–7, 3. 5, cf. Mitchell (1991), pp. 235–236.

17 Cicero, *ad Att*. 9. 6a; see also *ad Att*. 8. 13, 9. 13. 4, 15. 3, 16. 1–2, 9. 1. 2, 5. 4, 8. 1.

18 Cicero, *ad Att*. 9. 11a for Cicero's letter of 19 March; 9. 16 for Caesar's letter of 26 March; 9. 18 for the meeting.

19 Caesar, *BC* 1. 32–33, Dio 41. 15. 1–16. 4.

20 Caesar, *BC* 1. 32–33, Dio 41. 17. 1–3, Appian, *BC* 2. 41, Plutarch, *Caesar* 35, Pliny, *NH* 33. 56, Orosius 6. 15. 5.

21 See, for example, Cicero, *ad Att*. 10. 4. 8, *ad Fam*. 8. 16. 2–5.

22 Sallust, *Bell. Cat*. 59. 6, Pliny, *NH* 22. 11; Caesar, *BC* 1. 38–39.

23 Caesar, *BC* 1. 37, 39, Dio 41. 19. 1–4, Velleius Paterculus 2. 50. 3, Cicero, *ad Att*. 10. 8b.

24 For the quotation see Caesar, *BC* 1. 39; more generally see 1. 37–40.

25 Caesar, *BC* 1. 41–42.

26 Caesar, *BC* 1. 44–48.

27 Caesar, *BC* 1. 47–55, 59–61.

28 Caesar, *BC* 1. 61–65.

29 Caesar, *BC* 1. 66–76.

30 Caesar, *BC* 1. 77–87, for the siege of Massilia see 1. 56–58, 2. 1–16, 22, Varro 2. 17–21.

XIX Macedonia, November 49–August 48 BC

1   Cicero, *ad Fam*. 9. 9.

2   Caesar, *BC* 3. 68.

3   Suetonius, *Caesar* 56. 4, 72, Cicero, *ad Att*. 9. 18; on the partisans of both sides see R. Syme, *The Roman Revolution* (1939), pp. 50–51, 61–77; for 'what you need

is a civil war' see Suetonius, *Caesar* 27. 2; for the campaign in Sicily and Africa see Plutarch, *Cato the Younger* 53. 1–3, Caesar, *BC* 2. 23–44.

4   Appian, *BC* 2. 47, Dio 41. 26. 1–35. 5, Suetonius, *Caesar* 69.

5   Caesar, *BC* 3. 3–4, Plutarch, *Pompey* 63–64, Appian, *BC* 2. 40, 49–52.

6   Cicero, *ad Att.* 8. 11. 2, 9. 7, 9. 10. 2,10. 4, and for Cicero's attitude see T. Michell, *Cicero: The Senior Statesman* (1991), pp. 252–266.

7   Cicero, *ad Att.* 9. 9. 3, for Servilius see *CAH*² IX, p. 431, Dio 41. 36. 1–38. 3, Caesar, *BC* 3. 1–2, Plutarch, *Caesar* 37, Appian, *BC* 2. 48.

8   Caesar, *BC* 3. 2–8, Dio 41. 39. 1–40. 2, 44. 1–4, Appian, *BC* 2. 49–54, Plutarch, *Caesar* 37.

9   Caesar, *BC* 8–13, Appian, *BC* 2. 55–56.

10   Caesar, *BC* 3. 14; for death of Bibulus' sons see *BC* 3. 110 and Valerius Maximus 4. 1. 15; for Cicero's attitude to the Pompeians see Cicero, *ad Fam.* 7. 3. 2–3.

11   Caesar, *BC* 3. 15–17, 17 for the quote; on the properties of ancient warships see the very useful summary in B. Rankov, 'The Second Punic War at Sea' in T. Cornell, B. Rankov, & P. Sabin, *The Second Punic War: A Reappraisal* (London, 1996), pp. 49–57, as well as more generally J. Morrison & J. Coates, *Greek and Roman Oared Warships* (1996).

12   Caesar, *BC* 3. 19 for the meeting, 3. 18 for Bibulus' death and Pompey's comment; for the attempt to cross to Brundisium see Appian, *BC* 2. 50–59, Plutarch, *Caesar* 65, Dio 41. 46. 1–4.

13   Caesar, *BC* 3. 39–44, Dio 41. 47. 1–50. 4, Appian, *BC* 2. 58–60.

14   Caesar, *BC* 3. 45–49, Plutarch, *Caesar* 39, Appian, *BC* 2. 61.

15   Caesar, *BC* 3. 50–53; for Scaeva see Suetonius, *Caesar* 68. 3–4, Appian, *BC* 2. 60, Dio mentions a Scaevius who served with Caesar in Spain in 61 BC, Dio 38. 53. 3, and for the *ala Scaevae* CIL10. 6011 and comments in J. Spaul, *ALA 2* (1994), pp. 20–21; on Sulla's caution see A. Goldsworthy, 'Instinctive Genius: The depiction of Caesar the General', in K. Welch & A. Powell (eds.), *Julius Caesar as Artful Reporter: The War Commentaries as Political Instruments* (1998), pp. 193–219, esp. p. 205.

16   Caesar, *BC* 3. 54–58.

17   Caesar, *BC* 3. 59–61.

18   Caesar, *BC* 3. 61–65.

19   Caesar, *BC* 3. 66–70, quote from 69, Plutarch, *Caesar* 39, Appian, *BC* 2. 62.

20   Caesar, *BC* 3. 71–75, Appian, *BC* 2. 63–64, Dio 41. 51. 1.

21   Caesar *BC* 3. 77–81, Plutarch *Caesar* 41, Appian, *BC* 2. 63, Dio 41. 51. 4–5.

22   Caesar, *BC* 3. 72, 82–83, Cicero, *ad Fam.* 7. 3. 2; Plutarch, *Cato the Younger* 55, *Pompey* 40–41, Appian, *BC* 2. 65–67, Dio 41. 52. 1; in general for Pompey's strategy and attitude see R. Seager, *Pompey the Great* (2002), pp. 157–163, 166–167.

23   Caesar, *BC* 3. 84–85, quotation from 85; Appian, *BC* 2. 68–69, Plutarch, *Pompey* 68, *Caesar* 42, Dio 41. 52. 2–57. 4.

24   Caesar, *BC* 3. 86–88, Appian, *BC* 2. 70–71, 76, Frontinus, *Strategemata* 2. 3. 22; for a discussion of formations in this period see A. Goldsworthy, *The Roman Army at War 100 BC – AD 200* (1996), pp. 176–183.

25   Caesar, *BC* 3. 89.

26 Caesar, *BC* 3. 90–91, Dio 41. 58. 1–3, Appian, *BC* 2. 77–78, Plutarch, *Pompey* 71, *Caesar* 44.

27 For the battle and losses see Caesar, *BC* 3. 92–99, Appian, *BC* 2. 78–82, Plutarch, *Caesar* 42–47, and also Dio 41. 58. 1–63. 6 although he gives a vague, impressionistic account; Suetonius, *Caesar* 30. 4.

28 Caesar, *BC* 3. 102–104, Dio 42. 1. 1–5. 7, Plutarch, *Pompey* 72–80, Appian, *BC* 2. 83–86, Velleius Paterculus 2. 53. 3; and Seager (2002), pp. 167–168.

XX Cleopatra, Egypt and the East, Autumn 48–Summer 47 BC

1 Suetonius, *Caesar* 52. 1.

2 Dio 42. 34. 3–5 (Loeb translation by E. Cary (1916), p.169).

3 Caesar, *BC* 3. 106, Plutarch, *Caesar* 48, *Pompey* 80, Dio 42. 6. 1–8. 3, Appian, *BC* 2. 86, 88; see also M. Gelzer, *Caesar* (1968), pp. 246–247, and C. Meier, *Caesar* (1996), p. 406.

4 Caesar, *BC* 3. 106, *Alexandrian War* 17, 29, and 69.

5 On the wealth of Egypt and the impression it made on the Romans see Diodorus Siculus 28 b.3; on Egypt in this period see S. Walker & P. Higgs (eds.), *Cleopatra of Egypt: From History to Myth* (2001), especially the papers by A. Meadows, 'The Sins of the Fathers: The Inheritance of Cleopatra, Last Queen of Egypt', pp. 14–31, and J. Ray, 'Alexandria', pp. 32–37, and also S. Walker & S. Ashton, *Cleopatra Reassessed* (2003), esp. G. Grimm, 'Alexandria in the Time of Cleopatra', pp. 45–49.

6 See chapter 6; for Cleopatra's possible visit to Italy see G. Gouldaux, 'Cleopatra's Subtle Religious Strategy', in Walker & Higgs (2001), pp. 128–141, esp. 131–132.

7 On the history of the later Ptolemies see *CAH2* IX, pp. 310–326, esp. 323; on the low level of the Nile see Pliny, *NH* 5. 58; for the story of Cnacus Pompeius see Plutarch, *Antony* 25.

8 In general see M. Grant, *Cleopatra* (1972), and for a useful survey E. Rice, *Cleopatra* (1999); for her skill with languages see Plutarch, *Mark Antony* 27; on her support for Egyptian cults see Goudchaux (2001), pp. 128–141, and Walker & Ashton (2003), esp. J. Ray, 'Cleopatra in the Temples of Upper Egypt: The Evidence of Dendera and Armant', pp. 9–11, and S. Ashton, 'Cleopatra: Goddess, Ruler or Regent', pp. 25–30, D. Thompson, 'Cleopatra VII: The Queen of Egypt,' pp. 31–34.

9 On her appearance see Plutarch, *Mark Antony* 27, Dio 42. 34. 3–5, and also Grant (1972), pp. 65–67, Rice (1999), pp. 95–102, Walker & Higgs (2001), esp. S. Walker, 'Cleopatra's Images: Reflections of Reality', pp. 142–147, G. Goudchaux, 'Was Cleopatra Beautiful? The Conflicting Answers of Numismatics', pp. 210–214, and also in Walker & Ashton (2003), esp. S. Walker, 'Cleopatra VII at the Louvre', pp. 71–74, and F. Johansen, 'Portraits of Cleopatra – Do They Exist?', pp. 75–77.

10 See Ray (2001), Grimm (2003), pp. 45–49, and G. Goudchaux, 'Cleopatra the Seafarer Queen: Strabo and India', in Walker & Ashton (2003), pp. 109–112.

11 Caesar, *BC* 3. 106–112, *Alexandrian War* 1–3, Plutarch, *Caesar* 48, Appian, *BC* 2. 89.

12   *Alexandrian War* 4, Plutarch, *Caesar* 48–49, Dio 42. 34. 1–38. 2, 39. 1–2, Suetonius, *Caesar* 53. 1.

13   *Alexandrian War* 5–22, Plutarch, *Caesar* 49, Dio 42. 40. 1–6, Suetonius, *Caesar* 64, Appian, *BC* 2. 90.

14   *Alexandrian War* 23–32, Dio 42. 41. 1–43. 4, Josephus, *Jewish Antiquities* 14. 8. 12, *Jewish War* 1. 187–192.

15   *Alexandrian War* 33, Dio 42. 35. 4–6, 44. 1–45. 1, Suetonius, *Caesar* 52. 1, Appian, *BC* 90; for the bemused attitude of scholars to this cruise see Gelzer (1968), pp. 255–259 and also Meier (1995), pp. 408–410, 412.

16   For Caesar's baldness see Suetonius, *Caesar* 45. 2.

17   Suetonius, *Caesar* 76. 3, *Alexandrian War* 33, Plutarch, *Caesar* 49.

18   *Alexandrian War* 34–41.

19   *Alexandrian War* 65–78, Dio 42. 45. 1–48. 4, Josephus, *Jewish War* 1. 190–195, *Jewish Antiquities* 14. 8. 3–5, Plutarch, *Caesar* 50, Suetonius, *Caesar* 35. 2, 37. 2.

XXI   Africa, September 47–June 46 BC

1   Cicero, *ad Att.* 11. 17a. 3.

2   Plutarch, *Cato the Younger* 66. 2 (Loeb translation by B. Perrin (1919), p. 397).

3   Dio 42. 17. 1–19. 4, 22. 1–25. 3, Caesar, *BC* 3. 20–22, Velleius Paterculus 2. 68. 1–3, Livy *Pers.* 111; for discussion of Caelius' and Milo's unsuccessful rebellion see T. Rice Holmes, *The Roman Republic*, 3 (1923), pp. 223–225, M. Gelzer, *Caesar* (1968), pp. 227–228.

4   Dio 42. 21. 1–2, 26. 1–28. 4, Plutarch, *Antony* 8–10, Cicero, *Philippics* 2. 56–63, and in general see Holmes (1923), pp. 226–229, Gelzer (1968), pp. 253–254; for book on drinking see Pliny, *NH* 14. 148; on lions see Pliny, *NH* 8. 21, Plutarch, *Antony* 9.

5   Appian, *BC* 2. 92, Dio 42. 29. 1–32. 3, Plutarch, *Antony* 9, *Alexandrian War* 65, *African War* 54, Cicero, *ad Att.* 11. 10. 2, *Philippics* 6. 11, 11. 14; on the rumour of Pompeian attack on Italy see Cicero, *ad Att.* 11. 18. 1, Plutarch, *Cato the Younger* 58.

6   Dio 42. 19. 2–20. 5, Plutarch, *Brutus* 6, and *Cicero* 39; and T. Mitchell, *Cicero: The Senior Statesman* (1991), pp. 264–265.

7   Appian, *BC* 2. 92–94, Dio 42. 52. 1–55. 3, Suetonius, *Caesar* 70, Plutarch, *Caesar* 51, Frontinus, *Strategemata* 1. 9. 4. In Dio's version the troops were allowed into the city and the confrontation took place there rather than in a camp outside.

8   Dio 42. 49. 150. 5, Suetonius, *Caesar* 38. 2, 51. 2, Plutarch, *Antony* 10, Cicero, *Philippics* 2. 65, 71–73; and Gelzer (1968), p. 262, Holmes (1923), pp. 234–235.

9   Quote from *African War* 1; *African War* 60 for legion numbers; Suetonius, *Caesar* 59, Dio 42. 58. 3 for story of stumbling; for ignoring bad omens see Cicero, *de Divinatione* 2. 52, where he uses this for further evidence of the spurious nature of such predictions.

10   *African War* 1–3, 10–11, 19, 27, Appian, *BC* 2. 96.

11   *African War* 4–15.

12   *African War* 16.

13 *African War* 16–19, Dio 43. 2. 1–3, Appian, *BC* 2. 95, who implies that the
Pompeians deliberately withdrew, and Holmes (1923), pp. 242–245, J. Fuller,
Julius Caesar: Man, Soldier and Tyrant (1965), pp. 267–270; rallying the
standard-bearer, Suetonius, *Caesar* 62, Plutarch, *Caesar* 52.

14 *African War* 20–21, 24–26, 28, 33–35, 44–46; on seaweed used as fodder see
African War 24; on Scipio Salvito see Dio 42. 58. 1, Plutarch, *Caesar* 52,
Suetonius, *Caesar* 59.

15 *African War* 24–43, quotation from 31.

16 *African War* 48–55, Suetonius, *Caesar* 66.

17 *African War* 56–67.

18 *African War* 68–80.

19 *African War* 82–83.

20 Plutarch, *Caesar* 53.

21 *African War* 81–86, 91, 94–6, Appian, *BC* 2. 100.

22 *African War* 87–90, 97–98, Dio 43. 10. 1–13. 4, Appian, *BC* 2. 98–99, Plutarch,
Cato the Younger 56. 4, 59. 1–73. 1; on Queen Eunoe see Suetonius, *Caesar* 52. 1.

XXII Dictator, 46–44 BC

1 Cicero, *ad Fam.* 12. 18.

2 Velleius Paterculus, 2. 61. 1.

3 For accounts of the triumphs see Dio 43. 19. 1–21. 4, Appian, *BC* 2. 101–102,
Plutarch, *Caesar* 55, Suetonius, *Caesar* 37, Pliny, *NH* 7. 92, Cicero, *Philippics* 14.
23; see also comments in M. Gelzer, *Caesar* (1968), pp. 284–286, T. Rice Holmes,
The Roman Republic, 3 (1923), pp. 279–281, and S. Weinstock, *Divus Julius*
(1971), pp. 76–77, who suggests that the story of the chariot axle breaking was a
confused version of Caesar's superstitious mantra recited before travelling in a
chariot, Pliny, *NH* 28. 21.

4 Suetonius, *Caesar* 49. 4.

5 Suetonius, *Caesar* 51, Dio 43. 20. 2–4.

6 For celebrations and games see Dio 43. 22. 1–24. 4, Appian, *BC* 2. 102, Suetonius,
Caesar 38. 1, 39. 2, Plutarch, *Caesar* 55, Pliny, *NH* 8. 21–22, 181, Cicero, *ad Fam.*
12. 18. 2, Macrobius, *Saturnalia* 2. 7. 2–9, and also Gelzer (1968), pp. 285–287,
Holmes (1923), pp. 280–282.

7 On behaviour at games see Suetonius, *Augustus* 45. 1; one of the most useful
discussions of Caesar's legislation can be found in Z. Yazetz, *Julius Caesar and
His Public Image* (1983).

8 Caesar, *BC* 3. 57; for an introduction to the differing interpretations of Caesar
see Yazetz (1983), pp. 10–57.

9 Dio 43. 50. 3–4, Suetonius, *Caesar* 42. 1, 81, *Tiberius* 4. 1, Plutarch, *Caesar*
57–58, Strabo, *Geog.* 8. 6. 23, 17. 3. 15, Appian, *Punic History* 136, Cicero, *ad
Fam.* 9. 17. 2, 13. 4, 13. 5, 13. 8; also Yazetz (1983), pp. 137–149, E. Rawson,
CAH2IX , pp. 445–480, and Holmes (1923), pp. 320–324.

10 Suetonius, *Caesar* 41. 2, 76. 2, 80. 3, Dio 43. 46. 2–4, Plutarch, *Caesar* 58, Pliny,
NH 7. 181, Cicero, *ad Fam.* 7. 30. 1–2, Gelzer (1968), p. 309, 310–311, and
Holmes (1923), pp. 328–330.

11 Cicero, *ad Fam.* 6. 18. 1, *Philippics* 11. 5. 12, 13. 13. 27, Dio 43. 47. 3, Suetonius, *Caesar* 76. 2–3, 80. 2; for a detailed discussion of the origins of Caesar's senators see R. Syme, *The Roman Revolution* (1939), pp. 78–96.

12 On Sallust see Dio 43. 9. 2, 47. 4, Sallust, *Bell. Cat.* 3. 4, cf. Dio 43. 1. 3; on the refusal of a province to a follower see Dio 43. 47. 5, and Appian, *BC* 3. 89 for his cruelty.

13 Cicero, *pro Marcello* 3; cf. Titus Amplius Balbus, the 'trumpet of the Civil War' allowed back in November, Cicero, *ad Fam.* 6. 12. 3.

14 Suetonius, *Caesar* 42. 1, 44. 2.

15 Suetonius, *Caesar* 44. 2, Pliny, *NH* 18. 211, Plutarch, *Caesar* 59, Macrobius, *Saturnalia* 1. 14. 2–3, Holmes (1923), pp. 285–287, Gelzer (1969), p. 289, and Yazetz (1983), pp. 111–114.

16 Suetonius, *Caesar* 42. 1, 43. 1–2, Cicero, *ad Att.* 12. 35. 36. 1, 13. 6, 7, *ad Fam.* 7. 26, Dio 43. 25. 2, and Yazetz (1983), pp. 154–156 on sumptuary law; on the *collegia* see Suetonius, *Caesar* 42. 3, Josephus, *Jewish Antiquities* 14. 215–216, and Yazetz (1983), pp. 85–95.

17 Provincial law, Dio 43. 25. 3, and Cicero, *Philippics* 1. 8. 9 for approval; herders, Suetonius, *Caesar* 42. 1; on the municipia see discussion in Yazetz (1983), pp. 117–121.

18 Quotation from Cicero, *ad Fam.* 15. 19. 4; for Quintus Cassius in Spain see *Alexandrian War* 48–64, *Spanish War* 42, Appian, *BC* 2. 43, 103, Dio 43. 29. 1–31. 2, and Holmes (1923), pp. 293–295; the journey and the poem, Suetonius 56. 5, Strabo, *Geog.* 3. 4. 9, and Holmes (1923), p. 296.

19 *Spanish War* 2–27; for a more detailed discussion of the events of the war see Holmes (1923), pp. 297–306.

20 *Spanish War* 28–42, Appian, *BC* 2. 103–105, Plutarch, *Caesar* 56, Dio 43. 36. 1–41. 2, and Holmes (1923), pp. 306–308.

21 For honours see Dio 43. 42. 3, 44. 1–3; For Antony meeting Caesar see Plutarch, *Antony* 11; for Cicero's daughter see Cicero, *ad Att.* 13. 20. 1, and T. Mitchell, *Cicero: The Senior Statesman* (1991), p. 282; for Pontius Aquila see Suetonius, *Caesar* 78. 2, see also R. Holmes, p. 318.

22 Dio 43. 14. 7, 44. 1–46. 2, Cicero, *ad Att.* 12. 47. 3, 45. 3, *ad Fam.* 6. 8. 1, 6. 18. 1, Suetonius, *Caesar* 76. 1, and see Holmes (1923), pp. 315–316, Gelzer (1968), pp. 307–308, Mitchell (1991), pp. 282ff.

23 Cicero, *ad Att.* 13. 40. 1.

24 Cicero, *ad Att.* 12. 21. 1, 13. 40. 1, 46, 51. 1, *Orator* 10, 35, Plutarch, *Cato the Younger* 11. 1–4, 25. 1–5, 73. 4, *Cicero* 39. 2, *Caesar* 3. 2, Suetonius, *Caesar* 56. 5, and Gelzer (1968), p. 301–304, Holmes (1923), p. 311, and D. Stockton, *Cicero* (1971), p. 138.

25 Cicero, *ad Att.* 12. 40. 2, 51. 2, 13. 2. 1, 27. 1, 28. 2–3, 40. 1.

XXVIII The Ides of March

1 Suetonius, *Caesar* 86. 1–2.

2 Cicero, *pro Marcello* 8, 25.

3 Dio 43. 51. 1–2, 44. 1. 1, Appian, *BC* 2. 110, 3. 77, Plutarch, *Caesar* 58, Velleius Paterculus 2. 59. 4, Suetonius, *Caesar* 44. 3, T. Rice Holmes, *The Roman Republic*, 3 (1923), pp. 326–327.

4   Cicero, *ad Att.* 13. 52 for the visit, 14. 1 for calling on him in Rome; for the view that Caesar's character had changed profoundly, allegedly under the influence of Cleopatra see J. Collins, 'Caesar and the Corruption of Power', *Historia* 4 (1955), pp. 445–465.

5   Dio 43. 44. 1–45. 2, 44. 3. 1–6. 4, Suetonius, *Caesar* 76. 1; see also R. Carson, 'Caesar and the Monarchy', *Greece and Rome* 4 (1957), pp. 46–53, E. Rawson, 'Caesar's heritage: Hellenistic kings and their Roman equals', *Journal of Roman Studies* 65 (1975), pp. 148–159, S. Weinstock, *Divus Julius* (1971), esp. pp. 200–206; for the New Testament accounts of Jesus being questioned over taxation see Matthew 22. 17–21, Mark 12. 14–17, for the famous 'Render to Caesar the things that are Caesar's'.

6   Dio 43. 14. 6–7, 44. 6. 1, 5–6, Appian, *BC* 2. 106, Weinstock (1971), pp. 241–243, 276–286, 305–310.

7   Dio 44. 5. 3–7. 1, Cicero, *Philippics* 2. 43. 1; on Vespasian's last words see Suetonius, *Vespasian* 23; on the later imperial cult see S. Price, *Rituals and Power: The Roman Imperial Cult in Asia Minor* (1984).

8   Suetonius, *Caesar* 44. 2, Dio 43. 2, 44. 6. 1–3, Cicero, *de Divinatione* 1. 119, 2. 37; see also Weinstock (1971), pp. 271–3; on Cleopatra's visit see Dio 43. 27. 3, Appian, *BC* 2. 102; Suetonius, *Caesar* 52. 1 claims that Caesar summoned her, but falsely states that she left during his lifetime; Cicero's visit, *ad Att.* 15. 2; see also M. Grant, *Cleopatra* (1972), pp. 83–94, and E. Rice, *Cleopatra* (1999), pp. 41–44.

9   Suetonius, *Caesar* 52. 2, Plutarch, *Caesar* 49; however, note also Plutarch, *Antony* 52, which suggests that the boy was not born until after Caesar's death; for discussions see Grant (1972), pp. 83–85.

10 Suetonius, *Caesar* 83. 1–2, *Augustus* 8. 1–2, Appian, *BC* 2. 143, Pliny, *NH* 35. 21, Plutarch, *Antony* 11.

11 Plutarch, *Caesar* 61, *Antony* 12, Suetonius, *Caesar* 79. 1–2, Appian, *BC* 2. 108, Dio 44. 9. 2–10. 3, Cicero, *Philippics* 13. 31, Velleius Paterculus 2. 68. 4–5, Valerius Maximus 5. 7. 2.

12 Dio 44. 11. 1–3, Appian, *BC* 2. 109, Plutarch, *Caesar* 61, Antony 12, Cicero, *Philippics* 2. 84–87, *de Divinatione* 1. 52, 119, Suetonius, *Caesar* 79. 2; see also Weinstock (1971), pp. 318–341.

13 Bodyguard, see Dio 44. 7. 4, Suetonius, *Caesar* 84. 2, 86. 1–2, Appian, *BC* 2. 107; on justice and juries see Suetonius, *Caesar* 41. 2, 53. 1.

14 Dio 44. 8. 1–4, Plutarch, *Caesar* 60, Suetonius, *Caesar* 78. 1; see also the comments in Weinstock (1971), p. 276, M. Gelzer, *Caesar* (1968), p. 317, Rice Holmes (1923), pp. 333–334.

15 See R. Syme, *The Roman Revolution* (1939), p. 64, 95, for Galba, and also Suetonius, *Galba* 3; for Decimus Brutus being mentioned in Caesar's will see Suetonius, *Caesar* 83. 2, and also Dio 44. 14. 3–4; for Basilus see Dio 43. 47. 3, Appian, *BC* 3. 98; for Trebonius and Antony see Plutarch, *Antony* 13.

16 Plutarch, *Brutus* 6–13, *Caesar* 62, Appian, *BC* 2. 111–114, Dio 44. 11. 4–14. 4, Suetonius, *Caesar* 80. 1, 3–4, Velleius Paterculus 2. 58. 1–4; see also Syme (1939), p. 44–45, 56–60.

17 Suetonius, *Caesar* 52. 2–3, Appian, *BC* 2. 113, Plutarch, *Caesar* 62, *Brutus* 8, *Antony* 11.

18 Dio 43. 51. 7.

19 Plutarch, *Caesar* 63–65, Suetonius, *Caesar* 81. 14, Dio 44. 18. 1–4, Appian, *BC* 2. 115–116, Velleius Paterculus 2. 57. 2–3.

20 Plutarch, *Brutus* 14–15, *Caesar* 63, Suetonius, *Caesar* 80. 4, Cicero, *de Divinatione* 2. 9. 23, Dio 44. 16. 1–19. 1.

21 Plutarch, *Caesar* 66, *Brutus* 17, Dio 44. 19. 1–5, Appian, *BC* 2. 117, Suetonius, *Caesar* 82. 1–3; Dio and Suetonius both give Caesar's words to Brutus as 'You too, my son' (*kai sou teknon*); Suetonius gives his reply to Casca as 'What, this is violence!' (*Ista quidem vis est*).

22 Plutarch, *Caesar* 67–68, *Brutus* 18–21, *Antony* 14, Dio 44. 20. 1–53. 7, Appian, *BC* 2. 118–148, Suetonius, *Caesar* 82. 4–85.

23 Cicero, *ad Att.* 14. 1 for the quote from Caius Matius, and 14. 4 for prediction of rebellion in Gaul.

Epilogue

1 For British readers Kenneth Williams' portrayal of Caesar in *Carry on Cleo* (1964) – with the immortal line 'Infamy, infamy, they've all got it in for me.' – may be equally memorable, if not for reasons of historical accuracy. Similarly, for many, Caesar may be familiar from his regular appearances in the *Asterix* comics by Goscinny and Uderzo. Although the Romans are the principal villains of these stories, Caesar himself is a little formal and pompous, but still largely sympathetic.

INDEX